Edmund Spenser
Selected Shorter Poems

Longman Annotated Texts

General Editors:

Charlotte Brewer, Hertford College, Oxford
H. R. Woudhuysen, University College London
Daniel Karlin, University College London

Published Titles:

Michael Mason, *Lyrical Ballads*
Alexandra Barratt, *Women's Writing in Middle English*
Tim Armstrong, *Thomas Hardy: Selected Poems*
René Weis, *King Lear: A Parallel Text Edition*
James Sambrook, *William Cowper: The Task and Selected Other Poems*
Joseph Phelan, *Clough: Selected Poems*

Edmund Spenser
Selected Shorter Poems

Edited by
Douglas Brooks-Davies

LONGMAN
London and New York

1995

Longman Group Limited,
Longman House, Burnt Mill,
Harlow, Essex CM20 2JE, England
and Associated Companies throughout the world.

*Published in the United States of America
by Longman Publishing, New York*

© Longman Group Limited 1995

All rights reserved; no part of this publication may be
reproduced, stored in a retrieval system, or transmitted
in any form or by any means, electronic, mechanical,
photocopying, recording, or otherwise without either the
prior written permission of the Publishers or a licence
permitting restricted copying in the United Kingdom issued
by the Copyright Licensing Agency Ltd,
90 Tottenham Court Road, London W1P 9HE.

First published 1995

ISBN 0 582 089123 CSD
ISBN 0 582 089107 PPR

British Library Cataloguing-in-Publication Data
A catalogue record for this book is available from the British Library

Library of Congress Cataloging-in-Publication Data
Spenser, Edmund, 1552?–1599.
    [Selections. 1995]
        Selected shorter poems / Edmund Spenser; edited by Douglas Brooks
-Davies.
        p. cm. — (Longman annotated texts)
    Includes bibliographical references and index.
    ISBN 0–582–08912–3. — ISBN 0–582–08910–7
    I. Brooks-Davies, Douglas. II. Title. III. Series.
PR2352.B76   1995
821'.3—dc20   94–22616
                                                                                   CIP

Set by 8FF in 10/11pt Ehrhardt

Produced by Longman Singapore Publishers (Pte) Ltd.
Printed in Singapore

To A. C. Hamilton,
for his work on Spenser,
in admiration

Contents

Acknowledgements	ix
Abbreviations and references	xi
Chronology	xiii
Editorial procedure	xvii
General introduction	**1**
The Shepherds' Calendar	**7**
General headnote	7
Select bibliography	12
To His Book	16
[Dedicatory epistle]	18
The General Argument of the Whole Book	26
January	30
February	38
March	55
April	64
May	80
June	102
July	112
August	128
September	141
October	158
November	172
December	187
[*Epilogue*]	199
Amoretti and Epithalamion	**201**
Headnote	201
Select bibliography	210

Amoretti	214
[Dedicatory epistle]	214
[Dedicatory sonnets]	215
[*Amoretti*]	216
[Anacreontics]	287
Epithalamion	291
Four Hymns	**319**
Headnote	319
Select bibliography	323
[Dedicatory epistle]	324
An Hymn in Honour of Love	325
An Hymn in Honour of Beauty	340
An Hymn of Heavenly Love	354
An Hymn of Heavenly Beauty	368
Prothalamion	**385**
Headnote	385
Select bibliography	389
Prothalamion	390
Appendix	**403**
Illustrations: the woodcuts to The Shepherds' Calendar	**409**
Bibliography	**413**
Index	**427**

Acknowledgements

My overriding debt over the two and a half years it has taken to write this book is to Mary Brooks-Davies. Without her support, wisdom and help through a period of great difficulty for both of us, the project would not have been completed. I offer my heartfelt thanks to her.

The following Spenserians responded to my pleas with courtesy, kindness and promptness: Patrick Cheney, Haruhiko Fujii, Alastair Fowler, Bert Hamilton, Kent Hieatt, Robert Lane and David Miller. I am grateful to them all, especially to Alastair Fowler for his advice over the material that now constitutes the Appendix, and to Patrick Cheney and Robert Lane, who were gracious enough to entrust me with typescripts of their (then) forthcoming books: the extent to which I cite them in the notes is some sign of the excitement I felt on reading their work.

The Manchester University Research Support Fund granted me a year's leave (1992–3) to support research into Renaissance poetic language and to assist in the completion of this edition; the staff in charge of the University Library's rare book collection at Deansgate brought me my first editions and other texts with their customary (but never taken-for-granted) efficiency and courtesy; my doctoral student, Susan Chou, of the Department of Foreign Languages and Literature, National Taiwan University, Taipei, generously found time to instruct me in the finer points of word-processing and to undertake bibliographical searches for me; and the relevant LAT series editor, Henry Woudhuysen, scrutinised my texts with a patience and eagle-eyed thoroughness for which I am much in his debt.

My thanks again to all of you.

In addition to those listed above, and the scholars whose works are itemised in the bibliography, I have benefited enormously from the labours of previous editors of Spenser, in particular: W. L. Renwick; the editors of the *Variorum Spenser;* and the editors of the Yale edition of Spenser's shorter poems.

The woodcuts to *The Shepherds' Calendar* are from the edition in the Althorp Spencer Collection at the John Rylands University of

Manchester. They are reproduced here by courtesy of the Director and University Librarian.

D. B.-D.
1994

The publishers are grateful to the following for permission to reproduce copyright material: Oxford University Press for an extract from *Oxford English Dictionary*, 1933 edn Compact form, 2 vols, 1971.

Abbreviations and references

1. The following abbreviations have been used for Spenser's works:
   - Am — Amoretti
   - Epith — Epithalamion
   - FQ — The Faerie Queen
   - HB — An Hymn in Honour of Beauty
   - HHB — An Hymn of Heavenly Beauty
   - HL — An Hymn in Honour of Love
   - HHL — An Hymn of Heavenly Love
   - Proth — Prothalamion
   - SC — The Shepherds' Calendar
   - Three... Letters — Three Proper, and Witty, Familiar Letters: Lately Passed Between Two University Men

2. The following additional abbreviations have also been used in the notes:
   - DNB — The Dictionary of National Biography 1885–1900 (ed. Leslie Stephen and Sidney Lee), 63 vols, London
   - JEGP — Journal of English and Germanic Philology
   - OED — The Oxford English Dictionary 1933 (ed. J. A. H. Murray et al.), 12 vols and Supplement, Oxford; cumulative supplements, 4 vols 1972–86. Also consulted: 2nd edn (1989)
   - PQ — Philological Quarterly
   - PMLA — Publications of the Modern Language Association of America
   - SpE — Hamilton, A. C. et al. (eds) 1990 The Spenser Encyclopedia, Toronto, Buffalo and London
   - Var — Osgood, C. G. et al. (eds) 1943, 1947 The Works of Edmund Spenser: A Variorum Edition. The Minor Poems, 2 vols, Baltimore

3. Bible quotations are, unless stated otherwise, from the Geneva Bible (1560) in the London (1599) edition printed by Christopher Barker, designated: Geneva. Quotations have been modernised.

4. Greek and Latin references are to the respective Loeb Classical Library volumes unless otherwise stated.
5. Petrarch references are to *Petrarch's Lyric Poems: The 'Rime sparse' and Other Lyrics*, tr. R. M. Durling (1976), Cambridge, Mass., and London.

Chronology
⟨ 1552? ~ 1599 ⟩

1552?   Born, probably in London; nothing is known with certainty of his family origins, though his father may have been the John Spenser who moved from Lancashire to London and became a member of the Merchant Taylors' Company.
?–1569 Attends Merchant Taylors' School, London (founded 1561) under the headship of the celebrated educationist Richard Mulcaster.
1569   Contributes translations of epigrams from Petrarch, sonnets by Du Bellay and four sonnet paraphrases from the Book of Revelation to the English translation of Jan van der Noodt's Dutch Protestant *A Theatre for Worldlings*.
1569   20 May: matriculates at Cambridge, a sizar (i.e., poor scholar) at Pembroke Hall. Becomes friend of Gabriel Harvey (college fellow, 1570).
1573   Graduates B.A.
1576   Graduates M.A.
1578   Employed as secretary to John Young, Bishop of Rochester, formerly Master of Pembroke.
1579   Spring (?): enters employ of Earl of Leicester; acquainted with Philip Sidney and his circle. 27 October: an 'Edmounde Spenser' (presumably the poet) marries Machabyas Chylde at Westminster (she will bear him two children, Sylvanus and Katherine). 5 December: *The Shepherds' Calendar* entered in the Stationers' Register.
1580   The Gabriel Harvey-Spenser *Three . . . Letters* published; contain first reference to *The Faerie Queen*. Appointed secretary to Arthur, Lord Grey of Wilton, Lord Deputy of Ireland. August: arrives in Ireland with Grey; works as Clerk of the Privy Council at Dublin Castle; will remain in Ireland, with occasional trips to England.
1581   29 March: succeeds the poet Lodowick Bryskett as Clerk in the

	Chancery for Faculties (a sinecure) while remaining under Grey. December: leases castle and manor at Enniscorthy, County Wexford, for brief period; subsequently leases dissolved monastery at New Ross, County Wexford; a house in Dublin; and New Abbey, County Kildare (lease for the latter forfeited 1590 after failure to pay rent).
1583	Appointed Commissioner of Musters for County Kildare.
1585	Prebendary of Effin (non-resident living attached to Limerick cathedral).
1586	Assigned Kilcolman Castle, in Munster, with 3,000 acres (confiscated along with another 245,000 acres from the Irish Earl Desmond); undertakes to assist in colonisation of Munster by populating it with English immigrants; takes possession 1588(?); granted full perpetual lease to the property 1590.
1589	Succeeds Bryskett as Clerk of the Council in Munster (had been appointed his deputy in 1584). October: Spenser returns to England with Sir Walter Ralegh to present *The Faerie Queen*, Books 1–3, to Queen Elizabeth. 1 December: *The Faerie Queen*, Books 1–3 entered in the Stationers' Register.
1590	*The Faerie Queen*, Books 1–3, published by William Ponsonby in London. 29 December: *Complaints. Containing sundry small Poems of the World's Vanity* entered in the Stationers' Register.
1591	Returns to Ireland having been granted the considerable annual life pension of £50 by the queen (February); *Complaints* and *Daphnaida* published by William Ponsonby. 27 December: date of Dedicatory Epistle to Sir Walter Ralegh of *Colin Clout's Come Home Again* (not published until 1595).
1594	Appointed Queen's Justice for Cork. June: marries Elizabeth Boyle (they will have one child, Peregrine, who dies in 1642). 19 November: *Amoretti and Epithalamion* entered in the Stationers' Register.
1595	Publication of: *Colin Clout's Come Home Again* (published with *Astrophel. A Pastoral Elegy upon the Death of the most Noble and Valorous Knight, Sir Philip Sidney*); *Amoretti and Epithalamion*. Ponsonby published both sets of works.
1596	Publication of *The Faerie Queen*, Books 4–6 (published with Books 1–3), *Four Hymns* and *Prothalamion*, all by Ponsonby. King James VI claims that his mother, Mary Queen of Scots, is slandered in the figure of Duessa in *The Faerie Queen*, Book 5.
1598	Named Sheriff-designate for County Cork. April: *A View of the Present State of Ireland* entered in the Stationers' Register (not published until 1633). October: Kilcolman attacked and burned by forces led by Earl of Tyrone. Spenser takes refuge in Cork. 24 December: brings dispatches from Governor of Munster, Sir Thomas Norris, to the Privy Council in London.

1599	13 January: dies at Westminster; buried in Westminster Abbey; funeral paid for by Earl of Essex.
1609	Publication of *The Faerie Queen*, including *Two Cantos of Mutability*.
1611	Publication of folio works: *The Faerie Queen; The Shepherds' Calendar: Together with the Other Works of England's Arch-Poet, Edmund Spenser*.

Editorial procedure

This edition offers fully modernised texts, with the exception that archaisms and dialect forms are retained in their original spelling (for the rationale, see General Introduction, section 1). The copy text in each instance is the first edition. Original punctuation has been retained where possible, though in most cases this, too, has been modernised. Obvious misprints have been corrected, and it has not been thought necessary to indicate in the Textual Notes whether they have been corrected by the present editor or (in the case of *The Shepherds' Calendar*, of which there were several editions in Spenser's lifetime) by a contemporary. There are no holograph manuscripts of Spenser's poems, so the authority for his texts lies with the printed editions which were, by and large, produced with considerable care. The main resource here has been the copies in the Althorp Spencer collection in the John Rylands University Library of Manchester at Deansgate, though other copies have been consulted either in print or microfilm, and considerable use has been made of the tables of textual variants in the *Variorum Spenser*. Significant substantive departures from the copy texts, where they affect interpretation, are recorded in the footnotes. Other matters (excluding spelling differences and punctuation) are reserved for the Textual Notes.

General introduction

[Spenser's] *Shepherds' Calendar* hath much poetry in his eclogues indeed worthy the reading, if I be not deceived. That same framing [fashioning] of his style to an old, rustic, language I dare not allow, since neither Theocritus in Greek, Virgil in Latin, nor Sannazaro in Italian, did affect it.
(Philip Sidney, *Defence of Poesy*, 1595)

Spenser, in affecting the ancients, writ no language.
(Ben Jonson, *Timber; or Discoveries*; *Works*, vol. 2, 1640)

1 Why modernise Spenser?

Edmund Spenser – professional secretary, colonist, and poet – is one of the greatest and least read of English Renaissance writers. The loss is ours, though it is not entirely our fault. For one thing, Spenser found time in his busy and relatively brief life (he was probably born in 1552, though we do not know for certain, and died in 1599) to write too much: in 1590 he published the first three books of England's longest epic poem, *The Faerie Queen*, following this with another three books in 1596, by which time he had written a sufficient number of shorter poems (some critics prefer to call them 'minor', but that reveals an unfair bias) to fill a large volume. The epic overshadows the shorter works, and even it is so long that very few publishers can contemplate publishing it in its entirety. Then again, Spenser has become the property of the critics, who have made him the victim of well-meaning but often formidably obscurantist commentary. Questing for nuance upon nuance they have not only driven this learned, humane and readable author to the margins of his poems (and beyond); they have also possessed his texts to the extent of making it seem a betrayal to translate him into contemporary English.

The present edition is therefore radical in being the first large-scale attempt to modernise Spenser's texts so that we can read him as a contemporary would, without the artificialities of spelling differences or the older conventions of punctuation ambushing our attention. But even modernisation fails to solve the problem entirely, for *The Shepherds' Calendar* (and to a lesser extent *The Faerie Queen* and some of the other poems) is, as Sidney and Jonson testify in the quotations above, written in Spenser-speak, a mixture of mediaevalisms, dialect and neologisms. And this idiolect is, I suppose, the reason why, in the end, editors and critics have been reluctant to modernise. Tinker with the texts as they appeared in 1579, 1590 or whenever and, the argument goes, you risk major injury to authorial intention. Or do you?

I would argue that, unless we are fully familiar with sixteenth-century English, it *all* looks 'old' to us; so that it is actually with an unmodernised text that we miss the force of the archaisms and dialect words because we simply do not have the equipment to enable us to detect them. Whereas, if an editor modernises while leaving these forms as presented in the original, old-spelling text (the policy adopted in the present edition), they stand out as the signals Spenser intended them to be. As for the critical 'feeling' that Spenser should be read in old-spelling texts because it seems more appropriate, consider that we have no holograph manuscripts of the poems, so some at least (maybe even most) of the spellings editors tend to regard as authentic are, as is the case with other authors of the period, likely to be those of the compositors and/or of the publisher–booksellers for whom they worked. To modernise words like *pittie* and *annoied*, therefore, does no injustice to Spenser while helping the present-day reader enormously. It is also worth remembering that, in this period before spelling was fixed, Spenser's spelling forms could have differed from poem to poem, and within poems.

Although of the shorter poems *The Shepherds' Calendar* contains the greatest proportion of archaic and dialect forms, they are present in most of the other works. Therefore the notes in this edition give considerably more lexical information than has been available in previous editions. This means that, within the limits permitted by the *Oxford English Dictionary* (I have used the 1933 edition, cross-checking where relevant with the second edition of 1989: see Abbreviations and references), the reader is told when an archaic word was last used before Spenser, whether it was associated with a particular author (Chaucer or Langland, for example) and so on. Similarly, dialect words are identified, not least because the preferred poetic dialect of the time was that of the court and the environs of London, so that Spenser's choice was a deliberate affront to critical expectation: see the General headnote to *The Shepherds' Calendar*. Neologisms, too, are pinpointed: their number may well surprise the reader. Here, however, as with other linguistic matters, the information offered is at best provisional. Excellent though the *OED* is, we dearly need a Renaissance English dictionary.

2 How difficult is Spenser?

Apart from spelling and attendant lexical problems, historical difficulties are, I think, the main obstacle to the modern reader of Spenser: the fact that we have to be told what eclogues are and be persuaded that they, and the pastoral code to which they belong, were once relevant in a way they no longer are to our perception of the world; the fact that, pioneer though he was, the exciting newness of *Epithalamion*, *Prothalamion* and even *Amoretti* is inevitably lost on us and we can no longer respond to Spenser's language of love with ease; or the fact that Spenser wrote at a particular time and was immersed in (even if he did not always agree with) its dominant ideological concerns. But these are the problems besetting any 'old' artist and, provided that we are realistic, they should no more prevent our enjoyment of Spenser than of Shakespeare. The explanatory notes in this edition attempt to provide as much background information as is necessary to establish a historical context for each work, while the headnotes explain genre, verse forms, matters of particular historical relevance, and raise important critical questions. It is, however, worth reminding the reader that Spenser was, with Sidney and others, engaged in an attempt to establish the literary efficacy of the vernacular tongue so that it would not only supersede Latin as the medium for secular verse but aid in the creation of a literature that would equal, if not surpass, that of France and Italy. French achievements in this direction had been pioneered by the group of sixteenth-century poets known as the Pléiade. Led by Ronsard and Du Bellay, they fiercely championed the literary power of the vernacular tongue while recommending that its strengths be combined with imitation of the ancients in genre and subject-matter; their manifesto was Du Bellay's *Défense* of 1549: see *The Shepherds' Calendar* Dedicatory Epistle, p. 21, l. 95n. Italian vernacular literature, already encouraged by the fourteenth-century examples of Dante's *Divina Commedia* (*Divine Comedy*) and Petrarch's *Rime* (his vast sequence of sonnets and *canzoni*: see *Amoretti and Epithalamion* headnote), was nurtured by, among others, Ariosto (author of comedies, satires, and, above all, the romantic epic *Orlando Furioso* (1532)), and Tasso (whose sonnets were almost as influential as his epics *Rinaldo* (1562) and *Gerusalemme Liberata* (*Jerusalem Liberated*) (1581)).

The continental poets – and especially, perhaps, Dante, Petrarch and Du Bellay – were a major influence on Spenser's decision to organise his poems numerologically. Although other English contemporaries, Sidney among them, practised numerological structuring to some degree, with Spenser it was almost a compulsion. I draw attention to the more obvious numerological features in the headnotes to this edition, but it will help to offer some background here.

Despite its ancient and mediaeval history, numerology as applied to literary structures was very much a phenomenon of the Renaissance. Its origin in Christian poetic practice lay with the notion of the poet as a God-like creator whose works should mime the harmonious structure of the universe as inferred from the apocryphal Wisdom text that God made the universe in number, weight and measure (Wisdom 11: 21; the text was early on combined with the arithmetical recipe for the cosmic structure offered in Plato's *Timaeus* and elaborated by commentators on it). By the sixteenth century most numbers had developed a meaning or meanings derived from biblical or Graeco-Roman traditions, which meant that, in conjunction with the creator–poet concept, numerology as a compositional tool could easily take its place as an aspect of the decorums operating within the particular genres. When planning an epic, for instance, an author didn't just take account of registers of discourse, subject-matter, or characters' names but might also calculate the length of the action according to a numerological formula. When writing an elegy, he or she often took care to include the number eleven as a structural element (see *The Shepherds' Calendar, November* headnote). Information on numerological matters was available from the original Graeco-Roman sources and from more modern astrological and philosophical treatises (e.g., Henry Cornelius Agrippa's *Three Books of Occult Philosophy*, first published in Latin in 1531; English translation 1651: see *Amoretti and Epithalamion* headnote); but there was at least one numerological encyclopaedia, Pietro Bongo's *Numerorum mysteria* (cited in my notes in the Bergamo, 1599 edition). The more complex the literary structure an author produced – with the proviso that the complexity was concealed beneath a surface ease – the more it conformed to the prevailing mannerist style. Spenser's most brilliant innovation here occurs in *Epithalamion*, the gently fervent and lyrical narrative of which is underpinned by a numerological scheme encoding the day of the wedding itself (*Amoretti and Epithalamion* headnote). (For general background see Butler, C. 1970 *Number Symbolism*, Routledge, London; McQueen, J. 1985 *Numerology: Theory and Outline History of a Literary Mode*, Edinburgh U.P., Edinburgh; Shearman, J. 1967 *Mannerism*, Penguin, Harmondsworth.)

With Spenser, as with all writers from the past, we have to forget the present a little and try to listen to the author's voice. I hope the notes and headnotes to this edition will help the reader achieve this. I believe that Spenser was learned, but not abnormally so for an educated person of his time; hence I have cited as authorities in the notes well-known rather than obscure figures and have tried, wherever possible, to indicate when an idea was a commonplace. But, obtrusive as the notes are as they pursue Spenser's text sometimes word for word, my aim is that in the end you will forget my voice and hear, at least for a moment, Spenser's.

3 The contents of this edition

Within the limits imposed by publishing economics (which dictate the volume size) and the detail of annotation Spenser's work requires in order to make it accessible, I have included the better-known of the shorter poems for inclusion in this selection. *The Shepherds' Calendar* is printed complete with E.K.'s glosses and prefatory material and its accompanying illustrations. Not only is this work historically important as a statement about the directions the new poetry should take; it is also a fascinating and compelling interweaving of elegy, prophetic vision, political and theological realism, hard-hitting satire, pastoral nostalgia, and pro-monarchical propaganda. Modernised, as here, it no longer seems merely quaint and remote; and the notes reveal some hitherto unrecognised or undervalued layers of meaning in it.

I also include *Amoretti and Epithalamion* (1595), those moving and intricate testaments to Spenser's courtship of, and marriage to, his second wife, Elizabeth Boyle, which appeared at the height of the sonnet vogue of the 1590s. Together with the *Four Hymns* and *Prothalamion* (1596) they comprise the body of Spenser's love poetry, revealing its public as well as its private faces. No better introduction could be offered to late sixteenth-century humanist attitudes to love, as long as we remember that, however culturally determined a writer is, he or she always (*pace* the materialists) writes as an individual. The most public of these poems is *Prothalamion*, which celebrates at once a double engagement, London as New Troy, victory over the Spaniards, and the Order of the Garter; while meditating (as Spenser, like Hardy, nearly always does) on the transmutations wrought by passing time and the insignificance of the individual's place in history. The most private is *Amoretti* 89, with its poet–lover alone and grieving like Orpheus after the loss of Eurydice.

The Chronology reveals that Spenser wrote many more poems than there is room for in this volume. The omission of *Complaints* (1591), with its *Ruins of Time*, *Muiopotmos*, the earlier Du Bellay translations and various others, not to mention *Colin Clout's Come Home Again* (1595), does bias this selection against Spenser's concern with mutability, and his awareness of the fragility of civilisation in the face of exile and the ravages wrought by English colonialism in Ireland. Yet, within its limits, this volume offers a coherent Spenser and, with some exceptions, the 'best' Spenser. Even if he had not written *The Faerie Queen* he would be regarded as one of our great poets: the relative brevity of the 'shorter' poems says nothing adverse about their quality.

The Shepherds' Calendar,

Containing twelve eglogues proportionable to the twelve months.

Entitled

To the most noble and virtuous gentleman most worthy of all titles both of learning and chivalry Master Philip Sidney.

General headnote

SC was published in late 1579 by Hugh Singleton, the printer and bookseller who, only a short while earlier, in October, had been tried for being involved in the publication of John Stubbs's *The Discovery of a Gaping Gulf*, an attack on Queen Elizabeth's courtship of the French Catholic Duc d'Alençon, which had appeared anonymously in the late summer of the same year (see *January* headnote). Singleton was sentenced to amputation of the right hand, but was in the event pardoned. Earlier in 1579 Spenser had entered the household of the Earl of Leicester, also a strong opponent of the Alençon match (see Woudhuysen in *SpE*, pp. 432–3). These facts alert us to a primary element in *SC*: that it is a partisan work to which the three long ecclesiastical eclogues, *May*, *July* and *September*, are central because in them Spenser considers the role of the English Church and its responsibilities. This Church is Protestant, seeking, despite the retention of certain traditions and liturgies, a primitive Christian simplicity and purity that will shame the corrupt edifice of Romanism. Simultaneously, like all organisations, it contains those who oppose or resist: those for whom reform should go further; those for whom the old ways were best after all. By the Settlement of 1559 the queen had become the supreme head and governor of the Church, a fact which points to the close relationship between Church and State. Hence these three eclogues underline *SC*'s political message and thus its very *raison d'être*. For a man publishing his first long poem and intending to make a name for himself as a poet this message was dangerously risky. It was, simply, this address to the queen and her counsellors: don't betray your realm and your religion by espousing a French Catholic; remember and defend British liberty, so hard fought for against tyrant and invader. But the message was, in the tradition of contemporary pastoral theory, covert (see Dedicatory Epistle, p. 23n). Indeed, it was so encoded that critics only registered awareness of it this century (Higginson, J. J. (1912) *Spenser's 'Shepherd's Calendar' in Relation to Contemporary Affairs*; Parmenter 1936; McLane 1961; Lane 1993); until then *SC* was usually regarded as a puzzlingly directionless poem which was obviously important in terms of the English poetic renaissance (and English Renaissance poetry) but only really discussable in terms of style, source, genre, or Spenser's biography.

It is to the context of the poem's Protestantism, too, that the dedication to Philip Sidney also belongs, for like his uncle, the Earl of Leicester, to whom Spenser had originally intended to dedicate *SC*, he represents the particular form of Protestant humanist idealism that underlay Spenser's conception of himself as a poet: learned in the literature and philosophy of antiquity, assertive of nationalism (including the writing of good poetry in the vernacular as opposed to Latin), and deeply committed to the Reformation as a means of fostering the individual and discovering divine truth.

SC is, then, a pastoral poem with a message, recognisably and avowedly in the tradition of Mantuan and those other Renaissance and earlier poets (E.K.'s Dedicatory Epistle lists antecedents) who had been concerned in their eclogues (E.K. defines the word in the General Argument) to modulate the sheep and goats of classical pastoral, via the familiar biblical metaphor, into the faithful and the sinners of a Christian landscape; with the difference noted above that the expected ecclesiastical satire was enlarged to include specific political satire.

Before leaving the questions of political satire and the Alençon courtship, I should say that my own insistence on their relevance to *SC* runs counter to the emphasis of some modern scholars – notably A. C. Hamilton (Hamilton 1956) and Patrick Cullen (Cullen 1970) – and exceeds the emphasis placed on them by others – for example, Nancy Jo Hoffman (Hoffman 1977), L. S. Johnson (Johnson 1990) and S. K. Heninger (Heninger in *SpE*, pp. 645–51). I adduce my evidence for *SC*'s political commitment in the notes and headnotes where, I hope, it will be seen to coexist in balanced (if not untendentious) harmony with other relevant interpretative material.

To move from content to form, it should be noted that *SC* presented its readers with a teasing physical phenomenon: a modern poem with a half-familiar title (see Dedicatory Epistle, p. 24n) printed in black-letter (gothic-looking) type with prefatory material in contemporary Roman type, long glosses also in modern type, and woodcuts at the head of each eclogue which were, for the most part, in a fairly primitive popular style.

First and foremost, *SC* looked like an ancient classical text presented with the benefits of modern, humanist, scholarship. The illustrations have affinities with those to the Brant/Michel editions of Virgil (*January* headnote); the commentary, with its linguistic, rhetorical, and other explanatory matter, also looks like one belonging to an annotated Virgil or Homer. An obvious inference for a contemporary to draw is that this modern English poem is being promoted as having the importance of an ancient one: English poetry has, as it were, arrived.

Second, and more elusively, the whole set-up looked almost exactly like Francesco Sansovino's edition of Sannazaro's *Arcadia* published in Venice in 1571. This important discovery, made simultaneously by Henry Woudhuysen (Oxford D.Phil. thesis 1980, unpublished) and Bruce R. Smith (Smith 1980), has been amplified by Heninger (1988), who suggests that this is in rather abstruse compliment to the poem's dedicatee, Sidney, whose interest in Sannazaro was considerable because of his work on his own *Arcadia*. More to the point is Woudhuysen's suggestion that the format was designed to affirm for *SC* the classic status already accorded Sannazaro's work.

Beyond this it is perhaps foolish to speculate. Nevertheless it might be worth saying that, although black letter was still common in printed books of the 1570s and later, readers (prompted by *SC*'s linguistic archaisms) might have associated the typeface of the eclogues with reprints of old English authors such as Chaucer. In other words, the typeface confirmed to a certain extent the text's verbal message — that *SC* is a work indebted to old authors as a measure of stability and truth. Moreover, when we notice that the main authors alluded to — either directly, or by the use of words associated with those authors — are Chaucer and Langland, we see how closely antiquity and religious concern fuse in *SC*. For Spenser's Chaucer is the religious and political radical, supposed author of *The Plowman's Tale*, just as his Langland is the satirical author of *Piers Plowman* (see *May* headnote; Epilogue 10n). With E.K.'s introductions and glosses in their modern typeface accompanying it, the poem becomes not just a re-enactment of Sannazaro but an embedded antique text (both ancient classical and English mediaeval), a fossil of truth labelled in the fussy and concerned hand of modern humanist scholarship which teases out its meanings, *double entendres*, and rhetorical felicities in order that the world of 1579 will understand its simple proposition that truth is in danger of being lost as England seems set once again to embrace the corruptions of Catholicism by negotiating marriage with Alençon. As in the *Lyrical Ballads* — another revolutionary text born of a period of political revolution — the language and forms of the past function as reminders of the underlying strength and wisdom of the people and therefore of a truth lost to blinkered monarchs; with the additional function in *SC* that they associate the past with the reformed Church (primitive Christianity revived in Protestantism). How inaudible this message was to the modern courtly ear is demonstrated by George Puttenham's *Art of English Poesy*, the opening of Book 3 of which implicitly censures *SC* for its linguistic barbarity by forbidding poets to follow *Piers Plowman*, Lydgate and Chaucer, and to use 'the terms of northern men'. Instead, a good poet these days 'shall ... take the usual speech of the Court, and that of London and the shires lying about London within 60 miles, and not much above' (see Dedicatory Epistle, p. 19n). Those interested in this aspect of the poem will find in the notes copious examples of words taken from Langland, Lydgate and Chaucer, together with instances of northern dialect usage which was included in the poem as being more ancient and thus 'truer' than sophisticated southern forms with their continental accretions. The notes also point to Spenser's use of French forms, sometimes to satirical ends (e.g., *February* 209 gloss and n); sometimes to acknowledge indebtedness to Clément Marot who was a Protestant sympathiser: see *January*, *November*, *December* notes.

The calendar format, which alludes on one level to the popular almanac *The*

Calendar of Shepherds (Dedicatory Epistle, p. 24n), and on another to the familiar concept of the cycle of human life in relation to the circle of eternity (see Durr 1957; Heninger 1962), has in addition learned implications of a political/religious nature, indicating (like *SC*'s novel verse forms with their sometimes complex numerology) that the poem was urgently contemporary as well as rooted in the past. Calendar reform was in the air at the time, so that Spenser's decision to write a calendar (and, moreover, one that began in January rather than March) points to a controversial current debate, as E.K. notes in the General Argument. The debate involved a disagreement between England and Catholic Europe over the length of the year.

The first point to bear in mind is that there were two new-year dates in England, 1 January and 25 March. The former was popular and religious, the latter, originally religious (Lady Day), now marked the beginning of the legal year: *OED* style *sb* IV. 27. The second point is that, along with the rest of Europe, England followed the Julian calendar, which had been instituted by Julius Caesar in 44 B.C. With a new year that began in January, it was based on the 'tropical' year (the period it takes for the sun to return to the same point) of 365.25 days (Macrobius, *Saturnalia*, 1. 14. 3, 6), a calculation that was in fact 11 minutes 14 seconds too long. These quarter days were accumulated every four years as leap years; and the debate arose because of the inaccuracy of the Julian figure, which led to the regression of fixed dates at the rate of one day per 128 years. Therefore in 1578 Pope Gregory XIII circularised a proposal to correct the problem by omitting 10 days from the calendar and making other, smaller, adjustments. Catholic Europe accepted the proposal, instituting the change to the Gregorian calendar (which, like the Julian calendar, dated new year from 1 January) in 1582. England, however, refused to harmonise, remaining with the so-called 'Old-Style' (Julian) calendar until 1752.

The production of *SC* thus coincided with the heated consideration of calendrical reform alongside theological dispute (Elizabeth's leading ecclesiastics advised against Gregory's proposal), and E.K. was obviously worried that *SC*'s January beginning, with its rejection of the official English new-year month of March, might appear to some to favour the Gregorian reform by alluding to the new calendar. So he busily defended his poet's departure from the March new year, nudging his readers into awareness that January is not the property of the Catholics but is sanctioned as a beginning in England and elsewhere not only by long-standing custom but by Protestant practice (the *Book of Common Prayer* names 1 January – the Feast of the Circumcision, which marks the transition from the Old to the New Law through Christ's advent – as New Year's Day): Johnson (1990) ch. 5.

Finally, we must turn to the hoary old chestnut of *SC* criticism: the identity of E.K. Opinion is divided between those who think he was Spenser and those who think he was not. E.K.'s various errors – usually lexical – in glossing the text seem to argue against his being Spenser (though critical ingenuity can often, in these deconstructive days, turn an error into a subtlety that turns out to be the clue to the whole text . . .). On the other hand, his sympathy with the poem, and especially in *July* 33, 95, 127 and 147 glosses when his commentary opens up areas of political discourse only hinted at in the text itself, ensures that he and Spenser must have collaborated. It may well be that he was Spenser's Cambridge contemporary Edward Kirke or, as many have suspected,

Spenser's Cambridge friend Gabriel Harvey (and thus, in a joking way that would have been apppreciated by Erasmus or Rabelais, the recipient of his own dedicatory epistle). (On Harvey, see *September* 176 gloss.) For recent discussions of E.K.'s identity see: *SpE*, p. 231; Schleiner 1990; Waldman 1991.

On the present edition

1. Title

The title in original spelling is *The Shepheardes Calender*, which neatly poses (and refuses to answer) the question, is *Shepheardes* singular or plural? If the former, the poem is Colin's solo pastoral confession to the world; if the latter, it is the calendar of all the shepherds who participate within it and who receive its message. Given the public nature of that messsage, I have assumed that *Shepheardes* is plural: *Shepherds'*.

2. Copy text

With the provisos recorded in the 'Editorial procedure', the text follows the first edition, the quarto of 1579, identified as Q1. The four other quartos published in Spenser's lifetime – in 1581, 1586, 1591 and 1597 (designated Q2–5) – have little textual authority. Spenser was acknowledged publicly as the author only in the posthumous folio *Works* (London, 1611).

3. Order of the text and apparatus

The original eclogues were laid out as follows: woodcut; argument; poem; emblem(s); gloss (printed at the end with no line numbers to key gloss to text). In the present edition, the woodcuts are printed separately at the end of the volume; my explanatory notes are printed at the bottom of the page; and E.K.'s glosses are printed at the end of each eclogue as in the original, but are keyed into the text with line numbers. The relatively few mistakes in the ordering of the glosses in the original have been silently corrected.

To prevent time-wasting on the reader's part, footnotes will always indicate when there is a gloss to consult, thus: E.K. Where the glosses themselves are in need of commentary, these have been added within E.K.'s text inside square brackets.

This General headnote is supplemented by headnotes to each eclogue commenting on theme, structure, and other matters including an analysis of the relevant woodcut.

4. Modernisation

The effect of modernisation on the archaisms and dialect words in *SC* is commented on in the General Introduction, section 1.

Select bibliography

Note: This is a list of the books and articles cited in short form in the headnotes, glosses and notes to *SC*. A fuller bibliography of recommended reading on *SC* will be found at the end of the volume.

Aesop: see Chambry 1967
Agrippa, H. C. 1651 *Three Books of Occult Philosophy* (tr. J. F.). London
Alciati, A. 1551 *Emblematum liber*. Lyons
Allen, D. C. 1970 *Mysteriously Meant: The Rediscovery of Pagan Symbolism and Allegorical Interpretation in the Renaissance*. Baltimore
Ansell Robin, P. 1932 *Animal Lore in English Literature*. London
Aptekar, J. 1969 *Icons of Justice: Iconography and Thematic Imagery in Book V of 'The Faerie Queene'*. New York
Athanassakis, A. N. (tr. and ed.) 1977 *The Orphic Hymns*. Society of Biblical Literature Texts and Translations 12; Graeco-Roman Religion Series 4. Missoula, Montana
Barber, C. L. 1968 *Shakespeare's Festive Comedy: A Study of Dramatic Form in Relation to Social Custom*. Cleveland, Ohio and New York
Berger, H. 1983 'Orpheus, Pan, and the Poetics of Misogyny: Spenser's Critique of Pastoral Love and Art'. *ELH: A Journal of English Literary History* 50: 27–60
Berger, H. 1988 *Revisionary Play: Studies in Spenserian Dynamics*. Berkeley and Los Angeles
Bongo, P. 1599 *Numerorum mysteria*. Bergamo
Brooks-Davies, D. 1977 *Spenser's 'Faerie Queene': A Critical Commentary on Books I and II*. Manchester and Totowa, N.J.
Brooks-Davies, D. 1983 *The Mercurian Monarch: Magical Politics from Spenser to Pope*. Washington and Dover, N.H.
Brooks-Davies, D. (ed.) 1992a *Silver Poets of the Sixteenth Century: Wyatt, Surrey, Ralegh, Philip Sidney, Mary Sidney, Michael Drayton and Sir John Davies*. London and Rutland, Vermont
Brooks-Davies, D. 1992b ' "Shroude" versus "Shoulder" in the *June* Eclogue of Spenser's *Shepheardes Calender*'. *Notes and Queries*, n.s. 39: 292–3
Cain, T. H. 1968 'The Strategy of Praise in Spenser's "Aprill" '. *SEL: Studies in English Literature, 1500–1900* 8: 45–58
Cain, T. H. 1971 'Spenser and the Renaissance Orpheus'. *University of Toronto Quarterly* 41: 24–47
Cain, T. H. 1978 *Praise in 'The Faerie Queene'*. Lincoln, Nebraska
Chambry, É. (ed.) 1967 *Ésope: Fables*. Société d'édition Les Belles Lettres. Paris
Cheney, P. 1991 ' "The Nightingale is Sovereign of Song": The Bird as a Sign of the Virgilian Orphic Poet in *The Shepheardes Calender*'. *Journal of Medieval and Renaissance Studies* 21: 29–57
Cheney, P. 1994 *Spenser's Famous Flight: A Renaissance Idea of a Literary Career*. Toronto and Buffalo
Collinson, P. 1979 *Archbishop Grindal, 1519–1583: The Struggle for a Reformed Church*. London
Cooper, H. 1977 *Pastoral: Medieval into Renaissance*. Ipswich and Totowa, N.J.
Cullen, P. 1970 *Spenser, Marvell, and Renaissance Pastoral*. Cambridge, Mass.

Curtius, E. R. 1967 *European Literature in the Latin Middle Ages* (tr. W. R. Trask). Bollingen Series 36. Princeton, N.J.
D'Ancona, M. L. 1983 *Botticelli's 'Primavera': A Botanical Interpretation Including Astrology, Alchemy and the Medici*. Florence
de Vries, A. 1974 *Dictionary of Symbols and Imagery*. Amsterdam and London
Durr, R. A. 1957 'Spenser's Calendar of Christian Time'. *ELH: A Journal of English Literary History* 24: 269–95
Fowler, A. D. S. 1964 *Spenser and the Numbers of Time*. London
Fowler, A. D. S. 1970 *Triumphal Forms: Structural Patterns in Elizabethan Poetry*. Cambridge
Fowler, A. D. S. 1975 *Conceitful Thought: The Interpretation of English Renaissance Poems*. Edinburgh
Fraunce, A. 1592 *The Third Part of the Countess of Pembroke's Ivychurch*. London
Gafurius, F. 1969 *The Practica musicae of Franchinus Gafurius* (ed. I. Young). Madison, Milwaukee and London
Goldberg, J. 1986 *Voice Terminal Echo: Postmodernism and English Renaissance Texts*. New York and London
Gombrich, E. H. 1978 *Symbolic Images: Studies in the Art of the Renaissance II*. Oxford and New York
Heninger, S. K. Jr 1988 'The Typographical Layout of Spenser's *Shepheardes Calender*', in *Word and Visual Imagination* (ed. K. J. Höltgen *et al.*) Erlangen, pp. 33–71
Heninger, S. K. Jr 1989 *Sidney and Spenser: The Poet as Maker*. University Park, Pennsylvania and London
Hibbert, C. 1991 *The Virgin Queen: The Personal History of Elizabeth I*. London
Hughes, M. Y. 1923 'Spenser and the Greek Pastoral Triad'. *Studies in Philology* 20: 184–215
Hume, A. 1984 *Edmund Spenser: Protestant Poet*. Cambridge
Hutton, J. 1984 *Themes of Peace in Renaissance Poetry* (ed. R. Guerlac). Ithaca and London
Johnson, L. S. 1990 *'The Shepheardes Calender': An Introduction*. University Park, Pennsylvania and London
King, J. N. 1982 *English Reformation Literature: The Tudor Origins of the Protestant Tradition*. Princeton, N.J.
King, J. N. 1985 'Was Spenser a Puritan?'. *Spenser Studies: A Renaissance Poetry Annual* 6: 1–31
King, J. N. 1990 *Spenser's Poetry and the Reformation Tradition*. Princeton, N.J.
Klibansky, R., Saxl, F. and Panofsky, E. 1964 *Saturn and Melancholy: Studies in the History of Natural Philosophy, Religion and Art*. London
Lane, R. 1993 *Shepheards Devises: Edmund Spenser's 'Shepheardes Calender' and the Institutions of Elizabethan Society*. Athens, Ga. and London
Lemmi, C. W. 1929 'The Symbolism of the Classical Episodes in *The Faerie Queene*'. *Philological Quarterly* 8: 270–87
Linche, R. 1599 *The Fountain of Ancient Fiction*. London
de Lorris, G. and de Meun, J. 1962 *The Romance of the Rose* (tr. H. W. Robbins). New York
Lotspeich, H. G. 1932 *Classical Mythology in the Poetry of Edmund Spenser*. Princeton, N.J.

Luborsky, R. S. 1980 'The Allusive Presentation of *The Shepheardes Calender*'. *Spenser Studies: A Renaissance Poetry Annual* 1: 29–67
Luborsky, R. S. 1981 'The Illustrations to *The Shepheardes Calender*'. *Spenser Studies: A Renaissance Poetry Annual* 2: 3–53
Maclean, H. and Prescott, A. L. 1993 *Edmund Spenser's Poetry*, Norton Critical Edition (3rd edn). New York and London
Macrobius, A. A. T. (*Saturnalia* 1550) *In Somnium Scipionis Libri II; Saturnaliorum Libri VII*. Lyons
Macrobius, A. A. T. (*Saturnalia* 1969) *The Saturnalia* (tr. P. V. Davies). Records of Civilization Sources and Studies 79. New York and London
Mantuan (Mantuanus, B.) 1937 *The Eclogues of Mantuan* (tr. G. Turberville 1567 facsimile, ed. Douglas Bush). New York
Martianus Capella 1977 *The Marriage of Philology and Mercury*. In vol. 2 of *Martianus Capella and the Seven Liberal Arts* (tr. W. K. Stahl, R. Johnson and E. L. Burge), 2 vols. New York
McLane, P. E. 1961 *Spenser's 'Shepheardes Calender': A Study in Elizabethan Allegory*. Notre Dame, Indiana
Meyer-Baer K. 1970 *Music of the Spheres and the Dance of Death: Studies in Musical Iconology*. Princeton, N.J.
Miller, D. L. 1988 *The Poem's Two Bodies: The Poetics of the 1590 'Faerie Queene'*. Princeton, N.J.
Mustard, W. P. 1919 'E.K.'s Classical Allusions'. *Modern Lanagage Notes* 34: 193–203
Neale, J. E. 1934 *Queen Elizabeth*. London and Toronto
Neville Davies, H. 1970 'The Structure of Shadwell's *A Song for St Cecilia's Day 1690*'. In *Silent Poetry: Essays in Numerological Analysis* (ed. A. Fowler). London, pp. 201–33
Nichols, J. 1823 *The Progresses and Public Processions of Queen Elizabeth*, 3 vols. London
Norbrook, D. 1984 *Poetry and Politics in the English Renaissance*. London
Oram W. A., Bjorvand, E., Bond, R., Cain, T. H., Dunlop, A. and Schell, R. (eds) 1989 *The Yale Edition of the Shorter Poems of Edmund Spenser*. New Haven and London
Ovid 1965 *Ovid's 'Metamorphoses': The Arthur Golding Translation*, 1567 (ed. J. F. Nims). New York and London
Panofsky, E. 1955 *Meaning in the Visual Arts*. Garden City, New York
Panofsky, E. 1962 *Studies in Iconology: Humanistic Themes in the Art of the Renaissance*. New York and Evanston, Illinois
Parmenter, M. 1936 'Spenser's "Twelve Aeglogues Proportionable to the Twelve Monethes"'. *ELH: A Journal of English Literary History* 3: 190–217
Patterson, A. 1988 *Pastoral and Ideology: Virgil to Valéry*. Oxford
Prescott, A. L. 1978 *French Poets and the English Renaissance: Studies in Fame and Transformation*. New Haven and London
Puttenham, G. 1589 *The Art of English Poesy*. London
Renwick, W. L. (ed.) 1930 [Edmund Spenser] *The Shepherd's Calendar*. London
Richardson, J. M. 1989 *Astrological Symbolism in Spenser's 'The Shepheardes Calender': The Cultural Background of a Literary Text*. Studies in Renaissance Literature 1. Lewiston, N.Y., Queenston, Ontario, and Lampeter, Dyfed

Ripa, C. 1603 *Iconologia*. Rome, reprint Hildesheim and New York 1970
Robinson, J. 1815 *A Theological, Biblical, and Ecclesiastical Dictionary*. London
Ross, A. 1648 *Mystagogus Poeticus, Or The Muses' Interpreter*. London
Røstvig, M.-S. 1969 'The Shepheardes Calender: A structural Analysis'. *Renaissance and Modern Studies* 13: 49–75
Rydén, M. 1978 *Shakespearean Plant Names: Identifications and Interpretations*. Stockholm
Sacks, P. M. 1985 *The English Elegy: Studies in the Genre from Spenser to Yeats*. Baltimore
Schleiner, L. 1990 'Spenser's "E.K." as Edmund Kent (Kenned/of Kent): Kyth (Couth), Kissed, and Kunning-Conning'. *English Literary Renaissance* 20: 374–407
Servius, H. M. [Grammaticus] 1878–87 *Servii Grammatici qui feruntur in Vergilii Carmina commentarii* (ed. G. Thilo and H. Hagen), 3 vols. Leipzig
Smith, B. R. 1980 'On Reading *The Shepheardes Calender*'. *Spenser Studies: A Renaissance Poetry Annual* 1: 69–93
Smith, H. 1946 'English Metrical Psalms in the Sixteenth Century and their Literary Significance'. *Huntington Library Quarterly* 9: 249–71
Smith, C. G. 1970 *Spenser's Proverb Lore*. Cambridge, Mass.
Stewart, S. 1991 'Spenser and the Judgment of Paris'. *Spenser Studies: A Renaissance Poetry Annual* 9: 161–209
Strong, R. C. 1963 *Portraits of Queen Elizabeth I*. Oxford
Strong, R. C. 1987 *The Cult of Elizabeth: Elizabethan Portraiture and Pageantry*. London
Tervarent, G. de 1958 *Attributs et Symboles dans l'Art Profane, 1450–1600: Dictionnaire d'un Langage Perdu*. Travaux d'Humanisme et Renaissance 29. Geneva
Tooke, A. 1713 *The Pantheon*. London, reprint The Renaissance and the Gods 35. New York and London 1976
Tufte, V. 1970 *The Poetry of Marriage: The Epithalamium in Europe and Its Development in England* University of Southern California Studies in Comparative Literature 2. Los Angeles
Tuve, R. 1952 *A Reading of George Herbert*. London
Tuve, R. 1966 *Allegorical Imagery: Some Mediaeval Books and Their Posterity*. Princeton, N.J.
Valeriano Bolzani, G. P. 1602 *Hieroglyphica, seu de sacris Aegyptiorum aliarumque gentium literis commentarii*. Lyons, reprint The Renaissance and the Gods 17. New York and London
Waldman, L. 1991 'Spenser's Pseudonym "E.K." and Humanist Self-Naming'. *Spenser Studies: A Renaissance Poetry Annual* 9: 21–31
Wells, R. H. 1983 *Spenser's 'Faerie Queene' and the Cult of Elizabeth*. London
Whitaker, V. K. 1950 *The Religious Basis of Spenser's Thought*. Stanford
Whitney, G. 1586 *A Choice of Emblems, and Other Devices*. Leiden
Wilkins, E. 1969 *The Rose-Garden Game: The Symbolic Background to the European Prayer-Beads*. London
Wilson, E. C. 1939 *England's Eliza*. Cambridge, Mass.
Wind, E. 1967 *Pagan Mysteries in the Renaissance*, rev. edn. Harmondsworth, Middlesex
Yates, F. A. 1975 *Astraea: The Imperial Theme in the Sixteenth Century*. London and Boston

To His Book

Go, little book: thyself present
(As child whose parent is unkent)
To him that is the president
Of noblesse and of chivalry;
And if that Envy bark at thee,   5
As sure it will, for succour flee
  Under the shadow of his wing;
And asked who thee forth did bring,
A shepherd's swain say did thee sing,
All as his straying flock he fed;   10
And when his Honour has thee read,
Crave pardon for my hardihead.
But if that any ask thy name,
Say that thou wert base begot with blame,

---

1. Go ... book: echoing the envoy to Chaucer's *Troilus*, 5. 1786 ('Go, little book') as followed by, among others, John Lydgate's *Troy Book* (end of Book 5, addressed to Henry V) and John Skelton's *Garland or Chaplet of Laurel* (envoy to Henry VIII and Wolsey). See also *SC* Epilogue, 7.
2. unkent: unknown, untaught (a claim to humility recalling Lydgate's apology in his envoy for his lack of rhetorical skill): northern/Scots. Cf. *April* 21 gloss. This is *OED*'s first citation for the former sense in this spelling.
3. him: Philip Sidney as *SC*'s dedicatee and poet; also as Protestant dissident and opponent to the queen's proposed marriage to the Duc d'Alençon: *January* headnote.
3. president: guardian; but this is also a sixteenth-century spelling for *precedent* = (1) sign or token; (2) pattern: *OED* precedent *sb* 1e and 4.
4. noblesse: nobility (common mediaeval and Renaissance form); *chivalry*: knightly gallantry; the original spelling, *chevalry*, also denotes men-at-arms in the historical, mediaeval, sense (*OED* chivalry 1e), thus alluding to the chivalric revival at Elizabeth's court (Yates 1975). Cf. the title page dedication.
5. Envy bark: the dog is a traditional attribute of Envy: Ripa 1603: 242–3. Cf. Chaucer's *Troilus*, 5. 1789: 'no making [poetry] thou n'envy'.
10. All as: while.
11. his Honour: inappropriate as an address to Sidney, this is residual evidence of the original dedicatee, Leicester (as, presumably, are ll. 3–4): Woudhuysen in *SpE*, p 432. *read*: (1) perused; (2) discovered the meaning of (*OED* read *v* 2).
12. hardihead: daring (Spenserian neologism).
14. base ... blame: (1) published anonymously, *SC*'s parentage is unknown; (2) it is a Protestant reforming work in the popular (*base*) tradition (on which, see King 1982).

For-thy thereof thou takest shame. 15
And when thou art past jeopardy,
Come tell me what was said of me,
And I will send more after thee.
                                                    Immerito

15. For-thy: therefore (archaic).
16. jeopardy: the danger inherent in containing a religious/political messsage aimed in part at the queen.
19. Immerito: (1) undeserving; (2) guiltless (Italian/Latin).

[Dedicatory epistle]

To the most excellent and learned both
orator and poet, Master Gabriel Harvey,
his very special and singular good
friend E.K. commendeth the good
liking of this his labour,   5
and the patronage of
the new poet.

Uncouth unkissed, said the old famous poet Chaucer, whom, for his excellency and wonderful skill in making, his scholar Lydgate (a worthy scholar of so excellent a master) calleth the   10
loadstar of our language, and whom our Colin Clout in his *Eglogue* calleth Tityrus, the god of shepherds, comparing him to the worthiness of the Roman Tityrus, Virgil. Which proverb mine own good friend Master Harvey, as in that good old poet it served well Pandarus's purpose for the bolstering of his bawdy   15
brokage, so very well taketh place in this our new poet, who for that he is *uncouth* (as said Chaucer) is *unkissed* and, unknown to most men, is regarded but of few. But I doubt not, so soon as his name shall come into the knowledge of men and his worthiness be sounded in the trump of Fame, but that he shall be not only   20
kissed but also beloved of all, embraced of the most and wondered at of the best. No less, I think, deserveth his wittiness in devising, his pithiness in uttering, his complaints of love so lovely, his discourses of pleasure so pleasantly, his pastoral rudeness, his moral wiseness, his due observing of decorum   25

1. *Master . . . Harvey*: *January* 55 gloss.
8. *Uncouth unkissed*: unknown, unkissed: almost proverbial after Chaucer, *Troilus*, 1. 809 (*OED*, unkissed, *ppl a*, b).
9. *making*: poetry writing (*April* 19 gloss).
11. *loadstar*: John Lydgate, *Falls of Princes*, Prologue (1. 52): 'of our language he was the loadstar'.
11. *Colin Clout*: Spenser: see *January* argument gloss.
12. *Tityrus*: Virgil's *persona* in the *Eclogues* (invoked at *October*, 55–60); used for Chaucer at *June*, 81–96.
14–15. *poet . . . purpose*: the context of the phrase in Chaucer is Pandarus's encouraging of Troilus in his love of his niece, Cressida.
16. *brokage*: brokerage in the sense of pimping.
20. *trump*: trumpet, traditional emblem of Fame: Ripa 1603: 142–3.
24–25. *rudeness*: rustic 'roughness' and (apparent) lack of learning.
25. *decorum*: literary-theoretical concept of propriety: the matching of all the elements – diction, action, setting, characters, etc. – in a work.

everywhere: in personages, in seasons, in matter, in speech, and
generally in all seemly simplicity of handling his matter and
framing his words (the which of many things which in him be
strange I know will seem the strangest, the words themselves
being so ancient, the knitting of them so short and intricate, and 30
the whole period and compass of speech so delightsome for the
roundness and so grave for the strangeness).

And first of the words to speak, I grant they be something hard
and of most men unused: yet both English and also used of most
excellent authors and most famous poets, in whom, whenas this 35
our poet hath been much travailed and thoroughly read, how
could it be (as that worthy orator said) but that walking in the
sun, although for other cause he walked, yet needs he mought be
sunburnt; and having the sound of those ancient poets still ring-
ing in his ears he mought needs, in singing, hit out some of their 40
tunes. But whether he useth them by such casualty and custom,
or of set purpose and choice (as thinking them fittest for such
rustical rudeness of shepherds, either for that their rough sound
would make his rhymes more ragged and rustical, or else because
such old and obsolete words are most used of country folk), sure 45
I think – and think I think not amiss – that they bring great grace
and (as one would say) authority to the verse. For albe amongst
many other faults it specially be objected of Valla against Livy,
and of other against Sallust, that with overmuch study they affect

28–30. words ... ancient: for discussions of Spenser's archaisms and style generally, see *Var* 1. 614–30 and *SpE*, pp 52–3 (archaism), 215–16 (dialect) and 426–9 (language). For early adverse courtly criticism, see Puttenham (1589) 3. 4 ('Our maker therefore at these days shall not follow *Piers Plowman* nor Gower nor Lydgate nor yet Chaucer, for their language is now out of use with us: neither shall he take the terms of northern men') and Sidney, *Defence of Poesy* (1595): 'that same framing of his style to an old rustic language I dare not allow' (Duncan-Jones, K. and van Dorsten, J. (eds) 1973 *Miscellaneous Prose of Sir Philip Sidney*, Clarendon Press, Oxford, p. 112; see General headnote, p. 9).
36. travailed: learned, experienced; also, travelled.
37. orator: Cicero, *De oratore*, 2. 14. 60.
38. mought: must (from the archaic verb *mote* = may).
41. casualty: chance.
47. albe: although.
48–9. Valla ... Sallust: the fifteenth-century Italian humanist Laurentius Valla comments on the Roman historian Livy's style in his *Emendationes in Livium de bello Punico*, following a criticism by Asinius Pollio of Livy's lapses into native Paduan dialect (*Patavinitas*) reported in Quintilian, *Institutiones oratoriae*, 1. 5. 56, 8. 1. 3. The Roman historian Sallust's fondness for archaism had been noted most recently in Roger Ascham's *The Schoolmaster* (1570): Arber, E. (ed.) 1870: 154–9.

antiquity as coveting thereby credence and honour of elder years, yet I am of opinion (and eke the best learned are of the like) that those ancient solemn words are a great ornament both in the one and in the other, the one labouring to set forth in his work an eternal image of antiquity, and the other carefully discoursing matters of gravity and importance. For if my memory fail not, Tully, in that book wherein he endeavoureth to set forth the pattern of a perfect orator, saith that oft-times an ancient word maketh the style seem grave and, as it were, reverend: no otherwise than we honour and reverence grey hairs for a certain religious regard which we have of old age.

Yet neither everywhere must old words be stuffed in, nor the common dialect and manner of speaking so corrupted thereby, that (as in old buildings) it seem disorderly and ruinous; but all as in most exquisite pictures they use to blaze and portrait not only the dainty lineaments of beauty but also, round about it, to shadow the rude thickets and craggy cliffs that by the baseness of such parts more excellency may accrue to the principal. For oft-times we find ourselves, I know not how, singularly delighted with the show of such natural rudeness, and take great pleasure in that disorderly order: even so do those rough and harsh terms enlumine and make more clearly to appear the brightness of brave and glorious words. So, oftentimes, a discord in music maketh a comely concordance; so great delight took the worthy poet Alcaeus to behold a blemish in the joint of a well-shaped body. But if any will rashly blame such his purpose in choice of old and unwonted words, him may I more justly blame and condemn, or of witless headiness in judging, or of heedless hardiness in condemning: for, not marking the com-

---

51. *eke*: moreover, also.
56. *Tully*: i.e., Marcus Tullius Cicero, *De oratore*, 3. 38. 153 (old words give dignity); *Orator*, 23. 80 (defence of the occasional use of obsolete and archaic words).
60. *religious*: scrupulous
63. *all as*: just as.
64. *blaze*: depict. *portrait*: portray.
72. *maketh . . . comely concordance*: [helps] produce an agreeable harmony.
73. *Alcaeus*: Greek lyric poet, born late seventh century B.C. Most of his erotic verse (to which this remark pertains) is lost. E.K. recalls Cicero's quotation of a fragment in *De natura deorum*, 1. 28. 79 ('"a blemish on a part of a boy's body delighted" Alcaeus').
76. *or*: either. *headiness*: headstrongness.
77. *hardiness*: audacity.
77–8. *not . . . cast*: metaphor from archery: 'not noting the angle of his bow's elevation [and hence the flight path this determines], the critic will still disparage the length of the shot'.

pass of his bent, he will judge of the length of his cast. For in my opinion it is one special praise – of many which are due to this poet – that he hath laboured to restore, as to their rightful heritage, such good and natural English words as have been long time out of use and almost clear disherited; which is the only cause that our mother tongue (which truly of itself is both full enough for prose and stately enough for verse) hath long time been counted most bare and barren of both. Which default, whenas some endeavoured to salve and recure, they patched up the holes with pieces and rags of other languages – borrowing here of the French, there of the Italian, everywhere of the Latin – not weighing how ill those tongues accord with themselves, but much worse with ours. So now they have made our English tongue a gallimaufry or hodge-podge of all other speeches. Other some (no so well seem in the English tongue as perhaps in other languages), if they happen to hear an old word, albeit very natural and significant, cry out straightway that we speak no English, but gibberish – or, rather, such as (in old time) Evander's mother spake: whose first shame is that they are not ashamed in their own mother tongue strangers to be counted and aliens.

The second shame no less than the first: that what so they understand not they straightway deem to be senseless and not at all to be understood (much like the mole in Aesop's fable that, being blind herself, would in no wise be persuaded that any beast could see).

Textual note

91. no so well seem] not so well seene (Q5). The original makes sense so it is retained here, though other editions (e.g., *Var.* and Yale) adopt Q5.

80. restore . . . heritage: the language of the Protestant reformation, which insisted on return to a lost purity: King 1982.
90. gallimaufry: confused jumble (*OED* dates its first instance 1551–6).
90–1. hodge-podge: messy mixture.
91. no . . . seem: not seemly (i.e., conversant) enough.
92. if they: I follow Q3; Q1 reads *if the*; Q2 *if then*.
95. Evander's mother: Evander had emigrated to Italy (Latium) from Arcadia (*Aeneid*, 8. 51–4); in Aulius Gellius, *Noctes Atticae*, 1. 10. 2 a philosopher rebukes a young man for affecting archaic language 'as if [he] were talking today to Evander's mother'; but allusions in the General Argument indicate that E.K. recalls Macrobius, *Saturnalia*, 1. 5. 1. The argument of E.K.'s whole paragraph is a commonplace of humanist nationalist discourse: cf. Joachim Du Bellay, *Défense et Illustration de la langue française* (1549).
100. mole . . . fable: misremembering Aesop's fable 326 (The Mole and its Mother): Chambry 1967: 142.

The last, more shameful than both, that, of their own country and natural speech (which, together with their nurses' milk, they sucked) they have so base regard and bastard judgement that they will not only themselves not labour to garnish and beautify it, but also repine that of other it should be embellished: like to the dog in the manger that himself can eat no hay and yet barketh at the hungry bullock that so fain would feed; whose currish kind, though cannot be kept from barking, yet I con them thank that they refrain from biting.

Now for the knitting of sentences (which they call the joints and members thereof) and for all the compass of the speech: it is round without roughness, and learned without hardness; such, indeed, as may be perceived of the least, understood of the most, but judged only of the learned. For what in most English writers useth to be loose and, as it were, ungirt, in this author is well grounded, finely framed, and strongly trussed up together. In regard whereof I scorn and spew out the rakehelly rout of our ragged rhymers (for so themselves use to hunt the letter) which without learning boast, without judgement jangle, without reason rage and foam, as if some instinct of poetical spirit had newly ravished them above the meanness of common capacity and, being in the middest of all their bravery, suddenly (either for want of matter, or of rhyme, or having forgotten their former conceit) they seem to be so pained and travailed in their remembrance, as it were a woman in childbirth, or as that same Pythia when the trance came upon her:

Os rabidum fera corda domans, etc.

Natheless, let them a God's name feed on their own folly, so they seek not to darken the beams of others' glory. As for Colin,

---

107–8. dog in the manger: proverbial: Smith 1970: 82, #192.
110. con . . . thank: thank.
113. members: limbs. *compass*: measure, proportion.
116. useth to be: is customarily.
117. ungirt: not drawn together (*OED*'s first instance of this sense: ungirt *ppl a*, 2b).
119. rakehelly: utterly debauched (distinguished by Elizabethans from the weaker 'rascal').
120. hunt the letter: alliterate: cf. Sidney, *Defence* (ed. cit., note to ll. 28–30 above), p. 117, condemning poets' 'coursing of a letter, as if they were bound to follow the method of a dictionary'.
125. conceit: idea.
128. Os . . . domans: 'governing her raving mouth and wild heart': Virgil, *Aeneid*, 6. 80, the Cumaean Sibyl prophesying to Aeneas (*Pythia* from *Pytho*, the old Greek name for Delphi, site of the sun god Apollo's main oracle; she was an Apollonian sibyl).

under whose person the author self is shadowed, how far he is
from such vaunted titles and glorious shows both himself
showeth where he saith:

Of Muses, Hobbin, I con no skill, and:
*Enough is me to paint out my unrest,*etc. 135

And also appeareth by the baseness of the name, wherein (it
seemeth) he chose rather to unfold great matter of argument
covertly than professing it, not suffice thereto accordingly: which
moved him rather in eglogues than otherwise to write, doubting
perhaps his ability (which he little needed); or minding to furnish 140
our tongue with this kind, wherein it faulteth; or following the
example of the best and most ancient poets which devised this kind
of writing, being both so base for the matter and homely for the
manner, at the first to try their abilities – and as young birds, that
be newly crept out of the nest, by little first to prove their tender 145
wings before they make a greater flight. So flew Theocritus (as you
may perceive, he was already full-fledged). So flew Virgil, as not
yet well feeling his wings. So flew Mantuan, as being not full
summed. So Petrarch; so Boccaccio; so Marot, Sannazaro, and also
divers other excellent both Italian and French poets whose footing 150
this author everywhere followeth, yet so as few (but they be well
scented) can trace him out. So, finally, flieth this our new poet, as a

134–5. Of Muses . . . unrest: *June*, 65, 79.
137–8. argument covertly: cf. Puttenham (1589) 1. 18: '[it is the function of
eclogues] under the veil of homely persons, and in rude [rustic, untutored]
speeches to insinuate and glance at greater matters, and such as perchance had
not been safe to have been disclosed in any other sort'.
138. suffice: sufficient.
141. faulteth: lacks.
146–9. Theocritus . . . Sannazaro: Theocritus (third century B.C. Greek poet)
originated the eclogue as a literary genre with his 30 *Idylls*; he was imitated by
Virgil in his *Eclogues*, understood in the Renaissance to be pastoral pieces pre-
liminary to the agricultural/political *Georgics* and the epic *Aeneid* which
nevertheless concealed political coding; Battista Spagnoli (1448–1516), named
Mantuan after his birthplace, published eight of his ten often satirical eclogues
in 1498; Francesco Petrarca's (Petrarch's) (1304–74) twelve largely politically-
allegorical Latin eclogues were frequently reprinted; Giovanni Boccaccio
(*c*. 1313–75), like his friend Petrarch a humanist scholar, included sixteen alle-
gorical Latin eclogues in his considerable literary output; Clément Marot
(1496–1544) produced four eclogues in the vernacular, the two most important
of which are imitated in *November* and *December*; and Jacopo Sannazaro
(1456–1530) had a fundamental influence on Renaissance pastoral through his
prose and verse romance *Arcadia* and his Latin piscatory eclogues.
148–9. full summed: with plumage fully grown.

bird whose principals be scarce grown out, but yet as that in time shall be able to keep wing with the best.

Now, as touching the general drift and purpose of his eglogues, I mind not to say much, himself labouring to conceal it. Only this appeareth: that his unstaid youth had long wandered in the common labyrinth of love, in which time to mitigate and allay the heat of his passion, or else to warn – as he saith – the young shepherds (*scilicet* his equals and companions) of his unfortunate folly, he compiled these twelve eglogues which, for that they be proportioned to the state of the twelve months, he termeth the *Shepherds' Calendar*, applying an old name to a new work.

Hereunto have I added a certain gloss or scholion for the exposition of old words and harder phrases, which manner of glossing and commenting, well I wote, will seem strange and rare in our tongue. Yet for so much as I knew many excellent and proper devices, both in words and matter, would pass in the speedy course of reading (either as unknown, or as not marked), and that in this kind, as in other, we might be equal to the learned of other nations, I thought good to take the pains upon me (the rather for that, by means of some familiar acquaintance, I was made privy to his counsel and secret meaning in them, as also in sundry other works of his). Which, albeit I know he nothing so much hateth as to promulgate, yet thus much have I adventured upon his friendship (himself being for long time far estranged), hoping that this will the rather occasion him to put forth divers other excellent works of his which sleep in silence, as his *Dreams*, his *Legends*, his *Court of Cupid*, and sundry others, whose commendations to set out were very vain, the things (though worthy of many) yet being known to few.

These my present pains, if to any they be pleasurable or profitable, be you judge, mine own good Master Harvey, to whom I

---

153. *principals*: the main feathers in each wing.
157. *unstaid*: (1) undecided; (2) unregulated.
160. *scilicet*: namely.
163. *old name*: *The Calendar of Shepherds* (a translation of the French almanac *Le Compote et Calendrier des bergers* (1493)) was reprinted at least seven times between 1503 and 1559: Capp, B. 1979 *English Almanacs 1500 1800*, Cornell University Press, Ithaca.
166. *wote*: know.
167. *proper*: admirable.
168. *devices*: (1) things artistically devised; (2) intentions.
169. *marked*: noticed.
176. *estranged*: absent from his normal abode.
178. *Dreams . . . Cupid*: lost (or maybe merely projected) works: Oruch in *SpE*, pp 737–8. For the *Dreams* see also *November* 195 gloss. The list implies a parallel with Chaucer, whose apocryphal works included, in the sixteenth century, *Chaucer's Dream*, the legend *The Judgement of Paris* and *The Court of Cupid*.

have, both in respect of your worthiness generally and otherwise upon some particular and special considerations, vowed this my labour and the maidenhead of this our common friend's poetry, himself having already in the beginning dedicated it to the noble and worthy gentleman, the right worshipful Master Philip Sidney, a special favourer and maintainer of all kind of learning. Whose cause I pray you, sir, if Envy shall stir up any wrongful accusation, defend with your mighty rhetoric and other your rare gifts of learning (as you can), and shield with your good will (as you ought), against the malice and outrage of so many enemies as I know will be set on fire with the sparks of his kindled glory. And thus recommending the author unto you as unto his most special good friend, and myself unto you both (as one making singular account of two so very good and so choice friends), I bid you both most heartily farewell, and commit you and your most commendable studies to the tuition of the greatest.

*Your own assuredly to
be commanded* E.K.

Postscript
Now I trust, Master Harvey, that upon sight of your special friend's and fellow-poet's doings, or else for envy of so many unworthy *quidams* (which catch at the garland which to you alone is due), you will be persuaded to pluck out of the hateful darkness those so many excellent English poems of yours which lie hid, and bring them forth to eternal light. Trust me, you do both them great wrong in depriving them of the desired sun, and also yourself, in smothering your deserved praises, and all men generally, in withholding from them so divine pleasures which they might conceive of your gallant English verses, as they have already done of your Latin poems – which, in my opinion, both for invention and elocution, are very delicate and super-excellent. And thus again I take my leave of my good Master Harvey. From my lodging at London this 10 of April 1579.

---

189. can: know how.
203. quidams: certain people, nonentities.
205. those . . . English poems: unpublished.
211. your Latin poems: see *September* 176 gloss.

The General Argument of the Whole Book

Little, I hope, needeth me at large to discourse the first original of eglogues, having already touched the same. But, for the word *eglogues* (I know) is unknown to most, and also mistaken of some the best learned (as they think), I will say somewhat thereof, being not at all impertinent to my present purpose.

They were first of the Greeks (the inventors of them) called *aeglogai*, as it were *aigon* or *aigonomon logoi*, that is, goatherds' tales. For although in Virgil and others the speakers be most shepherds and goatherds, yet Theocritus (in whom is more ground of authority than in Virgil, this specially from that deriving, as from the first head and well-spring, the whole invention of his eglogues) maketh goatherds the persons and authors of his tales. This being, who seeth not the grossness of such as, by colour of learning, would make us believe that they are more rightly termed *eclogai* (as they would say): extraordinary discourses of unnecessary matter (which definition, albe in substance and meaning it agree with the nature of the thing, yet no whit answereth with the *analysis* and interpretation of the

Textual note

8–9. most shepherds and goatherds] more shepheards, then Goteheards (Q5). Again, editors usually prefer Q5; Q1 is retained here because it, too, makes excellent sense (most = mostly).

7. aeglogai: the etymological discussion is a commonplace of Renaissance critical theory. An early *Life* of Virgil offered the incorrect *aix* = goat etymology, as did Petrarch (Mustard 1919: 195). *Aigos* = pen (here, for goats); *aigonomon* = place where goats graze; *logoi* = words, utterances (Q1 prints all three words in Greek; they were anglicised in subsequent quartos). The correct etymon (which E.K., along with other theorists, dismisses) is Greek *eklogē* = selection (alternative names are *bucolic* and *idyll*).
8. most: mostly. See Textual note.
9. Theocritus: Dedicatory Epistle, p. 23n.
13. grossness: stupidity.
14. colour: pretence.
16. albe: although.
18. analysis: printed in Greek; apparently the first recorded instance of its use in English (*OED* analysis 1b).

word). For they be not termed *eclogues* but *eglogues*: which sentence this author very well observing, upon good judgement (though indeed few goatherds have to do herein), natheless doubteth not to call them by the used and best-known name. Other curious discourses hereof I reserve to greater occasion.

These twelve eglogues, everywhere answering to the seasons of the twelve months, may be well divided into three forms or ranks: for either they be *plaintive* (as the first, the sixth, the eleventh, and the twelfth), or *recreative* (such as all those be which conceive matter of love or commendation of special personages), or *moral*, which for the most part be mixed with some satirical bitterness (namely the second, of reverence due to old age; the fifth, of coloured deceit; the seventh and ninth, of dissolute shepherds and pastors; the tenth, of contempt of poetry and pleasant wits). And to this division may everything herein be reasonably applied, a few only except, whose special purpose and meaning I am not privy to. And thus much generally of these twelve eglogues.

Now will we speak particularly of all, and first of the first, which he calleth by the first month's name, January: wherein to some he may seem foully to have faulted in that he erroneously beginneth with that month which beginneth not the year. For it is well known, and stoutly maintained with strong reasons of the learned, that the year beginneth in March: for then the sun reneweth his finished course and the seasonable spring refresheth the earth, and the pleasance thereof being buried in the sadness of the dead winter now worn away, reliveth. This opinion maintain the old astrologers and philosophers, namely the reverend Andalo, and Macrobius in his *Holidays of Saturn* – which account also was generally observed both of Grecians and Romans.

But, saving the leave of such learned heads, we maintain a custom of counting the seasons from the month January, upon a more special cause than the heathen philosophers ever could conceive: that is, for the incarnation of our mighty saviour and eternal redeemer, the Lord Christ, who, as then renewing the

22. *best-known name*: 'the pastoral poesy, which we commonly call by the name of *Eglogue*': Puttenham (1589) 1. 18.
25. *three . . . ranks*: perhaps hinting at a hierarchy based on Renaissance tripartite schemes culminating in divine wisdom: Johnson 1990: 38–47.
39. *month . . . year*: see *SC* General headnote.
42. *seasonable*: (1) opportune; (2) suitable for the time of year.
43. *pleasance*: pleasantness, with overtones of *OED* sense 5, pleasure garden.
46. *Andalo . . . Saturn*: Andalo di Negro instructed Boccaccio (Dedicatory Epistle, p. 23n) in astronomy; the fifth-century polymath Ambrosius Aurelius Theodosius Macrobius's influential series of dialogues *Saturnalia* begins with an account of the festivals of Janus and Saturn and of the Roman calendar.

state of the decayed world and returning the compass of expired
years to their former date and first commencement, left to us his
heirs a memorial of his birth in the end of the last year and the   55
beginning of the next; which reckoning, beside that eternal mon-
ument of our salvation, leaneth also upon good proof of special
judgement. For, albeit that in elder times (when as yet the count
of the year was not perfected, as afterward it was by Julius
Caesar) they began to tell the months from March's beginning,   60
and according to the same God (as is said in scripture) com-
manded the people of the Jews to count the month Abib (that
which we call March) for the first month in remembrance that in
that month he brought them out of the land of Egypt: yet,
according to tradition of latter times, it hath been otherwise   65
observed, both in government of the church and rule of mightiest
realms. For from Julius Caesar (who first observed the leap year,
which he called *bissextilem annum*, and brought into a more cer-
tain course the odd wandering days which of the Greeks were
called *hyperbainontes*, of the Romans *intercalares* (for in such mat-   70
ter of learning I am forced to use the terms of the learned)) the
months have been numbered twelve which, in the first ordinance
of Romulus, were but ten, counting but 304 days in every year
and beginning with March. But Numa Pompilius, who was the
father of all the Roman ceremonies and religion, seeing that reck-   75
oning to agree neither with the course of the sun nor of the
moon, thereunto added two months, January and February,
wherein it seemeth that wise king minded upon good reason to

62. *Abib*: means corn-spike; the first month of the Jewish ecclesiastical, and
the seventh of the civil, year, hence equivalent to March (since the civil year
begins in September); later called Nisan. E.K. alludes to Exodus 12 and 13 on
the liberation from the Egyptian bondage and the institution of the Passover.
Cf. 13: 4: 'This day come ye out in the month of Abib' (Geneva gloss:
'Containing part of March and part of April, when corn began to ripe in that
country'), and the gloss on Exodus 12: 2 ('This month shall be unto you the
beginning of months: it shall be to you the first month of the year'): 'Called
Nisan, containing part of March, and part of April'.
68–70. bissextilem . . . intercalares: Latin *bis-sextus* = twice six; so called
because the *intercalary* day in the *bissextile* (or leap year) was inserted immedi-
ately before the last five days of February, thus doubling the sixth day before
the Calends of March: Macrobius, *Saturnalia*, 1. 13. 15, 1. 14. 6.
Hyperbainontes: Macrobius, 1. 13. 10.
73–4. *Romulus . . . Numa Pompilius*: Macrobius, 1. 12 for Romulus, whom
Numa followed as second king of Rome: he instituted the month Januarius
(named after the ancient god of entrances and beginnings, two-faced Janus:
Macrobius, 1. 9 and 1. 13). See *ibid*. 1. 12. 3–5 for the 304-day year beginning
in March.

begin the year at January, of him therefore so called *tanquam Janua anni* (the gate and entrance of the year) or of the name of the god Janus, to which god (for that the old paynims attributed the birth and beginning of all creatures new coming into the world) it seemeth that he therefore to him assigned the beginning and first entrance of the year. Which account, for the most part, hath hitherto continued, notwithstanding that the Egyptians begin their year in September for that (according to the opinion of the best rabbins and very purpose of the scripture itself) God made the world in that month, that is called of them Tisri, and therefore he commanded them to keep the feast of pavilions in the end of the year, in the fifteenth day of the seventh month which, before that time, was the first.

But our author, respecting neither the subtlety of the one part nor the antiquity of the other, thinketh it fittest, according to the simplicity of common understanding, to begin with January (weening it, perhaps, no decorum that shepherd should be seen in matter of so deep insight, or canvass a case of so doubtful judgement). So, therefore, beginneth he, and so continueth he throughout.

79-80. tanquam . . . anni: as it were, the gate of the year (probably echoing Macrobius 1. 13. 3: *tanquam bicipitis Dei mense, respicientem ac prospicientem transacti anni finem, futurusque* ('as the month of the two-faced god who looks back to the past year and forward to the beginnings of the one to come')).
81. paynims: pagans.
87. rabbins: rabbis.
89. Tisri: the Babylonian name for the first month of the Jewish civil year.
89-90. feast of pavilions: (or tabernacles): Leviticus 23: 34: 'Speak unto the children of Israel, and say, In the fifteenth day of this seventh month, shall be for seven days the feast of Tabernacles unto the Lord' (cf. Numbers 29: 12).
95. weening: believing, supposing.
95. seen: versed (in an art or science): *OED* seen *ppl a* 2.

January

A love complaint uttered by Colin containing Petrarchan elements and based on Virgil's *Eclogue* 2 and Thomas Sackville's *Induction* to *A Mirror for Magistrates* (1563): see l. 19n. The soliloquy is answered by *December*, which shares *January*'s stanza form. (Used also in *The Tears of the Muses* (in *Complaints* (1591), the six-line stanza rhyming ababcc, each line with a stately iambic pentameter beat, is found in the work of other poets of the period. (The iambic foot consists of an unstressed followed by a stressed syllable.) Examples from Sidney include 'You living powers' and 'Over these brooks' from *Arcadia*, Book 2, both of which, incidentally, conform to C. H. Herford's characterisation of the stanza as suitable for 'impassioned monologue': cit. *Var* 1. 638. A variant is used in *August*.) Colin's name – as E.K.'s opening gloss implies – contains clues to the eclogue's covert meaning. In deriving from Skelton it encodes a populist anti-prelatical message; in deriving also from Clément Marot it is more teasing. As a Protestant exile (and pastoral poet) whose psalm translations were endorsed by Calvin, Marot is invoked to support *SC*'s Protestant stance (Patterson 1988: 106–18; for a different view see Prescott 1978: 15–17). But the fact that Spenser's Colin is a *lover* with a French name may possibly suggest an allusion to the queen's proposed marriage to the French Catholic Duc d'Alençon (see also *March* headnote and emblem n): proposals that Elizabeth should marry him were originally mooted in 1572, but developed in intensity in 1578 when he offered to aid the Dutch in their revolt against Spain, thus opening up the possibility of an Anglo-French alliance against Spain which marriage might make a certainty. Colin fails with Rosalind as Spenser, Sidney, Leicester, Walsingham and many others – including preachers and ballad-writers – hoped that Alençon would fail with Elizabeth (and note that Marot's *Eglogue* . . . *de ma Dame Louise de Savoye* introduces its Colin as *Colin d'Anjou*: François, Duc d'Alençon, assumed his elder brother Henri's title of Duc d'Anjou in 1576. See Neale (1934) ch 15; McLane 1961: 13–26.) This riddling allegorical doubleness accords with the symbolism of January's deity, twin-headed Janus (General Argument, pp. 28–9nn), patron of mysteries and secrets (Wind 1967: 230–1).

The woodcut (fig. 1) derives from the illustration for *Eclogue* 1 in S stian Brant's edition of Virgil's *Opera* (1502 and often reprinted) via th .mpler woodcut in Guillaume Michel's edition of Virgil, *Oeuvres* (Paris 1540): Colin's stance is that of Brant's/Michel's Meliboeus, Virgil's exiled goatherd; the entwined trees echo the leafy beech (symbol of royal patronage) under which Tityrus rests; the buildings to the left recall Brant's/Michel's distant Rome. In the *SC* woodcut the trees, embracing and barren, divide the picture, separating a disaffected Colin/Meliboeus, spokesman of the people, from a city which, it may be, he perceives as containing a queen about to make a marriage choice hostile to the people's interest. At the trees' feet lies Colin's broken bagpipe, emblem of his (or courtly patronage's) rejection of poetry (*January*, 72). The instrument, common to both English and French pastoral traditions, was also an emblem of lust (Winternitz, E. 1967 *Musical Instruments and their Symbolism in Western Art*, Faber and Faber, London, ch. 4). On an alternative and less obscure reading Colin, the aspiring Virgilian poet, turns his back on pastoral (the shepherd's hut) to gaze at Rome, symbol of epic achievement: Luborsky 1981: 29. See also Luborsky 1980: 29–68; Smith B. R. 1980; Patterson 1988: 121–4.

January
Aegloga prima

Argument

In this first eglogue, Colin Clout, a shepherd's boy, complaineth him of his unfortunate love, being but newly (as seemeth) enamoured of a country lass called Rosalind; with which strong affection being very sore travailed, he compareth his care-full case to the sad season of the year, to the frosty ground, to the frozen trees, and to his own winter-beaten flock. And lastly, finding himself robbed of all former pleasance and delights, he breaketh his pipe in pieces and casteth himself to the ground.

Colin Clout

A shepherd's boy (no better do him call),
When Winter's waste-full spite was almost spent,
All in a sunshine day (as did befall)
Led forth his flock that had been long ypent.
So faint they woxe and feeble in the fold   5
That now uneaths their feet could them uphold.

All as the sheep, such was the shepherd's look,
For pale and wan he was (alas the while):
May seem he loved, or else some care he took
(Well couth he tune his pipe and frame his style).   10
Tho to a hill his fainting flock he led,
And thus him plained the while his sheep there fed:

Argument: *Colin Clout*: E.K.; *Rosalind*: E.K., 60 gloss; *care-full*: full of grief or care.
2. *waste-full*: causing desolation. Cf. *June* 50n.
4. *ypent*: penned; cf. *July* 216n, *April* 155 and *October* 72 glosses.
5. *woxe*: waxed (grew): a contemporary form.
6. *uneaths*: E.K.
9. *care*: sorrow; *took*: suffered (*OED* take *v* VI. 34b).
10. *couth*: E.K. *frame* . . . *style*: (1) articulate his discourse; (2) direct his pen: *OED* style *sb* I. 1, II. 13 and Curtius 1967: 313–14. Cf. Epilogue 9n.
11. *Tho*: then (not archaic). *fainting*: sluggish, feeble.
12. *plained*: lamented (note the paronomasia [61 gloss] *hill/plain*).

Ye gods of love that pity lovers' pain
(If any gods the pain of lovers pity),
Look from above, where you in joys remain,   15
And bow your ears unto my doleful ditty:
And Pan, thou shepherds' god, that once didst love,
Pity the pains that thou thyself didst prove.

Thou, barren ground (whom Winter's wrath hath wasted),
Art made a mirror to behold my plight: 20
Whilom thy fresh spring flowered, and after hasted
Thy summer proud with daffadillies dight;
And now is come thy winter's stormy state,
Thy mantle marred wherein thou masked'st late.

Such rage as Winter's rageth in my heart,   25
My life-blood freezing with unkindly cold:
Such stormy stours do breed my baleful smart
As if my year were waste and woxen old.

13–14. pity . . . pity: rhetorical figure of chiasmus (inversion of word order in succeeding clause, etc.).
17. Pan: half goat, half man, son of Mercury (god of eloquence, grammar, sheep, music, etc.) and Penelope, wife of Odysseus. Named from Greek *paein* = to pasture, later understood as derived from *pan* = everything. His frustrated passion for Syrinx led to his invention of the shepherd's pipe (*April* 50 gloss). God of woods, shepherds and music: Virgil, *Eclogues*, 2. 31–3. His invocation is appropriate to *January* since his alternative name, Inuus (from Latin *ineo* = enter, begin) equates him with Janus: Macrobius, *Saturnalia*, 1. 22. 2.
18. prove: suffer; learn of by experience.
19. Thou . . . wasted: Bush 1932: 62n compares Sackville's *Induction*, 1, 5, 13, 16–17 with *January*, 19, 24, 31, 35. The allusions to Sackville's wintry landscape, prelude to the narrator's encounter with Sorrow and his entry into the underworld, are an index of Colin's melancholy and serve the more public function of reminding the reader that, just as the *Induction* prefaces a series of cautionary tales on the falls of those in power, *SC* too is in part a 'mirror' for its particular magistrate, Elizabeth. Renwick 1930: 178–9 compares Petrarch, *Rime*, 66 (about winter and the lover's melancholy).
21. Whilom: *August* 8 and *October* 4 glosses.
22. daffadillies: not *daffodil* (a spring flower) but *white* or *yellow asphodel*, the leaves of which provide sheep fodder (for the Elizabethan confusion of the forms *affodil(ly)/daffodil(ly)* see *OED* asphodel 1a; affodill; daffodilly). *dight*: *April* 29 gloss.
24. masked'st: concealed, hinting at masquerade revels.
26. unkindly: (1) unnatural; (2) hurtful.
27. stormy stours: *January* 51 gloss and *May* 156. *baleful smart*: painful suffering (first and only *OED* instance of *baleful* in this sense since *c*. 1200).

And yet, alas, but now my spring begun,
And yet, alas, it is already done.   30

You naked trees (whose shady leaves are lost),
Wherein the birds were wont to build their bower,
And now are clothed with moss and hoary frost
Instead of blooms, wherewith your buds did flower:
I see your tears that from your boughs do rain,   35
Whose drops in dreary icicles remain.

All so my lustful leaf is dry and sere,
My timely buds with wailing all are wasted:
The blossom which my branch of youth did bear
With breathed sighs is blown away and blasted,   40
And from mine eyes the drizzling tears descend
As, on your boughs, the icicles depend.

Thou feeble flock (whose fleece is rough and rent,
Whose knees are weak through fast and evil fare),
Mayest witness well by thy ill government   45
Thy master's mind is overcome with care:
Thou weak, I wan; thou lean, I quite forlorn;
With mourning pine I, thou with pining mourn.

A thousand sithes I curse that care-full hour
Wherein I longed the neighbour town to see,   50
And eke ten thousand sithes I bless the stour
Wherein I saw so fair a sight as she.
Yet all for nought: such sight hath bred my bane.
Ah, God, that love should breed both joy and pain!

29. *spring*: youth.
31–4. *You . . . flower*: common analogy: *Var* 1. 249.
34. *blooms*: the original spelling *bloosmes* also conveys the idea of *blossom* as a mass of flowers: *OED* blossom *sb* 1b.
37. *sere*: E.K.
42. *depend*: hang down (second *OED* instance; first dated *c*. 1510: depend *v* 1, 1).
44. *Whose . . . fast*: Psalms 109: 24: 'My knees are weak through fasting, and my flesh hath lost all fatness' (Geneva gloss: 'For hunger, that came of sorrow . . . '). In Petrarchising vein Colin identifies religious with secular emotions. *evil*: unwholesome (*OED* evil *a* and *sb* A II. 7a).
48. *mourning . . . mourn*: chiasmus again. *pine*: waste from grief. Cf. *August*, 18.
49. *sithes*: E.K.
50. *neighbour town*: E.K.
51. *stour*: E.K.
53. *bane*: (1) woe; (2) ruin.

It is not Hobbinol wherefore I plain, 55
Albe my love he seek with daily suit:
His clownish gifts and court'sies I disdain,
His kids, his cracknels and his early fruit.
Ah, foolish Hobbinol, thy gifts bene vain:
Colin them gives to Rosalind again. 60

I love thilk lass (alas, why do I love?),
And am forlorn (alas, why am I lorn?).
She deigns not my goodwill but doth reprove,
And of my rural music holdeth scorn:
Shepherd's device she hateth as the snake, 65
And laughs the songs that Colin Clout doth make.

Wherefore, my pipe, albe rude Pan thou please
(Yet for thou pleasest not where most I would),
And thou, unlucky Muse, that wont'st to ease
My musing mind (yet canst not when thou should), 70
Both pipe and Muse shall sore the while aby:
So broke his oaten pipe, and down did lie.

---

55. Hobbinol: Gabriel Harvey. See E.K.
57. His . . . gifts: E.K. *clownish*: rustic (*OED* first citation 1570). *court'sies*: (1) courteous acts; (2) (gifts in) moderate quantities: *OED* curtsy *sb* 4.
58. cracknels: thin crisp biscuits of hollow shape.
59. bene: are; mediaeval (Chaucerian) or possibly midland dialect form: *OED* be *v* A I. 1, 1–3 plural, b.
60. Colin . . . again: parodic disruption of the triple rhythm of giving and receiving operated by the three Graces: Johnson 1990: 169–70. Answered at *April*, 109. *Rosalind*: E.K.
61. I love: E.K. *thilk*: *May* 1 gloss.
62. lorn: *September* 57 gloss.
63. deigns not: does not graciously accept: *OED* deign *v* 2b.
65. device: (1) (poetic) structure; (2) desire; (3) talk; (4) motto or emblem (with a glance at Colin's affirmation of hope in *Anchôra speme*). *hateth . . . snake*: cf. *FQ*, 1. 2. 9 and Horace, *Odes*, 1. 8. 9 (one of the effects of love on Sybaris is that he shuns wrestling oil more warily than viper's blood).
71. sore . . . aby: dearly pay the penalty.
72. broke . . . pipe: cf. *April*, 3, 15, *November*, 71 and contrast with *December*, 141.

By that the welked Phoebus 'gan avail
His weary wain, and now the frosty Night
Her mantle black through heaven 'gan overhale: 75
Which seen, the pensive boy, half in despite,
Arose, and homeward drove his sunned sheep
Whose hanging heads did seem his care-full case to weep.

Colin's emblem:
Anchôra speme.

GLOSS

Colin Clout) is a name not greatly used, and yet have I seen a poesy of Master Skelton's under that title [John Skelton's attack on church corruption, *Colin Clout* (1521–2?). See Scattergood J. (ed.) 1983 *Skelton: Complete Poems.* Penguin, Harmondsworth, p. 466 on the derivation of *Colin* from Latin *colonus* (husbandman) and *clout* as 'rag' or 'patch'; also King 1982: 254–61 for Skelton's significance as a native poet and supposed prophet of the Protestant Reformation]. But, indeed, the word *Colin* is French, and used of the French poet, Marot (if he be worthy of the name of a poet) in a certain eglogue [*Eglogue . . . de ma Dame Louise de Savoye*: see *November* headnote; E.K. follows Du Bellay's dismissal of Marot in the *Défense* (Dedicatory Epistle, p. 21n) as antiquated and unlearned, thus deflecting attention from his Protestantism and glancing ironically at Spenser's own poetic programme], under which name this poet secretly shadoweth himself (as sometime did Virgil under the name of Tityrus [Dedicatory Epistle, p. 18n]), thinking it much fitter than such Latin names, for the great unlikelihood of the language [i.e., French suits the English pastoral and its setting better than Latin].
6] **uneaths**) scarcely [not archaic, though *uneath* was arguably more common].
10] **couth**) cometh of the verb *con*, that is, to know or to have skill [*OED* can *v* 1 II. 3; archaic]: as well interpreteth the same the worthy Sir Thomas Smith in his book of government, whereof I have a perfect copy in writing lent me by his kinsman, and my very singular good friend, Master Gabriel Harvey, as also of

73–5. *By . . . overhale*: common closing topos of eclogues: Virgil, *Eclogues*, 1. 83; 2. 67; 6. 85–6, etc.; Curtius 1967: 90–1. *welked* = waned, diminished in brightness (cf. *November* 13 gloss).
73–4. *Phoebus . . . wain*: for the chariot of the sun god see, e.g., Ovid, *Metamorphoses*, 2. 107–77, etc.
73. *avail*: E.K.
74–5. *Night . . . overhale*: for Night's mantle, see Ripa 1603: 360–3.
75. *overhale*: E.K.
Anchôra speme: Italian *ancóra* (still) + *speme* (hope), punning on *àncora* = anchor, emblem of religious hope: 'Which hope we have, as an anchor of the soul' (Hebrews 6: 19). An anchor accompanied by the Latin motto *anchora spei* (anchor of hope) was also a familiar printer's device (it would be used by William Ponsonby on the title pages of the *Four Hymns* and of the 1596 *FQ*); so that Spenser/Colin here reinforces his public role as poet by signifying his intention to publish. See also E.K.

some other his most grave and excellent writings [Sir Thomas Smith, *De republica Anglorum*, 1. 19, published 1581 and so only available to E.K. in manuscript. Quoted by Renwick 1930: 180–1.].

37] **sere**) withered [not archaic].

49] **sithe**) time [archaic but not uncommon. Spenser also puns on *sithe* = sigh.]

50] **neighbour town**) the next town [i.e., farm or village: *OED* town *sb* 1–3]: expressing the Latin *vicina* [a current adjectival use, though this is *OED*'s first citation in this precise sense: neighbour *sb* 4b and *June*, 52 below].

51] **stour**) a fit [misleading: usually meant conflict, but archaic in sixteenth century; Spenser reintroduced it to mean time of turmoil: *OED* stour *sb* 1, 3].

55] **Hobbinol**) is a feigned country name whereby (it being so common and usual) seemeth to be hidden the person of some his very special and most familiar friend, whom he entirely and extraordinarily beloved, as peradventure shall be more largely declared hereafter [Gabriel Harvey: *September* 176 gloss; the name derives from *hob* = rustic + *noll* = head (*OED* hobbinoll); note also *hoball* = clown, idiot (first citation 1553)]. In this place seemeth to be some savour of disorderly love, which the learned call *paederastikē* [love of boys: Greek *pais* (boy) + *erastes* (lover): see Theocritus, *Idyll* 23 and Virgil, *Eclogue* 2. *OED* cites Gabriel Harvey's use of the word in 1593]: but it is gathered beside [i.e., is above and beyond] his meaning. For who that hath read Plato his dialogue called *Alcibiades* [1. 130E–131D], Xenophon [*Symposium*, 8. 6–43] and Maximus Tyrius [*Dissertationes*, 21. 8H] of Socrates' opinions may easily perceive that such love is much to be allowed and liked of, specially so meant as Socrates used it – who sayeth that indeed he loved Alcibiades extremely, yet not Alcibiades' person but his soul, which is Alcibiades' own self. And so is *paederastikē* much to be preferred before *gynerastikē* (that is, the love which enflameth men with lust toward womankind): but yet let no man think that herein I stand with Lucian [Syrian–Greek, second century A.D.] or his devilish disciple Unico Aretino [i.e., Pietro Aretino (1492–1556), infamous for his erotic verses *Sonnetti lussuriosi*] in defence of execrable and horrible sins of forbidden and unlawful fleshliness, whose abominable error is fully confuted of Perionius and others [Joachim Perion (d. 1559) had opposed Aretino in his *In Petrum Aretinum Oratio* of 1551].

57] **His clownish gifts**) imitateth Virgil's verse, *Rusticus es, Corydon, nec munera curat Alexis* ['You are a clown, Corydon, and Alexis does not care for your gifts': *Eclogues*, 2. 56].

60] **Rosalind**) is also a feigned name which, being well ordered, will bewray [disclose] the very name of his love and mistress whom by that name he coloureth [disguises; on Rosalind see *April* 26 gloss]: so as Ovid shadoweth his love under the name of Corinna [*Amores*, 1. 5, 11; 2. 12, 13, 17; *Tristia*, 4. 10. 60, etc.], which of some is supposed to be Julia, the emperor Augustus his daughter, and wife to Agrippa [married M. Vipsanius Agrippa 23 B.C.; after his death married Tiberius. Noted for her wit and sexual promiscuity]; so doth Aruntius Stella everywhere call his lady *Asteris* [Star] and *Ianthis* [Violet], albe it is well known that her right name was Violantilla, as witnesseth Statius in his *Epithalamium* [*Epithalamium in Stellam et Violentillam* in *Silvae*, 1. 2, written to celebrate the marriage of Arruntius. His wife is named Asteris at ll. 197–8 and Martial names her Ianthis in *Epigrams*, 6. 21 and 7. 14]. And so the famous paragon of Italy, Madonna Celia, in her letters envelopeth herself under the name of Zima [prefatory note to *Lettre Amorose di Madonna Celia Gentildonna Romana* (1562)], and Petrona [unidentified] under the name of Bellochia. And this generally hath been a common custom of counterfeiting the names of secret personages.

61] **I love**) a pretty epanorthosis [the recalling and/or correction of a word] in these two verses, and withall a paranomasia, or playing with the word, where he sayeth 'I love thilk lass (alas . . .)', etc.

73] **avail**) bring down [archaic: cf. *February*, 8].

75] **overhale**) draw over [apparently a Spenserian neologism in this sense: *OED*].

Emblem.

His emblem (or poesy) is hereunder added in Italian: *anchôra speme*: the meaning whereof is, that notwithstanding his extreme passion and luckless love, yet, leaning on hope, he is somewhat recomforted [strengthened].

February

A pastoral debate on the youth/age topos, the ideal of which, classically and biblically, was wisdom in youth and/or an unscathed wise old age: Curtius 1967: 98–101. There are hints, too, of Ephesians 4: 22, 24 ('cast off . . . that old man . . . and put on the new man') interpreted as a conflict between the generations. But generational debate is also political disagreement, and so *February* focuses itself thematically in a religiously- and politically-coded quasi-Aesopic fable on corruption and envy within the Elizabethan court. Metrically, as well as in subject-matter, the eclogue anticipates the theological/ecclesiastical satirical eclogues *May*, *July* and *September* (in contrast to the smoothness of Colin's verse in *January*, *February*'s metre conveys the impression of rough and antiquated rusticity by juxtaposing iambs (see *January* headnote) and anapaests (two unstressed syllables followed by a stressed syllable) to give the impression of couplets in mediaeval four-beat (tetrameter) form). Linguistically, too, *February* shares with the theological eclogues a higher proportion of archaisms and (particularly northern) dialect words than appears in the other eclogues in order to emphasise its political meanings (see, e.g., *May* 18 and 224nn).

The woodcut (fig. 2) again alludes to the illustrations to Virgil's *Eclogue* 1 in the Brant/Michel editions (*January* headnote) which portrayed a woodcutter back centre (Patterson 1988: 95, 124): woodcutting is one of the traditional labours associated with February (Luborsky 1981: 21 and fig. 14). The tree presumably alludes to the oak in Thenot's fable of the Oak and the Briar and hence partakes of its complex symbolism (see *February* 103n), though its positioning back right as a symbolic complement to the church (back left, clearly signifying English Protestantism) may suggest that it represents Catholicism. In the foreground youthful Cuddy, right (in part perhaps representing the supporters of young, Catholic Alençon) is opposed by Thenot, left (named after Colin's interlocutor in Marot's *Eglogue . . . de ma Dame Louise de Savoye* and who thus again suggests the voice of Protestant wisdom: *January* headnote and *February* 25 gloss). The hands of the opponents almost touch in friendship, miming the embrace of *January*'s two trees and the entwined fish of February's zodiacal sign Pisces (top centre) which, as the sign marking the exaltation of Venus, signifies both loving accord and youthful lust (Richardson 1989: 165–6).

February
Aegloga secunda

Argument

This eglogue is rather moral and general than bent to any secret or particular purpose. It specially containeth a discourse of old age in the person of Thenot, an old shepherd, who, for his crookedness and unlustiness, is scorned of Cuddy, an unhappy herdsman's boy. The matter very well accordeth with the season of the month, the year now drooping and, as it were, drawing to his last age. For as in this time of year so then in our bodies there is a dry and withering cold which congealeth the cruddled blood and freezeth the weatherbeaten flesh with storms of Fortune and hoar frosts of Care. To which purpose the old man telleth a tale of the Oak and the Briar so lively and so feelingly as, if the thing were set forth in some picture before our eyes, more plainly could not appear.

                     Cuddy.   Thenot.
Ah, for pity! Will rank Winter's rage
These bitter blasts never 'gin to assuage?
The keen cold blows through my beaten hide
All as I were through the body gride;
My ragged runts all shiver and shake   5
As doen high towers in an earthquake:
They wont in the wind wag their wriggle-tails
Perk as a peacock, but now it avails.

                            Thenot.
Lewdly complainest thou, lazy lad,
Of Winter's wrack, for making thee sad.   10
Must not the world wend in his common course

Argument: *Thenot*: E.K., 25 gloss. *unlustiness*: lack of health and strength. *Cuddy*: abbreviation of Cuthbert: northern. *year . . . last age*: the vernal equinox occurs in the next month, March, the beginning of the legal year: see General Argument, and *SC* General headnote, p. 10. The equation of the four seasons of the year and the four ages of man was a commonplace. *cruddled*: i.e., curdled, congealed (with cold): a favourite word with Spenser, who always uses this form. *OED* curdled *ppl a* 1a, c offers it as a Spenserian neologism, ignoring this instance and citing *FQ* 1590 and *Astrophel* 1595.
2. *'gin*: begin; *gin* is Spenser's normal (and probably archaising) form in *SC*: *begin* was just current.
3. *keen*: E.K.
4. *gride*: E.K.
5. *runts*: E.K.
6. *doen*: archaic form (*OED* do *v* A 2d).
7. *wont . . . tails*: their habit was to shake their curly tails.
8. *perk*: brisk, lively (*OED*'s first citation of the word as an adjective). *avails*: lowers, drops (*January* 73 gloss): i.e., they have dropped the habit (with a pun on drooping tails).
9. *Lewdly*: foolishly (mediaevalism; last *OED* citation in this sense 1477).
10. *wrack*: E.K.
11–14. *world . . . fall*: for the commonplace of historical cyles, see, e.g., Hutton (1984) ch 6 and cf. *May*, 103–31. Here it has apocalyptic overtones: the world runs down before it reforms and renews politically and theologically.

From good to bad and from bad to worse,
From worse unto that is worst of all,
And then return to his former fall?
Who will not suffer the stormy time, 15
Where will he live till the lusty prime?
Self have I worn out thrice thretty years,
Some in much joy, many in many tears,
Yet never complained of cold nor heat,
Of Summer's flame, nor of Winter's threat; 20
Ne ever was to Fortune foeman,
But gently took that ungently came,
And ever my flock was my chief care:
Winter or Summer they mought well fare.

      Cuddy.
No marvel, Thenot, if thou can bear 25
Cheerfully the Winter's wrathful cheer,
For Age and Winter accord full nigh:
This chill, that cold, this crooked, that wry;
And as the louring weather looks down,

In such a time (signalled by the revolt of youth against age's authority) natural order is reversed and trees can talk (the fable that follows): Curtius 1967: 94–8.
11. wend: change from one state to another: *OED* wend *v* II. 7 cites this as the last instance of this sense.
14. former: either *earlier* or *first* (the fall of Adam and Eve: *OED* former *a* 1a, c).
15. Who: he who.
16. lusty prime: cheerful (pleasant) spring (with *prime* also meaning first age: i.e., the return of primitive simplicity).
17. thretty: possibly archaic. *thrice thretty*: 90 is a biblical number of renewal (Enosh and Sarah both become parents at that age: Genesis 5: 9, 17: 17).
21. Fortune: the goddess of cycles whose emblem is a ball or wheel: Alciati 1551: 133. *foeman*: E.K.
22. gently: mildly (first *OED* citation 1548); but primarily gentility in the Adamic sense: 'When Adam delved and Eve span,/Who was then the gentleman' (Resnikov, S. 1937 The Cultural History of a Democratic Proverb, *JEGP* 36: 391–405).
25. Thenot: E.K.
26. cheer: face.
27. accord full nigh: parallel each other exactly.
28. wry: bent.
29. louring weather: the original's spelling and capitalisation (Wether) suggests the punning possibility: not just sullen weather but a frowning Aries, or Ram (the spring sign of March renewal, still a long way off): *OED* wether 2.

So seemest thou like Good Friday to frown.   30
But my flowering youth is foe to frost,
My ship unwont in storms to be tossed.

       Thenot.
The sovereign of seas he blames in vain
That, once sea-beat, will to sea again:
So, loitering, live you little herd-grooms,   35
Keeping your beasts in the budded brooms,
And when the shining Sun laugheth once
You deemen the Spring is come at once.
Then 'gin you, fond flies, the cold to scorn
And, crowing in pipes made of green corn,   40
You thinken to be Lords of the Year.
But eft, when ye count you freed from fear,
Comes the breme Winter with chamfered brows,
Full of wrinkles and frosty furrows,
Drearily shooting his stormy dart   45
Which cruddles the blood and pricks the heart.
Then is your care-less courage accoyed:
Your care-full herds with cold bene annoyed.
Then pay you the price of your surquedry
With weeping, and wailing, and misery.   50

30. Good . . . frown: alludes to the tradition that the sky becomes overcast as the time of the crucifixion approaches (following Luke 23: 44–5 etc.).
33. The . . . seas: E.K.
35–50. So . . . misery: following Mantuan 6. 19–25 (Turberville (tr.) 1567: 53–4), for whose reputation as a prophet of the Reformation see Norbrook 1984: 59–60, and Aesop's fable 336 (The Grasshopper and the Ants): Chambry 1967: 146.
35. herd-grooms: E.K.
36: brooms: the shrub broom (*Cytisus* and *Genista*) which grows profusely in pastures.
38. at once: once for all.
39. fond flies: E.K.
41. Lords . . . Year: summer lords of misrule, upstarts rejecting religious solemnity: *OED* lord *sb* II. 14 citing Grindal (*May* 75n), *Injunction at York*: 'The Minister and churchwardens shall not suffer any Lords of Misrule or Summer Lords . . . to come unreverently into any Church'. See also McLane 1961: 153.
42. But eft, when: E.K. (*eft* = afterwards: *OED* eft *adv* giving 1559 as last instance).
43. breme: E.K. *chamfered*: E.K.
46. cruddles: *February* Argument n above.
47. courage: (1) vigour; (2) lust (see 80n below); (3) bravado. *accoyed*: E.K.
49. surquedry: E.K.

                                    Cuddy.
Ah, foolish old man, I scorn thy skill
That wouldest me my springing youngth to spill.
I deem thy brain emperished be
Through rusty eld that hath rotted thee;
Or siker thy head veray totty is,   55
So on thy corbe shoulder it leans amiss.
Now thyself hast lost both lop and top,
Als my budding branch thou wouldest crop.
But were thy years green as now bene mine,
To other delights they would incline: 60
Tho wouldest thou learn to carol of love,
And hery with hymns thy lass's glove;
Tho wouldest thou pipe of Phyllis' praise;
But Phyllis is mine for many days:
I won her with a girdle of gelt   65
Embossed with bugle about the belt.
Such an one shepherds would make full fain:
Such an one would make thee young again.

52. *youngth*: I have kept the archaism since it may be deliberate (and see 87n); however, Cuddy uses the modern form at l. 31. *spill*: destroy (*OED* spill *v* I. 3); or possibly a dialect form of *spoil* (*OED* lists *spile*).
53. *emperished*: enfeebled (*OED* cites only two examples before this and one after, all sixteenth-century).
54. *eld*: E.K.
55. *siker*: E.K. *veray:* truly. *totty*: E.K.
56. *corbe*: E.K.
57. *lop and top*: the smaller branches and twigs of a tree (as opposed to the timber): *OED* top *sb* 1 II. 6, noting it as a phrase. That is, Thenot has been heavily pruned but, unlike the Briar, Cuddy does not want him felled.
58. *Als*: northern form of *also* = wholly. Cf. *July* 8 gloss.
61. *carol*: sing joyously.
62. *hery*: E.K. *glove*: a common fetish: e.g., Wyatt's 'What needs these threatening words', entitled in *Tottel's Miscellany* (1557), 'To his love from whom he had her gloves'.
63. *Phyllis*: E.K.
65–6: *girdle . . . belt*: a gilded waist-band (*gelt* = either an archaism or a Kentish dialect form: *OED* gilt *ppl a*) embossed [studded] with tubular glass beads (*OED* bugle *sb* 3, 1 citing this as the first instance). *Belt* (see E.K.) is syntactically redundant. The girdle/cestus symbolises marriage, chastity and love (via Venus's girdle: *Iliad* 14; cf. Florimell's girdle at *FQ*, 3. 7. 31, 4. 5. 2–6).
67. *fain*: glad.

> Thenot.
> Thou art a fon of thy love to boast:
> All that is lent to love will be lost. 70
>
> Cuddy.
> Seest how brag yon bullock bears
> So smirk, so smooth, his pricked ears?
> His horns bene as broad as rainbow bent,
> His dewlap as lithe as lass of Kent.
> See how he venteth into the wind: 75
> Weenest of love is not his mind?
> Seemeth thy flock thy counsel can,
> So lustless bene they, so weak, so wan,
> Clothed with cold and hoary with frost.
> Thy flock's father his courage hath lost; 80
> Thy ewes, that wont to have blown bags,
> Like wailful widows hangen their crags;
> The rather lambs bene starved with cold:
> All for their master is lustless and old.
>
> Thenot.
> Cuddy, I wote thou kennest little good 85
> So vainly t'advance thy headless hood.
> For youngth is a bubble blown up with breath

69. *fon*: E.K.
71. *brag*: haughtily (*OED* brag *a* 3, giving this as its last citation).
72. *smirk*: trimly (*OED* gives before 1530 as date of first use; this is its second citation). *pricked*: erect, alert.
74. *dewlap*: fold of loose skin hanging from throat. *lithe*: E.K.
75. *venteth*: E.K.
76. *Weenest*: do you think.
77. *can*: have learned.
78. *lustless*: without vigour (*OED*'s last instance is 1612).
80. *Thy . . . father*: E.K. *courage*: sexual appetite, erection (*OED* courage *sb* 3c; later sixteenth-century slang of short duration: *OED*'s citations span only 1541–1615).
81. *blown bags*: full udders.
82. *crags*: E.K.
83. *rather lambs*: E.K. *starved*: perished (*OED* starved *ppl a* 4, first citation 1581).
85. *wote*: know (northern). *kennest*: *April* 21 gloss.
86. *headless hood*: empty hood; hence *stupidity*.
87. *youngth*: E.K. (and see 52n above). *bubble*: a common emblem: Tervarent (1958) col 56; Smith 1970: 46–7. Thenot also suggests that Cuddy forgets Ecclesiastes 12: 1: 'Remember now thy Creator in the days of thy youth'.

Whose wit is weakness, whose wage is death,
Whose way is wilderness, whose inn Penance,
And stoop-gallant Age the host of Grievance.   90
But shall I tell thee a tale of truth
Which I conned of Tityrus in my youth,
Keeping his sheep on the hills of Kent?

      Cuddy.
To nought more, Thenot, my mind is bent
Than to hear novels of his devise: 95
They bene so well-thewed and so wise
Whatever that good old man bespake.

      Thenot.
Many meet tales of youth did he make,
And some of love, and some of chivalry,
But none fitter than this to apply.   100
Now listen awhile, and hearken the end:

  There grew an aged tree on the green,
A goodly Oak sometime had it been,

88. wit: power of understanding. *wage . . . death*: Romans 6: 23 ('For the wages of sin is death').
89–90. Whose . . . Grievance: for the pilgrimage allegory, see Tuve (1966) ch 3. *Wilderness* evokes 2 Corinthians 11: 26 ('In journeying I was often . . . in perils in wilderness'); the House of Holiness contains Penance in *FQ*, 1. 10. 27; *Age* is *stoop-gallant* because it lays gallants low (also a sixteenth-century term for the sweating sickness: *OED*); and it is the lodging place (*OED* host *sb* 3, a [archaic]) of disease (*OED* grievance 4). On penance in Protestant thought, see King 1990: 64.
92. conned: learned. *Tityrus*: E.K.
95. novels: short stories (a new word in this sense: *OED*'s first citation is 1566). *devise*: devising.
96. well-thewed: E.K.
98. meet: suitable.
101. hearken the end: (1) attend (listen) to the moral of the tale; (2) listen (and learn) thy own end.
102. There grew: E.K.
103. Oak: its meanings include kingship, fortitude and genealogy. It also evokes the (supposed) ancient British religion of Druidism which was, in the Renaissance, seen as a precursor of Christianity in its belief in the divinity of the sun, the immortality of the soul, etc.: Clarke, R. A., Wright, A. and Barnett, R. 1987 *The Blasted Oak: The Oak Tree: Natural History, Art and Myth in European Culture*, Herbert Art Gallery and Museum, Coventry; Owen, A. L. 1962 *The Famous Druids: A Survey of Three Centuries of English Literature on the Druids*, Clarendon Press, Oxford. See also 209n below. An

With arms full strong and largely displayed,
But of their leaves they were disarrayed; 105
The body big and mightily pight,
Thoroughly rooted and of wondrous height:
Whilom had been the king of the field
And mochel mast to the husband did yield,
And with his nuts larded many swine. 110
But now the grey moss marred his rine,
His bared boughs were beaten with storms,
His top was bald and wasted with worms,
His honour decayed, his branches sere.
    Hard by his side grew a bragging Briar 115

analogue to Spenser's oak appears in John Harington's (Protestant) elegy on the execution of Thomas Seymour (1549), 'Erst in Arcadia's land', in which Seymour is a shading oak axed through envy: Harington, H. and Park, T. (eds) 1804 *Nugae Antiquae* (2 vols), London, 2: 330–2. Contradicting this favourable reading is the Reformation allegorical tradition in which trees are felled because of their corruption. Thus the felling of the Oak could represent the overthrow of Catholicism and/or the purging of Catholic elements within English Protestantism (as itemised in *May*, *July* and *September*) on the authority of Matthew 3: 10: 'And now also is the axe put to the root of the trees: therefore every tree which bringeth not forth good fruit, is hewn down, and cast into the fire'; cf. Luke 3: 9. See also Turner, J. 1979 *The Politics of Landscape*, Harvard University Press, Cambridge, Mass., p 97 and cf. Spenser's *Ruins of Rome*, sonnet 28 (translating Du Bellay, who in turn draws on Lucan's *Pharsalia*, 1. 136–43), where Rome is a dead oak, bedecked with ancient trophies, which nevertheless gives birth to 'many young plants'. On tree-felling as a profiteering episcopal abuse, see Long, P. W. 1916 'Spenser and the Bishop of Rochester', *PMLA* 31: 732–3.

105. disarrayed: stripped of (*OED*'s first instance of this specific sense: disarray *v* 2c).
106. pight: set fast (archaic past participle of *pitch*: *OED* pitch *v* 1, B I. 1).
109. mochel: archaic form of *mickle* = much, cf. *July* 16 gloss. *mast*: collective name for oak, beech and other forest-tree fruits when used as food for swine.
110. larded: fattened (*OED*'s first citation for this sense: lard *v* 2).
111. rine: bark (common form of *rind*).
114. sere: *January* 37 gloss.
115. Briar: any thorny bush; but here the wild rose (eglantine or sweet-briar). In Aesop's fable of the Bush and the Briar (102 gloss) it is humble; Spenser's fable is closer to Whitney 1586: 34 (in which a pine tree reminds an upstart gourd that it will die with the first frost) or 220 (in which an oak destroyed by Envy's blasts is blamed for not bending like the reeds). A primary meaning of the briar rose was 'love won through difficulty' (Whitney 1586: 165), though the adverse meaning of thorns as a consequence of the Fall (Geneva gloss on Genesis 3: 18, 'Thorns also and thistles' reads 'These . . . proceed of the corruption of sin') is central to Spenser's fable (in Whitney 1586: 221 thorns and briars symbolise the wicked threatening the virtuous lily). But in view of the

Which proudly thrust into the element
And seemed to threat the firmament.
It was embellished with blossoms fair,
And thereto aye wonned to repair
The shepherds' daughters to gather flowers   120
To paint their garlands with his colours,
And in his small bushes used to shroud
The sweet nightingale singing so loud;
Which made this foolish Briar wax so bold
That on a time he cast him to scold   125
And sneb the good Oak for he was old:
  'Why standest there (quoth he) thou brutish block?
Nor for fruit nor for shadow serves thy stock.
Seest, how fresh my flowers bene spread,
Dyed in lily white and crimson red,   130
With leaves engrained in lusty green:

sweet-briar's significance as an emblem of Queen Elizabeth as the rose of love from at least as early as 1574 (Strong 1987: 68–71 and plates 44–9), the Briar would seem to represent corruption within court and monarch (the latter, maybe, as wooer of Alençon and enemy of the radical Protestant reformers) that threatens to destroy the oak of constancy and ancient national strengths. An emblem of some ten years later would depict a sweet-briar embracing a tree: Strong 1987: 70, 75, 153; while a probable source for Spenser's fable, George Gascoigne's *Princely Pleasures of Kenilworth Castle*, depicts the oak of Constancy and the briar of Contention metamorphosed by Queen Complacida (she who pleases everyone; she who has favourites): Friedland, L. S. 1954 'A Source of Spenser's "The Oak and the Briar"', *PQ* 33: 222–4.
116. element: air.
118. embellished: *April* 63 gloss.
119. aye: ever. *wonned*: E.K.
121. garlands: the Elizabethan spelling, girlond, which Spenser uses, contains an obvious pun on *girl*. Cf. *November* 75n.
123. nightingale: emblem of poetry (*August* 183–6n): hence, presumably, flattering court poets.
125. cast: resolved (possibly Chaucerian; obsolete by 1662: *OED* cast *v* V. 34).
126. sneb: E.K.
127. Why standest: E.K.
128. stock: (1) trunk (without branches); (2) stupidity; (3) source of a line of descent and the line of descent itself.
130–3. lily . . . queen: white and red roses signify the Tudor inheritance (union of the red rose of Lancaster and white rose of York with the marriage of Henry VII and Elizabeth of York: *April* 68 gloss); *engrained*: E.K.; *maiden queen* = a phrase used by Spenser of Elizabeth (e.g., *April*, 57; *FQ*, 1. 12. 8), thus implicating the queen in the description.
131. lusty: bright, gay.

Colours meet to clothe a maiden queen.
Thy waste bigness but cumbers the ground
And dirks the beauty of my blossoms round;
The mouldy moss which thee accloyeth   135
My cinnamon smell too much annoyeth.
Wherefore, soon (I rede thee) hence remove,
Lest thou the price of my displeasure prove'.
So spake this bold Briar with great disdain:
Little him answered the Oak again,   140
But yielded, with shame and grief adawed
That of a weed he was overawed.
  It chanced after, upon a day,
The husbandman self to come that way
Of custom for to surview his ground   145
And his trees of state in compass round.
Him when the spiteful Briar had espied
Causeless complained and loudly cried
Unto his lord, stirring up stern strife:
'O my liege lord, the god of my life,   150
Pleaseth you ponder your suppliant's plaint,
Caused of wrong and cruel constraint
Which I, your poor vassal, daily endure:
And, but your goodness the same recure,
Am like for desperate dool to die   155

Textual note

142. overawed] some editors (but not *Var.*) prefer Q3's overcrawed (= crowed over). Q1 is retained here because it makes good sense, appears to be another Spenserian neologism (this is *OED*'s first citation for *overawe*), and because Q3 has no obvious authority. (But note: *OED*'s second instance of *overcraw* comes from *FQ*, 1. 9. 50; so this may be an authorial revision.)

133. waste: (1) serving no purpose; (2) superfluous (*OED* waste *a* 4a, 6). *cumbers*: troubles, via Luke 13: 7 in Tyndale's translation: 'Cut it down: why cumbereth it the ground?' (The Briar should remember that the tree should be cut down only if, after being fertilised, it continues to be barren: Luke 13: 9.)
134. dirks: darkens (archaic form).
135. accloyeth: E.K.
137. rede: advise.
141. adawed: E.K.
145. surview: archaic form of *survey*.
146. trees of state: E.K.; also, nobler trees. *in . . . round*: all around.
149. stern strife: E.K.
150. O my liege: E.K.
154. recure: cure (from something).
155. dool: grief (obsolete by end of sixteenth century).

Through felonous force of mine enemy'.
Greatly aghast with this piteous plea
Him rested the goodman on the lea
And bade the Briar in his plaint proceed.
With painted words tho 'gan this proud weed   160
(As most usen ambitious folk)
His coloured crime with craft to cloak:
  'Ah, my sovereign, lord of creatures all,
Thou placer of plants both humble and tall,
Was not I planted of thine own hand   165
To be the primrose of all thy land,
With flowering blossoms to furnish the prime
And scarlet berries in summer time?
How falls it, then, that this faded Oak
(Whose body is sere, whose branches broke,   170
Whose naked arms stretch unto the fire)
Unto such tyranny doth aspire,
Hindering with his shade my lovely light
And robbing me of the sweet Sun's sight?
So beat his old boughs my tender side   175
That oft the blood springeth from wounds wide,
Untimely my flowers forced to fall
That bene the honour of your coronal.
And oft he lets his canker-worms light
Upon my branches to work me more spite;   180
And oft his hoary locks down doth cast,
Wherewith my fresh flowerets bene defaced.
For this and many more such outrage,
Craving your goodlihead to assuage
The rancorous rigour of his might,   185

156. felonous: (1) mischievous (Chaucerian; obsolete by 1590s); (2) thievish (only one *OED* citation, from 1570).
158. Him: i.e., the goodman. *lea*: maybe *ground* (untilled land); but more likely *scythe* (a northernism: *OED* lea *sb* 3).
162. coloured crime: deceitful accusation (*OED* crime *sb* 3; first used by Chaucer).
163. sovereign . . . all: the Briar addresses the woodsman as Adamic lord of the earth (Genesis 1: 26–9).
166. primrose: E.K.
167. prime: spring.
171. naked arms: E.K.
176. blood: E.K.
178. coronal: E.K.
181. hoary locks: E.K.
182. flowerets: E.K.

Nought ask I but only to hold my right,
Submitting me to your good sufferance
And praying to be guarded from grievance'.
To this the Oak cast him to reply
Well as he couth; but his enemy 190
Had kindled such coals of displeasure
That the goodman nould stay his leisure
But home him hasted with furious heat,
Increasing his wrath with many a threat.
His harmful hatchet he hent in hand 195
(Alas that it so ready should stand!)
And to the field alone he speedeth
(Aye little help to harm there needeth!).
Anger nould let him speak to the tree
Enaunter his rage mought cooled be, 200
But to the root bent his sturdy stroke
And made many wounds in the waste Oak.
The axe's edge did oft turn again
As half unwilling to cut the grain:
Seemed the senseless iron did fear, 205
Or to wrong holy eld did forbear.
For it had been an ancient tree,
Sacred with many a mystery,
And often crossed with the priests' crew,

187. sufferance: indulgence; but punning on the legal meaning (first attributed to Spenser by *OED* citing *May*, 106), the condition of holding an estate (or kingdom) which one has inherited lawfully, even after the title has ceased to be valid (*OED* sufferance *sb* II. 6).
188. grievance: injury, oppression (*OED*'s sense 1; cf. 89–90n).
190. couth: *January* 10 gloss.
192. nould: E.K.
195. hent: E.K.
198. Aye: E.K.
200. Enaunter: E.K.
202. wounds: E.K.
206. eld: 54 gloss.
207. ancient: (1) aged; (2) ancestor (*OED* ancient *sb* 1 and *a* III. 4).
209. crossed . . . crew: had the sign of the cross made over it with a *crew* (see E.K.). Berger 1988: 427 sees a general allusion to Druidism here (Greek *drūs* = oak), which would identify the tree as a symbol of ancient British liberties and a reminder that Druidic monotheism was seen by some reformers as a precursor of Christianity (its 'fancies' can be rejected now that Christianity is a fact): Brooks-Davies (1983) ch 4; Norbrook 1984: 41. But *crew* also suggests a different reading: as an apparently unique instance of a French loan word, it signals that the Oak's problems lie with French Catholicism (and hence, presumably, Alençon again).

And often hallowed with holy water due.   210
But sike fancies weren foolery
And broughten this Oak to this misery,
For nought mought they quitten him from decay,
For fiercely the goodman at him did lay.
The block oft groaned under the blow,   215
And sighed to see his near overthrow.
In fine the steel had pierced his pith,
Tho down to the earth he fell forthwith.
His wondrous weight made the ground to quake,
The earth shrank under him and seemed to shake: 220
There lieth the Oak, pitied of none.
   Now stands the Briar like a lord, alone,
Puffed up with pride and vain pleasance:
But all this glee had no continuance,
For eftsoons Winter 'gan to approach.   225
The blustering Boreas did encroach
And beat upon the solitary Briar
For now no succour was seen him near.
Now 'gan he repent his pride too late
For, naked left and disconsolate,   230
The biting frost nipped his stalk dead,
The watery wet weighed down his head,
And heaped snow burdened him so sore
That now upright he can stand no more
And, being down, is trod in the dirt   235
Of cattle, and bruised, and sorely hurt.
Such was the end of this ambitious Briar
For scorning eld—

                    Cuddy.
   Now I pray thee, shepherd, tell it not forth:
Here is a long tale, and little worth.   240

210. due: the original spelling (*dewe*) allows for the two senses: fulfilled as an obligation *and* droplets.
211. sike: such (northern/Scots).
213. quitten: deliver. *decay*: destruction.
215. The block oft groaned: E.K. *block*: (1) tree trunk; (2) the 'block' of his own execution.
217. In fine: in the end, at last.
223. pleasance: delight.
224. glee: E.K.
226. Boreas: E.K. (possibly alluding to the reformist zeal of Scots Calvinism).
236. bruised: i.e., mangled (*OED* bruise *v* 1); but the original spelling *brouzed* is also a contemporary form of *browsed* (= cropped).
238. For scorning eld: E.K.

So long have I listened to thy speech
That graffed to the ground is my breech.
My heart's-blood is well nigh frorne, I feel,
And my galage grown fast to my heel;
But little ease of thy lewd tale I tasted. 245
Hie thee home, shepherd, the day is nigh wasted.

> Thenot's emblem:
> *Iddio perche è vecchio,*
> *Fa suoi al suo essempio.*
>
> Cuddy's emblem:
> *Niuno vecchio*
> *Spaventa Iddio.*

GLOSS

3] **keen**) sharp [not archaic, dialectal, or obviously problematic].

4] **gride**) pierced: an old word much used of Lydgate, but not found (that I know of) in Chaucer [*OED* gride *v* confirms that Spenser was the first to use it after Lydgate].

5] **runts**) young bullocks [northern/Scots].

10] **wrack**) ruin or violence, whence cometh *shipwrack*: and not *wreak* (that is, vengeance or wrath) [an instance of E.K.'s interest in etymology as a clue to meaning].

21] **foeman**) a foe [archaic].

25] **Thenot**) the name of a shepherd in Marot his eglogues [see *February* headnote].

33] **The sovereign of seas**) is Neptune, the god of the seas. The saying is borrowed of Mimus Publianus, which used this proverb in a verse: *Improbe Neptunum accusat, qui iterum naufragium facit* ['It is shameful for a man who is shipwrecked more than once to blame Neptune': Smith 1970: 205. Erasmus's edition of the moral sayings of the first-century B.C. Publilius Syrus was published in 1514. See also *March* emblem n.].

35] **herd-grooms**) Chaucer's verse almost whole [*House of Fame*, 1225–6: 'As han these little herd-grooms,/That kepen beasts in the brooms'. The echo reinforces Thenot's obsession with the vanity of human aspirations. Line 39, 'crowing in pipes made of green corn', repeats *House of Fame*, 1224: 'And pipes made of green corn'].

242. graffed: grafted (Cuddy uses the archaic word).
243. frorne: frozen (mediaevalism).
244. galage: E.K.
245. lewd: (1) foolish; (2) unholy and unlettered, ignorant (*OED* lewd 4, 1 and 2 respectively). Cf. 9n above.
248–9. Iddio . . . essempio: Because he is an old man, God makes his own to his own pattern; or: Because God is an old man, take him for your example (see E.K.'s translation in gloss): Italian.
251–52. Niuno . . . Iddio: No old man fears God: Italian. E.K.

39] **fond flies**) he compareth careless sluggards or ill husbandmen to flies that, so soon as the sun shineth, or it waxeth anything warm, begin to fly abroad, when suddenly they be overtaken with cold.

42] **But eft, when**) a very excellent and lively description of Winter so as may be indifferently taken either for Old Age, or for Winter season.

43] **breme**) chill, bitter [*OED* breme *a* II. 6 notes the word's revival by Spenser, as an adjective for winter, from Lydgate's *Troy Book*, 2. 16. Cf. *gride* (4 gloss above) and *December* 148 gloss].

43] **chamfered**) chapped, or wrinkled [used in Thomas Cooper's *Thesaurus linguae Romanae et Britannicae* (1565) to translate *striatus*; new in the 1570s].

47] **accoyed**) plucked down and daunted [not archaic].

49] **surquedry**) pride [not archaic; but E.K. may have thought Spenser got it from Lydgate's *Troy Book*, 1. 452].

54] **eld**) old age [archaic].

55] **siker**) sure [northern/Scots after 1500: *OED*].

55] **totty**) wavering [i.e., physically or mentally unstable; not archaic].

56] **corbe**) crooked [or humped; archaic].

62] **hery**) worship [another mediaevalism revived by Spenser: cf. *November* 10 gloss].

63] **Phyllis**) the name of some maid unknown whom Cuddy (whose person is secret) loved. The name is usual in Theocritus, Virgil and Mantuan [not in the first, but in the others: e.g., Virgil, *Eclogues*, 3. 78), and common in the secular love lyric: e.g., Wyatt's 'If waker Care'].

66] **belt**) a girdle or waist-band.

69] **a fon**) a fool [*OED*'s last citation before Spenser is from Skelton].

74] **lithe**) soft and gentle [mediaevalism revived by Spenser].

75] **venteth**) snuffeth in the wind [*OED* vent *v* 2 III. 14 dates first instance of this meaning 1538].

80] **Thy flock's father**) the ram.

82] **crags**) necks [northern/Scots].

83] **rather lambs**) that be ewed early in the beginning of the year [*rathe* = early is not an archaism; E.K. is explaining a 'pastoral' point to learned and courtly readers].

87] **youth is** [note E.K.'s – or the compositor's – modernised spelling in contrast to the original's] a very [truly] moral and pithy allegory of Youth and the lusts thereof compared to a weary wayfaring man.

92] **Tityrus**) I suppose he mean Chaucer, whose praise for pleasant tales cannot die so long as the memory of his name shall live and the name of poetry shall endure [cf. Dedicatory Epistle, p. 18n and *June* 81 gloss, and note Spenser's invocation of Chaucer's spirit in *FQ*, 4. 2. 32–4].

96] **well-thewed**) that is, *bene moratae*, full of moral wiseness [or 'of good moral character': *OED* thewed *ppl a* 1a: archaic; Spenser was the last to use it, according to *OED*].

102] **There grew**) this tale of the Oak and the Briar he telleth as learned of Chaucer; but it is clean [completely] in another kind, and rather like to Aesop's fables [e.g., fable 143, The Reed and the Olive Tree: Chambry 1967: 64. E.K.'s citation of Aesop signals the presence of political comment, since the fable tradition was almost invariably used in this way: Patterson and Coiro in *SpE*, pp 257–8]. It is very excellent for pleasant descriptions, being altogether a certain

icon [image] or hypotyposis [vivid outline] of disdainful younkers [young gentlemen].
118] **embellished**) beautified and adorned [*OED*'s first instance in this sense since Caxton, 1474].
119] **To wonne**) to haunt or frequent [wrong. E.K. confuses two meanings of the archaic verb *wone* = to dwell; to be accustomed].
126] **sneb**) check [a less common form of *snib* = snub].
127] **Why standest**) the speech is scornful and very presumptuous.
131] **engrained**) dyed in grain [thoroughly].
135] **accloyeth**) encumbreth [rare rather than archaic; but used by Lydgate, so for Spenser it has the force of an archaism].
141] **adawed**) daunted and confounded [a sixteenth-century false archaism: *OED* adaw *v* 2].
146] **trees of state**) taller trees fit for timber wood.
149] **stern strife**) said Chaucer, *scilicet* [namely] fell and sturdy [in *The Plowman's Tale*, 55, printed as Chaucer's in the sixteenth century: 'A stern strife is stirred new'. Since the work was strongly anti-Catholic, the allusion is another pointer to Spenser's reformist intent: King 1982: 51–2, 323; Norbrook 1984: 42–3, 59–60; King 1990: 21].
150] **O my liege**) a manner of supplication wherein is kindly coloured [naturally revealed] the affection and speech of ambitious men.
166] **the primrose**) the chief and worthiest [Spenser exploits an etymological pun: *primrose* = *prima rosa*, the first (or spring) rose (Latin)].
171] **naked arms**) metaphorically meant of the bare boughs, spoiled of leaves. This colourably [metaphorically] he speaketh, as adjudging him to the fire.
176] **the blood**) spoken of a block [tree stump] as it were of a living creature, figuratively, and, as they say, *kat'eikasmon* [as a comparison; Q1 prints in Greek].
178] **coronal**) garland [usually means *coronet* in the aristocratic sense; *OED* cites this as the first instance of the meaning *flower garland*].
181] **hoary locks**) metaphorically for withered leaves.
182] **flowerets**) young blossoms [*November* 83 gloss].
192] **nould**) for *would not* [slightly archaic; usual form = *nold(e)*; this is *OED*'s first cited instance of *nould*].
195] **hent**) caught [archaic; cf. *November*, 169].
198] **Aye**) evermore [the usual meaning in the sixteenth century; E.K. glosses it to distinguish it from *aye* = certainly, which emerged around 1575: *OED*].
200] **Enaunter**) lest that [or, in case; archaic. Cf. *May*, 78 and *September* 161 glosses].
202] **wounds**) gashes.
209] **the priests' crew**) holy water pot [Old French *crue*; the only instance in English cited by *OED*], wherewith the popish priest used to sprinkle and hallow [bless] the trees from mischance. Such blindness was in those times, which the poet supposeth to have been the final decay of this ancient Oak.
215] **The block oft groaned**) a lively figure, which giveth sense and feeling to unsensible creatures, as Virgil also saith: *Saxa gemunt gravido* etc. ['The rocks groaned at the heavy blow'; not in Virgil].
224] **glee**) cheer and jollity [no *OED* citation between 1460 and 1598: glee *sb* 3].
226] **Boreas**) the northern wind, that bringeth the most stormy weather.
238] **For scorning eld**) and minding (as should seem) to have made rhyme to the

former verse, he is cunningly cut off by Cuddy, as disdaining to hear any more.
244] **galage**) a startup [rustic boot] or clownish [rustic] shoe [a variant of *galosh*
= shoe with wooden sole and leather-thonged upper].

Emblem.

This emblem is spoken of Thenot as a moral of his former tale: namely, that God (which is himself most aged, being before all ages, and without beginning) maketh those whom he loveth like to himself, in heaping years unto their days, and blessing them with long life. For the blessing of age is not given to all, but unto those whom God will so bless; and albeit that many evil men reach unto such fulness of years, and some also wax old in misery and thraldom, yet therefore is not age ever the less blessing. For even to such evil men such number of years is added, that they may in their last days repent and come to their first home. So the old man checketh the rash-headed boy for despising his grey and frosty hairs.

Whom Cuddy doth counterbuff with a biting and bitter proverb [e.g., John Florio 1591 *Giardino di ricreatione* sig R2v], spoken indeed at the first in contempt of old age generally. For it was an old opinion (and yet is continued in some men's conceit [thinking]), that men of years have no fear of God at all, or not so much as younger folk; for that, being ripened with long experience, and having passed many bitter brunts [blows] and blasts of vengeance, they dread no storms of Fortune, nor wrath of gods, nor danger of men, as being either by long and ripe wisdom armed against all mischances and adversity, or with much trouble hardened against all troublesome tides: like unto the Ape, of which is said in Aesop's fables that, oftentimes meeting the Lion, he was at first sore aghast and dismayed at the grimness and austerity of his countenance, but at last being acquainted with his looks, he was so far from fearing him that he would familiarly gibe and jest with him [E.K. changes the Fox in Aesop's fable 42 (Chambry 1967: 22) to an Ape presumably in allusion to Alençon's representative Simier, whom Elizabeth nicknamed her *singe* (ape): Neale 1934: 239]: such long experience breedeth in some men security. Although it please Erasmus (a great clerk [ecclesiastic] and good old [(1) skilled; (2) belonging to a former time] father [priest]) more fatherly and favourably to construe it in his *Adages* for his own behoof, that by the proverb *nemo senex metuit Jovem* ['no old person fears Jove'] is not meant that old men have no fear of God at all, but that they be far from superstition and idolatrous regard of false gods, as is Jupiter [not in the *Adagia*]. But his great learning notwithstanding, it is too plain to be gainsaid that old men are much more inclined to such fond fooleries than younger heads.

March

Like *February*, *March* is a bipartite poem, this time structured with exact symmetry about its mid-point: Willy divides past from future at line 59 – central out of the total of 117 – and Thomalin then begins his tale of Cupid based on the third century B.C. pastoral poet Bion's *Idyll* 4, probably via Politian's Latin translation (79 gloss) and Pierre Ronsard's paraphrase *L'Amour oiseau* (1560): Spitzer L. 1950 'Spenser, *Shepheardes Calender*, March', *Studies in Philology* 47: 494–505. On mid-point symbolism, see Fowler (1970). The theme of the dangers of love harks back to *January* and anticipates Elizabeth as queen of love in *April*, while the metrical and rhyme patterns may allude to Chaucer's romance parody *Sir Thopas*: *Var* 1. 267–8. (Like Chaucer's stanzas, Spenser's consist of six lines grouped in two sets of two tetrameter (four-beat) lines and one trimeter (three-beat) line.) The covert (political) meaning of the eclogue would appear to emerge retrospectively, from the emblems: for Willy's statement about the folly of lovers seems to assume a dangerously treasonable quality when read in the light of Thomalin's gall/Gaul pun (see emblem footnote), and both emblems together invite the reader to interpret *March* as a warning against marriage to Alençon (see *January* headnote). The woodcut (fig. 3) emphasises the entrapment of Cupid (ll. 106–14), probably with a glance at the netting of Mars by Vulcan when he was making love to Venus (March was named after Mars: Ovid, *Fasti*, 3. 1–4). Their union – an ideal conjunction of valour and beauty, according to the mythographers – resulted in the offspring Harmonia (Harmony: Panofsky 1962: 162–4; Luborsky 1981: 21–4). Maybe one of the points of the woodcut is that harmony is the opposite of what Protestants expected from the union of Elizabeth and Alençon.

March
Aegloga tertia

Argument

In this eglogue two shepherds' boys, taking occasion of the season, begin to make purpose of love and other pleasance which to springtime is most agreeable. The special meaning hereof is, to give certain marks and tokens to know Cupid (the poets' god of love). But more particularly, I think, in the person of Thomalin is meant some secret friend who scorned Love and his knights so long till at length himself was entangled and unawares wounded with the dart of some beautiful regard, which is Cupid's arrow.

Argument: *make purpose*: discourse, or propose the subject. *secret friend*: not identified (though when Thomalin reappears in *July* he is apparently Thomas Cooper, Bishop of Lincoln). *regard*: glance.

                    Willy.   Thomalin.
Thomalin, why sitten we so,
As weren overwent with woe,
    Upon so fair a morrow?
The joyous time now nigheth fast
That shall alegge this bitter blast   5
And slake the Winter's sorrow.

                        Thomalin.
Siker, Willy, thou warnest well,
For Winter's wrath begins to quell
    And pleasant Spring appeareth:
The grass now 'gins to be refreshed,   10
The swallow peeps out of her nest,
    And cloudy welkin cleareth.

                         Willy.
Seest not thilk same hawthorn stud,
How bragly it begins to bud
    And utter his tender head?   15
Flora now calleth forth each flower
And bids make ready Maia's bower,
    That new is uprist from bed.
Tho shall we sporten in delight
And learn with Lettice to wax light   20
    That scornfully looks askance;

2. *overwent*: E.K.
4. *nigheth*: approaches.
5. *alegge*: E.K.
7. *Siker*: *February* 55 gloss.
8. *quell*: E.K.
11. *swallow*: E.K.
12. *welkin*: E.K.
13. *stud*: wooden post; as *tree trunk* the usage originates with Spenser here (*OED* stud *sb* 1 I. 4a).
14. *bragly*: ostentatiously (this passage cited by *OED* as a nonce use; but cf. *February*, 71).
15. *utter*: shoot.
16. *Flora*: E.K.
17. *Maia*: E.K.
18. *uprist*: uprisen, Spenserian archaising form (*OED*).
20. *Lettice*: E.K. *wax light*: grow frivolous and wanton.
21. *askance*: E.K.

Tho will we little Love awake
That now sleepeth in Lethe lake,
   And pray him leaden our dance.

                  Thomalin.
Willy, I ween thou be assot,   25
For lusty Love still sleepeth not
   But is abroad at his game.

                  Willy.
How kennest thou that he is awoke?
Or hast thyself his slumber broke,
   Or made privy to the same?   30

                  Thomalin.
No, but haply I him spied
Where in a bush he did him hide
   With wings of purple and blue;
And were not that my sheep would stray,
The privy marks I would bewray   35
   Whereby by chance I him knew.

                  Willy.
Thomalin, have no care for-thy:
Myself will have a double eye
   Ylike to my flock and thine;
For als at home I have a sire,   40
A stepdame eke as hot as fire
   That duly a-days counts mine.

22. *Love*: Cupid.
23. *Lethe*: E.K.
25. *ween*: think. *assot*: foolish (and see E.K.).
26. *lusty*: lively. *still*: always (i.e., he never sleeps).
28. *kennest*: *April* 21 gloss; cf. *February*, 85.
29. *his slumber*: E.K.
31. *haply*: by chance.
33. *wings*: E.K.
35. *privy*: peculiar, belonging to him alone. *bewray*: disclose.
37. *for-thy*: E.K.
38–9. *Myself . . . thine*: a pastoral commonplace: e.g., Virgil, *Eclogues*, 5. 12 ('You begin, and Tityrus will watch the grazing kids').
39. *Ylike*: alike; archaic spelling.
40. *For als*: E.K. (*als*: *February* 58n).
41. *hot*: choleric.

####### Thomalin.

Nay, but thy seeing will not serve:
My sheep for that may chance to swerve
   And fall into some mischief;   45
For sithens is but the third morrow
That I chanced to fall asleep with sorrow
   And waked again with grief:
The while, thilk same unhappy ewe
(Whose clouted leg her hurt doth show)   50
   Fell headlong into a dell
And there unjointed both her bones:
Mought her neck bene jointed at once
   She should have need no more spell.
The elf was so wanton and so wood   55
(But now, I trow, can better good)
   She mought ne gang on the green—

####### Willy.

Let be as may be, that is past:
That is to come, let be forecast.
   Now, tell us what thou hast seen.   60

####### Thomalin.

It was upon a holiday,
When shepherds' grooms han leave to play,
   I cast to go a-shooting.
Long wandering up and down the land
With bow and bolts in either hand   65
   For birds in bushes tooting,

43–57. Cf. *January*, 43–6 and the theme of (monarchical?) 'motherly care' at *May* 180n.
44. swerve: deviate from their path.
46. sithens: since the time that (archaic).
49. unhappy: (1) unfortunate; (2) troublesome.
50. clouted: bandaged.
51. dell: E.K.
53. jointed: broken (*OED* joint *v* 3a). *at once*: February 38n.
54. spell: E.K.
55. elf: mischievous creature (*OED* elf *sb* 2b). *wood*: (1) insane; (2) reckless.
56. trow: believe (archaic). *can*: knows (*January* 10 gloss and cf. *February*, 85).
57. gang: E.K. (i.e., with the other sheep).
62. grooms: servants, 'boys'. *han*: have.
63. cast: February 125n.
65. bolts: arrows.
66. tooting: peeping, spying (probably already archaic: *OED* toot *v* 1, 2a–c).

At length, within an ivy tod
(There shrouded was the little god),
   I heard a busy bustling.
I bent my bolt against the bush,   70
Listening if anything did rush,
   But then heard no more rustling.
Tho, peeping close into the thick,
Might see the moving of some quick
   Whose shape appeared not: 75
But, were it fairy, fiend or snake,
My courage earned it to awake
   And manfully thereat shot.
With that sprang forth a naked swain,
With spotted wings like peacock's train,   80
   And laughing lope to a tree;
His gilden quiver at his back,
And silver bow (which was but slack),
   Which lightly he bent at me.
That seeing, I levelled again   85
And shot at him with might and main
   As thick as it had hailed:
So long I shot that all was spent.
Tho pumice stones I hastily hent
   And threw, but nought availed,   90
He was so wimble and so wight:
From bough to bough he leaped light
   And oft the pumice latched.
Therewith, afraid, I ran away,

---

67. *ivy tod*: E.K.
74. *quick*: living creature.
77. *earned*: strongly desired: *OED* earn *v* 3, 1 citing this and *FQ*, 1. 1. 3 as its only instances.
79. *swain*: E.K.
80. *peacock*: the bird of vigilance and marital concord: Ovid, *Metamorphoses*, 1. 720–3; Tervarent (1958) col 298: a detail from Ronsard's *L'Amour oiseau* (see headnote).
81. *lope*: leaped, sprang.
82. *gilden quiver*: in Moschus, *Idylls*, 1. 20.
89. *pumice*: presumably Aetna lava, because Spenser's landscape is Theocritean-Sicilian. The original reads *pumie* (and at l. 93, *pumies*), a form used between 1565 and 1595 according to *OED*. *hent*: February 195 gloss.
90. *availed*: (1) succeeded; (2) brought him down (*January* 73 gloss).
91. *wimble . . . wight*: E.K.
93. *latched*: E.K.

But he, that erst seemed but to play, 95
   A shaft in earnest snatched
And hit me, running, in the heel.
For-then I little smart did feel,
   But soon it sore increased,
And now it rankleth more and more, 100
And inwardly it festereth sore,
   Ne wote I how to cease it.

                         Willy.
Thomalin, I pity thy plight:
Perdy with Love thou diddest fight –
   I know him by a token; 105
For once I heard my father say
How he him caught upon a day
   (Whereof he will be wroken)
Entangled in a fowling net
Which he for carrion crows had set 110
   That in our pear tree haunted:
Tho said, he was a winged lad,
But bow and shafts as then none had
   Else had he sore be daunted.
But see: the welkin thicks apace 115
And stooping Phoebus steeps his face:
   It's time to haste us homeward.

        Willy's emblem:
   To be wise and eke to love
  Is granted scarce to God above. 120

---

95. *erst*: at first (archaism). Cf. *September* 6n.
97. *heel*: E.K.
98. *For-then*: as a result. *smart*: sharp pain (as of a sting).
102. *wote*: know (archaism; *OED* wot *v*).
104. *Perdy*: truly (literally 'by God').
105. *token*: sign.
108. *wroken*: E.K.
111. *haunted*: frequented.
115. *welkin thicks*: sky [see 12 gloss] darkens.
116. *stooping Phoebus*: E.K. *steeps*: bathes (*OED*'s first instance of this sense: steep *v* 1, 1c).
119–20. *To be . . . above*: popular Latin tag by Publilius Syrus in *Sententiae*, 22: Duff, J. W. and A. M. (tr.) 1934, 1. 16. Cf. *ibid.*, #131: 'When you love you can't be wise; when you're wise you're not in love'.

Thomalin's emblem:
Of honey and of gall in love there is store:
The honey is much, but the gall is more.

GLOSS

This eglogue seemeth somewhat to resemble that same of Theocritus [actually Bion, *Idyll* 4], wherein the boy likewise telling the old man that he had shot at a winged boy in a tree was by him warned to beware of mischief to come.

2] **overwent**) overgone [or overwhelmed; archaic].

5] **alegge**) to lessen or assuage [mediaevalism; alegge = abate was replaced by *allay* from around 1400: *OED* allay *v* 1 II].

8] **to quell**) to abate [*OED*'s first citation with this spelling, which is a Spenserian form of the intransitive verb *quail*: cf. *November*, 91].

11] **The swallow**) which bird useth to be counted the messenger and, as it were, the forerunner of spring [Ovid, *Fasti*, 2. 853–4: 'the swallow, harbinger of spring'].

12] **welkin**) the sky [poetical, and Lancashire dialectal, from the sixteenth century: *OED*].

16] **Flora**) the goddess of flowers, but indeed (as saith Tacitus) a famous harlot which, with the abuse of her body having gotten great riches, made the people of Rome her heir; who, in remembrance of so great beneficence, appointed a yearly feast for the memorial of her, calling her, not as she was, nor as some do think, Andronica, but Flora, making her the goddess of all flowers, and doing yearly to her solemn sacrifice [not in Tacitus, but from Boccaccio, *De genealogia deorum*, 4. 61 (citing Lactantius, *Institutiones divinae*, 1. 20. 6), or other common sources: *Var* 1. 273 (the phrase 'Flora was a famous harlot' appears in Stephen Batman's *The Golden Book of the Leaden Gods* (1577) p 13). *Andronica* remains untraced, but presumably alludes to her power over men as lover or prostitute: Greek *andros* (man) + *nikē* (victory). For the earlier part of her history as Chloris, see *April* 122 gloss. Chloris/Flora became a cult name for Elizabeth, though it was not established this early.].

17] **Maia's bower**) that is, the pleasant field, or rather the May bushes. Maia is a goddess and the mother of Mercury [messenger of the gods, god of eloquence and, most appropriately for this context, god of shepherds who was occasionally depicted bearing a ram (March's zodiacal sign: see fig. 3): Linche 1599: sig R3], in honour of whom the month of May is of her name so called, as saith Macrobius [*Saturnalia*, 1. 12. 19. At paragraph 20 he reports 'Maia . . . is the Earth'.].

121–2. *Of honey . . . more*: another Latin tag, originating with Plautus, *Cistellaria*, 69 ('love is most abundant in honey and gall') and repeated at *FQ*, 4. 10. 1. In the *FQ* instance the spelling is *gall*, whereas the original spelling of the emblem here (which could well preserve Spenser's own spelling) is *Gaule*, thus apparently suggesting a warning about the queen's mooted marriage to the Gallic (and Catholic) Duc d'Alençon: see *January* headnote. There is also a reference to the Platonic–Orphic tradition of the bitterness underlying love's sweetness: *Amoretti* Anacreontics 4 (below); Theocritus, *Idyll* 19; Whitney 1586: 219; Wind 1967: 161–5. See also E.K.

20] **Lettice**) the name of some country lass [Italian *letizia* = gladness; may hint at Lettice Knollys, the widowed Countess of Essex who, to the queen's displeasure, secretly married the Earl of Leicester in 1578 after an earlier ceremony in 1576; though in view of Spenser's connection with the Leicester-Sidney circle, this seems unlikely. Indeed, it suggests that Spenser was unaware of the marriage (Kent Hieatt, private communication).]

21] **askance**) askew or asquint [but Spenser implies disdain, and *OED* records this as the first instance of this meaning].

23] **Lethe**) is a lake in hell which the poets call the lake of forgetfulness (for *Lethe* signifieth forgetfulness) wherein the souls being dipped did forget the cares of their former life [Virgil, *Aeneid*, 6. 703–51, where souls are reported as drinking from the river Lethe]; so that by Love sleeping in Lethe lake, he meaneth he was almost forgotten and out of knowledge by reason of winter's hardness, when all pleasures, as it were, sleep and wear out of mind.

25] **assot**) to dote [mediaevalism: as a form of *assotted* this is *OED*'s only instance after Gower].

29] **his slumber**) to break Love's slumber is to exercise the delights of love and wanton pleasures.

33] **wings of purple**) so is he feigned of the poets [a commonplace: Mustard 1919: 196 cites Ovid, *Remedia amoris*, 701; *purple* could mean bright, shining (Latin *purpureus*)].

37] **for-thy**) therefore [archaic].

40] **For als**) he imitateth Virgil's verse, *Est mihi namque domi pater, est injusta noverca*, etc. ['For at home I have a father and a severe stepmother': *Eclogues*, 3. 33].

51] **a dell**) a hole in the ground [in this meaning, rare: *OED*'s only earlier instance is from Sir Thomas Eliot, 1531].

54] **spell**) is a kind of verse or charm that in elder times they used often to say over everything that they would have preserved – as the night-spell for thieves, and the wood-spell. And herehence, I think, is named the gospel: as it were, God's spell, or word. And so saith Chaucer: 'Listeneth, lordings, to my spell' [*Sir Thopas*, opening of fitt 1: 'Listeth, lordes' (or: 'Listeneth Lordings' in 1561–2 *Chaucer*) and fitt 2: 'Now hold your mouth . . . And hearkeneth to my spell': *Var*. 1. 274 and Kent Hieatt, private communication].

57] **gang**) go [archaic and probably already northern].

67] **an ivy tod**) a thick bush [*tod* = bushy mass, usually in the phrase *ivy-tod* (= ivy bush), *OED*'s first citation of which is 1553 (tod *sb* 2 II. 2)].

79] **swain**) a boy; for so is he described of the poets to be a boy: *scilicet* [namely] always fresh and lusty [lively; handsome]; blindfolded because he maketh no difference of personages; with divers [vari-] coloured wings (*scilicet* full of flying fancies); with bow and arrow (that is, with glance of beauty which pricketh as a forked arrow). He is said also to have shafts, some leaden, some golden (that is, both pleasure for the gracious and loved, and sorrow for the lover that is disdained or forsaken). But who list more at large to behold Cupid's colours and furniture [equipment], let him read either Propertius [*Elegies*, 2. 12] or Moschus his *Idyllion* of wandering Love [*Idyll* 1], being now most excellently translated into Latin by the singular learned man Angelus Politianus [*Epigrammata graeca* (1512)], which work I have seen amongst other of this poet's doings very well translated also into English rhymes [E.K. alludes to an apparently lost work by Spenser: Oruch in *SpE*, pp 737-8; for a full iconography of Cupid, see Panofsky (1962) ch 4].

91] **wimble and wight**) quick and deliver [*wimble* = nimble, a northernism adopted by Spenser (*OED*); *wight* = swift (archaic); *deliver* = agile].

93] **latched**) caught [or grasped: mediaevalism: *OED* latch *v* 1, 1a, 2a].

97] **in the heel**) is very poetically spoken, and not without special judgement. For I remember that in Homer it is said of Thetis that she took her young babe Achilles (being newly born) and, holding him by the heel, dipped him into the river of Styx, the virtue whereof is to defend and keep the bodies washed therein from any mortal wound. So Achilles, being washed all over save only his heel by which his mother held, was in the rest invulnerable [not in Homer's *Iliad* but in Boccaccio's *De genealogia deorum*, 12. 52]: therefore by Paris was feigned to be shot with a poisoned arrow in the heel whiles he was busy about the marrying of Polyxena in the temple of Apollo. Which mystical fable Eustathius, unfolding, saith: that by wounding in the heel is meant lustful love [Eustathius was a twelfth-century allegorising commentator on Homer; but E.K. still draws on Boccaccio, 12. 52: Lotspeich 1932: 31; Mustard 1919: 196–7]. For from the heel (as say the best physicians) to the privy parts there pass certain veins and slender sinews, as also the like come from the head and are carried like little pipes behind the ears; so that (as saith Hippocrates [*On the Nature of Man*, 11]) if those veins there be cut asunder, the party [part] straight becometh cold and unfruitful: which reason our poet well weighing maketh this shepherd's boy of purpose to be wounded by Love in the heel.

106] **For once**) in this tale is set out the simplicity of shepherds' opinion of love.

108] **wroken**) revenged [mediaeval form of *wreak*: cf. *February* 10 gloss].

116] **stooping Phoebus**) is a periphrasis of the sun setting.

Emblem.

Hereby is meant that all the delights of love, wherein wanton youth walloweth, be but folly mixed with bitterness, and sorrow sauced with repentance. For besides that the very affection of love itself tormenteth the mind and vexeth the body many ways (with unrestfulness all night and weariness all day, seeking for that we cannot have, and finding that we would not have), even the self [same] things which best before us liked, in course of time and change of riper years (which also therewithal changeth our wonted liking and former fantasies) will then seem loathsome and breed us annoyance when youth's flower is withered and we find our bodies and wits answer not to such vain jollity and lustful pleasure [pleasure].

April

The love theme of *March* now modulates into two keys: the minor key of Colin's frustrations over Rosalind, and the complementary major key of his encomium on Elizabeth as queen of love. The latter is recited by Hobbinol as an inset ode linguistically and structurally differentiated from his and Thenot's pastoral dialogue (the dialogue consists of iambic pentameter quatrains; the ode of thirteen more rhythmically complex nine-line stanzas). But note that a Colin and a Thenot converse in Marot's elegy on a ruler's death, thus potentially darkening and qualifying the picture: see *January*, *February* and *November* headnotes. Monarchical panegyric in the eclogue genre begins with Theocritus, *Idyll* 17, 'Encomium: to Ptolemy' (where already, as in *April*, we find the topos of the divine pedigree); but praise of the Virgin Queen within a springlike and hence Golden-Age landscape in *SC*'s fourth eclogue signals specific imitation of Virgil's *Eclogue* 4, with its celebration of the restoration of the Golden Age with the return of the virgin goddess of justice, Astraea: *iam redit et virgo, redeunt Saturnia regna* ('now too returns the virgin, and Saturn's kingdoms' [*Eclogue*, 4. 6]; for Astraea as a cult name for Elizabeth, see Yates 1975). Emphasis on the queen's virginity expresses a preference for her mystical marriage to the realm (McLane 1961: 39–40; Tufte 1970: 167–78; Hibbert 1991: 78) as opposed to Alençon; a matter further encoded in the iconographic details that render her a composite figure based both on virginal Diana and Venus, goddess of love (see emblem gloss): such a combination signifies chaste love, i.e., a figure created to symbolise the reciprocity of love between monarch and people rather than physical sexual activity. In other words, *April* promotes Elizabeth as the virgin that her birth sign said she was (she was born on 7 September 1533, under Virgo). Its monarchical panegyric is supported by echoes of the discourse of court pageant; by introduction of the Protestant queen-church-bride analogy from the biblical Song of Solomon; and by a complex numerological structure, a feature considered appropriate to praise of monarchs because of its intricacy: Cain 1968: 45–58; Cain 1978; Brown, J. N. 1980 'A Note on Symbolic Numbers in Spenser's "April" ', *Notes and Queries* 225: 301–4; and headnotes to *August*, *October* and *November* below.

The woodcut (fig. 4) depicts Elizabeth as queen of harmony surrounded by musicians and placed directly under Taurus. Since harmony, like Taurus and April itself, is dedicated to Venus (Bongo 1599: 267; Richardson (1989) ch 4), the emphasis is on the queen as love-object and generator of concord within the realm. The Venerean references also fulfil a dynastic function, since Elizabeth was, according to the propagandists who favoured the 'British' myth, descended from Brutus, the namer of Britain and great-grandson of Aeneas, whose mother was Venus: MacLachlan in *SpE*, p 113. However, Taurus was also understood to be the metamorphosed Io/Isis, Dianan goddess of the Egyptians who was important in the virginal cult of Elizabeth (Fowler 1964: 154–5; Brooks-Davies 1983: 56–62, 159–60; *July* 154 gloss); so that its symbolism is again Dianan-Venerean. The sun (back right) sets because he cannot compete with Elisa's beauty (*April*, 73–81) and to recall Venus's command that the sun set early on 15 April so that Augustus – whose own dynastic ancestor she was –

might be proclaimed emperor earlier the following day: Ovid, *Fasti*, 4. 20, 673–6; Richardson 1989: 280. Finally, the centrality of Elisa alludes to the position of the triumphator in Renaissance revisions of the ancient Roman triumph, a feature that duplicates the elevation of Elisa as goddess in the inset lay's central stanza: Fowler 1970 and Cain and Brown as above.

April
Aegloga quarta

Argument

This eglogue is purposely intended to the honour and praise of our most gracious sovereign, Queen Elizabeth. The speakers herein be Hobbinol and Thenot, two shepherds, the which Hobbinol being before mentioned greatly to have loved Colin, is here set forth more largely, complaining him of that boy's great misadventure in love, whereby his mind was alienate and withdrawn not only from him who most loved him, but also from all former delights and studies, as well in pleasant piping as cunning rhyming, and singing, and other his laudable exercises: whereby he taketh occasion, for proof of his more excellency and skill in poetry, to record a song which the said Colin sometime made in honour of her majesty, whom abruptly he termeth Elisa.

<blockquote>

Thenot. Hobbinol.
Tell me, good Hobbinol, what gars thee greet?
What, hath some wolf thy tender lambs ytorn?
Or is thy bagpipe broke, that sounds so sweet?
Or art thou of thy loved lass forlorn?

Or bene thine eyes attempered to the year,   5
Quenching the gasping furrows' thirst with rain?
Like April shower so streams the trickling tears
Adown thy cheek to quench thy thristy pain.

</blockquote>

Argument: *Hobbinol . . . Colin*: *January* 55 and *September* 176 glosses. *cunning*: expert and learned. *record*: repeat from memory; sing (a mid-to-late sixteenth-century use). *abruptly*: suddenly terminated or abbreviated.
1. *gars . . . greet*: E.K.
2. *ytorn*: 155 gloss below.
3. *bagpipe*: cf. *August*, 3, 6: *January* headnote.
4. *forlorn*: E.K.
5. *attempered*: E.K.
8. *thristy*: archaic form: cf. *February* 17n. (Q2 emends to *thirsty*.)

                    Hobbinol.
Nor this nor that so much doth make me mourn,
But for the lad whom long I loved so dear   10
Now loves a lass that all his love doth scorn:
He, plunged in pain, his tressed locks doth tear.

Shepherds' delights he doth them all forswear:
His pleasant pipe, which made us merriment,
He wilfully hath broke, and doth forbear   15
His wonted songs, wherein he all outwent.

                    Thenot.
What is he for a lad you so lament?
Is Love such pinching pain to them that prove?
And hath he skill to make so excellent,
Yet hath so little skill to bridle Love?   20

                    Hobbinol.
Colin thou kennest, the southern shepherd's boy:
Him Love hath wounded with a deadly dart.
Whilom on him was all my care and joy,
Forcing with gifts to win his wanton heart;

But now from me his madding mind is start   25
And woos the widow's daughter of the glen:

9–28. *Nor . . . fren*: general echoes of Virgil, *Eclogues*, 2 and 10; and cf. *January*.
10. *lad*: E.K.
11. *lass*: E.K.
12. *tressed locks*: E.K. (the tearing of hair was traditionally a sign of grief).
14–15. *pipe . . . broke*: *January*, 67–72.
17. *is . . . lad*: E.K.
18. *prove*: experience (suffer) it.
19. *make*: E.K.
20. *bridle*: emblem of rational control of libido or bestial love: Wind 1967: 145 and 147 nn and plate 41.
21. *Colin . . . kennest*: E.K. *southern . . . boy*: in connection with E.K.'s gloss, recalls that by 1578 Spenser was (apparently) secretary to John Young, Bishop of Rochester, formerly Master of Pembroke Hall, Cambridge, while Spenser was an undergraduate there in the early 1570s (and cf. *September* 171 gloss).
23. *Whilom*: *January* 21n.
24. *wanton*: rebellious (rather than amorous).
25. *start*: deserted.
26. *widow's . . . glen*: E.K.

So now fair Rosalind hath bred his smart;
So now his friend is changed for a fren.

      Thenot.
But if his ditties bene so trimly dight
I pray thee, Hobbinol, record some one   30
The whiles our flocks do graze about in sight
And we close shrouded in this shade alone.

      Hobbinol.
Contented I. Then will I sing his lay
Of fair Elisa, queen of shepherds all,
Which once he made as by a spring he lay   35
And tuned it unto the water's fall:

Ye dainty nymphs, that in this blessed brook
 Do bathe your breast,
Forsake your watery bowers, and hither look
 At my request;   40
And eke you virgins that on Parnass' dwell
(Whence floweth Helicon, the learned well)
 Help me to blaze
 Her worthy praise
Which in her sex doth all excel.   45

Of fair Elisa be your silver song,
 That blessed wight:
The flower of virgins, may she flourish long
 In princely plight.

---

28. *fren*: E.K.
29. *dight*: E.K. (trimly dight = cleverly composed or constructed).
30. *record*: Argument n.
33. *lay*: E.K.
36. *tuned . . . fall*: motif originating with Theocritus, *Idylls*, 1. 7–8. Cf. *June* 6–8n.
37. *Ye dainty*: E.K. *nymphs*: traditionally water deities: cf. 120 gloss.
41. *eke*: also. *virgins . . . Parnass'*: E.K.
42. *Helicon*: E.K.
43. *blaze*: (1) proclaim; (2) describe heraldically (*OED* blaze *v* 2, 2, 3).
46. *silver song*: E.K.
47. *wight*: person, but with special reference to supernatural beings (*OED* wight *sb* 1a, b; 2a; archaic).
49. *plight*: state, condition (*OED* plight *sb* 2, II. 4a).

For she is Syrinx' daughter, without spot, 50
Which Pan, the shepherds' god, of her begot:
   So sprung her grace
   Of heavenly race;
No mortal blemish may her blot.

See where she sits upon the grassy green, 55
   (O seemly sight!)
Yclad in scarlet, like a maiden queen,
   And ermines white.
Upon her head a crimson coronet
With damask roses and daffadillies set: 60
   Bay leaves between
   And primroses green
Embellish the sweet violet.

50–1. Syrinx . . . Pan: E.K. (who, however, omits the identification of Syrinx with Elizabeth's mother, Anne Boleyn).
50. without spot: literally, immaculate like the (Protestant) bride-Church of the Song of Solomon 4: 7 and the Virgin Mary, whose iconography was based largely on the Song (see Wilson 1939: 200–29; King 1982: 368–71; Johnson 1990: 156–71); but also alluding to the ermine (57–8n below). Spenser's account is broadly neo-Platonic in its emphasis on divine origins: cf. *Am* 8, 61, 79, etc.
52. grace: in the senses of (1) divine favour and influence; (2) gracefulness (with a pun on the Graces: 109 gloss); (3) virtue; (4) clemency; (5) courtesy title bestowed on monarchs (*OED* grace *sb*).
57–8. scarlet . . . white: *scarlet* = rich cloth not necessarily of scarlet colour (*OED* scarlet *sb* and *a*. A 1a), though scarlet is the colour of Venus's robe in, e.g., Botticelli's *Primavera*; *maiden queen*: February 130–3n; *ermines*: i.e., ermine trimmings: the ermine traditionally signified purity, becoming associated with the phrase 'rather dead than spotted [or sullied]': cf. 50, 54 above. It became an emblem of Elizabeth probably earlier than the 'Ermine' portrait of 1585: Strong 1963: 82; Strong 1987: 147–9.
59. crimson coronet: E.K. (possibly of red roses, to recall Venus and her Graces, or the Virgin Mary, or Isis, all of whom were associated with the red rose: Wilkins (1969) ch 7 and, for Elizabeth and Isis, *April* headnote).
60. damask . . . daffadillies: the *damask rose* = a red or deep pink semi-double flower (as opposed to the single rose or sweet-briar: *February* 115n). It has Tudor connections because it was first imported by Thomas Linacre, physician to Henry VII and Henry VIII. *Daffadillies*: maybe daffodils, but possibly white asphodel (see red and white motif at 68): *January* 22n.
61–3. Bay . . . violet: the *bay* signifies virginity (see 104 gloss below); the *sweet violet* (*viola odorata*: traditionally paired with the spring-welcoming *primrose*) symbolises both virginal modesty and Venus: D'Ancona 1983: 94–5, citing Politian and Petrarch.
63. Embellish: E.K.

Tell me, have ye seen her angelic face,
   Like Phoebe fair? 65
Her heavenly haviour, her princely grace,
   Can you well compare?
The red rose meddled with the white yfere
In either cheek depincten lively cheer:
   Her modest eye, 70
   Her majesty,
Where have you seen the like but there?

I saw Phoebus thrust out his golden head
   Upon her to gaze;
But when he saw how broad her beams did spread, 75
   It did him amaze:
He blushed to see another Sun below,
Ne durst again his fiery face out-show:
   Let him, if he dare,
   His brightness compare 80
With hers, to have the overthrow.

Show thyself, Cynthia, with thy silver rays,
   And be not abashed:
When she the beams of her beauty displays,
   O how art thou dashed! 85
But I will not match her with Latona's seed:
Such folly great sorrow to Niobe did breed.
   Now she is a stone
   And makes daily moan,
Warning all other to take heed. 90

Pan may be proud that ever he begot
   Such a bellibone,

65. *Phoebe*: E.K.
66. *haviour*: bearing.
68. *meddled . . . yfere*: E.K.
69. *depincten*: depict (*OED depeinct v*, citing this as first instance, and one other in *FQ*).
73. *Phoebus*: E.K.
77. *another Sun*: Petrarchan motif: e.g., *Rime* 115; Sidney's 'When two suns do appear' from the *Old Arcadia*; *FQ*, 5. 3. 19.
81. *to . . . overthrow*: to be defeated (*OED* instances of the phrase span 1553–1601: overthrow *sb* I. 1b).
82. *Cynthia*: E.K.
86–7. *Latona's seed . . . Niobe*: E.K.
92. *bellibone*: E.K.

And Syrinx rejoice that ever was her lot
    To bear such an one.
Soon as my younglings cryen for the dam,   95
To her will I offer a milk-white lamb:
    She is my goddess plain,
    And I her shepherd swain,
Albe forswonk and forswat I am.

I see Calliope speed her to the place   100
    Where my goddess shines;
And after her the other Muses trace,
    With their violins.
Bene they not bay branches which they do bear
All for Elisa in her hand to wear?   105
    So sweetly they play
    And sing all the way
That it a heaven is to hear.

Lo, how finely the Graces can it foot
    To the instrument: 110
They dancen deftly and singen soot
    In their merriment.
Wants not a fourth Grace, to make the dance even?
Let that room to my lady be yeven:
    She shall be a Grace   115
    To fill the fourth place
And reign with the rest in heaven.

96. *milk-white lamb*: pastoral prize (as in *August*); but also emblem of innocence and humility associated with the St George legend: Brooks-Davies 1977: 15–16.
99. *forswonk . . . forswat*: E.K.
100. *Calliope*: E.K.
102. *trace*: tread.
103. *violins*: this is *OED*'s first reference. The instrument was occasionally attributed to Clio (Muse of History) and Thalia (Muse of Comedy): Tervarent (1958) cols 280–1. Violins were specifically courtly instruments: Boyden, D. D. 1965 *The History of Violin Playing from its Origins to 1761*, Oxford University Press, London, p 57.
104. *bay branches*: E.K.
109. *Graces*: E.K.
111. *deftly . . . soot*: E.K.
112. *merriment*: E.K.
113. *fourth Grace*: 109 gloss. The Graces traditionally danced around Venus.
114. *yeven*: given (mediaevalism).

And whither rens this bevy of ladies bright
  Ranged in a row?
They bene all Ladies of the Lake behight   120
  That unto her go.
Chloris, that is the chiefest nymph of all,
Of olive branches bears a coronal:
  Olives bene for peace
  When wars do surcease: 125
Such for a princess bene principal.

Ye shepherds' daughters, that dwell on the green,
  Hie you there apace:
Let none come there but that virgins bene
  To adorn her grace.   130
And when you come, whereas she is in place,
See that your rudeness do not you disgrace:
  Bind your fillets fast,
  And gird in your waist
(For more finesse) with a tawdry lace.   135

Bring hither the pink and purple columbine,
  With gillyflowers:
Bring coronations, and sops-in-wine,
  Worn of paramours.
Strew me the ground with daffadowndillies,   140

118. *rens*: mediaeval form of *runs. bevy*: E.K.
120. *Ladies . . . Lake*: E.K. *behight*: E.K.
122. *Chloris*: E.K. (another cult name for Elizabeth).
123. *coronal*: circlet, wreath.
124. *olives*: E.K.
125. *surcease*: cease.
126. *principal*: of greatest value.
133. *bind*: E.K.
135. *finesse*: delicacy, refinement. *tawdry lace*: silk tie or band (*OED*).
136–44. *Bring . . . flower de lis*: E.K. Columbines and carnations symbolise love (Rydén 1978), and the latter appears in the 'Rainbow' portrait of Elizabeth; the daffodil (first *OED* citation of *daffadowndilly* is 1573) is Venerean (Richardson 1989: 276) and appears in the Hardwick Hall portrait; *cowslip* and *kingcup* (marsh marigold or buttercup) function here, like the primrose (61–3n), as spring flowers (but note that yellow is a colour identified with Venus: Ptolemy, *Tetrabiblos*, 2. 9); *paunce* = pansy (symbol of thought); *chevisaunce*: not a known plant but a Spenserianism (*OED* chevisance 2). For the word see *May* 92 gloss; probably meant to convey general knightly (*chevalric*) qualities.

And cowslips, and kingcups, and loved lilies:
  The pretty paunce
  And the chevisaunce
Shall match with the fair flower de lis.

Now rise up, Elisa, decked as thou art   145
  In royal array;
And now ye dainty damsels may depart,
  Each one her way:
I fear I have troubled your troops too long.
Let dame Elisa thank you for her song;   150
  And if you come hither
  When damsons I gather
I will part them all you among.

            Thenot.
And was thilk same song of Colin's own making?
Ah, foolish boy, that is with love yblent.   155
Great pity is he be in such taking,
For nought caren that bene so lewdly bent.

            Hobbinol.
Siker I hold him for a greater fon
That loves the thing he cannot purchase;
But let us homeward, for night draweth on   160
And twinkling stars the daylight hence chase.

       Thenot's emblem:
    O quam te memorem virgo?

       Hobbinol's emblem:
       O dea certe.

GLOSS
1] **gars thee greet**) causeth thee weep and complain [*gar* = cause is a northern/Scots usage; *greet* = grieve was also largely northern/Scottish by the

145. Now rise: E.K.
152. damsons: E.K.
153. part: divide.
155. yblent: E.K.
156. taking: plight.
157. lewdly: February 9n.
158. Siker: February 55 gloss. *fon*: February 69 gloss.
163–5. O quam . . . certe: E.K.

mid-sixteenth century. Syntactically and in terms of spelling-forms the alternative meaning *jars [discords] are accosting you* is possible].

4] **forlorn**) left and forsaken [in this sense, i.e., *forsaken by* someone, this is the first citation by *OED* since 1150: forlorn *a* and *sb* 4b].

5] **attempered to the year**) agreeable to the season of the year, that is, April, which month is most bent to showers and seasonable rain; **to quench** [line 8], that is, to delay [i.e., mitigate and/or soak] the drought caused through dryness of March winds.

10] **the lad**) Colin Clout. 11] **the lass**) Rosalinda.

12] **tressed locks**) wreathed and curled [obviously suspected by E.K. of being a mediaevalism though it had sixteenth-century currency].

17] **is he for a lad**) a strange manner of speaking: *scilicet* [namely] what manner of lad is he? [cf. Shakespeare, *Much Ado*, 1. 3: 'What is he for a fool'].

19] **to make**) to rhyme and versify; for in this word *making* our old English poets were wont to comprehend all the skill of poetry, according to the Greek word *poiein*, to make, whence cometh the name of *poets* [cf. Puttenham (1589) 1. 1: 'A poet is as much to say as a maker. And our English name well conforms with the Greek word . . . '].

21] **Colin thou kennest**) knowest [northern/Scots]. Seemeth hereby that Colin pertaineth to some southern nobleman, and perhaps in Surrey or Kent, the rather because he so often nameth the Kentish downs and, before, *As lithe as lass of Kent* [*February* 74; see also *June* 18 gloss].

26] **the widow's**) he calleth Rosalind 'the widow's daughter of the glen', that is, of a country hamlet or borough [Scots and actually = narrow mountain valley with stream running through it; according to *OED* Spenser was responsible for its introduction into literary English], which I think is rather said to colour [disguise] and conceal the person than simply spoken. For it is well known, even in spite of Colin and Hobbinol, that she is a gentlewoman of no mean house, nor endued with any vulgar and common gifts both of nature and manners; but such, indeed, as need neither Colin be ashamed to have her made known by his verses, nor Hobbinol be grieved that so she should be commended to immortality for her rare and singular virtues: specially deserving it no less than either Myrto (the most excellent poet Theocritus his darling [*Idylls*, 7. 97]), or Lauretta (the divine Petrarch's goddess [for this form of the name see, e.g., *Rime*, 5]), or Himera, the worthy poet Stesichorus his idol, upon whom he is said so much to have doted that, in regard of her excellency, he scorned and wrote against the beauty of Helena. For which his presumptuous and unheedy hardiness [audacity] he is said by vengeance of the gods (thereat being offended) to have lost both his eyes [Himera was his birthplace, not his beloved; but E.K.'s 'error' may be a deliberate reminder of the jealousy and unpredictability of queens: for Elizabeth as Helen see *August* 138 gloss. For the bibliography on Rosalind, see *Var* 1. 651-5 and Mallette in *SpE*, p 622. McLane 1961: 27-46 argues convincingly that Elizabeth as the Tudor rose is intended].

28] **fren**) a stranger. The word, I think, was first poetically put, and afterward used in common custom of speech for *foreign* [*OED* frenne/fren lists this as the first substantive use of the word].

29] **dight**) adorned [cf. *January*, 22; clearly thought of by E.K. as a mediaevalism, though frequent in Wyatt and Surrey].

33] **lay**) a song [mediaeval], as *roundelays* [short song with refrain; first citation in *OED* 1573 from Gabriel Harvey; see *August*, 53–124] and *virelays* [revived in the late sixteenth century in imitation of the French fourteenth-century form, these were short lyrics based on two rhymes only: cf. *November*, 21]. In all this song is not to be respected what the worthiness of Her Majesty deserveth, nor what to the highness of a prince is agreeable, but what is most comely for the meanness of a shepherd's wit, or [either] to conceive or to utter. And therefore he calleth her Elisa (as through rudeness [artlessness] tripping in her name), and a shepherd's daughter, it being very unfit that a shepherd's boy brought up in the sheepfold should know, or ever seem to have heard, of a queen's royalty [*Elisa* suggests *Elissa*, one of Elizabeth's cult names: Bono in *SpE*, pp 218–19].

37] **Ye dainty**) is, as it were, an *exordium ad preparandos animos* ['preface to prepare the passions'; and since *animus* also means *soul* or *spirit*, E.K. may be drawing attention to the Orphic quality of the 'lay' which is, in fact, rather a hymn to various divine powers on the Orphic model: Orphic Footnote to *Epith* headnote].

41] **virgins**) the nine Muses, daughters of Apollo and Memory, whose abode the poets feign to be on Parnassus, a hill in Greece; for that in that country specially flourished the honour of all excellent studies [Jupiter/Zeus was traditionally the preferred father of the Muses and Apollo, god of poetry and music, their leader: Hesiod, *Theogony*, 56; but Spenser, following a statement in *Natalis Comes*, made them Apollo's 'brood' in *Tears of the Muses* (1591), 2: Lemmi 1929: 274].

42] **Helicon**) is both the name of a fountain at the foot of Parnassus, and also of a mountain in Boeotia, out of which floweth the famous spring Castalius, dedicate also to the Muses: of which spring it is said that when Pegasus the winged horse of Perseus (whereby is meant fame and flying renown) struck the ground with his hoof, suddenly thereout sprang a well of most clear and pleasant water which from thenceforth was consecrate to the Muses and ladies of learning [Tooke 1713: 218, 357].

46] **your silver song**) seemeth to imitate the like in Hesiodus: *argureon melos* [Greek for 'silver song'; printed in Greek; not in Hesiod].

50] **Syrinx**) is the name of a nymph of Arcady whom, when Pan [*January* 17n], being in love, pursued, she, flying from him, of [by] the gods was turned into a reed. So that Pan, catching at the reeds instead of the damsel, and puffing hard (for he was almost out of wind), with his breath made the reeds to pipe: which he, seeing, took of them and, in remembrance of his lost love, made him a pipe thereof [Ovid, *Metamorphoses*, 1. 689–712]. But here by Pan and Syrinx is not to be thought that the shepherd simply meant those poetical gods; but, rather, supposing (as seemeth) her grace's progeny to be divine and immortal (so as the paynims [pagans] were wont to judge of all kings and princes, according to Homer's saying: *Thumos dē megas esti diotrepheōs basileōs,/timē d'ek Dios esti, philei de ho mētieta Zeus* [printed in Greek in Q1; *Iliad*, 2. 196–7: 'For the anger of heaven-fostered kings is terrible; for their honour is from Zeus, and Zeus, god of counsel, loves them']), could devise no parents in his judgement so worthy for her as Pan, the shepherds' god, and his best-beloved Syrinx. So that by Pan is here meant the most famous and victorious king, her highness's father, late of worthy memory, King Henry the Eighth. And by that name [Pan] ofttimes, as hereafter appeareth, be noted [denoted] kings and mighty potentates and, in some place, Christ himself, who is the very Pan and god of shepherds

[Marot uses Pan to denote Francis I in his *Eglogue* . . . *au Roi* and *Eglogue* . . . *de ma Dame Louise de Savoye* (see *January* and *December* headnotes) and Christ in his *Complaint d'un pasteur chrétien*; and see *May*, 54 and *July* 49 and 179 glosses].

59] **crimson coronet**) he deviseth her crown to be of the finest and most delicate flowers instead of pearls and precious stones, wherewith princes' diadems use to be [are customarily] adorned and embossed.

63] **Embellish**) beautify and set out [cf. *February*, 118; apparently unusual in the sixteenth century, though common enough earlier].

65] **Phoe**be) the Moon, whom the poets feign to be sister unto Phoebus, that is, the Sun [Phoebe is, as the planet of virginity and chastity, the main emblem of Elizabeth as Virgin Queen: Wilson (1939) chs 5, 7, 8. For the parentage of Phoebe and Phoebus see 86–7 gloss below.].

68] **meddled**) mingled [still a main meaning in the sixteenth century, but perhaps felt by E.K. to be an archaism; or maybe his pedantry compelled him to discriminate].

68] **yfere**) together [common as a rhyming word in mediaeval poetry (*OED*), and current in the sixteenth century before Spenser; but clearly thought of by E.K. as an archaism]. By the mingling of the red rose and the white is meant the uniting of the two principal houses of Lancaster and of York, by whose long discord and deadly debate this realm many years was sore travailed [afflicted] and almost clean decayed [the Wars of the Roses, which ended in August 1485 with Henry Tudor's victory over Richard III at Bosworth Field and his subsequent coronation (in October) as Henry VII], till the famous Henry the Seventh, of the line of Lancaster, taking to wife the most virtuous Princess Elizabeth, daughter to the fourth Edward [1442–83] of the House of York, begat the most royal Henry the Eighth aforesaid, in whom was the first union of the white rose and the red. [Any reader would have known this; but E.K. is at pains to explicate the function of *April* as political propaganda at a particularly sensitive moment. Rose symbolism based on white/red as a particular feature of the Elizabeth cult, signifying Elizabeth as Marian virgin (Wilkins (1969) ch 6; also Wilson 1939: 134–5) as well the union of opposing political forces (York and Lancaster: Strong 1987: 68–71). For the conjunction of red and white roses as a symbol of alchemical union, see Brooks-Davies 1983: 23–5.]

73] **I saw Phoebus**) the sun. A sensible [perceptible to the senses] narration and present view of the thing mentioned, which they call *parousia* [printed in Greek; making a thing seem present].

82] **Cynthia**) the Moon, so called of Cynthus, a hill where she was honoured [on Delos, the island of Diana-Phoebe's, and her brother Phoebus Apollo's, birth].

86–7] **Latona's seed**) was Apollo and Diana whom, whenas Niobe (the wife of Amphion) scorned in respect of the noble fruit of her womb, namely her seven sons and so many daughters, Latona, being therewith displeased, commanded her son Phoebus to slay all the sons, and Diana all the daughters. Whereat the unfortunate Niobe being sore dismayed, and lamenting out of measure, was feigned of the poets to be turned into a stone upon the sepulchre of her children; for which cause the shepherd saith he will not compare her to them for fear of like misfortune. [Ovid, *Metamorphoses*, 6. 146–312. E.K. suppresses the obvious, as Lane 1993: 18–20 points out: the Phrygian Queen Niobe actually forbade her subjects to worship Latona, requiring that they prefer her as a deity. Although the analogy involves Colin, quasi-divine Elisa is clearly implicated, as she is in *February*'s husbandman.]

92] **a bellibone**) or a bonibell: homely spoken for a fair maid or bonny-lass [cf. *August*, 61; *OED* cites only these instances together with one from 1586; perhaps a reversal of *bonibell* [*bonny* + *belle* or *bonne* + *belle*], but *OED*'s first citation for this is also these two Spenser passages. Presumably they are both Spenserian neologisms.]

99] **forswonk and forswat**) overlaboured and sunburnt [the former is archaic, though *OED* cites an example from 1589; the latter appears to mean 'covered in sweat', though E.K. takes it as a form of *forswart* (sunburnt): *OED* forswart and for- *pref.* 5. Echoing *The Plowman's Tale*, Prologue, 14: 'He was forswonk and all forswat'. Cf. *February* 149 gloss.]

100] **Calliope**) one of the nine Muses, to whom they assign the honour of all poetical invention and the first glory of the heroical verse [e.g., Hesiod, *Theogony*, 79]. Other say that she is the goddess of rhetoric [e.g., Tooke 1713: 216]; but by Virgil it is manifest that they mistake the thing, for there in his *Epigrams* that art seemeth to be attributed to Polymnia, saying:

> *Signat cuncta manu, loquiturque Polymnia gestu*

[from *De Musarum inventis* (or *Nomina Musarum*) by Ausonius (fourth century A.D.), attributed to Virgil by Renaissance scholars and printed in editions of his works. It means: 'Polymnia expresses everything with the hand and speaks through gesture'], which seemeth specially to be meant of action and elocution, both special parts of rhetoric. Beside that, her name (which, as some construe it, importeth *great remembrance* [a commonplace: e.g., Tooke 1713: 217, repeating the etymology from Greek *polus* = much and *mneia* = remembrance]), containeth another part. But I hold rather with them which call her Polymnia or Polyhymnia of her good singing [*polus* + *hymnos* = hymn, ode; cf. Spenser, *Tears of the Muses*, 547–8].

104] **bay branches**) be the sign of honour and victory, and therefore of mighty conquerors worn in their triumphs, and eke [also] of famous poets, as saith Petrarch in his *Sonnets*:

> *Arbor vittoriosa triomphale,*
> *Honor d'Imperadori et di Poeti*, etc.

[*Rime*, 263: 'Victorious triumphal tree,/ Honour of emperors and poets'. The bay (laurel) belongs to Apollo, god of poetry, through the Daphne myth, which yields the victory symbolism (Ovid, *Metamorphoses*, 1. 559–61) as well as celebrating virginity, a significance primary to Petrarch's mythologisation of his beloved 'laurel', Laura: hence its further appropriateness here as a gift for Elisa.]

109] **the Graces**) be three sisters, the daughters of Jupiter (whose names are Aglaia, Thalia, Euphrosyne [Greek for Beauty (or Splendour), Abundance and Mirth respectively], and Homer only addeth a fourth, *scilicet* [namely] Pasithea [= Shining on All; *Iliad*, 14. 276]), otherwise called Charites, that is, Thanks; whom the poets feigned to be the goddesses of all bounty and comeliness which therefore, as saith Theodontius [although not cited in Boccaccio's chapter on the Graces, *De genealogia deorum*, 5. 35, Theodontius seems to be known only by the frequent citation of him in that work: Mustard 1919: 197–8], they make three: to wit, that men first ought to be gracious and bountiful to other freely; then to receive benefits at other men's hands courteously; and thirdly, to requite them thankfully: which are the three sundry actions in liberality. And Boccaccio saith [*ibid.*] that they be painted naked (as they were, indeed, on the tomb of C. Julius Caesar), the one having her back toward us and her face fromward [turned away], as proceeding from us; the other two toward us, noting double thank to be due to us for the benefit we have done. [A major source for the iconography of the Graces is Seneca's *De beneficiis*: Wind (1967) ch 2. In neo-Platonic thought the qualities represented separately by the Graces were understood to be infolded into the mystery of the composite Venus–Virgo (see emblem gloss below): Wind pp 75, 205.]

111] **deftly**) finely and nimbly [apparently a neologism in 1579, the date of *OED*'s first quotations (this and one other)].

111] **soot**) sweet [still just in use].

112] **merriment**) mirth [*OED*'s first citation 1576].

118] **bevy**) a bevy of ladies is spoken figuratively for a company or troop. The term is taken of larks; for they say *a bevy of larks* even as *a covey of partridge*, or *an eye of pheasants* [*OED* confirms E.K.'s explanation; it offers no citation between 1486 and this gloss of 1579].

120] **Ladies of the Lake**) be nymphs. For it was an old opinion amongst the ancient heathen that of every spring and fountain was a goddess the sovereign; which opinion stuck in the minds of men not many years sithence [since] by means of certain fine fablers and loud liars, such as were the authors of *King Arthur the Great*, and suchlike, who tell many an unlawful leasing [lie] of the Ladies of the lake, that is, the nymphs; for the word *nymph* in Greek signifieth *well water*, or, otherwise, a *spouse* or *bride* [E.K.'s scorn of Arthurian romance reflects Reformation rejection of its lack of moral seriousness: cf. Roger Ascham's dismissal of the *Morte d'Arthur* as comprising 'manslaughter and bold bawdry' (King 1982: 176–7 and 213–14); as such it opposes Spenser's mythopoeic intention here which seems rather to support the Arthurian (as well as other) aspects of the cult of Elizabeth: cf. George Gascoigne's 1575 *Kenilworth* entertainment (*February* 115n) in Nichols (1823) 1. 485–523 and MacLachlan in *SpE*, pp 64–6].

120] **behight**) called or named [cf. *May*, 201 and *December*, 54. A misunderstanding of its true meaning (vow, promise, etc.) perpetrated by Spenser and his followers as the word became obsolete (*OED* behight *v* II. 6)].

122] **Chloris**) the name of a nymph, and signifieth *greenness* [Greek *chl‾oros*], of whom it is said that Zephyrus, the western wind, being in love with her, and coveting her to wife, gave her for a dowry the chiefdom and sovereignty of all flowers and green herbs [plants] growing on earth [Ovid, *Fasti*, 5. 183–374 and *March* 16 gloss. Note the emphasis on marriage (with hints of Elizabeth and Alençon again?); E.K. suppresses the fact that Zephyrus took Chloris by force.].

124] **Olives bene**) the olive was wont to be the ensign of Peace and Quietness, either for that it cannot be planted and pruned and so carefully looked to, as it ought, but in time of peace, or else for that the olive tree (they say) will not grow near the fir tree, which is dedicate to Mars, the god of battle, and used most for spears and other instruments of war [Tervarent (1958) cols 131, 290 and, for Elizabeth and the olive, Strong 1963: 111–12 and Yates 1975: 58, 72. Patterson 1988: 122 notes that E.K. draws on Servius's gloss on Virgil's *Georgics*, 1. 11–13. For the fir as a weapon see Apollodorus, *Library*, 2. 5. 4.]. Whereupon is finely feigned that, when Neptune and Minerva strove for the naming of the city of Athens, Neptune, striking the ground with his mace, caused a horse to come forth, that importeth war; but at Minerva's stroke sprang out an olive, to note that it should be a nurse of learning and such peaceable studies [Pliny, *Natural History*, 16. 89. 240, but probably drawing on Servius on *Georgics* 1. 12: Mustard 1919: 198)].

133] **Bind your**) spoken rudely, and according to shepherds' simplicity.

136] **Bring**) all these be names of flowers: *sops-in-wine* a flower in colour much like to a *coronation*, but differing in smell and quantity [size; coronation was a common sixteenth-century variant for carnation, or cultivated pink, particularly appropriate for the decking of Elisa; so named because the tooth-edged petals made the flower look like a coronet (*OED*). The colour is, of course, pink (Latin *carnis* = flesh). *Sops-in-wine* entered the pastoral catalogue via Spenser (cf. *May*, 14) and appear to be another name for the *gillyflower*, itself a name for the carnation (William Salmon, *Pharmacopoeia Londinensis, or The New London Dispensatory* (1678) 1. 5. 14: '*Caryophylli rubri, Tunicae, Flores Vetonicae*, Clove-gilly flowers or Carnations'; also *OED*, sops-in-wine, citing Sylvester's *Du Bartas* (1605).]. *Flower de lis* [line 144], that which they use to [i.e., customarily] misterm *flower-de-luce*, being in Latin called *flos delitiarum*. [See *OED* for the etymologies; *flower-de-luce* = flower of light; *flos delitiarum* = flower of delights. It is the lily, emblem of purity (Tervarent (1958) col 248), of Juno, goddess of marriage (hence of the Virgin Queen's marriage to her realm; Linche (1599) sig M1v-2r), and of France; so that the flower could symbolise the Alençon marriage since *match* at line 44 = marry or encounter as an adversary: Tufte 1970: 176–8. Note that carnations and lilies, together with olive branches, roses and laurel, adorn the coffin of the dead queen mother in Marot's *Eglogue . . . de ma Dame Louise de Savoye*, ll. 230–1, 234, 239–40: see *April* headnote.]

145] **Now rise**) is the conclusion; for having so decked her with praises and comparisons, he returneth all the thank of his labour to the excellency of her Majesty [punning on the idea of the reciprocity symbolised by the Charites: 109 gloss].

152] **When damsons**) a base reward of a clownish giver.

155] **yblent**) *y* is a poetical addition [a mediaevalism, but still in Wyatt and Surrey]; *blent*: blinded [a mediaevalism used again in *FQ*, 1. 2. 5].

Emblem.

This poesy is taken out of Virgil, and there of him used in the person of Aeneas to his mother Venus, appearing to him in likeness of one of Diana's damsels, being there most divinely set forth [*Aeneid*, 1. 314–20]. To which similitude of divinity Hobbinol comparing the excellency of Elisa and being, through the worthiness of Colin's song, as it were overcome with the hugeness of his imagination, bursteth out in great admiration, *O quam te memorem virgo?* [*Aeneid*, 1. 327], being otherwise unable than by sudden silence to express the worthiness of his conceit [idea, image]. Whom Thenot answereth with another part of the like verse, as confirming by his grant and approvance that Elisa is no whit inferior to the majesty of her of whom the poet so boldly pronounced, *O dea certe* [*Aeneid*, 1. 328; the Venus–Diana symbolism of this passage spawned a neo-Platonic tradition in which the opposites were combined to embody chaste love: Wind 1967: 75–9 and plate 14. Spenser uses it in connection with Una in *FQ*, 1 (Brooks-Davies 1977: 64–5). It is appropriate in 1579, under the shadow of the Alençon marriage, as an affirmation of the Virgin Queen's betrothal to her realm: see *April* headnote.].

May

April's Virgilian 'Messianic' Virgin Queen of love is the successor to and inheritor of the Reformation initiated by Henry VIII's Act of Supremacy of 1534 and continued under Edward VI. That Reformation was itself re-formed after Mary Tudor's restoration of Catholicism (1553–8) by the Elizabethan Settlement of 1559 and its establishment of the English Church with the queen as its 'supreme governor'. Hence *May*, the month in which love in the form of the pagan festivals of Venus and Flora was traditionally celebrated, is structured as a dialogue concerning Elizabethan Protestantism's rejection of the licentiousness and frivolity (as well as the 'Catholic' taint) of traditional May festivities. It thus picks up the theme of *February*, which it mirrors also in its division into dialogue + fable and its metrical form of tetrameter rhyming couplets (see *February* headnote). *Piers* – inherited by Spenser from William Langland's late fourteenth-century ecclesiastical satire *Piers Plowman* and the reformist tradition it spawned (King (1982) ch 7; Norbrook 1984: 41–2; King 1990: 20–31) – is a form of *Peter*, the rock upon whom Christ founded the Church (Matthew 16: 18) which Protestants saw themselves as redeeming from centuries of Roman corruption. He speaks for the radical (or zealous) Protestantism of the 1570s as embodied in Archbishop Grindal, the Algrind of l. 75. (The possibility of an allusion to John Piers, Bishop of Salisbury, who preceded Young (*April* 21n) as Bishop of Rochester, suggested by McLane 1961: 175–87, has been dismissed by King 1985: 16 on the grounds of his religious conservatism.) *Palinode* = retraction or recantation. He objects to what Piers says not because he is formally a Catholic but because he sees continuing Protestant reform as a threat to the secularism that some Elizabethan clerical converts borrowed from their old Church and that had long been the topic of Catholic anti-prelatical satire in the pastoral mode by Petrarch, Chaucer, Mantuan, Marot, Skelton and others. For the best accounts of Spenser's religious position see Hume 1984; Norbrook (1984) ch 3; King 1985: 1–31. See also Whitaker 1950.

The sun enters Gemini in May, and since the Ptolemaic star total for the constellation (which symbolises concord) is 18, it is worth noting that *May* opens with a series of 4×18 line exchanges between the opposed Piers and Palinode (four is also a number of friendship and accord): on the symbolisms see Fowler 1964: 24–33 and 177–82, also *Proth* headnote.

The woodcut (fig. 5) parallels *April*'s woodcut in that both share two shepherd interlocutors (back left); a similar hilly background; and a sun setting by a leafy tree. This suggests in turn that the foreground elements may comment on each other – that *May*'s depict a May festal pageant (the kind of thing supported by Palinode) which is reminiscent of a monarchical progress or triumph and thus parallels Elisa and her maidens in the foreground of *April*'s woodcut, thereby raising the question of the relationship between the iconography of monarchical display and Protestant reformist attitudes to such display. Note that the wagon is drawn by winged horses – an allusion to Pegasus as the emblem of poetic fame or worldly glory, but also as the emblem of fleeting time (a symbolism underlined by the sun, which has set even further than in *April*'s woodcut): Tervarent (1958) cols 92–3.

May
Aegloga quinta

Argument

In this fifth eglogue, under the persons of two shepherds, Piers and Palinode, be represented two forms of pastors or ministers (or, the Protestant and the Catholic), whose chief talk standeth in reasoning whether the life of the one must be like the other: with whom, having showed that it is dangerous to maintain any fellowship or give too much credit to their colourable and feigned good will, he telleth him a tale of the fox that, by such a counterpoint of craftiness, deceived and devoured the credulous kid.

Palinode. Piers.

Is not thilk the merry month of May,
When love-lads masken in fresh array?
How falls it, then, we no merrier bene,
Ylike as others, girt in gaudy green?
Our blunket liveries bene all too sad   5
For thilk same season when all is yclad
With pleasance: the ground with grass, the woods
With green leaves, the bushes with blooming buds.

Textual note

Argument, opening line *fifth*] Q5; firste Q1–4.

Argument: *pastors*: shepherds in the Christian metaphorical sense. *Minister* is politically loaded, implying a firmly Protestant servant of God (as opposed to priest or clergyman): Palinode would strongly object that he was *not* a minister (for Grindal's use of the word see *February* 41n). *fellowship*: another loaded word. Contemporary meanings included: 'political alliance' and 'admission to membership of and communion within a [Protestant] church' (cf. Galatians 2: 9, 'the right hands of fellowship'; Geneva gloss: 'They gave us their hand in token that we agreed wholly to the doctrine of the Gospel'). *credit*: belief. *colourable*: deceptive. *counterpoint*: exact opposite (i.e., completely successful deception).
1. *thilk*: E.K.
4. *Ylike*: *March* 39n. *gaudy green*: bright green (mediaeval phrase). Green was the colour of hope and spring.
5. *blunket*: E.K.
6. *yclad*: E.K.
7. *pleasance*: that which awakens pleasure (cf. *February* 223n); also hinting at pleasure garden.
8. *blooming*: *January* 34n.

Yougthes-folk now flocken in everywhere
To gather May buskets and smelling briar, 10
And home they hasten the posts to dight,
And all the kirk pillars ere daylight,
With hawthorn buds and sweet eglantine,
And garlands of roses and sops-in-wine:
Such merry-make holy saints doth queme. 15
But we here sitten as drowned in a dream.

Piers.

For younkers, Palinode, such follies fit;
But we tway bene men of elder wit.

Palinode.

Siker this morrow – ne lenger ago –
I saw a shoal of shepherds outgo 20
With singing, and shouting, and jolly cheer.
Before them yode a lusty taborer
That to the many a hornpipe played,

---

9. *Yougthes-folk*: the spelling here, which may be Spenser's, is perhaps slightly more modern than *February*'s youngth: see *February* 52n. *in everywhere*: E.K.
10. *buskets*: E.K.
11. *dight*: *April* 29 gloss.
12. *kirk*: E.K. (the northern usage is ironic as it is applied to a lax church: see 18n on dialect).
13. *eglantine*: hedge rose or sweet briar (*February* 115n).
14. *garlands . . . wine*: *April* 59n and 136 gloss (note the way Palinode's speech interweaves allusions to both *February* and *April*).
15. *merry-make*: merry-making (*OED* cites *November*, 9 as first instance). *saints*: in the traditional Catholic sense followed by conservative members of the Elizabethan Church, as opposed to the more usual Protestant sense, 'the elect'. Cf. *July*, 113–24. *queme*: E.K.
17. *younkers*: young men (with a hint of class bias: youths of fashion).
18. *tway*: northern/Scots form. *elder wit*: (1) the knowledge belonging to age; (2) the wisdom belonging to a true minister (*elder* translates Greek *presbyteros* and here alludes to the office in the early church that radical Protestants saw themselves as restoring: Titus 1: 5: 'thou . . . shouldest ordain Elders in every city as I appointed thee'. Piers hints at the model followed in Scotland by Calvin's disciple John Knox and reinforced here, as in *July* and *September*, by the adoption of northern/Scots linguistic forms which complement the 'plowman' *persona* signalled in the headnote).
19. *Siker*: *February* 55 gloss. *lenger*: archaic form.
20. *shoal*: E.K. *outgo*: go forth (archaic).
22. *yode*: E.K. *lusty*: *February* 16 and 131nn. *taborer*: drummer.
23. *many*: company.

Whereto they dancen, each one with his maid:
To see those folks make such jouissance 25
Made my heart after the pipe to dance.
Tho to the green wood they speeden hem all
To fetchen home May with their musical,
And him they bringen in a royal throne,
Crowned as king; and his queen at one 30
Was Lady Flora, on whom did attend
A fair flock of fairies and a fresh band
Of lovely nymphs (O that I were there
To helpen the ladies their May bush bear!).
Ah, Piers, bene not thy teeth on edge to think 35
How great sport they gainen with little swink?

       Piers.
Perdy, so far am I from envy
That their fondness inly I pity:
Those faitours little regarden their charge
While they, letting their sheep run at large, 40
Passen their time, that should be sparely spent,
In lustihead and wanton merriment.
Thilk same bene shepherds for the devil's stead
That playen while their flocks be unfed:

---

25. *jouissance*: E.K.
27. *hem*: them, a colloquial and possibly archaic form.
28. *May*: the May-lord who was chosen to preside over the May-day festivities, embodiment of the may tree (hawthorn): Barber 1968: 18–24. Cf. Grindal's attack on festive lords, *February* 41n. *musical*: musical performance (*OED* musical *a* and *sb* B 1 cites only this and one other instance).
29. *him*: all editions print *home*, which I have treated as a variant of *heom*, a form of *him*: *OED*.
30. *at one*: in concord (almost 'companion in harness').
31. *Flora*: the female May deity and Roman fertility goddess, metamorphosed from Chloris: *March* 16 and *April* 122 glosses.
32. *band*: the original spelling *bend* preserves the rhyme.
36. *swink*: E.K.
37. *Perdy*: *March* 104n.
38. *fondness*: folly. *inly*: E.K.
39. *faitours*: E.K.
41. *sparely*: frugally (*OED* cites Arthur Golding (tr.) 1571 *The Psalms of David . . . with J. Calvin's Commentaries*, Psalm 37: 25: 'By their living sparely, they have always enough').
42. *lustihead*: (1) vigour; (2) pleasure; (3) lustfulness.
43. *stead*: place.

Well is it seen, their sheep bene not their own 45
That letten them run at random alone;
But they bene hired for little pay
Of other that caren as little as they
What fallen the flock, so they han the fleece
And get all the gain, paying but a piece. 50
I muse what account both these will make –
The one for the hire which he doth take,
And the other for leaving his Lord's task –
When great Pan account of shepherds shall ask.

                      Palinode.
Siker now I see thou speakest of spite 55
All for thou lackest somedeal their delight.
I, as I am, had rather be envied –
All were it of my foe – than fonly pitied;
And yet, if need were, pitied would be
Rather than other should scorn at me: 60
For pitied is mishap that n'as remedy,
But scorned bene deeds of fond foolery.
What shoulden shepherds other things tend
Than, sith their God his good does them send,
Reapen the fruit thereof (that is, pleasure) 65

45–50. Well . . . piece: the appointing of inadequate curates or deputies as a consequence of pluralism and resultant absenteeism was a common abuse within the English Church, as the Puritans were not alone in pointing out: cf. *July*, 173–80 (on the Roman Church) and *Var* 1. 298 citing Philip Stubbes, *The Anatomy of Abuses* (1583) 2. 2. The key biblical text is John 10: 11–12: 'I am that good shepherd: that good shepherd giveth his life for his sheep. But an hireling, and he which is not the shepherd, neither the sheep are his own, seeth the wolf coming, and he leaveth the sheep, and fleeth, and the wolf catcheth them, and scattereth the sheep' (cf. 54 gloss).
50. piece: (1) coin; (2) portion.
54. great Pan: E.K. *account*: cf. Matthew 12: 36: 'But I say unto you, that of every idle word that men shall speak, they shall give account thereof at the day of judgement'.
55. of: out of.
56. somedeal: somewhat.
57. I . . . am: E.K.
58. fonly: foolishly.
61. n'as: E.K.
64. sith: seeing that.
65. Reapen: ironically recalling Galatians 6: 8: 'For he that soweth to his flesh, shall of the flesh reap corruption: but he that soweth to the spirit, shall of the spirit reap life everlasting'.

The while they here liven, at ease and leisure?
For when they bene dead their good is ygo:
They sleepen in rest well as other mo'.
Tho with them wends what they spent in cost,
But what they left behind them is lost: 70
Good is no good but if it be spend:
God giveth good for none other end.

               Piers.
Ah, Palinode, thou art a world's child:
Who touches pitch mought needs be defiled.
But shepherds – as Algrind used to say – 75
Mought not live ylike as men of the lay:
With them it sits to care for their heir
Enaunter their heritage do impair:
They must provide for means of maintenance
And to continue their wont countenance. 80
But shepherd must walk another way:
Sike worldly sovenance he must forsay;

68. *other mo'*: many others.
69. *Tho . . . them*: E.K. *Tho*: then. *wends*: departs.
74. *Who . . . defiled*: Ecclesiasticus 13: 1 (Old Testament apocrypha). Geneva gloss: 'The companies of the proud and of the rich are to be eschewed'.
75. *Algrind*: anagram of *Grindal*: i.e., Edmund Grindal, formerly Archbishop of York and, since 1576, Archbishop of Canterbury. Appointed at Burghley's urging and because of his sympathy with radical Protestantism (he was one of the Marian exiles and involved in the Bishops' Bible and John Foxe's history and martyrology *Acts and Monuments* (1563)), he subsequently refused to suppress the clerical meetings on the interpretation of scripture known as 'prophesyings' (which involved lay participation and were Puritan in origin) and was suspended from his duties from May 1577 until late in 1582. See E.K.; *July*, 213–30; Collinson 1979; Bednarz in *SpE*, pp 342–3.
76. *men . . . lay*: E.K.
78. *Enaunter*: E.K.
80. *wont countenance*: customary appearance.
81–94. *But . . . overflow*: Piers propounds the extreme Protestant doctrine of 'living by faith' which originates with Matthew 6 (cf. Luke 12): 'Lay not up treasures for yourselves upon the earth. . . . Therefore take no thought, saying, What shall we eat? or what shall we drink? or wherewith shall we be clothed? (For after all these things seek the Gentiles) for your heavenly Father knoweth that ye have need of all these things'. His concept of *inheritance* is the Pauline one of the inheritance of the spirit (Acts 26: 18; Galatians 3: 18 and Geneva gloss; Colossians 1: 12, etc.).
82: *Sike*: such. *sovenance*: E.K. *forsay*: renounce. Cf. *July* 69n.

The son of his loins why should he regard
To leave enriched with that he hath spared?
Should not thilk God that gave him that good 85
Eke cherish his child, if in his ways he stood?
For, if he mislive in lewdness and lust,
Little boots all the wealth and the trust
That his father left by inheritance:
All will be soon wasted with misgovernance. 90
But through this, and other their miscreance,
They maken many a wrong chevisance,
Heaping up waves of wealth and woe
The floods whereof shall them overflow.
Sike men's folly I cannot compare 95
Better than to the ape's foolish care,
That is so enamoured of her young one
(And yet, God wote, such cause hath she none)
That with her hard hold and strait embracing
She stoppeth the breath of her youngling: 100
So, oftentimes, when as good is meant,
Evil ensueth of wrong intent.
 The time was once, and may again return
(For aught may happen that hath bene beforn),
When shepherds had none inheritance – 105
Ne of land, nor fee – in sufferance,
But what might arise of the bare sheep
(Were it more, or less) which they did keep.

83–6. The . . . stood: concerning one of the problems attending on the Protestant affirmation of the right of the clergy to marry.
84. spared: (1) refrained from using; (2) saved up: *October* 9n.
88. boots: does good, cures. *trust*: property entrusted.
90. misgovernance: mismanagement (archaic).
91. miscreance: E.K.
92. chevisance: E.K.
94. floods . . . overflow: Psalm 69: 15: 'Let not the water floods drown me . . .'.
96. ape's . . . care: familiar fable originating with Pliny, *Natural History*, 8. 80. 215–16. Cf. Whitney 1586: 188 ('With kindness, lo, the Ape doth kill her whelp,/Through clasping hard . . . /Even so, the babes, whose nature, Art should help:/The parents fond do hazard them with harms . . . '). Alongside the fable of the Goat and Kid, this offers a warning about the limits of monarchical power (see 180n).
98. wote: *February* 85n.
99. strait: tight, constricting.
103. The . . . return: *February* 11–16n.
106. fee: revenue. *sufferance*: *February* 187n.

Well, ywis, was it with shepherds tho:
Nought having, nought feared they to forgo; 110
For Pan himself was their inheritance,
And little them served for their maintenance.
The shepherds' God so well them guided
That of nought they were unprovided:
Butter enough, honey, milk, and whey, 115
And their flocks' fleeces them to array.
But tract of time, and long prosperity
(That, nurse of vice, this of insolency)
Lulled the shepherds in such security
That, not content with loyal obeisance, 120
Some 'gan to gape for greedy governance
And match themself with mighty potentates,
Lovers of lordship, and troublers of states.
Tho 'gan shepherds' swains to look aloft
And leave to live hard, and learn to ligge soft. 125
Tho, under colour of shepherds, somewhile

109. ywis: archaic form of *iwis* = indeed. *tho*: 69n above.
110. forgo: do without.
111. Pan: E.K.
115. Butter . . . whey: mixes biblical primitivism (e.g., Genesis 18: 8) and prophecy (Joshua 5: 6: 'the land, which the Lord had sworn unto their fathers, that he would give us, even a land that floweth with milk and honey'). Note 'that sincere milk of the word' (1 Peter 2: 2) and Psalm 119: 103, on God's word: 'How sweet are thy promises unto my mouth! yea, more than honey unto my mouth'; and cf. Isaiah 7: 15: 'Butter and honey shall he eat, till he have knowledge to refuse the evil and to choose the good'.
116. array: attire.
117. tract: passage.
121. Some 'gan: E.K. *governance*: mode of living.
123. Lovers of lordship: Piers may voice the Puritan objection to the English Church's retention of the episcopate (and hence the equation of lords spiritual and temporal), or he may simply repeat radical Protestant objections to episcopal worldliness. Cf. 1 Peter 5: 1–4: 'The Elders which are among you, I beseech which am also an Elder. . . . Feed the flock of God, which dependeth upon you, caring for it not by constraint, but willingly: not for filthy lucre, but of a ready mind: Not as though ye were Lords over God's heritage, but that ye may be examples to the flock. And when that chief Shepherd shall appear, ye shall receive an incorruptible crown of glory'.
125. ligge: lie (archaic northern form): cf. 217 gloss.
126. colour: disguise.

There crept in wolves, full of fraud and guile,
That often devoured their own sheep,
And often the shepherds that did hem keep.
This was the first source of shepherds' sorrow,   130
That now nill be quit with bail nor borrow.

                     Palinode.
Three things to bear bene very burdenous,
But the fourth to forbear is outrageous.
Women, that of love's longing once lust,
Hardly forbearen, but have it they must: 135
So, when choler is inflamed with rage,
Wanting revenge is hard to assuage;
And who can counsel a thristy soul
With patience to forbear the offered bowl?
But, of all burdens that a man can bear,   140
Most is, a fool's talk to bear and to hear:
I ween the giant has not such a weight
That bears on his shoulders the heavens' height.
Thou findest fault where n'is to be found,
And buildest strong wark upon a weak ground: 145
Thou railest on right withouten reason
And blamest hem much for small encheason.
How shoulden shepherds live, if not so?
What, should they pinen in pain and woe?

---

127. wolves: cf. the fable in *September*, 146–225. The biblical basis for this favourite Renaissance pastoral motif is Matthew 7: 15 : 'Beware of false prophets, which come to you in sheep's clothing, but inwardly they are ravening wolves' (Geneva gloss: 'False teachers must be taken heed of, and they are known by false doctrine and evil living'). The next verse suggests a link between *May* and the Briar of *February*: 'Ye shall know them by their fruits. Do men gather grapes of thorns?'.
129. hem: see 27n above.
130. source: E.K.
131. nill: will not (ne + will): possibly archaic. *bail*: release (on security). *borrow*: E.K.
132–3. Three . . . fourth: for the formula, cf., e.g., Proverbs 30: 18, 21, 29.
133. forbear: refrain from. *outrageous*: exceeding proper limits.
137. Wanting: lacking.
138. thristy: *April* 8n.
141. fool's talk: Proverbs 18: 6–7, 29: 11, Ecclesiastes 5: 3, 10: 14 etc.
142. giant: E.K.
144. n'is: archaic: cf. 61 gloss and *June*, 19.
145. wark: E.K.
147. encheason: E.K.

Nay said I thereto, by my dear borrow: 150
If I may rest, I nill live in sorrow.
Sorrow ne need be hastened on,
For he will come without calling anon.
While times enduren of tranquillity,
Usen we freely our felicity; 155
For when approachen the stormy stours
We mought with our shoulders bear off the sharp showers.
And, sooth to sayn, nought seemeth sike strife
That shepherds so witen each other's life
And layen her faults the world beforn 160
The while their foes done each of hem scorn.
Let none mislike of that may not be mended:
So conteck soon by concord mought be ended.

      Piers.
Shepherd, I list none accordance make
With shepherd that does the right way forsake, 165
And of the twain (if choice were to me)
Had lever my foe than my friend he be:

150. borrow: E.K.
156. stours: *January* 51 gloss.
157. bear off: thrust away (*OED* bear *v* 1, III. 26b citing only one instance, from 1627).
158–63. And . . . ended: the call for peace in the Church, frequent at the time, was based on 1 Corinthians 11: 16: 'But if any man lust to be contentious, we have no such custom, neither the Churches of God' (Geneva gloss: 'Against such as are stubbornly contentious we have to oppose this, that the Churches of God are not contentious') and Galatians 5: 26: 'Let us not be desirous of vain glory, provoking one another, envying one another' (Geneva gloss: 'He addeth peculiar exhortations according as he knew the Galatians subject to divers vices: and first of all he warneth them to take heed of ambition, which vice hath two fellows, backbiting and envy, out of which two it cannot be but many contentions must needs arise').
158. nought seemeth: E.K.
159. witen: E.K.
160. her: E.K. *beforn*: mediaeval form.
161. done: archaic: cf. *February* 6n.
162. that: that which.
163. conteck: E.K. The phrase, like others in Palinode's speech (e.g., 144–5, 152–3), is proverbial, rooting him in a conservative, Catholic, past. *SC*'s reformers, on the other hand, speak the reformist language of the prophetic past: that of Langland and Chaucer complemented by northern/Scots forms (*May* headnote and 18n, *SC* Epilogue 10n).
164. list: choose. *accordance*: agreement.
167. lever: rather (mediaeval form of *liefer*).

For what concord han light and dark sam?
Or what peace has the lion with the lamb?
Such faitours, when their false hearts bene hid,   170
Will do as did the Fox by the Kid.

      Palinode.
Now, Piers, of fellowship tell us that saying,
For the lad can keep both our flocks from straying.

      Piers.
Thilk same Kid (as I can well devise)
Was too very foolish and unwise,   175
For on a time in summer season
The Gate, her dame, that had good reason,
Yode forth abroad unto the green wood
To browse, or play, or what she thought good.
But, for she had a motherly care   180
Of her young son, and wit to beware,

---

168. han . . . sam: E.K. *concord . . . dark*: 2 Corinthians 6: 14: 'Be not unequally yoked with the infidels: for what fellowship hath righteousness with unrighteousness? and what communion hath light with darkness?'
169. peace . . . lamb: as in the case of 168, an uncompromisingly Protestant position, this time based on Micah 5: 8, where 'the Lion whelp among the flocks of sheep, who, when he goeth through, treadeth down and teareth in pieces' is an emblem of God's destruction of 'all things wherein thou puttest thy confidence, as thy vain confidence and idolatry' (Geneva gloss). The eirenic promise of Isaiah 11: 6 ('The wolf also shall dwell with the lamb'; Geneva gloss: 'Men because of their wicked affections are named by the names of beasts, wherein the like affections reign: but Christ by his Spirit shall reform them, and work in them such mutual charity, that they shall be like lambs, favouring and loving one another, and cast off all their cruel affections') is for Piers a prophecy still to be fought for. Before the Fall the animals were at peace: Hutton 1984: 233–7.
170. faitours: 39 gloss.
172. fellowship: cf. *May* Argument n and 168n.
173. lad . . . straying: *March* 38–9n.
174. E.K. *devise*: imagine.
177. Gate: E.K. *her*: his (dialectal). *dame*: primary meaning = female ruler (with a glance at Elizabeth); its subsidiary meaning = mistress of a household: *OED* dame *sb* I. 1, 2.
178. Yode: E.K.
180. motherly care: hinting at Elizabeth's relationship with the realm via Isaiah 49: 23: 'And Kings shall be thy nursing fathers, and Queens shall be thy nurses' (a fundamental text for patriarchal/matriarchal theories of monarchical power and responsibility).
181. wit to beware: sense to be cautious.

She set her youngling before her knee
That was both fresh and lovely to see,
And full of favour, as kid mought be:
His vellet head began to shoot out, 185
And his wreathed horns 'gan newly sprout;
The blossoms of lust to bud did begin
And spring forth rankly under his chin.
   'My son', quoth she (and with that 'gan weep,
For care-full thoughts in her heart did creep) 190
'God bless thee, poor orphan, as he mought me,
And send thee joy of thy jollity.
Thy father —' (that word she spake with pain,
For a sigh had nigh rent her heart in twain)
'Thy father, had he lived this day 195
To see the branch of his body display,
How would he have joyed at this sweet sight!
But ah, false Fortune such joy did him spite,
And cut off his days with untimely woe,
Betraying him into the trains of his foe. 200
Now I, a wailful widow behight,
Of my old age have this one delight:
To see thee succeed in thy father's stead,
And flourish in flowers of lustihead;
For even so thy father his head upheld, 205
And so his haughty horns did he wield'.
   Tho, marking him with melting eyes,
A thrilling throb from her heart did arise,
And interrupted all her other speech

182. She set: E.K.
184. favour: good appearance.
185. vellet: velvet (northern/Scots form).
187. The . . . lust: E.K.
188. rankly: proudly, vigorously.
189. and with: E.K.
191. orphan: E.K. *mought*: may (not archaic).
193. that word: E.K.
196. the branch: E.K.
200. trains: snares.
201. behight: *April* 120 gloss.
203. stead: place.
204. lustihead: lustiness (i.e., vigour, lustfulness).
205. For even so: E.K.
206. haughty: (1) high (a sense frequent only between 1570 and 1621: *OED* haughty *a* 3); (2) stately (sense 1b, first instance 1585). *wield*: the original spelling *weld* maintains the rhyme.
208. thrilling throb: E.K.

With some old sorrow that made a new breach: 210
Seemed she saw in the youngling's face
The old lineaments of his father's grace.
At last her sullen silence she broke
And 'gan his new-budded beard to stroke:
   'Kiddy,' quoth she, 'thou kennest the great care 215
I have of thy health and thy welfare
Which many wild beasts liggen in wait
For to entrap in thy tender state;
But most the Fox, master of collusion
(For he has vowed thy last confusion). 220
For-thy, my Kiddy, be ruled by me
And never give trust to his treachery.
And if he chance come when I am abroad
Spar the yate fast for fear of fraud:
Ne for all his worst, nor for his best, 225
Open the door at his request'.
   So schooled the Gate her wanton son,
That answered his mother, all should be done.
Tho went the pensive dam out of door
And chanced to stumble at the threshold floor. 230
Her stumbling step somewhat her amazed
(For such, as signs of ill luck, bene dispraised)
Yet forth she yode thereat half-aghast,
And Kiddy the door sparred after her fast.
It was not long after she was gone 235
But the false Fox came to the door anon:
Not as a fox (for then he had be kenned)
But all as a poor pedlar he did wend,
Bearing a truss of trifles at his back,

213. sullen: (1) gloomy; (2) lonely (the original spelling *solein* – perhaps Spenser's – may be intentionally archaic).
215. kennest: *April* 21 gloss.
217. liggen: E.K.
219. master . . . collusion: E.K.
220. confusion: destruction.
221. For-thy: *March* 37 gloss.
224. Spar the yate: E.K.: note the use of northern forms in a reformist context again: 18n above.
232. For such: E.K. *dispraised*: blamed.
234. fast: firmly.
238. wend: travel.
239. truss: bundle.

As bells, and babes, and glasses in his pack. 240
A biggin he had got about his brain,
For in his head-piece he felt a sore pain;
His hinder heel was wrapped in a clout,
For with great cold he had got the gout.
There at the door he cast me down his pack 245
And laid him down and groaned 'Alack! alack!
Ah, dear Lord, and sweet Saint Charity,
That some good body would once pity me!'.
Well heard Kiddy all this sore constraint
And lenged to know the cause of his complaint. 250
Tho, creeping close behind the wicket's clink,
Privily he peeped out through a chink –
Yet not so privily but the Fox him spied,
For deceitful-meaning is double eyed.
'Ah, good young master' (then 'gan he cry), 255
'Jesus bless that sweet face I espy,
And keep your corpse from the care-full stounds
That in my carrion carcase abounds'.
The Kid, pitying his heaviness,
Asked the cause of his great distress, 260
And also who, and whence, that he were.
Tho he (that had well yconned his lere)

240. *As bells*: E.K.
241. *biggin*: night-cap tied under the chin (but an authoritarian symbol in that it also denoted the headgear of a serjeant-at-law: *OED* biggin 1, 2).
243. *clout*: rag.
244. *great cold*: E.K.
245. *me*: the ethical dative (expressive of the narrator's interest in the detail narrated).
247. *Saint Charity*: E.K.
249. *constraint*: distress. *OED*'s last citation of a usage that starts with Chaucer: constraint *sb* 3a. Cf. *November*, 205.
250. *lenged*: longed (apparently a false northern dialect form: should for accuracy read *langed*).
251. *wicket*: small door or gate. *clink*: E.K.
252. *Privily*: stealthily.
254. *deceitful . . . eyed*: Deceit has two heads and thus two pairs of eyes: Ripa 1603: 173–5.
257. *stounds*: E.K.
258. *carrion*: putrefying with illness; also *fleshly* in the Pauline sense of *sinful* (e.g., 2 Corinthians 7: 1 and, bearing in mind the pun on *corpse* = *corpus* = *body* in 257, Colossians 2: 11: 'the sinful body of the flesh'). In addition, Spenser invokes the familiar fable of the fox who feigns death: Ansell Robin 1932: 16.
259. *heaviness*: dejection.
262. *yconned*: learned. *lere*: E.K. (punning also on *leer* = sly glance and *lere* = destruction (*OED* lure *sb* 1)).

Thus meddled his talk with many a tear:
'Sick, sick, alas, and little lack of dead,
But I be relieved by your beastlihead. 265
I am a poor sheep, albe my colour dun,
For with long travail I am brent in the sun;
And if that my grandsire me said be true,
Siker I am very sib to you.
So be your goodlihead, do not disdain 270
The base kindred of so simple swain:
Of mercy and favour then I you pray
With your aid to forestall my near decay'.

   Tho out of his pack a glass he took
Wherein, while Kiddy unwares did look, 275
He was so enamoured with the newel
That nought he deemed dear for the jewel.
Tho opened he the door, and in came
The false Fox as he were stark lame
(His tail he clapped betwixt his legs twain 280
Lest he should be descried by his train).

   Being within, the Kid made him good glee
All for the love of the glass he did see.
After his cheer the pedlar 'gan chat
And tell many leasings of this and that, 285
And how he could show many a fine knack.
Tho showed his ware, and opened his pack –
All save a bell, which he left behind
In the basket for the Kid to find;
Which, when the Kid stooped down to catch, 290
He popped him in and his basket did latch:
Ne stayed he once the door to make fast,
But ran away with him all in haste.

263. meddled: E.K.
264. lack of: short of [being].
265. But: unless. *beastlihead*: E.K.
267. travail: (1) exertion; (2) suffering; (3) journey. *brent*: burned (mediaeval form).
269. Siker: February 55 gloss. Punning on *siker* = safe, trustworthy. *sib*: E.K.
273. forestall: E.K.
276. newel: E.K.
280–1. tail . . . train: for the fox's tail as a specific emblem of deceit, see Aptekar 1969: 143 and Duessa in *FQ*, 1. 8. 48. *train* = (1) tail; (2) lure; (3) trickery.
282. glee: E.K.
284. After . . . cheer: in response to his gaiety.
285. leasings: lies.

Home when the doubtful dam had her hied
She mought see the door stand open wide: 295
All aghast, loudly she 'gan to call
Her Kid, but he nould answer at all.
Tho on the floor she saw the merchandise
Of which her son had set too dear a price.
What help? Her Kid she knew well was gone: 300
She wept, and wailed, and made great moan.
Such end had the Kid for he nould warned be
Of craft coloured with simplicity:
And such end, perdy, does all hem remain
That of such falsers' friendship bene fain. 305

      Palinode.
Truly, Piers, thou art beside thy wit,
Furthest fro' the mark, weening it to hit.
Now, I pray thee, let me thy tale borrow
For our Sir John to say tomorrow
At the kirk when it is holiday, 310
For well he means but little can say:
But and if foxes bene so crafty, as so,
Much needeth all shepherds hem to know.

      Piers.
Of their falsehood more could I recount;
But now the bright Sun 'ginneth to dismount 315

294. doubtful: full of fear. *hied*: hastened.
297. nould: *February* 192 gloss, and cf. 131n above.
298. merchandise: the Catholics defile the house/temple as the money changers did: John 2: 16: 'Take these things hence: make not my father's house, an house of merchandise'. But equivalent corruption in the English Church is also implied: cf. the Geneva gloss on Matthew's version (21: 12–13): 'Under the pretence of religion hypocrites seek their own gain, and spoil God of his true worship'.
299. price: E.K. Hinting – via *borrow* at 131 and 150 – at Christ's purchase of our salvation as at 1 Corinthians 6: 20: 'For ye are bought for a price'.
304. such end: E.K.
305. fain: E.K.
306. art . . . wit: have misunderstood.
308. borrow: Palinode has, perhaps, used up his spiritual credit: 299n.
309. Sir John: E.K. *say*: in the sense 'to say mass'.
311. can: knows (what or how to): Palinode appropriates Piers's radical tale as an anodyne homily for a Catholic-style (or middle-way English Church) *holy-day* (saint's day) festival (310). On *kirk* see 12n above.
315. dismount: E.K.

And, for the dewy Night now doth nigh,
I hold it best for us home to hie.

>Palinode's emblem:
>*Pas men apistos apistei.*

>Piers his emblem: 320
>*Tis d'ara pistis apistō.*

GLOSS

1] **thilk**) this same month. It is applied to the season of the month when all men delight themselves with pleasance [enjoyment] of fields, and gardens and garments [*thilk* is archaic but passes without gloss at *January*, 61].

5] **blunket liveries**) grey coats [*blunket* = grey was common in the sixteenth century].

6] **yclad**) arrayed; *y* redoundeth [returns] as before [*April* 155 gloss].

9] **in everywhere**) a strange yet proper kind of speaking [E.K. comments on the substantival use of *where* (everywhere = every place), though it is quite common in the sixteenth century: *OED* where III. 14].

10] **buskets**) a diminutive, *scilicet* [namely] little bushes of hawthorn [*OED*'s only citation].

12] **kirk**) church [northern/Scots].

15] **queme**) please [mediaevalism].

20] **a shoal**) a multitude: taken of fish, whereof some going in great companies are said to swim in a shoal [first citation of this meaning in *OED* shoal sb 2, which notes an almost contemporaneous use of it in North's *Plutarch* to denote a flock of birds].

22] **yode**) went [archaic but not infrequent in sixteenth-century literary texts].

25] **jouissance**) joy [*OED*'s first instance of this sense, citing also *November*, 2].

36] **swink**) labour [mediaevalism; cf. *April* 99 gloss].

38 **inly**) entirely [i.e., straight to the heart].

39] **faitours**) vagabonds [specifically means impostors, which fits Spenser's meaning better; archaic].

54] **great Pan**) is Christ, the very God of all shepherds [cf. *April* 50 gloss], which calleth himself the great and good shepherd [John 10: 14; Hebrews 13: 20]. The name is most rightly, methinks, applied to him, for *Pan* signifieth *all* or *omnipotent*, which is only the Lord Jesus. And by that name, as I remember, he is called of Eusebius in his fifth book *De Preparat. Evang.*, who thereof telleth a proper story to that purpose [Eusebius, *Praeparatio Evangelica*, 5. 17. 6–9], which story is first recorded of Plutarch in his book *Of the Ceasing of Oracles* [*De Defectu Oraculorum*, 17], and of Lavater translated in his book of walking spirits [Ludwig Lavater, *De Spectris*, tr. R[obert] H[arrison] as *Of Ghosts and Spirits Walking by Night* (1572), 1. 19, which also supplies E.K. with his two references]: who saith, that about the same time that our Lord suffered his most bitter Passion for the redemption of man, certain passengers sailing

316. nigh: E.K.
319–21. Pas . . . apistō: E.K.

from Italy to Cyprus and passing by certain isles called Paxae, heard a voice calling aloud, 'Thamus, Thamus'. Now Thamus was the name of an Egyptian which was pilot of the ship, who, giving ear to the cry, was bidden, when he came to Palodes, to tell that the great Pan was dead: which he doubting to do, yet, for that when he came to Palodes there suddenly was such a calm of wind that the ship stood still in the sea unmoved, he was forced to cry aloud that Pan was dead. Wherewithal there was heard such piteous outcries and dreadful shrieking as hath not been the like. By which Pan, though of some be understood the great Satan, whose kingdom at that time was by Christ conquered, the gates of hell broken up, and death by death delivered to eternal death (for at that time, as he saith, all oracles surceased, and enchanted spirits, that were wont to delude the people, thenceforth held their peace), and also, at the demand of the Emperor Tiberius, who that Pan should be, answer was made him by the wisest and best learned that it was the son of Mercury and Penelope, yet I think it more properly meant of the death of Christ, the only and very [true] Pan, then suffering for his flock.

57] **I, as I am**) seemeth to imitate the common proverb, *malim invidere mihi omnes quam miserescere* ['I would prefer to have everyone envy rather than pity me'; precise source unknown, but there are close parallels in Pindar, *Pythian Odes*, 1. 85 ('envy is better than pity') and Herodotus, 3. 52 ('consider how much better a thing it is to be envied than to be pitied'): Mustard 1919: 198 citing Erasmus, *Adagia*, 1044B].

61] **n'as**) is a syncope [contraction] for *ne has*, or *has not*: as *nould* for *would not* [see *February* 192 gloss].

69] **Tho with them**) doth imitate the epitaph of the riotous king Sardanapalus [ninth century B.C. king of the Assyrian empire] which caused to be written on his tomb in Greek (which verses be thus translated by Tully):

> *Haec habui quae edi, quaeque exaturata libido*
> *Hausit, at illa manent multa ac praeclara relicta.*

Which may thus be turned into English:

> All that I ate did I 'joy, and all that I greedily gorged;
> As for those many goodly matters, left I for others.

[Cicero, *Tusculanae Disputationes*, 5. 35. 101; Spenser's own translation into quantitative (hexameter: emblem gloss) verse: see his preliminary address to *Three . . . Letters* (1580)]. Much like the epitaph of a good old Earl of Devonshire which, though much more wisdom bewrayeth [reveals] than Sardanapalus, yet hath a smack of his sensual delights and beastliness. The rhymes be these:

> Ho, ho, who lies here?
> I, the good Earl of Devonshire,
> And Maud my wife, that was full dear.
> We lived together lv [fifty-five] year:
>> That we spent, we had;
>> That we gave, we have;
>> That we left, we lost.

75] **Algrind**) the name of a shepherd [see 75n above].
76] **men of the lay**) laymen [as opposed to 'men of the faith': *OED* lay *sb* 3].
78] **Enaunter**) lest that [*February* 200 gloss].
82] **sovenance**) remembrance [*November* 5 gloss].
91] **miscreance**) despair or misbelief [rare but not archaic].
92] **chevisance**) sometime of Chaucer used for *gain*, sometime of other for *spoil*, or *booty*, or *enterprise*, and sometime for *chiefdom* [common in the sixteenth century].
111] **Pan himself**) God, according as is said in Deuteronomy [10: 9], that in division of the land of Canaan, to the tribe of Levi [the priests] no portion of heritage should be allotted, for God himself was their inheritance.
121] **Some 'gan**) meant of the Pope and his Antichristian [i.e., belonging to Antichrist] prelates which usurp a tyrannical dominion in the Church and, with Peter's [note the omission of 'saint'] counterfeit keys, open a wide gate to all wickedness and insolent government. Nought here spoken as of purpose to deny fatherly rule and godly governance (as some maliciously of late have done to the great unrest and hindrance of the Church) but to display the pride and disorder of such as, instead of feeding their sheep, indeed feed off their sheep.
130] **source**) wellspring and original [in its literal sense, a mediaevalism, first cited in *OED* from Chaucer; Spenser's is apparently an early example of its metaphorical use: *OED*'s first citation (source *sb* 3c) is dated 1581].
131] **borrow**) pledge or surety [archaic; see 150 gloss].
142] **the giant**) is the great Atlas, whom the poets feign to be a huge giant that beareth heaven on his shoulders – being, indeed, a marvellous high mountain in Mauretania (that now is Barbary [the Moslem countries on the north-African coast]) which to man's seeming pierceth the clouds and seemeth to touch the heavens. Other think, and they not amiss, that this fable was meant of one Atlas, king of the same country (of whom, maybe, that that hill had his denomination), brother to Prometheus, who, as the Greeks say, did first find out the hidden courses of the stars by an excellent imagination, wherefore the poets feigned that he sustained the firmament on his shoulders. Many other conjectures, needless to be told hereof. [E.K. repeats commonplaces: Fraunce 1592: 9, Ross 1648: 36–7.]
145] **wark**) work [northern/Scots form].
147] **encheason**) cause, occasion [*OED*'s first citation after 1450].
150] **dear borrow**) that is, our Saviour, the common pledge of all men's debts to death.
158] **nought seemeth**) is unseemly.
159] **witen**) blame [archaic; northern/Scots overtones].
160] **her**) their, as useth Chaucer [and thus a southern/south midland form; *her* was obsolete by 1500].
163] **conteck**) strife, contention [mediaevalism; cf. *September* 86 gloss].
168] **han**) for *have* [midland form; see *March*, 62, which passes without gloss].
168] **sam**) together [this is *OED*'s first citation after *c*. 1525].
174] This tale is much like to that in Aesop's *Fables* [The Wolf and the Kid: Chambry 1967: 49], but the catastrophe [denouement; *OED*'s first instance of this usage] and end is far different. By the Kid may be understood the simple sort of the faithful and true Christians; by his Dam, Christ, that hath already with careful watchwords (as here doth the goat) warned his little ones to beware

of such doubling deceit; by the Fox, the false and faithless papists, to whom is no credit to be given, nor fellowship to be used. [Foxes, a type of the devil after Luke 13: 32, were frequently identified in Protestant polemic with English clergy who secretly favoured Roman doctrines; while wolves represented Roman priests: Hume 1984: 21–6.]

177] **The Gate**) the Goat: northernly spoken, to turn *o* into *a*.

178] **yode**) went: aforesaid [22 gloss].

182] **She set**) a figure called fictio, which useth to attribute reasonable [rational] actions and speeches to unreasonable creatures.

187] **The blossoms of lust**) be the young and mossy hairs which then begin to sprout and shoot forth when lustful heat beginneth to kindle.

189] **and with**) a very poetical pathos [pathetic utterance. Printed in Greek in Q1 but anglicised in Q2–5. Noted by *OED* as first instance of a rare usage].

191] **orphan**) a youngling or pupil that needeth a tutor and governor.

193] **that word**) a pathetical parenthesis to increase a care-full hyperbaton ['To all their speeches which wrought by disorder the Greeks gave a general name [hyperbaton] as much as to say as the trespasser . . . [there are many varieties, several of which are 'foul and intolerable']. Your first figure of tolerable disorder is [parenthesis] or by an English name the [inserter] and is when ye will . . . piece or graft in the middest of your tale an unneccessary parcel [part] of speech, which nevertheless may be thence without any detriment to the rest': Puttenham (1589) 2. 12. Commentators from Renwick 1930: 196 to Cain in Oram *et al.* 1989: 103 have misunderstood E.K.'s point: the hyperbaton is the interruption of 'Thy father' by the parenthesis.].

196] **the branch**) of the father's body is the child.

205] **For even so**) alluded to the saying of Andromache to Ascanius in Virgil: *Sic oculos, sic ille manus, sic ora ferebat* ['Thus were his eyes, thus was his very hand, thus was his face': Hector's wife Andromache comparing her dead son Astyanax to Aeneas's son Ascanius: *Aeneid*, 3. 490].

208] **A thrilling throb**) a piercing sigh [*OED* notes these as the first instances of *thrilling* = piercing, penetrating, and *throb* = 'violent beat or pulsation of the heart or an artery' respectively].

217) **liggen**) lie [cf. 125n].

219) **master of collusion**) *scilicet* [namely] coloured guile, because the fox of all beasts is most wily and crafty.

224) **Spar the yate**) shut the door [the original spelling here and in the text, *sperre*, is the normal mediaeval one: this is *OED*'s first instance after 1483; *yate* = door or gate is a northern/Scots form].

232] **For such**) the goat's stumbling is here noted as an evil sign: the like to be marked in all histories, and that not the least of the Lord Hastings in King Richard the Third his days. For, beside his dangerous dream (which was a shrewd prophecy of his mishap that followed), it is said that in the morning riding toward the Tower of London, there to sit upon matters of council, his horse stumbled twice or thrice by the way; which of some that, riding with him in his company, were privy to his near destiny, was secretly marked, and afterward noted for memory of his great mishap that ensued. For being then as merry as man might be, and least doubting any mortal danger, he was, within two hours after, of the tyrant put to a shameful death [story in *The Mirror for Magistrates* (1563), 'Lord Hastings': Campbell, L. B. (ed.) 1938: 284ff. The reference to monarchical tyranny may implicate Elizabeth for her increasingly authoritarian attitude towards the puritans].

240] **As bells**) by such trifles are noted the relics and rags of popish superstition, which put no small religion in bells, and babies (*scilicet* [namely] idols), and glasses (*scilicet* paxes [plates of glass, gold, etc. bearing sacred images – e.g., of the crucifixion – passed from priests to congregation to be kissed at the appropriate point in the mass]) and suchlike trumperies.

244] **great cold**) for they boast much of their outward patience and voluntary sufferance as a work of merit and holy humbleness.

247] **sweet Saint Charity**) the Catholics' common oath and only speech, to have charity always in their mouth, and sometime in their outward actions, but never inwardly in faith and godly zeal [frequently invoked as a saint: e.g., *Hamlet* 4. 5. 59].

251] **clink**) a key hole; whose diminutive is *clicket*, used of Chaucer for a key [a unique instance: *OED* clink *sb* 4].

257] **stounds**) fits: aforesaid [stound = sharp (or fierce) attack was a northernism; E.K.'s 'aforesaid' misremembers *January* 51 gloss].

262] **his lere**) his lesson [mediaevalism; *OED*'s first instance since 1450].

263] **meddled**) mingled [*April* 68 gloss].

265] **beastlihead**) agreeing to the person of a beast [i.e., a courtesy title; a Spenserian coinage].

269] **sib**) of kin [not obviously archaic or remarkable].

273] **to forestall**) to prevent [*OED*'s first citation in this sense].

276] **newel**) a new thing [*OED* newel 2 cites only three instances of which this is the second; first dated *c*. 1475].

282] **glee**) cheer, aforesaid [*February* 224 gloss].

299] **dear a price**) his life, which he lost for those toys.

304] **such end**) is an epiphonema [moralising conclusion or 'consenting close': Puttenham (1589) 3. 19; cf. *October* emblem gloss] or, rather, the moral of the whole tale, whose purpose is to warn the Protestant beware how he giveth credit to the unfaithful Catholic: whereof we have daily proofs sufficient, but one most famous of all, practised of late years in France by Charles the Ninth [refers to the massacre of Huguenots in Paris on St Bartholomew's Day (24 August) 1572; the reference presumably glances at Alençon, collateral heir to the French throne].

305] **fain**) glad or desirous [archaic].

309] **our Sir John**) a popish priest: a saying fit for the grossness of a shepherd, but spoken to taunt unlearned priests [*OED* John 3, which explains that *Sir* renders Latin *Dominus* (modern *don*) as a title at Oxford and Cambridge].

315] **dismount**) descend or set.

316] **nigh**) draweth near [rare after 1500: *OED* nigh *v*].

Emblem.

Both these emblems [printed in Greek in original editions] make one whole hexameter [a line of six feet containing five dactyls (one long syllable and two short) and a trochee (one long syllable, one short) or spondee (two long syllables)]: the first spoken of Palinode, as in reproach of them that be distrustful, is a piece of Theognis's verse [not actually traceable in Theognis] intending [meaning] that who doth most mistrust is most false. For such experience in falsehood breedeth mistrust in the mind, thinking no less guile to lurk in others than in himself. But Piers thereto strongly replieth with another piece of the same verse, saying (as in his former fable), what faith then is there in the faithless? For if faith be the ground of religion, which faith they daily false, what hold then is there of their religion? [Cf. Mantuan, *Eclogues*, 4. 15: *Qui non credit, inops fidei* ('He who does not believe is weak in faith'): Renwick 1930: 197.] And this is all that they say.

June

At the centre of *SC* Spenser opposes, as in a diptych, its two main themes: *June*'s topic is Colin's love and its failure (Rosalind now favours Menalcas); *July*'s is the condition of the Church. Both are linked in addition by the question of the location of the paradisal place (or *locus amoenus*): whether it resides in the dales as the seat of pastoral ease, as favoured by Hobbinol (*June*, 1–24), or in the dales as a symbol of priestly humility, as advocated by Thomalin (*July*, 13–14). *June*, which contains Colin's lament for Rosalind's infidelity as well as his elegy for the death of Tityrus/Chaucer (ll. 81–96), has 15 stanzas, a feature which links it with the 15-stanza elegy for Dido-Elizabeth in *November* and could be seen as reinforcing Rosalind's identification as Elizabeth (in which case Menalcas is Alençon again): McLane 1961: 36–40. Colin's move towards rejection of Hobbinol/Gabriel Harvey and acceptance of a fate which impels him 'from coast to coast' (l. 15) suggests Spenser's decision to move from Cambridge (his and Harvey's university) into employment in the wider world. It also affirms his Meliboeus pose (*January* headnote) and the uneasiness underlying his, as also Colin's, perception of the poet's role as interrogator of social, political and religious ills.

June's line total, 120, which it shares with *October* (another eclogue to contain an elegy on Tityrus), supports Colin's sense of his reforming purpose, for it signifies penitence (because 120 years was the maximum human life span between the Fall and the Flood: Bongo 1599: 586 citing Genesis 6: 3). Metrically, *June* shares a regular iambic pentameter beat with Colin's *January* eclogue, though the rhyme scheme – as befits this dialogue between the *personae* of two educated friends – is more testing: the pattern ababbaba offers almost as great a challenge to the poet's ingenuity as *August*'s sestina (*August* 151–89n).

The woodcut (fig. 6) depicts Hobbinol firmly ensconced in his tree-shaded *locus amoenus* complete with stream (for details of the topos see Curtius 1967: 195–200), while Colin, backed by June's traditional harvesters, points beyond their haycocks to the difficult journey to the summit of the hill of Truth (cf. Donne, *Satires*, 3. 79–80: 'On a huge hill,/Cragged, and steep, Truth stands').

June
Aegloga sexta

Argument

This eglogue is wholly vowed to the complaining of Colin's ill success in his love. For being (as is aforesaid) enamoured of a country lass, Rosalind, and having (as seemeth) found place in her heart, he lamenteth to his dear friend Hobbinol that he is now forsaken unfaithfully, and in his stead Menalcas, another shepherd, received disloyally. And this is the whole argument of this eglogue.

Argument: *Menalcas*: see E.K., 102 gloss.

Hobbinol.   Colin Clout.

Lo, Colin, here the place, whose pleasant site
From other shades hath weaned my wandering mind.
Tell me, what wants me here to work delight?
The simple air, the gentle warbling wind,
So calm, so cool, as nowhere else I find: 5
The grassy ground with dainty daisies dight;
The bramble bush, where birds of every kind
To the waters' fall their tunes attemper right.

Colin.

O happy Hobbinol, I bless thy state,
That paradise hast found which Adam lost.   10
Here wander may thy flock early or late
Withouten dread of wolves to bene ytossed:
Thy lovely lays here mayest thou freely boast.
But I (unhappy man) whom cruel fate
And angry gods pursue from coast to coast,   15
Can nowhere find to shoulder my luckless pate.

Hobbinol.

Then if by me thou list advised be,
Forsake the soil that so doth thee bewitch:
Leave me those hills where harbrough n'is to see,
Nor holly bush, nor briar, nor winding wych,   20

---

1. *site*: E.K.
3. *wants*: lacks.
6–8. *grassy . . . right*: a typical *locus amoenus* (see headnote) with the full complement of ingredients: shade, water, birdsong, flowers, breeze. Daisies are traditionally paradisal (de Vries 1974: 127) and Venerean (D'Ancona 1983: 78); the roses signify love (thus undoing the braggart Briar of *February*): Ovid, *Fasti*, 4. 138.
8. *attemper*: bring into harmony (*OED*'s first citation for this sense): cf. *April* 5 gloss and 36n.
9–16. *O . . . pate*: echo Virgil, *Eclogues*, 1. 1–5, Tityrus unconcerned in the shade while Meliboeus has to flee his homeland: cf. headnote.
10. *paradise*: E.K.
12. *ytossed*: agitated.
16. *shoulder*: quartos read *shouder* (i.e., shoulder = prop); later editors uniformly follow the folios' *shroude*. Brooks-Davies 1992b defends *shoulder*.
17. *list*: choose.
18. *Forsake . . . soil*: E.K.
19. *Leave me*: *May* 245n. *those hills*: E.K. *harbrough*: the spelling, possibly Spenser's, is a contemporary variant of both harbour and arbour. *n'is*: E.K.
20. *wych*: wych elm, with its pliant branches.

And to the dales resort, where shepherds rich
And fruitful flocks bene everywhere to see.
Here no night ravens lodge more black than pitch,
Nor elvish ghosts, nor ghastly owls do flee;

But friendly fairies, met with many Graces,   25
And lightfoot nymphs, can chase the lingering night
With hay-de-guys and trimly-trodden traces,
Whilst sisters nine, which dwell on Parnass' height,
Do make them music for their more delight,
And Pan himself, to kiss their crystal faces,   30
Will pipe and dance when Phoebe shineth bright:
Such peerless pleasures have we in these places.

              Colin.
And I, whilst youth and course of care-less years
Did let me walk withouten links of love,
In such delights did joy amongst my peers.   35
But riper age such pleasures doth reprove,
My fancy eke from former follies move
To stayed steps; for Time, in passing, wears
(As garments doen, which waxen old above)
And draweth new delights with hoary hairs.   40

Tho couth I sing of love, and tune my pipe
Unto my plaintive pleas in verses made;

Textual note

23. ravens] F, correcting Ravene (Q1–2); Raven (Q3–5).

21. the dales: E.K.
23. night ravens: E.K.
24. elvish: (1) supernatural; (2) mischievous. *ghastly owls*: ghastly = terrible (etymologically separate from, but just being influenced by, *ghost*: *OED* ghastly *a* 1); *owls* have a similar significance to that of ravens: Agrippa (1651) 1. 54, 55.
25. fairies: E.K. *Graces*: E.K.
26. lightfoot nymphs: a common Spenserian phrase (e.g., *Epith*, 67), but probably echoing Horace, *Odes*, 1. 1. 31, with its context of poetic ambition and withdrawal.
27. hay-de-guys: E.K. *trimly . . . traces*: elegantly-trodden steps (or dances): cf. *April* 102n.
28–31. Whilst . . . bright: cf. *April* 41, 50 and 65 glosses.
34. links: chains.
35. peers: E.K.
39. doen: *February* 6n. *waxen . . . above*: grow old (i.e., show wear) on the surface.
41. couth: *January* 10 gloss.

Tho would I seek for queen-apples unripe
To give my Rosalind; and in summer shade
Dight gaudy garlands was my common trade   45
To crown her golden locks. But years more ripe,
And loss of her – whose love as life I weighed –
Those weary wanton toys away did wipe.

       Hobbinol.
Colin, to hear thy rhymes and roundelays
(Which thou were wont on waste-full hills to sing)   50
I more delight than lark in summer days:
Whose Echo made the neighbour groves to ring,
And taught the birds (which in the lower spring
Did shroud in shady leaves from sunny rays)
Frame to thy song their cheerful chirruping,   55
Or hold their peace for shame of thy sweet lays.

I saw Calliope, with Muses mo',
Soon as thy oaten pipe began to sound,

43. *queen-apples unripe*: E.K. The apple is an attribute of Venus and thus a symbol of love: Tervarent (1958) cols 311–12; *unripe* suggests Colin's impatience or the stage of his love.
45. *Dight*: to make (archaic: last *OED* citation of this sense is 1607: dight *v* II. 7a). *gaudy*: cf. *May* 4n.
48. *toys*: amorous sport, trifles (cf. 1 Corinthians 13: 11: ' . . . but when I became a man, I put away childish things'; Geneva gloss: 'But when we become men, to what purpose should we desire that stammering, those childish toys, and suchlike things, whereby our childhood is framed by little and little?').
49. *roundelays*: *April* 33 gloss.
50. *waste-full*: desolate: *OED* wasteful *a* 3; first citation 1572. Cf. *January* 2n.
51. *lark*: cf. *November* 71n.
52. *Echo . . . ring*: imitates Virgil, *Eclogues*, 1. 4–5: 'You, Tityrus, unconcerned in the shade, teach the woods to echo [ring with] *Beautiful Amaryllis*' (cf. 9–16n); anticipates the refrain to *Epithalamion*; and recalls the Echo/Narcissus myth, in which the nymph Echo, spurned by Narcissus, fades away into an insubstantial echo (*September* emblem and gloss; Rosalind is known in *SC* only by the voicing of her name). For an adverse comparison between Colin and Narcissus see Johnson 1990: 104–14; for Orphic implications see Cullen 1970: 86 (and cf. *October* 28 gloss).
53. *spring*: E.K.
55. *frame*: fashion. *chirruping*: an onomatopoeic extension of *chirp* (which had been known since the 1440s) and a Spenserian neologism, this is *OED*'s only instance until 1774.
57–64. *I . . . outgo*: cf. *December*, 43–8.
57. *Calliope*: E.K.

Their ivory lutes and tambourines forgo
And, from the fountain where they sat around,   60
Run after hastily thy silver sound.
But when they came where thou thy skill didst show
They drew aback, as half with shame confound
Shepherd to see them in their art outgo.

                    Colin.
Of Muses, Hobbinol, I con no skill,   65
For they bene daughters of the highest Jove
And holden scorn of homely shepherd's quill.
For sith I heard that Pan with Phoebus strove –
Which him to much rebuke and danger drove –
I never list presume to Parnass' hill   70
But, piping low in shade of lowly grove,
I play to please myself, albeit ill.

Nought weigh I who my song doth praise or blame,
Ne strive to win renown, or pass the rest:
With shepherd sits not follow flying Fame   75
But feed his flock in fields, where falls hem best.
I wote my rhymes bene rough, and rudely dressed,
The fitter they my care-full case to frame.

---

59. *tambourines*: E.K. For the iconography of the Muses, see Tervarent (1958) cols 279–81; Ripa 1603: 346–51.
64. *outgo*: surpass.
65. *Of. . . skill*: Dedicatory Epistle, p. 23, and *January* 10 gloss.
66. *daughters . . . Jove*: the commonest tradition: their mother was Mnemosyne (Memory).
67. *quill*: (1) hollow cane, and hence musical pipe made therefrom (*OED* quill sb 1, 1a, c); (2) pen made from bird feather; plectrum for stringed instrument (senses 3b, c).
68. *sith*: since. *Pan . . . Phoebus*: E.K.
70–1. *Parnass' . . . grove*: cf. the hill/dale dichotomy of 19–21: Colin opts for pastoral rather than the more strenuous labour of heroic verse.
72. *play . . . myself*: Narcissus (52n) as well as the bereaved archetypal poet Orpheus after his failure to redeem Eurydice from the underworld: Ovid, *Metamorphoses*, 10. 1–85; Virgil, *Georgics*, 4. 465 (Orpheus sang 'of thee to himself' [*te solo*]). Calliope (l. 57) was Orpheus's mother (Virgil, *Eclogues*, 4. 55–7 where the poet, unlike Colin, offers a challenge to Pan: 'Pan, judged by Arcadia, would admit defeat').
74. *pass*: surpass.
75. *sits not*: is not fitting: *November* 26n. *flying Fame*: Ripa 1603: 142–5. Note also flying = fleeting (hence of brief duration).
76. *falls . . . best*: it befits them best to be.

Enough is me to paint out my unrest
And pour my piteous plaints out in the same. 80

The god of shepherds, Tityrus, is dead,
Who taught me, homely as I can, to make.
He, whilst he lived, was the sovereign head
Of shepherds all that bene with Love ytake:
Well couth he wail his woes, and lightly slake 85
The flames which Love within his heart had bred,
And tell us merry tales to keep us wake
The while our sheep about us safely fed.

Now dead he is, and lieth wrapped in lead
(Oh why should Death on him such outrage show?); 90
And all his passing skill with him is fled,
The fame whereof doth daily greater grow.
But if on me some little drops would flow
Of that the spring was in his learned head,
I soon would learn these woods to wail my woe, 95
And teach the trees their trickling tears to shed.

Then should my plaints (caused of discourtesy),
As messengers of all my painful plight
Fly to my love, wherever that she be,
And pierce her heart with point of worthy wite: 100
As she deserves, that wrought so deadly spite.

79. *paint out*: depict vividly: *OED* paint *v* 11, giving 1556 as date of first and only earlier instance.
81. *Tityrus*: E.K.
82. *make*: E.K.
84. *Love*: e.g., in *Troilus and Criseyde*, *The Knight's Tale*, the *Romance of the Rose* translation, etc.
87. *merry tales*: the *Canterbury Tales*. Cf. Lydgate's *Fall of Princes*, Prologue (1. 246–7): 'My master Chaucer, with his fresh comedies,/Is dead, alas . . . '.
89. *lead*: cf. *October*, 61–3.
90. *Oh why*: E.K.
91. *passing*: (1) surpassing (*OED* passing *ppl a* 3); (2) transient.
93–6. *drops . . . shed*: the *spring* (Heliconian: *April* 42 gloss) is also the *well spring* or *source* of poetic inspiration, its drops descending like divine grace and also mirroring the tears of Colin's grief. Cf. the metempsychotic stanzas of *FQ*, 4. 2. 32–4 where Spenser invokes Chaucer as 'well of English undefiled' and begs his spirit 'infuse' him. Learn = teach was good sixteenth-century usage. The power to move trees is also Orphic: cf. 52n.
97. *discourtesy*: E.K.
100. *point . . . wite*: E.K.

And thou, Menalcas, that by treachery
Didst underfong my lass to wax so light,
Shouldest well be known for such thy villainy.

But since I am not as I wish I were, 105
Ye gentle shepherds (which your flocks do feed,
Whether on hills, or dales, or other-where),
Bear witness all of this so wicked deed,
And tell the lass (whose flower is wox' a weed,
And faultless faith is turned to faithless fere) 110
That she the truest shepherd's heart made bleed
That lives on earth, and loved her most dear.

Hobbinol.

O care-full Colin, I lament thy case:
Thy tears would make the hardest flint to flow.
Ah faithless Rosalind (and void of grace) 115
That art the root of all this ruthful woe!
But now is time, I guess, homeward to go.
Then rise ye, blessed flocks, and home apace,
Lest Night with stealing steps do you forslow
And wet your tender lambs, that by you trace. 120

Colin's emblem:
Gia speme spenta.

GLOSS

1] **site**) situation and place [*OED*'s first citation for this sense].

10] **paradise**) a paradise in Greek signifieth a *garden of pleasure* or *place of delights* [Greek *paradeisos* = enclosure, orchard, pleasure garden]. So he compareth the soil wherein Hobbinol made his abode to that earthly paradise in scripture called Eden [Gen. 2, 3; *Eden* in Hebrew = pleasure (Geneva table of names)], wherein Adam in his first creation was placed [Gen. 2: 8]: which of the most learned is thought to be in Mesopotamia, the most fertile and pleasant country in the world (as may appear by Diodorus Siculus' description of it in the history of Alexander's conquest thereof [*Library of History*, 17. 53. 3]), lying between the two famous rivers (which are said in scripture to flow out of

102. *Menalcas*: E.K.
103. *underfong*: E.K.
109. *wox'*: i.e., woxen (become). A normal sixteenth-century form.
110. *fere*: companion (with overtones of *wife*).
119. *forslow*: delay.
120. *trace*: proceed, tread.
122. *Gia . . . spenta*: 'Hope [is] indeed extinguished' (Italian): E.K. In view of *January*'s emblem and its religious overtones, suggesting the depths of Colin's despair.

paradise) Tigris and Euphrates [Gen. 2: 10–14], whereof it is so denominate [i.e., Greek *mesos* = middle + *potamos* = river].

18] **Forsake the soil**) this is no poetical fiction but unfeignedly spoken of the poet self who, for special occasion of private affairs (as I have been partly of himself informed), and for his more preferment removing out of the north parts, came into the south, as Hobbinol [Gabriel Harvey] indeed advised him privately ['north' may be relative, and refer to Spenser's move from Cambridge to London after his graduation (MA, 1576); or it may refer to a visit to relatives: his father may have been the John Spenser whose family came from Hurstwood in Lancashire: Mohl in *SpE*, pp 668–71].

19] **those hills**) that is, the north country where he dwelt [for the arguments over what E.K. means, see *Var* 1. 312–15, and 21 gloss].

19] **n'is**) is not [cf. *May* 144n].

21] **the dales**) the south parts where he now abideth which, though they be full of hills and woods (for Kent is very hilly and woody and therefore so called; for *kantsh* in the Saxons' tongue signifieth *woody* [see William Lambarde, *Perambulation of Kent* (1576) p 7: '*Cainc*, a word that (in the language of the Britons . . .) signifieth *boughs*, or woods': Renwick 1930: 199. E.K.'s mistaken attribution of the word to the Saxons as opposed to the Celtic Britons may be accounted for by his possibly pro-Saxon stance at *July* 33 gloss]), yet in respect of the north parts they be called dales, for, indeed, the north is counted the higher country [clearly more applicable to the contrast between, for example, Lancashire and Kent than Kent and Cambridgeshire's predominantly flat landscape].

23] **night ravens, etc.**) by such hateful birds he meaneth all misfortunes (whereof they be tokens) flying everywhere [see Agrippa (1651) 1. 54].

25] **friendly fairies**) the opinion of fairies and elves is very old, and yet sticketh very religiously in the minds of some. But, to root that rank opinion of elves out of men's hearts, the truth is that there be no such things, nor yet the shadows of the things, but only by a sort of bald friars and knavish shavelings [tonsured monks] so feigned which, as in all other things, so in that, sought to nousel [i.e., nuzzle = nurture a belief in] the common people in ignorance lest, being once acquainted with the truth of things, they would in time smell out the untruth of their packed pelf [bundled-up wealth or booty] and Mass-penny religion [mass-penny = money offering made at mass: *OED*'s first citation is from Langland, 1362; but E.K. puns on amassing money]. But the sooth [truth] is, that when all Italy was distract [torn apart] into the factions of the Guelphs and Ghibellines, being two famous houses in Florence, the name began, through their great mischiefs and many outrages, to be so odious (or, rather, dreadful) in the people's ears that, if their children at any time were froward [difficult] and wanton [unruly], they would say to them that the Guelph or the Ghibelline came; which words now from them (as many thing else) be come into our usage, and for 'Guelphs' and 'Ghibellines' we say 'elves' and 'goblins' [the Guelphs supported the popes and the Ghibellines the imperial faction in mediaeval Italian politics. The etymology is consciously false and jesting. E.K. represents a characteristic Reformation attitude to fairies: cf. *April* 120 gloss and, on Spenser's fairy lore in general, *SpE*, pp 295–6]. No otherwise than the Frenchmen used to say of that valiant captain, the very scourge of France, the Lord Talbot, afterward Earl of Shrewsbury, whose *noblesse* bred such a terror in the hearts of the French that oft-times even great armies were defeated and put to flight at the only hearing of his name: insomuch that the French women, to affray their children, would tell them that the Talbot cometh [John Talbot, first Earl of Shrewsbury, 1388(?)–1453, particularly active against the French 1427–44; a major character in Shakespeare's *I Henry VI*].

25] **many Graces**) though there be indeed but three Graces or Charites (as afore is said [*April* 109 gloss]), or at the utmost but four, yet in respect of many gifts of bounty there may be said more. And so Musaeus saith that in Hero's either eye there sat a hundred Graces [Musaeus, *De Herone et Leandro*, 63–5]; and by that authority this same poet in his *Pageants* saith: 'An hundred Graces on her eyelid sat', etc [the only reference to an apparently lost work by Spenser: Oruch in *SpE*, pp 737–8; for the commonplace, cf. *FQ*, 2. 3. 25 and *Am* 40].

27] **hay-de-guys**) a country dance or round. The conceit [idea] is that the Graces and nymphs do dance unto the Muses and Pan his music all night by moonlight to signify the pleasantness of the soil.

35] **peers**) equals and fellow shepherds.

43] **queen-apples unripe**) imitating Virgil's verse: *Ipse ego cana legam tenera lanugine mala* ['I myself will pick the delicate and downy quince']: *Eclogues*, 2. 51; for the queen-apple – a type of apple we can no longer identify – see Sidney's 'What tongue can her perfections tell', l. 25: Robertson, J. (ed) 1973 *Old Arcadia*, p 238].

52] **neighbour groves**) a strange phrase in English, but word for word expressing the Latin *vicina nemora* [*OED*'s first citation for this usage: neighbour *sb* 4c; cf. *January* 50 gloss].

53] **spring**) not of water, but of young trees springing [*OED* spring *sb* 1 III. 10c].

57] **Calliope**) aforesaid [*April* 100 gloss]. This staff [stanza] is full of very poetical invention.

59] **tambourines**) an old kind of instrument which of some is supposed to be the clarion [what this refers to is a mystery: *OED*. A clarion is a trumpet. There is a suggestion that it could allude to a wind instrument in Drayton's *Endymion and Phoebe* (1595), 15n in Brooks-Davies (ed.) 1992a: 450].

68] **Pan with Phoebus**) the tale is well known how that Pan and Apollo, striving for excellency in music, chose Midas for their judge, who, being corrupted with partial affection, gave the victory to Pan undeserved, for which Phoebus set a pair of ass's ears upon his head, etc. [Ovid, *Metamorphoses*, 11. 146–93, though E.K. makes a familiar error in calling Midas the judge: he was punished for disputing the judgement].

81] **Tityrus**) that by Tityrus is meant Chaucer hath been already sufficiently said [Dedicatory Epistle], and by this more plain appeareth, that he saith he told merry tales (such as be his *Canterbury Tales*): whom he calleth the god of poets for his excellency, so as Tully calleth Lentulus *deum vitae suae, scilicet* [namely] the god of his life [Cicero, *Post Reditum, in Senatu Oratio*, 4. 8].

82] **to make**) to versify [*April* 19 gloss].

90] **Oh why**) a pretty epanorthosis or correction [cf. *January* 61 gloss].

97] **discourtesy**) he meaneth the falseness of his lover, Rosalind, who, forsaking him, had chosen another [first *OED* citation 1555].

100] **point of worthy wite**) the prick of deserved blame [wite = archaic and already northern/Scots].

102] **Menalcas**) the name of a shepherd in Virgil [*Eclogues*, 3, 5]; but here is meant a person unknown and secret, against whom he often bitterly inveigheth [see headnote].

103] **underfong**) undermynde [undermine: see Textual note] and deceive by false suggestion [a rare usage: this is *OED*'s first citation in the more precise sense of seduce, entrap].

Emblem.

You remember that in the first eglogue Colin's poesy was *anchôra speme*, for that as then there was hope of favour to be found in time. But now, being clean forlorn and rejected of her, as whose hope (that was) is clean extinguished and turned into despair, he renounceth all comfort and hope of goodness to come: which is all the meaning of this emblem.

Textual note

Gloss 103. *undermynde*] available (if archaic) form of undermine (which is the modernised reading adopted by Q5). Q3–4 offer the intermediate form underminde.

July

The second of the three theological/ecclesiastical debates, each of which is separated by an eclogue devoted to Colin (*May / June* [Colin] // *July* // *August* [Colin] / *September*), *July* complements *June* in its emphasis on low versus high while privileging the latter by offering various different readings of high places (it is also, in effect, a meditation on Isaiah 40: 4: 'Every valley shall be exalted, and every mountain and hill shall be made low'). For Thomalin (who almost certainly stands for Archbishop Grindal's supporter Thomas Cooper, Bishop of Lincoln: McLane 1961: 203–15; King 1985: 15–16), they are merely memorials of the lives of saints. His general position is the progressive Protestant one of Piers in *May*, and the eclogue's emphasis on sanctity – which occupies its centre – makes a specific doctrinal point: saints are not intercessors to be prayed to, and possible workers of miracles, as they are for Catholics (functions which, reinforced by the Counter-Reformation, led to the Protestant misunderstanding of icons and relics as idolatry mingled with black magic); they are simply the holy departed, revered exemplars of the virtuous Christian life in action: cf. Hume 1984: 30 citing William Tyndale's *Obedience of a Christian Man*: 'let us take the Saints for an example only'. Morrell adopts a more literal (Catholic) stance consonant with the attitudes of *May*'s Palinode (for the identification of Morrell with John Aylmer/Elmore, Bishop of London, see McLane, pp 188–202 and King as above): saints preside over the holy places connected with them; and in his enthusiasm he links Catholic shrine and pagan demigod (much as *May* links pagan festival with Catholic worldliness) when he invokes the century-old Loretto shrine alongside fauns and sylvans (74, 77–8). Yet Morrell's mythopoeic response to the Kentish landscape is one that will be characteristic of the later Spenser; so that *July* is also the site of Spenser's pioneering of his poetics of nationalistic Protestantism as he attempts to reconcile the visionary and imaginary (with its links with faerie, mythology and, inevitably, the 'Catholic' view of the world as full of images to be wondered at and read allegorically) with the sparer Reformation view of truth and the linguistic means of declaring it (on the Reformation background see King 1982: 144–60).

July's main source is Mantuan, *Eclogues*, 8, the Argument to which in Turberville's 1567 translation (Mantuan 1937), reads: 'Two Shepherds met yfere [together],/one likes the mountains most,/And t'other did commend the vale/above the hilly coast./The praise of Pollux Saint/is intermingled here/And sacred feasts, with holy days/that happen in the year' (its influence is particularly strong in ll. 1–92; in the succeeding 70 lines Spenser is occasionally indebted to Mantuan's seventh eclogue). E.K.'s glosses are of interest, particularly at ll. 33 and 147, where he clearly amplifies the political signals in Spenser's text. *July*'s verse form is that of the popular but obsolete fourteener (divided 8/6), perhaps most familiar from its use by Sternhold and Hopkins for their metrical psalm translations: Smith 1946. It is worth noting, however, that Turberville also used the metre for his Mantuan translation. In modernising *July* I have retained the sixteenth-century convention of beginning the second half of each line with a lower-case letter.

The woodcut (fig. 7) is one of *SC*'s simplest: Morrell occupies the mount of ambition (a modulation of *June*'s hill of Truth), while Thomalin confronts him with July's zodiacal sign Leo above him, presumably signifying Christ in Judgement as the lion of apocalyptic wrath: glosses to 17 and 21.

July
Aegloga septima

Argument

This eglogue is made in the honour and commendation of good shepherds, and to the shame and dispraise of proud and ambitious pastors, such as Morrell is here imagined to be.

                 Thomalin. Morrell.
Is not thilk same a goatherd proud
   that sits on yonder bank,
Whose straying herd themself doth shroud
   among the bushes rank?

                 Morrell.
What ho, thou jolly shepherd's swain,   5
   come up the hill to me:
Better is than the lowly plain
   als for thy flock, and thee.

                 Thomalin.
Ah, God shield, man, that I should climb,
   and learn to look aloft: 10
This rede is rife, that oftentime
   great climbers fall unsoft.
In humble dales is footing fast –
   the trod is not so trickle;

Textual note

14. trickle] Q1–4; *Var*, Yale and others adopt Q5's tickle, even though *trickle* is the more unusual and likely word.

1. *thilk*: *May* 1 gloss. *goatherd*: E.K.
2. *bank*: E.K.
3. *straying herd*: E.K.
4. *rank*: (1) haughty (*OED* rank *a* A I. 1; last instance *c.* 1560); (2) luxuriant. Cf. 211n below.
8. *als*: E.K.   9. *God shield*: God forbid. *climb*: E.K.
11. *rede is rife*: proverb is widespread, or frequently uttered.
12. *great climbers*: E.K.
14. *trod*: path (*September* 92 gloss). *trickle*: treacherous (*OED*'s first of only two instances).

And though one fall through heedless haste, 15
  yet is his miss not mickle.
And now the Sun hath reared up
  his fiery-footed team,
Making his way between the Cup
  and golden Diadem: 20
The rampant Lion hunts he fast,
  with Dog of noisome breath,
Whose baleful barking brings in haste
  pine, plagues, and dreary death.
Against his cruel scorching heat 25
  where hast thou coverture?
The waste-full hills unto his threat
  is a plain overture.
But, if thee lust to holden chat
  with seely shepherd's swain, 30
Come down and learn the little what
  that Thomalin can sayen.

                    Morrell.
Siker, thou's but a lazy lord,
  and recks much of thy swink
That with fond terms and weetless words 35
  to blear mine eyes dost think:
In evil hour thou hentest in hond
  thus holy hills to blame,

16. *mickle*: E.K.
17. *Sun*: E.K.
19–20. *Cup, Diadem*: E.K.
21. *Lion*: E.K.
24. *pine*: affliction.
26. *coverture*: refuge.
27. *waste-full*: *June* 50n.
28. *overture*: E.K.
29. *lust*: wish (archaic; *OED*'s last citation in this sense is 1586: lust *v* 3). *chat*: E.K.
30. *seely*: innocent, simple.
33. *Siker*: *February* 55 gloss. *lord*: E.K.
34. *recks . . . swink*: E.K.
35. *fond*: foolish. *weetless*: E.K.
36. *blear . . . eyes*: hoodwink.
37. *hentest . . . hond*: *February* 195 and gloss. The spelling *hond* (as opposed to *February*'s *hand*) is archaic.

For sacred unto saints they stond,
   and of them han their name.   40
St Michael's Mount who dost not know,
   that wards the western coast?
And of St Bridget's Bower, I trow,
   all Kent can rightly boast;
And they that con of Muses' skill   45
   sayen most what, that they dwell
(As goatherds wont) upon a hill,
   beside a learned well.
And wonned not the great god Pan
   upon Mount Olivet,   50
Feeding the blessed flock of Dan,
   which did himself beget?

                              Thomalin.
O blessed sheep, O shepherd great,
   that bought his flock so dear,
And them did save with bloody sweat   55
   from wolves that would them tear!

                              Morrell.
Beside, as holy fathers sayen,
   there is a hilly place
Where Titan riseth from the main
   to ren his daily race,   60
Upon whose top the stars bene stayed
   and all the sky doth lean:
There is the cave where Phoebe laid

41. St Michael's Mount: E.K.
43. St Bridget's Bower: unidentified; but St Bridget, patroness of Ireland, built her cell under a large oak, so Morrell may simply mean Kentish oaks: cf. *June* 21 gloss.
43. trow: believe (archaic).
47. hill: E.K. Cf. *FQ*, 1. 10. 53–4.
49. wonned: dwelled; cf. *February* 119 gloss. *Pan*: E.K.
50. Olivet: e.g., Matthew 24: 3.
51. Dan: E.K. *Feeding . . . flock*: perhaps alluding to Ezekiel 34: 14: 'I will feed them in a good pasture, and upon the high mountains of Israel shall their fold be'.
55. bloody sweat: life blood (also perspiration). The phrase refers specifically to Christ's agony in the garden: Luke 22: 44; *OED* sweat *sb* II 2 c.
59. Titan: E.K.
60. ren: *April* 118n.
63. There: E.K.

             the shepherd long to dream.
Whilom there used shepherds all 65
   to feed their flocks at will,
Till by his folly one did fall
   that all the rest did spill;
And sithence shepherds bene forsaid
   from places of delight: 70
For-thy I ween thou be afraid
   to climb this hill's height.
Of Sinai can I tell thee more,
   and of Our Lady's bower:
But little needs to strew my store – 75
   suffice this hill of our.
Here han the holy fauns resource,
   and silvans haunteth rathe:
Here has the salt Medway his source,
   wherein the nymphs do bathe – 80
The salt Medway that trickling streams
   adown the dales of Kent
Till with his elder brother, Thames,
   his brackish waves be ment.
Here grows melampod everywhere, 85
   and terebinth, good for goats:
The one, my madding kids to smear,
   the next, to heal their throats.
Hereto, the hills bene nigher heaven

64. *shepherd*: E.K.
68. *spill*: bring to death (archaic).
69. *sithence*: subsequently. *forsaid*: prohibited (*OED* instances only from Spenser): cf. *May* 82n.
70. *places of delight*: i.e., Edens: *June* 10 gloss.
73. *Sinai*: E.K.
74. *Our Lady's bower*: E.K.
75. *strew my store*: display my store [of examples]: *OED*'s only instance of this specific sense: strew *v* 1d.
77–8. *fauns . . . silvans*: E.K.
77. *resource*: (their) uprising, or return (into the landscape and history, etc.): antedating *OED*'s first instance by over 30 years and a Spenserian coinage from the French *resourdre* = rise again; *OED* resource 1a.
78. *haunteth*: resort. *rathe*: early (also: with speed).
79. *Medway*: E.K.
84. *ment*: E.K.
85–6. *melampod . . . terebinth*: E.K.
89. *nigher heaven*: E.K.

    and thence the passage eath,   90
As well can prove the piercing levin
    that seldom falls beneath.

                            Thomalin.
Siker thou speaks like a lewd lorel,
    of heaven to deemen so:
Howbe I am but rude and borrel,   95
    yet nearer ways I know.
To kirk the narre, from God more farre
    has been an old-said saw;
And he that strives to touch the stars
    oft stumbles at a straw.   100
Alsoon may shepherd climb to sky
    that leads in lowly dales
As goatherd proud that, sitting high,
    upon the mountain sails.
My seely sheep like well below,   105
    they need not melampod;
For they bene hale enough, I trow,
    and liken their abode.
But if they with thy goats should yede
    they soon might be corrupted,   110
Or like not of the frowy feed,
    or with the weeds be glutted.
The hills, where dwelled holy saints,
    I reverence and adore –
Not for themself but for the saints,   115
    which han be dead of yore:
And now they bene to heaven forewent
    their good is with them go',

90. eath: easy: *September* 17 gloss.
91. levin: E.K.
93. lorel: E.K.
95. borrel: E.K.
97. To kirk . . . farre: proverbial: *Var* 1. 331. *narre*: E.K.
101. Alsoon: as soon (mediaevalism; *OED*'s last cited instance).
105–12. My . . . glutted: cf. the parable cited at 1 gloss.
105. seely: 30n above.
107. hale: E.K.
109. yede: E.K.
111. Or: either. *frowy*: E.K.; perhaps recalling 'the leaven [i.e., sour dough] of the Pharisees and Sadducees' which is their corrupt doctrine: Matthew 16: 6, 12; also 1 Corinthians 5: 6–8.
116. yore: E.K.
117. forewent: E.K.

Their sample only to us lent
    that als we mought do so.   120
Shepherds they weren of the best,
    and lived in lowly leas;
And sith their souls bene now at rest,
    why done we them disease?
Such one he was (as I have heard   125
    old Algrind often sayen)
That whilom was the first shepherd,
    and lived with little gain:
As meek he was as meek mought be,
    simple as simple sheep: 130
Humble, and like in each degree
    the flock which he did keep.
Often he used of his keep
    a sacrifice to bring,
Now with a kid, now with a sheep,   135
    the altars hallowing.
So louted he unto his Lord,
    such favour couth he find,
That sithens never was abhorred
    the simple shepherds' kind.   140
And such, I ween, the brethren were
    that came from Canaan:
The brethren twelve that kept yfere
    the flocks of mighty Pan.
But nothing such thilk shepherd was   145
    whom Ida hill did bear,
That left his flock to fetch a lass

---

119. sample: example.
122. leas: grassland.
124. done: cause; see 186n. *disease*: disturbance.
126. Algrind: *May* 75n.
127. whilom: *January* 21n. *the first shepherd*: E.K.
129–56. As . . . brass: cf. Mantuan, *Eclogues*, 7. 14–31.
133. keep: E.K.
135. kid . . . sheep: Abel only sacrificed sheep (Genesis 4: 4), but Old Testament instances of the sacrifice of kids include Numbers 15: 11: 'Thus shall it be done . . . for a lamb, or for a kid'.
137. louted: E.K.
141. the brethren: E.K.
143. yfere: together (archaic).
146. whom Ida: E.K.
147. a lass: E.K.

   whose love he bought too dear:
For he was proud that ill was paid
   (no such mought shepherds be)   150
And with lewd lust was overlaid:
   tway things doen ill agree.
But shepherd mought be meek and mild,
   well-eyed (as Argus was),
With fleshly follies undefiled,   155
   and stout as steed of brass.
Sike one (said Algrin') Moses was,
   that saw his maker's face –
His face more clear than crystal glass –
   and spake to him in place.   160
This had a brother (his name I knew),
   the first of all his cote:
A shepherd true, yet not so true
   as he that erst I hote.
Whilom all these were low and lief,   165
   and loved their flocks to feed:
They never stroven to be chief,
   and simple was their weed.
But now (thanked be God therefore)
   the world is well amend: 170
Their weeds bene not so nighly wore,
   such simplesse mought them shend:
They bene yclad in purple and pall,
   so hath their god them blessed;
They reign and rulen over all,   175

152. tway: *May* 18n. *doen*: *February* 6n.: northern/Scots forms again support a radical Protestant case: *May* 18n.
154. Argus: E.K.
156. steed of brass: perhaps recalling Chaucer's *Squire's Tale*, 81, etc.
157. Moses: Exodus 34: 30–5: 'And the children of Israel saw the face of Moses, how the skin of Moses' face shone bright . . . '.
161. his name: E.K.
162. cote: house, cottage.
163. not so true: E.K.
164. hote: named; past tense of Spenser's pseudo-archaic *hight*: cf. *April* 120 gloss and *OED* hight *v* 1, III. 6.
165. low: humble. *lief*: (1) willing; (2) beloved (of the Lord).
170. amend: amended.
171. nighly: sparingly, meanly: this is the second of *OED*'s two instances.
172. shend: disgrace, reprove.
173. in purple: E.K. *pall*: woollen vestment worn by the Pope and other high-ranking ecclesiastics.

and lord it, as they list –
Ygirt with belts of glitterand gold
  (mought they good shepherds bene)
Their Pan their sheep to them has sold,
  I say (as some have seen).   180
For Palinode – if thou him ken –
  yode late on pilgrimage
To Rome (if such be Rome) and then
  he saw thilk misusage.
For shepherds (said he) there doen lead   185
  as lords done other-where:
Their sheep han crusts and they the bread,
  the chips, and they the cheer;
They han the fleece and eke the flesh
  (O seely sheep the while!):   190
The corn is theirs – let other thresh,
  their hands they may not file.
They han great stores and thrifty stocks,
  great friends and feeble foes:
What need hem caren for their flocks? –   195
  their boys can look to those.
These wizards welter in wealth's waves,
  pampered in pleasures deep:
They han fat kerns and leany knaves
  their fasting flocks to keep.   200
Sike mister men bene all misgone –

---

177. glitterand: E.K.
179. Their Pan: E.K.
181. Palinode: E.K.
182. yode: May 22 gloss.
184. misusage: abuse, corrupt practice (last of only three *OED* instances, the first dated 1532).
185. lead: behave, act (mediaevalism: *OED* lead *v* 1, I. 9b).
186. lords: looking back to 33 (lord = lout), though in this context the particular point is that lord originally = keeper/dispenser of the bread (*OED* lord *sb* I. 1), which here suggests eucharistic bread. *done*: common plural form: *OED* do *v* A 2d.
188. chips: bread-crust parings (second of *OED*'s two instances, the first dated *c*. 1440: chip *sb* 1, 2a). *cheer*: (good) food.
192. file: defile.
197. wizards: E.K. *welter*: E.K.
199. kerns: E.K. *leany*: lean (second of three *OED* instances, the first fifteenth-century, the last (1602) an imitation of Spenser). *knaves*: male servants, 'boys'.
201. sike . . . men: E.K. *misgone*: astray.

they heapen hills of wrath;
Sike surly shepherds han we none:
they keepen all the path.

Morrell.

Here is great deal of good matter, 205
lost for lack of telling.
Now siker I see thou dost but clatter:
harm may come of melling.
Thou meddlest more than shall have thank
to witen shepherds' wealth: 210
When folk bene fat and riches rank,
it is a sign of health.
But say me, what is Algrin' he,
that is so oft benempt?

Thomalin.

He is a shepherd great in gree 215
but hath bene long ypent.
One day he sat upon a hill
as now thou wouldest me
(But I am taught by Algrin's ill
to love the low degree); 220
For, sitting so with bared scalp,
an eagle soared high
That, weening his white head was chalk,
a shellfish down let fly:

202. heapen . . . wrath: prophecy of the end of Catholicism based on Revelation 6: 15–17: 'And the kings of the earth, and the great men, and the rich men . . . hid themselves in dens, and among the rocks of the mountains, And said . . . Fall on us, and hide us . . . from the wrath of the Lamb. For the great day of his wrath is come . . .'. Cf. *May*, 51–4 and n.
203. surly: E.K.
207. clatter: babble.
208. melling: E.K.
210. witen: censure: cf. *June* 100 gloss.
211. rank: (1) abundant; (2) excessive; (3) corrupt. See 4n.
213. Algrin': E.K.
214. benempt: E.K.
215–28. He . . . pain: daring allegory of Elizabeth's disagreement with Grindal: *May* 75n. The eagle = the queen; the shellfish = the instrument effecting his suspension.
215. gree: E.K.
216. ypent: imprisoned: cf. *January* 4n. The *SC* instances are *OED*'s first after two citations from the pseudo-Chaucerian *Plowman's Tale* (*SC* Epilogue 10n).

She weened the shellfish to have broke, 225
    but therewith bruised his brain.
So now astonied with the stroke
    he lies in lingering pain.

                    Morrell.
Ah, good Algrin', his hap was ill,
    but shall be bett' in time. 230
Now farewell, shepherd, sith this hill
    thou hast such doubt to climb.

            Thomalin's emblem:
            In medio virtus.

            Morrell's emblem: 235
            In summo felicitas.

GLOSS

1] **a goatherd**) by goats in scripture be represented the wicked and reprobate whose pastor also must needs be such [Matthew 25: 31–46; apocalyptic Protestantism, since the passage describes the separation of sheep from goats at the Last Judgement].

2] **bank**) is the seat of honour [*OED* bank *sb* 2; E.K. carefully distinguishes it from sense 1, sloping ground].

3] **straying herd**) which wander out of the way of truth.

8] **als**) for *also* [northern but also archaic: *February* 58n].

9] **climb**) spoken of ambition [cf. John 10: 1: 'He that entereth not in by the door into the sheepfold, but climbeth up another way, he is a thief and a robber'].

12] **Great climbers**) according to Seneca his verse: *Decidunt celsa graviore lapsu* [not Seneca; E.K. presumably thinks it is in Seneca's *De vita beata*, but he misremembers Horace, *Odes*, 2. 10. 10–11 (*celsae graviore casu/Decidunt turres*) which is, significantly, on the advantages of the golden mean. The E.K. quote translates: 'lofty things tumble with a heavier fall'].

16] **mickle**) much [archaic, also northern].

17] **the Sun**) a reason why he refuseth to dwell on mountains, because there is no shelter against the scorching sun: according to the time of the year, which is the hottest month of all [thus at the centre of *SC* Thomalin alludes to the mid-

227. *astonied*: stunned, paralysed. *stroke*: (1) blow of judgement (*OED* stroke *sb* 1, 3a); (2) apoplectic seizure: *ibid.*, 6a.

230. *bett'*: E.K. The text in all quartos reads *better* while the prompt to the gloss reads *bett*. Because it maintains the metre and seems to preserve Spenser's spelling, I follow the gloss: see Herford in *Var* 1. 718.

234–6. *In medio . . . felicitas*: E.K. The first is ascribed wrongly to Palinode in all early edns; E.K. gets the attribution right. Note that the emphasis on *middle* and *height* at the end of this second central eclogue accords with the decorum of 'triumphal' mid-point symbolism: *April* headnote.

day Sun of Judgement: 'For behold, the day cometh that shall burn as an oven, and all the proud, yea, and all that do wickedly, shall be stubble, and the day that cometh shall burn them up' (Malachi 4: 1); for the tradition of Christ as the avenging sun, see Panofsky 1955: 261–2. Cf. the opening of Mantuan, *Eclogues*, 8, tr. Turberville: '. . . the Sun/Is in the highest point of heaven/that he is wont to run'.]

19–20] the Cup and Diadem) be two signs in the firmament through which the sun maketh his course in the month of July [Crater and Corona borealis: Fowler 1975: 69–70n].

21] Lion) this is poetically spoken, as if the sun did hunt a Lion with one dog: the meaning whereof is, that in July the sun is in Leo, at which time the Dog star, which is called Sirius or Canicula, reigneth with immoderate heat causing pestilence, drought, and many diseases [the Dog days, frequently thought of as beginning in mid-July with the heliacal rising of the Dog star, were often seen as times of social and political ferment: *OED* citing John Philpot, 1555. For the lion of wrath, see Ripa 1603: 75, and, for Christ as the avenging lion (based on Revelation 5: 5), Panofsky 1955: 262 citing Pierre Bersuire: 'In summer, when he is in the Lion, the sun withers the herbs . . . . So shall Christ, in that heat of the Judgement, appear as a man fierce and leonine; He shall wither sinners'. Lane 1993: 116–18 identifies the lion with the oppressive Crown and nobility.].

28] overture) an open place. The word is borrowed of the French and used in good writers [already in use to mean aperture; but this is *OED*'s only citation in this sense].

29] to holden chat) to talk and prate [*OED*'s first citation of *chat* in the sense *easy talk* is from Gabriel Harvey, 1573].

33] a lord) [i.e., lout] was wont among the old Britons to signify a Lord; and therefore the Danes, that long time usurped their tyranny here in Britain, were called (for more dread and dignity) *Lurdanes* (*scilicet* [namely] Lord Danes), at which time it is said that the insolency and pride of that nation was so outrageous in this realm that, if it fortuned a Briton to be going over a bridge and saw the Dane set foot upon the same, he must return back till the Dane were clean over, or else abide the price of his displeasure, which was no less than present [immediate] death. But, being afterward expelled, that name of lurdane became so odious unto the people whom they had long oppressed that, even at this day, they use, for more reproach, to call the quartan ague the *fever lurdane* [Renwick 1930: 205 cites the story from Holinshed, 7. 3, and see *Var* 1. 336. Since *lord* = master is Anglo-Saxon in origin, E.K.'s *Britons* are the Saxon Britons rather than the native Celtic Britons. The point of the anecdote (in support of *SC*'s reformist favouring of old and dialect forms) is to recall the Reformation insistence on Saxon (as well as Celtic) as the mother tongue (cf. King 1982: 55, 67–8, 430 and *February* 209n on Druids): linguistic origins are an analogue to the original Church, and Danish overlordship is a yoke equivalent to that of 'Roman' Catholicism (and cf. 147 gloss). *Lurdane* actually derives from Old French *lourdin* = heavy, dull; *OED* traces the false etymology from 1529. *Fever-lurden* = laziness (*OED*).].

34] recks much of thy swink) counts much of thy pains [*OED*'s first citation of *reck* in this sense since 1481; *swink*: *May* 36 gloss. But the spelling of the original – *rekes* – also suggests reeks = exhale sweat.]

35] weetless) not understood [= meaningless; Spenserian coinage. From weet

= to know, which was archaic by the mid-sixteenth century: *OED.*].
41] **St Michael's Mount**) is a promontory in the west part of England.
47] **a hill**) Parnassus, aforesaid [*April* 41, 42 glosses; cf. *June*, 70–1].
49] **Pan**) Christ [*May* 54 gloss].
51] **Dan**) one tribe is put for the whole nation *per synecdochen* [part standing for the whole: i.e., Judah: Numbers 1: 38–9].
59] **Where Titan**) the sun: which story is to be read in Diodorus Siculus of the hill Ida [17. 7. 6–7], from whence (he saith) all night time is to be seen a mighty fire as if the sky burned, which, toward morning, beginneth to gather into a round form, and thereof riseth the sun, whom the poets call Titan [the sun god Hyperion was a Titan; Morrell uses the name which suggests rebellion and parricide: Apollodorus, *Library*, 1. 1–4. On Ida see further 146 gloss.].
63] **There**) that is, in paradise, where, through error of shepherd's understanding, he saith that all shepherds did use to feed their flocks till one (that is, Adam) by his folly and disobedience made all the rest of his offspring be debarred and shut out from thence [Genesis 3: 23–4].
64] **the shepherd**) is Endymion, whom the poets feign to have been so beloved of Phoebe (*scilicet* [namely] the Moon) that he was by her kept asleep in a cave by the space of thirty years for to enjoy his company [a myth interpreted by neo-Platonists as signifying initiation into the mystery of love through death: Wind 1967: 154. Euhemeristic readings saw him as an early astronomer, relevant in view of the astronomical references in the eclogue. Endymion was in fact a shepherd on Latmos, not Ida.].
73] **Sinai**) a hill in Arabia where God appeared [Exodus 19: 2–3, 24: 15–18. But Morrell is introducing covert Catholicism, for Sinai was the burial place of St Catherine: *Var* 1. 329.].
74] **Our Lady's bower**) a place of pleasure so called [E.K.'s tone, as a Protestant, is dismissive (bower = chamber or arbour); but the phrase suggests the shrine of Our Lady at Loretto named at Mantuan, *Eclogues*, 8. 52. The shrine was a sufficiently recent miracle to prompt Protestant scepticism.].
77–8] **fauns or silvans**) be of poets feigned to be gods of the wood [and traditionally mischievous and lustful: St Augustine, *City of God*, 15. 23, identifying them as incubi].
79] **Medway**) the name of a river in Kent which, running by Rochester, meeteth with Thames, whom he calleth 'his elder brother' both because he is greater and also falleth sooner into the sea [Spenser was secretary to John Young, Bishop of Rochester, 1578–9; the Medway, at the mouth of which Rochester lies, was of supreme strategic and naval importance, so Morrell fakes the pose of a patriotic Elizabethan. Spenser celebrates the marriage of the Thames and the Medway at *FQ*, 4. 11.].
84] **ment**) mingled [third person plural of meng; archaic].
85–6] **melampod and terebinth**) be herbs good to cure diseased goats. Of the one speaketh Mantuan [*Eclogues*, 8. 15–17; tr. Turberville ll. 42–8], and of the other Theocritus: *terminthou trōgōn eschaton akremona* [printed in Greek in the quartos; misquoting Theocritus (attrib.), *Epigrams*, 1. 6: '[The white he-goat] is eating the ends of the terebinth twigs'. E.K. has *tragōn* (goat) instead of *trōgōn* (eating): *Var* 1. 337. *Melampod* = black hellebore, a purge for melancholy and its effects (including madness); *terebinth* (the turpentine tree) purged phlegm and the 'clammy humours': Salmon (1678) 1. 1. 62 and 132 respectively. Both

grow best in high places: Richardson 1989: 449.].

89] **nigher heaven**) note the shepherd's simpleness, which supposeth that from the hills is nearer way to heaven.

91] **levin**) lightning [archaic]; which he taketh for an argument to prove the nighness to heaven because the lightning doth commonly light on high mountains, according to the saying of the poet: *feriuntque summos fulmina montes* [Horace, *Odes*, 2. 10. 11–12: 'lightning strikes mountain tops'. E.K. misremembers *fulgura* (lightning) as *fulmina* (thunderbolt): this completes the quotation cited at 12 gloss above.].

93] **lorel**) a losel [rogue; but both etymologically mean 'lost ones', the damned. Not archaic, but *lewd lorel* appears in Langland, *Piers Plowman*, A 8. 123 (*OED*) and in Chaucer: *Var* 1. 330.].

95] **a borrel**) a plain fellow [current usage; but E.K.'s gloss draws attention by omission to Thomalin's Protestant irony, since the alternative meaning of borrel = layman (as opposed to Latin-learned priest): i.e., God is on the side of the Protestants in their championing of the vernacular and plain speaking. Cf. Chaucer's *Franklin's Prologue*, 8: 'I am a burel man'.].

97] **narre**) nearer [northern/Scots].

107] **hale**) for *whole* [i.e., healthy; northern/Scots].

109] **yede**) go [*May* 22, 178 glosses].

111] **frowy**) musty or mossy [i.e., sour: *OED*'s first citation: froughy *a*].

116] **of yore**) long ago [archaic].

117] **forewent**) gone afore [common usage].

127] **the first shepherd**) was Abel the righteous, who (as scripture saith) bent his mind to keeping of sheep, as did his brother Cain to tilling the ground [Genesis 4: 1–15; and cf. Matt. 23: 35 (Jesus attacking the Pharisees and invoking 'the blood of Abel the righteous'). E.K. reinforces the apocalyptic Protestantism of Spenser's passage. At Hebrews 12: 24 Abel is a type of Christ.].

133] **his keep**) his charge (*scilicet* [namely] his flock) [*OED*'s only instance in this sense: keep *sb* 2b].

137] **louted**) did honour and reverence [archaic].

143] **The brethren**) the twelve sons of Jacob, which were sheepmasters and lived only thereupon [Genesis 46, esp. verse 32].

146] **whom Ida**) Paris, which, being the son of Priamus, king of Troy, for his mother Hecuba's dream which, being with child of him, dreamed she brought forth a firebrand that set all the tower of Ilium on fire, was cast forth on the hill Ida where, being fostered of shepherds, he eke in time became a shepherd and lastly came to knowledge of his parentage [Apollodorus, *Library*, 3. 12. 5; see 147 gloss].

147] **a lass**) Helena, the wife of Menelaus, king of Lacedaemonia, was by Venus for the golden apple to her given, then promised to Paris, who thereupon with a sort of lusty Trojans, stole her out of Lacedaemonia and kept her in Troy: which was the cause of the ten years' war in Troy, and the most famous city of all Asia most lamentably sacked and defaced [for the Judgement of Paris, see Stewart 1991: 161–209; and for Paris as a shepherd exiled by his wrong choice from paradisal Ida, see *ibid.*, p 177 (Paris thus becomes an analogue of Christian pastors who have lost touch with the 'true' Church). Note E.K.'s interweaving of the Trojan myth – the official Tudor story of Britain's origins in Aeneas's descendant Brutus – with the tale of subsequent conquest and oppression (33 gloss above).].

154] **Argus**) was of the poets devised to be full of eyes, and therefore to him was committed the keeping of the transformed cow Io: so called because that in the print of a cow's foot there is figured an I in the middest of an O [Ovid, *Metamorphoses*, 1. 649–50. Ovid doesn't name the I and O, but at least one Renaissance commentator did: Mustard 1919: 199–200.].

161] **his name**) he meaneth Aaron, whose name (for more decorum) the shepherd saith he hath forgot, lest his remembrance and skill in antiquities of holy writ should seem to exceed the meanness of the person [Moses's brother (Exodus 4: 14); first high priest of the Jews (Exodus 28–30) and the exemplar of priestly perfection and type of Christ (Tuve 1952: 153–6). His name means *teacher* (Geneva table of names), and, appropriately, *mountain*: John Robinson 1815, *A Theological...Dictionary*, s.v. Aaron.].

163] **not so true**) for Aaron in the absence of Moses started aside and committed idolatry [the making and worshipping of the golden calf: Exodus 32. The Geneva gloss on Exodus 32: 1 explains the heinousness from the Protestant viewpoint: 'The root of idolatry is, when men think that God is not at hand, except when they see him carnally'; that on verse 4 explains E.K.'s interest in the Io myth (154 gloss): 'They [the Jews] smell of their leaven of Egypt, where they saw calves, oxen and serpents worshipped'. Io, metamorphosed from cow back to girl, was worshipped by the Egyptians as a goddess.].

173] **in purple**) spoken of the popes and cardinals, which use such tyrannical colours and pompous painting [in the list of Aaron's priestly garments the ephod and breastplate of judgement contain purple and scarlet (Exodus 28: 5–6, 15); and in the context of the vestiarian controversy of the 1560s and 70s (the Puritan objection to surplice, chasuble, cope, etc., with which Grindal had some sympathy: Wall in *SpE*, p 157; McLane 1961: 141–2) Aaron, despite his function as type of priestly perfection, could be seen as embodying a tendency to 'papistical' deviation. The *purple* links Catholic vestments with Aaron's via (e.g.) the Geneva gloss on Revelation 17: 3–4: 'a red and purple garment: and surely it was not without cause that the Romish clergy were so much delighted with this colour'.].

177] **glitterand**) glittering: a participle used sometime in Chaucer but altogether in John Gower [in the apocryphal Chaucerian *Plowman's Tale*, 134, 162 (cf. *February* 149 gloss); a common mediaeval form].

179] **Their Pan**) that is the Pope, whom they count their god and greatest shepherd [Spenser and E.K. now forget the typology – Pan as Christ – and recall that he is the lustful and therianthropic goat-god, apt emblem for the leaders of the Roman – and aspects of the English – Church].

181] **Palinode**) a shepherd, of whose report he seemeth to speak all this [not the pro-Roman Palinode of *May* but a visitor who takes the opposite – palinode – point of view to the Roman].

197] **wizards**) great learned heads [often contemptuous: *OED*. But Spenser also intends the meaning *conjuror*, a common charge levelled by Protestants at Catholic priests.].

197] **welter**) wallow [*OED* dates its first citation in this sense 1530].

199] **kern**) a churl or farmer [first instance of this contemptuous use is dated 1553 in *OED*: kern *sb* 1, 2. But Thomalin (and Spenser) manifest a conscious

Protestant linguistic imperialism: a *kern* is primarily an Irish peasant, or lightly armed foot soldier from the peasantry (and thus by definition wild and Catholic!): *OED*, sense 1.].

201] **sike mister men**) such kind of men [archaic: *September* 103 gloss; but E.K. ignores the possibility that Spenser recalls the original meaning: men of a particular profession or mystery].

203] **surly**) stately and proud [first citation in *OED* in this sense is dated *c.* 1572; it also cites a 1573 instance from Gabriel Harvey].

208] **melling**) meddling [E.K.'s gloss distinguishes one of several possible contemporary meanings].

213] **Algrin'**) the name of a shepherd aforesaid [see 126, also *May* 75n], whose mishap he alludeth to the chance that happened to the poet Aeschylus that was brained with a shellfish [Pliny, *Natural History*, 10. 3. 7–8. The reference is to Grindal's suspension from his duties in 1577.].

214] **benempt**) named [*OED*'s only citation in this precise sense: bename *v* 2. See also *November* 46 gloss.].

215] **gree**) for *degree* [an acceptable contemporary usage: *OED* gree *sb* 1, 4].

230] **bett'**) better.

Emblem.

By this poesy Thomalin confirmeth that which in his former speech by sundry reasons he had proved: for, being both himself sequestered [the word glances at Grindal's suspension or sequestration] from all ambition and also abhorring it in others of his coat [profession], he taketh occasion to praise the mean [middle as well as low] and lowly state as that wherein is safety without fear and quiet without danger, according to the saying of old philosophers that virtue dwelleth in the midst [centre], being environed with two contrary vices [Aristotle, *Nicomachean Ethics*, 2. 9. 1–4 (1109A)]. Whereto Morrell replieth with continuance of the same philosopher's opinion that, albeit all bounty [virtue] dwelleth in mediocrity [Latin *mediocritas* = middle state; also insignificance], yet perfect felicity dwelleth in supremacy. For they say (and most true it is) that happiness is placed in the highest degree, so as if anything be higher or better, then that straight way ceaseth to be perfect happiness: much like to that which once I heard alleged in defence of humility out of a great doctor [teacher of the church; unidentified]: *suorum Christus humillimus* ['Christ [is] the humblest of his own [people]']. Which saying a gentleman in the company, taking at the rebound, beat back again with like saying of another doctor as he said: *suorum Deus altissimus* ['God is the highest of his own people'].

August

A singing match on the theme of love in the tradition of Theocritus (*Idylls* 5, 6, 8, 9 and 27) and Virgil (*Eclogues* 3, 5, 7, 8 and 9) but transmitted into English via French modulations of the tradition by the Pléiade, *August* presents a bravura tripartite display of stanzaic technique: the 6-line stanzas of lines 1–52 (reminiscent of those voiced by Colin in *January*, but with frequent 4-beat lines to recall the rustic tetrameters of *February* and *May*) yield to a central 72-line roundelay (53–124; the metrical pattern here recalls the divided fourteeners of *July*) which, after another group of 6-line stanzas, is superseded by one of the first sestinas to be written in English (see 151–89n). To a greater degree than other *SC* eclogues, *August* supports technical display with numerological wit as Spenser follows the native Reformation tradition of *July* with signals of his ability to imitate the complexities of continental humanist poetry. Thus, the emphasis on 6 (6-line stanzas; a roundelay of 6 × 12 lines; a sestina of 6 × 6-line stanzas followed by 6 concluding lines) reminds us that in the calendar eschewed by *SC* with its March new year (see General Argument above) August is the sixth month; it reminds us more wittily that six is the number of Venus, goddess of love (because 6 is the product of the multiplication of the first male number (3) by the first female number (2)) and mother of harmony (because there are six whole tones in the harmonious octave; and note that August is the 'octave' – eighth – month of the *SC*'s actual year). Note, too, that Willy and Perigot speak in the octave ratio of 2:1 (Willy has 4 lines to Perigot's 2 up to line 24; then Willy has 2 stanzas to Perigot's 1 before they equalise at line 43; at ll. 125–50 the ratios continue): see Agrippa 1651: 2. 9, and Martianus Capella, *The Marriage of Philology and Mercury* in Stahl, W. H., Johnson, R. and Burge, E. C. (eds) 1977 *Martianus Capella and the Seven Liberal Arts*, 2 vols, Columbia University Press, New York: 2: 280–1 for the symbolisms, and March headnote on Venus and Harmony. In addition, the roundelay is framed by the 2:1 ratio since it is preceded by a 52-line exchange between Perigot and Willy and succeeded by a 26-line exchange between them and Cuddy (ll. 125–50).

The woodcut (fig. 8), following, like the others, the old sign-per-month tradition (Gombrich 1978: 109–18, plates 113–14), gives the sovereign position to August's sign, Virgo. Since this was Elizabeth's birth sign (see *April* headnote), we may suspect that *August* complements *April* as a piece of anti-Alençon propaganda: the queen must remain *semper virgo*, always virgin. Hence the denigration of love culminating in Colin's sestina, and, before that, the evocation by Willy and Perigot in their roundelay of a maiden very like *April*'s Elisa (and note the introduction of the queen's primary emblem, the virginal moon, at ll. 89–92). The combination of Venerean 6 and virginal presiding sign supports *April*'s message of a virginal queen of love chastely married to her realm, not to Catholic Alençon.

The woodcut's other most notable feature – the woman to the left of the main foreground group of Willy, Perigot, Cuddy and the prizes – supports this reading. She is clearly the winner of the golden apple in the Judgement of Paris, a myth that links *July* (see 146 and 147 glosses) with *August* (glosses to 138) and is thus Venus holding the apple of beauty that is, simultaneously, the orb of world rule (see the painting *Queen Elizabeth and the Three Goddesses* (1569) in Wilson 1939, facing p. 238; Wind 1967: 82–3). But she is backed by rows of corn sheaves, emblems of Astraea/Virgo (who can just be seen holding her traditional *spica* [ear of corn] top centre); so that this Venus, like *April*'s queen of love, is *semper virgo* too. On the iconography see Stewart 1991: 161–209, esp. 197–202.

August
Aegloga octava

Argument

In this eglogue is set forth a delectable controversy made in imitation of that in Theocritus, whereto also Virgil fashioned his third and seventh eglogue. They choose for umpire of their strife Cuddy, a neatherd's boy, who, having ended their cause, reciteth also himself a proper song whereof Colin (he saith) was author.

               Willy. Perigot. Cuddy.
Tell me, Perigot, what shall be the game
Wherefore with mine thou dare thy music match?
Or bene thy bagpipes ren far out of frame?
Or hath the cramp thy joints benumbed with ache?

               Perigot.
Ah, Willy, when the heart is ill assayed   5
How can bagpipe or joints be well apaid?

               Willy.
What the foul evil hath thee so bestad?
Whilom thou was peregal to the best
And, wont to make the jolly shepherds glad
With piping and dancing, didst pass the rest.   10

Argument: *delectable*: delightful. *neatherd's*: cowherd's.
proper: (1) belonging to someone (Colin); (2) distinctive; (3) fitting the circumstances (*OED* proper *a* I. 2, III. 9).
2. *music*: the harmonious subject of *August*, along with love (hence the sixes: see headnote).
3. *bagpipes*: *April* 3n. *ren*: *April* 118n. *frame*: order (i.e., tune, harmonious accord).
5. *assayed*: tried with afflictions (*OED*'s last instance is from *FQ*).
6. *apaid*: satisfied.
7. *bestad*: E.K.
8. *Whilom, peregal*: E.K.
10. *pass*: *June*, 74.

Perigot.
Ah, Willy, now I have learned a new dance,
My old music marred by a new mischance.

Willy.
Mischief mought to that new mischance befall
That so hath raft us of our merriment.
But rede me, what pain doth thee so appall –   15
Or lovest thou, or bene thy younglings miswent?

Perigot.
Love hath misled both my younglings and me:
I pine for pain, and they my pain to see.

Willy.
Perdy and wellaway: ill may they thrive;
Never knew I lover's sheep in good plight.   20
But and if in rhymes with me thou dare strive,
Such fond fancies shall soon be put to flight.

Perigot.
That shall I do, though mochel worse I fared:
Never shall be said that Perigot was dared.

Willy.
Then lo, Perigot, the pledge which I plight: 25
A mazer ywrought of the maple warre,
Wherein is enchased many a fair sight

---

14. raft: E.K.
15. rede: advise (archaic). *appall*: dismay, make pale.
16. miswent: E.K.
18. pine: January 48n.
19. wellaway: alas. *ill may*: E.K.
20. plight: condition, state.
23. mochel: February 109n.
24. dared: daunted (*OED* dare *v* 2, II. 6), punning on dare = challenge.
25. pledge: promise.
26. mazer: E.K. Wooden drinking bowl originally (as here) made of maple: *OED* mazer *sb* 1, 2; cf. *FQ*, 2. 12. 49. *warre*: burr, knot (obsolete; last *OED* instance 1530): i.e., burr-maple.
27 enchased: E.K.

Of bears and tigers that maken fierce war;
And over them spread a goodly wild vine
Entrailed with a wanton ivy twine. 30

Thereby is a lamb in the wolf's jaws:
But see how fast renneth the shepherd swain
To save the innocent from the beast's paws –
And here with his sheephook hath him slain.
Tell me, such a cup hast thou ever seen? 35
Well mought it beseem any harvest queen.

                Perigot.
Thereto will I pawn yonder spotted lamb:
Of all my flock there n'is sike another,
For I brought him up without the dam;
But Colin Clout raft me of his brother, 40
That he purchased of me in the plain field:
Sore against my will was I forced to yield.

                Willy.
Siker make like account of his brother.
But who shall judge the wager won or lost?

                Perigot.
That shall yonder herd-groom and none other, 45
Which over the pousse hitherward doth post.

28–30. *bears . . . twine*: bears and tigers symbolise wrath: Tervarent (1958) col 292; Ripa 1603: 243–4; de Vries 1974: 467; the vine and ivy are both Bacchic (hence lustful, amorous, *wanton*): the excesses of the latter pair counteract those of the former. But maybe the mazer is devoted totally to Bacchus, since tigers were attributed to him (Horace, *Odes*, 3. 3. 13–15) and bears were associated with lust (Tervarent, cols 291–2). The mazer in Theocritus, *Idylls*, 1. 27–9 is bordered with ivy; those in Virgil, *Eclogues*, 3. 38–9 are embossed with vine and ivy.
30. *Entrailed*: E.K.
31. *lamb...jaws*: traditional opposites again (meekness, innocence; destructiveness).
32. *renneth*: for the form see *OED* run *v* A II. 11.
36. *mought*: might. *beseem*: befit. *harvest queen*: E.K.
40. *raft*: 14 gloss.
41. *purchased*: obtained. *plain*: open (i.e., he got it from me without trickery).
43. *Siker . . . brother*: certainly the same will happen to his brother.
45. *herd-groom*: February 35 gloss.
46. *pousse*: E.K.

                    Willy.
But for the sunbeam so sore doth us beat,
Were not better to shun the scorching heat?

                    Perigot.
Well agreed, Willy. Then sit thee down, swain:
Sike a song never heardest thou but Colin sing.   50

                    Cuddy.
'Gin when ye list, ye jolly shepherds twain:
Sike a judge as Cuddy were for a king.

Perigot. It fell upon a holy eve
Willy.   (hey ho holiday)
Perigot. When holy fathers wont to shrive   55
Willy.   (now 'ginneth this roundelay),
Perigot. Sitting upon a hill so high
Willy.   (hey ho the high hill),
Perigot. The while my flock did feed thereby
Willy.   (the while the shepherd self did spill!),   60
Perigot. I saw the bouncing bellibone
Willy.   (hey ho bonibell)
Perigot. Tripping over the dale alone
Willy.   (she can trip it very well),
Perigot. Well decked in a frock of grey   65
Willy.   (hey ho grey is greet)
Perigot. And in a kirtle of green say
Willy.   (the green is for maidens meet):
Perigot. A chaplet on her head she wore
Willy.   (hey ho chaplet),   70

---

53. *It . . . upon*: E.K.
55. *wont . . . shrive*: customarily hear confession: the feast could be that of the Assumption of the Blessed Virgin, 15 August or, under the auspices of Virgo, the Nativity of the Blessed Virgin, 8 September, on the eve of which Queen Elizabeth was born. Note that this *roundelay* (cf. *April* 33 gloss) is thus located in a Cranmerian rather than progressive Protestant landscape: on saints' days in the reformed Church, see Wall in *SpE*, pp 153–60, esp. p 155; also *July* headnote.
60. *spill*: squander.
61. *bellibone*: *April* 92 gloss.
66. *greet*: E.K.
67. *kirtle*: skirt. *say*: fine-textured woollen cloth.
68. *meet*: proper.
69. *chaplet*: E.K.

Perigot. Of sweet violets therein was store
Willy.   (she sweeter than the violet).
Perigot. My sheep did leave their wonted food
Willy.   (hey ho seely sheep),
Perigot. And gazed on her as they were wood   75
Willy.   (wood as he that did them keep!).
Perigot. As the bonny lass passed by
Willy.   (hey ho bonny lass)
Perigot. She roved at me with glancing eye
Willy.   (as clear as the crystal glass)   80
Perigot. All as the sunny beam so bright
Willy.   (hey ho the sunbeam)
Perigot. Glanceth from Phoebus' face forthright
Willy.   (so love into thy heart did stream);
Perigot. Or as the thunder cleaves the clouds   85
Willy.   (hey ho the thunder)
Perigot. Wherein the lightsome levin shrouds
Willy.   (so cleaves thy soul asunder);
Perigot. Or as Dame Cynthia's silver ray
Willy.   (hey ho the moonlight)   90
Perigot. Upon the glittering wave doth play
Willy.   (such play is a piteous plight),
Perigot. The glance into my heart did glide
Willy.   (hey ho the glider).
Perigot. Therewith my soul was sharply gride   95
Willy.   (such wounds soon waxen wider).
Perigot. Hasting to ranch the arrow out
Willy.   (hey ho Perigot),
Perigot. I left the head in my heart-root
Willy.   (it was a desperate shot):   100
Perigot. There it rankleth aye more and more

Textual note

84. *thy*] F; correcting quartos' *my*.

71. *violets*: love and modesty: *April* 61–3n.
73. *wonted*: customary.
74. *seely*: poor.
75. *wood*: mad.
79. *roved*: shot (as with arrows at a target): a sixteenth-century usage.
87. *lightsome . . . shrouds*: bright lightning [*levin*: E.K.] conceals itself.
89. *Cynthia*: E.K.
92. *plight*: folding, waving: *OED* plight *sb* 2, I. 1.
95. *gride*: E.K.
97. *ranch*: pull, pluck (the first of two instances in *OED*: ranch *v* 3).
100. *desperate*: very dangerous: *OED* desperate *a* A II. 5b.

Willy.   (hey ho the arrow)
Perigot. Ne can I find salve for my sore
Willy.   (love is a careless sorrow).
Perigot. And though my bail with death I bought   105
Willy.   (hey ho heavy cheer),
Perigot. Yet should thilk lass not from my thought
Willy.   (so you may buy gold too dear);
Perigot. But whether in painful love I pine
Willy.   (hey ho pinching pain)   110
Perigot. Or thrive in wealth, she shall be mine
Willy.   (but if thou can her obtain).
Perigot. And if for graceless grief I die
Willy.   (hey ho graceless grief),
Perigot. Witness, she slew me with her eye   115
Willy.   (let thy folly be the prief),
Perigot. And you that saw it, simple sheep
Willy.   (hey ho the fair flock),
Perigot. For prief thereof my death shall weep
Willy.   (and moan with many a mock):   120
Perigot. So learned I love on a holy eve
Willy.   (hey ho holiday),
Perigot. That ever since my heart did grieve
Willy.   (now endeth our roundelay).

                    Cuddy.
Siker sike a roundel never heard I none: 125
Little lacketh Perigot of the best;
And Willy is not greatly overgone,
So weren his undersongs well addressed.

104. careless: having no regard or thought (thus all editions before Bathurst's of 1732; all subsequent editions follow its emendation to *cureless*, including *Variorum* and Yale: see *Var* 1. 718).
105. bail: release: the original spelling, *bale*, permits a pun on *bale* = destruction.
107. should . . . thought: would not leave my mind.
110. pinching: painful, withering.
112. but if: E.K.
113. graceless: lacking [the girl's] favour (last *OED* instance of what appears to be a mediaevalism: graceless *a* 2).
116. prief: proof (archaic form).
127. overgone: surpassed.
128. undersongs: burdens, accompaniments (first *OED* instance). *addressed*: ordered, arranged.

Willy.

Herd-groom, I fear me thou have a squint eye:
Aread uprightly, who has the victory?   130

Cuddy.

Faith of my soul, I deem each have gained:
For-thy let the lamb be Willy his own,
And (for Perigot so well hath him pained)
To him be the wroughten mazer alone.

Perigot.

Perigot is well pleased with the doom: 135
Ne can Willy wite the witeless herd-groom.

Willy.

Never dempt more right of beauty, I ween,
The shepherd of Ida, that judged beauty's queen.

Cuddy.

But tell me, shepherds, should it not yshend
Your roundels fresh to hear a doleful verse   140
Of Rosalind (who knows not Rosalind?)
That Colin made, ilk can I you rehearse.

Perigot.

Now say it, Cuddy, as thou art a lad:
With merry thing it's good to meddle sad.

---

129. *squint eye*: E.K.
130. *Aread uprightly*: adjudge fairly (pseudo-archaism; antedates *OED*'s first instance of this sense (1593): aread *v* II. 8).
131. *each have*: E.K.
133. *pained*: as at 109; also: taken trouble (in giving the lead in the roundelay).
135. *doom*: E.K.
136. *wite . . . witeless*: E.K.
137. *dempt*: E.K.
138. *shepherd*: E.K. *beauty's queen*: E.K.
139. *yshend*: archaic prefix + shend (*July* 172n).
140. *fresh*: new, invigorating.
142. *ilk*: the same.
144. *meddle*: *April* 68 gloss (note the theme of harmonious mingling again).

Willy.
Faith of my soul, thou shalt ycrowned be 145
In Colin's stead if thou this song aread;
For never thing on earth so pleaseth me
As him to hear, or matter of his deed.

Cuddy.
Then list'neth each unto my heavy lay,
And tune your pipes as rufthful as ye may: 150

Ye waste-full woods, bear witness of my woe,
   Wherein my plaints did oftentimes resound;
   Ye care-less birds are privy to my cries,
   Which in your songs were wont to make a part;
   Thou, pleasant spring, hast lulled me oft asleep, 155
   Whose streams my trickling tears did oft augment.

Resort of people doth my griefs augment,
   The walled towns do work my greater woe:
   The forest wide is fitter to resound
   The hollow Echo of my care-full cries. 160
   I hate the house since thence my love did part,
   Whose wailful want debars mine eyes from sleep.

---

146. stead: place. *aread*: (1) utter (*OED* aread *v* I. 3); (2) interpret, solve (as of a riddle): sense 5.

148. matter: subject-matter. *deed*: making, with overtones of *formal written document* to contrast his wrought text with the oral simplicities of the roundelay.

151–89. Ye ... augment: Colin's poem (probably a late addition in view of E.K.'s lack of comment on it) is a sestina: i.e., a poem of 6 × 6 line stanzas, each stanza utilising the same end words usually in accordance with the scheme 123456, 615243, 364125, etc. with an obligatory 6-line envoy in which the terminal words are recapitulated. The form was invented by the troubadour Arnaut Daniel, and Petrarch included nine influential examples in the *Rime*. Spenser's simple end-word scheme (123456, 612345, 561234, etc.) is perhaps borrowed from the sixteenth-century Spanish poet Gutierre de Cetina, though his sestina as a whole is indebted to Sannazaro via *SC*'s dedicatee Philip Sidney: Sidney, *Poems* ed Ringler 1962: 416; Shapiro in *SpE*, pp 637–8; *SC* General headnote, p. 9 above. For this sestina as a sterile echo of Colin's lay to Elisa, see Johnson 1990: 173–4.

160. Echo: *June* 52, 72nn.

161. part: depart.

162. want: lack.

Let streams of tears supply the place of sleep;
   Let all that sweet is, void; and all that may augment
   My dole, draw near. More meet to wail my woe   165
   Bene the wild woods my sorrows to resound
   Than bed or bower, both which I fill with cries
   When I them see so waste, and find no part

Of pleasure past. Here will I dwell apart
   In ghastful grove therefore, till my last sleep   170
   Do close mine eyes: so shall I not augment
   With sight of such a change my restless woe.
   Help me, ye baneful birds whose shrieking sound
   Is sign of dreary death, my deadly cries

Most ruthfully to tune. And as my cries   175
   (Which of my woe cannot bewray least part)
   You hear all night (when nature craveth sleep)
   Increase, so let your irksome yells augment.
   Thus all the night in plaints, the day in woe,
   I vowed have to waste till safe and sound   180

She home return whose voice's silver sound
   To cheerful songs can change my cheerless cries.
   Hence with the nightingale will I take part –
   That blessed bird that spends her time of sleep

164. void: leave.
165. dole: grief.
167. bower: bedchamber: *July* 74 gloss.
170. ghastful: fearsome.
173. baneful birds: ravens and owls: *June* 23–4nn.
174. deadly: subject to death, mortal.
175. ruthfully: piteously.
176. bewray: divulge.
178. irksome: distressing.
183–6. nightingale . . . woe: Philomela, raped by her brother-in-law Tereus who ripped out her tongue so that she would not tell her sister Procne what had happened, wrote her tale in blood. Subsequently fleeing him, she escaped his grip by being metamorphosed into a nightingale: Ovid, *Metamorphoses*, 6. 424–674. She became a type of the poet because of her song and love of solitude: Philip Sidney *Certain Sonnets*, 4; but Colin's adoption of the *persona* suggests an identification with (rather than appropriation of) female violation and grief and his recognition of the power of writing to overcome voicelessness: Brooks-Davies 1992a: xv; and Goldberg 1986: 12–13 and ch. 3 *passim*. For the nightingale as a sign of Colin's Orphic status (*June* 72n; *October* 28 gloss), see Cheney 1991: 29–57. Cf. *November* 141 gloss.

In songs and plaintive pleas the more t'augment 185
The memory of his misdeed that bred her woe.

And you that feel no woe,/ whenas the sound
  Of these my nightly cries/ ye hear apart,
  Let break your sounder sleep/ and pity augment.

Perigot.

O Colin, Colin, the shepherds' joy, 190
  How I admire each turning of thy verse;
And Cuddy, fresh Cuddy, the liefest boy,
  How dolefully his dole thou didst rehearse.

Cuddy.

Then blow your pipes, shepherds, till you be at home:
The night nigheth fast, it's time to be gone. 195

Perigot his emblem:
Vincenti gloria victi.

Willy's emblem:
Vinto non vitto.

Cuddy's emblem: 200
Felice chi può.

GLOSS

7] **bestad**) disposed, ordered [archaic form of bested, used only in the passive; Spenser, uniquely, makes it active].
8] **Whilom**) once [*January* 21n].
8] **peregal**) equal [archaic].
14] **raft**) bereft, deprived [reft was in common use; E.K.'s gloss alerts us to Spenser's use of a mediaeval form].

189. sounder: punning on sound (187); and on sounder = sunder (the sleep that sets you *apart* (see 188) from me).
191. turning . . . verse: an unoriginal etymological pun hinted at in the balancing of *roundel* and *verse* at 140: verse = line (from Latin *vertere* = turn) is named from the act of turning pen and hand to begin another line. Note the pun on turn = revolve with reference to the changes rung on the sestina's terminal words.
192. liefest: dearest.
197–201. Vincenti . . . può: Perigot's emblem = 'the conqueror [obtains] the glory of the conquered one' (Latin); Willy's = 'excelled yet uncomquered' (Italian); Cuddy's = either '[let him be] happy who can' or 'happy [is he] who can' (also Italian). Each has the pithy linguistic ambiguity of epigram (see Kennedy in *SpE*, p 653) and E.K.'s gloss is as good as any, terminating as it does on a note of ethical balance that accords with the eclogue's theme of harmony.

16] **miswent**) gone astray [from miswend; literary archaism].
19] **ill may**) according to Virgil: *Infelix o semper ovis pecus* ['O that flock of sheep is always unfortunate': *Eclogues*, 3. 3].
26] **A mazer**) so also do Theocritus [*Idylls*, 1. 27–56 for the mazer; 5. 20–30 for the pledging of animals] and Virgil [*Eclogues*, 3. 28–51: heifer and beechwood mazers] feign pledges of their strife.
27] **enchased**) engraven [*OED*'s first citation in this sense: enchase *v* 2, 4b]. Such pretty descriptions everywhere useth Theocritus to bring in his *Idyllia*, for which special cause indeed he by that name termeth his eglogues: for *idyllion* in Greek signifieth the *shape* or *picture* of anything, whereof his book is full; and not (as I have heard some fondly [foolishly] guess) that they be called, not *Idyllia*, but *Haedilia*, of the goatherds in them [for the use of the iconic motif in Pléiade poetry, see Hughes, M. Y. 1923 'Spenser and the Greek Pastoral Triad', *Studies in Philology* 20: 184–215].
30] **Entrailed**) wrought between [early instance of a rare verb: *OED*'s first citation 1577].
36] **harvest queen**) the manner of country folk in harvest time [E.K. defers to the presumed ignorance of country customs by the 'learned'].
46] **pousse**) peas [dialect form of pulse]: i.e., pea-field.
53] **It fell upon**) Perigot maketh his song in praise of his love, to whom Willy answereth every under-verse. By Perigot who is meant I cannot uprightly [honestly] say; but if it be who is supposed, his love deserveth no less praise than he giveth her [unidentified].
66] **greet**) weeping and complaint [cf. *April* 1 gloss].
69] **chaplet**) a kind of garland like a crown [a common usage, so E.K. hints that we look for monarchical symbolism in the eclogue. The reference is particularly appropriate to August's Virgo because those born when Corona borealis rises in the fifth degree of Virgo will be makers of wreaths: Gombrich 1978: 111–12 citing Firmicus. This explains as well the appropriateness of a *roundelay* to *August*.].
87] **levin**) lightning [*July* 91 gloss].
89] **Cynthia**) was said to be the Moon [*April* 82 gloss].
95] **gride**) pierced [*February* 4 gloss].
112] **but if**) not unless.
129] **squint eye**) partial judgement [*OED*'s first citation, noting that early instances usually imply envy].
131] **each have**) so saith Virgil: *Et vitula tu dignus, et hic*, etc. ['You are deserving of the heifer, and so is he': *Eclogues*, 3. 109]. So, by interchange of gifts, Cuddy pleaseth both parts [parties].
135] **doom**) judgement [archaism].
136] **wite the witeless**) blame the blameless [*June* 100 gloss; *July*, 210].
137] **dempt**) for *deemed, judged* [mediaeval form].
138] **The shepherd of Ida**) was said to be Paris [*July* 146 gloss].
138] **beauty's queen**) Venus, to whom Paris adjudged the golden apple as the prize of her beauty [*July* 147 gloss and *August* headnote. For the Venus-Queen Elizabeth association, see Wilson 1939: 148, 238–9.].

Emblem.

The meaning hereof is very ambiguous, for Perigot by his poesy claiming the conquest, and Willy not yielding, Cuddy (the arbiter of their cause and patron of his own) seemeth to challenge it as his due, saying, that he is happy which can — : so abruptly ending. But he meaneth either him that can win the best, or moderate himself being best, and leave off with the best.

September

The third and last of the ecclesiastical/theological eclogues' opening quarter is indebted to Mantuan's bitterly satirical *Eclogue* 9 on Roman corruption, the Argument to which in Turberville's translation reads: 'Here Faustul' having throughly tried/the nature of the Roman ground:/The vileness of the soil, and Shep/herds' filthy manners doth expound'. Diggon Davie is almost certainly Richard Davies, Bishop of St David's 1561-81, one of the Marian exiles and a friend of Grindal as well as of Spenser's employer, John Young, Bishop of Rochester (*September*'s Roffy: 171 gloss): McLane 1961: 216-34. Along with *July*'s Thomalin, he had signed a letter to the queen supporting Grindal at the time of his suspension. Diggon/Diccon was a Welsh form of Richard/Dick; but in fact Diggon Davey's idiolect is largely northern/Scots like that of SC's other reformist Protestant speakers in *May* and *July*. Thus, significantly, his name also derives from the millennialist visionary Davy Diker [original spelling, Dycar] in Thomas Churchyard's *Davy Diker's Dream* (*c.* 1552). Diker = ditcher; and he originates with 'Dave the diker' in Langland's *Piers Plowman*, B 5. 320, hence connecting with the radical ploughman tradition again: King 1990: 25; *May* headnote. An account of corruption in the English Church, largely on the matter of temporalities (properties and revenues), yields to a fable (as in *February* and *May*) on the threat from the Douai missionaries (154-61n below); but underlying the whole eclogue is a concern for the social ills - poverty, vagrancy, the exploitation of the poor by the rich - resulting from the many economic pressures, particularly those caused by enclosures, in later sixteenth-century England: Lane (1993) ch 5. Metrically, *September*'s tetrameter couplets recall those of *February* and *May*.

In the woodcut (fig. 9) a prostrated Diggon (identified by his pilgrim's scrip or pouch) sits in parody of Tityrus comfortable under his beech tree as depicted in the illustration to the Brant edition of Virgil's *Eclogue* 1, while Hobbinol adopts the pose of Meliboeus: cf. Patterson 1988: 95 and *January* headnote. Above left, September's zodiacal sign, Libra, emblem of the justice executed by August's Virgo-Astraea, sign of Queen Elizabeth (Yates 1975), itself leans crazily to the left as a reminder of a world that is skewed sinisterly far from earthly - let alone heavenly - rectitude and just action.

September
Aegloga nona

Argument

Herein Diggon Davy is devised to be a shepherd that, in hope of more gain, drove his sheep into a far country, the abuses whereof, and loose living of popish prelates, by occasion of Hobbinol's demand, he discourseth at large.

                    Hobbinol.   Diggon Davy.
Diggon Davy, I bid her god day:
Or Diggon her is, or I missay.

                         Diggon.
Her was her, while it was daylight,
But now her is a most wretched wight;
For day, that was, is wightly past,   5
And now at erst the dirk night doth haste.

                         Hobbinol.
Diggon, aread, who has thee so dight?
Never I wist thee in so poor a plight.
Where is the fair flock thou was wont to lead:
Or bene they chaffered, or at mischief dead?   10

                         Diggon.
Ah, for love of that is to thee most lief,
Hobbinol, I pray thee gall not my old grief:
Sike question rippeth up cause of new woe,
For one opened mote unfold many mo'.

                         Hobbinol.
Nay, but sorrow close shrouded in heart   15
(I know) to keep is a burdenous smart.
Each thing imparted is more eath to bear:
When the rain is fallen, the clouds wexen clear.
And now, sithence I saw thy head last,
Thrice three moons bene fully spent and past,   20
Since when thou hast measured much ground
And wandered, I ween, about the world round,

---

1. bid: E.K. *her*: him; Welsh form: *OED* her *pers pron* 2b. *god*: archaic form of good (or perhaps intended to reflect Welsh pronunciation).
5. wightly: E.K.
6. at erst: at once, suddenly: archaic; a Spenserian misunderstanding of now at erst = now and not sooner: *OED* erst *a* and *adv*, A 2. *dirk*: *February* 134n.
7. aread: tell (*August* 146n). *dight*: dressed: *April* 29 gloss.
8. wist: knew (sixteenth-century pseudo-archaism).
10. chaffered: E.K. *mischief dead*: E.K.
11. lief: E.K.
17. eath: E.K.
19. sithence: since.
20. thrice..moons: E.K.
21. measured: E.K.

So as thou can many things relate:
But tell me first of thy flock's astate.

Diggon.

My sheep bene wasted (wae is me, therefore): 25
The jolly shepherd that was of yore
Is now nor jolly nor shepherd more.
In foreign coasts, men said, was plenty –
And so there is, but all of misery.
I dempt there much to have eked my store, 30
But such eking hath made my heart sore.
In tho' countries whereas I have bene,
No being for those that truly mean;
But for such as of guile maken gain,
No such country as there to remain: 35
They setten to sale their shops of shame,
And maken a mart of their good name.
The shepherds there robben one another,
And layen baits to beguile her brother;
Or they will buy his sheep out of the cote, 40
Or they will carven the shepherd's throat.
The shepherd's swain you cannot well ken
(But it be by his pride) from other men:

24. astate: archaic form of estate = condition.
25. wasted: destroyed; diminished (in number and/or strength). *wae:* E.K.
26. yore: July 116 gloss.
30. dempt: decided; but for this specific sense, decide to do something, *OED* registers only one instance, from *c*. 1340 (deem *v* 4b); if Diggon means *hoped*, then that is equally rare: *OED* cites one instance from *c*. 1400 (sense 8). Cf. *August* 137 gloss. *eked:* E.K.
33. being: livelihood. *mean:* speak, tell: *OED* mean *v* 1, 6b; northern/Scots.
36–7. shops . . . mart: May 298n, with specific reference to the selling of benefices; *of shame:* shameful; shamefully.
38–41. shepherds . . . throat: referring (1) to the system of unjust fines; (2) the ejection of clergy from rich benefices when the queen or her favourites demanded the appointment of their nominees.
39. her: their: *May* 160 gloss.
40. cote: shelter.
41. carven: E.K.
42. ken: E.K.

They looken big as bulls that bene bait,
And bearen the crag so stiff and so state 45
As cock on his dunghill crowing crank.

                  Hobbinol.
Diggon, I am so stiff and so stank
That uneath may I stand any more;
And now the western wind bloweth sore,
That now is in his chief sovereignty, 50
Beating the withered leaf from the tree.
Sit we down here under the hill:
Tho may we talk and tellen our fill
And make a mock at the blustering blast.
Now say on, Diggon, whatever thou hast. 55

                  Diggon.
Hobbin, ah Hobbin, I curse the stound
That ever I cast to have lorn this ground:
Wellaway the while I was so fond
To leave the good that I had in hand
In hope of better that was uncouth: 60
So lost the dog the flesh in his mouth.
My seely sheep (ah, seely sheep)
That here by there I whilom used to keep –
All were they lusty, as thou didst see –

---

44. *bulls*: image of pride based on Psalm 22: 12–13 (and see 124–6 below): 'mighty bulls of Bashan have closed me about. They gape upon me with their mouths . . . ' (Geneva gloss: 'He meaneth, that his enemies were so fat, proud, and cruel, that they were rather beasts than men'). Also Amos 4: 1: 'Hear this word, ye kine of Bashan . . . which oppress the poor, and destroy the needy'; where 'kine' is glossed as 'princes and governors'. *bait*: fed.
45. *crag*: E.K. *state*: E.K.
46. *cock*: traditional emblem of pride. *crank*: lustily, triumphantly.
47. *stank*: E.K.
48. *uneath*: scarcely.
49. *And now*: E.K.
54. *mock*: E.K.
56. *stound*: occasion.
57. *cast*: resolved. *lorn*: E.K.
58. *Wellaway*: alas.
60. *uncouth*: E.K.
61. *dog . . . mouth*: Aesop, *Fables*, 185; Chambry 1967: 81.
62. *seely*: *July* 30n.
63. *here by there*: E.K. *whilom*: *January* 21n.

Bene all sterved with pine and penury: 65
Hardly myself escaped thilk pain,
Driven for need to come home again.

                Hobbinol.
Ah fon, now by thy loss art taught
That seldom change the better brought:
Content who lives with tried state 70
Need fear no change of frowning Fate;
But who will seek for unknown gain
Oft lives by loss and leaves with pain.

                Diggon.
I wote ne, Hobbin, how I was bewitched
With vain desire and hope to be enriched: 75
But siker so it is, as the bright star
Seemèth aye greater when it is far,
I thought the soil would have made me rich.
But now I wote it is nothing sich,
For either the shepherds bene idle and still 80
And led of their sheep what way they will;
Or they bene false and full of covetise,
And casten to compass many wrong emprise.
But the more bene freight with fraud and spite,
Ne in good nor goodness taken delight 85
But kindle coals of conteck and ire
Wherewith they set all the world on fire;
Which, when they thinken again to quench

---

65. *sterved*: dying (dead) of a lingering death. *pine*: (1) affliction; (2) famine: archaic; *OED* pine *sb* 1, 2a, 4. Cf. *January* 48n.
68. *fon*: foolish (man): favourite Spenserian archaism: cf. *February* 69 gloss.
74. *wote ne*: know not; but the normal grammatical formulation was *ne wote*: cf. *February* 85n.
76. *bright star*: E.K.
79. *sich*: archaic/dialect form.
81. *of*: by.
83. *casten to compass*: decide to contrive. *emprise*: E.K.
84. *freight*: filled, laden.
86. *kindle*: cf. James 3: 5–6: 'the tongue is a little member, and boasteth of great things: behold, how great a thing a little fire kindleth . . . the tongue [is] set among our members, that it defileth the whole body, and setteth on fire the course of nature, and is set on fire of hell'. *conteck*: E.K.

With holy water, they doen hem all drench.
They say they con to heaven the highway;   90
But, by my soul, I dare undersay
They never set foot in that same trod,
But balk the right way and strayen abroad.
They boast they han the devil at command –
But ask hem therefore what they han pawned: 95
Marry, that great Pan bought with dear borrow
To quit it from the black bower of sorrow.
But they han sold thilk same long ago,
For they woulden draw with hem many mo'.
But let hem gang alone, a God's name: 100
As they han brewed, so let hem bear blame.

      Hobbinol.
Diggon, I pray thee speak not so dirk:
Such mister saying me seemeth to mirk.

      Diggon.
Then plainly to speak of shepherds most what,
Bad is the best (this English is flat):   105
Their ill haviour gars men missay

---

89. holy water: *February* 209 gloss. *doen*: *July* 152n. *drench*: drown (archaic). The imagery (anger, fire, drowning) is apocalyptic so that the attack on Romanism within the English Church broadens to include Rome itself.
90. con: know. *heaven . . . highway*: Matthew 7: 13–15: 'Enter in at the strait gate: for it is the wide gate, and broad way that leadeth to destruction. . . . Beware of false prophets, which come to you in sheep's clothing, but inwardly they are ravening wolves'. Also John 14: 6: 'Jesus said unto him, I am that Way, that Truth, and that Life. No man cometh unto the Father, but by me'.
91. undersay: say by way of answer; counter (*OED* cites this as a unique instance).
92. trod: E.K.
93. balk: miss, ignore.
94. devil: Protestant charges of Catholic black magic: cf. *July* 197 gloss.
95. pawned: pledged as security (i.e., like Marlowe's Faustus, their souls).
96. Marry: E.K. *Pan . . . borrow*: *May* 54 and 150 glosses.
97. quit: redeem: cf. *February*, 213. *black*: E.K.
100. gang: E.K.
101. brewed: brought about (evil): *OED* brew *v* 4a, giving 1578 as date of last instance.
102. dirk: riddlingly: cf. 6n above.
103. mister: E.K. *mirk*: E.K.
104. most what: matter most relevant (to shepherds).
106. haviour: *April* 66n. *gars*: *April* 1 gloss. *missay*: speak evil against.

Both of their doctrine and of their fay.
They sayen the world is much war than it wont
All for her shepherds bene beastly and blunt;
Other sayen (but how truly I n'ote)   110
All for they holden shame of their cote;
Some stick not to say (hot coal on her tongue)
That sike mischief grazeth hem among
All for they casten too much of world's care
To deck her dame and enrich her heir.   115
For such encheason, if you go nigh,
Few chinmeys reeking you shall espy:
The fat ox that wont ligge in the stall
Is now fast stalled in her crumenal.
Thus chatten the people in their steads,   120
Ylike as a monster of many heads.
But they that shooten nearest the prick
Sayen, other the fat from their beards doen lick:
For big bulls of Bashan brace hem about
That with their horns butten the more stout,   125

107. fay: faith: archaic; Spenser supplies *OED*'s last instances: fay *sb* 1, 1.
108. war: E.K.
109. All for: because. *beastly*: 44n. *blunt*: stupid, ignorant.
110. n'ote: know not: cf. 74n.
111. cote: fold (i.e., the Church to which they belong); or coat (the vestments of their vocation).
112. stick not: do not hesitate. *coal*: cf. 86n; but, because the attack is justified, see more especially Isaiah 6: 6–7 (hot coal on the mouth purges sin) and 30: 27: '[the Lord's] lips are full of indignation, and his tongue is as a devouring fire'.
114. casten . . . care: reckon too much by worldly things.
115. dame: i.e., mistress. *heir*: cf. *May*, 75–94.
116–24. For . . . about: Diggon alludes, via Isaiah 6: 11–13 (on the dereliction of towns and desolation of the countryside), to the deprivation consequent upon land enclosure for landlords' private benefit: Lane 1993: 138–9.
116. encheason: E.K.
117. reeking: smoking.
118. ligge: *May* 125n.
119. crumenal: E.K.
120. steads: (1) hamlets; (2) villages; (3) farms.
121. monster . . . heads: the Lernaean hydra killed by Hercules, which became an emblem of falsehood: Alciati 1551: 149. But Diggon's irony also encompasses the fact that it was an anti-democratic image of 'the people'.
122. prick: the bull's-eye in archery.
123. other: others (i.e., the patrons of the clergy and the big landowners). *fat . . . lick*: proverbial: Smith 1970: 169. Means to cheat someone out of property, etc.
124. bulls: 44n. *brace*: E.K.

But the lean souls treaden underfoot.
And to seek redress mought little boot,
For liker bene they to pluck away more
Than aught of the gotten good to restore;
For they bene like foul quagmires overgrassed 130
That, if thy galage once sticketh fast,
The more to wind it out thou dost swink,
Thou mought aye deeper and deeper sink:
Yet better leave off with a little loss
Than by much wrestling to leese the gross. 135

            Hobbinol.
Now, Diggon, I see thou speakest too plain:
Better it were a little to feign,
And cleanly cover that cannot be cured:
Such ill as is forced mought needs be endured.
But of sike pastors how done the flocks creep? 140

            Diggon.
Sike as the shepherds, sike bene her sheep,
For they n'ill listen to the shepherd's voice
But, if he call hem, at their good choice
They wander at will and stray at pleasure,
And to their folds yield at their own leisure: 145
But they had be better come at their call,
For many han into mischief fall
And bene of ravenous wolves yrent
All for they n'ould be buxom and bent.

127. *boot*: remedy.
130. *quagmires*: the original spelling, *wagmoires*, is an apparently unique instance of a word which had various forms at the time, *quagmire* being first recorded in 1579: *OED* quagmire, wagmoire. *overgrassed*: E.K.
131. *galage*: E.K.
132. *wind*: lift (*OED* wind *v* 1, 3b). *swink*: toil: *May* 36 gloss.
135. *leese*: lose. *gross*: E.K.
136–7. *speakest . . . feign*: in conjunction with 102–3, suggests the problems of coding criticism of Church and state in a period of increasing censorship.
139. *forced*: compelled.
140. *creep*: manage.
145. *yield*: submit. The 1611 folio reading *yead* (from yode/yede, archaic past of go – cf. *July* 109 gloss) is tempting.
149. *buxom . . . bent*: E.K.

Hobbinol.

Fie on thee, Diggon, and all thy foul leasing: 150
Well is known that, sith the Saxon king,
Never was wolf seen – many nor some –
Nor in all Kent, nor in christendom;
But the fewer wolves (the sooth to sayen)
The more bene the foxes that here remain. 155

Diggon.

Yes, but they gang in more secret wise,
And with sheep's clothing doen hem disguise:
They walk not widely (as they were wont)
For fear of rangers and the great hunt,
But privily prowling to and fro 160
Enaunter they mought be inly know.

Hobbinol.

Or privy or pert if any bene
We han great bandogs will tear their skin.

Diggon.

Indeed thy ball is a bold big cur,
And could make a jolly hole in their fur; 165

---

150. leasing: lying.
151. Saxon king: E.K.
153. Kent . . . christendom: E.K.
154–61. But . . . know: for the symbolism of the papist fox, see *May* 174 gloss. The reference is almost certainly to the mission against English Protestantism during the 1570s, part of a fervent and continuing attempt of Jesuits, and particularly Douai seminary priests (the seminary had been founded in 1568), to regain England for Rome. The disappearance of the wolves alludes to the abolition of Catholicism as the state religion with Elizabeth's accession at the death of Catholic Mary Tudor (but some – recusants – remain); foxes – those pretending outward conformity – have now infiltrated and, in order to attain their evangelical ends, have adopted the wolves' traditional disguise (90n above).
154. sooth: truth.
156. gang: 100n.
158. widely: openly.
159. great hunt: E.K.
161. Enaunter: E.K. *inly*: E.K.
162. privy . . . pert: E.K.
163. bandogs: chained (guard) dogs, hence mastiffs, bloodhounds; also metaphorical for law-enforcement officers.
164. ball: weapon, missile.
165. jolly: 'fine old'.

But not good dogs hem needeth to chase,
But heedy shepherds to discern their face:
For all their craft is in their countenance,
They bene so grave and full of maintenance.
But shall I tell thee what myself know   170
Chanced to Roffin not long ago?

      Hobbinol.
Say it out, Diggon, whatever it hight,
For not but well mought him betight,
He is so meek, wise and merciable,
And with his word his work is convenable.   175
Colin Clout, I ween, be his self boy
(Ah for Colin, he whilom my joy!):
Shepherds sich God mought us many send
That doen so carefully their flocks tend.

      Diggon.
Thilk same shepherd mought I well mark.   180
He has a dog to bite or to bark:
Never had shepherd so keen a cur,
That waketh and if but a leaf stir.
Whilom there wonned a wicked wolf
That with many a lamb had glutted his gulf,   185
And ever at night wont to repair
Unto the flock, when the welkin shone fair,
Yclad in clothing of seely sheep
When the good old man used to sleep.
Tho at midnight he would bark and bawl   190
(For he had eft learned a cur's call)
As if a wolf were among the sheep.
With that the shepherd would break his sleep

169. maintenance: bearing, upright behaviour.
171. Roffin: E.K.
172. hight: *July* 164n.
173. betight: betide (befall): cf. *November* 174 gloss.
174. merciable: merciful: a mediaevalism (this is *OED*'s last citation).
175. convenable: consistent, in agreement (rare; second of *OED*'s two citations in this sense).
176. Colin Clout: E.K. *self*: own.
180–225. E.K.
184. wonned: E.K.
185. gulf: insatiable appetite.
187. welkin: E.K.
188. clothing . . . sheep: 90n.

And send out Lowder (for so his dog hote)
To range the fields with wide open throat;   195
Tho, whenas Lowder was far away,
This wolfish sheep would catchen his prey –
A lamb, or a kid, or a weanel waste;
With that to the wood would he speed him fast.
Long time he used this slippery prank   200
Ere Roffy could for his labour him thank.
At end, the shepherd his practice spied
(For Roffy is wise and as Argus eyed),
And when at even he came to the flock
Fast in their folds he did them lock   205
And took out the wolf in his counterfeit coat,
And let out the sheep's blood at his throat.

                   Hobbinol.   207a
Marry, Diggon, what should him affray
To take his own wherever it lay?
For had his weasand bene a little wider,   210
He would have devoured both hidder and shidder.

                   Diggon.
Mischief light on him, and God's great curse
Too good for him had bene a great deal worse:
For it was a perilous beast above all,
And eke had he conned the shepherd's call,   215
And oft in the night came to the sheepcote
And called 'Lowder!' with a hollow throat,
As if it the old man self had bene.
The dog his master's voice did it ween,
Yet half in doubt he opened the door   220

Textual note

207a. Hobbinol] Q2; Diggon Q1.

194. hote: *July* 164n. *Lowder*: Hugh *Lloyd* was the Rochester diocese's Chancellor; though Renwick 1930: 213 suggests that Lowder's function would suit an archdeacon better.
198. weanel waste: E.K.
203. Argus: Ovid, *Metamorphoses*, 1. 624–7; 670–88; 713–23. Cf. *July* 154 gloss. Diggon emphasises Roffin's watchfulness: 230n below.
208. affray: frighten.
210. weasand: windpipe.
211. hidder and shidder: E.K.
215. conned: learned (*January* 10 gloss): echoing John 10: 3–5 concerning the sheep who follow their keeper because they know his voice.

And ran out, as he was wont of yore.
No sooner was out but, swifter than thought,
Fast by the hide the wolf Lowder caught,
And had not Roffy ren to the steven,
Lowder had be slain thilk same even. 225

Hobbinol.
God shield, man, he should so ill have thrive
All for he did his devoir belive.
If sike bene wolves, as thou hast told,
How mought we, Diggon, hem behold?

Diggon.
How but, with heed and watchfulness, 230
Forstallen hem of their wiliness?
For-thy with shepherds sits not play,
Or sleep (as some doen) all the long day,
But ever liggen in watch and ward
From sudden force their flocks for to guard. 235

Hobbinol.
Ah, Diggon, thilk same rule were too straight
All the cold season to watch and wait.
We bene of flesh – men as other be:
Why should we be bound to such misery?
Whatever thing lacketh changeable rest 240
Mought needs decay when it is at best.

Diggon.
Ah but, Hobbinol, all this long tale
Nought easeth the care that doth me forhale.
What shall I do? What way shall I wend

---

224. ren: *April* 118, *July* 60nn. *steven*: E.K.
226. shield: forbid.
227. devoir: duty. *belive*: E.K.
229. behold: (1) watch; (2) restrain: *OED* behold *v* I. 1a.
230. watchfulness: biblically loaded word: e.g., Matthew 24: 42: 'Watch therefore: for ye know not what hour your master will come'.
234. liggen: 118n. *ward*: guardianship.
236. straight: strict.
237. wait: also biblically loaded: e.g., Luke 12: 36: 'like unto men that wait for their master [God]'.
240. Whatever . . . changeable: as a change; alternating (with activity): *OED* changeable *adv* (archaism). E.K.
243. forhale: E.K.

My piteous plight, and loss, to amend? 245
Ah, good Hobbinol, mought I thee pray
Of aid or counsel in my decay.

                Hobbinol.
Now, by my soul, Diggon, I lament
The hapless mischief that has thee hent.
Netheless, thou seest my lowly sail 250
That froward Fortune doth ever avail;
But were Hobbinol as God mought please,
Diggon should soon find favour and ease.
But if to my cottage thou wilt resort,
So as I can, I will thee comfort: 255
There mayest thou ligge in a vetchy bed
Till fairer Fortune show forth her head.

                Diggon.
Ah Hobbinol, God mought it thee requite:
Diggon on few such friends did ever light.

             Diggon's emblem: 260
            Inopem me copia fecit.

GLOSS
The dialect and phrase of speech in this dialogue seemeth somewhat to differ from the common, the cause whereof [i.e., of the dialogue] is supposed to be by occasion of the party herein meant, who, being very friend of the author hereof, had been long in foreign countries and there seen many disorders, which he here recounteth to Hobbinol.

1] **bid her**) bid good morrow; for *to bid* is to pray, whereof cometh *beads* for *prayers*. And so they say *to bid his beads*, *scilicet*, *to say his prayers* [bead = prayer was obsolescent by the mid-sixteenth century when it attracted the primary notion of [rosary] beads. E.K.'s gloss is etymologically correct but linguistically unnecessary, since bid = offer was common usage. It thus has the thematic

---

249. *hapless*: unfortunate (first *OED* citation 1568). *hent*: *February* 195 gloss.
251. *froward*: adverse. *avail*: *January* 73 gloss.
256. *vetchy*: E.K.
257. *her*: the Pforzheimer copy of the first quarto reads *her*, but at least three of the six extant copies (Bodleian, Houghton, Huntington) read *his*. I have adopted *her* because Fortune is female: see *Var* 1. 719. *OED* his *poss pron* B 2c notes instances of the substitution of *his* for *her* as the result of scribal or typographical error.
258. *requite*: repay, reward.
261. *Inopem . . . fecit*: 'Plenty makes me poor': see E.K.

function of underpinning the eclogue's anti-Catholicism.].

5] **wightly**) quickly or suddenly [archaic: cf. *March* 91 gloss].

10] **chaffered**) sold [archaic; *OED* cites no sixteenth-century examples before Spenser].

10] **dead at mischief**) an unusual speech, but much usurped of [used by] Lydgate, and sometime of Chaucer [i.e., dead of some misfortune: *OED* mischief *sb* 1c cites an instance from Lydgate's *Bochas*, 8. 1].

11] **lief**) dear [archaic; cf. *August* 192n].

17] **eath**) easy [archaic; cf. *July* 90n].

20] **Thrice three moons**) nine months.

21] **measured**) for *travelled* [a favourite of Spenser's, to whom *OED* attributes the first instance since Chaucer].

25] **wae**) woe (northernly) [i.e., northern/Scots].

30] **eked**) increased [mediaevalism; also northern/Scots].

41] **carven**) cut [mediaevalism].

42] **ken**) know [mediaevalism; also Scots; *April* 21 gloss].

45] **crag**) neck [*February* 82 gloss; northern/Scots].

45] **state**) stoutly [i.e., proudly, 'state(li)ly'; but *OED* state *a* 2 cites this as a unique instance].

47] **stank**) weary or faint [neologism from Ital. *stanco*; *OED* cites only this instance and one from Florio (1598)].

49] **And now**) he applieth it to the time of the year, which is in the end of harvest, which they call *the fall of the leaf*: at which time the western wind beareth most sway.

54] **a mock**) imitating Horace: *Debes ludibrium ventis* ['[Beware lest] you become the laughing-stock of the wind': Horace, *Odes*, 1. 14. 15–16; addressed, significantly, to the endangered ship of state].

57] **lorn**) left [cf. *January*, 62. Incorrect usage unique to Spenser (normal sense = lose, destroy): *OED* leese *v* 1, 6, citing only *FQ* instances. Cf. *April* 4 gloss.].

Soot) sweet [not in *September*; but if its positioning between *lorn* and *uncouth* is correct, then it seems to have been the original for *good* at l. 59. *Soot* is glossed as an adjective at *April* 111 and *October* 90, but it was also a substantive: that which is sweet. Maybe the compositor misread Spenser's handwriting and the text's *good* should be *soot*; or maybe *soot* was revised to *good* in the text but was overlooked in the gloss.].

60] **uncouth**) unknown [archaic; cf. Dedicatory Epistle, opening line].

63] **here by there**) here and there.

76] **as the bright**) translated out of Mantuan [*Eclogues*, 7. 8–9].

83] **emprise**) for enterprise: *per syncopen* ['by omission of a syllable'; but in fact a mediaevalism apparently revived by Spenser (= chivalric undertaking). *Enterprise* is an independent word dated by *OED* from *c.* 1430.].

86] **conteck**) strife [*May* 163 gloss].

92] **trod**) path [dialect; *OED* trod *sb* 2 cites first instance from 1570 and two other instances from the 1570s. Cf. *July*, 14 where it passes without comment.].

96] **Marry, that**) that is, their souls, which, by popish exorcisms and practices

Textual note

Gloss 20. Thrice] Q5; These Q1–4.

they damn to hell [Diggon's point is reinforced by using the (Catholic) interjection derived from [the Virgin] *Mary*].
97] **black**) hell.
100] **gang**) go [*March* 57 gloss].
103] **mister**) manner [Spenserian archaism based on misunderstanding of mister = craft, trade: *OED* mister *sb* 1, I. 5. See *July* 201 gloss.].
103] **mirk**) obscure [Spenser's spelling preserves the northern/Scots form, hence the gloss].
108] **war**) worse [northern/Scots].
116] **encheason**) occasion [*May* 147 gloss.].
119] **crumenal**) purse [Spenserian neologism from Latin *crumena* = pouch, purse].
124] **brace**) compass [independent form from embrace; mediaevalism but also apparently Scots: *OED* brace *v* 1, 2 and 3].
130] **overgrassed**) overgrown with grass [Spenserian neologism: *OED*, citing this passage].
131 **galage**) shoe [*February* 244 gloss.].
135] **the gross**) the whole [*OED*'s first citation in this sense: gross *a* and *sb* 4, B. 4 c].
149] **buxom and bent**) meek and obedient [*buxom* in this sense is a mediaevalism, but not *bent*].
151] **Saxon king**) King Edgar, that reigned here in Britain in the year of our Lord   [left blank by E.K. or compositor in error; he reigned 959–75]: which king caused all the wolves, whereof then was store in this country, by a proper policy to be destroyed; so as never since that time there have been wolves here found unless they were brought from other countries. And therefore Hobbinol rebuketh him of untruth for saying there be wolves in England [Holinshed, *Chronicles*, 6. 23. Part of *SC*'s pro-Saxon subtext: cf. *July* 33 gloss.].
153] **nor in christendom**) this saying seemeth to be strange and unreasonable but, indeed, it was wont to be an old proverb and common phrase, the original [origin] whereof was for that most part of England in the reign of King Ethelbert [under-king of Kent 855; king of Wessex 860, thus reuniting Kent with the rest of southern England; died 866] was christened, Kent only except, which remained long after in misbelief and unchristened; so that Kent was counted no part of christendom [for the proverb, see Smith 1970: 160].
159] **great hunt**) executing of laws and justice [i.e., penalties against Catholics].
161] **Enaunter**) lest that [*February* 200 and *May* 78 glosses].
161] **inly**) inwardly: aforesaid [*May* 38 gloss].
162] **privily** [*sic*] **or pert**) openly, saith Chaucer [the apocryphal Chaucerian *La Belle Dame sans Mercy*, 175: 'privy no' [noe] pert', with 'nor' for 'noe' in the 1561 *Chaucer: Var* 1. 365–6].
171] **Roffy** [*sic*]) the name of a shepherd in Marot his eglogue of Robin and the king, whom he here commendeth for great care and wise governance of his flock [not in his *Eclogue* 3, *au Roi, sous les noms de Pan et Robin*, but mentioned rather in *Eclogue* 1, *sur le Trépas de ma Dame Louise de Savoye*, 42 (the celebrated

Textual note

Gloss 151   here found] Q2; here souude Q1.

lute maker *Raffy Lyonnais*): see *January*, opening gloss, and *November* and *December* headnotes. The reference is in fact to John Young, Bishop of Rochester (title in ecclesiastical Latin, *episcopus Roffensis*), for whom Spenser/Colin worked from 1578: *April* 21n; McLane 1961: 158–9.].

176] **Colin Clout**) now I think no man doubteth but by Colin is ever meant the author self, whose especial good friend Hobbinol saith he is, or, more rightly, Master Gabriel Harvey, of whose special commendation, as well in poetry as rhetoric and other choice learning, we have lately had a sufficient trial in diverse his works; but specially his *Musarum lachrymae* [a volume of elegies (1577) in memory of Sir Thomas Smith of Audley End, Saffron Walden: cf. *January* 10 gloss] and his late *Gratulationum Valdinensium* (which book, in the progress at Audley in Essex, he dedicated in writing to Her Majesty, afterward presenting the same in print unto Her Highness at the worshipful Master Capell's in Hertfordshire [Arthur Capell of Hadham; E.K. refers to the royal progress which arrived at Audley End on 26 July 1578; for full details, see Nichols, J. 1823 *The Progresses and Public Processions of Queen Elizabeth I* 3 vols. 2: 110–15]): beside other his sundry most rare and very notable writings, partly under unknown titles and partly under counterfeit names; as his *Tyrannomastix*, his *Ode natalitia*, his *Rameidos*, and especially that part of Philomusus [Muse-lover; a pseudonym] his divine [most excellent] *Anticosmopolita* [lost, apart from the *Ode* (1575); but *Rameidos* was presumably, like the *Ode*, in praise of the logician Petrus Ramus (1515–72), and the last was a British epic in Latin verse subtitled *Britanniae apologia*], and diverse other of like importance [Harvey (1552–1631), himself from Essex, was Spenser's close friend at Cambridge; he later became the University's Professor of Rhetoric. He was known also as a scholar and bibliophile.]. As also by the names of other shepherds he covereth the persons of diverse other his familiar friends and best acquaintance.

180–225] This tale of Roffy seemeth to colour [conceal] some particular action of his, but what I certainly know not. [Suggestions that the tale refers to an event concerning Thomas Watson, Bishop of Lincoln under Mary Tudor and the chief English Catholic cleric under Elizabeth, who had been placed under the care of the Bishop of Rochester, have been disputed by Mclane 1961: 158–67, who uses the reformist interpretation of wolves as Catholic false prophets to identify the Wolf with the Dutch Anabaptist Henry Nicolas whom, in 1579, Young had exposed as a Catholic. But this depends on a particular (late) dating of *SC*'s composition and has not won wide acceptance.].

184] **wonned**) haunted [archaic; cf. *July* 49n].

187] **welkin**) sky: aforesaid [*March* 12 gloss].

198] **a weanel waste**) a weaned youngling [*OED*'s first instance of weanel = weanling is 1488–9; for *waste* see *February* 133n. E.K. is presumably explaining a rustic term again.].

211] **hidder and shidder**) he and she; male and female [*OED*'s first citation of both: s.v. heder, sheder].

224] **steven**) noise [archaic].

227] **belive**) quickly [archaic].

240] **Whatever**) Ovid's verse translated: *Quod caret alterna requie, durabile non est* ['What lacks alternating periods of rest will not endure': *Heroides*, 4. 89].

243] **forhale**) draw or distress [this is *OED*'s first cited example: for- *pref* 1, 5b)].

256] **vetchy**) of pease straw [*vetch* was commonly used of cornfield weeds (i.e., tares); but *pea-straw* was pea-stalks etc. used as fodder. This is *OED*'s first citation of vetchy.].

Emblem.
This is the saying of Narcissus in Ovid [*Metamorphoses*, 3. 466]; for when the foolish boy, by beholding his face in the brook, fell in love with his own likeness and, not able to content himself with much looking thereon, he cried out that plenty made him poor (meaning that much gazing had bereft him of sense). But our Diggon useth it to other purpose: as, who that by trial of many ways had found the worst and, through great plenty, was fallen into great penury. This poesy I know to have been much used of the author, and to such like effect as first Narcissus spake it [he used it later in, e.g., *Am* 35. Cf. *June* 52 and 72nn.].

October

A discourse on the state of poetry – its decline (cf. Spenser's *Tears of the Muses* (1591)), its inspirational origin, its epideictic function as monarchical panegyric – *October* is in part dedicated to the memory of Virgil, 'the Romish Tityrus' (l. 55), who was born in mid-October, 70 B.C. (hence, perhaps, his mention at the middle of the *October* eclogue (ll. 55–60 out of a total of 120: Cain in Oram *et al.* 1989: 168)). By invoking Virgil, Spenser recalls a career exemplar as important to him, prospectively at least, as that other Tityrus, Chaucer (mourned in *June*): Virgil proceeded to write epic in praise of Augustus; and Cuddy/Spenser is invited by Piers to aspire to heroic verse (ll. 37–54). Note the splitting of the poetic *persona* into Cuddy and Colin: the latter is 'with love so ill bedight' (l. 89) that he is incapacitated from poetic utterance as he is also (with one exception) from appearing in the poem – except for quotation at second hand – in all but the darkest winter months of January, November and December (the exception is *June*, the midsummer light of which he darkens, characteristically, with an elegy). *October* seems to suggest that Colin's failure lies in his refusal to separate private from public, Rosalind from Elisa; or, to put it another way, it lies in his inability to move from his dominant love melancholy into that inspirational melancholy presided over by Saturn that places the poet in true communion with the Muses thus enabling him to become the writer of epic (see Klibansky *et al.* 1964: 241–74; Richardson 1989: 101–5. But through Piers the eclogue offers an alternative view: all love leads to the divine; Colin is blessed through his pain. Hence the line total, 120, the number of the completeness of human life, albeit defined by sin (see *June* headnote), and the eternal blessedness of the elect (Bongo 1599: 586 citing Acts 1: 15). *October*'s theme is thus the traditional Platonic and neo-Platonic one of the disjunction between sensual and heavenly love and the rapture of divine (poetic) inspiration, or 'enthusiasm' (a resolution is offered in *Four Hymns*: see *Hymns* headnote). In view of the eclogue's emphasis on poetry's musical power (ll. 25–30, etc.), the use of a smoothly 'harmonious' 6-line stanza (cf. *August* headnote) is significant. It also doubtless relates to the implicit reconciliation of Mars and Venus detected in *October* by Richardson 1989: 251.

The woodcut (fig. 10) is divided between Piers and Cuddy, its iconography drawn yet again from the illustration to Virgil's first eclogue in the Brant/Michel editions (*January* headnote). Piers, proponent of heroic and religious verse and crowned with the bay of immortality and poetic fame, substitutes for Tityrus, standing rather than reclining, his backdrop classical (Augustan) Rome (the same city shadows reclining Tityrus in Brant/Michel). He thus tells of poetry's dependence on patronage, in the modern as in the ancient world. Cuddy also stands, for there is no recognition of pastoral ease in this eclogue, just as there is no tree to shade him from the influence of October's sign, destructive and maleficent Scorpio (on which, see Richardson 1989: 244–8). Cuddy is apparently in retreat yet defiant; the prophetic birds fly from him as from Rome, their destiny some unknown place; the centre foreground is occupied by pastoral poetry's instrument the pan-pipes, wrested by Piers from Cuddy, perhaps. In any case, they are the focus of attention, sign of pastoral's status as a form devoted to radical critique, its refusal to succumb to the convenient silences demanded by patrons. See also Luborsky 1981: 36–7; Goldberg 1986: 61–2.

October
Aegloga decima

Argument

In Cuddy is set out the perfect pattern of a poet which, finding no maintenance of his state and studies, complaineth of the contempt of poetry and the causes thereof: specially having been in all ages, and even amongst the most barbarous, always of singular account and honour, and being indeed so worthy and commendable an art – or, rather, no art but a divine gift and heavenly instinct not to be gotten by labour and learning but adorned with both, and poured into the wit by a certain *enthousiasmos* and celestial inspiration (as the author hereof elsewhere at large discourseth in his book called *The English Poet* – which book, being lately come to my hands, I mind also by God's grace upon further advisement to publish).

Pierce.   Cuddy.

Cuddy, for shame, hold up thy heavy head,
And let us cast with what delight to chase,
And weary this long lingering Phoebus' race.
Whilom thou wont the shepherds' lads to lead

Argument: *Cuddy*: may be the Cuddy of *February* and *August*. *contempt of poetry*: cf. Spenser's *Tears of the Muses*. *instinct*: prompting. *wit*: mind, understanding (for the water image – pour – cf. *June* 93–6n). *enthousiasmos*: printed in Greek in the original; means divine possession; *inspiration*: literally, breathing into (again, divine possession). *English Poet*: lost, or never existed: see Orluch in *SpE*, p 737.

Names: *Pierce* (i.e., *Piers*): in *May* he is the progressive Protestant. Here he defends the career of poet. Cf. *July* headnote on Spenser and the reconciliation of Protestantism with the poetic imagination. Uniquely in *SC*, his name is metamorphic (a feature retained in the present edition): as *Piers* he is the Protestant rock (with hints of *Pieria*, home of the Muses); as *Pierce* and *Pires* he is piercingly perceptive (pire = peer closely, scrutinise: *OED* pire v). The variation of Cuddy from *Cuddye* to *Cuddie*, though, seems merely to register the characteristic randomness of Elizabethan orthography.

1. *Cuddy*: E.K. *heavy*: downcast.
2. *cast*: *February* 125n. *chase*: run (not hunt).
3. *Phoebus' race*: course of the sun (i.e., day).
4. *Whilom*: E.K.

In rhymes, in riddles, and in bidding base: 5
Now they in thee, and thou in sleep, art dead.

Cuddy.

Piers, I have piped erst so long with pain
That all mine oaten reeds bene rent and wore,
And my poor Muse hath spent her spared store:
Yet little good hath got, and much less gain. 10
Such pleasance makes the grasshopper so poor
And ligge so laid when Winter doth her strain.

The dapper ditties that I wont devise
To feed youth's fancy and the flocking fry
Delighten much – what I the bett' for-thy? 15
They han the pleasure, I a slender prize:
I beat the bush, the birds to them do fly:
What good thereof to Cuddy can arise?

Pires.

Cuddy, the praise is better than the prize,
The glory eke much greater than the gain: 20
Oh what an honour is it to restrain

---

5. *bidding base*: singing competition (cf. Shakespeare, *Two Gentlemen of Verona*, 1. 2); also game in which you challenge your opponent to run from home-base: described at *FQ*, 5. 8. 5; see also 3.11.5.
7. *erst*: until recently; a favourite Spenserian word: *OED* erst *a* and *adv* B 5b.
8. *oaten reeds*: E.K.
9. *spared*: saved up: this is *OED*'s first instance of the usage; but see *May* 84n.
11. *pleasance*: frivolous delight(s). *grasshopper*: Aesop's Fable 336 of the grasshopper who sings all summer and fails to provide for winter: Chambry 1967: 146. Also an emblem of poets who sing, forgetful of food or drink: Plato, *Phaedrus*, 259 cit. Goldberg 1986: 46.
12. *ligge so laid*: E.K. *strain*: afflict: *OED*'s last instance before an eighteenth-century revival: strain *v* 1, I. 6.
13. *dapper*: E.K.
14. *fry*: E.K.
17. *birds*: probably related to the bird of learning in the emblem of Cupid as bird catcher: *December* 79n.
19–20. *prize . . . gain*: cf. 1 Corinthians 9: 24–5: 'they which run in a race, run all, yet one receiveth the prize . . . so run that ye may obtain. And every man that proveth masteries, abstaineth from all things: and they do it to obtain a corruptible crown: but we for an incorruptible'; and 1 Peter 5: 4: 'And when that chief Shepherd shall appear, ye shall receive an incorruptible crown of glory'. Cf. also *Tears of the Muses*, 453–4: 'his deserved meed,/Due praise, that is the spur of doing well'.
21. *restrain*: E.K.

The lust of lawless youth with good advice,
Or prick them forth with pleasance of thy vein,
Whereto thou list their trained wills entice.

Soon as thou 'ginnest to set thy notes in frame,   25
Oh how the rural routs to thee do cleave!
Seemeth thou dost their soul of sense bereave,
All as the shepherd that did fetch his dame
From Pluto's baleful bower withouten leave:
His music's might the hellish hound did tame.   30

            Cuddy.
So praisen babes the peacock's spotted train,
And wondren at bright Argus' blazing eye:
But who rewards him ere the more for-thy,
Or feeds him once the fuller by a grain?
Sike praise is smoke that sheddeth in the sky,   35
Sike words bene wind, and wasten soon in vain.

            Piers.
Abandon then the base and viler clown:
Lift up thyself out of the lowly dust
And sing of bloody Mars, of wars, of jousts.
Turn thee to those that wield the awe-full crown,   40

---

23. *prick*: spur. *pleasance . . . vein*: the Horatian dictum of *utile dulci* (poetic moral utility through delight): *Ars Poetica*, 343.
24. *trained*: drawn: cf. the Gallic Hercules who was depicted drawing people with the chains of his eloquence: Alciati 1551: 194.
25. *frame*: *August* 3n.
26. *routs*: companies, bands.
27. *sense bereave*: E.K.
28. *All as*: just as. *shepherd*: E.K.
29. *baleful bower*: deadly dwelling.
30. *hellish hound*: Cerberus, triple-headed dog who guarded the entrance to the underworld.
32. *Argus*: E.K.
33. *ere*: ever.
35. *sheddeth*: pours forth; disperses.
37. *viler clown*: low (in social degree, but also implying moral depravity) rustic (with a hint of the primal Adam, 'of the earth, earthly': 1 Corinthians 15: 47; Geneva gloss: 'Wallowing in dirt, and wholly given to an earthly nature').
39. *Mars*: the subject of the *Iliad* and of the *Aeneid*, 1. 1: *Arma virumque cano*, 'I sing of arms and the man'.
40. *wield*: have at command: archaic: *OED* wield *v* B 2.

To doubted knights, whose woundless armour rusts
And helms unbruised wexen daily brown.

There may thy Muse display her fluttering wing
And stretch herself at large from east to west:
Whether thou list in fair Elisa rest   45
Or, if thee please, in bigger notes to sing,
Advance the worthy whom she loveth best,
That first the white bear to the stake did bring.

And when the stubborn stroke of stronger stounds
Has somewhat slacked the tenor of thy string,   50
Of love and lustihead tho mayest thou sing,
And carol loud, and lead the millers round,
All were Elisa one of thilk same ring:
So mought our Cuddy's name to heaven sound.

                        Cuddy.
Indeed, the Romish Tityrus, I hear,   55
Through his Maecenas left his oaten reed

---

41. doubted: dreaded, redoubted: *OED* doubted *ppl a* 1 cites this as its last of only three instances, the first dated *c.* 1485. *woundless armour*: E.K.
42. unbruised: uncrushed.
43. display: E.K.
44. east . . . west: the traditional (Roman) direction of the spread of learning and empire (*translatio studii et imperii*) as also of Elizabethan imperial claims: Curtius 1967: 29; Yates 1975.
47–8. worthy . . . bring: E.K.
49. stounds: blows (cf. *May* 257 gloss) of battle; also: on the strings of his Orphic lute/lyre.
50. slack: E.K.
51. love: anticipating Spenser's epic programme in *FQ* 1 proem where, in the phrase 'sing of knights' and ladies' gentle deeds', the Virgilian proposition of singing of 'arms and the man' is modified in the light of Ariosto's 'Of ladies, cavaliers, arms, and loves . . . I sing': *Orlando Furioso* (1532) 1. 1.
52. millers: E.K.
53. ring: E.K. *All*: even though.
55. Tityrus: E.K.
56. Maecenas: patron of Virgil, Horace, and others, and Octavian's vice-regent in charge of Italy at the time of the defeat of Antony at the battle of Actium (31 B.C.) which was decisive in leading to Octavian's emergence as first emperor of the Roman empire and his honorific surname Augustus (29 B.C.).
56–9. oaten . . . dread: Virgil's career from pastoral *Eclogues* through the farming *Georgics* (named from Greek *geōrgos* = farm labourer) to the epic *Aeneid* as summarised in the opening of the *Aeneid* as printed in Renaissance editions: 'I am the poet who formerly created the light music of pastoral verse. In my next

(Whereon he erst had taught his flocks to feed,
And laboured lands to yield the timely ear),
And eft did sing of wars and deadly dread
So as the heavens did quake his verse to hear. 60

But ah! Maecenas is yclad in clay,
And great Augustus long ago is dead;
And all the worthies liggen wrapped in lead
That matter made for poets on to play:
For ever who, in derring-do were dread, 65
The lofty verse of hem was loved aye.

But after Virtue 'gan for age to stoop,
And mighty manhood brought a-bed of ease,
The vaunting poets found nought worth a pease
To put in press among the learned troop: 70
Tho 'gan the streams of flowing wits to cease,
And sunbright Honour penned in shameful coop.

And if that any buds of Poesy
Yet of the old stock 'gan to shoot again,
Or it men's follies mote be forced to feign 75
And roll with the rest in rhymes of ribaldry,
Or, as it sprung, it wither must again:
Tom Piper makes us better melody.

      Piers.
O peerless Poesy, where is then the place?
If nor in prince's palace thou do sit 80

poem I abandoned the woods for the neighbouring farmlands. . . . But now I turn to the fierce battles of Mars'.
57. *Whereon*: E.K.
59. *eft*: afterwards.
63. *liggen*: *September* 234n. *lead*: *June* 89n, *November* 59n.
65. *For ever*: E.K. *derring-do*: E.K.
67. *But after*: E.K. *Virtue*: manliness, courage: Latin *virtus* from *vir* = man.
69. *pease*: commonly used as a singular (pea).
70. *press*: crowd: i.e., they found no subject that could place them among the crowd of the ancient learned poets.
71. *wits*: people of learning and talent.
72. *penned*: E.K.
74. *stock*: cf. *February* 128n.
75. *Or*: either. *feign*: disguise, conceal; Spenser was the last to use it in this sense: *OED* feign *v* II. 6.
78. *Tom Piper*: E.K.
79. *the*: this is the reading of the first and second quartos; Q3's emendation to *thy* (followed, e.g., by *Var* and Yale) seems unnecessary.

(And yet is prince's palace the most fit),
Ne breast of baser birth doth thee embrace,
Then make thee wings of thine aspiring wit
And, whence thou camest, fly back to heaven apace.

Cuddy.
Ah, Percy, it is all too weak and wan   85
So high to soar and make so large a flight –
Her pieced pinions bene not so in plight.
For Colin fits such famous flight to scan:
He (were he not with Love so ill bedight)
Would mount as high, and sing as soot, as swan.   90

Pires.
Ah fon, for Love does teach him climb so high,
And lifts him up out of the loathsome mire:
Such immortal mirror as he doth admire
Would raise one's mind above the starry sky
And cause a caitiff courage to aspire,   95
For lofty Love doth loathe a lowly eye.

82. *Ne breast*: E.K.
87. *pieced pinions*: E.K. *plight*: (physical) condition.
88. *fits*: is suitable. *scan*: climb: rare Latinism; *OED* scan *v* 7 attributes its first instance to *FQ*, ignoring this earlier Spenser instance. Punning on scan = analyse verse; judge; interpret.
89. *bedight*: (1) governed; (2) abused, maltreated: *OED* dight *v* I. 3, 4; be- *prefix* 1, 2.
90. *soot*: *April* 111 gloss. *swan*: E.K.
91–102. *Ah . . . hand*: the argument is based on the Platonic and neo-Platonic distinction between sensual and heavenly love: *Four Hymns* headnote. Piers argues for the effectiveness of the neo-Platonic ladder of ascent through love from earth to heaven, flesh to divine beauty; Cuddy sees only the disastrous effects of love.
91. *fon*: *September* 68n.
93. *immortal mirror*: reflection of the immortal world: Elizabeth is 'Mirror of grace and majesty divine' at *FQ*, 1 proem. See also E.K. and *HL* 190–6n.
94. *starry sky*: the sphere of the fixed stars, above those of the planets and adjacent to the *primum mobile*; thus, near God.
95. *caitiff*: base; but originally *captive*: hence a pun here on the Platonic notion of the imprisoning of the soul – and of courage, seated in the heart according to Platonic thought – within the body: E.K.
96. *lofty Love*: E.K.

                                Cuddy.   96a
All otherwise the state of poet stands,
For lordly Love is such a tyrant fell
That, where he rules, all power he doth expel.
The vaunted verse a vacant head demands,   100
Ne wont with crabbed care the Muses dwell:
Unwisely weaves, that takes two webs in hand.

Whoever casts to compass weighty prize,
And thinks to throw out thundering words of threat,
Let pour in lavish cups, and thrifty bits of meat;   105
For Bacchus' fruit is friend to Phoebus wise,
And when with wine the brain begins to sweat,
The numbers flow as fast as spring doth rise.

Thou kennest not, Percy, how the rhyme should rage:
Oh, if my temples were distained with wine   110
And girt in garlands of wild ivy twine,
How could I rear the Muse on stately stage,
And teach her tread aloft in buskin fine
With quaint Bellona in her equipage!

But ah, my courage cools ere it be warm: 115
For-thy, content us in this humble shade,

Textual note

96a. Cuddy] Q3; omitted Q1–2.

98. fell: savage.
100. vaunted: highly praised. *vacant head*: E.K.
103. casts to compass: decides to grasp (gain): cf. *September* 83n.
105. lavish cups: E.K. *thrifty . . . meat*: food that is decent (appropriate) or food of good quality; the meaning 'only small amounts of food' is unlikely: *OED* thrifty *a* 1, 2b.
106. Bacchus . . . Phoebus: Bacchus (Dionysus), god of wine, inspires a particular quality of poetic inspiration (110–11 glosses); Phoebus Apollo is god of poetry and leader of the Muses: *April* 41 gloss.
108. numbers: (1) poetic metrics; (2) the poem's numerological content (headnote). *spring*: Spenser's favourite metaphor of poetic conception: *June* 93–6n.
109. kennest: *April* 21 gloss.
110. Oh, if: E.K.
111. wild ivy: E.K.: cf. *August* 30.
113. buskin: E.K.: the *Muse* (l. 112) of tragedy is Melpomene: cf. *Tears of the Muses*, 115–74.
114. quaint: E.K. *equipage*: E.K.

Where no such troublous tides han us assayed:
Here we our slender pipes may safely charm.

Pires.

And when my gates shall han their bellies laid,
Cuddy shall have a kid to store his farm.   120

Cuddy's emblem:
Agitante calescimus illo etc.

GLOSS

This eglogue is made in imitation of Theocritus his sixteenth *Idyllion*, wherein he reproved the tyrant Hiero of Syracuse for his niggardise [niggardliness] toward poets [not Hiero I, known as 'the tyrant' (5th century B.C.), but Hiero II (3rd century B.C.)], in whom is the power to make men immortal for their good deeds or shameful for their naughty life [*Idylls*, 16. 29–59]; and the like also is in Mantuan [*Eclogue* 5, a debate between Candidus and Silvanus on the place and function of poetry, and the main source for *October*]. The style hereof (as also that in Theocritus) is more lofty than the rest, and applied to the height of poetical wit.

1] **Cuddy**) I doubt whether by Cuddy be specified the author self or some other; for in the eighth eglogue the same person was brought in singing a *cantion* [song; Latin] of Colin's making, as he saith [*August*, 139–93]: so that some doubt that the persons be different [*January* opening gloss].

4] **Whilom**) sometime [archaic; *August* 8 gloss].

8] **oaten reeds**) *avena* [Latin for oats, thence reed-pipe: Virgil, *Eclogues*, 1. 2].

12] **ligge so laid**) lie so faint and unlusty [unlusty = feeble, listless; for ligge see *May* 125n; laid = past participle of lay = prostrate].

13] **dapper**) pretty [first *OED* instance of its application to a thing rather than a person].

14] **fry**) is a bold metaphor, forced from the spawning fishes, for the multitude of young fish be called the *fry* [the word had been current at least since 1389; the metaphor directs attention to the fish of (youthful) lust: Alciati 1551: 83].

21] **to restrain**) this place seemeth to conspire [agree] with Plato who, in his first Book *De legibus* [Of laws], saith that the first invention of poetry was of very vir-

117. *tides*: E.K.
118. *charm*: E.K.
119. *gates*: *May* 177 gloss. *bellies laid*: given birth.
120. *store*: stock.
122. *Agitante . . . etc.* Ovid, *Fasti*, 6. 5, with the *etc.* implying that we should recall the surrounding lines: '[there is a god in us.] When he stirs, our breast glows; [it is his impulse that sows the seeds of inspiration: I have a particular right to see the faces of the gods, either because I am a bard [seer: *vates*] or because I sing of sacred things]'. Ovid is then, as historian of the Roman year, granted a vision of Juno, queen of heaven, who gave her name to the month June (l. 26): interesting in view of the substantive and structural links between *October* and *June*. See also E.K.

tuous intent; for at what time [i.e., at the time when] an infinite number of youth usually came to their great solemn feasts called *Panegyrica* (which they used every five years to hold), some learned man being more able than the rest for special gifts of wit and music would take upon him to sing fine verses to the people in praise either of virtue, or of victory, or of immortality, or suchlike: at whose wonderful gift all men being astonied [astonished] and, as it were, ravished with delight (thinking – as it was indeed – that he was inspired from above), called him *vatem* [seer; the preceding, a series of commonplaces, is not in the *Laws*]. Which kind of men afterward framing their verses to lighter music (as of music be many kinds, some sadder, some lighter, some martial, some heroical; and so diversely eke affect the minds of men) found out lighter matter of poesy also (some playing with love, some scorning at men's fashions, some poured out in pleasures), and so were called *poets* or *makers* [*April* 19 gloss].

27] **sense bereave**) what the secret working of music is in the minds of men – as well appeareth hereby – that some of the ancient philosophers (and those the most wise, as Plato and Pythagoras) held for opinion that the mind was made of a certain harmony and musical numbers for [because of] the great compassion [sympathy] and likeness of affection in the one and in the other as also by that memorable history of Alexander: to whom, whenas Timotheus the great musician played the Phrygian melody, it is said that he was distraught with such unwonted fury that, straightway rising from the table in great rage, he caused himself to be armed as ready to go to war (for that music is very warlike); and immediately whenas the musician changed his stroke into the Lydian and Ionic harmony, he was so far from warring that he sat as still as if he had been in matters of council [on music and the passions, see Plato, *Timaeus*, 47A; *Phaedo*, 86B; Aristotle, *Politics*, 1340B. It became a commonplace. The story comes from the ancient lexicographer Suidas, *s.v.* Alexander, Timotheos. On the qualities of the modes, see Gafurius (1969) Book 1]. Such might is in music: wherefore Plato and Aristotle forbid the Arabian [Q3; Q1, 2 read *Aradian*, which may be a misprint for *Arcadian*] melody from children and youth for that, being altogether on the fifth and seventh tone, it is of great force to mollify and quench the kindly [natural] courage which useth to burn [customarily burns] in young breasts [untraced]. So that it is not incredible which the poet here saith, that music can 'bereave the soul of sense'.

28] **the shepherd that**) Orpheus, of whom is said that, by his excellent skill in music and poetry, he recovered his wife Eurydice from hell [Orpheus, one of the traditional founders of music and poetry who had the power to move rocks, trees, etc., did regain Eurydice from the underworld; he also lost her again: see Virgil, *Georgics*, 4. 454–527; Ovid, *Metamorphoses*, 10. 1–85, 11. 1–84; also *June* 52 and 72nn; *Epith* 16–18nn; Cain 1971; Berger 1983; Cheney 1991].

32] **Argus' eyes**) of Argus is before said [*July* 154 gloss] that Juno to him committed her husband Jupiter his paragon Io because he had an hundred eyes. But afterward Mercury, with his music lulling Argus asleep, slew him and brought Io away, whose eyes (it is said that) Juno for his eternal memory placed in her bird the peacock's tail; for those coloured spots indeed resemble eyes [*March* 80n. Note that, like the tale of Orpheus, this is a tale of the origin of poetry: Mercury beguiles Argus by playing 'an oaten reed' (*Metamorphoses*, 1. 842 in Golding's 1567 translation) and then narrating the reed's origins in Syrinx: *April* 50 gloss.].

41] **woundless armour**) unwounded in war, do rust through long peace [see *FQ*, 5. 9. 30 for Mercilla-Elizabeth's rusty sword as an emblem of peace].

43] **display**) a poetical metaphor, whereof the meaning is, that if the poet list show his skill in matter of more dignity than is the homely eglogue, good occasion is him offered of higher vein and more heroical argument in the person of our most gracious sovereign, whom, as before [*April*], he calleth Elisa. Or, if the matter of knighthood and chivalry please him better, that there be many noble and valiant men that are both worthy of his pain in their deserved praises and also favourers of his skill and faculty [power, ability].

47] **the worthy**) he meaneth, as I guess, the most honourable and renowned the Earl of Leicester whom, by his cognisance [emblem] (although the same be also proper to other) rather than by his name he bewrayeth [reveals], being not likely that the names of noble princes be known to country clown [on Robert Dudley, Earl of Leicester, Sidney's uncle and intended dedicatee of *SC*, whose crest portrayed a bear and ragged staff, and for whom Spenser worked from early 1579 until mid-1580, see *SpE*, pp 432–3].

50] **slack**] that is, when thou changest thy verse from stately discourse to matter of more pleasance [pleasure] and delight [see *Epith* 9n below for similar instances; here, *slackening the tenor* (condition, state: i.e., tuning) suggests a tuning down from the Phrygian mode associated with Mars and war to the Hypolydian of Venus and love: Gafurius (1969) frontispiece].

52] **the millers**) a kind of dance [only reference cited by *OED* miller 7b].

53] **ring**) company of dancers [maybe E.K. suspects this is a rusticism].

55] **the Romish Tityrus**) well known to be Virgil, who by Maecenas's means was brought into the favour of the Emperor Augustus and by him moved to write in loftier kind than he erst had done [see Dedicatory Epistle, and *June* 81 gloss].

57] **Whereon**) in these three verses are the three several works of Virgil intended: for in 'teaching his flocks to feed' is meant his *Eglogues*; in 'labouring of lands' is his *Georgics* [Q3; corrected from *Bucolics* (another term for eclogue) in Q1, 2]; in 'singing of wars and deadly dread' is his divine [excellent; inspired by the gods] *Aeneis* figured [the Virgilian career pattern is framed by Piers's Christianised version: from pastoral and epic (ll. 37–50) to secular love lyric (ll. 51–4) to hymn (79–84): Cheney 1991: 53–6].

65] **For ever**) he showeth the cause why poets were wont be had in such honour of noblemen: that is, that by them their worthiness and valour should, through their famous poesies, be commended to all posterities. Wherefore it is said that Achilles had never been so famous as he is but for Homer's immortal verses, which is the only advantage which he had of Hector. And also that Alexander the Great, coming to his tomb in Sigeus, with natural tears blessed him that ever was his hap [luck] to be honoured with so excellent a poet's work, as so renowned and ennobled only by his means; which, being declared in a most eloquent oration of Tully's [Cicero, *Pro Archia Poeta*, 10. 24], is of Petrarch no less worthily set forth in a sonnet:

> *Giunto Alexandro a la famosa tomba*
> *Del fero Achille sospirando disse:*
> *O fortunato che si chiara tromba.*
> *Trovasti, etc.*

[*Rime*, 187: 'When Alexander reached the famous tomb of fierce Achilles, he sighing said: "O fortunate man who found so clear a trumpet . . . "'.] And that such account hath been always made of poets as well showeth this, that the worthy Scipio, in all his wars against Carthage and Numantia, had evermore in his company (and that in a most familiar sort) the good old poet Ennius [Cicero, *op. cit.*, 9. 22]; as also that Alexander, destroying Thebes, when he was informed that the famous lyric poet Pindarus was born in that city, not only commanded straitly [strictly] that no man should, upon pain of death, do any violence to that house by fire or otherwise, but also specially spared most, and some highly rewarded, that were of his kin. So favoured he the only name of a poet; which praise otherwise was in the same man no less famous that, when he came to ransacking of King Darius's coffers (whom he lately had overthrown), he found in a little coffer of silver the two books of Homer's works, as laid up there for special jewels and riches; which he, taking thence, put one of them daily in his bosom, and the other every night laid under his pillow. Such honour have poets always found in the sight of princes and noblemen; which this author here very well showeth, as elsewhere more notably [for the Alexander stories, see Plutarch, *Alexander*, 11. 4–6; 26. 1–4; and cf. Pliny, *Natural History*, 7. 29. 108–9; if 'this author' is Spenser, then the allusion seems to be to another lost work: for a list, see Oruch in *SpE*, pp. 737–8].

65] **in derring-do**) in manhood and chivalry [first instance of this favourite Spenser archaism; based on misunderstanding of its occurrence in Chaucer and particularly Lydgate: *OED*. For *chivalry* see *SC* dedicatory poem 4n.].

67] **But after**) he showeth the cause of contempt of poetry to be idleness and baseness of mind.

72] **penned**) shut up in sloth, as in a coop or cage [first *OED* instance since 1393: pen *v* 1, 2. However, the original reads *pend* whereas E.K.'s prompt reads *pent*: ypent passes without gloss at *January*, 4, and *OED* cites an instance of pent from 1555: pent *pa pple* 1. Note the pun on pen = quill = writing instrument.].

78] **Tom Piper**) an ironical *sarcasmus* spoken in derision of these rude wits which make more account of a rhyming ribald than of skill grounded upon learning and judgement [generic name for village piper; but Spenser's satire is aimed rather at the decline in aristocratic virtue and its effect on poetry].

82] **Ne breast**) the meaner sort of men.

87] **Her pieced pinions**) unperfect skill [i.e., repaired flight feathers]: spoken with humble modesty [the Platonic flight metaphor is common in Spenser: e.g. *HHB*, 26–8. Cf. Plato, *Phaedrus*, 249.].

90] **as soot, as swan**) the comparison seemeth to be strange, for the swan hath ever won small commendation for her sweet singing. But it is said of the learned that the swan, a little before her death, singeth most pleasantly, as prophesying by a secret instinct her near destiny, as well saith the poet elsewhere in one of his sonnets:

> The silver swan doth sing before her dying day
> As she that feels the deep delight that is in death,

etc. [the sonnet is lost. The conjunction of song with death is a neo-Platonic mystery: Wind 1967: 156–7. For Orpheus (28 gloss above) and the swan, see Virgil, *Eclogues*, 8. 55–6; Valeriano 1602: 230, and 228–9 on the swan and death.].

93] **immortal mirror**) Beauty, which is an excellent object of poetical spirits, as appeareth by the worthy Petrarch's saying:

> *Fiorir faceva il mio debile ingegno*
> *A la sua ombra, et crescer ne gli affanni*

['[The noble tree (i.e., the laurel, Laura)]...made my weak wit flourish in its shade and grow in griefs': *Rime*, 60.]

95] **a caitiff courage**) a base and abject mind.

96] **For lofty Love**) I think this playing with the letter to be rather a fault than a figure [appropriate device], as well as in our English tongue as it hath been always in the Latin, called *cacozelon* [rather, a Greek term, the Latin form of which = *cacozelia*, bad imitation: Quintilian, 2. 3. 9].

100] **a vacant**) imitateth Mantuan's saying: *vacuum curis divina cerebrum/Poscit* ['divine [poetry] demands a brain free from cares'; not in Mantuan in this form, though cf. *Eclogues*, 5. 18–19, 90–1; also Juvenal, *Satires*, 7. 59–66; Ovid, *Heroides*, 15. 14; Cicero, *ad Quintum fratrem*, 3. 4 (*Var* 1. 389, 394)].

105] **lavish cups**) resembleth that common verse *Faecundi calices quem non fecere disertum* ['Who is he whom overflowing goblets have not made eloquent?': Horace, *Epistles*, 1. 5. 19].

110] **Oh, if my**) he seemeth here to be ravished with a poetical fury [i.e., Dionysian/Bacchic possession: see Plato, *Ion*, 534A and Agrippa (1651) 3. 47]; for (if one rightly mark) the numbers [metrics] rise so full, and the verse groweth so big, that it seemeth he hath forgot the meanness of shepherd's state and style.

111] **wild ivy**) for it is dedicated to Bacchus, and therefore it is said that the Maenads (that is, Bacchus's frantic priests) used in their sacrifice to carry thyrsos, which were pointed staves or javelins wrapped about with ivy [Philostratus, *Imagines*, 1. 18, 23].

113] **in buskin**) it was the manner of poets and players in tragedies to wear buskins [high thick-soled boots], as also in comedies to use stocks [stockings] and light shoes [i.e., the comic actor's sock]; so that the *buskin* in poetry is used for tragical matter, as it said in Virgil: *Solo Sophocleo tua carmina digna cothurno* ['Your songs are worthy of the Sophoclean buskin alone': *Eclogues*, 8. 10]; and the like in Horace: *Magnum loqui, nitique cothurno* ['[Aeschylus taught actors] to speak grandly and strive in buskins': *Ars poetica*, 280].

114] **quaint**) *strange* Bellona: the goddess of battle; that is, Pallas, which may therefore well be called *quaint* for that (as Lucian saith [*Dialogi deorum*, 225–6]) when Jupiter her father was in travail [labour] of her, he caused his son Vulcan with his axe to hew his head, out of which leaped forth lustily [energetically] a valiant damsel armed at all points; whom Vulcan seeing so fair and comely, lightly leaping to her, proffered her some courtesy which the lady, disdaining, shaked her spear at him and threatened his sauciness [Pallas/Minerva, armed goddess of virginity and wisdom, is classically distinct from Bellona the Roman warrior goddess, wife (or sister) to Mars (and hence companion to Tragedy): Ovid, *Fasti*, 6. 201; though the two were conflated in the Renaissance. In view of the reference to Bacchus, and Cuddy's repudiation of heroic poetry, note

Textual note

Gloss 114. Vulcan seeing] Q3; seeing Vulcan Q1–2.

that the priests of Bellona let blood in order to inspire a warlike spirit: Lucan, *De bello civili*, 1. 565–6.]. Therefore such strangeness is well applied to her [but *quaint* clearly means ingenious, cunning: *OED* quaint *a* I. 1, 2].

114] **equipage**) order [*OED* cites this as the first instance of its use in English, giving it the meaning retinue, attendants: equipage *sb* III. 11. But its use in *FQ*, 2. 9. 17 as a verb meaning to accoutre or equip (another Spenserian first) suggests that in the present instance it also means equipment, attire, a sense dated by *OED* only from 1633 (sense II. 4): i.e., Bellona in her (Melpomene's) retinue; Bellona in her (own) attire].

117] **tides**) seasons [a current meaning; but E.K. wishes to distinguish it from other possibilities].

118] **charm**) temper and order [first *OED* instance of this sense: charm *v* 1, 7a]; for charms [chanted verses with occult powers] were wont to be made by verses, as Ovid saith: *Aut si carminibus* ['Or if in songs': Renwick 1930: 220 suggests that E.K. is remembering Ovid, *Amores*, 3. 7. 27–30 on charms but mistakenly misquotes *Aeneid*, 4. 487: *haec se carminibus*, 'by her spells'].

Emblem.

Hereby is meant, as also in the whole course of this eglogue, that poetry is a divine instinct and unnatural rage passing the reach of common reason. Whom Piers answereth *epiphonematicos* [with a summary: *May* 304 gloss] as admiring the excellency of the skill whereof in Cuddy he had already had a taste [but Piers's emblem is missing from all editions].

November

November is an elaborate pastoral elegy in the tradition initiated by Theocritus, *Idylls*, 1, Bion, *Idylls*, 1 ('Lament for Adonis'), and Moschus, *Idylls*, 3 ('Lament for Bion') and followed by Virgil, *Eclogues*, 5 and 10 as well as by various continental Renaissance poets, including Petrarch, Boccaccio and Marot. Indeed, it is the latter's *Eglogue sur le Trépas de ma Dame Louise de Savoye* (1531; published 1532) in memory of the French king's mother that Spenser now closely imitates, having recalled it earlier by taking Colin's and Thenot's names from it (*January, February* headnotes): Colin and Thenot both come from Marot's eclogue; and Colin's elegy derives many details from that sung by Marot's Colin. Like Sidney's 'Since that to death is gone the shepherd high' from the *Arcadia*, *November* is an early instance of the formal pastoral elegy in English (as opposed to neo-Latin examples). Attribution of an elegy to the eleventh month accords with recognised numerological decorum, since eleven was the ritual Roman number of grief for dead kin (Ovid, *Fasti*, 2. 567–8): note that Sidney's model for 'Since that to death' was the elegiac *eleventh* eclogue in Sannazaro's *Arcadia*: Sidney, *Old Arcadia*, ed. Robertson 1973: 344–8; 477 (and see *SC* General headnote on the influence of Sannazaro's *Arcadia* on *SC*). Formally, *November* answers *April* in its dialogue + song structure, with the difference that this time the song is performed by Colin himself, who emerges to prove Piers's point in *October* that love is not so much incapacitating as poetically liberating. The identity of Dido is still open to debate, though the source in Marot's elegy for a queen, the parallels with *April*, and the fact that 'Dido' was a familiar cult name for Elizabeth, suggest a strong element of anticipatory elegy for the English queen: either because the marriage to Catholic Alençon would make her 'dead' to her largely Protestant realm which revered her as the Virgin Queen (cf. Parmenter 1936: 214; McLane 1961:47–60); or because her power as monarch, reinforced by twenty years on the throne, encouraged, in the month in which her accession day, 17 November (and hence her marriage to England) was celebrated, a symbolic review of her death and regeneration as an emblem of the revival of the realm achieved under her (the day was actually celebrated as a new-year rebirth, as at *FQ*, 2. 2. 42: cf. Yates 1975: 90 and Cooper 1977: 208). However, the surname of Marot's Colin (d'Anjou), together with Marot's Protestantism (*January* headnote), strengthens the former suggestion: this is the climactic eclogue in Spenser's war against the Alençon/Anjou marriage. Note further that, since the alternative name for Carthaginian Dido in Virgil and Ovid was *Elissa*, we have another link between *April* with its Elisa and *November*'s dead queen; while the name Dido itself must recall the reprehensible dalliance between the Carthaginian queen and Aeneas at the beginning of *Aeneid*, 4 and thus at least glance at the Alençon affair: Johnson 1990: 175 (on this reading the 'turn' which begins at l. 163, imagining Dido walking 'in Elysian fields', depicts her – in contrast to the Dido of *Aeneid*, 6. 453ff. – as a happy queen who has escaped her wrongful lover). It is worth recalling, too, that in *November* as elsewhere in *SC* Spenser gets very near to treason: imaging the Queen's death was treasonable by an act of 1571 (13 Eliz. cap. 1: Lane 1993: 22). The inset elegy's numerological structure emphasises regeneration because the number of lines per stanza – 10 – signals the cycle of renewal and return: 'This number . . . being heaped together, returns into a unity...[so] the spirit shall return to God that gave it': Agrippa (1651) 2. 13; while the stanza total – 15 – yields the number of approach to a deity: Røstvig 1969: 70 (but the elegy itself turns from lament to rejoicing at the end of its eleventh stanza: on eleven, see above). More particularly, in view of Marian aspects in the virginal cult of Elizabeth (*April* 50n; Wells 1983), it is noteworthy that the number 15 and the month of November coincide in the Feast of the Presentation of the Virgin in the Temple (21 November); for the temple steps are usually depicted in paintings of the event as 15 in number: Neville Davies 1970: 215–16 (and see Prescott 1978: 46–7 on Spenser, Du Bellay, and 15). Metrically the inset elegy's stanzas are composed of a group of iambic pentameter lines (like the preceding dialogue and Colin's soliloquies in *January* and *December*), framed by a 6-foot iambic line (an alexandrine) and a sequence beginning at the sixth line which comprises two iambic tetrameters, a dimeter, a pentameter, and another dimeter. In other words, the elegy has as complicated a stanzaic structure as *April*'s ode (which also contains iambic pentameter, dimeter and tetrameter lines).

In the woodcut (fig. 11) Thenot bestows a laurel garland on Colin, whose cloak is sufficiently French in style to underpin the range of Marot allusions noted above (and see Luborsky 1981: 52–3). Behind Colin, Dido's coffin is borne to a church; behind Thenot, in the far distance, is a large building that may be a royal palace. The two buildings oppose heavenly and earthly glory and encode the political battle that is *November*'s subject: the custodial relationship between the House of Tudor and the English Church that the Alençon marriage threatened.

November
Aegloga undecima

Argument
In this eleventh eclogue he bewaileth the death of some maiden of great blood, whom he calleth Dido. The personage is secret, and to me altogether unknown, albe of himself I often required the same. This eglogue is made in imitation of Marot his song which he made upon the death of Louise, the French queen – but far passing his reach, and (in mine opinion) all other the eglogues of this book.

Thenot. Colin.
Colin, my dear, when shall it please thee sing,
As thou were wont, songs of some jouissance?
Thy Muse too long slumbereth in sorrowing,

Argument: *required*: asked (archaic).
2. *jouissance*: E.K.

Lulled asleep through Love's misgovernance:
Now somewhat sing, whose endless sovenance 5
Among the shepherds' swains may aye remain –
Whether thee list thy loved lass advance,
Or honour Pan with hymns of higher vein.

Colin.

Thenot, now n'is the time of merry-make,
Nor Pan to hery, nor with Love to play: 10
Sike mirth in May is meetest for to make,
Or summer shade under the cocked hay.
But now sad Winter welked hath the day,
And Phoebus, weary of his yearly task,
Ystabled hath his steeds in lowly lay 15
And taken up his inn in Fishes' hask.
Thilk sullen season sadder plight doth ask,
And loatheth sike delights as thou dost praise.
The mournful Muse in mirth now list ne mask,
As she was wont in youngth and summer days; 20
But if thou algate lust light virelays
And looser songs of love to underfong,
Who but thyself deserves sike poet's praise?
Relieve thy oaten pipes, that sleepen long.

---

4. *misgovernance*: (1) mismanagement (*May* 90n); (2) lack of restraint: *OED* sense 4 citing only fifteenth-century examples.
5. *somewhat*: a certain thing. *sovenance*: E.K.
7–8. *Whether . . . vein*: recalling Virgil, *Eclogues*, 5. 10–11: 'Begin first, Mopsus, either with Phyllis's flames, or praises of Alcon, or disputes with Codrus'.
8. *Pan: January* 17n.
9. *n'is: June* 19 gloss. *merry-make: May* 15n.
10. *hery*: E.K.
11. *make*: punning on make = write poetry.
12. *cocked*: in cocks (conical stacks).
13. *welked*: E.K.
15–16. *lowly lay . . . hask*: E.K.
17. *plight*: mood: *OED* plight *sb* 2 II. 6.
19. *Muse*: see 53 gloss.
20. *youngth: February* 52n.
21. *algate*: in any case (archaic). *lust*: desire. *virelays*: E.K.
22. *underfong*: undertake; mediaevalism: *OED* underfo *v* 2, citing last instance from Gower. Cf. *June* 103 gloss for a Spenserian neologism based on the verb.
24. *Relieve*: raise up; mediaevalism: last *OED* citation 1533: relieve *v* II. 6a.

                    Thenot.
The nightingale is sovereign of song –   25
Before him sits the titmouse silent be:
And I, unfit to thrust in skilful throng,
Should Colin make judge of my foolery.
Nay, better learn of hem that learned be
And han be watered at the Muses' well: 30
The kindly dew drops from the higher tree,
And wets the little plants that lowly dwell.
But if sad Winter's wrath and season chill
Accord not with thy Muse's merriment,
To sadder times thou mayest attune thy quill,   35
And sing of sorrow, and death's dreariment:
For dead is Dido – dead, alas, and drent –
Dido, the great shepherd his daughter sheen:
The fairest may she was that ever went;
Her like she has not left behind, I ween.   40
And if thou wilt bewail my woeful teen,
I shall thee give yond' cosset for thy pain;
And if thy rhymes as round and rueful bene
As those that did thy Rosalind complain,

25. *nightingale*: despite its gender, Philomel with her freight of grief (*August* 183–6n). The gender is probably influenced by the translation of Marot's *Eglogue . . . de ma Dame Louise*, 29: *Le rossignol de chanter est le maître* ['The nightingale is lord of singing'], which opens Thenot's second speech, as in *November*. See 141 gloss.
26. *sits*: it is seemly (that): *OED*'s last instance of this usage: sit *v* B II. 17a; cf. *June* 75n. *titmouse*: tomtit; the opposition of nightingale and tit was commonplace: in George Gascoigne's *Complaint of Philomene* (1576), 25–6, Philomel says: 'sometimes I weep/To see Tom Tittimouse so much set by'.
30. *watered*: E.K.
31. *kindly*: natural, benevolent. *dew*: cf. *June* 93–6n.
34. *merriment*: *April* 112 gloss.
35. *quill*: *June* 67n.
36. *dreariment*: E.K.
37. *drent*: common form of drenched = drowned; perhaps a nod in the direction of pastoral elegiac convention: e.g., Theocritus, *Idylls*, 1. 139–41, where Daphnis is drowned in what may be Acheron, the river of death.
38. *great shepherd*: E.K. *sheen*: E.K.
39. *may*: E.K.
41. *teen*: E.K.
42. *cosset*: E.K.: the offer echoes Theocritus, *Idylls*, 1. 23; Marot, *Eglogue* 1 (*de ma Dame Louise*), 37–44, etc.
43. *round*: full. *rueful*: arousing sorrow.

Much greater gifts for guerdon thou shalt gain 45
Than kid or cosset, which I thee benempt.
Then up, I say, thou jolly shepherd swain:
Let not my small demand be so contempt.

                    Colin.
Thenot, to that I choose thou dost me tempt;
But, ah! too well I wot my humble vein, 50
And how my rhymes bene rugged and unkempt:
Yet as I con, my conning I will strain.

Up, then, Melpomene, thou mournfullest Muse of nine:
Such cause of mourning never hadst afore!
Up, grisly ghosts, and up, my rueful rhyme! – 55
Matter of mirth now thou shalt have no more,
For dead she is that mirth thee made of yore:
    Dido my dear, alas, is dead,
      Dead, and lieth wrapped in lead:
        O heavy hearse; 60
Let streaming tears be poured out in store:
        O care-full verse.

Shepherds that by your flocks on Kentish downs abide,
Wail ye this woeful waste of Nature's wark;
Wail we the wight whose presence was our pride; 65
Wail we the wight whose absence is our cark.

45. *guerdon*: E.K.
46. *benempt*: E.K.
48. *contempt*: contemptuously disregarded: *OED* contemn *v* 2 cites this as first instance of past participle in this sense.
50. *vein*: aptitude: *OED* vein *sb* III. 11, first citation 1577.
51. *rugged*: harsh to the ear: a Spenserian sense (*OED* rugged *a* 1, 5 cites *FQ*, 3. 2. 3). *unkempt*: E.K.
52. *con, conning*: *January* 10 gloss. *strain*: (1) extend to its limits; (2) utter in song (*OED* strain *v* 1, V. 22, first instance 1580).
53. *Melpomene*: E.K.
55. *grisly ghosts*: E.K.
58–9. *dead, Dead*: elegiac formula: Sacks (1985) ch. 1.
59. *lead*: *June* 89n; also the metal of Saturn, god of melancholy and death: Agrippa (1651) 1. 25 (p. 55).
60. *hearse*: E.K.
61. *store*: plenty.
64. *waste*: E.K. *wark*: *May* 145 gloss.
65. *wight*: *April* 47n.
66. *cark*: E.K.

The sun of all the world is dim and dark:
  The earth now lacks her wonted light,
  And all we dwell in deadly night:
    O heavy hearse;   70
Break we our pipes that shrilled as loud as lark:
    O care-full verse.

Why do we longer live (ah, why live we so long)
Whose better days Death hath shut up in woe?
The fairest flower our garland all among   75
Is faded quite and into dust ygo':
Sing now ye shepherds' daughters, sing no mo'
  The songs that Colin made in her praise,
  But into weeping turn your wanton lays:
    O heavy hearse,   80
Now is time to die – nay, time was long ygo':
    O care-full verse.

Whence is it that the floweret of the field doth fade
And lieth buried long in Winter's bale
Yet, soon as Spring his mantle doth display,   85
It flowereth fresh as it should never fail –
But thing on earth that is of most avail
  (As Virtue's branch and Beauty's bud)
  Reliven not for any good?
    O heavy hearse,   90

71. *lark*: song bird of dawn, hence traditional opposite of darkness and the nightingale (25): cf. *June*, 51; Shakespeare, *Romeo and Juliet*, 3. 5. 2–7; Bawcutt, P. 1972 'The Lark in Chaucer and Some Later Poets', *Yearbook of English Studies* 2: 8–10. On the breaking of pipes, cf. Marot, *Eglogue* 1. 105; *January*, 72; *April*, 3 and *FQ*, 6. 10. 18.
73. *ah, why*: E.K.
75. *garland*: the original's (possibly Spenser's) preferred spelling (here, gyrlond; cf. girlonds at 108 and girlond at 144), from Italian *ghirlanda* and Greek *gyros* = circle, invariably contains a pun on *girl*. Cf. *February* 121n.
76. *ygo'*: gone.
77. *sing no mo'*: the 'no more' topos derives from Theocritus, *Idylls*, 1. 116–17 and Moschus, *Idylls*, 3. 20–1 ('sings . . . no more').
78. *songs . . . praise*: the *April* song to Elisa (?).
79. *wanton*: lively: *OED* wanton *a* A 3d dates first instance of this sense 1583. *lays*: *April* 33 gloss.
83. *floweret*: E.K. Cf. 1 Peter 1: 24 ('all flesh is as grass, and all the glory of man is as the flower of grass. The grass withereth, and the flower falleth away'); Moschus, *Idylls*, 3. 99–104 (flowers die but live again; man dies for ever).
89. *Reliven not*: E.K.

The branch once dead, the bud eke needs must quail:
    O care-full verse.

She, while she was (that *was* a woeful word to sayen)
For beauty's praise and pleasance had no peer:
So well she couth the shepherds entertain   95
With cakes and cracknels and such country cheer.
Ne would she scorn the simple shepherd's swain,
    For she would call hem often heme
    And give hem curds and clotted cream.
        O heavy hearse: 100
Als' Colin Clout she would not once disdain;
    O care-full verse.

But now sike happy cheer is turned to heavy chance,
Such pleasance now displaced by Dolour's dint:
All music sleeps where Death doth lead the dance,   105
And shepherds' wonted solace is extinct.
The blue in black, the green in grey is tinct:
    The gaudy garlands deck her grave,
    The faded flowers her corse embrave.
        O heavy hearse: 110

---

91. The branch: E.K. Ct. Job 14: 7 ('For there is hope of a tree, if it be cut down, that it will yet sprout . . . '). *quail*: fade.
93. was . . . was: epanorthosis again (73 gloss).
94. pleasance: the disposition to please: *OED* pleasance 1, 2a, last instance 1599.
95. couth: *January* 10 gloss.
96. cakes: E.K. *cracknels*: *January* 58n. *cheer*: food.
98. heme: E.K. (who spells it *heame*).
99. cream: note that *cream* was a mediaeval variant of *chrism*, the mixture of oil and balm used in sacramental anointing, including extreme unction even after it had ceased to be a sacrament in the English Church: *OED* cream *sb* 1.
103. chance: happening, (mis)fortune.
104. pleasance: (1) delight; (2) agreeableness. *dint*: blow.
105. music . . . dance: the dance of death in fact had its own music: Meyer-Baer 1970.
106. extinct: perhaps suggested by Virgil, *Eclogues*, 5. 20 (143n below).
107. blue . . . grey: blue symbolised hope, as also did green (Brooks-Davies 1977: 95); cf. *May* 4n.; for grey see *August*, 66 and gloss. *tinct*: E.K.
108. gaudy: E.K.
109. embrave: adorn beautifully: *OED* embrave *v* 1, citing this line; Spenserian neologism.

Mourn now, my Muse, now mourn with tears besprint;
    O care-full verse.

O thou great shepherd, Lobbin, how great is thy grief!
Where bene the nosegays that she dight for thee –
The coloured chaplets wrought with a chief,   115
The knotted rush rings and gilt rosemary
(For she deemed nothing too dear for thee)?
    Ah, they bene all yclad in clay –
    One bitter blast blew all away:
        O heavy hearse;   120
Thereof nought remains but the memory:
    O care-full verse.

Ay me, that dreary Death should strike so mortal stroke
That can undo Dame Nature's kindly course:
The faded locks fall from the lofty oak,   125
The floods do gasp (for dried is their source),
And floods of tears flow in their stead perforce;
    The mantled meadows mourn,
    Their sundry colours turn:
        O heavy hearse;   130
The heavens do melt in tears without remorse:
    O care-full verse.

111 besprint: besprinkled: Chaucerianism, though current in the sixteenth century: *OED* besprent *ppl a*, a.
113. O . . . grief: translating Marot, *Eglogue* 1. 61: *O grand pasteur, que tu as de souci* ['O great shepherd, what care possesses you']. *Lobbin*: E.K.
114. dight: made: *OED* dight *v* II. 7.
115. chief: (flower) head.
116. rush rings: E.K. *gilt rosemary*: the habit of gilding vegetation was a Graeco-Roman triumphal custom; *rosemary* = remembrance (as at *Hamlet* 4. 5); as *ros marinus* (dew of the sea) it reinforces the poem's water imagery (30–1, 37, 111, etc.); as *rose-mary* it relates to the *may* of 39 and gloss. Cf. Marot, *Eglogue* 1. 231, where *romarin vert* ('[ever]green rosemary') is brought to adorn Louise's coffin.
125–35. faded locks . . . wood: commonplaces of pastoral elegy, as at Theocritus, *Idylls*, 1. 71–5, 132–6; Moschus, *Idylls*, 3. 1–12; Virgil, *Eclogues*, 5. 25–39, and particularly active in French Pléiade elegies: Hughes 1923 citing Ronsard and Baïf.
125. faded locks: E.K. *oak*: symbol of permanence.
126. source: E.K.
128. mantled meadows: E.K.; also translating Marot, *Eglogue* 1. 103: *Du manteau vert les prés se dévêtirent* ['The meadows divest themselves of their green mantle'].
131. remorse: mitigation; *OED*'s first citation in this sense: remorse *sb* 3c.

The feeble flocks in field refuse their former food,
And hang their heads as they would learn to weep;
The beasts in forest wail as they were wood   135
(Except the wolves, that chase the wandering sheep
Now she is gone that safely did hem keep).
　The turtle on the bared branch
　　Laments the wound that Death did launch:
　　　O heavy hearse;   140
And Philomel her song with tears doth steep:
　　　O care-full verse.

The water nymphs, that wont with her to sing and dance,
And for her garland olive branches bear,
Now baleful boughs of cypress doen advance;   145
The Muses, that were wont green bays to wear,
Now bringen bitter elder branches sere;

135. wood: *August* 75n.
138. turtle: turtle dove, emblem of love, and fidelity in grief: Tervarent (1958) cols 104–6; Virgil, *Eclogue* 1. 58: 'Nor will the turtle cease to mourn from the airy elm', echoed by Marot, *Eglogue* 1. 127.
139. launch: (1) discharge (with his emblematic dart); (2) cause by piercing: *OED* launch *v* 1a.
141. Philomel: E.K.; also in Marot, *Eglogue* 1. 125: *Sous arbre sec s'en complaint Philomène* ['Beneath a gaunt tree Philomel laments'].
143. water nymphs: Virgil, *Eclogues*, 5. 20–1: 'The nymphs weep for Daphnis, destroyed [*exstinctum*] by cruel death'. Contrast the celebratory nymphs of *April*, 37.
144. olive branches: the olive of peace (Ripa 1603: 375–8) found also in Marot, *Eglogue* 1. 239–40, where it is brought to adorn Louise's coffin: *Et n'oubliez force branches d'olive,/ Car elle était la bergère de paix* ['Be sure not to forget olive branches,/For she was the shepherdess of peace']; but answering, like the other shrubs and trees, the flower catalogue of *April*, 122–6 (and see *April* 124 gloss).
145. baleful: mournful. *cypress*: E.K.
146. green bays: emblem of immortality because evergreen (and thus decorates Louise's coffin: Marot, *Eglogue* 1. 230), and worn by the Muses because it is the emblem of their leader Apollo: cf. *April* 104 gloss.
147. elder: the black-berried shrub, dedicated to Saturn as god of death, as are all 'those things . . . which bring forth berries of a dark colour': Agrippa (1651) 1. 25 (p 56), and cf. Shakespeare, *Titus Andronicus*, 2. 3. 272; hence linked with grief (as in Shakespeare's *Cymbeline*, 4. 2. 59); it represents the winter solstitial month (25 November–22 December); and was misused for *alder* (*OED* elder *sb* 1, 4), which itself is Saturnian because fruitless (Agrippa, *ibid*.; Pliny *Natural History* 16. 45. 108), and associated with death in, e.g. Virgil, *Eclogues*, 6. 62–3, which reports that the sisters of Phaethon were metamorphosed into alders, also mentioning the *bitter* moss on the alders' bark. *sere*: *January* 37 gloss.

The Fatal Sisters eke repent
Her vital thread so soon was spent:
   O heavy hearse;   150
Mourn now, my Muse, now mourn with heavy cheer:
   O care-full verse.

O trustless state of earthly things, and slipper hope
Of mortal men, that swink and sweat for nought
And, shooting wide, do miss the marked scope: 155
Now have I learned (a lesson dearly bought)
That n'is on earth assurance to be sought:
   For what might be in earthly mould,
   That did her buried body hold
     (O heavy hearse),   160
Yet saw I on the bier when it was brought:
   O care-full verse.

But maugre Death, and dreaded Sisters' deadly spite,
And gates of hell, and fiery Furies' force,
She hath the bonds broke of eternal Night,   165
Her soul unbodied of the burdenous corpse:
Why then weeps Lobbin so without remorse?
   O Lobb, thy loss no longer lament –
   Dido n'is dead, but into heaven hent:

---

148. Fatal Sisters: E.K.
151. heavy: October 1n. *cheer*: face.
153. trustless: E.K. *slipper*: slippery, unstable.
154. swink . . . sweat: *April* 99 and *May* 36 glosses.
155. scope: target: cf. *September*, 122.
158. mould: (1) object of imitation, pattern (*OED* mould *sb* 2, I. 5, first citation *c*. 1547); (2) soil, particularly that of the grave (mould *sb* 1, 2); (3) the substance of the human body: *ibid*. 4 (cf. 1 Corinthians 15: 47).
161. Yet: I still saw that perfection in her corpse. *bier*: E.K.
163. maugre: in spite of.
164. Furies: E.K.
165. eternal Night: E.K.
167. remorse: see 131n.
169. Dido . . . dead: the peripeteia originates with the astral immortality of Daphnis in Virgil, *Eclogues*, 5. 52, 56–64, followed by Marot, *Eglogue* 1. 189–92: *Elle est aux champs Elisiens reçue*. See also *November* headnote above. *hent*: *February* 195 gloss.

    O happy hearse; 170
Cease now, my Muse, now cease thy sorrow's source:
    O joyful verse.

Why wail we, then? Why weary we the gods with plaints
As if some evil were to her betight?
She reigns a goddess now among the saints 175
That whilom was the saint of shepherds' light,
And is installed now in heaven's height:
    I see thee, blessed soul, I see,
    Walk in Elysian fields so free:
    O happy hearse; 180
Might I once come to thee (oh that I might!) –
    O joyful verse.

Unwise and wretched men to weet what's good or ill:
We deem of Death as doom of ill desert;
But knew we fools what it us brings until, 185
Die would we daily, once it to expert.
No danger there the shepherd can astart:
    Fair fields and pleasant leas there bene,
    The fields aye fresh, the grass aye green:
    O happy hearse; 190
Make haste, ye shepherds, thither to revert:
    O joyful verse.

Dido is gone afore (whose turn shall be the next?):
There lives she with the blessed gods in bliss,

---

170. happy hearse: the change of refrain derives from Theocritus, *Idylls*, 1. 127 and Moschus, *Idylls*, 3. 119–20, where dead Bion is exhorted to sing a melodious bucolic to the Maid (Persephone, queen of the underworld; cf. the similar change in Spenser's *Epith*).
174. betight: E.K.
175. saints: the holy dead: cf. *July*, 113–24. (*Goddess* is either an instance of pastoral naivety or of syncretism – the characteristic Renaissance marrying of 'pagan' with Christian.)
176. saint . . . light: the illuminating living exemplar of perfection to shepherds.
178. I see: E.K.
179. Elysian fields: E.K.
184. doom of: judgement for: cf. *August* 135 gloss.
185. until: unto.
186. Die would: E.K. *expert*: experience: *OED expert v*, last example 1587.
187. astart: E.K.
188. leas: meadows: cf. *July* 122n.

There drinks she nectar with ambrosia mixed, 195
And joys enjoys that mortal men do miss.
The honour now of highest gods she is
  That whilom was poor shepherds' pride
  While here on earth she did abide:
    O happy hearse; 200
Cease now, my song, my woe now wasted is:
    O joyful verse.

                           Thenot.
Ay, frank shepherd, how bene thy verses meynt
With doleful pleasance, so as I ne wot
Whether rejoice or weep for great constraint? 205
Thine be the cosset – well hast thou it got.
Up, Colin, up! Ynough thou mourned hast:
Now 'gins to mizzle; hie we homeward fast.

                    Colin's emblem:
                    La mort ny mord. 210

GLOSS

2] **jouissance**) mirth [*May* 25 gloss].

5] **sovenance**) remembrance [*OED* cites three earlier instances, two from Caxton, one from *c*. 1550; Spenser's linguistic francophilia in the opening lines is attributable to his indebtedness to Marot though, like *jouissance*, the word also appears in *May*: 82 and gloss].

10] **hery**) honour [apart from an adjectival instance in Stanyhurst's *Aeneis* (1583), *OED*'s only example since *c*. 1450: *February* 62 gloss].

13] **welked**) *shortened* or *impaired*: as the moon, being in the wane, is said of Lydgate to *welk* [still current with reference to the fading of flowers, etc.; but a mediaevalism in the sense that E.K. explains it and a Spenserian first in its transitive application: welk *v* 1, 2, 3].

15] **in lowly lay**) according to the season of the month November when the

195. nectar . . . ambrosia: E.K. Cf. Marot, *Eglogue* 1. 197: *Car toute odeur ambrosienne y fleurent* ['For every ambrosial fragrance flowers there'].

201. wasted: spent.

203–5. Ay..constraint: translating Marot's conclusion (261–2): *O franc pasteur, combien tes vers sont pleins/De grand douceur et de grand amertume* ['O loyal shepherd, how full of great sweetness and bitterness your lines are'].

203. frank: unburdened: *OED* frank *a* 2, 1e gives 1558 as date of last instance. But the French meaning is probably intended as well. *meynt*: E.K.

205. constraint: *May* 249n (but appears here because of Marot's l. 263: *mon coeur tu contrains* ['you constrain my heart'; original reads *constraincts*]).

208. mizzle: drizzle.

210. La mort ny mord: E.K. The motto under which Marot's *Oeuvres* (Paris 1539) were published. Luborsky 1981: 53 describes a 1576 portait of him with the motto.

sun draweth low in the south toward his tropic or return [earlier than *OED*'s first instance of lay = lodging, lair which is 1590: lay *sb* 7, 2].

16] **in Fishes' hask**) the sun reigneth, that is, in the sign Pisces all November (a *hask* is a wicker pad [basket] wherein they use [it is the custom] to carry fish) [first instance of only three *OED* examples of hask, one of the others being Florio's translation of Italian *cavagna* (1598). But see *OED* hassock *sb* 3. E.K.'s gloss is astrologically wrong and compounds a Spenserian crux. See Appendix.].

21] **virelays**) a light kind of song [*April* 33 gloss].

30] **be watered**) for it is a saying of poets that they have drunk of the Muses' well Castalias (whereof was before sufficiently said [*April* 42 gloss]).

36] **dreariment**) dreary and heavy cheer [Spenserian neologism].

38] **the great shepherd**) is some man of high degree and not (as some vainly suppose) god Pan [on whom, see *January* 17n]. The person both of the shepherd and of Dido is unknown and closely buried in the author's conceit [imagination]. But out of doubt I am that it is not Rosalind, as some imagine; for he speaketh soon after of her also [despite E.K. the shepherd could = Pan = Henry VIII, as at *April* 50 gloss].

38] **sheen**) *fair* and *shining* [E.K. distinguishes the two main current senses: *OED* sheen *a* 1a, 2a].

39] **may**) for *maid* [a common contemporary form; E.K. is perhaps (pretending to be) worried that it is also a pet form of *Mary* and thus hints at the Marian cult of Elizabeth: *November* headnote; Wells 1983. Modernisation removes the initial capital of the original.].

41] **teen**) sorrow [archaic].

42] **cosset**) a lamb brought up without the dam [i.e., by hand. First instance in *OED*.].

45] **guerdon**) reward [archaic].

46] **benempt**) bequeathed [or promised with an oath: *OED*, bename *v* 1; first instance since *c*. 1315. For its other sense, see *July* 214 gloss.].

51] **unkempt**) *incompti* [Latin], *not combed*: that is, *rude* and *unhandsome* [the Latin usage leads to English incompt by 1631 (*OED*), but Spenser's *unkempt* does not require the pedantry: although a first in this sense (*OED* unkempt 2), it is merely a metaphorical extension of unkembed].

53] **Melpomene**) the sad and wailful Muse used of poets in honour of tragedies, as saith Virgil: *Melpomene tragico proclamat maesta boatu* ['Melpomene calls out with the loud voice of sorrowful tragedy': not Virgil, but Ausonius's *Nomina musarum*: *April* 100 gloss].

55] **Up, grisly ghosts**) the manner of tragical poets, to call for help of Furies and damned ghosts: so is Hecuba of Euripides [Polydorus's ghost appears at the opening of Euripides's *Hecuba*], and Tantalus brought in of Seneca [his ghost opens *Thyestes*] – and the rest of the rest.

60] **hearse**) is the solemn obsequy [rites] in funerals [a unique sense (*OED* hearse *sb* 6) and perhaps an error of E.K.'s: the contemporary meanings of (1) framework for carrying tapers over the coffin of distinguished people (senses 2a–c) and (2) corpse (sense 7) are both appropriate. But note that *rehearse* = rehearsal = recitation was a current northern/Scots substantive. The original spelling – *herse* – may also suggest herse = glorify, a verb related to hery (10 gloss above; *OED* herse *v*): the hearse is thus the elegiac verse itself, extolling Dido's fame and memory: Berger 1988: 401.].

64] **waste of**) decay of so beautiful a piece [*OED* waste *sb* II. 9].

66] **cark**) care [archaic].

73] **ah, why**) an elegant epanorthosis [*June* 90 gloss]; as also soon after: 'nay, time was long ygo'' [81].
83] **floweret**) a diminutive for a *little flower* [*OED* cites only one instance before this, from *c.* 1400; cf. *February* 182 gloss]. This is a notable and sententious comparison – *a minore ad maius* [from less to greater].
89] **Reliven not**) live not again [relive is used by E.K. in the General Argument]: *scilicet* [namely] not in their earthly bodies; for in heaven they enjoy their due reward.
91] **The branch**) he meaneth Dido, who, being (as it were) the main branch (now withered) the buds (that is, beauty, as he said afore) can no more flourish [cf. *May*, 196].
96] **With cakes**) fit for shepherds' banquets.
98] **heame**) for *home*, after the northern pronouncing.
107] **tinct**) *dyed* or *stained* [Spenserian neologism from Latin *tinctus*: *OED* tinct *ppl a*].
108] **The gaudy**) the meaning is that the things which were the ornaments of her life are made the honour of her funeral, as is used [is the custom] in burials [gaudy = fine, gay: *OED* gaudy *a* 2, dates first citation 1583. Cf. *May* 4n.].
113] **Lobbin**) the name of a shepherd which seemeth to have been the lover and dear friend of Dido [commentators favour an identification with the Earl of Leicester, the queen's favourite and, at one time, an apparent possible husband: Parmenter 1936: 214–16].
116] **rush rings**) agreeable for such base gifts.
125] **faded locks**) dried leaves, as if Nature herself bewailed the death of the maid.
126] **source**) spring [*May* 130 gloss].
128] **mantled meadows**) for the sundry flowers are like a mantle or coverlet wrought with many colours.
141] **Philomel**) the nightingale, whom the poets feign once to have been a lady of great beauty till, being ravished by her sister's husband [Tereus, husband of Procne], she desired to be turned into a bird of her name [*August* 183–6n]: whose *Complaints* be very well set forth of Master George Gascoigne, a witty gentleman and the very chief of our late rhymers who, and if some parts of learning wanted [lacked] not (albe it is well known he altogether wanted not learning), no doubt would have attained to the excellency of those famous poets; for gifts of wit and natural promptness appear in him abundantly [Gascoigne, *Complaint of Philomene*: see 26n above].
145] **cypress**) used of the old paynims [pagans] in the furnishing of their funeral pomp, and properly the sign of all sorrow and heaviness [Agrippa (1651) 1. 25].
148] **The Fatal Sisters**) Clotho, Lachesis and Atropos, daughters of Herebus and the Night [this is the parentage cited in, e.g., Cicero, *De natura deorum*, 3. 17. 44], whom the poets feign to spin the life of man as it were a long thread which they draw out in length till his fatal hour and timely death be come; but if by other casualty his days be abridged, then one of them (that is, Atropos) is said to have cut the thread in twain. Hereof cometh a common verse: *Clotho*

Textual note

Gloss 145. *the sign of*] Q3; *the of* Q1–2.

colum baiulat, Lachesis trahit, Atropos occat ['Clotho carries the burden of the web, Lachesis draws it out, Atropos cuts it': in the *Anthologia Latina*, 792R: Mustard 1919: 202)].

153] **O trustless**) a gallant exclamation moralised with great wisdom and passionate with great affection.

161] **bier**) a frame whereon they use to lay the dead corse [E.K. distinguishes this from the other contemporary sense, tomb].

164] **Furies**) of poets be feigned to be three: Persephone, Allecto and Megera, which are said to be the authors of all evil and mischief [Persephone, as queen of the underworld, is the infernal goddess of death (Apollodorus, *Library*, 1. 3. 1) and the Furies were her daughters by the god of the underworld (Orphic *Hymn to Persephone*, 6: Athanassakis 1977: 41). E.K. has perhaps been misled by Spenser's *Virgil's Gnat* (also 1579?), 422–3 ('Persephone... [and] her fellow Furies') into regarding her as a Fury and thus putting her name for Tisiphone's. For a description see *Aeneid*, 12. 845–8.].

165] **eternal Night**) is death or darkness of hell [in context Spenser also means Night herself, who inhabited the underworld (Hesiod, *Theogony*, 123, 744) and was interpreted neo-Platonically as an emblem of worldly existence].

174] **betight**) happened [from betide; first instance in *OED* since *c*. 1430].

178] **I see**) a lively icon or representation, as if he saw her in heaven present.

179] **Elysian fields**) be devised of poets to be a place of pleasure like paradise, where the happy souls do rest in peace and eternal happiness [e.g., *Aeneid*, 6. 638–59].

186] **Die would**) the very express saying of Plato *in Phaedone* [*Phaedo*, 5, Socrates on the wish for death but forbidding suicide].

187] **astart**) befall unwares [in this sense *OED*'s first and only example after Gower (1393): astart *v* 2].

195] **nectar and ambrosia**) be feigned to be the drink and food of the gods: ambrosia they liken to manna in scripture, and nectar to be white like cream; whereof is a proper tale of Hebe that spilt a cup of it and stained the heavens, as yet appeareth [Hebe = goddess of youth and cupbearer to the gods; but this tale remains untraced]. But I have already discoursed that at large in my commentary upon the *Dreams* of the same author [neither is extant, but they are mentioned in *Three... Letters*, postscript].

203] **meynt**) mingled [*July* 84 gloss].

Emblem.

Which is as much to say as death biteth not. For although by course of nature we be born to die and, being ripened with age – as with a timely harvest – we must be gathered in time (or else of ourselves we fall like rotted ripe fruit from the tree); yet death is not to be counted for evil nor, as the poet said a little before, as 'doom of ill desert' [l. 184]. For, though the trespass of the first man brought death into the world as the guerdon of sin, yet, being overcome by the death of one that died for all [1 Cor. 15: 21–2], it is now made, as Chaucer saith, the green pathway to life [E.K. paraphrases the opening of the *Parson's Tale* (itself translated from Jeremiah 6: 16): 'seeth... which is the good way, and walketh in that way, and ye shall find refreshing for your souls']. So that it agreeth well with that was said, that *Death biteth not* (that is, *hurteth not) at all* [the emblem also refers – via Marot (see note to gloss above) – to poetic immortality, as at *December* emblem gloss].

December

Colin utters a farewell to Rosalind that is also a recognition of the failure of his love. But his adieu, intoned by a self-conscious sufferer from love melancholy, does not just belong to his secret history: it signals in addition Spenser's recognition that love for another human being *per se* must no longer be the subject of his verse (cf. *October*). The eclogue includes a conventional survey of the four ages of man compared to the seasons, though Colin's insistence that his growth through maturity to old age is defined and determined by his love for Rosalind underlines his morbid introspection: unrequited love leads nowhere except deeper into the self (we remember the hints of the Narcissus myth at *June* 52n and *September* emblem and gloss). Spenser's source, Marot's *Eglogue ... au Roi, sous les noms de Pan et Robin* (1539), reinforces our sense of Colin's introversion. Here the poet, under the name Robin, considers the stages/seasons of his life and appeals to the king (Pan/Francis I) for his continuing patronage, which will enable him to sing better than ever. Colin, on the other hand, can only look back and inward (to Rosalind). (Note how *December* shares *January*'s stanzaic structure as well as its solitary speaker, so that the poem ends as it began, reiterating a circle of sterile self-involvement.) The imitation of Marot also generates political significances. For Spenser knew that Marot's expression of gratitude for patronage and the hope for its continuance was built on his earlier banishment by Francis because of his Protestantism (he was exiled in 1535; he returned, after a formal re-espousal of Catholicism, in 1537, only two years before the eclogue was composed). If Colin speaks as Marot's Robin speaks, then he assumes the mantle of one who, while addressing the sovereign, nevertheless remains a covert Protestant rebel. Furthermore, when we recall that *Marot*'s Colin is Colin d'Anjou (*January* and *November* headnotes), we see that the farewell to Rosalind is in effect a daring adieu from the Duc d'Anjou/Alençon to Elizabeth (thus continuing the message of *November*), an adieu that ensures the integrity of English Protestantism. From a different perspective, however, *December* marks Spenser's farewell to pastoral as a mode, and the note of closure is echoed in a numerological feature that links *January* and *December* and exploits the positive meaning of the circle as perfection and completion; for *December* is exactly twice *January*'s length (156 lines to the latter's 78). This places the eclogues in a 2:1 ratio with each other, and since this is the ratio that produces the octave (*August* headnote), we are to infer that Spenser (as distinct from Colin) has happily emerged from the limited pastoral modality of his 'green cabinet' (17) in order to move into a more heroic mode by literally enclosing his exercise in pastoral within a diapason of completion and integration: that circle perfected, he can proceed to another. (For the circle here as an emblem of eternity see Røstvig 1969: 63–4; Fowler 1970: 159–60 notes the observance of the 2:1 ratio between introduction and envoy in Renaissance verse without citing this *SC* instance.)

The woodcut (fig. 12) encodes a landscape of desolation, its main feature being the tree of patronage, now bare of leaves, under which Colin, like Virgil's Tityrus, sits (see *January* headnote; Marot's *Eglogue ... au Roi* opens with an echo of Virgil's first eclogue, comparing Robin implicitly to Tityrus). Fragments of his pipe lie at his feet (compare *January* woodcut), in contradiction to the text which states that Colin (like Marot's Robin) suspends his instrument from a tree: 141n and Luborsky 1981: 40–1. Structurally the woodcut is closest to that for *September*, though the opposition of court and country, palace and cottage, that informs the background to *January*'s woodcut is perhaps satirically alluded to here in the balancing of hovel (back left) against water tank (right foreground), the leonine gargoyles to which suggest a diminishing of the monarchical lion inherited by the Tudors from Aeneas's descendant Brutus (Yates (1975) plates 8a, b, d): a touch of grotesquerie that demonstrates the monarchy's loss of status as a result of its dalliance with French Catholicism through Alençon.

December
Aegloga duodecima

Argument

This eglogue – even as the first began – is ended with a complaint of Colin to god Pan wherein, as weary of his former ways, he proportioneth his life to the four seasons of the year, comparing his youth to the springtime (when he was fresh, and free from love's folly), his manhood to the summer (which, he saith, was consumed with great heat and excessive drouth caused through a comet or blazing star – by which he meaneth love, which passion is commonly compared to such flames and immoderate heat); his riper years he resembleth to an unseasonable harvest wherein the fruits fall ere they be ripe; his latter age to winter's chill and frosty season, now drawing near to his last end.

The gentle shepherd sat beside a spring
(All in the shadow of a bushy briar)
That Colin hight, which well could pipe and sing,
For he of Tityrus his songs did lere.
   There as he sat in secret shade alone   5
   Thus 'gan he make of love his piteous moan:

Argument: *drouth*: drought.
1–18. The . . . Colinet: paraphrasing the opening of Marot's *Eglogue* 3 (*au Roi*), itself imitating the opening of Virgil's first eclogue (Robin sitting in the shade of beeches sings to Pan).
3. hight: called.
4. Tityrus: E.K. *lere*: learn.

O sovereign Pan, thou god of shepherds all,
Which of our tender lambkins takest keep
And, when our flocks into mischance mought fall,
Dost save from mischief the unwary sheep   10
   (Als of their masters hast no less regard
   Than of the flocks, which thou dost watch and ward):

I thee beseech (so be thou deign to hear
Rude ditties tuned to shepherd's oaten reed,
Or if I ever sonnet sang so clear   15
As it with pleasance mought thy fancy feed),
   Harken awhile from thy green cabinet
   The rural song of care-full Colinet:

Whilom in youth, when flowered my joyful Spring,
Like swallow swift I wandered here and there,   20
For heat of heedless lust me so did sting
That I of doubted danger had no fear:
   I went the waste-full woods and forest wide
   Withouten dread of wolves to bene espied.

I wont to range amid the mazy thicket   25
And gather nuts to make me Christmas game,
And joyed oft to chase the trembling pricket,

7–10. *O . . . sheep*: combining Marot as above with the invocation to his pro-Protestant *Complainte d'un Pastoureau Chrétien*, published posthumously in 1549: 'Pan, great god of shepherds, who protects our sheep . . . ' (where Pan is God).
8. *lambkins*: E.K.
11. *Als . . . their*: E.K. *Als*: *July* 8 gloss.
13. *deign*: E.K.
14. *oaten reed*: *October* 8 gloss.
15. *sonnet*: short lyrical poem, not necessarily of 14 lines.
17–18. *cabinet, Colinet*: E.K.
19–36. *Whilom . . . life*: closely following Marot's *Eglogue* 3. 19–36: parallels include the swallow, the recklessness of youth, the wolves, the nut-gathering, and the dislodging of birds from their nests.
20. *swallow swift*: a pun is historically impossible; the swiftness of the swallow (emblem of spring and lust) was proverbial.
22. *doubted*: *October* 41n.
25. *mazy*: E.K.
27. *pricket*: buck in its second year having unbranched horns (not in Marot): there are overtones of the love hunt: Thiébaux, M. 1974 *The Stag of Love*, Cornell U.P., Ithaca and London.

Or hunt the heartless hare till she were tame.
   What recked I of wintry Age's waste:
   Tho deemed I my Spring would ever last.   30

How often have I scaled the craggy oak,
All to dislodge the raven off her nest!
How have I wearied with many a stroke
The stately walnut tree, the while the rest
   Under the tree fell all for nuts at strife –   35
   For ylike to me was liberty and life!

And – for I was in thilk same looser years
(Whether the Muse so wrought me from my birth,
Or I too much believed my shepherd peers)
Somedeal ybent to song and music's mirth –   40
   A good old shepherd (Wrenock was his name)
   Made me by art more cunning in the same.

Fro' thence I durst in derring-do compare
With shepherd's swain whatever fed in field;
And, if that Hobbinol right judgement bear,   45
To Pan his own self pipe I need not yield:
   For, if the flocking nymphs did follow Pan,
   The wiser Muses after Colin ran.

Textual note

43. derring-do] reading admitted by Morris and Hales, 1869 on the authority of *Gloss 43*. Quartos and F read derring to.

28. heartless: timid; for the *hare* as an emblem of Venus and lust see Tervarent (1958) cols 241–2 (Marot's Robin hunted rabbits).
31. craggy: (1) rough (-barked, etc.): first instance of this sense 156ᶜ *OED* craggy *a* 2); (2) difficult (to climb): sense 3a, first *OED* citation 1583.
32. raven: magpie and jay at Marot, *Eglogue* 3. 30.
36. ylike: March 39n.
38. Whether . . . birth: Marot, *Eglogue* 3. 45: *Ou la nature aux Muses inclinée* ['Whether my disposition inclined me to the Muses'].
39. peers: E.K.
40. Somedeal: somewhat. *music*: E.K.
41. Wrenock: maybe Spenser's headmaster at Merchant Taylors', Richard Mulcaster. At the equivalent point (*Eglogue* 3. 49) Marot acknowledges the influence of his father.
42. cunning: learned.
43. derring-do: E.K.
47–8. nymphs . . . Muses: suggesting the urge to abandon pastoral for higher genres.

But ah, such pride at length was ill repaid –
The shepherd's god (perdy god was he none!)   50
My hurtless pleasance did me ill upbraid:
My freedom lorn, my life he left to moan.
    'Love' they him called that gave me checkmate;
    But better mought they have behote him 'Hate'.

Tho 'gan my lovely Spring bid me farewell,   55
And Summer season sped him to display
(For Love then in the Lion's house did dwell)
The raging fire that kindled at his ray:
    A comet stirred up that unkindly heat
    That reigned (as men said) in Venus' seat.   60

Forth was I led – not as I wont afore,
When choice I had to choose my wandering way,
But whither luck and Love's unbridled lore
Would lead me forth on Fancy's bit to play:
    The bush my bed, the bramble was my bower –   65
    The woods can witness many a woeful stour.

Where I was wont to seek the honey bee
Working her formal rooms in wexen frame,

---

51. hurtless pleasance: harmless delight.
52. lorn: *September* 57 gloss: perhaps here in its correct sense, destroyed.
53. checkmate: often used as a metaphor for love difficulties, as in Chaucer's *Book of the Duchess*.
54. behote: a form of behight = named: see *April* 120 gloss.
57. Lion's house: E.K.
58. ray: E.K.
59. comet: E.K. *unkindly*: unnatural.
60. reigned: was astrologically dominant. *Venus' seat*: E.K.
63–4. Love's . . . bit: recalling the unbridled Platonic horse of the passions: Wind 1967: 145.
65. bower: bedchamber (*July* 74 gloss).
66. stour: *January* 51 gloss.
67. Where I was: E.K. *honey bee*: emblem of lyric poetry (Plato, *Ion*, 534A and especially Philostratus, *Imagines*, 2. 12) as well as of love (*March* emblem n).
68. formal: symmetrical (*OED formal a* A 9 dates first instance 1597).

The grisly toadstool grown there mought I see,
And loathed paddocks lording on the same;   70
   And where the chanting birds lulled me asleep,
   The ghastly owl her grievous inn doth keep.

Then, as the Spring gives place to elder time,
And bringeth forth the fruit of Summer's pride,
Also my age, now passed youngthly prime,   75
To things of riper reason self applied,
   And learned of lighter timber cotes to frame
   Such as might save my sheep and me fro' shame.

To make fine cages for the nightingale
And baskets of bulrushes was my wont: 80
Who to entrap the fish in winding sale
Was better seen, or hurtful beasts to hunt?
   I learned als the signs of heaven to ken –
   How Phoebe fails, where Venus sits, and when.

---

69. grisly: ugly; fear-inducing.
69–72. toadstool . . . owl: traditionally either poisonous and/or of ill omen: for the poisonous toad (paddock) see Pliny, *Natural History*, 8. 48. 110 (it is also an emblem of lust: de Vries 1974: 468); for the owl, see *June* 24n. Both toad and owl are Saturnine, hence melancholic: Agrippa (1651) 1. 25 (p. 56); and since the toadstool has hallucinatory power, the passage signifies Colin's entry into the fantasies of love melancholy.
70. lording: E.K.
72. inn: abode.
73–82. echoing Marot, *Eglogue* 3. 107–23.
73. Then, as: E.K.
75. youngthly: cf. *February* 52, 87nn.
77. cotes: E.K. *frame*: build.
79. nightingale: *November* 141 gloss. For the caged nightingale as an emblem of the man of learning enclosed by the book of knowledge, see Allen 1970: 275–7.
81. fish: emblem of lust because of Venus's metamorphosis into a fish: Ovid, *Metamorphoses*, 5. 331. Cf. *November*, 16. *sale*: E.K.
83–90. I . . . sleep: imitating Marot, *Eglogue* 3. 124–33: *J'apprends les noms des quatre parts du monde;/J'apprends les noms des vents qui de là sortent,/Leurs qualités, et quels temps ils apportent,/Dont les oiseaux, sages devins des champs,/M'avertissent par leurs vols et leurs chants./Je apprends aussi . . . A éviter les dangereux herbages . . .* ['I learned the names of the four parts of the world; I learned the names of the winds which issue from them, their qualities and the seasons they bring, which the birds (wise soothsayers) would inform me of by their flight and their songs. I learned also to avoid poisonous herbs . . .'].
84. Phoebe fails: E.K. *Venus*: E.K.

And tried time yet taught me geater things: 85
The sudden rising of the raging seas,
The sooth of birds by beating of their wings,
The power of herbs – both which can hurt and ease,
   And which be wont to enrage the restless sheep,
   And which be wont to work eternal sleep. 90

But ah, unwise and witless Colin Clout,
That kiddest the hidden kinds of many a weed,
Yet kiddest not ene to cure thy sore heart-root,
Whose rankling wound as yet does rifely bleed:
   Why livest thou still, and yet hast thy death's wound? 95
   Why diest thou still, and yet alive art found?

Thus is my Summer worn away and wasted;
Thus is my harvest hastened all too rathe –
The ear that budded fair is burnt and blasted,
And all my hoped gain is turned to scathe: 100
   Of all the seed that in my youth was sown
   Was nought but brakes and brambles to be mown.

My boughs with blooms that crowned were at first,
And promised of timely fruit such store,

---

86. raging seas: E.K.
87. sooth of birds: E.K.
88. herbs: E.K.
92. kiddest: E.K.
93. not ene: not on one (single) occasion (*OED ene adv* 1 gives 1325 as date of last instance).
94. rifely: abundantly.
97–126. Thus . . . wind: Spenser's text abandons Marot's at the point where Marot supplicates for Francis I's patronage.
97–8. Thus . . . my: E.K.
98. rathe: early in relation to its proper time: *OED* rathe *adv* 2b, with citations spanning only 1565–98.
99. ear: E.K.
100. scathe: E.K.
102. brakes: perhaps bracken (*OED* brake *sb* 1), but probably clumps of briars (*OED* brake *sb* 2): cf. Isaiah 5: 6 and 32: 13 (where the growth of 'briars and thorns' symbolises divine punishment for sin); Hebrews 6: 7–8: 'For the earth . . . which beareth thorns and briars, is reproved, and is near unto cursing, whose end is to be burned'; Matthew 13: 5–7, the seed cast on stony ground and amid thorns.
103. blooms: original spelling = bloosmes (*January* 34n).

Are left both bare and barren now at erst: 105
The flattering fruit is fallen to ground before,
    And rotted ere they were half mellow-ripe:
    My harvest waste my hope away did wipe.

The fragrant flowers that in my garden grew
Bene withered, as they had bene gathered long: 110
Their roots bene dried up for lack of dew,
Yet dewed with tears they han be ever among:
    Ah, who has wrought my Rosalind this spite
    To spill the flowers that should her garland dight?

And I, that whilom wont to frame my pipe 115
Unto the shifting of the shepherd's foot,
Sike follies now have gathered as too ripe,
And cast hem out as rotten and unsoot.
    The looser lass I cast to please no more:
    One, if I please, enough is me therefore. 120

And thus of all my harvest-hope I have
Nought reaped but a weedy crop of care
Which, when I thought have threshed in swelling sheaf,
Cockle for corn, and chaff for barley bare:
    Soon as the chaff should in the fan be fined, 125
    All was blown away of the wavering wind.

105. at erst: September 6n.
106. flattering: pleasing to the imagination: *OED flattering ppl a* 2.
107. mellow: soft and juicy.
109. The . . . flowers: E.K.
111. dew: cf. the metaphor at *June* 93–6 and n.
112. ever among: E.K.
114. spill: February 52n. *flowers . . . garland*: playing with the common posy/poesy pun and the familiar title of poetic anthologies, *garland*. *dight*: *April* 29 gloss.
115. frame: August 3n.
118. unsoot: unsweet (only three instances noted by *OED unsoot a*: this and two from Lydgate): cf. *April* 111 and *October* 90 glosses.
119. cast: February 125n.
124–6. Cockle . . . wind: nemesis for 101. Cf. Job 31: 38–40: 'If my land cry against me . . . Let thistles grow in stead of wheat, and cockle in the stead of barley' (cockle = a corn-weed: *OED cockle sb* 1); Isaiah 33: 11 ('Ye shall conceive chaff, and bring forth stubble . . .'; Geneva gloss: 'he showeth that their enterprise shall be in vain'); Psalms 1: 4 ('The wicked . . . are as the chaff which the wind driveth away') and 35: 5 ('Let them be as chaff before the wind, and let the Angel of the Lord scatter them').
125. fined: refined.

So now my year draws to its latter term:
My Spring is spent, my Summer burnt up quite,
My harvest hastes to stir up Winter stern
And bids him claim with rigorous rage his right: 130
   So now he storms with many a sturdy stour;
   So now his blustering blast each coast doth scour.

The care-full cold hath nipped my rugged rind,
And in my face deep furrows Eld hath pight:
My head besprent with hoary frost I find, 135
And by mine eye the crow his claw doth write;
   Delight is laid abed and pleasure past;
   No sun now shines; clouds han all overcast.

Now leave, ye shepherds' boys, your merry glee:
My Muse is hoarse, and weary of this stound. 140
Here will I hang my pipe upon this tree –
Was never pipe of reed did better sound:
   Winter is come that blows the bitter blast –
   And after Winter dreary Death does haste.

Gather ye together, my little flock 145
(My little flock that was to me so lief);
Let me, ah, let me in your folds ye-lock
Ere the breme Winter breed you greater grief:
   Winter is come that blows the baleful breath –

---

127. So . . . year: E.K.
131. stour: 66n above.
133. care-full cold: E.K. *rugged rind*: wrinkled skin: *OED* rugged *a* 1, 3 citing *FQ*, 4 proem 1 as first instance.
134. Eld: Old Age (*February* 54 gloss). *pight*: pierced: mediaevalism; last *OED* citation 1398: pitch *v* 1, B 2. Cf. *February* 106n.
135. besprent: *November* 111n. *hoary frost*: E.K.
136. crow . . . write: not necessarily colloquial at this time and perhaps borrowed from Chaucer (this is *OED*'s second citation, its first being from Chaucer's *Troilus*: crow's foot 1).
139. glee: E.K.
140. stound: *September* 56n.
141. hang my pipe: borrowed from Marot, *Eglogue* 3. 205: *Vois ma musette, à un arbre pendue* ['Behold my bagpipe, hanging from a tree']. The action signifies the relinquishing of a stage of life now outgrown: cf. *FQ*, 6. 5. 37. Ct. the broken pipe of grief at *January* 72 and n.
146. lief: *September* 11 gloss.
148. breme: E.K.
151. Adieu, delights: E.K.

And after Winter cometh timely Death. 150

Adieu, delights, that lulled me asleep;
Adieu, my dear, whose love I bought so dear;
Adieu, my little lambs and loved sheep;
Adieu, ye woods that oft my witness were:
   Adieu, good Hobbinol, that was so true – 155
   Tell Rosalind, her Colin bids her adieu.

                Colin's emblem:

GLOSS

4] **Tityrus**) Chaucer, as hath been oft said [*June* 81 gloss].

8] **lambkins**) young lambs [first *OED* citation].

11] **Als of their**) seemeth to express Virgil's verse: *Pan curat oves oviumque magistros* ['Pan cares for sheep and the keepers of sheep': *Eclogues*, 2. 33; translated by Marot, *Eglogue* 3 (*au Roi*). 6–8, where Pan is King Francis].

13] **deign**) vouchsafe [undergoing active shifts in meaning in the late sixteenth century: cf. *January* 63n].

17–18] **cabinet, Colinet**) diminutives [*OED* earliest date for *cabinet* = hut, cottage, etc. is 1572; but Spenser pillages Marot, *Eglogue* 3. 13–14: *Écoutez un peu, de ton vert cabinet/ Le chant rural du petit Robinet* ['Listen a while, from your green room,/To the country song of little Robinet'. For lexical complexities see Patterson 1988: 128–30.].

25] **mazy**) for they be like to a maze whence it is hard to get out again [*OED*'s first instance of this sense: mazy *a* 1a; usual meaning = giddy].

39] **peers**) fellows and companions [*OED* attributes the first use of this sense since 1467 to Spenser: peer *sb* 3].

40] **music**) that is, poetry, as Terence saith: *Qui artem tractant musicam* (speaking of poets) ['Those who pursue the musical art': *Phormio*, prologue, 17].

43] **derring-do**) aforesaid [*October* 65 gloss].

57] **Lion's house**) he imagineth simply that Cupid (which is Love) had his abode in the hot sign Leo, which is in middest of summer [*July* 21 gloss]: a pretty allegory whereof the meaning is that Love in him wrought an extraordinary heat of lust.

58] **his ray**) which is Cupid's beam (or flames) of love.

59] **A comet**) a blazing star – meant of beauty, which was the cause of his hot love [cf. *FQ*, 3. 1. 16, Florimell's beauty compared to that of a comet, the point of the comparison being (a) the etymology of the word from Greek *komētēs* = long haired, and thus particularly applicable to women, and (b) the rarity of comets].

emblem: missing in all editions, despite E.K.'s gloss. Spenser must have noticed, so the omission may be deliberate (as at the end of *Hamlet*, 'the rest is silence'); but it could be an oversight. J. Hughes (edition of 1715) ingeniously supplied the motto from the clues in E.K.'s gloss: *Vivitur ingenio, caetera mortis erunt* ('He survives through his talents, the remainder was mortal': pseudo-Virgilian *in Maecenatis obitum, elegeia*, 37–8 (*Var* 1. 425–6)).

60] **Venus**) the goddess of beauty or pleasure; also a sign in heaven, as it is here taken. So he meaneth that beauty, which hath always aspect to Venus, was the cause of all his unquietness in love [Venus herself isn't a *sign*, of course. Spenser's phrase presumably means *Venus's abode*, i.e., her late spring/early summer zodiacal house Taurus and (metaphorically) Colin's heart.].

67] **Where I was**) a fine description of the change of his life and liking; for all things now seemed to him to have altered their kindly [proper] course.

70] **lording**) spoken after the manner of paddocks [toads] and frogs sitting, which is indeed lordly, not removing nor looking once aside unless they be stirred.

73] **Then, as**) the second part: that is, his manhood.

77] **cotes**) sheepcotes: for such be the exercises of shepherds [current usage; E.K. explains yet another rusticism].

81] **sale**) or *sallow*: a kind of wood like willow, fit to wreath and bind in leaps [baskets] to catch fish withal [see *OED* sallow *sb* 1 and saugh (northern/Scots form of sallow), b: rope made of twisted sallow-withes].

84] **Phoebe fails**) the eclipse of the moon, which is always in *Cauda* [Tail] or *Capite Draconis* [Head of the Dragon], signs in heaven [see *OED s.v.*].

84] **Venus**) *scilicet* [namely] Venus star [i.e., the star Venus], otherwise called Hesperus and Vesper [Greek and Latin respectively for evening star] and Lucifer [Latin for light-bearer, i.e., Venus as the morning star] both because he seemeth to be one of the brightest stars and also first riseth and setteth last: all which skill in stars being convenient for shepherds to know, as Theocritus and the rest use [Theocritus, *Idylls*, 7. 52–3, 13. 25–6, 24. 10–11].

86] **raging seas**) the cause of the swelling and ebbing of the sea cometh of the course of the moon, sometime increasing, sometime waning and decreasing.

87] **sooth of birds**) a kind of soothsaying used in elder times which they gathered by the flying of birds: first (as is said) invented by the Tuscans and from them derived to the Romans, who (as is said in Livy) were so superstitiously rooted in the same that they agreed that every nobleman should put his son to the Tuscans, by them to be brought up in that knowledge [Livy 9. 36. 3–4 and, more precisely, Cicero, *De divinatione*, 1. 41. 92].

88] **of herbs**) that wondrous things be wrought by herbs as well appeareth by the common working of them in our bodies as also by the wonderful enchantments and sorceries that have been wrought by them: insomuch that it is said that Circe (a famous sorceress) turned men into sundry kinds of beasts and monsters, and only by herbs, as the poet saith: *Dea saeva potentibus herbis, etc* ['the savage goddess through powerful herbs': Virgil, *Aeneid*, 7. 19].

92] **kiddest**) knewest [a mediaevalism glossed as recently as 1570: *OED* kithe *v* B 4].

97–8] **Thus is my**) the third part, wherein is set forth his ripe years as an untimely harvest that bringeth little fruit.

99] **ear**) of corn.

Textual note

Gloss 97–8. Thus is] corrected by Todd 1805 from the text; quartos and F read This is.

100] **scathe**) loss, hindrance [*OED*'s post-mediaeval pre-Spenserian examples are Scottish: scathe *sb* 2a].
109] **The fragrant flowers**) sundry studies and laudable parts of learning wherein how our poet is seen, be they witness which are privy to his study.
112] **ever among**) ever and anon [from time to time: *OED* among B 2; scarce archaic usage].
127] **So now my year**) the last part, wherein is described his age by comparison of wintry storms.
133] **care-full cold**) for care is said to cool the blood.
135] **hoary frost**) a metaphor of hoary hairs scattered like to a grey frost.
139] **glee**) mirth [*February* 224 and *May* 282 glosses].
148] **breme**) sharp and bitter [*February* 43 gloss].
151] **Adieu, delights**) is a conclusion of all, where, in six verses, he comprehendeth briefly all that was touched in this book: in the first verse his delights of youth generally; in the second, the love of Rosalind; in the third, the keeping of sheep (which is the argument of all eglogues); in the fourth, his complaints; and in the last two his professed friendship and good will to his good friend Hobbinol.

Emblem.

The meaning whereof is that all things perish and come to their last end, but works of learned wits and monuments of poetry abide for ever. And therefore Horace of his *Odes* (a work though full indeed of great wit and learning, yet of no so great weight and importance) boldly saith:

> *Exegi monumentum aere perennius,*
> *Quod nec imber nec aquilo vorax, etc.*

[misquoting *Odes*, 3. 30. 1 and 3: *nec* for *non* and *vorax* for *impotens* ('I have completed a monument more lasting than bronze ... which neither pelting rain nor ravenous north wind [can destroy])']. Therefore let not be envied that this poet in his Epilogue saith he hath made a Calendar that shall endure as long as time, etc., following the example of Horace and Ovid in the like:

> *Grande opus exegi quod nec Iovis ira nec ignis,*
> *Nec ferrum poterit nec edax abolere vetustas, etc.*

[slightly misquoting *Metamorphoses*, 15. 871–2 by transposing *ferrum* and *poterit*: 'I have completed a great work which neither Jove's anger nor fire nor sword nor devouring time can erase'].

Textual notes

Emblem, Horace quote: *Quod*] Q3; quae Q1–2.
Ovid quote: *ferrum*] Q3; ferum Q1–2.

[Epilogue]

With the same number of syllables per line as it has lines (12 × 12, the calendrical number), the poem conforms to the prescription for a 'square' poem, the figure itself signifying constancy and firmness: '[because] for his own stay and firmity [the square] requireth none other base than himself...so is [he] for his inconcussible [unshakeable] steadiness likened to the earth': Puttenham (1589) 2. 11. Spenser thus affirms the moral steadfastness of *SC* through a symbol that expresses its rootedness in pastoral and georgic (from Greek *gē* = earth) traditions. By conjoining it with *SC*'s overall circular structure (*December* headnote) Spenser suggests that he has 'squared the circle' (an impossibility mathematically until the discovery of Pi).

> Lo, I have made a *Calendar* for every year
> That steel in strength and Time in durance shall outwear.
> And if I marked well the stars' revolution,
>   It shall continue till the world's dissolution
> To teach the ruder shepherd how to feed his sheep,   5
> And from the falser's fraud his folded flock to keep.
>   Go, little *Calendar*, thou hast a free passport;
> Go but a lowly gait amongst the meaner sort:
> Dare not to match thy pipe with Tityrus his style,
>   Nor with the pilgrim that the ploughman played awhile,   10

2–4. *steel . . . dissolution*: cf. Horace and Ovid as cited in *December* emblem gloss. Heninger 1989: 316–19 comments on the use here of the topos of astronomy as an aid to understanding God.

5. *teach . . . sheep*: alludes to the instruction within the ecclesiastical eclogues and to *SC* as a manifesto for the humanist revolution in English poetry. Cf. John 10: 1–16.

7. *Go*: cf. *SC*'s dedicatory poem, 1 and n. *passport*: a sixteenth-century word with various meanings: (1) document granting safe passage in foreign lands; (2) dismissal; (3) permit for paupers etc. to beg alms (*OED* passport *sb* 1).

9. *Tityrus . . . style*: Chaucer's (*June* 81 gloss) or Virgil's (*October* 55 gloss) literary mannerisms, etc. with an etymological pun on *stylus* = writing/incising implement (*OED* style *sb* I. 1, II. 13).

10. *pilgrim . . . ploughman*: alluding to the pseudo-Chaucerian *Pilgrim's Tale* and *Plowman's Tale* (both reformist works), with hints of Langland's *Piers Plowman*, the origin of the 'plowman' tradition: Norbrook 1984: 43, 59–60 and *May* headnote.

But follow them far off, and their high steps adore.
The better please, the worse despise: I ask no more.

Merce non mercede.

---

11. *follow . . . adore*: echoing Chaucer's *Troilus* envoy, 1791–2: 'And kiss the steps, where as thou seest pace/Virgil, Ovid, Homer, Lucan, and Stace [Statius]' (Miller 1988: 43).
13. *Merce non mercede:* 'for [just] reward, not bribe' (Latin; particularly applicable to a politically sensitive work); or 'grace [mercy], not wages' (Italian). Other suggestions are: 'for reward, not for hire' (Latin; Maclean and Prescott 1993: 542n, but see Kennedy in *SpE*, p. 654) and '[judge] by the goods, not the price' (Latin; Cain in Oram *et al.* 1989: 213n).

Amoretti and Epithalamion

Written not long since by Edmund Spenser

Headnote

Entered in the Stationers' Register 19 November 1594, the volume *Amoretti and Epithalamion. Written not long since by Edmunde Spenser*, published in a small octavo volume by William Ponsonby in 1595, comprises four sections: (1) dedicatory epistle from Ponsonby to Sir Robert Needham and two dedicatory sonnets to Spenser; (2) 89 *Amoretti* sonnets (their title is Italian for 'little loves' in allusion to Cupid, the infant god of love, who was frequently understood as not one but many to symbolise the various erotic desires of men: Philostratus, *Imagines*, 1. 6); (3) 4 'anacreontic' poems (see 2 below); (4) *Epithalamion*. It is now generally agreed that the volume celebrates Spenser's courtship of, and marriage to, his second wife, Elizabeth Boyle (for details see *Var* 2: 631–8, 647–52).

1. *Amoretti*

Criticism has traditionally found the sonnet sequence difficult to handle: what, simply, does one say about apparently random accumulations of individual lyric utterances? Critical reactions to Francesco Petrarca's (Petrarch's) 366 *Rime sparse* (or *Canzoniere*), completed by the mid-1350s and the inspirational model for subsequent sequences (itself inspired by Dante's *Vita nuova*), provide an answer. The *Rime* chart, first, Petrarch's love for Laura from the moment he fell in love with her one Good Friday to her death on Easter Sunday some twenty-one years later (*Rime*, 1–263); and, second, his relationship with her after her death (*Rime*, 264–366; an inscription on the flyleaf of Petrarch's copy of Virgil gives dates and some supplementary information: Durling 1976: 5–6). Clearly, the *Rime* invited biographical speculation, and Giacomo Colonna, a friend of Petrarch, set the ball rolling by doubting whether Laura ever existed and suggesting she was merely a symbol. Later commentators affirmed and further probed the autobiographical status of the *Rime* while also developing a tradition of allegorical readings which included the application of neo-Platonic schemes to the poems' imagery. The *Rime* thus emerged as precisely-focused statements about the poet's relationship with God, beauty, intellect, appetite, and so on.

In similar fashion Spenser's earlier critics, like those of Sidney's *Astrophil and Stella* (1591 but written some eight to ten years earlier) and Shakespeare's *Sonnets* (1609), tended to scrutinise *Am* for the autobiographical detail it (supposedly) conceals (an approach often combined with source-hunting). Equally, *Am* was (and to some extent still is) read as a neo-Platonic structure charting the lover's attainment of, and failure to attain, recognition of his beloved as a manifestation of divine Beauty (Bhattacherje 1935 and Casady 1941; important modifications of our understanding of Spenser's relationship with neo-Platonism have subsequently been offered by, among others, Ellrodt 1960; Nelson 1963; Hankins 1971; Quitslund 1973; Hyde 1986; Bieman 1988; Gibbs 1990. See also Quitslund in *SpE*, pp 546–8 and *Four Hymns* headnote.) Broadly speaking, the neo-Platonism in *Am* falls within the ideologies manifested in Ficino 1944 and Book 4 of Baldassare Castiglione's influential courtesy book *Il Cortegiano* (*The Courtier*; 1528, English translation 1561), though it probably also results from Spenser's indebtedness to the Italian sonneteer Torquato Tasso (1544–95), himself a Platonist writer: Scott 1927; Kostić 1959.

My notes signal those individual sonnets obviously demonstrating the influence of neo-Platonic doctrines of love (they include *Am* 1, 3, 7, 10, 11, 26, 35, 39, 40, 45, 61, 72, 79, 81, 88). But to limit one's understanding of *Am*'s neo-Platonism to its love-content is, we have realised for some time now, too restrictive. As a way of explaining the world and its relation, mediated by the human intellect, to the deity, neo-Platonism was a complete symbolic system that saw the effects of the divine percolating through angels, constellations, planets, plants, and music (to list but a few). Thus *Am*'s numerology (see below) belongs to that system, and so does much of its imagery: the rose of *Am* 64. 6 signifies transience and the fragility of love; but as the flower of Venus it also signifies love as the manifestation of the procreative urge (Plato's and neo-Platonism's earthly Venus or Aphrodite Pandemos) and/or as the manifestation of our longing to be at one with the divine (Plato's Aphrodite Ourania, or Heavenly Venus). Hence in the notes the reader will discover, more so than is the case with *SC* (for Spenser's interest in Platonism increased with that of his contemporaries as well as reflecting the ideological commitment of his individual works), attempts to explain *Am*'s symbolic coding not just through references to contemporary emblematists but through references to Agrippa 1651 (the English translation of the work of a celebrated – even notorious – early sixteenth-century 'occult philosopher' who combined numerological, astrological, medical, animal and plant lore, together with the Jewish mystical interpretative tradition known as cabbala, and angelology, into what is in many ways a typical neo-Platonic mix). I also invoke Wind 1967 – an exemplary textbook on Renaissance neo-Platonic mysteries that is the best single introduction to that aspect of the period. Simply, *Am*'s very fabric is neo-Platonic because neo-Platonism lay at the root of much learned contemporary thought, especially that of the Sidney circle with which Spenser was at least briefly in direct touch. (Sidney combined firm Protestantism with a considerable interest in Platonism. On the relationship, see Robertson in *SpE*, pp. 656–7 and Waller in *SpE*, pp. 658–9.)

Yet Spenser reveals himself in *Am* – as Sidney and Shakespeare do in their sonnets – to be a ludic pragmatist. If he echoes Petrarch with an eye on the neo-Platonising commentators, he can also deconstruct neo-Platonic attitudinising with considerable glee: the reader is never fully sure how serious Spenser is because his narrating *persona* is so aware of the essential ludicrousness of the rituals of courtship and the contemporary vocabulary that the Petrarchan/neo-Platonic vogue demanded for it. Is *Am* 88 serious neo-Platonism or not? And what about 76 and 77, those companion blazons on his beloved's body, the first of which undermines the neo-Platonic code-word 'ravish'; the second of which, despite its allegorising of myth, fruit and precious materials, expresses all too plainly a zeal to manhandle that body with lascivious physicality?

Protestantism provides another major component of *Am*'s thinking (King 1990). Though in the post-Reformation English Church marriage was no longer a sacrament, it may have assumed increasing significance as a repudiation of Roman Catholicism's commitment to monasticism and a celibate priesthood (the evidence is, however, conflicting, and it is certainly true that Elizabeth's failure to marry and her strong objection to clerical marriage still tended to privilege the celibate ideal: Dubrow (1990) ch 1). Whatever the theoretical position, we miss much of *Am*'s underlying seriousness if we fail to appreciate that the bride and bridegroom of the Reformation English Church were instructed that their relationship replicated not only Adam and Eve's in paradise but that between Christ and his Church as well: 'matrimony . . . signif[ies] unto us the mystical union that is bewixt Christ and his Church' (Marriage Service in *Prayer-book* 1559: 122). The notes direct attention to *Am*'s many echoes of the Service (they begin in sonnet 1 with a reference to the wedding ring). And, too, the various puns on *will* evoke the controversies engendered by the Reformation over the freedom of human will, just as the lover's doubts that he merits his mistress's love recall the Calvinistic assurance that one cannot earn divine grace – it is either bestowed, or not (e.g., *Am* 10, 38, 41, 46, 48, 69, 84).

Thus *Am* celebrates courtship (sonnets 1–67), betrothal (68–89), and marriage (*Epith*) as a triad that emulates, like the dance of the three Graces, humanity's relationship, through love, with God. Yet the lover-poet knows that marriage involves compromises of individual liberty and (male) fantasies of capture (e.g., 67), as well as misogyny (e.g., 2, 53). For if Spenser is the first English poet to address a sonnet sequence to his bride (thereby reversing the convention that the beloved should be unattainable by being already married, as is the case with Petrarch and Sidney), he was also awesomely aware of the power base upon which marriage was built.

Most recently, critics have concentrated on the spatial structure of the sonnet sequence. In the case of *Am*, the pioneer was Dunlop 1969, 1970, who discovered that *Am* was structured (like Petrarch's *Rime*, only more precisely) in accordance with numerological principles derived from the church calendar for the period from Ash Wednesday (the beginning of Lent) to Easter Sunday. Specifically, Dunlop demonstrated that *Am* follows a scheme derived from the liturgical calendar for 1594: *Am* 62 marks the new year beginning on 25 March; each sonnet following signifies a day leading to the Easter Day sonnet, 68

(Easter Sunday was on 31 March in 1594). Counting backwards (one day per sonnet) to 22 ('This holy season, fit to fast and pray') we reach 13 February, the day on which Ash Wednesday was celebrated in 1594. Overall, this yields the symmetrical (chiastic) scheme: 21 sonnets (1–21); 47 sonnets (22–68, the Lent–Easter sequence); 21 sonnets (69–89).

Whereas Dunlop was content to describe the structure of *Am* alone, however, his successors have emphasised its place in a structural scheme that includes the anacreontic verses and *Epith*. Noting that sonnets 35 and 83 are identical, and including the anacreontics and *Epith*, Fowler 1970 modified the symmetry as follows: 34 + 1 (*Am* 35) + 47 (36–82) + 1 (*Am* 83) + 34 (i.e., 6 (sonnets 84–89) + 4 anacreontics + 24 (the stanza total of *Epith*)). Furthermore, argued Fowler, *Am*'s total of 89 sonnets represents the winter quarter of the year (89 days according to Renaissance authorities); a total which, when the 4 anacreontics are added, becomes 93, the number of days in the spring quarter. *Epith*, naturally enough, encodes summer, its stanzas being subdivided by short lines into a total of 92 long-line sections, 92 being the number of days in the summer quarter (Fowler 1970: 167). (Liturgical echoes have been pursued by Johnson 1974; Kaske 1977; Larson (edition as yet unpublished, but see King 1990: 165); the numerology has been questioned and refined by Brown 1973; Hieatt 1973; Hunter 1975; Kaske 1978; Thompson 1985; Loewenstein 1990; Kaske 1990; Fukuda 1991.)

Fukuda has made the crucial additional discovery that the *Am* sonnets are paired in precise ways in the original, 1595, volume: printed one per page, sonnet 1 stands alone, while 2 and 3 face each other (and so on through the volume). Thus 58 and 59 (the assurance sonnets) confront each other in mirror fashion, as do the name and name-erasure sonnets 74–5. We may add that the links are closer in the later part of the sequence, which suggests that the pairings are designed to reflect the increasing closeness of the sequence's subject-pair, the lover and his beloved. On structure (numerological and otherwise) in Renaissance sonnet sequences as a whole, see Fowler 1970; Webster 1981; Roche 1989.

Am is, then, a sequence charting courtship patterned according to a numerological–calendrical *schema* that simultaneously relates courtship and betrothal to the winter, spring (and, together with *Epith*, summer) seasons as well as to that part of the liturgical calendar that concerns fasting, penitence and rebirth. (Brown 1973 adds a lunar *schema* deriving from the epactal number for 1594, 18, as given in the *Prayer-book*'s calendar.) Interwoven throughout are myths, allusions and echoes relating the lover and his beloved to the bride and bridegroom of the Song of Solomon; to such avatars of love and self-love as Orpheus and Narcissus; and to the certainties and fragilities of Protestant humanism (the belief that God is good and approachable and his love manifest in our earthly power to love; all of which is undercut by the Calvinist certainty that he is forbidding and unknowable and that we can never merit grace. Hence, when one's beloved frowns and rejects, this is an emblem of one's vulnerability to damnation.)

Finally, there is the elusive matter of the relation of *Am* to external politics (e.g., Marotti 1982; Hazard 1987). Spenser interrupted the composition of *FQ* (*Am* 33, 80) in order to produce his sequence, permitting private love to supersede affirmation of public love for his monarch. Yet his private beloved was also called Elizabeth (*Am* 74); so that *Am*'s constant reiteration of distance and desire somehow mimes the relationship between Spenser and his queen, with the poet again seeking favour, sometimes being granted it, yet potentially (like his friend Ralegh) under threat of disfavour. Therefore *Am*'s author compensates by creating, controlling, vituperating, adoring and (textually) mastering his beloved, fantasising as he does so about both Elizabeths. The Cynthia who peeps in at the window on the marriage night (*Epith*, 372–7) is the monarch in one of her celebrated guises, nosily busying herself in matters that shouldn't concern her, jokingly manipulated and domesticated into the moon's other roles of patroness of virginity about-to-be-lost and of childbirth, the seeds of which are about to be sown. Similarly, the waves that wash away the inscribed name 'Elizabeth' in *Am* 75 are at once an image of temporal process and an assertion of authorial power to erase the mightiest name in the land – to achieve in script and on paper an act of unnaming that compensates for the months and years spent creating Queen Elizabeth through the fictions of the *FQ*. Thus, the queen is one of the 'baser things' destined 'to die in dust' in this sonnet, and Elizabeth Boyle is the woman destined to live eternally in her lover's verse. This sonnet will surprise those who thought that Donne was the first Elizabethan to undermine convention with egotistical and politically-barbed wit.

2. [Anacreontics]

This is the title now given by editors to the verses that mediate between *Am* and *Epith* in the original editions. The verses were untitled in the original and unnumbered, 1 and 2 being printed on the verso of *Am* 89, with 3 facing 1 and 2 on the recto of the next page. The stanzas that comprise 4 are printed one per page, like the *Am* sonnets, starting on the verso of 3. Following the practice of many previous editors, I have treated 4 as a separate longer poem. Note that 1 has a unique rhyme scheme; that 2 and 3 share a rhyme scheme; and that the stanzas comprising 4 also share a (different) rhyme scheme. The poems imitate the light-hearted, frequently mythopoeic, vein of odes attributed to the sixth-century B.C. Greek poet Anacreon (60 in number, they were discovered in 1549 by Henri Estienne, who published the Greek text, with Latin translation of 31 of them, at Paris in 1554). Estienne's friend, Ronsard, wrote imitations, and anacreontics (as a metrical or, as in Spenser's case, thematic exercise) soon became something of a vogue (Hutton 1941a, 1941b repr. 1980; Levarie 1973). Like Spenser, Shakespeare appends anacreontics as a coda to his sonnet sequence; and as with the case of Shakespeare, critics have traditionally remained dismissive of their function or validity, immune as the poems are to obvious psychological or (auto)biographical readings. (Exceptions include Cummings 1971; Kaske 1978; Miola 1980; Warkentin in *SpE*, pp 34–5.)

In the case of *Am* the verses revise, in a mythological mode, the preceding sonnets' preoccupations with love's pain, bitter-sweetness, and the Venerean/Dianan beauty of the beloved, as well as offering a light-hearted interlude between *Am*'s desolate end and *Epith*'s dark and solitary beginning. They also serve to emphasise (by contrast) *Am*'s liturgical underpinning and mediate between it and the Graeco-Roman formulae utilised in *Epith*; so that Spenser's volume *Amoretti and Epithalamion* offers a taxonomy of contemporary modes of describing and analysing love, Petrarchan, neo-Platonic, biblical, Christian, anacreontic–pagan and emblematic–psychological all contributing their part. The focus of the verses is, of course, Cupid – the one, ultimate, *amoretto* or 'little Love'; a baby who acts as midwife to the marriage celebrated in *Epith* and anticipates the hoped-for infant offspring of Elizabeth and Spenser themselves.

3. *Epithalamion*

The title is Spenser's Graeco–Latin form from Latin *epithalamium*, itself derived from Greek *epithalamos* = [song sung] before the bridal chamber (originally only one of several songs sung at successive stages of the wedding day). *Epith* celebrates Spenser's marriage to Elizabeth Boyle possibly at Cork, Kilcolman, or Youghal (see *Var* 2. 647–52) on St Barnabas's Day, 11 June 1594. The day coincided in the Old Style calendar with the longest day or summer solstice (see *Epith* 265–6n). Formally the poem is a *canzone*; thematically it marks the culmination of the courtship charted in *Am* by celebrating the Protestant ideal of marriage and married love. Hence *Epith* rewrites its classical antecedents and contemporary Continental analogues (both neo-Latin and vernacular) and the prescriptions for epithalamia offered, for example, by Julius Caesar Scaliger, *Poetics*, 3. 101 (the chapter has been translated by Jackson Bryce in Dubrow 1990: 271–96), or, less learnedly, Puttenham 1589: the pagan world is there, but assimilated, in accordance with Renaissance syncretistic practice, into that of Protestant Christianity. For Spenser, marriage is not a matter of reluctantly abandoning your boy lover and an excuse for spinning multiple fescennine (bawdy) jokes (Catullus, 61. 122–6; Scaliger tr. Bryce, p. 275); neither is his epithalamion sung to cover 'the shrieking and outcry of the young damsel' as her lover makes his assault on her (Puttenham (1589), 1. 26). Marriage is, rather, the result of mutual choice and love, the re-enactment of the paradisal state and thus literally a state of pleasure (*Am* 76. 3n; *Epith* 392n). It also gives Spenser the power to overgo Orpheus, the archetypal poet whose own bride died on her wedding day (*Epith* 16n). To affirm his view of marriage's – and *his* marriage's – supreme place in the universal scheme, Spenser devised an elaborate and essentially original structural pattern for his poem: *Am* had celebrated courtship through Lenten–Easter patterns; *Epith* symbolises at once the wedding day on the longest (solstitial) day, and the solar year. For, as Hieatt 1960 brilliantly demonstrated, its 24 stanzas correspond to the hours of Spenser's wedding day; its short lines mark the passing of the quarter hours; its total of long lines (365) corresponds to the number of days in the solar year; the change from positive to negative refrain in stanza 17, preluded as it is by the announcement 'Now night is come' at the stanza's quarter point, marks the duration of daylight hours – $16\frac{1}{4}$ – on the wedding day (this is the figure given for the latitude nearest to southern Ireland in handbooks available to Spenser). The remaining stanzas and a fraction ($7\frac{3}{4}$) mark the number of night hours. (For modifications to these and Hieatt's other findings – particularly his argument that the poem's stanzas are paired 1/13; 2/14, etc. in order to symbolise the sidereal hours – see Hieatt 1961; Welsford 1967; Fowler 1970; Eade 1972.) Additional symmetries worth noting here are (1) the poem's recessed (chiastic) stanzaic structure, outlined by Wickert 1968 as follows: 1 / 3 / 4 / 3 // 2 // 3 / 4 / 3 / 1 (this makes the actual wedding ceremony at the altar at stanzas

12–13 a central, triumphal, focus); and (2) Fowler's reminder that the ratio between the 16 day and 8 night stanzas – 2:1 – marks the relationship of reason to concupiscence according to the Renaissance neo-Platonist Pico della Mirandola (Fowler 1970: 159–60; marriage was ordained in part 'for a remedy against sin and to avoid fornication': *Prayer-book* 1559: 122).

Epith's classical sources include Catullus, 61, 62, 64; Statius, *Epithalamium in honour of Stella and Violentilla* (*Thebaid*, 1. 2); Claudian, *Epithalamium of Honorius and Maria* and *Epithalamium of Palladius and Celerina* (*Epith* shows no apparent awareness of Theocritus, *Idyll* 18); Renaissance vernacular and neo-Latin precedents include poems by Gioviano Pontano, Francesco Giorgio, Giovanni Battista Marino, Marc-Claude de Buttet, Joachim Du Bellay, George Buchanan and Philip Sidney (whose epithalamium 'Let mother Earth' appeared in the *Arcadia*, third eclogues). These antecedent epithalamia were, however, for the most part written for royalty and the aristocracy: Spenser's marriage belongs to a different social stratum, and in his appropriation of the epithalamic genre he anticipates seventeenth-century gestures towards its democratisation.

For a survey of influences and precedents, see McPeek 1936; Greene 1957; also McPeek, J. A. S. 1939 *Catullus in Strange and Distant Britain*, Harvard U.P., Cambridge, Mass. Outstanding modern studies of the genre are: Tufte 1970; Schenck 1988; Dubrow 1990. A gloss on the ceremonies Spenser describes can be found in Ben Jonson, *Hymenaei* (1606) and his copious notes to it (in Orgel, S. (ed.) 1969 *Complete Masques*), supplemented by Gordon, D. J. 1945 '*Hymenaei*: Ben Jonson's Masque of Union', *Journal of the Warburg and Courtauld Institutes* 8: 107–45.

4. Orphic Footnote

I have referred to 'Orpheus' in the preceding pages, and in the notes to *SC*, as the poet of Graeco-Roman mythology. However, he was equally important in Renaissance neo-Platonic thought as the founder of the ancient mystery religion known as Orphism. I shall first explain the term, and then suggest ways in which Orphism may have influenced *Am* and *Epith*. This will provide a background for the footnotes that accompany these texts.

Orphism is the philosophy contained in the extant writings – especially the *Hymns* and Orphic *Argonautica* – that were supposedly written by Orpheus as the founder of a mystery religion based on his descent to Hades to regain Eurydice and the arcane knowledge that was revealed to him there. The first manuscript of the Orphic texts reached the west from Constantinople in 1423; the first printed edition (containing the *Hymns* and Orphic *Argonautica*) was published in 1500, to be followed by five more editions by 1600 (including one – Paris 1566 – by the Estienne we have encountered in connection with the anacreontics): see Wind (1967) Introduction; *Thomas Taylor* 1969: 198–205; Friedman 1970; Athanassakis 1977; Vian 1987; Brown in *SpE*, pp 519–20. Spenser's association of himself with Orpheus the poet is well known (Cain 1971). However, the possibility that he was interested in the literature of the Orphic mysteries has so far remained unexplored, despite hints in Bieman 1988: 147–9 and Brooks-Davies in *SpE*, pp 485–7.

The *Hymns* address various deities, supplicating their blessing and influence (as such, they mesh readily with the practices of Renaissance white magic or 'occult philosophy': see Walker 1953, 1958, 1972; Shumaker 1972; Yates 1978, 1979). Awareness of their content, and of the general aura of Renaissance Orphism that Spenser – as a poet absorbed by the philosophies of love and keen to prove himself a leading English poet aware of all modern movements and areas of knowledge – can be supposed to have been alert to, provokes the following reading of the *Am–Epith* volume:

Spenser, through Orphically blind Cupid (*Am* 8), explores the psychological and philosophical consequences of human love asking, essentially, how it relates to divine love. What makes *Am* more than incidentally Orphic is its Cupid symbolism: the fact that each sonnet is, as it were, a darting Cupid (*amoretto*) embodying a struggle between darkness and light and reaching out, through frustration and bafflement, to understanding and illumination. Moreover, *Am* develops to the point of betrothal, yet proceeds to stress uncertainty, fragmentation, and failure to reach illumination, until it climaxes in agonised separation and solitude (*Am* 86–9), a mood remembered at the beginning of *Epith* with the statement that the poet will sing 'unto [him]self alone'. Now, since this statement is preceded by an allusion to Orpheus and his bride, it seems that we are to link the references to solitude to Orpheus's own after Eurydice was killed on their wedding day by a snake bite (see *Epith* 10, 16, 17, 18nn) – a snake already recalled, by implication at least, at the opening of *Am* 86 ('Venomous tongue, tipped with vile adder's sting'). Then, in *Am* 88, the lover 'wander[s] as in darkness of the night' – but, we are to infer, without the illumination that should, in Orphic thought, lie at the heart of night (see *Epith* 315–27n).

The anacreontics follow. Their main character is again blind Cupid, who enacts a symbolic ritual of reunion through the neo-Platonic/Orphic idea of love's bitter-sweetness (honey and bee sting: see Wind (1967) ch. 10) as a preparation for *Epith*, the first stanza of which marks a return to the solitary Orphic poet who then proceeds to sing reunion into existence through a wedding that, despite its echoes of ancient epithalamia and its strong Protestant flavour, is also an Orphic mystery. Prepared for by various clues (the naming of Orpheus, the invocations of the Hours and Graces, etc.: see *Epith* 10–18nn and 98–102, 103nn), the Orphic rationale becomes dominant with the advent of Night (to whom Orphic *Hymn* 3 is addressed). This is succeeded by the roll-call of evil spirits, inauspicious Hadean birds, etc. (st. 19), which suggests on the one hand the exorcism of the folk fear of the dark and, on the other, a landscape of death – a death beyond which the lovers will unite (in Renaissance Orphism love was equated with Night and Death because only through dying to imperfection could the perfect union of love be achieved: Wind (1967) ch 10.) But note Spenser's joke: he and his bride enjoy an ecstatic *physical* union, not an Orphic post-mortem one. So that, although the three figures invoked in st. 20 – Silence, Peace, Sleep – were all, like Night, central to Orphic ritual and thus contribute to the poem's Orphic cast (*Epith* 353, 354, 355nn), we sense that Spenser's handling of the Orphic mystery of Eros and Death is, in the end, even more jesting than Shakespeare's in *Romeo and Juliet*. And yet it is also much more serious. For his Orphic invocations are deeply personal and heartfelt charms against the unthinkable horror of the first Orpheus who was left alone to mourn after his wedding but before the wedding night.

It may be worth concluding by remarking that *Epith*'s frequent use of the Song of Songs (in which it complements *Am*, itself full of echoes of the Song: e.g., *Am* 64, 65, 67, 70, 77; *Epith* 23–5, 74–8, 167nn, etc.) is consonant with the Orphic reading offered here, since the Song was read by, for example, Pico della Mirandola as an ecstatic expression of Solomon's desire for union with the divine (Wind 1967: 155 and n).

5. Verse forms

The sonnet was a thirteenth-century invention with a fairly complex history, particularly in Italy, where Petrarch may be considered, for our purposes here, the main practitioner. The Petrarchan sonnet was divided into a group of eight lines (octet) rhyming abbaabba, followed by a group of six (sestet) typically rhyming cdecde (the pattern varies but never includes a rhyming couplet). English antecedents for *Am*, usually with the iambic pentameter line as their norm, include the sonnets by Wyatt and Surrey, the latter having established what became known as the 'Shakespearean' sonnet, with its three linked quatrains and terminal couplet rhyming: abab cdcd efef gg.

This was a favourite form with Elizabethan practitioners of the sonnet long after Surrey's death in 1547 and the publication of his and Wyatt's lyrics in *Tottel's Miscellany* (1557). Of the best-known of the sequences that emerged from the sonnet vogue that followed the publication of Philip Sidney's *Astrophil and Stella* in 1591, Samuel Daniel's *Delia* (1592) adheres to it throughout, as does Michael Drayton in *Idea's Mirror* (1594), and Fulke Greville in *Caelica* (written in the 1590s though not published complete until 1633). Sidney himself had preferred the Petrarchan form (with occasional modifications), while Henry Constable in *Diana* (1592) had adopted variants of the Petrarchan pattern on the lines of: abba acca dedeff.

Spenser didn't invent the form he uses in *Am* (abab bcbc cdcd ee, the quatrains being interlinked in a manner reminiscent of the rhyme-royal stanza (see *Four Hymns* headnote)). Nevertheless, he is its most skilful and celebrated practitioner. It should also be noted that, although there appears to be no precedent for a sequence concluded by an epithalamion, the sonnet sequence as practised by Sidney, Greville and others – including Shakespeare himself – was a mixed affair: *Astrophil and Stella* is interspersed with songs, as was *Caelica*; Shakespeare's sonnets (probably written in the late 1590s even though not published until 1609) end with anacreontics.

Epith, like *Proth*, has a stanzaic structure that derives from the Italian and Provençal *canzone*: a fairly long poem with stanzas of varying length (from seven to twenty lines in Petrarch's examples of the form), each stanza divided into three parts, the first two similar, the last dissimilar. The poem ended with a short *commiato*, or envoy-stanza, and there was no set rhyme-scheme or metre. While *Proth* uses an eighteen-line stanza throughout, the stanza length of *Epith* varies slightly (seventeen to eighteen lines, excluding the one-line refrain) and, unlike *Proth*, it has a *commiato* (of seven lines). *Epith* is metrically variable, too, with the basic iambic pentameter unit interrupted by the three symmetrically-spaced short (trimeter) lines per stanza and the refrain's alexandrine (the twelve-beat line familiar from French sixteenth-century verse). It would, however, be misleading to refer *Epith* and *Proth* to the *canzone* without mentioning that the *canzone* is a close relative of the ode; for in the end it is a moot point whether Spenser's two poems should be called *canzoni* or odes. (An ode is, briefly, a ceremonious lyric of considerable length with an elaborate stanza structure of varying line totals and line lengths.) In addition, *Epith* and *Proth* are influenced by ancient epithalamia (see 3. *Epithalamion* above, and the footnotes to *Epith*). It is to Catullus 61 and 62, specifically, that Spenser is indebted to the idea of refrains in marriage songs: the device is foreign to both *canzone* and ode. For a fuller description, see *SpE*, pp 662–5 (Warkentin on *sonnet, sonnet sequences*) and pp 710–13 (Woods on *versification*).

Select bibliography

Note: this is a bibliography of works cited in short form in *Am–Epith* headnote and notes to the texts; works already listed under *SC* General headnote bibliography are excluded. As with *SC*, a supplementary bibliography of recommended reading will be found at the end of the volume.

Batman, S. 1577 *The Golden Book of the Leaden Gods*. London
Bhattacherje, M. 1935 *Platonic Ideas in Spenser*. London
Bieman, E. 1988 *Plato Baptized: Towards the Interpretation of Spenser's Mimetic Fictions*. Toronto, Buffalo and London
Braden, G. 1986 'Beyond Frustration: Petrarchan Laurels in the Seventeenth Century'. *SEL: Studies in English Literature, 1500–1900* 26: 5–23
Brown, J. N. 1973 '"Lyke Phoebe": Lunar Numerical and Calendrical Patterns in Spenser's *Amoretti*'. *Gypsy Scholar* 1: 5–15
Campbell, G. 1987 '"The Crab Behind His Back": Astrology in Spenser's *Epithalamion*'. *Notes and Queries* 232: 200–1
Casady, E. 1941 'The Neo-Platonic Ladder in Spenser's *Amoretti*'. *Philological Quarterly* 20: 284–95
Castiglione, B. 1986 *The Book of the Courtier* (tr. G. Bull). Harmondsworth, Middlesex
Cummings, R. M. (ed.) 1971 *Spenser: The Critical Heritage*. London
DeNeef, A. L. 1982 *Spenser and the Motives of Metaphor*. Durham, North Carolina
Doob, P. R. 1990 *The Idea of the Labyrinth from Classical Antiquity through the Middle Ages*. Ithaca and London
Dubrow, H. 1990 *A Happier Eden: The Politics of Marriage in the Stuart Epithalamium*. Ithaca and London
Dunlop, A. 1969 'Calendar Symbolism in the "Amoretti"'. *Notes and Queries* 214: 24–6
Dunlop, A. 1970 'The Unity of Spenser's *Amoretti*'. In *Silent Poetry: Essays in Numerological Analysis* (ed. A. Fowler). London, pp. 116–40
Eade, J. C. 1972 'The Pattern in the Astronomy of Spenser's *Epithalamion*'. *Review of English Studies* n.s. 23: 173–8
Eade, J. C. 1984 *The Forgotten Sky: A Guide to Astrology in English Literature*. Oxford
Edwards, C. R. 1977 'The Narcissus Myth in Spenser's Poetry'. *Studies in Philology* 74: 63–88

Ellrodt, R. 1960 *Neoplatonism in the Poetry of Edmund Spenser* Travaux d'Humanisme et Renaissance 35. Geneva
Ferguson, G. 1961 *Signs and Symbols in Christian Art*. New York
Ficino, M. 1944 *Commentary on Plato's 'Symposium'* (tr. and ed. S. R. Jayne). The University of Missouri Studies 19. Columbia, Missouri
Freccero, J. 1975 'The Fig Tree and the Laurel: Petrarch's Poetics'. *Diacritics* 5: 35–40
Friedman, J. B. 1970 *Orpheus in the Middle Ages*. Cambridge, Mass
Fukuda, S. 1991 'The Numerological Patterning of *Amoretti and Epithalamion*'. *Spenser Studies: A Renaissance Poetry Annual* 9 (1988): 33–48
Gibbs, D. 1990 *Spenser's 'Amoretti': A Critical Study*. Aldershot, Hampshire
Greene, T. M. 1957 'Spenser and the Epithalamic Convention'. *Comparative Literature* 9: 215–28
Hankins, J. E. 1971 *Source and Meaning in Spenser's Allegory: A Study of 'The Faerie Queene'*. Oxford
Hardison, O. B. 1972 '*Amoretti* and the *Dolce Stil N[u]ovo*'. *English Literary Renaissance* 2: 208–16
Hazard, M. E. 1987 'Absent Presence and Present Absence: Cross-Couple Convention in Elizabethan Culture'. *Texas Studies in Literature and Language* 29: 1–27
Helgerson, R. 1986 'The Land Speaks: Cartography, Chorography, and Subversion in Renaissance England'. In *Representing the English Renaissance* (ed. S. Greenblatt 1988). Berkeley, Los Angeles and London, pp. 327–61
Heninger, S. K. Jr 1977 *The Cosmographical Glass: Renaissance Diagrams of the Universe*. San Marino, California
Hieatt, A. K. 1960 *Short Time's Endless Monument: The Symbolism of the Numbers in Edmund Spenser's 'Epithalamion'*. New York
Hieatt, A. K. 1961 'The Daughters of Horus: Order in the Stanzas of *Epithalamion*'. In *Form and Convention in the Poetry of Edmund Spenser* (ed. W. Nelson). New York, pp. 103–21
Hieatt, A. K. 1973 'A Numerical Key for Spenser's *Amoretti* and Guyon in the House of Mammon'. *Yearbook of English Studies* 3: 14–27
Hieatt, C. B. 1983 'Stooping at a Simile: Some Literary Uses of Falconry'. *Papers on Language and Literature* 19: 339–60
Hone, W. 1826 *The Every-Day Book; or, Everlasting Calendar of Popular Amusements*. 2 vols. London
Hunter, G. K. 1975 '"Unity" and Numbers in Spenser's *Amoretti*'. *Yearbook of English Studies* 5: 39–45
Hutton, J. 1941a '*Amor Fugitivus*: The First Idyl of Moschus in Imitations to the Year 1800'. In J. Hutton 1980 *Essays on Renaissance Poetry* (ed. R. Guerlac). Ithaca and London, pp. 74–105
Hutton, J. 1941b 'Cupid and the Bee'. In J. Hutton 1980 *Essays on Renaissance Poetry* (ed. R. Guerlac). Ithaca and London, pp. 106–31
Hyde, T. 1986 *The Poetic Theology of Love: Cupid in Renaissance Literature*. Newark, Delaware
Jacobs E. C. and Jacobs, K. R. 1983 '*Amoretti* 79 and 1 Peter 3: 1–4'. *University of Mississippi Studies in English* 4: 187–90
Johnson, W. C. 1974 'Spenser's *Amoretti* and the Art of the Liturgy'. *SEL: Studies in English Literature 1500–1900* 14: 47–61

Jonson, B. 1969 *The Complete Masques* (ed. S. Orgel). The Yale Ben Jonson 4. New Haven and London

Kaske, C. V. 1977 'Another Liturgical Dimension of "Amoretti" 68'. *Notes and Queries* 222: 518–19

Kaske, C. V. 1978 'Spenser's *Amoretti and Epithalamion* of 1595: Structure, Genre, and Numerology'. *English Literary Renaissance* 8: 271–95

Kaske, C. V. 1990 'Rethinking Loewenstein's "Viper Thoughts"'. *Spenser Studies: A Renaissance Poetry Annual* 8: 325–9

Kastner, L. E. 1908–9 'Spenser's *Amoretti* and Desportes'. *Modern Language Review* 4: 65–9

Kostić, V. 1959 'Spenser's *Amoretti* and Tasso's Lyrical Poetry'. *Renaissance and Modern Studies* 3: 51–77

Leonard, C. A. 1984 *Flora's Bargain: A Study of Gender Relations in the Poetry of Edmund Spenser*. University of California, Santa Cruz, Ph.D. thesis

Levarie, J. 1973 'Renaissance Anacreontics'. *Comparative Literature* 25: 221–39

Lievesay, J. L. 1941 'Greene's Panther'. *Philological Quarterly* 20: 298–303

Loewenstein, J. 1984 *Responsive Readings: Versions of Echo in Pastoral, Epic, and the Jonsonian Masque*. New Haven and London

Loewenstein, J. 1986 'Echo's Ring: Orpheus and Spenser's Career'. *English Literary Renaissance* 16: 287–302

Loewenstein, J. 1990 'A Note on the Structure of Spenser's *Amoretti*: Viper Thoughts'. *Spenser Studies: A Renaissance Poetry Annual* 8: 311–23

Marotti, A. F. '"Love is not Love": Elizabethan Sonnet Sequences and the Social Order'. *ELH: A Journal of English Literary History* 49: 396–428

Martz, L. L. 1961 'The *Amoretti*: "Most Goodly Temperature"'. In *Form and Convention in the Poetry of Edmund Spenser* (ed. W. Nelson). New York, pp. 146–68

McPeek, J. A. S. 1936 'The Major Sources of Spenser's *Epithalamion*'. *Journal of English and Germanic Philology* 35: 183–213

Miola, R. S. 1980 'Spenser's Anacreontics: A Mythological Metaphor'. *Studies in Philology* 77: 50–66

Nelson, W. 1963 *The Poetry of Edmund Spenser*. New York

Neumann, E. 1955 *The Great Mother: An Analysis of the Archetype* (tr. R. Manheim). Bollingen Series 47. New York

Neuse, R. 1966 'The Triumph over Hasty Accidents: A Note on the Symbolic Mode of the "Epithalamion"'. *Modern Language Review* 61: 161–74

Nitzsche, J. C. 1975 *The Genius Figure in Antiquity and the Middle Ages*. New York and London

Nohrnberg, J. 1976 *The Analogy of 'The Faerie Queene'*. Princeton, N.J.

Panofsky, D. and Panofsky, E. 1956 *Pandora's Box: The Changing Aspects of a Mythical Symbol* (rev. edn 1962). Bollingen Series 52. Princeton, N.J.

Prayer-book 1559 *The Prayer-Book of Queen Elizabeth 1559* (introd. E. Benham 1909). Edinburgh

Prescott, A. L. 1985 'The Thirsty Deer and the Lord of Life: Some Contexts for *Amoretti* 67–70'. *Spenser Studies* 6: 33–76

Quitslund, J. A. 1973 'Spenser's *Amoretti* VIII and Platonic Commentaries on Petrarch'. *Journal of the Warburg and Courtauld Institutes* 36: 256–76

Renwick, W. L. (ed.) 1929 Spenser, E. *Daphnaida and Other Poems*. London

Roche, T. P. Jr 1989 *Petrarch and the English Sonnet Sequences*. New York

Salmon, W. (tr.) 1678 *Pharmacopoeia Londinensis, or the New London Dispensatory*. London
Scott, J. G. 1927 'The Sources of Spenser's "Amoretti"'. *Modern Language Review* 22: 189–95
Schenck, C. M. 1988 *Mourning and Panegyric: The Poetics of Pastoral Ceremony*. University Park, Pennsylvania
Shumaker, W. 1972 *The Occult Sciences in the Renaissance: A Study in Intellectual Patterns*. Berkeley, Los Angeles and London
Smith, B. 1992 'Greece'. In *The Feminist Companion to Mythology* (ed. C. Larrington). London, pp. 65–101
Tasso, T. 1898–1902 *Le Rime di Torquato Tasso* (ed. A. Solerti) 4 vols. Bologna
Thomas Taylor 1969 *Thomas Taylor the Platonist: Selected Writings* (ed. K. Raine and G. M. Harper). Bollingen Series 88. Princeton, N.J.
Thiébaux, M. 1974 *The Stag of Love: The Chase in Medieval Literature*. Ithaca and London
Thompson, C. 1985 'Love in an Orderly Universe: A Unification of Spenser's Amoretti, "Anacreontics", and Epithalamion'. *Viator* 16: 277–85
Trapp, J. B. 1968 'The Iconography of the Fall of Man'. In *Approaches to 'Paradise Lost'* (ed. C. A. Patrides). London, pp. 223–65
Twycross, M. 1972 *The Mediaeval Anadyomene: A Study in Chaucer's Mythography*. Medium Aevum Monographs 9. Oxford
Vian, F. (ed.) 1987 *Les Argonautiques Orphiques*. Paris
Walker, D. P. 'Orpheus the Theologian and Renaissance Platonists'. *Journal of the Warburg and Courtauld Institutes* 16: 100–20
Walker, D. P. 1958 *Spiritual and Demonic Magic from Ficino to Campanella*. London
Walker, D. P. 1972 *The Ancient Theology: Studies in Christian Platonism from the Fifteenth to the Eighteenth Century*. London
Warner, M. 1985 *Alone of All Her Sex: The Myth and Cult of the Virgin Mary*. London
Webster, J. 1981 '"The Methode of a Poete": An Inquiry into Tudor Conceptions of Poetic Sequence'. *English Literary Renaissance* 11: 22–43
Welsford, E. 1967 *Spenser: 'Fowre Hymnes', 'Epithalamion': A Study of Edmund Spenser's Doctrine of Love*. Oxford
Wickert, M. A. 1968 'Structure and Ceremony in Spenser's *Epithalamion*'. *ELH: A Journal of English Literary History* 35: 135–57
Yates, F. A. 1966 *The Art of Memory*. London
Yates, F. A. 1969 *Theatre of the World*. London
Yates, F. A. 1978 *Giordano Bruno and the Hermetic Tradition*. London, Henley and Chicago
Yates, F. A. 1979 *The Occult Philosophy in the Elizabethan Age*. London, Henley and Boston
Ziegler, G. 1992 'Penelope and the Politics of Woman's Place in the Renaissance'. In *Gloriana's Face: Women, Public and Private, in the English Renaissance* (ed. S. P. Cerasano and M. Wynne-Davies). New York, London, Toronto, Sydney, Tokyo and Singapore, pp. 25–46

Amoretti

[Dedicatory epistle]
To the Right Worshipful Sir Robert Needham, Knight.

Sir, to gratulate your safe return from Ireland, I had nothing so ready, nor thought anything so meet, as these sweet-conceited sonnets, the deed of that well-deserving gentleman Master Edmund Spenser, whose name sufficiently warranting the worthiness of the work, I do more confidently presume to publish it   5
in his absence under your name, to whom (in my poor opinion) the patronage thereof doth in some respects properly appertain. For, besides your judgement and delight in learned poesy, this gentle Muse, for her former perfection long wished-for in England, now at length crossing the seas in your happy company   10
(though to yourself unknown) seemeth to make choice of you as meetest to give her deserved countenance after her return. Entertain her, then, Right Worshipful, in sort best beseeming your gentle mind and her merit, and take in worth my goodwill herein, who seek no more but to show myself yours in all dutiful   15
affection.

                                                         W.P.

---

1. Sir Robert Needham: native of Shropshire, a cavalry captain knighted in Ireland 1 September 1594; left Ireland for England 25 September 1594, returned to Ireland 7 April 1596 (Renwick 1929: 196).
3. sweet-conceited: pleasingly ingenious, witty: *OED* conceited *ppl a* I. 1 b, c; II. 6.
13. meetest: fittest.
18. W.P.: William Ponsonby, publisher of all of Spenser's works of the 1590s including *FQ*.

[Dedicatory sonnets]

[1]
G.W. Senior, to the Author

Dark is the day when Phoebus' face is shrouded,
   And weaker sights may wander soon astray;
   But when they see his glorious rays unclouded,
   With steady steps they keep the perfect way:
So, while this Muse in foreign lands doth stay,   5
   Invention weeps and pens are cast aside,
   The time like night, deprived of cheerful day,
   And few do write but (ah) too soon may slide.
Then hie thee home, that art our perfect guide,
   And with thy wit illustrate England's fame,   10
   Daunting thereby our neighbours' ancient pride
   That do for poesy challenge chiefest name:
So we that live, and ages that succeed,
   With great applause thy learned works shall read.

[2]
Ah, Colin, whether on the lowly plain,
   Piping to shepherds thy sweet roundelays;
   Or whether singing in some lofty vein
   Heroic deeds of past or present days;
Or whether in thy lovely mistress' praise   5
   Thou list to exercise thy learned quill,
   Thy Muse hath got such grace, and power to please
   With rare invention beautified by skill,
As who therein can ever joy their fill?
   Oh therefore let that happy Muse proceed   10

[1] *G.W. Senior*: probably Geoffrey Whitney, father of the author of sonnet 2, Geoffrey Whitney Junior. The latter's *A Choice of Emblems* (1586) was dedicated to Leicester. For other possible links with Spenser, see *Var* 2: 418.
1. *Phoebus'*: the sun's.
6. *Invention*: the finding out and selection of topic(s), traditionally the first step in creating a literary work.
11. *Daunting*: taming.
14. *read*: *SC* dedicatory poem 11n.
[2] 1–6. *Ah . . . quill*: recalling *SC June* and *October*, 38–48.
1. *Colin*: *SC January* headnote.
2. *roundelays*: *SC April* 33 gloss.
4. *Heroic . . . days*: *FQ* (1590) and (possibly) Spenser's elegy for Sidney, *Astrophel* (1595).
9. *who . . . fill?* : who can ever be sated by your works? (*joy* = enjoy).

To climb the height of Virtue's sacred hill,
Where endless honour shall be made thy meed
Because no malice of succeeding days
   Can rase those records of thy lasting praise.
                                            G.W.J.

[*Amoretti*]

SONNET 1

Happy, ye leaves, whenas those lily hands
   (Which hold my life in their dead-doing might)
   Shall handle you and hold in love's soft bands,
   Like captives trembling at the victor's sight;
And happy lines, on which with starry light   5
   Those lamping eyes will deign sometimes to look,
   And read the sorrows of my dying spright
   Written with tears in heart's close bleeding book;
And happy rhymes, bathed in the sacred brook

---

12. meed: reward.
14. rase . . . records: erase (originally by scraping) the written testaments; *records* also = memorials.
Sonnet 1 *1–3. hands . . . hold . . . hold*: cf. the Marriage Service's 'to have and to hold' (*Prayer-book* 1559: 123).
1. leaves: pages; anticipating the laurel of *Am* 28, 29. *whenas*: when. *lily*: the hands are cupped like a lily, the flower of purity and marriage (*SC April* 136 gloss, *Epith* 43n).
2. dead-doing: death-dealing.
3. bands: (1) the fingers as symbols of confinement as well as of union; (2) the cords binding the *leaves* of a book together (*OED band sb* 1 I. 2b, but first instance 1759); (3) the rings exchanged in the Marriage Service (band *sb* 2).
4. captives: introducing the (conventional) military metaphor (e.g., *Am* 29, 52) and the ritual submission of the male to the female in the courtly love tradition. *trembling*: in *Am* 67. 11 the doe trembles at the hands of her lover.
5. lines: (1) of print; (2) of the angler catching the fish/beloved in the *brook* (l. 10): cf. Donne's 'The Bait'.
6. lamping: shining, beaming: *OED lamping ppl a* cites *FQ* (1590), 3. 3. 1 as its first instance, where the subject is again stars, heaven and love. *deign*: condescend.
7. read: dedicatory sonnets, 1. 14n above. *spright*: original spelling (possibly Spenser's), first *OED* instance of which is dated 1536; variant of sprite = spirit = soul, one's immaterial part. But in connection with *heart* and *soul* (ll. 8, 12) may suggest the neo-Platonic notion of spirit as vapour produced by the heart and mediating between soul and body: Agrippa (1651) 3. 37 (pp. 465–6).
8–9. heart's . . . brook: hints at the deer and brook at *Am* 67 headnote and 7n and introduces the heart/hart pun.
8. close: secret, private. *book*: book of the heart topos, deriving from 2

> Of Helicon (whence she derived is), 10
>   When ye behold that angel's blessed look,
>   My soul's long-lacked food, my heaven's bliss:
> Leaves, lines and rhymes, seek her to please alone
>   Whom, if ye please, I care for other none.

SONNET 2

> Unquiet thought, whom at the first I bred
>   Of the inward bale of my love-pined heart,
>   And sithence have with sighs and sorrows fed
>   Till greater than my womb thou woxen art:
> Break forth at length out of the inner part 5
>   (In which thou lurkest like to viper's brood),
>   And seek some succour both to ease my smart
>   And also to sustain thyself with food.
> But if in presence of that fairest proud
>   Thou chance to come, fall lowly at her feet, 10
>   And with meek humblesse and afflicted mood
>   Pardon for thee, and grace for me, entreat
> Which, if she grant, then live, and my love cherish:
>   If not, die soon, and I with thee will perish.

Corinthians 3. 2–3 ('Ye are our epistle, written in our hearts . . . ye are manifest, to be the Epistle of Christ, ministered by us, and written, not with ink, but with the Spirit of the living God, not in tables of stone, but in fleshly tables of the heart'); cf. Curtius 1967: 319.

10. Helicon: *SC April* 42 gloss: the beloved is his Muse. Cf. *Am*. 34. 10n.

11. angel's: cf. *Am* 8. 7, 17. 1, 61. 6: Hardison 1972: 210 compares the Dantean/Petrarchan *donna angelicata* (idealized lady) motif, noting that it is usually prominent after the lady's death.

14. other none: none other.

Sonnet 2 *2. bale*: torment, grief; traditionally opposed to *bliss* (cf. *Am* 1. 12 and *OED* bale *sb* 1). *pined*: *SC January* 48n, *September* 65n. *heart*: noting a pun on *hart*, Bieman 1988: 171 records that harts traditionally killed snakes (l. 6).

3. sithence: *SC March* 46n.

4. woxen: *SC January* 5n.

6. viper's brood: young vipers were believed to eat their way out of the womb, thus killing their mother: Ansell Robin 1932: 29–31. The opening octave suggests a parallel with the serpent-woman Error and her brood (*FQ*, 1. 1. 15–26); so that the *unquiet thought* = a *viper* = the *lady* seen now as the opposite of angelic.

11. humblesse: mediaevalism revived by Spenser: *OED*, citing *FQ*, 1. 3. 26. *afflicted*: downcast (physically in the sense of modestly casting eyes to the ground); humble: *OED* afflicted *ppl a*, 3 citing this as first instance. *mood*: (1) mind, heart (archaic senses); (2) state of feeling.

12. grace: in the theological sense, and see *SC April* 52n.

13. cherish: (1) hold dear; (2) (glancing at the motherhood image) nurse, foster: *OED* cherish *v* 1, 2.

SONNET 3

The sovereign beauty which I do admire,
  Witness the world how worthy to be praised,
  The light whereof hath kindled heavenly fire
  In my frail spirit (by her from baseness raised)
That, being now with her huge brightness dazed, 5
  Base thing I can no more endure to view
  But, looking still on her, I stand amazed
  At wondrous sight of so celestial hue.
So, when my tongue would speak her praises due,
  It stopped is with thought's astonishment; 10
  And when my pen would write her titles true,
  It ravished is with fancy's wonderment:
Yet in my heart I then both speak and write
  The wonder that my wit cannot indite.

SONNET 4

New Year, forth looking out of Janus' gate,
  Doth seem to promise hope of new delight

Sonnet 3   Scott 1927: 194 compares Tasso, *Rime*, ed Solerti, 2. 52, no. 35 ('Veggio quando tal vista'). Cf. Petrarch, *Rime*, 20, 49.
1. sovereign: (1) excelling others of her kind; (2) queen. *beauty*: viper thought forgotten, the lady becomes a manifestation of a Platonic/neo-Platonic abstract: cf. *HB*, *HHB*. In Petrarch, *Rime*, 20 the poet is similarly silenced by Laura's beauty. *admire*: wonder at.
4. spirit: vital or animating principle: original spelling retained (*Am* 1. 7n). *raised*: elevated; but the original spelling, *raysed*, suggests also *erase*: *OED* raise *v* 2. 2.
5. That: so that. *dazed*: stupefied, dazzled: both effects of divine beauty on the mortal lover. Cf. *HB*, 99–140, *HHB*, 1–7, etc., and Plato's *Phaedrus*, 250D–252B.
7. amazed: stunned (sign of possession by the divine in neo-Platonic thought).
8. hue: (1) shape or figure; (2) apparition.
9. her . . . due: praises due to her.
10. astonishment: (1) insensibility (first *OED* citation 1576); (2) overpowering sense of wonder (first citation 1594).
11. pen: the pen/penis pun is historically possible: cf. Bieman 1988: 169. *titles*: (1) appellations of honour because of her high rank (as Queen Beauty): *OED* title *sb* 5, citing *FQ*, 2. 7. 43 as first instance; (2) *title-deeds* (substantiating her claim to her kingdom).
12. ravished: seized in the technical neo-Platonic sense of divine possession (*raptus*) leading to return to heaven: Wind 1967: 37–8, 42n; there are also sexual undertones. *fancy's*: fancy = the fantasy or imagination (the image-receiving and -creating faculty). *wonderment*: object of wonder.
14. wit: (1) mind; (2) understanding. *indite*: put into words and literary form.
Sonnet 4   *1. New Year*: marks the beginning of the sequence's calendrical

And, bidding the Old 'adieu', his passed date
   Bids all old thoughts to die in dumpish spright;
And, calling forth out of sad Winter's night   5
   Fresh Love (that long hath slept in cheerless bower),
   Wills him awake, and soon about him dight
   His wanton wings and darts of deadly power.
For lusty Spring, now in his timely hour,
   Is ready to come forth him to receive,   10
   And warns the Earth with diverse-coloured flower
   To deck herself and her fair mantle weave:
Then you, fair flower, in whom fresh youth doth reign,
   Prepare yourself new love to entertain.

SONNET 5
Rudely thou wrongest my dear heart's desire
   In finding fault with her too portly pride:

structure with January: see headnote and *Am* 62. 1–2n. *Janus' gate*: Janus as the sun god guards the two gates of heaven, east and west, symbol of his progress through the day and also the year: Linche (1599) sig. D1 v; Macrobius, *Saturnalia*, 1. 9. 9. Cf. *SC* General Argument, p. 28n. But there may be an allusion to the neo-Platonic concept of Cancer and Capricorn as the 'gates' through which souls descend to, and ascend from, the material world: *Janua* in Latin = gate, so January's sign, Capricorn, reminds one of the soul's return to its 'pristine felicity': Porphyry in *Thomas Taylor* 1969: 312.
4. dumpish spright: low spirit[s], appropriate to melancholy Saturn's zodiacal house Capricorn, which also covers part of December, last month of the old year. Cf. *Am* 52. 11.
6. Fresh Love: youthful Cupid, emblem of the poet/lover's lust. *bower*: *SC August* 167n.
7. dight: put on; *SC April* 29 gloss.
8. wanton . . . power: for the iconography of Cupid, see *SC March* 33 and 79 glosses.
9. lusty: (1) merry; (2) gaily dressed (traditional epithet of Spring). The sonnet celebrates January as the beginning of the cycle of renewal, 'as when the sun unlocketh the spring from the stubborn embracements of the winter, enamelling the pleasant verdure of the earth with so many delicate and diverse-coloured flowers' (Linche as at 1n above).
10. him: Cupid.
11. diverse . . . flower: flowers of various colours. But flowers result from Chloris/earth's rape by Zephyrus, the wind of spring: after the rape she is Flora (Flower Maiden): *SC March* 16 and *April* 122 glosses.
13. flower: anticipates the garden image of *Am* 64.
Sonnet 5 Scott 1927: 194 compares Tasso, *Rime*, ed Solerti, 2. 54, no. 36 ('Questa rara bellezza').
1. Rudely: ignorantly. *thou*: an imagined observer; maybe the lover addressing himself.
2. portly pride: stately (dignified) awareness of her own position and worth.

The thing which I do most in her admire
   Is of the world unworthy most envied;
For in those lofty looks is close implied   5
   Scorn of base things and sdeign of foul dishonour,
   Threatening rash eyes which gaze on her so wide
   That loosely they ne dare to look upon her.
Such pride is praise, such portliness is honour
   That boldened innocence bears in her eyes,   10
   And her fair countenance like a goodly banner
   Spreads in defiance of all enemies:
Was never in this world aught worthy tried
   Without some spark of such self-pleasing pride.

SONNET 6

Be nought dismayed that her unmoved mind
   Doth still persist in her rebellious pride:
   Such love, not like to lusts of baser kind,
   The harder won, the firmer will abide.
The dureful oak, whose sap is not yet dried,   5
   Is long ere it conceive the kindling fire;
   But when it once doth burn it doth divide

---

4. world unworthy: the unworthy world; or, she is unworthily envied by the world. *envied*: regarded with displeasure.
5. close: *Am* 1. 8n.
6. sdeign: the original's idiomatic spelling (hence, probably Spenser's), importing Italian *sdegno* (*OED* sdeign *sb* and *v*). The current form *disdeigne* is the spelling used at *Am* 20. 7.
7. so wide: i.e., she threatens the rash eyes over such a long distance.
8. loosely: immorally. *ne*: not.
10. boldened: emboldened, encouraged (*OED*'s first citation for *bolden* = 1526; for *embolden*, 1571). *innocence*: traditionally depicted as a virgin dressed in white and crowned either with flowers or palm leaves, accompanied by the lamb of innocence: Ripa 1603: 235–6.
11. banner: cf. Song of Solomon 6: 4 (the bride/Church 'terrible as an army with banners') and Petrarch's *Triumph of Death* as translated by Mary Sidney, 1. 19–21 (in ed. Brooks-Davies 1992a: 291): the company of virgins symbolised through an unfurled banner.
Sonnet 6 *3. kind*: natural disposition.
5. dureful: durable, enduring: the first of *OED*'s three citations. *oak*: emblem of moral force and constancy: Tervarent (1958) col 91 and cf. *SC February* 103n.
6. kindling: (1) igniting; (2) giving birth to (*OED* kindle *v* 2), punning on *conceive* and (more remotely) *kind*.
7. divide: give forth in various directions: *OED* divide *v* 8c citing this as the first of only two instances. Note also divide = share (*OED* sense 8b), so that the two lovers share the 'great heat' of love's flames: Fowler 1975: 90.

Great heat, and makes his flames to heaven aspire.
So, hard it is to kindle new desire
   In gentle breast that shall endure for ever: 10
   Deep is the wound that dints the parts entire
   With chaste affects that nought but death can sever:
Then think not long in taking little pain
   To knit the knot that ever shall remain.

SONNET 7
Fair eyes, the mirror of my mazed heart,
   What wondrous virtue is contained in you
   The which both life and death forth from you dart
   Into the object of your mighty view?
For when ye mildly look with lovely hue, 5
   Then is my soul with life and love inspired;

8. aspire: breathe desire towards (Latin *adspiro*); influenced by *spire* to mean mount upwards: *OED* aspire *v* III. 5, citing Spenser, *Ruins of Time*, 408 as first instance. In both the *Am* and *Ruins* instances Spenser puns on *pire* as an Elizabethan form for Greek *pyr* = fire, flame as at *HL*, 80.

10. gentle: courteous, noble (manner rather than birth). *endure*: punning (via Latin *durus* = hard) on *hard* in l. 9; cf. 11. 4–5 (*harder, dureful*). The notion is proverbial: Smith 1970: 122–3. On puns in *Am* 6 see Johnson, W. C. 1971 *Explicator* 29 #5, item 38.

11. dints: makes an impression in: *OED* dint *v* 2; rare usage of a favourite Spenserian word. *parts entire*: intact organs, but see *HHL*, 271n.

12. affects: tendencies, general disposition.

14. knot: symbol of union (love-knot) and hinting at the Herculean knot of marriage, the undoing of which guarantees children: Ben Jonson, *Hymenaei* (1606), 175 and note in Orgel, S. (ed) 1969 *Complete Masques*. Note the puns that anticipate it: nought (ll. 1, 12), not (ll. 3, 5, 13); also the fact that the oak's wood is knotty. The knot is tightened at *Am* 67. 11–12.

Sonnet 7 *1. eyes . . . mirror*: at *Am* 1. 6 they light the lover's way; for the neo-Platonic mirror image, see *HL*, 192–6 and n. Also Ficino, *Commentary*, 7. 1 (just as a mirror receives a ray of the sun and, reflecting it, sets a piece of wool on fire, so that part of a lover's soul called memory receives through the eyes an image of Beauty and makes another image from it, a reflection of the first, by which desire is kindled; in Ficino 1944: 216). Cf. *HL*, 192–6 and n and *Am* 35 on Narcissus. *mazed*: stupefied, dazed (and punning on the *maze* as symbol of perplexity, hence confused: *OED* maze *v* 3): cf. *Am* 3. 7n (though *maze* is independent of *amaze* as a verb, albeit related to it). Given that both eyes and heart mirror each other as containers (l. 2), there is probably a pun on *mazer*: *SC August* 26 gloss.

3. dart: the rays from the lady's eyes are also Cupid's darts: *Am* 4. 8 and *HL*, 117–24.

5. lovely: loving; worthy of love. *hue*: *Am* 3. 8n.

6. inspired: breathed into, animated (cf. *Am* 6. 8n) in the specific sense of aroused by divine agency.

But when ye lour, or look on me askew,
  Then do I die, as one with lightning fired.
But since that life is more than death desired,
  Look ever lovely, as becomes you best,   10
  That your bright beams, of my weak eyes admired,
  May kindle living fire within my breast:
Such life should be the honour of your light;
  Such death the sad ensample of your might.

SONNET 8

More than most fair, full of the living fire
  Kindled above unto the Maker near:
No eyes, but joys in which all powers conspire,
  That to the world nought else be counted dear.
Through your bright beams doth not the blinded guest   5
  Shoot out his darts to base affection's wound?
But angels come to lead frail minds to rest
  In chaste desires on heavenly Beauty bound.
You frame my thoughts and fashion me within;
  You stop my tongue, and teach my heart to speak;   10
  You calm the storm that passion did begin,
  Strong through your cause, but by your virtue weak:

---

8. lightning fired: cf. the oak of *Am* 6. Lightning is an attribute of Cupid: Tervarent (1958) cols 194–5.
12. kindle . . . breast: cf. *Am* 6. 9–10.
14. ensample: pattern (of conduct).
Sonnet 8   Influenced by Petrarch, *Rime*, 151, 154: Renwick 1929: 197. Quitslund 1973 argues for the influence of Andrea Gesualdo's Platonising commentary on the *Rime*, especially that on 154.
1–2. fire . . . near: cf. *HL* 64–5n (on the birth of Cupid); but the lover's hyperbole probably refers to Ficino's account of God's first creation, Angelic Mind, which turns to God with desire and is set on fire with the glow of his radiance: *Commentary*, 1. 3 (Ficino 1944: 127).
5–6. bright . . . wound: cf. *Am* 7. 3n and Petrarch, *Rime*, 151. 5–11. The effect of Cupid is to encourage lust, a moral implication of his blindness: Panofsky (1962) ch 4; contrast this with the lover's dazed/dazzled state at *Am* 3. 5.
7–8. angels . . . bound: cf. *HHB*, 15–28, 85–119; also *FQ*, 2. 8. 1–6 (the descent of the angel, a celestial Cupid signifying divine love, to Guyon); and cf. Panofsky 1962: 101–2.
9. frame: *SC January* 10, *June* 55, *August* 3 and *December* 77 nn.
10. stop: prevent, but punning on *stop* = act of closing a hole in a wind instrument or pressing a finger on a string of a stringed instrument to alter its pitch: *OED* stop *sb* 2, 15.

Dark is the world where your light shined never;
   Well is he born that may behold you ever.

SONNET 9
Long while I sought to what I might compare
   Those powerful eyes which lighten my dark spright,
   Yet find I nought on earth to which I dare
   Resemble the image of their goodly light:
Not to the sun, for they do shine by night;   5
   Nor to the moon, for they are changed never;
   Nor to the stars, for they have purer sight;
   Nor to the fire, for they consume not ever;
Nor to the lightning, for they still persevere;
   Nor to the diamond, for they are more tender;   10
   Nor unto crystal, for nought may them sever;

---

13. Dark: cf. *HL*, 57–73; also John 1: 5: 'And that light shineth in the wilderness, and the darkness comprehendeth it not'.
14. Well . . . born: sight of the lady promotes him into the aristocracy of lovers; or (since the original spelling, *borne*, is ambiguous): he is carefully carried (by angels) into her heaven.
Sonnet 9 A series of comparisons (cf. *Am* 55) following the rhetorical scheme of *expeditio*, 'a manner of speech . . . when we do briefly set downe all our best reasons . . . and reject all of them saving one': Puttenham (1589) 3. 19 (p 195).
2. eyes: cf. *Am* 1. 6, 8. 5–6nn, and the role of Venus at *HL*, 71–3. *spright*: *Am* 1. 7n.
5–6. sun . . . moon: the wit of the comparison resides in the fact that Apollo and Diana were, like the eyes, twinned: cf. *SC April* 73, 82, 86–7 glosses. *Sun* anticipates the argument's resolution at ll. 13–14: Christ is the sun who illuminates the world for the full 24 hours (Bongo 1599: 448). The *moon* is the traditional emblem of fortune and instability, but also of Diana and chastity: Tervarent (1958) cols 253–4. *Changed never* recalls Queen Elizabeth's motto *semper eadem*, always the same (cf. the queen in *Am* 74).
7. stars: the sphere of the fixed stars is 'purer' because near to God in the Ptolemaic scheme; being fixed (as opposed to the 'wandering' seven planets) it signifies constancy.
8. fire: highest of the four elements, it is the motivating force of the seraphim, highest of the angelic hierarchy: *HHB* 94–5n.
9. lightning: here an attribute of the divinity: Macrobius, *Saturnalia*, 1. 23. 12; Matthew 28: 3: 'the angel of the Lord descended . . . .and his countenance was like lightning'. (But cf. *Am* 7. 8n.)
10. diamond: hard (Greek *adamas* = unconquerable); also symbol of fortitude, good faith, Christ, and associated with the sun: Brooks-Davies 1977: 76–8.
11. crystal: symbol of purity and the durability of true faith: Brooks-Davies 1977: 94; the Heavenly Jerusalem shines 'clear as crystal' at Revelation 21: 11.

Nor unto glass: such baseness mought offend her.
Then to the Maker's self they likest be,
  Whose light doth lighten all that here we see.

SONNET 10

Unrighteous Lord of love, what law is this
  That me thou makest thus tormented be,
  The whiles she lordeth in licentious bliss
  Of her free will, scorning both thee and me?
See how the tyranness doth joy to see   5
  The huge massacres which her eyes do make,
  And humbled hearts brings captives unto thee,
  That thou of them mayest mighty vengeance take.
But her proud heart do thou a little shake,
  And that high look (with which she doth control   10
  All this world's pride) bow to a baser make,
  And all her faults in thy black book enrol,
That I may laugh at her in equal sort
  As she doth laugh at me, and makes my pain her sport.

SONNET 11

Daily, when I do seek and sue for peace,
  And hostages do offer for my truth,

---

12. glass: last and least of the three 'transparency' comparisons. Cf. Ripa 1603: 328, where Earthly Misery (*Miseria Mondana*) is portrayed as a woman with her head inside a glass globe because 'glass demonstrates the vanity of earthly things because of its fragility'. *mought* = might.

13–14. Maker . . . lighten: Luke 2: 32: 'A light to be revealed to the gentiles'; John 1: 4: 'In it [the Word] was life, and that life was the light of men' (Geneva gloss on *light*: 'That force of reason and understanding, which is kindled in our minds to knowledge him, the author of so great a benefit'). Cf. *Am* 8. 13n.

Sonnet 10 Based (loosely) on Petrarch, *Rime*, 121. The love-as-warfare theme is commonplace (see *Am* 11, 12, 14, 52, 57, 69) and follows, broadly, the Platonic tradition that Venus (and Cupid) are stronger than Mars, god of strife: Plato, *Symposium*, 196D; Wind 1967: 89–96.

3. licentious: lawless (from Latin *licere* = to be lawful: cf. *law* at l. 1).

4. free will: alluding to the Calvinist denial of freedom of the will.

5. tyranness: Spenserian coinage, first *OED* example from *FQ*, 1. 5. 46.

7. humbled . . . captives: brings humbled (abased) hearts as captives.

11. make: (1) peer or equal; (2) mate, companion (i.e., the poet himself).

12. black book: book of ill deeds (proverbial), but implying a connection with Cupid's dark (as opposed to golden) arrows, identified with the lady's pride, *hauteur*, etc.: Panofsky 1962: 102n.

Sonnet 11 *2. truth*: troth, or pledge of one's faith in support of an agreement.

She, cruel warrior, doth herself address
   To battle and the weary war reneweth;
Ne will be moved with reason or with ruth   5
   To grant small respite to my restless toil,
   But greedily her fell intent pursueth
   Of my poor life to make unpitied spoil.
Yet my poor life, all sorrows to assoil,
   I would her yield, her wrath to pacify: 10
   But then she seeks with torment and turmoil
   To force me live, and will not let me die.
All pain hath end, and every war hath peace –
   But mine no price nor prayer may surcease.

SONNET 12

One day I sought with her heart-thrilling eyes
   To make a truce and terms to entertain,
   All fearless then of so-false enemies
   Which sought me to entrap in treason's train.
So, as I then disarmed did remain,   5
   A wicked ambush (which lay hidden long
   In the close covert of her guileful eyen)
   Thence breaking forth did thick about me throng.
Too feeble, I, to abide the brunt so strong,

---

3. *cruel warrior*: modification of Petrarch's *o dolce mia guerrera* (O my gentle warrior: *Rime*, 21. 1) followed by, e.g., Du Bellay, *L'Olive*, 70 (*o ma douce guerrière*). Spenser turns his beloved into a *Venus armata* signifying the cruelty of the warfare of love (Venus, having conquered Mars, adopts his weapons for her own): Wind as in *Am* 10 headnote. The beloved's cruelty and beauty are a constant topic in *Am*: cf. Castiglione, *Courtier*, 4: 329 (beautiful women are called cruel when they don't grant what you want).
5. *Ne*: nor. *ruth*: pity; remorse (*OED* ruth 2).
7. *fell*: cruel.
9. *assoil*: discharge, get rid of (*OED* assoil *v* II. 10 cites only two instance of this rare usage, from *FQ*, 3. 1. 58 and 4. 5. 30).
14. *surcease*: put an end to.
Sonnet 12 Renwick 1929: 198 compares Petrarch, *Rime*, 2 and 3.
1. *thrilling*: penetrating (as of a dart): *OED* thrill *v* 1, I; the meaning 'cause an emotional tremor' was just current (sense II. 5, first instance 1592). Note also thrilling = enthralling, enslaving (*OED* thrill *v* 2).
4. *train*: (1) guile; (2) trap.
5. *disarmed*: the poet as Mars stripped of his armour again.
6. *ambush*: cf. Cupid's ambush of Thomalin, *SC March*, 67–84.
7. *close covert*: hiding place.
9. *brunt*: attack, with overtones of the mediaeval sense *sharp blows*: *OED* brunt *sb* 1, 1, 2.

Was forced to yield myself into their hands 10
Who, me captiving straight with rigorous wrong,
Have ever since me kept in cruel bands:
So, Lady, now to you I do complain
Against your eyes, that justice I may gain.

SONNET 13

In that proud port, which her so goodly graceth,
    Whiles her fair face she rears up to the sky
    And to the ground her eyelids low embaseth,
    Most goodly temperature ye may descry:
Mild humblesse mixed with awe-full majesty. 5
    For, looking on the earth whence she was born,
    Her mind remembereth her mortality
    (Whatso is fairest shall to earth return);
But that same lofty countenance seems to scorn
    Base thing, and think how she to heaven may climb, 10
    Treading down earth as loathsome and forlorn,
    That hinders heavenly thoughts with drossy slime:
Yet lowly, still vouchsafe to look on me:
    Such lowliness shall make you lofty be.

11. captiving: taking captive (normal usage).
Sonnet 13 Scott 1927: 194 compares Tasso, *Rime*, ed. Solerti, 2. 316, no. 15 ('Quell'alma ch'immortal'). Renwick 1929: 198 compares Petrarch, *Rime*, 215.
1. port: bearing, mien (cf. *Am* 5. 2n).
2. face . . . sky: cf. Ovid's description of humanity created with an uplifted face, commanded to stand erect with eyes turned towards the stars, in contrast to the other animals who gaze upon the earth (*Metamorphoses*, 1. 84–6).
3. ground . . . embaseth: the posture of Shamefastness, or Modesty, regarded as an essential virginal virtue: Ripa 1603: 420; *FQ*, 2. 9. 41. *embaseth* = lowers.
4. temperature: (1) mixture (of elements); (2) temperate balance (in body and soul).
6. earth . . . born: 2 Corinthians 15: 47: 'The first man [Adam] is of the earth, earthly' (Geneva gloss: 'Wallowing in dirt, and wholly given to an earthly nature'). The Pauline context – human mortality, resurrection through Christ – is relevant to the sonnet, as also is Paul's source, Genesis 2: 7 ('The Lord God also made the man of the dust of the ground').
8. return: Genesis 3: 19: 'to dust shalt thou return'.
9. lofty: (1) exalted in dignity; (2) haughty: *OED* lofty *a* 2.
10. Base . . . climb: the neo-Platonic notion of ascent: cf. *HHL*, 267–87.
11. forlorn: *SC April* 4 gloss.
12. drossy: containing impure matter (ct. the 'goodly temperature' of l. 4).
14. lofty: (1) exalted (in comparison); (2) aiming high.

SONNET 14

Return again, my forces late dismayed,
  Unto the siege by you abandoned quite:
  Great shame it is to leave (like one afraid)
  So fair a piece for one repulse so light.
'Gainst such strong castles needeth greater might   5
  Than those small forts which ye were wont belay:
  Such haughty minds, inured to hardy fight,
  Disdain to yield unto the first assay.
Bring, therefore, all the forces that ye may,
  And lay incessant battery to her heart: 10
  Plaints, prayers, vows, ruth, sorrow and dismay –
  Those engines can the proudest love convert;
And if those fail, fall down and die before her:
  So, dying, live, and, living, do adore her.

Sonnet 14 *1. dismayed*: (1) daunted; (2) vanquished (first *OED* citation, *FQ*, 5. 2. 8 (1596)).
4. piece: (1) fortress: *OED* piece *sb* II. 10b; (2) individual; when applied to a female apparently often derogatory: sense II. 9b.
5. castles: for the siege of love commonplace cf. *FQ*, 4. 10 and Guillaume de Lorris and Jean de Meun 1962 *Romance of the Rose*, sections 64, 76, 95, etc.
6. wont belay: (1) accustomed to besiege; (2) (of a person) waylay.
7. inured: accustomed.
8. assay: attack.
11. Plaints . . . dismay: cf. de Lorris and de Meun 1962, *Romance of the Rose*, 10. 196–201 (let her hear your groans and complaints; unless she is hard-hearted she will be moved). This self-abasing reversal of the six-stage ladder of love (in which the lover assumes the postures normally asociated with the woman) is typical of the courtly love tradition: for the ladder see Friedman, L. J. 1965–6 'Gradus Amoris', *Romance Philology* 19: 167–77. *ruth*: lamentation, grief: *OED* ruth 3. *dismay*: in its etymological sense of fainting: Spenser provides *OED* with its first instances of *dismay* as a substantive.
12. convert: in the literal sense, cause to turn round (this is the original's spelling, but the rhyme requires the contemporary pronunciation, *convart*).

SONNET 15

Ye tradeful merchants that, with weary toil,
   Do seek most precious things to make your gain
   And both the Indias of their treasures spoil,
   What needeth you to seek so far in vain?
For lo, my love doth in herself contain   5
   All this world's riches that may far be found:
   If sapphires, lo, her eyes be sapphires plain;
   If rubies, lo, her lips be rubies sound;
If pearls, her teeth be pearls both pure and round;
   If ivory, her forehead ivory ween;   10

Sonnet 15 A blazon, or listing of the beloved's physical attributes by means of quasi-heraldic emblems (cf. *Am* 64, 76–7, *Epith* 167–180, and ct. *Am* 9); like all blazons, it has its roots in the Song of Songs, especially 5: 10–16. Pléiade parallels include Desportes, *Diane*, 1. 32 and Du Bellay, *XIII Sonnets de l'Honnête Amour*, 2: *Var* 2: 424–5. The sonnet allegorises the lady as an iconic object of desire through metaphorical jewels via biblical passages such as Ezekiel 28: 13–14, where the former perfection of the king of Tyre is conveyed in terms of precious stones and metal (ruby, sapphire, gold, etc.) which are in turn identified by the Geneva gloss as 'my people Israel, which shined as precious stones'.
1. tradeful: engaged in trade (this is *OED*'s first citation). *merchants*: condemned for their greed at Revelation 18: 11–19 as they lose 'gold, and silver, and . . . precious stone, and . . . pearls' with the fall of the corrupt earthly city Babylon. Their dross is replaced by the bridal Heavenly Jerusalem's gold, sapphire and pearl, etc.: Revelation 21. Cf. Ezekiel 27–8 (the destruction of Tyre and its merchants' wealth because of its king's pride).
3. both . . . Indias: East and West; synonymous with wealth.
5. in . . . contain: for the female body mapped as country/empire, see the frontispiece to Michael Drayton's *Poly-Olbion* (1612) and cf. the 'Ditchley' portrait of Elizabeth I: Helgerson 1986 repr. 1988. Cf. the balancing of opposites in 'goodly temperature' in *Am* 13.
7. sapphires: attribute of Venus (Agrippa (1651) 1. 28 (p 59)); the belly of the male beloved (identified with Christ) is 'covered with sapphires' at Song of Solomon, 5: 14. The gem was particularly good for the eyes: Salmon (1678) 3. 13 (p 418).
8–9. rubies . . . pearls: conventional comparisons. *Rubies* symbolise love (de Vries 1974: 394), and restrain lust (Salmon, 3. 13 (p 417)); a ruby is featured in the first row of stones in the priest's breastplate of judgement (a sapphire is placed in the second row): Exodus 28: 17–18. *Pearls* signify wisdom (Proverbs 3: 15, Matthew 7: 6) and female virtue (Proverbs 31: 10). The best pearls reputedly came from India: Pliny, *Natural History*, 9. 54. 106ff.
10. ivory: emblem of Venus (Tooke 1713: 124) and an attribute of the lovers in Song of Solomon 5: 14, 7: 4. *ween*: think, suppose.

If gold, her locks are finest gold on ground;
If silver, her fair hands are silver sheen.
But that which fairest is, but few behold:
Her mind, adorned with virtues manifold.

SONNET 16

One day, as I unwarily did gaze
   On those fair eyes, my love's immortal light
   (The whiles my 'stonished heart stood in amaze
   Through sweet illusion of her look's delight),
I mote perceive how, in her glancing sight,   5
   Legions of Loves with little wings did fly,
   Darting their deadly arrows fiery bright
   At every rash beholder passing by.
One of those archers closely I did spy,
   Aiming his arrow at my very heart –   10
   When suddenly, with twinkle of her eye,
   The damsel broke his misintended dart.
Had she not so done, sure I had been slain:
   Yet, as it was, I hardly 'scaped with pain.

11. gold . . . ground: the colour of Laura's hair (*Rime*, 90), and cf. Song of Solomon 5: 11: 'his head is as fine gold'; traditional symbol of temperance and perfection. *Ground* (1) earth; (2) the cloth on which threads were embroidered, or the underlying surface (as in heraldic decoration): *OED* ground *sb* II. 6a, b.
12. silver: usually attributed to Diana, virgin moon goddess; also Venerean: Agrippa (1651) 1. 24, 28 (pp 54, 59). *sheen*: (1) beautiful (applied to women); (2) shining.
Sonnet 16 *2. eyes*: *Am* 1. 6n, etc.
3. 'stonished: stunned, paralysed. *amaze*: *Am* 7. 1n.
4. illusion: (1) mockery; (2) deception.
5. mote: might. *glancing*: (1) of a weapon, hitting and gliding off (the lady's eyes as Cupid's arrows: *Am* 7. 3n); (2) flashing, gleaming. *FQ*, 5. 6. 38 gives *OED* its first instance of the adjectival participle.
6. Loves: Cupids; *Amoretti* in Italian.
11. twinkle: wink.
12. misintended: maliciously aimed (*OED*'s only instance of the adjectival participle; it also cites only two instances of the verb, both from the 1590s).
14. hardly: (1) forcibly; (2) with difficulty (*OED* hardly 1, 6). But he was still wounded.

SONNET 17

The glorious portrait of that angel's face –
   Made to amaze weak men's confused skill
   And this world's worthless glory to embase –
   What pen, what pencil can express her fill?
For though he colours could devise at will,   5
   And eke his learned hand at pleasure guide
   (Lest, trembling, it his workmanship should spill),
   Yet many wondrous things there are beside:
The sweet eye-glances that like arrows glide,
   The charming smiles that rob sense from the heart,   10
   The lovely pleasance and the lofty pride
   Cannot expressed be by any art:
A greater craftsman's hand thereto doth need
   That can express the life of things indeed.

SONNET 18

The rolling wheel that runneth often round,
   The hardest steel in tract of time doth tear;
   And drizzling drops that often do redound
   The firmest flint doth in continuance wear:
Yet cannot I, with many a dropping tear   5
   And long entreaty, soften her hard heart
   That she will once vouchsafe my plaint to hear,

Sonnet 17 The portrait is a conventional topos: cf. Sir John Davies, *Hymns of Astraea* (1599), no. 12. Renwick 1929: 198 compares Petrarch, *Rime*, 77, 78.
1. *glorious*: (1) splendidly beautiful; (2) meriting renown; (3) brilliant with light.
2. *skill*: the faculty of reason: *OED* skill *sb* 1 (archaic).
3. *glory*: (1) vainglory; (2) ambition: *OED* sense 1. *embase*: *Am* 13. 3n.
4. *pencil*: brush. *fill*: (1) to her satisfaction; (2) fullness (in the sense of complete perfection).
7. *spill*: *SC February* 52n.
11. *pleasance*: agreeableness, courtesy: *OED* pleasance 1, 2. *lofty*: *Am* 13. 14n.
Sonnet 18 Parallels in Ovid, *Tristia*, 4. 6. 1–16, *Ars amatoria*, 1. 471–7; Petrarch, *Rime*, 265; Desportes, *Les Amours d'Hippolyte*, no. 51.
1. *rolling wheel*: suggesting in part the cartwheel on which Fortune stands as sign of her mutable nature: Alciati 1551: 133. The phrasing is proverbial: Smith 1970: 283.
2. *steel*: emblem of durability: cf. *SC* Epilogue 2 and n. *tract of time*: proverbial: *OED* tract *sb* 3, I. 1a. *tear*: split: *OED* tear *v* 1, B I. 1c (first citation 1582). The whole line is proverbial: Smith 1970: 136.
3. *redound*: overflow. For the image, cf. Petrarch, *Rime*, 265. 9–11; also Smith 1970: 83–4.
7. *plaint*: (1) lamentation; (2) (legal) statement of grievance.

Or look with pity on my painful smart.
But when I plead, she bids me play my part;
    And when I weep, she says tears are but water;   10
    And when I sigh, she says I know the art;
    And when I wail, she turns herself to laughter.
So do I weep, and wail, and plead in vain,
    Whiles she as steel and flint doth still remain.

SONNET 19
The merry cuckoo, messenger of spring,
    His trumpet shrill hath thrice already sounded
That warns all lovers wait upon their king,
    Who now is coming forth with garland crowned:
With noise whereof the choir of birds resounded   5
    Their anthems sweet devised of Love's praise,
That all the woods their echoes back rebounded,
    As if they knew the meaning of their lays.
But 'mongst them all which did Love's honour raise
    No word was heard of her that most it ought;   10
But she his precept proudly disobeys,

---

8. *smart*: (1) wound; (2) sorrow.
11. *I . . . art*: (1) the lady says the lover knows how to woo; (2) she says she sees the tricks of his trade.
12. *laughter*: in deflating the lover's ritual postures the lady assumes the Venerean characteristic, mirth: Hesiod, *Theogony*, 989.
14. *flint*: symbol of hardness of heart; but note that fire (= love) can be struck from it. A proverbial end to match the beginning: Smith 1970: 250 (cf. *Am* 56. 9–10).
Sonnet 19 Traditional spring poem: e.g., Petrarch, *Rime*, 310. Cf. *Am* 4, 70.
1. *cuckoo*: emblem of Juno as goddess of marriage (Valeriano 1602: 254–5); of spring (*ibid*.); and of adulterous lust: Shakespeare, *Love's Labour's Lost*, 5. 2 (song).
3–4. *king . . . crowned*: for garlanded and enthroned Cupid, see Panofsky 1962: 101 and plate 73; the original spelling, *girland*, contains the usual pun: *SC November* 75n.
5. *choir of birds*: mediaeval convention: e.g., *Romance of the Rose*, 613ff.: de Lorris and de Meun (1962) 3. 84–106. Cf. *Epith*, 78–91.
6. *anthems*: only *songs of praise* in loose sense from 1591 (*OED* anthem *sb* 3); probably here in original sense of antiphonal song (because of the way the echo responds). *devised*: fashioned, constructed. *of*: indicating the origin of an action: *OED* of *prep* 13.
7. *woods . . . echoes*: *SC June* 52n; *Epith*'s refrain. *rebounded*: re-echoed (sixteenth-century usage).
8. *lays*: *SC April* 33 gloss.

And doth his idle message set at nought.
Therefore, O Love, unless she turn to thee
   Ere cuckoo end, let her a rebel be.

SONNET 20

In vain I seek, and sue to her for, grace,
   And do mine humbled heart before her pour,
   The whiles her foot she in my neck doth place,
   And tread my life down in the lowly floor;
And yet the lion – that is lord of power,   5
   And reigneth over every beast in field –
   In his most pride disdaineth to devour
   The silly lamb that to his might doth yield.
But she, more cruel and more savage wild
   Than either lion or the lioness,   10
   Shames not to be with guiltless blood defiled,
   But taketh glory in her cruelness:
Fairer than fairest, let none ever say
   That ye were blooded in a yielded prey.

SONNET 21

Was it the work of Nature or of Art
   Which tempered so the feature of her face
   That pride and meekness, mixed by equal part,
   Do both appear to adorn her beauty's grace?

---

12. idle: (1) useless; (2) encouraging indolence.
14. let: (1) permit (her to be); (2) prevent her from being (*OED* let *v* 2).
Sonnet 20   3. *foot . . . neck*: traditional position of (monarchical) triumphator: cf. *FQ*, 6. 7. 26 (also in connection with lion); Yates 1975: 43–4, plates 4a, c, 5a, 7a.
5–8. lion . . . yield: the power and clemency of the lion (emblem of kingship) were traditional (Tervarent (1958) cols 245–6) and proverbial: Smith 1970: 172.
8. silly: (1) deserving of compassion; (2) defenceless; usual epithet for sheep: *OED* silly *a* A 1. *lamb*: innocence, gentleness, humility: Tervarent, cols 2–3.
14. blooded: smeared, stained, with blood (*OED*'s first instance of this meaning: blood *v* 2). You shouldn't kill a *prey* that has *yielded* (given up).
Sonnet 21   Scott 1927: 194 compares Tasso, *Rime*, ed. Solerti, 2. 115 no. 80 ('Qualor madonna') and 2. 315, no. 14 ('Non regna brama'). Cf. Petrarch, *Rime*, 154.
1. Nature . . . Art: the complementariness of the two is a Renaissance commonplace: Nature fell from perfection with the Fall of Man; Art (in some measure) redeems that fallenness.
2. tempered: mixed in equal balance: cf. *Am* 13. 4n.

For with mild pleasance, which doth pride displace,   5
   She to her Loves doth lookers' eyes allure,
   And with stern countenance back again doth chase
   Their looser looks that stir up lusts impure.
With such strange terms her eyes she doth inure
   That with one look she doth my life dismay,   10
   And with another doth it straight recure:
   Her smile me draws, her frown me drives away.
Thus doth she train and teach me with her looks:
   Such art of eyes I never read in books.

SONNET 22

This holy season, fit to fast and pray,
   Men to devotion ought to be inclined.
Therefore I likewise, on so holy day,
   For my sweet saint some service fit will find:
Her temple fair is built within my mind,   5
   In which her glorious image placed is
   On which my thoughts do day and night attend
   Like sacred priests that never think amiss.
There I to her, as the author of my bliss,

---

5. *pleasance*: *Am* 17. 11n.
6. *Loves*: see *Am* 16. 6. *lookers'*: those who look: first *OED* citation, 1556. Develops the proverb 'Love is bred by looking': Smith 1970: 177–8.
9. *With . . . terms*: within (or to) such extreme limits. *inure*: (1) accustom: cf. *Am* 14. 7n; (2) put into effect.
10. *life*: (1) life force; (2) soul. *dismay*: *Am* 14. 1n.
11. *recure*: restore.
13. *train*: (1) instruct; (2) draw (me on): *OED* train *v* 1, II. 4, III. 6.
Sonnet 22 The beginning of the Lenten/Easter sequence: see headnote. Sources include Desportes, *Les Amours de Diane*, 1. 43 (Kastner 1908–9: 67–8) and the Easter symbolism of Petrarch's *Rime* (Petrarch fell in love with Laura on Good Friday (*Rime*, 3): Roche 1989: 32–3, 42–4.
4. *saint*: suggests the Petrarchan veneration of the beloved's holiness (in *Rime*, 4 Laura is a 'sun' sent by Christ) and the biblical sense of 'the elect'. See *SC July* headnote.
5–8. *temple . . . amiss*: the poet creates a mental image which is at once a testament to his worship of her (cf. the psychological symbolism of the Temple of Venus at *FQ*, 4. 10) and a memory construct which will enable him to recall her image in times of doubt (see Yates 1966 on the building as memory aid).
5. *temple*: implying the Pauline idea of the body as the temple of the Holy Spirit: 1 Corinthians 3: 16, 6: 19, etc.
6. *glorious*: *Am* 17. 1n.
9. *author*: used of Christ as saviour at Hebrews 5: 9: Gibbs 1990: 127. Refers also to the poet as writer of *Am* and recorder of the 'bliss' achieved in *Epith*.

Will build an altar to appease her ire, 10
　And on the same my heart will sacrifice,
　Burning in flames of pure and chaste desire,
The which vouchsafe, O goddess, to accept,
　Amongst thy dearest relics to be kept.

SONNET 23

Penelope, for her Ulysses' sake,
　Devised a web her wooers to deceive,
　In which the work that she all day did make
　The same at night she did again unreave.
Such subtle craft my damsel doth conceive 5
　The importune suit of my desire to shun:
　For all that I in many days do weave,
　In one short hour I find by her undone.
So, when I think to end that I begun,
　I must begin and never bring to end: 10
　For with one look she spills that long I spun,
　And with one word my whole year's work doth rend.
Such labour like the spider's web I find,
　Whose fruitless work is broken with least wind.

---

11. heart: the lover's heart identified with the sinner's Lenten heart: cf. Psalm 51, recited in full as part of the 'Commination against Sinners' appointed for Ash Wednesday (see verses 10, 17 and 19, the last two of which read: 'a contrite and a broken heart, O God, thou wilt not despise. . . . Then shalt thou accept the sacrifices of righteousness, even the burnt offering and oblation'); the heart is also prominent in the Collect and Epistles (Joel 2: 12–17, Matthew 6: 16–21) for Ash Wednesday: *Prayer-book 1559*: 144–5, 67.
12. flames: Dunlop (Oram *et al.* 1989: 614n) compares the purifying fire of Dante, *Purgatorio*, 25. 112–139.
Sonnet 23 *1. Penelope*: emblem of the chaste and obedient wife because she resisted the suitors who pursued her during the twenty-year absence of her husband, Odysseus (Ulysses), by promising to listen to them when she finished the shroud she was weaving. However, each night she unravelled the previous day's work: Homer, *Odyssey*, 2. 93–105. She became proverbial: Smith 1970: 215–16. Neo-Platonically the product of weaving (web, tapestry, etc.) symbolises the material universe veiling us from the world of the spirit and the divine: Porphyry in *Thomas Taylor* 1969: 305 and cf. *Am* 77. 1n. See also Ziegler 1992: 25–46.
4. unreave: unravel; first *OED* citation 1593.
7. I . . . weave: the lover appropriates the traditionally female role: cf., in addition to Penelope, Arachne (Ovid, *Metamorphoses*, 6. 1–145; note the reference to *spider* at l. 13).
11. spills: *Am* 17. 7n.
14. wind: (1) puff of air; (2) action of winding.

SONNET 24

When I behold that beauty's wonderment,
  And rare perfection of each goodly part
  (Of Nature's skill the only complement),
  I honour and admire the maker's art.
But when I feel the bitter baleful smart   5
  Which her fair eyes unwares do work in me
  That death out of their shiny beams do dart,
  I think that I a new Pandora see,
Whom all the gods in council did agree
  Into this sinful world from heaven to send   10
  That she to wicked men a scourge should be
  For all their faults with which they did offend:
But since ye are my scourge, I will entreat
  That for my faults ye will me gently beat.

SONNET 25

How long shall this like-dying life endure
  And know no end of her own misery,
  But waste and wear away in terms unsure,
  'Twixt fear and hope depending doubtfully?
Yet better were at once to let me die,   5
  And show the last ensample of your pride,

Sonnet 24 *1. beauty's wonderment*: wonderful quality of beauty (*OED* sense 3, citing the same phrase from *FQ*, 4. 5. 20 as its first instance); more probably wonderful example (of beauty): *OED* sense 2b, first citation 1606.
4. maker's: no initial capital in original. Possibly God, but maybe an allusion to the lady as a statue fashioned by a sculptor (e.g., Pygmalion and Galathea: cf. *Am* 51. 10n).
5. baleful smart: *SC January* 27n.
6. unwares: (1) unexpectedly; (2) unintentionally.
8. Pandora: = all gifts (or gifts of all): the first woman, fashioned by Vulcan, blacksmith of the gods, and given an attribute or accomplishment by each of them. When Prometheus, the creator of man, stole fire from heaven for his creation, angry Jupiter sent Pandora to become the wife of Prometheus's brother, Epimetheus, bearing a large jar containing all the diseases and evils that would afflict mankind and which she eventually released. Hesiod's phrase for Pandora, *kalon kakon* (beautiful evil; *Theogony*, 585), sums up Spenser's ambivalent attitude. On the myth, see Panofsky 1956 (rev. 1962). Cf. *Am* 61. 8n.
Sonnet 25 Scott 1927: 194 compares Petrarch, *Rime*, 134.
2. her: life's.
3. terms: (1) circumstances; (2) periods of time.
4. depending: hanging, suspended. *doubtfully*: uncertainly.
6. ensample: instance.

            Than to torment me thus with cruelty
            To prove your power which I too well have tried.
        But yet if in your hardened breast ye hide
            A close intent at last to show me grace, 10
            Then all the woes and wrecks which I abide
            As means of bliss I gladly will embrace,
        And wish that more and greater they might be,
            That greater meed at last may turn to me.

SONNET 26

Sweet is the rose, but grows upon a briar;
    Sweet is the juniper, but sharp his bough;
    Sweet is the eglantine, but pricketh near;
    Sweet is the fir bloom, but his branches rough;
Sweet is the cypress, but his rind is tough; 5
    Sweet is the nut, but bitter is his pill;
    Sweet is the broom flower, but yet sour enough;

---

8. *tried*: tested.
10. *close*: *Am* 1. 8n.
11. *wrecks*: overthrowing(s) of the normal order of things: *OED* sense 10, first instance 1577. *abide*: endure.
14. *meed*: reward. *turn*: (1) transfer; (2) return, revert: *OED* turn *v* IV. 15, 21.
Sonnet 26 Based on the neo-Platonic/Orphic theme of love's bitter-sweetness, often symbolised through the idea of dying into love, as in *Romeo and Juliet*: Wind 1967: 160–65. The sonnet also emphasises smell, taste and touch – the last two associated with lust (on smell, see *Am* 64. 1n). This flower catalogue, 4th after the Ash Wednesday sonnet, corresponds to the garden sonnet *Am* 64, 4th before the Easter Day sonnet, 68.
1. *rose*: emblem of Venus and love (D'Ancona 1983: 104, 145); the thorny *briar* symbolises (1) the difficulty of attaining the beloved; (2) the fallen world (*SC February* 115n). The phrasing is proverbial: Smith 1970: 262.
2. *juniper*: sweet-berried and sweetly-scented but prickly-leaved: Pliny, *Natural History*, 13. 11. 52–3.
3. *eglantine*: hedge rose: *SC February* 115n. *near*: extremely.
4. *fir . . . rough*: not the coniferous tree but *furze*, i.e., gorse or whin (*OED* fur *sb* 3), sweet-scented but prickly (*OED* rough *a* B I. 1 citing the phrase 'rougher than thorns'). Like the rose and eglantine, associated with spring and love: de Vries 1974: 206. (But the ambiguity is useful: *firs* are placed by Politian in the Garden of Love: D'Ancona 1983: 60.)
5. *cypress*: sweet-smelling again; *rind* = bark.
6. *pill*: shell. The line is proverbial: Smith 1970: 208.
7. *broom*: related to the furze (de Vries 1974: 66): sweet-smelling but bitter, it was used as a diuretic and for vomits: Salmon (1678) 1. 4 (p 59).

And sweet is moly, but his root is ill:
So every sweet with sour is tempered still
   That maketh it be coveted the more,   10
   For easy things that may be got at will
   Most sorts of men do set but little store.
Why then should I account of little pain
   That endless pleasure shall unto me gain?

SONNET 27

Fair proud, now tell me why should fair be proud,
   Sith all world's glory is but dross unclean
And in the shade of death itself shall shroud,
   However now thereof ye little ween?
That goodly idol, now so gay beseen,   5
   Shall doff her flesh's borrowed fair attire,
   And be forgot as it had never been,
   That many now much worship and admire.
Ne any then shall after it enquire,
   Ne any mention shall thereof remain   10
But what this verse (that never shall expire)
   Shall to you purchase with her thankless pain:
Fair, be no longer proud of that shall perish,
   But that which shall you make immortal, cherish.

---

8. *moly*: shrub given to Odysseus by Hermes/Mercury to enable him to overcome the lusts offered by Circe (hence = reason, eloquence): white-flowered, it had a black root (*Odyssey*, 10. 302–6) – hence (perhaps) 'ill'.
9. *sweet . . . still*: proverbial: Smith 1970: 256. *tempered*: modified.
11–12. *easy . . . store*: proverbial: Smith 1970: 138–9.
13. *account of*: make much of.
Sonnet 27 On the traditional vanity theme; the promise of immortality through verse is developed through the laurel/poetry/immortality connection in *Am* 28, 29.
2. *Sith*: since. *glory*: (1) honour; (2) glittering splendour. *dross*: cf. *Am* 13. 12n.
3. *shade of death*: shadow of death (common phrase: *OED* shade *sb* I. 1b).
4. *ween*: think.
5–6. *idol . . . attire*: traditional attack on female vanity (cf. *Hamlet*, 5. 1). *Idol* contrasts with *saint* (*Am* 22. 4n), evoking biblical passages such as Ezekiel 23: 37 ('with their idols have they committed adultery'). Line 6 also alludes to the neo-Platonic and Christian idea of the escape of the soul from the body.
5. *goodly*: comely. *gay beseen*: gaily dressed.
6. *doff*: put/take off clothing.
9–10. *Ne . . . Ne*: neither . . . nor.
11. *But*: except.
12. *Shall . . . pain*: shall gain for you with thankless effort.
13. *that*: that which.

SONNET 28

The laurel leaf, which you this day do wear,
   Gives me great hope of your relenting mind;
   For, since it is the badge which I do bear,
   Ye, bearing it, do seem to me inclined;
The power thereof, which oft in me I find,   5
   Let it likewise your gentle breast inspire
   With sweet infusion, and put you in mind
   Of that proud maid whom now those leaves attire:
Proud Daphne, scorning Phoebus' lovely fire,
   On the Thessalian shore from him did flee,   10
   For which the gods (in their revengeful ire)
   Did her transform into a laurel tree:
Then fly no more, fair love, from Phoebus' chase,
   But in your breast his leaf and love embrace.

SONNET 29

See how the stubborn damsel doth deprave
   My simple meaning with disdainful scorn,
   And by the bay which I unto her gave
   Accounts myself her captive quite forlorn:
'The bay', quoth she, 'is of the victors borne,   5

Sonnet 28 Like all Elizabethan sonnets to the laurel (cf. *Am* 29), indebted to Petrarch's characterisation of Laura as the virgin laurel that resulted from Daphne's metamorphosis after Apollo's pursuit of her: *Rime*, 5; Ovid, *Metamorphoses*, 1. 452–567. The laurel/bay became Phoebus Apollo's emblem in his role as god of poetry and music (*Metamorphoses*. 1. 518), as well as the emblem of victory and immortality (*ibid.*, 558–64; cf. *SC April* 104 gloss; Braden 1986; Roche (1989) ch 1). Neo-Platonically, Daphne's rejection of Apollo marks a rejection of divine illumination.

1–4. laurel . . . inclined: the poet misreads the lady's wearing of his laurel as a sign of submission (whereas –*Am* 29. 1–4 – it is actually a sign of her victorious independence from male domination).

7. infusion: literally, pouring in (Daphne was daughter of the river-god, Peneus); in connection with *inspire*, suggests the infiltration of divine grace: *OED* infusion sb 2, quote 1526.

8. proud: perhaps influenced by Ronsard, *Astrée*, 11 (Lotspeich 1932: 52); but probably merely an accusation against the lady's insistence on retaining her virginity. *leaves*: of laurel as poetic fame, hence the pages of *Am*, as at 1. 1.

9. fire: flame of love; punning on Apollo as sun god.

14. leaf: punning on *lief* = beloved.

Sonnet 29 *1. deprave*: (1) pervert; (2) corrupt a text.

2. disdainful: cf. *Am* 5. 6n.

4. forlorn: *Am* 13. 11n.

Yielded them by the vanquished as their meeds,
And they therewith do poets' heads adorn
To sing the glory of their famous deeds'.
But sith she will the conquest challenge needs,
   Let her accept me as her faithful thrall,   10
   That her great triumph (which my skill exceeds)
   I may in trump of Fame blaze over all:
Then would I deck her head with glorious bays,
And fill the world with her victorious praise.

SONNET 30

My love is like to ice, and I to fire:
   How comes it, then, that this her cold so great
   Is not dissolved through my so-hot desire,
   But harder grows the more I her entreat?
Or, how comes it that my exceeding heat   5
   Is not delayed by her heart frozen cold,
   But that I burn much more in boiling sweat
   And feel my flames augmented manifold?
What more miraculous thing may be told
   That fire, which all thing melts, should harden ice,   10
   And ice, which is congealed with senseless cold,
   Should kindle fire by wonderful device?
Such is the power of love in gentle mind,
That it can alter all the course of kind.

SONNET 31

Ah, why hath Nature to so hard a heart
   Given so goodly gifts of beauty's grace,
   Whose pride depraves each other better part,

6. *meeds*: *Am* 25. 14n.
9. *will . . . needs*: feels compelled to.
10. *thrall*: (1) captive; (2) servant.
12. *trump of Fame*: see Ripa 1603: 142–3; also the emblem of the epic poet: *FQ*, 1 proem 1. In view of the triumphal symbolism, the phrase puns on the title of Petrarch's *Triumph of Fame* (cf. *Am* 5. 11 and 20. 3nn). *blaze*: blow (of a trumpet, etc.); hence, proclaim. The first sense is a mediaevalism: *OED* blaze *v* 2, 1.
Sonnet 30   *1. ice . . . fire*: deriving from Petrarch, *Rime*, 202 (and cf. 134).
6. *delayed*: (1) mitigated; (2) tempered: *OED* delay *v* 2.
11–12. *ice . . . fire*: proverbial: Smith 1970: 107.
11. *senseless*: devoid (and depriving) of sensation.
12. *device*: ingenuity, contrivance.
14. *kind*: nature.
Sonnet 31   Scott 1927: 194 compares Desportes, *Cléonice*, 74.
3. *depraves*: spoils the character of.

And all those precious ornaments deface
(Sith to all other beasts of bloody race 5
   A dreadful countenance she given hath
   That, with their terror, all the rest may chase
And warn to shun the danger of their wrath)?
But my proud one doth work the greater scathe
   Through sweet allurement of her lovely hue, 10
   That she the better may in bloody bath
Of such poor thralls her cruel hands imbrue:
But did she know how ill these two accord,
   Such cruelty she would have soon abhorred.

SONNET 32

The painful smith, with force of fervent heat,
   The hardest iron soon doth mollify
   That with his heavy sledge he can it beat
And fashion to what he it list apply.
Yet cannot all these flames in which I fry 5
   Her heart more hard than iron soft a whit,
   Ne all the plaints and prayers with which I
Do beat on the anvil of her stubborn wit:
But still the more she fervent sees my fit,
   The more she freezeth in her wilful pride, 10
   And harder grows the harder she is smit
With all the plaints which to her be applied.

---

4. *deface*: defaces.
5. *Sith*: *Am* 27. 2n. *beasts . . . race*: i.e., carnivorous predators.
6. *dreadful countenance*: cf. *Am* 49, 53.
9. *scathe*: hurt.
10. *hue*: *Am* 3. 8n.
12. *imbrue*: defile.
13. *ill . . . accord*: charge of intemperance: ct. *Am* 13. 4n, 21. 2n, 26. 9.
Sonnet 32 1. *painful*: taking extreme care. *smith*: perhaps hinting at Pandora's origin: *Am* 24. 8n. *fervent*: glowing.
2. *mollify*: soften (from Latin *mollis*, which provides the root for *mulier* = woman).
3. *sledge*: blacksmith's heavy hammer.
4. *fashion*: make. *list*: wishes. *apply*: bend.
5. *fry*: am tortured by burning.
6. *a whit*: at all.
7. *plaints*: *Am* 18. 7n.
9. *fit*: (1) section of poem; (2) paroxysm (*OED* fit *sbs* 1, 2).
11. *harder . . . smit*: proverbial: Smith 1970: 157.

What then remains but I to ashes burn,
　And she to stones at length all frozen turn?

SONNET 33

Great wrong I do, I can it not deny,
　To that most sacred Empress, my dear dread,
　Not finishing her *Queen of Faery*,
　That mote enlarge her living praises dead.
But, Lodwick, this of grace to me aread:　　　　　　　　　　5
　Do ye not think the accomplishment of it
　Sufficient work for one man's simple head,
　All were it as the rest but rudely writ?
How, then, should I, without another wit,
　Think ever to endure so tedious toil,　　　　　　　　　　　10
　Since that this one is tossed with troublous fit
　Of a proud love that doth my spirit spoil?
Cease, then, till she vouchsafe to grant me rest,
　Or lend you me another living breast.

SONNET 34

Like as a ship that through the ocean wide
　By conduct of some star doth make her way,

14. stones: hailstones (*OED* stone *sb* 9); but also glancing (ironically) at the stones cast by Deucalion and Pyrrha (son and daughter respectively of Prometheus and Epimetheus) which 'soften' into human form: Ovid, *Metamorphoses*, 1. 398–415: note the link with the Pandora myth (*Am* 24. 8n) and the fact that in Ovid this myth immediately precedes the Apollo-Daphne myth (*Am* 28 headnote). The hint at metamorphosis implicates Narcissus at *Am* 35, 83, suggesting the sterility of self-change in contrast to the children resulting from the change brought about by marriage: *Epith* 357–9, 384–7nn, etc.
Sonnet 33 *2. Empress*: the 1590 *FQ* was dedicated to Elizabeth as 'the most mighty and magnificent empress' (on the empire she claimed, see Yates 1975). *dread*: someone revered, held in awe: cf. *FQ*, 1 proem 4: the queen as 'dearest dread'. For a complementary sonnet, see *Am* 80.
4. mote: might. *living . . . dead*: posthumous reputation.
5. Lodwick: Lodowick Bryskett, friend of Sidney and Spenser, who worked with Spenser in Ireland and contributed an elegy on Sidney to *Astrophel*. *aread*: tell, advise.
7. simple: humble.
8. All: even. *rudely*: unskilfully.
9. wit: intellect.
11. this one: the lover['s wit]. *fit*: (1) hardship; (2) section of poem.
12. spoil: destroy.
Sonnet 34 Based on a common Petrarchan metaphor: *Rime*, 189 (translated by Wyatt as 'My galley charged with forgetfulness') and 235. Cf. *FQ*, 3. 4. 53.
2. conduct: guidance.

Whenas a storm hath dimmed her trusty guide
Out of her course doth wander far astray:
So I – whose star (that wont with her bright ray   5
  Me to direct) with clouds is overcast –
  Do wander now in darkness and dismay
  Through hidden perils round about me placed.
Yet hope I well that, when this storm is past,
  My Helice, the lodestar of my life,   10
  Will shine again, and look on me at last
  With lovely light to clear my cloudy grief.
Till then I wander care-full comfortless
  In secret sorrow and sad pensiveness.

SONNET 35

My hungry eyes, through greedy covetise
  Still to behold the object of their pain,
  With no contentment can themselves suffice,
  But having, pine, and having not, complain:
For, lacking it, they cannot life sustain,   5
  And, having it, they gaze on it the more,

8. hidden perils: Petrarch, *Rime*, 189 – closer to the traditional allegory of the tempted ship of the body – names Scylla and Charybdis from *Odyssey*, 10, (lust and greed: Allen 1970: 150.) For the sea and storm of sensual temptation, see Porphyry in *Thomas Taylor* 1969: 331.

10. Helice: = winding (Greek); name given to Ursa Major and, by extension, to Ursa Minor (which contains the pole star), it signifies their apparent circling motion round the north pole. The allusion is witty because (1) Ursa Major is the stellified nymph Callisto, raped by Jupiter, metamorphosed into a bear by Juno, elevated to heaven by Jupiter (Ovid, *Metamorphoses*, 2. 409–530): cf. the metamorphic themes at *Am* 28 and 32. 14n; (2) Diana banished Callisto/Helice for her unchastity (cf. Dante, *Purgatorio*, 25. 130–2); (3) *Helice* recalls *Helicon* (*Am* 1. 10); (4) *Helice* sounds like *Elise/Elisa*: *Am* 74. 13n. *Lodestar* was a common name for the pole star.

Sonnet 35 Repeated (with one substantive variant) as *Am* 83. For the numerological function of the repetition, see headnote.

1. covetise: lust: cf. 1 John 2: 16 on 'lust of the eyes' as a worldly – as opposed to spiritual – attribute. Chaucer, *Parson's Tale*, 850 calls it 'covetise of eyen'. *hungry . . . greedy* lead to lustful *covetise* because gluttony and lust are close cousins (*Parson's Tale*, 836). The insatiability of covetousness was proverbial: Smith 1970: 64.

4. pine: *SC January* 48n.

In their amazement like Narcissus vain,
   Whose eyes him starved: so plenty makes me poor.
Yet are mine eyes so filled with the store
   Of that fair sight that nothing else they brook,   10
But loathe the things which they did like before,
   And can no more endure on them to look:
All this world's glory seemeth vain to me,
   And all their shows but shadows, saving she.

SONNET 36
Tell me, when shall these weary woes have end?
   Or shall their ruthless torment never cease,
But all my days in pining languor spend
   Without hope of assuagement or release?
Is there no means for me to purchase peace,   5
   Or make agreement with her thrilling eyes,
But that their cruelty doth still increase,
   And daily more augment, my miseries?

7. amazement: *Am* 3. 7n.
7–8. Narcissus . . . poor: *SC September* emblem gloss. Often interpreted as an emblem of greed: Ross 1648: 307, noting also that 'the name *Narcissus* sheweth, that it causeth stupidity' (senselessness, or *amazement*). Unlike the poet, however, Narcissus loved an unattainable beloved (his reflection; in some accounts, his twin sister: Pausanias, *Description of Greece*, 9. 31. 8). On Narcissus, Petrarch and Laura, see Leonard 1984: 16–21, 66–9 and Freccero 1975.
8. starved: caused to die of grief (*OED* starve *v* I. 1); also used of the withering of plants (sense I. 3): appropriate, because Narcissus was metamorphosed into a daffodil.
9. store: abundance.
10. brook: (1) endure; (2) enjoy; (3) digest (*OED* brook *v* 2), linking with *greedy*, *store*.
13–14. glory . . . shadows: apparent Platonist rejection of the world in favour of the soul (cf. *Am* 27. 2) with overtones of 1 John 2: 15: 'Love not this world, neither the things that are in this world' (cf.l. 1n). But his fixation on the lady for herself (rather than as a symbol of Beauty) suggests he is committing the sin of Narcissus as interpreted by Ficino, *Commentary*, 6. 17 (Ficino 1944: 212): pursuing the shadow of his reflection, Narcissus represents the soul attracted by the beauty of the physical body rather than its own (spiritual) beauty, hence remaining unfulfilled. The water on which Narcissus gazed is the element of confusion and parallels the ocean of error in the preceding sonnet. For a slightly different application of Ficino, see Edwards 1977: 70–4.
Sonnet 36 Cf. war/peace/eyes in Petrarch, *Rime*, 21 and 150; also *Am* 12.
6. thrilling: *Am* 12. 1n.

But when ye have showed all extremities,
   Then think how little glory ye have gained   10
   By slaying him whose life, though ye despise,
   Mote have your life in honour long maintained:
But by his death (which some, perhaps, will moan)
   Ye shall condemned be of many a one.

SONNET 37

What guile is this, that those her golden tresses
   She doth attire under a net of gold,
   And with sly skill so cunningly them dresses
   That which is gold or hair may scarce be told?
Is it that men's frail eyes, which gaze too bold,   5
   She may entangle in that golden snare
   And, being caught, may craftily enfold
   Their weaker hearts, which are not well aware?
Take heed, therefore, mine eyes, how ye do stare
   Henceforth too rashly on that guileful net   10
   In which, if ever ye entrapped are,
   Out of her bands ye by no means shall get:
Fondness it were for any, being free,
   To covet fetters, though they golden be.

---

9. extremities: intense passions.
12. Mote: might.
Sonnet 37 *1. golden tresses*: cf. *Am* 81 and Petrarch, *Rime*, 90 (Laura'a golden hair was spread out in the breeze).
2. attire: dress (the head): *OED*'s only sixteenth-century example of this sense.
6. entangle: a further instance of the poet/lover's insistent misreading of the lady's body language and signals: bound hair was emblematic of chastity: Wind 1967: 117. He sees her as an enchaining Venus: Wind, fig. 77 and *Am* 10 headnote. Cf. Penelope's *web* at *Am* 23. The hair-as-trap motif originates with Song of Solomon 7: 5 and is frequent in Petrarch (e.g., *Rime*, 59, 196, 253). Cf. *Am* 73.
13–14. Fondness . . . be: proverbial: Smith 1970: 105; cf. *FQ*, 3. 9. 8.
13. Fondness: folly. *any . . . free*: (1) any free being; (2) anyone who is free (but the lover isn't).

SONNET 38

Arion, when through tempest's cruel wrack
   He forth was thrown into the greedy seas,
   Through the sweet music which his harp did make
   Allured a dolphin him from death to ease:
But my rude music, which was wont to please   5
   Some dainty ears, cannot with any skill
   The dreadful tempest of her wrath appease,
   Nor move the dolphin from her stubborn will.
But in her pride she doth persever still,
   All careless how my life for her decays –   10
   Yet with one word she can it save or spill.
   To spill were pity, but to save were praise:
Choose rather to be praised for doing good
   Than to be blamed for spilling guiltless blood.

SONNET 39

Sweet smile, the daughter of the queen of love,
   Expressing all thy mother's powerful art
   With which she wonts to temper angry Jove
   When all the gods he threats with thundering dart:
Sweet is thy virtue as thyself sweet art,   5
   For when on me thou shinedst late in sadness,
   A melting pleasance ran through every part

Sonnet 38 *1. Arion*: Greek musician-poet, often paired with Orpheus, who was robbed while on a sea journey but played to the thieves on his lyre before throwing himself overboard. He was borne to land by a dolphin attracted by his playing; it was rewarded by being immortalised as the constellation Delphinus, controller of the sea and navigation (Valeriano 1602: 274–6): cf. the sea dangers of *Am* 34. But Ovid reports that the dolphin was stellified because it was 'a happy guide in love-intrigues': *Fasti*, 2. 81. The lover's introduction of the *tempest* marks his appropriation of the legend to his psychology of storm and torment (e.g., *Am* 34, 36, 40). *wrack*: (1) violence; (2) retributive punishment.
5. *rude*: *Am* 33. 8n. *was . . . please*: customarily pleased.
6. *dainty*: of delicate sensibility: first *OED* citation, 1576.
9. *persever*: the normal sixteenth-century spelling preserves the pronunciation.
10. *careless*: uncaring.
11. *spill*: destroy (the soul): *OED* spill *v* 2b; also (14), shed blood.
12. *spill . . . praise*: proverbial: Smith 1970: 139–40. Cf. *Am* 49. 4.
Sonnet 39 *1. smile . . . love*: Venus is traditionally associated with laughter: *Am* 18. 12n.
3. *wonts*: is accustomed. *temper*: temperance again: *Am* 13. 4, 26. 9, 31. 13nn. *Jove*: king of heaven, one of whose emblems is the thunderbolt.
7. *pleasance*: delight.

And me revived with heart-robbing gladness
Whilst, rapt with joy resembling heavenly madness,
   My soul was ravished quite as in a trance   10
   And, feeling thence no more her sorrow's sadness,
   Fed on the fulness of that cheerful glance:
More sweet than nectar or ambrosial meat
   Seemed every bit which thenceforth I did eat.

SONNET 40

Mark when she smiles with amiable cheer,
   And tell me, whereto can ye liken it
   When on each eyelid sweetly do appear
   An hundred Graces as in shade to sit?
Likest it seemeth (in my simple wit)   5
   Unto the fair sunshine in summer's day
   That, when a dreadful storm away is flit,
   Through the broad world doth spread his goodly ray,
At sight whereof each bird that sits on spray,
   And every beast that to his den was fled,   10
   Comes forth afresh out of their late dismay,
   And to the light lift up their drooping head:
So my storm-beaten heart likewise is cheered
   With that sunshine, when cloudy looks are cleared.

8. heart . . . gladness: blood leaves the heart (so it was thought) when one blushes with joy (the meaning of the Grace Euphrosyne's name: *SC April* 109 gloss).
9–10. rapt . . . trance: neo-Platonic (*Am* 3. 12n), with suggestions that he is flirting with, but ignoring, the rapture (or frenzy) induced by Venus that 'doth by a fervent love convert, and transmute the mind to God, and makes it altogether like to God': Agrippa 1651: 3. 49 (p 507).
13. nectar: the drink of the gods (*ambrosia* is the food or *meat*): cf. *SC November* 195 gloss. But neo-Platonically nectar was identified with honey, the *sweetness* (ll. 1, 5, 13) of which could signify the soul's entrapment in the pleasures of the body: Porphyry in *Thomas Taylor* 1969: 305–8 (cf. the bee in *Am* 71 and anacreontics 4).
14. bit: mouthful.
Sonnet 40 Cf. Laura's power over nature in *Rime*, 192, originating in Lucretius, *On the Nature of Things*, 1. 1 ff., where the influence of Venus disperses clouds, diminishes winds, persuades the earth to put forth flowers, encourages the birds to sing and mate, etc.
1. cheer: (1) face; (2) jollity.
3–4. eyelid . . . Graces: *SC June* 25 gloss.
7. storm: *Am* 34. 8, 38. 1nn. *flit*: past.
9. spray: slender branch.
11. dismay: terror (and see *Am* 14. 11n).
12. light . . . head: neo-Platonic image of illumination: cf. Porphyry in *Thomas Taylor* 1969: 302.

SONNET 41

Is it her nature, or is it her will,
   To be so cruel to an humbled foe?
   If nature, then she may it mend with skill;
   If will, then she at will may will forgo.
But if her nature and her will be so   5
   That she will plague the man that loves her most,
   And take delight to increase a wretch's woe,
   Then all her nature's goodly gifts are lost;
And that same glorious beauty's idle boast
   Is but a bait such wretches to beguile   10
   As, being long in her love's tempest tossed,
   She means at last to make her piteous spoil:
O fairest fair, let never it be named
   That so fair beauty was so foully shamed.

SONNET 42

The love which me so cruelly tormenteth
   So pleasing is in my extremest pain,
   That all the more my sorrow it augmenteth,
   The more I love and do embrace my bane.
Ne do I wish (for wishing were but vain)   5
   To be acquit from my continual smart,
   But joy her thrall for ever to remain,
   And yield for pledge my poor captived heart –
The which (that it from her may never start)
   Let her, if please her, bind with adamant chain,   10
   And from all wandering loves which mote pervart

Sonnet 41 For the cruelty/will theme, see *Am* 10.
1. nature: innate disposition. *will*: in the weak form, wish; or the stronger theological sense, will infected by original sin.
2. humbled foe: cf. yielded prey, *Am* 20. 14.
Sonnet 42 *2. pleasing . . . pain*: cf. love as bitter-sweet and a painful gift: Wind 1967: 162 and *Am* 26 headnote.
4. bane: (1) murderer; (2) poison (= the bitterness of love).
6. acquit: freed (in the legal sense, discharged).
7. joy: rejoice. *thrall*: *Am* 29. 10n, and *Am* 10–12 and 37nn (on Venus as imprisoner).
9. start: (1) recoil; (2) escape; (3) leave its hiding place (pun on *hart*: *Am* 1. 8–9n, 67, 73, etc.).
10. adamant chain: with which the cosmos is bound together by love: *HL*, 89. Cf. the *diamond* of *Am* 9. 10n.
11. pervart: common alternative spelling of *pervert*.

His safe assurance, strongly it restrain:
Only let her abstain from cruelty
     And do me not before my time to die.

SONNET 43
Shall I then silent be, or shall I speak?
     And if I speak, her wrath renew I shall;
     And if I silent be, my heart will break,
     Or choked be with overflowing gall.
What tyranny is this both my heart to thrall,   5
     And eke my tongue with proud restraint to tie,
     That neither I may speak nor think at all,
     But like a stupid stock in silence die?
Yet I my heart with silence secretly
     Will teach to speak, and my just cause to plead;   10
     And eke mine eyes with meek humility
     Love-learned letters to her eyes to read,
Which her deep wit, that true heart's thought can spell,
     Will soon conceive, and learn to construe well.

SONNET 44
When those renowmed noble peers of Greece
     Through stubborn pride amongst themselves did jar,

---

12. *assurance*: formal pledge: cf. *Am* 58–9.
14. *do . . . die*: cause me to die; proverbial: Smith 1970: 79.
Sonnet 43   Imitates Tasso, *Rime*, ed. Solerti, 2. 246, no. 164 ('Vuol che l'ami costei') and 2. 248, no. 166 ('Se taccio, il duol s'avanza'): Kostić 1959: 53–4. The sonnet plays with the Pythagorean and subsequently neo-Platonic idea of mystic silence assisting contemplation of the soul's origins (Wind 1967: 12–13n; *Epith* 353n), and the traditional Silence with bound mouth: Ripa 1603: 453.
1. *Shall . . . speak*: echoing Erasmus, *Praise of Folly*, 429D: Smith 1970: 247.
4. *gall*: the bitterness of love again: *Am* 42. 2, 4nn; *SC March* emblem n.
5. *thrall*: enslave.
8. *stock*: *SC February* 128n: as tree trunk it relates to the metamorphic theme (*Am* 28, 32): he is stunned by the lady so that he either becomes stupid or loses his senses so that his soul will be liberated.
13. *wit*: understanding. *spell*: (1) speak; (2) read.
14. *conceive*: understand. *construe*: interpret.
Sonnet 44   *1. renowmed*: common form of renowned. *peers*: equally-matched companions; here, the fifty heroes, including Orpheus and Hercules, who, led by Jason, sailed in the Argo questing for the Golden Fleece (remnant of a ram sacrificed to Jupiter in Colchis). Jason was aided in his attempt to get the Fleece by the witch Medea, daughter of the king of Colchis. For the quarrel (*jar*) of the heroes appeased by Orpheus, see Apollonius Rhodius, *Argonautica*,

Forgetful of the famous Golden Fleece,
  Then Orpheus with his harp their strife did bar.
But this continual cruel civil war 5
  (The which myself against myself do make
  Whilst my weak powers of passions warrayed are)
  No skill can stint nor reason can aslake:
But when in hand my tuneless harp I take,
  Then do I more augment my foe's despite, 10
  And grief renew, and passions do awake
  To battle fresh against myself to fight:
'Mongst whom, the more I seek to settle peace,
  The more I find their malice to increase.

SONNET 45

Leave, lady, in your glass of crystal clean
  Your goodly self for evermore to view,
  And in myself – my inward self, I mean –
  Most lively-like behold your semblant true.
Within my heart, though hardly it can show 5
  Thing so divine to view of earthly eye,
  The fair Idea of your celestial hue,
  And every part, remains immortally;
And were it not that through your cruelty
  With sorrow dimmed and deformed it were, 10
  The goodly image of your visnomy

---

1. 492–515; and on Orpheus, *SC June* 72n, *October* 28 gloss, *Epith* 16n. Since Medea killed her brother and, eventually, her children by Jason, the allusion glances at the poet's charge of the lady's cruelty; while the Fleece's colour relates it to *Am*'s neo-Platonic theme of solar illumination: *Am* 40. 12n (for the Fleece as immortality and the goal of the alchemical quest, see Ross 1648: 195).
7. *of . . . warrayed*: are ravaged by my passions (Spenser was the last to use *warray* with any frequency: see *OED*).
8. *aslake*: alleviate; with hints of *slacken* (*OED* sense 3), anticipating the *tuneless* (slack-stringed) *harp* of 9.
10. *despite*: disdain, aversion (Italian *dispetto*).
Sonnet 45 *1. glass*: mirror: *Am* 7. 1n. *clean*: completely (qualifies *leave*).
4. semblant: likeness.
6. view: sight.
7. Idea: suggests the Platonic Idea of Beauty; but as the lover is still immersed in bodily passions, actually signifies mental picture. *hue*: *Am* 3. 8n.
11. image: (1) likeness; (2) mental picture or idea; (3) optical appearance (as in mirror); (4) icon or picture (thus recalling *Am* 27. 5–6nn). *visnomy*: contemporary form of *physiognomy* = face.

Clearer than crystal would therein appear.
But if yourself in me ye plain will see,
   Remove the cause by which your fair beams darkened be.

SONNET 46

When my abode's prefixed time is spent,
   My cruel fair straight bids me wend my way:
   But then from heaven most hideous storms are sent,
   As willing me against her will to stay.
Whom, then, shall I, or heaven or her, obey?   5
   The heavens know best what is the best for me,
   But as she will – whose will my life doth sway,
   My lower heaven – so it perforce must be.
But ye high heavens, that all this sorrow see,
   Sith all your tempests cannot hold me back,   10
   Assuage your storms, or else both you and she
   Will both together me too sorely wrack:
Enough it is for one man to sustain
   The storms which she alone on me doth rain.

SONNET 47

Trust not the treason of those smiling looks
   Until ye have their guileful trains well tried,
   For they are like but unto golden hooks
   That from the foolish fish their baits do hide:

12. Clearer . . . crystal: proverbial: Smith 1970: 54; cf. *SC July*, 159, *August*, 80.
Sonnet 46 *1. abode's*: visit's.
4. willing . . . will: cf. *Am* 41. 1n.
5. or . . . or: either . . . or.
10. tempests: symbols of divine punishment (Isaiah 29: 6) as well as of the passions: cf. *Am* 34. 8n and 41. 11.
12. wrack: (1) variant of wreck; (2) punish (rare: *OED* wrack *v* 1, 1); (2) torture, as on a rack (*OED* rack *v* 3).
Sonnet 47 Scott 1927: 194 compares Tasso, *Rime*, ed. Solerti, 2. 128, no. 88 ('M'apre talor madonna').
1–2. Trust . . . tried: proverbial: Smith 1970: 270.
2. trains: (1) wiles or stratagems (*OED* train *sb* 2); (2) trails, lines (that draw one towards something: *OED* train *sb* 1 and *v* 1): alluding here to contemporary drawings of the way optical images are received by the eye by tracing lines between it and the object viewed. Then, by extension, angling lines (ll. 3–4: see *Am* 1. 5n). *tried*: *Am* 25. 8n.
3–4. hooks . . . hide: proverbial: Smith 1970: 35.

So she, with flattering smiles, weak hearts doth guide 5
    Unto her love, and tempt to their decay;
    Whom, being caught, she kills with cruel pride,
    And feeds at pleasure on the wretched prey.
Yet, even whilst her bloody hands them slay,
    Her eyes look lovely and upon them smile 10
    That they take pleasure in her cruel play
    And, dying, do themselves of pain beguile:
O mighty charm, which makes men love their bane,
    And think they die with pleasure, live with pain.

SONNET 48

Innocent paper – whom too cruel hand
    Did make the matter to avenge her ire
    And, ere she could thy cause well understand,
    Did sacrifice unto the greedy fire –
Well worthy thou to have found better hire 5
    Than so bad end for heretics ordained:
    Yet heresy nor treason didst conspire,
    But plead thy master's cause unjustly pained,
Whom she, all careless of his grief, constrained
    To utter forth the anguish of his heart, 10
    And would not hear when he to her complained
    The piteous passion of his dying smart:
Yet live for ever, though against her will,
    And speak her good though she requite it ill.

---

6. *decay*: (1) erosion; (2) destruction.
7–8. *cruel . . . prey*: the emphasis on smiles evokes Venus (*Am* 18. 12 and 39. 1nn), so the lady is not so much a predatory animal here as a hunter *via* the Venus/venery (= hunting and pursuit of lust) pun: cf. *Am* 41. 2n.
10. *lovely*: lovingly: *OED*'s last citation is from *FQ*, 4. 3. 49.
12. *beguile*: cheat.
13. *bane*: *Am* 42. 4n.
Sonnet 48   Compare Desportes, *Diane* 2. 75: Kastner 1908–9: 69.
2. *matter*: cause.
5. *hire*: reward.
8. *plead*: past tense. *pained*: punished: *OED* pain *v* I. 1.
9. *careless*: uncaring.
11. *when . . . complained*: either (1) transitive (he laments his passion to her) or (2) intransitive (she won't hear, when he laments, the passion).
12. *passion*: affliction. *smart*: suffering.
14. *speak . . . good*: speak of her goodness; speak well of her.

SONNET 49

Fair cruel, why are ye so fierce and cruel?
   Is it because your eyes have power to kill?
   Then know that mercy is the mighties' jewel,
   And greater glory think to save than spill.
But if it be your pleasure and proud will 5
   To show the power of your imperious eyes,
   Then, not on him that never thought you ill,
   But bend your force against your enemies:
Let them feel the utmost of your cruelties,
   And kill with looks, as cockatrices do. 10
   But him that at your footstool humbled lies,
   With merciful regard give mercy to:
Such mercy shall you make admired to be,
   So shall you live by giving life to me.

SONNET 50

Long languishing in double malady
   Of my heart's wound and of my body's grief,
   There came to me a leech that would apply
   Fit medicines for my body's best relief.
'Vain man', quod I, 'that hast but little prief 5
   In deep discovery of the mind's disease:

Sonnet 49 Scott 1927: 194 compares Tasso, *Rime*, ed. Solerti, 2: 107 no. 74 ('O più crudel').

3. mercy . . . jewel: mercy is the jewel of those who are mighty, for it was the virtue of emperors: Thomas Elyot, *The Book named The Governor* (1531), 2. 7: note *imperious* at l. 6. But possibly 'the Almighty's' is intended: Cook 1918: 289.

4. spill: kill. Cf. *Am* 38. 12n.

10. cockatrices: fabulous creatures with body of cock and serpent's tail, supposedly born from a cock's egg; identified with the basilisk; had the power to kill with its glance: Ansell Robin 1932: 84–95. The cock is an emblem of pride; the serpent inevitably alludes to the lady as a daughter of Eve: cf. the paradisal serpent depicted with female head and torso in Trapp 1968: 262–3.

11. footstool . . . lies: *Am* 20. 3n.

Sonnet 50 Indebted to Desportes' *Les Amours d'Hippolyte*, sonnet 53: Kastner 1908–9: 68–9.

1. languishing: (1) suffering from sickness; (2) pining with love.

3. leech: physician. But the poem hinges on the fact that the word often referred to Christ: 13n below.

5. prief: knowledge, experience (*OED* proof *sb* II. 5; a favourite with Spenser; last citation 1613).

Is not the heart of all the body chief,
  And rules the members as itself doth please?
Then with some cordials seek first to appease
  The inward languor of my wounded heart,   10
  And then my body shall have shortly ease:
  But such sweet cordials pass physicians' art'.
Then, my life's leech, do you your skill reveal,
  And with one salve both heart and body heal.

SONNET 51

Do I not see that fairest images
  Of hardest marble are of purpose made,
  For that they should endure through many ages,
  Ne let their famous monuments to fade?
Why then do I, untrained in lovers' trade,   5
  Her hardness blame which I should more commend,
  Sith never aught was excellent assayed
  Which was not hard to achieve and bring to end?

---

7. heart . . . chief: true in the sense that it controls the body's life force and is the organ by which the soul supposedly entered the body: Agrippa (1651) 3. 37 (p. 465); but the body is in turn governed by understanding, will, memory and judgement: as the physiology of Alma's castle makes clear (*FQ*, 2. 9), the brain is more obviously 'chief', whereas the heart is seat of the hierarchically lower passions and affections (or moods) – concupiscence and irascibility.
9. cordials: stimulating medicines (from Latin *cor* = heart).
10. languor: sickness.
13. life's leech: cf. Chaucer, *Summoner's Tale*, 3 (D). 1892: 'high God, that is our life's leech'; but the idea was also applied (as here) to the beloved: 'My heart's delight, my sorrow's leech, mine earthly goddess here': Surrey, 'If care do cause men cry'.
14. salve: healing ointment; also (continuing the physical/spiritual ambiguity) spiritual remedy: *OED* salve *sb* 1, 2a, last citation *c.* 1610.
Sonnet 51 *1. images: Am* 45. 11n.
2. marble: cf. Stella's marble face in Sidney's *Astrophil and Stella*, 9.
4. Ne: nor.
6. hardness: suggests a hardnesss of heart (l. 11) which, on the lover's reading, corresponds to spiritual hardness as in Mark 3: 5, Romans 2: 5.
7–8. Sith . . . end: proverbial: Smith 1970: 132–3 (excellent things are the most difficult).
7. assayed: attempted (*OED* assay *v* III. 16); punning on try by touch (sense I. 3).
8. achieve: (1) bring to an end (*OED* achieve I. 3, last citation 1599): i.e., the lover has his revenge on the lady's cruelty by imagining her death and subsequent marble effigy (pun on *hard*); (2) bring to successful issue.

Ne aught so hard, but he that would attend
   Mote soften it and to his will allure: 10
   So do I hope her stubborn heart to bend,
   And that it then more steadfast will endure.
Only my pains will be the more to get her
   But, having her, my joy will be the greater.

SONNET 52

So oft as homeward I from her depart
   I go like one that, having lost the field,
   Is prisoner led away with heavy heart,
   Despoiled of warlike arms and knowen shield:
So do I now myself a prisoner yield   5
   To sorrow and to solitary pain,
   From presence of my dearest dear exiled,
   Long while alone in languor to remain.
There let no thought of joy or pleasure vain
   Dare to approach, that may my solace breed,   10
   But sudden dumps and dreary sad disdain
   Of all world's gladness more my torment feed:
So I her absence will my penance make
   That of her presence I my meed may take.

9–10. Ne . . . allure: proverbial: Smith 1970: 79–80.
9. attend: (1) wait; (2) turn his energies to.
10. Mote: might. *soften*: hints at Pygmalion and the sculpture that came to life (Ovid, *Metamorphoses*, 10. 243–97) and recalls *Am* 32. 2, 14nn. *allure*: win over, entice: derived from *lure* = fake bird on string used to train hawks with· f. and ct. the bird imagery at *Am* 72 and 89.
11. bend: in the normal sense (cause someone to incline to one's will: the lover is having his revenge for the lady's assertion of her will at, e.g., *Am* 46); also bind, or fetter and cause to relent (*OED* bend *v* II. 11).
13. pains: (1) sufferings; (2) troubles (in achieving).
Sonnet 52 The absence topos is conventional: Petrarch, *Rime*, 242; *Am* 46; Sidney, *Astrophil and Stella*, 60, 106. For the rhetoric and strategies involved, see Hazard 1987. The sonnet is based mainly on the idea of the lady as triumphator, with hints of the enchaining Venus: *Am* 10–12, 20, 37nn.
4. knowen: known, familiar (referring to the crest depicted on a shield).
8. languor: woeful state: *OED* langour *sb* 2, citing *FQ*, 3. 3. 35 (1590) as last instance; also sense 3, sorrow.
11. dumps: (1) fit(s) of abstraction; (2) dejection.
14. meed: reward.

SONNET 53

The panther, knowing that his spotted hide
  Doth please all beasts, but that his looks them fray,
  Within a bush his dreadful head doth hide
  To let them gaze whilst he on them may prey:
Right so my cruel fair with me doth play,   5
  For with the goodly semblant of her hue
  She doth allure me to mine own decay,
  And then no mercy will unto me show.
Great shame it is thing so divine in view,
  Made for to be the world's most ornament,   10
  To make the bait her gazers to imbrue:
  Good shames to be to ill an instrument,
But mercy doth with beauty best agree,
  As in their maker ye them best may see.

SONNET 54

Of this world's theatre in which we stay,
  My love like the spectator idly sits,
  Beholding me that all the pageants play,

Sonnet 53 Based on the familiar legend that the panther attracts prey by its sweet scent and hides its head, aware that its ferocity repels them: Pliny, *Natural History*, 8. 23; Valeriano 1602: 111, interpreting it as an emblem of deceit; Lievesay 1941.

1. spotted hide: emphasised rather than the scent because, along with tigers, the panther's colours were regarded as attractive to other animals (Valeriano 1602: 110): cf. the vanity theme of *Am* 27, and note that *spotted* suggests moral contagion through contrast with Song of Solomon 4: 7 ('there is no spot in thee') and Ephesians 5: 27 ('a glorious Church, not having spot'). Valeriano, p 113 also notes the ferocity of the female panther (cf. l. 5: 'cruel fair').

2. fray: frighten.
6. semblant: appearance. *hue*: *Am* 3. 8n.
7. allure: *Am* 51. 10n.
9. view: appearance.
10. most: greatest.
11. make: make herself. *imbrue*: stain with blood (cf. *Am* 31. 12n.)
12. shames: is ashamed.

Sonnet 54 Scott 1927: 195 and Kostić 1959: 68–9 compare Tasso, *Rime*, ed. Solerti, 3. 265, no. 213 ('Riede la stagion lieta').

1. world's theatre: common topos, usually emphasising life's vanities and miseries: Curtius 1967: 138–44; Yates (1969) ch 9. The lover gives the lady the spectating role usually attributed to God or to Satan and the sins: Yates, pp. 165–6.

3. pageants: (1) parts played in life's drama; (2) scenes; (3) tricks, deceptions: *OED* pageant *sb* 1.

Disguising diversely my troubled wits.
Sometimes I joy when glad occasion fits, 5
   And mask in mirth like to a comedy;
   Soon after, when my joy to sorrow flits,
   I wail, and make my woes a tragedy.
Yet she, beholding me with constant eye,
   Delights not in my mirth nor rues my smart; 10
   But when I laugh she mocks, and when I cry
   She laughs, and hardens evermore her heart.
What, then, can move her? If nor mirth nor moan,
   She is no woman, but a senseless stone.

SONNET 55

So oft as I her beauty do behold,
   And therewith do her cruelty compare,
   I marvell of what substance was the mould
   The which her made at once so cruel fair:
Not earth, for her high thoughts more heavenly are; 5
   Not water, for her love doth burn like fire;
   Not air, for she is not so light or rare;

---

5. *joy*: rejoice.
6. *mask*: act as in a masque (with overtones of disguising one's real feelings), hinting at the mask as Roman emblem of the theatre and of sexual intrigue: Tervarent (1958) col 262.
7. *flits*: changes direction.
9. *constant*: steady.
10. *smart*: *Am* 48. 12n.
14. *senseless*: *Am* 30. 11n. For the stone as emblem of the lowest form on the chain of being, see Heninger 1977: 162–3. Ct. the softening at *Am* 51. 10n
Sonnet 55 For the rhetorical structure, see *Am* 9 headnote.
3. *mould*: earth regarded as the substance out of which the body is made (*OED* mould *sb* 1, 4a): cf. *Am* 13. 6n.
5–8. *earth . . . fire*: the elements are enumerated in their traditional order counting from earth upwards.
5. *earth . . . are*: *Am* 13. 2n.
6. *water . . . fire*: the naming of water and fire together anticipates the lover's ultimate goal, marriage, since the *auspices* at a Roman marriage carried the two elements to signify the joining of female (water) and male (fire): Plutarch, *Roman Questions*, 1, 263E; *FQ*, 1. 12. 37. More specifically, the lover here contrasts Venus's flame (Tervarent (1958) col 185) with the water of moral instability, lust, and sloth: Brooks-Davies 1977: 139.
7. *air*: the element of woman (by a false but popular etymology Latin *mulier* was derived from *mollis aer*: cf. *Am* 32. 2n); of Juno, goddess of marriage (Ripa 1603: 121); and of the lustful sanguinic temperament (Peacham, H. 1612 *Minerva Britanna*, p 127); hence *light*, which puns on the meanings: (1) of little weight; (2) of little worth; (3) unchaste.

Not fire, for she doth freeze with faint desire.
Then needs another element inquire
  Whereof she mote be made: that is the sky;   10
  For to the heaven her haughty looks aspire,
  And eke her mind is pure, immortal, high:
Then sith to heaven ye likened are the best,
Be like in mercy as in all the rest.

SONNET 56

Fair ye be sure; but cruel and unkind
  As is a tiger that, with greediness,
  Hunts after blood when he by chance doth find
A feeble beast doth felly him oppress.
Fair be ye sure; but proud and pitiless   5
  As is a storm that all things doth prostrate,
  Finding a tree alone all comfortless
Beats on it strongly it to ruinate.
Fair be ye sure, but hard and obstinate,
  As is a rock amidst the raging floods,   10

8. *fire . . . desire*: suggesting the Petrarchan commonplace (*Am* 30). *Faint* puns on the meanings (1) weak; (2) feigned.
9. *Then . . . inquire*: then must [I] search for (*OED* inquire *v* 6). *another element*: the fifth element or quintessence, of which the heavens were thought to be composed (see 10–11).
11. *haughty*: (1) elevated (*OED* haughty *a* 2); (2) disdainful.
12. *eke*: in addition. *mind*: soul.
13. *likened . . . best*: you are best likened.
14. *mercy*: God's attribute; and see *Am* 49. 3n.
Sonnet 56 Scott 1927: 193, 195 compares Tasso, *Rime*, ed. Solerti, 4. 69, no. 523 ('Voi sête bella, ma . . . ').
1. *unkind*: (1) lacking in kindness; (2) unnatural.
2. *tiger*: connected with the panther for its attractive (*fair*) coat and destructiveness by, e.g., Valeriano 1602: 110. Cf. *Am* 53. 1n.
4. *felly*: exceedingly; possibly also fiercely.
6. *storm*: cf. *Am* 34. 8, 46. 10nn.
7. *tree*: cf. *Am* 43. 1n. For the ancient and Renaissance tradition of the man metamorphosed into a tree, see *Aeneid*, 3. 27–68 and *FQ*, 1. 2. 28–44. *comfortless*: desolate (*OED* sense 1).
8. *ruinate*: destroy (*OED* ruinate *v* 4, first citation 1560s).
9–10. *hard . . . rock*: *Am* 18. 14n.
9. *obstinate*: stubborn; but exploiting the etymon, Latin *obstare* = stand in the way of.
10–11. *rock . . . ship*: drawing on the traditional image of the ship/body wrecked by floods of passion: e.g., Whitney 1586: 129, 137, and *Am* 34. 8n on the rocks Scylla and Charybdis.

'Gainst which a ship of succour desolate
  Doth suffer wreck both of herself and goods:
That ship, that tree, and that same beast am I,
  Whom ye do wreck, do ruin and destroy.

SONNET 57

Sweet warrior, when shall I have peace with you?
  High time it is this war now ended were,
  Which I no longer can endure to sue,
  Ne your incessant battery more to bear:
So weak my powers, so sore my wounds appear,   5
  That wonder is how I should live a jot,
  Seeing my heart through-launched everywhere
  With thousand arrows which your eyes have shot.
Yet shoot ye sharply still, and spare me not,
  But glory think to make these cruel stours: 10
  Ye cruel one, what glory can be got
  In slaying him that would live gladly yours?
Make peace, therefore, and grant me timely grace
  That all my wounds will heal in little space.

11. of . . . desolate: devoid of help.
Sonnet 57 *1. Sweet warrior*: recalls love's bitter-sweetness (*Am* 42. 2n) and the armed Venus (*Am* 11. 3n).
3. sue: pursue.
4. incessant battery: confirmation that the lady has taken the initiative: the lover's forces were going to 'lay incessant battery to her heart' at *Am* 14. 10.
7. launched: pierced (*OED* launch *v* 1).
8. arrows: the Venerean beloved now wounds with Cupid's weapons (*Am* 7. 3n).
10. stours: in its normal sense, battles: ct. *SC January* 51 gloss.
12. slaying: hints at Cupid as god of death: Orphic Footnote to headnote, above.
13. timely: in time.
14. all . . . space: proverbial: Smith 1970: 263; cf. *SC July* 229–30.

SONNET 58

By her that is most assured to herself.

Weak is the assurance that weak flesh reposeth
   In her own power, and scorneth others' aid:
   That soonest falls whenas she most supposeth
   Herself assured and is of nought afraid.
All flesh is frail and all her strength unstayed,   5
   Like a vain bubble blowen up with air:
   Devouring Time and changeful Chance have preyed
   Her glory's pride, that none may it repair.
Ne none so rich or wise, so strong or fair,
   But faileth trusting on his own assurance;   10

Sonnet 58 A rejection of the vanity of the flesh (cf. *Am* 27. 5–6n) apparently attributed by the lover to the lady as if she were addressing herself. Its most significant stylistic feature is the preponderance of platitudes. It can be read as a rejection of the flesh implying the lady's recognition of, and need for, God; or as a statement of the folly of her self-sufficiency when she could receive the support, in marriage, of the lover. However, interpretative problems disappear if we understand *By* as meaning concerning, with regard to (*OED by prep* A IV. 26), as Martz 1961: 163 suggests.

Heading: *assured*: the sonnet plays with various meanings of the word: here, confident (with overtones of presumption); later (and in *Am* 59) the word means: (1) pledged for marriage; (2) to guarantee peace (thus glancing back at *Am* 57. 13); (3) formal pledge in a general sense: see *OED* assurance/ assure/assured.

1. Weak . . . flesh: statement about the weakness of the flesh (as opposed to the strength of the spirit) supported by 1 John 3. 18–19: ('let us . . . love . . . indeed and in truth. For thereby we know that we are of the truth, and shall before him assure our hearts'). For the general idea, cf. 2 Corinthians 1: 9: 'we should not rest in our selves, but in God, which raised the dead'. The lover's secular subtext is: she needs a man.

3. soonest falls: in connection with the feminine gender attributed to *flesh* here, suggests Eve, cause of the Fall into fleshly appetites (Genesis 3). The idea of falling when secure is proverbial: Smith 1970: 237.

5. All . . . frail: cf. Job 34: 15 ('All flesh shall perish together, and man shall return unto dust'), Isaiah 40: 6–8 ('All flesh is grass . . . .The grass withereth, the flower fadeth: but the word of our God shall stand for ever'). Proverbial: Smith 1970: 108. *unstayed*: unsupported, unstable: *OED* unstayed *ppl a* 3, first citation 1594 (the year *Am* was written). Ct. *Am* 59. 11n.

6. vain: (1) worthless; (2) conceited. *bubble*: *SC February* 87n.

7. Devouring: traditional epithet of Time; for his iconographical link with Occasion/Fortune (*Chance*) see Panofsky 1962: 72. *preyed*: plundered, spoiled: *OED* prey *v* 1.

9. Ne none: nor is there anyone.

10. faileth . . . assurance: Smith 1970: 208.

And he that standeth on the highest stair
  Falls lowest, for on earth nought hath endurance.
Why, then, do ye, proud fair, misdeem so far
  That to yourself ye most assured are?

SONNET 59

Thrice-happy she that is so well assured
  Unto herself and settled so in heart,
  That neither will for better be allured,
  Ne feared with worse to any chance to start;
But, like a steady ship, doth strongly part   5
  The raging waves and keeps her course aright,
  Ne aught for tempest doth from it depart,
  Ne aught for fairer weather's false delight:
Such self-assurance need not fear the spite
  Of grudging foes, ne favour seek of friends,   10
  But in the stay of her own steadfast might
  Neither to one herself nor other bends:
Most happy she that most assured doth rest;
  But he most happy who such one loves best.

11–12. he . . . lowest: proverbial: Smith 1970: 146; cf. *SC July*, 11–12.
12. on . . . endurance: another proverb: Smith 1970: 50, 165 citing *SC November*, 153, *FQ*, 1. 9. 11, etc.
13. proud fair: not the lover (*pace* Dunlop in Oram *et al*. 1989: 635n) but the lady. *misdeem*: hold the wrong opinion.
14. That . . . are: the lover accuses the lady of self-sufficiency, implying (through puns on *assured*) that she should trust in him.
Sonnet 59 A palinode (or reversal) of 58: the lover (or the lady) now apparently reads the lady's self-sufficiency as a positive virtue – either as part of some elaborate game the lover is playing with himself or in genuine recognition that her qualities are superior to his own and worth aspiring to.
1. Thrice-happy: Latin *ter felix* with (perhaps) an ironic glance at Ovid, *Metamorphoses*, 8. 51, where Nisus's daughter, Scylla, exclaims her love for his enemy, Minos, before betraying her father: 'I should be thrice happy if I could confess my love to Minos'. If there is an allusion, it would link up with the complaints against the lady's cruelty.
3. allured: *Am* 51. 10n.
4. Ne . . . start: nor ever caused through fear of worse [things] to recoil: *to any chance* is a form of the obsolete *for any chance* (*OED* chance *sb* II. 9); for *start*, see also *Am* 42. 9n.
5–8. ship . . . delight: cf. the lover at *Am* 56. 10–12n.
11. stay: reliance (*OED* stay *sb* 2 1c); but note *stay sb* 1, large rope to support mainmast of ship. The line describes a state of temperate balance between extremes: *Am* 39. 3n.

SONNET 60

They that in course of heavenly spheres are skilled
  To every planet point his sundry year
  In which her circle's voyage is fulfilled,
  As Mars in three score years doth run his sphere:
So, since the winged god his planet clear   5
  Began in me to move, one year is spent,
  The which doth longer unto me appear
  Than all those forty which my life outwent.
Then by that count, which lovers' books invent,
  The sphere of Cupid forty years contains,   10
  Which I have wasted in long languishment,
  That seemed the longer for my greater pains.
But let my love's fair planet short her ways
  This year ensuing, or else short my days.

Sonnet 60 Kastner 1908–9: 69 compares Desportes, *Cléonice*, 4. Petrarch dates the progress of his love in, e.g., *Rime*, 79, 212.
1–4. They . . . sphere: the number is the problem. No one has bettered R. E. Neil Dodge's suggestion that Spenser misremembered Ptolemy's figure of 79+ (solar) years for the time it would take Mars to depart from and return to a given position in relation to the sun: cit. *Var* 2. 440. *Three* is thus an error for *four*. But note the self-referring element: this is sonnet 60.
2. point: ordain, determine: *OED* point *v* 2, 2. *sundry*: (1) specific; (2) set apart (sundered: the lover from his beloved).
3. her: their (i.e., the planets'): archaic form of third person plural possessive pronoun.
5. winged god: Cupid. *clear*: distinctly.
6. one year: the figure for the revolution period of Venus was 348 days, often rounded up to a (solar) year: Eade 1984: 22; Thomas Wyatt, 'Iopas's Song', 55–7. This painful year of courtship is answered by the solar year mimed in *Epith*'s 365 long lines: Kaske 1978: 286–7 and *Epith* 318n.
8. forty: numerologically suggesting the lover's desperation since it is an important marriage number (Bongo 1599: 501 citing Isaac's marriage to Rebecca when he was forty (Genesis 25: 20), a marriage referred to in the Marriage Service: *Prayer-book* 1559: 124; Plato's upper limit for the male marriage age was 35: *Laws* 785B); or maybe it is a simple factual statement. *outwent*: has passed through.
11–12. long . . . pains: proverbial: Smith 1970: 169–70.
11. languishment: *Am* 50. 1n.
13. planet: the lady as Venus. *short*: shorten. *ways*: (1) path; (2) orbit.

SONNET 61

The glorious image of the Maker's beauty,
   My sovereign saint, the idol of my thought,
   Dare not henceforth above the bounds of duty
   To accuse of pride, or rashly blame for aught:
For being (as she is) divinely wrought,   5
   And of the brood of angels heavenly born,
   And with the crew of blessed saints upbrought,
   Each of which did her with their gifts adorn –
The bud of joy, the blossom of the morn,
   The beam of light, whom mortal eyes admire –   10
   What reason is it, then, but she should scorn
   Base things that to her love too bold aspire?
Such heavenly forms ought rather worshipped be
   Than dare be loved by men of mean degree.

SONNET 62

The weary Year his race now having run,
   The New begins his compassed course anew:

Sonnet 61 *1–3. The . . . Dare*: I dare not accuse this glorious image.
1. glorious image: cf. *Am* 22. 5–8 and 6nn. Dunlop (Oram *et al.* 1989: 636n) cites Ficino *Commentary* 7. 1 (Ficino 1944: 216–17): the lover's fancy retains a particular image, which is then reflected in the mind as a general image of the human race as a whole and raises him to the contemplative life (the passage follows that cited at *Am* 7. 1n). *the Maker's*: the original's *the* could be a form of *thi*, itself a form of *thy*. If it is simply the definite article, then *makers* (no initial capital in the original) needs to be modernised to indicate God; if not, it should be left uncapitalised to suggest statue- or image-maker (see l. 2).
2. saint . . . idol: *Am* 27. 5–6n.
3–4. Dare . . . blame: proverbial: Smith 1970: 43–4.
3. Dare: [I] dare.
6. brood: parentage: a Spenserian usage: *OED* brood *sb* 2b citing *FQ*, 1. 3. 8; 5. 7. 21 (the former instance refers to Una's heavenly lineage). Cf. *Am* 79. 9–12.
7. crew: company. *upbrought*: reared: *OED* upbrought *pa pple* cites *FQ* as yielding last recorded instances.
8. their gifts: laudatory revision of the Pandora image (*Am* 24. 8n): the queen is 'Pandora of all heavenly graces' in Spenser's *Tears of the Muses* (1591), 578; see also Panofsky 1962: 68–70.
9–10. bud . . . light: describing the lady (*her*) rather than the gifts.
11–12. scorn . . . things: proverbial: Smith 1970: 236; cf. *Am* 5. 6.
13. forms: (1) shapes; (2) examples (*OED* form *sb* I. 7); (3) the essential quality of a thing (= soul: *OED* sense I. 4a).
Sonnet 62 *1–2. Year . . . anew*: in the sequence's calendrical structure (*Am* headnote) marks the traditional civil new year of 25 March: *SC* General headnote, p. 10; and cf. the January sonnet, *Am* 4.
2. compassed: circular.

With show of morning mild he hath begun,
  Betokening peace and plenty to ensue.
So let us, which this change of weather view,   5
  Change eke our minds, and former lives amend:
  The Old Year's sins forepast let us eschew,
  And fly the faults with which we did offend.
Then shall the New Year's joy forth freshly send
  Into the glooming world his gladsome ray,   10
  And all these storms, which now his beauty blend,
  Shall turn to calms and timely clear away:
So likewise, love, cheer you your heavy spright,
  And change Old Year's annoy to new delight.

SONNET 63
After long storms' and tempests' sad assay
  (Which hardly I endured heretofore
  In dread of death and dangerous dismay)
  With which my silly bark was tossed sore,
I do at length descry the happy shore   5
  In which I hope ere long for to arrive:
  Fair soil it seems from far, and fraught with store
  Of all that dear and dainty is alive.
Most happy he that can at last achieve

4. *peace and plenty*: phrase associated with Ceres, spring and autumn goddess of ploughing, sowing, and fruitfulness: Brooks-Davies 1983: 121–2n. Cf. *Epith* 354n.
6–8. *amend . . . offend*: as Easter Day approaches (*Am* 68), the lover uses spring to focus his sin and hope of spiritual renewal which is identified with his beloved's acceptance of him (spring is equated with renewal through Christ in Song of Solomon 2: 11–12: *Am* 70. 5–6n; an equation particularly appropriate here since 25 March is Lady Day, the day on which the Annunciation to Mary of her motherhood was announced by the angel). Note the absence of such phrases from January New Year sonnet 4.
10. *gladsome ray*: the impregnating Holy Spirit was often depicted as a sunbeam piercing Mary's womb in paintings of the Annunciation: Warner 1985: 40, 44.
11–12. *storms . . . calms*: proverbial: Smith 1970: 250.
11. *blend*: conceal: rare usage; only *OED* instance from Lydgate, 1430 (blend *v* 1, 3).
13. *spright*: disposition; and see *Am* 1. 7n.
Sonnet 63 *1–4. storms' . . . bark*: cf. *Am* 34, 38, and 56. 10–12n, 59. 5–8n.
1. *assay*: trial.
2. *hardly*: with difficulty.
4. *silly*: (1) deserving of compassion; (2) helpless (*OED* senses A 1 a, b). *sore*: with great distress.
7. *fraught*: abundant with. *store*: *Am* 35. 9n.
8. *dainty*: choice, excellent. *alive*: in the world.

The joyous safety of so sweet a rest, 10
Whose least delight sufficeth to deprive
Remembrance of all pains which him oppressed:
All pains are nothing in respect of this,
All sorrows short that gain eternal bliss.

SONNET 64

Coming to kiss her lips, such grace I found,
   Me seemed I smelled a garden of sweet flowers
   That dainty odours from them threw around
   For damsels fit to deck their lovers' bowers:
Her lips did smell like unto gillyflowers; 5
   Her ruddy cheeks like unto roses red;
   Her snowy brows like budded bellamours;

---

11. delight: one of the meanings of paradise/Eden (*SC June* 10 gloss): a reminder that the spiritual and erotic are one: see *Am* 64 headnote.

14. eternal bliss: the eternal sabbath that succeeds the 6 ages of the world. Prescott in Maclean and Prescott 1993: 612 notes that a common meaning offered for the name Elizabeth was Hebrew *eli-sabbath* = Lord's rest.

Sonnet 64 Cf. the blazon sonnet, *Am* 15. This time, jewels are replaced by flowers to iconise the beloved as a garden (1) because Venus was goddess of gardens (so the garden is to be visited and the flowers – in imagination at least – plucked; cf. Agrippa (1651) 1. 30 (p. 61): 'every thing that bears flowers is from Venus') and (2) because of the exegetical tradition deriving from Song of Solomon 4: 12 ('My sister, my spouse, is as a garden enclosed'), which interpreted the enclosed garden as the Virgin Mary and as the soul filled with flower-virtues (Tuve 1966: 22–4, 108–10). Venus (gardens, flowers) now displaces Ceres (goddess of fields, fruits, grasses).

1. kiss: the Song of Solomon opens 'Let him kiss me with the kisses of his mouth', interpreted as a sign of spiritual union (Castiglione, *Courtier*, 4: 336). For the erotic power of smell (l. 2; third in the hierarchy of senses), see George Chapman, *Ovid's Banquet of Sense* (1595) 280–360. *grace*: *SC April* 52n; note that most of the flowers listed appear in the *April* blazon for Elisa. *Grace* also suggests the kiss's pleasant flavour: *OED* grace *sb* I. 1a.

4. bowers: bedchambers.

5. gillyflowers: *SC April* 136 gloss. As a form of carnation they symbolise love (*ibid.* note) and, specifically, marriage: D'Ancona 1983: 74; Ferguson 1961: 29. Salmon (1678) 1. 5. 14 notes that they 'are a great cordial, and exhilarate the heart'.

6. roses red: dedicated to Venus: *SC April* 59–60nn.

7. bellamours: the name = 'beautiful loves', a Spenserian nonce word first used in the pejorative erotic context of *FQ*, 2. 6. 16. As a flower, unidentified (cf. *chevisaunce* at *SC April*, 143). Fowler 1975: 96 interprets them as 'love glances' on the (later) authority of Giles Fletcher.

Her lovely eyes like pinks but newly spread;
Her goodly bosom like a strawberry bed;
   Her neck like to a bunch of columbines;   10
   Her breast like lilies ere their leaves be shed;
   Her nipples like young-blossomed jessamines:
Such fragrant flowers do give most odorous smell,
   But her sweet odour did them all excel.

SONNET 65

The doubt which ye misdeem, fair love, is vain,
   That fondly fear to lose your liberty
   When, losing one, two liberties ye gain,
   And make him bond that bondage erst did fly.
Sweet be the bands the which true love doth tie,   5
   Without constraint or dread of any ill:
   The gentle bird feels no captivity
   Within her cage, but sings and feeds her fill.
There Pride dare not approach, nor Discord spill
   The league 'twixt them, that loyal love hath bound,   10

---

8. pinks: a form of carnation.

9. strawberry: emblem of love and sensuality: D'Ancona 1983: 93; also associated with the Virgin Mary and humility: Ferguson 1961: 38. There is a pun on *bed*.

10. columbines: *SC April* 136n. The name derives from Latin *columba* = dove, emblem of Venus and of sensual caresses: Tervarent (1958) cols 104–5; also in Song of Solomon (e.g., 4: 1). But because the dove is the emblem of the Holy Spirit (Matthew 3: 16), the flower can symbolise the gifts of the Holy Spirit: de Vries 1974: 108. Spenser puns in addition on Latin *collum* = neck and *colligo* = bind together (*bunch* of columbines).

11. lilies: *SC April* 136 gloss and *Am* 1. 1n. Ubiquitous in Song of Solomon (e.g., 2: 1, 2), also emblem of the quest for the eternal: D'Ancona 1983: 84.

12. jessamines: jasmine, emblem of love, grace, amiability: D'Ancona 1983: 82–3.

Sonnet 65 *1. misdeem*: hold mistakenly.

2. fondly: foolishly.

4. bond: playing with the ideas of *bond/bondage* as (1) imprisonment; (2) restraint; (3) obligation; (4) maintenance of a union (especially marriage); (5) serf or slave. *erst*: *SC March* 95n.

5. bands: binding shackles or rope (but see *Am* 1. 3 and 37. 6nn) which now produce a *true love* knot: *Am* 6. 14n.

7–8. bird . . . cage: emblem of soul in body; but see *Am* 73. 5n.

9. spill: destroy.

10. league: covenant, alliance.

> But simple truth and mutual goodwill
> Seeks with sweet peace to salve each other's wound:
> There Faith doth fearless dwell in brazen tower,
> And spotless Pleasure builds her sacred bower.

SONNET 66

> To all those happy blessings which ye have,
>   With plenteous hand by heaven upon you thrown,
>   This one disparagement they to you gave,
>   That ye your love lent to so mean a one:
> Ye – whose high worths, surpassing paragon,   5
>   Could not on earth have found one fit for mate,
>   Ne but in heaven matchable to none –
>   Why did ye stoop unto so lowly state?
> But ye thereby much greater glory gate
>   Than had ye sorted with a prince's peer,   10
>   For now your light doth more itself dilate,
>   And in my darkness greater doth appear:

11. mutual: marriage 'was ordained . . . for the mutual society, help, and comfort, that the one ought to have of the other': Marriage Service in *Prayer-book* 1559: 122.
12. salve: heal, put ointment on: cf. *Am* 50. 14n.
13. brazen tower: brass signifies durability; the tower, divine strength (Psalm 61: 3: 'For thou hast been . . . a strong tower against the enemy'). Recalls the myth of Danaë (who was shut up in a brazen tower by her father, Acrisius, but was nevertheless impregnated by Jupiter disguised as a shower of gold): Ross 1648: 90.
14. spotless Pleasure: for Pleasure, see *HL* 287n (the lovers here thus recall Cupid and Psyche, Eros and Soul). It amplifies the *delight* of *Am* 63. 11n. *spotless*: Song of Solomon 4: 7 ('Thou art all fair my love, and there is no spot in thee') and ct. *Am* 53. 1n.
Sonnet 66 *1. blessings*: cf. *Am* 61. 8n.
3. disparagement: lowering in estimation; but *OED*'s sense 1 is the dishonour involved in marriage to one of inferior rank, citing *FQ*, 3. 8. 12.
5. paragon: (1) person of supreme excellence; (2) consort in marriage.
6. mate: marriage companion (*OED* mate *sb* 2, 3a).
8. lowly state: cf. references to the lady's condescension at *Am* 61 (and ct. the 'lofty looks' of *Am* 5). But in religious terms, marriage 'is an honourable state . . . signifying unto us the mystical union that is betwixt Christ and his Church' (*Prayer-book* 1559: 122); so that the lady's heavenly qualities are Christ-like, and the lover signifies the body of the Church.
9. gate: northern/Scots form of *get*.
10. sorted: consorted, matched. *peer*: equal.
11–14. light . . . be: neo-Platonism conflated with John 1: *Am* 8. 13, 9. 13–14nn.
11. dilate: spread abroad.

Yet, since your light hath once enlumined me,
    With my reflex yours shall increased be.

SONNET 67
Like as a huntsman after weary chase,
    Seeing the game from him escaped away,
    Sits down to rest him in some shady place
    With panting hounds beguiled of their prey:
So, after long pursuit and vain assay,   5
    When I, all weary, had the chase forsook,
    The gentle deer returned the self same way,
    Thinking to quench her thirst at the next brook.

13. enlumined: archaic alternative to *illumined*: see *HL*, 108n.
14. reflex: reflection of light: *OED* reflex *sb* 1. Cf. *Am* 7.
Sonnet 67 Influenced in part by Petrarch, *Rime*, 190 (imitated by Wyatt in 'Whoso list to hunt') via Psalm 42: 1 ('As the hart brayeth for the rivers of water, so panted my soul after thee, O God') which was sung by the newly converted as they proceeded to baptism on Easter eve (along with Whitsun, the traditional time for baptism from the early Christian period on, as the *Prayer-book* 1559: 107 recalled): Prescott 1985: 33–76, especially p. 55, citing Johnson 1974: 57 and noting also that the psalm is prominent in the Sarum Missal's liturgy for that day. Other possible influences include Tasso, *Rime*, ed. .Solerti, 2. 429, no. 1 (Scott 1927: 195; Kostić 1959: 56–7), Horace, *Odes*, 3. 23, and Marguerite de Navarre, *Chansons spirituelles* (1547), no. 6 (discussed by Prescott (1985) *passim*).
1. huntsman: the hunt of love again (*Am* 47. 7–8n; cf. Thiébaux 1974), with hints of Actaeon, the hunter who spies on Diana bathing in her sacred grove and is punished for his vision of the divine mystery by being metamorphosed into a deer and devoured by his own hounds: Ovid, *Metamorphoses*, 3. 155–252; Ross 1648: 6–7.
4. beguiled: cheated, disappointed.
5. assay: attempt: cf. *Am* 63. 1n; with the additional meanings (1) trial by drinking or tasting (hence cup of assay: *OED* assay *v* II. 12; so that the lover/huntsman – unlike Psalm 42's deer – has drunk prematurely and unsatisfactorily); (2) trial of 'grease of deer': i.e., their fitness for hunting and killing: *OED* sense II. 9.
7. deer: dedicated to the huntress Diana, goddess of virginity: Valeriano 1602: 70. The bridegroom (allegorically, Christ) is a deer at Song of Solomon 2: 9 ('My beloved is like a roe, or a young hart'), and the ideal wife whom the husband should not reject is 'as the loving hind and pleasant roe' at Proverbs 5: 19 (where, incidentally, water is emblematic of godliness and purity: verses 15–16). Whitney 1586: 43 depicts the hart's drinking as a sign of longing for God, while the accompanying text comments on the seaman's determined navigation of difficulties: suggesting that *Am* 67 resolves the image complex of *Am* 34, 56 etc.
8. next: nearest, most convenient.

There she, beholding me with milder look,
  Sought not to fly, but fearless still did bide,   10
  Till I in hand her yet half-trembling took,
  And with her own goodwill her firmly tied:
Strange thing, me seemed, to see a beast so wild
  So goodly won, with her own will beguiled.

SONNET 68

Most glorious Lord of life that, on this day,
  Didst make Thy triumph over death and sin
  And, having harrowed hell, didst bring away
  Captivity thence captive, us to win:

9–12. she . . . tied: Petrarch's deer remains free because she belongs to a greater lord (her collar – sign of belonging – is inscribed 'Touch me not, for I am Caesar's'); Spenser's submits – perhaps like Christ, willingly incarnate and sacrificed (Prescott 1985: 47); but more like the submissive woman forced to admit her lover's fantasy of Caesar-like greatness: *take in hand* (11) = take responsibility for and apply discipline to.
12. goodwill: voluntary yielding, the lover's response to which is the love (and nuptial) knot (*tied*: cf. *Am* 65. 5n). Cf. Ephesians 5 and Colossians 3 as cited in the marriage liturgy: 'Ye wives, submit yourselves unto your own husbands' (*Prayer-book* 1559: 127–8).
14. So goodly: so easily (adverbial); or may be adjectival (a beast so wild, so comely, won). *beguiled*: charmed, willingly persuaded; but cf. l. 4.
Sonnet 68 Easter Day, and the end of the Lenten/Easter sequence. As the final sonnet of the second section of *Am* (see headnote) it marks the lover's betrothal to the lady which, through the Easter symbolism, assumes considerable spiritual significance.
1. glorious . . . day: *glorious*: *Am* 17. 1 and 22. 6nn, with additional biblical resonances: e.g., John 13: 31–2 ('Now is the son of man glorified . . . '). *Lord of life*: Acts 3: 15: ('And killed the Lord of life'). Prescott 1985: 56 notes the echo of the Sarum Missal's main Easter prayer: 'Lord who, on this very day, through your only–begotten son, unlocked for us the gateway of eternity having conquered death' (*Deus qui hodierna die per unigenitum tuum aeternitatis nobis aditum devicta morte reserasti*).
2. triumph . . . sin: displaces earlier triumphalism (*Am* 20. 3n) with biblical texts such as Exodus 15: 1 ('I will sing unto the Lord: for he hath triumphed gloriously'). For the victory over death and sin, see 1 Corinthians 15, especially 54–6 ('Death is swallowed up into victory . . . .The sting of death is sin').
3. harrowed hell: Christ's descent to hell from Good Friday to Easter Day to break open its gates and free its prisoners who are bound in original sin: apocryphal Gospel of Nicodemus, 2. 6 (in Lightfoot J. B., James M. R. and Swete H. B., *Excluded Books of the New Testament*. London, n.d., p. 95).
4. Captivity . . . captive: Ephesians 4: 8 ('he [Christ] led captivity captive'), quoting Psalm 68: 18, the Geneva gloss to which explains: 'As God overcame the enemies of his Church, took them prisoners . . . so Christ . . . subdued Satan and sin under us'.

This joyous day, dear Lord, with joy begin,   5
   And grant that we, for whom Thou didest die,
   Being with Thy dear blood clean-washed from sin,
   May live for ever in felicity;
And that Thy love, we weighing worthily,
   May likewise love Thee for the same again;   10
   And for Thy sake, that all like-dear didst buy,
   With love may one another entertain:
So let us love, dear love, like as we ought:
   Love is the lesson which the Lord us taught.

SONNET 69

The famous warriors of the antique world
   Used trophies to erect in stately wise,
   In which they would the records have enrolled
   Of their great deeds and valorous emprise:
What trophy, then, shall I most fit devise   5
   In which I may record the memory
   Of my love's conquest, peerless Beauty's prize,
   Adorned with honour, love and chastity?

---

7. blood . . . sin: Revelation 1: 5 (Christ 'washed us from our sins in his blood').
9. weighing worthily: cf. Revelation 3: 4 ('they shall walk with me in white: for they are worthy'): i.e., we, being worthy to weigh (feel the true weight of) his love, may . . . . For the *weight*, cf. 2 Corinthians 4: 17 ('an eternal weight of glory').
11. dear: also qualifies *buy*: you bought (redeemed) at great cost.
13–14. love . . . taught: John 15: 12 ('This is my commandment, that ye love one another, as I have loved you'), the verse which began the gospel for Holy Communion on Spenser's wedding day (St Barnabas's day, 1594): Kaske 1977: 518–19; *Epith* headnote above. See *Am* 66. 8n for further religious overtones.
Sonnet 69 The lover is now the triumphator: cf. Du Bellay's *L'Olive*, 34: Renwick 1929: 202. Also indebted to Desportes, *Cléonice*, 11: Kastner 1908–9: 68. The appurtenances – trophies, monuments – are usually associated with the evanescence of earthly glory: e.g., Spenser's *Ruins of Rome*, sonnets 7, 27, etc. (translations of Du Bellay).
4. emprise: *SC September* 83 gloss.
7. peerless . . . prize: the original spelling – *prise* – is also a form of *price*; so that in being matchless Beauty's prize (reward, cost) the lady is problematic: Paris awarded the prize of the golden apple to Venus (Beauty), not Juno or Minerva; his prize was sensual Helen, the price for whom was the Trojan war: see *SC July* 146–7 glosses, *August* headnote and 138n.
8. honour . . . chastity: cf. the triplets of female virtues in *FQ*, 3: Nohrnberg 1976: 461–70.

>Even this verse, vowed to eternity,
>>Shall be thereof immortal monument,   10
>>And tell her praise to all posterity
>>That may admire such world's rare wonderment –
>The happy purchase of my glorious spoil,
>>Gotten at last with labour and long toil.

SONNET 70

>Fresh Spring – the herald of love's mighty king,
>>In whose coat-armour richly are displayed
>>All sorts of flowers the which on earth do spring
>>In goodly colours gloriously arrayed –
>Go to my love, where she is care-less laid   5
>>Yet in her winter's bower not well awake:
>>Tell her the joyous Time will not be stayed

9. eternity: on the immortality bestowed by verse, see *Am* 27 headnote, *SC December* gloss and Epilogue nn.

10. monument: (1) chronicle, record: *OED* sense 2; (2) surviving (exemplary) vestige (sense 4).

12. wonderment: object of wonder: cf. *Am* 24. 1n.

13. purchase: somewhat uneasily places the lover in the position of Christ: *Am* 68. 11. *glorious spoil*: triumphalism at the lady's expense: all meanings of *spoil* include *plunder, booty*.

14. Gotten . . . toil: the lover's perception: in fact the lady offered herself willingly (like Christ to mankind), and the lover's 'works' (to adopt the Calvinist concept which is to the fore here) did very little – if anything – to merit her. The line echoes a proverb on the spoils of valour making labour a pleasure: Smith 1970: 163.

Sonnet 70 Another spring sonnet: cf. *Am* 19. For the possible influence of Sarum Missal Whitsun texts, see Prescott 1985: 57; mainly influenced by Song of Solomon 2 (the lover seeing himself again as the Christ/bridegroom to the lady's Church) and the libertine *carpe diem* (seize the day) topos (on which see, e.g., *FQ*, 2. 12. 74–5).

1. Spring: cf. *SC May*, 1–36. *king*: *Am* 19. 3–4n.

2. coat-armour: vest embroidered with heraldic emblems worn over armour by knights, heralds, etc.

5–6. Go . . . awake: Song of Solomon 2: 10–12: 'My well-beloved spake and said unto me, Arise, my love, my fair one, and come thy way. For behold, winter is past. . . . The flowers appear in the earth' (Geneva gloss on *winter is past*: 'That is, sin and error is driven back by the coming of Christ, which is here described by the spring time, when all things flourish': a reading which the Spenserian lover perhaps largely ignores in favour of the male-biased Zephyrus/Flora reading of the season: *Am* 4. 11, 13nn).

6. bower: *Am* 64. 4n.

7. stayed: detained, with hints of *captured* (Spenserian meaning: *OED* stay *v* 1 III. 20d citing only *FQ*, 1. 10. 40).

Unless she do him by the forelock take.
Bid her, therefore, herself soon ready make
   To wait on Love amongst his lovely crew,   10
   Where everyone that misseth then her make
   Shall be by him amerced with penance due:
Make haste, therefore, sweet love, whilst it is prime,
   For none can call again the passed time.

SONNET 71

I joy to see how, in your drawen work,
   Yourself unto the bee ye do compare,
   And me unto the spider that doth lurk
   In close await to catch her unaware:
Right so yourself were caught in cunning snare   5
   Of a dear foe, and thralled to his love,
   In whose strait bands ye now captived are

---

8. forelock: for devouring Time's appropriation of bald Opportunity's forelock, see Panofsky 1962: 72.
10. crew: *Am* 61. 7n.
11. make: mate (the identical rhyme – cf. l. 9 – is common in Spenser).
12. amerced: punished (with a specified penalty).
13–14. Make . . . time: not an attempt at seduction after all (ct. the warning that failure to love now leaves you open to death's perpetual sleep: Catullus, 5. 1–6): rather, a characteristic Spenserian concern with the timely (opportune) moment. Cf. *Epith* 386n.
13. prime: (1) spring; (2) beginning (of the lovers' new life); (3) time of maximum physical vigour.
Sonnet 71   *1. drawen work*: drawn-thread work: the creating of patterns in a fabric from pulled-out threads of warp and woof (first *OED* citation 1595). Cf. Penelope and Arachne at *Am* 23. 1 and 7nn. The lady offers her text of the courtship which the lover (mis)interprets.
2. bee: emblem of love's bitter-sweetness (see *Am* 42. 2n and anacreontics [1] and [4] below); of sovereignty; of the female sweetness that pleases men; of the prostitute; and of chastity (Valeriano 1602: 261–5); also of the mother goddess (Neumann 1955: 262–7).
3. spider: traditionally female, and emblem of Arachne's power to weave compelling tales, hence identified with Minerva and her wisdom: Tervarent (1958) col 31; also emblem of the sense of touch: *ibid.*; cf. *Am* 26 headnote. The opposition of spider and bee was a commonplace: e.g., Whitney 1586: 51, where the former is associated with poison and death, the latter with eternal life through the gospel.
4. In . . . await: in secret ambush: *OED* await *sb* 1b.
5. snare: cf. Shakespeare, *2 Henry VI*, 3. 1: 'My brain, more busy than the labouring spider,/Weaves tedious snares to trap mine enemies'.
7. strait: tight; *bands*: cf. *Am* 67. 12n. *captived*: imprisoned.

So firmly that ye never may remove.
But, as your work is woven all above
   With woodbind flowers and fragrant eglantine,   10
   So, sweet your prison you in time shall prove,
   With many dear delights bedecked fine,
And all thenceforth eternal peace shall see
   Between the spider and the gentle bee.

SONNET 72

Oft when my spirit doth spread her bolder wings,
   In mind to mount up to the purest sky,
   It down is weighed with thought of earthly things
And clogged with burden of mortality,
Where, when that sovereign beauty it doth spy   5
   (Resembling heaven's glory in her light),
   Drawn with sweet Pleasure's bait it back doth fly
And unto heaven forgets her former flight.
There my frail fancy, fed with full delight,
   Doth bathe in bliss and mantleth most at ease,   10

---

8. remove: depart.
9. woven: cf. knots in *Am* 6. 14n. *above*: see Textual Notes, p. 318.
10. woodbind: form of *woodbine*, i.e., honeysuckle, emblem of love: de Vries 1974: 256. *eglantine*: love again: *SC February* 115n.
11. prove: discover.
13. peace: the bee is an emblem of concord: Valeriano 1602: 264–5.
Sonnet 72 Lines 1–5 imitate Tasso, *Rime*, ed. Solerti, 2. 98, no. 67 ('L'alma vaga di luce e di bellezza'): Scott 1927: 191–2.
1–4. spirit . . . mortality: cf. *HL*, 176–89 and *Am* 1. 7n. For the bird/soul see Plato, *Phaedrus*, 246C–247C and cf. *Am* 65. 7–8n, *SC October* 87 gloss. *Wings* picks up the idea of poetic fame (Cheney (1994) ch. 4) and is influenced by the *bee* as the emblem of the lyric poet (Plato, *Ion*, 534B) and of the soul: Porphyry in *Thomas Taylor* 1969: 307.
3. earthly things: 1 Corinthians 7: 33 ('he that is married, careth for the things of the world, how he may please his wife'): Kaske 1978: 275.
4. clogged: impeded by a clog (block of wood attached to neck or leg of an animal or man to prevent escape: *OED* clog *sb* 2; cf. Alciati 1551: 132).
7. Pleasure's bait: not the Pleasure of *Am* 65. 14n (aspect of the pleasure [*voluptas*] experienced as the last phase of the neo-Platonic triad that induces the soul to return in joy to heaven: Wind 1967: 43–52; cf. *Am* 74. 14n), but earthly Pleasure, attracted by such sensuous things as flowers, jewels, Venerean music, etc.: Ripa 1603: 398–400.
9. fancy: *Am* 3. 12n.
10. mantleth: stagnates (literally, becomes covered in scum): *OED* mantle *v* 4b, first citation 1596; punning on sense 3, from falconry: habit of stretching one wing then the other for exercise when perched, particularly after bathing: Constance Hieatt 1983: 349.

Ne thinks of other heaven but how it might
   Her heart's desire with most contentment please:
Heart need not wish none other happiness
   But here on earth to have such heaven's bliss.

SONNET 73

Being myself captived here in care,
   My heart (whom none with servile bands can tie
   But the fair tresses of your golden hair),
   Breaking his prison, forth to you doth fly:
Like as a bird that in one's hand doth spy   5
   Desired food, to it doth make his flight,
   Even so my heart, that wont on your fair eye
   To feed his fill, flies back unto your sight.
Do you him take and, in your bosom bright,
   Gently encage, that he may be your thrall: 10
   Perhaps he there may learn with rare delight
   To sing your name and praises over all,
That it hereafter may you not repent
   Him lodging in your bosom to have lent.

SONNET 74

Most happy letters, framed by skilful trade,
   With which that happy name was first designed,
   The which three times thrice happy hath me made

12–13. heart's . . . Heart: for the heart as seat of the affections, see *Am* 50. 7n.
Sonnet 73 Modelled on Tasso, *Rime*, ed. Solerti, 2. 319, no. 222 ('Donna, poiché fortuna'): Scott 1927: 192, 195; Kostić 1959: 58–9.
1. care: sorrow.
2. heart . . . tie: the original spelling, *hart*, points up the punning relationship with *Am* 67. 9–12. *bands*: cf. *Am* 71. 7n.
3. golden hair: alludes to Petrarch's Laura; yellow was also a colour of Venus: Ptolemy, *Tetrabiblos*, 2. 9 and *Am* 37. 1 and 6nn.
5. bird: recalling the caged bird as emblem of lustful youth's hopefulness: Tervarent (1958) col. 59 (note the gluttonous emphasis on *food*, *feed*).
9. bright: beautiful.
10. encage: confine: *OED*'s first instance, 1593. *thrall*: *Am* 29. 10n.
11. rare: especially intense.
Sonnet 74 *1. framed*: fashioned. *trade*: application, practice (rare usage: *OED* trade *sb* I. 4 listing three examples between 1575 and 1608).
2. designed: indicated (*OED* design *v* I. 1 citing this as its second instance); also sense 3, signified (first citation 1627).
3. three . . . thrice: not just because of mother, queen, and beloved, but because the name Elizabeth contains 9 letters (the number of the spirit: Bongo 1599: 567).

With gifts of body, fortune, and of mind:
The first my being to me gave by kind,   5
  From mother's womb derived by due descent;
  The second is my sovereign Queen most kind,
  That honour and large richesse to me lent;
The third my love, my life's last ornament,
  By whom my spirit out of dust was raised   10
  To speak her praise and glory excellent,
  Of all alive most worthy to be praised:
Ye three Elizabeths, forever live,
  That three such Graces did unto me give.

SONNET 75

One day I wrote her name upon the strand,
  But came the waves and washed it away;

---

4. *body . . . mind*: a neo-Platonic hierarchy, as at *Am* 1. 7n. The division into body (birth)/worldly fortune/spirit also recalls the neo-Platonic attribution of the individual human's life to 'a threefold good Demon' (or Genius) who governs nativity, profession (overseeing success, good patrons, etc.), and the rational soul, derived from God and 'direct[ing] the life of the soul . . . being always active in illuminating of us, although we do not always take notice of it; but when we are purified . . . then it doth . . . speak with us . . . and studieth daily to bring us to a sacred perfection': Agrippa (1651) 3. 22 (pp. 410–11). Cf. Ficino's reading of the three Graces as soul/body/fortune: Wind 1967: 40.
5. *kind*: birth.
7. *kind*: (1) belonging by right of birth; (2) noble; (3) favourably disposed.
8. *richesse*: wealth. *lent*: gave, granted.
9. *life's*: the original spelling, *lives*, is a normal genitive singular form.
10. *spirit . . . dust*: *Am* 1. 7n, 13. 6 and 8nn.
11. *praise and glory*: a biblical phrase (e.g., Philippians 1: 11), confirming the lady as his spiritual guide.
13. *Elizabeths*: the only occasion on which Spenser names his mother and second wife.
14. *Graces*: *SC April* 109 gloss. In neo-Platonic thought they signified the rhythm by which the soul receives the overflowing (*emanatio*) of divine influence, is seized by it (*raptio*), and then returns to its source in the divine (*remeatio*): Wind (1967) ch. 3.
Sonnet 75 *1. wrote . . . strand*: shore, implying the instability of sand. For sand-writing cf. Cleophila's 'Over these brooks' in Sidney's *Old Arcadia*, Book 2.
2. *waves . . . away*: punning on *strand* = sea (a Spenserianism: *OED* strand *sb* 2, 2). For the erasure motif, cf. Chaucer, *House of Fame*, 3. 1136–47, the ice mountain engraved with names of the famous which has partly melted 'so/That of the letters one or two/Was molt [melted] away of every name,/So infamous was woxe their fame'.

Again I wrote it with a second hand,
But came the tide, and made my pains his prey.
'Vain man', said she, 'that dost in vain assay   5
A mortal thing so to immortalise;
For I myself shall like to this decay,
And eke my name be wiped out likewise'.
'Not so', quod I, 'let baser things devise
To die in dust, but you shall live by fame: 10
My verse your virtues rare shall eternise,
And in the heavens write your glorious name
Where, whenas Death shall all the world subdue,
Our love shall live, and later life renew'.

SONNET 76
Fair bosom fraught with Virtue's richest treasure,
The nest of Love, the lodging of delight,
The bower of bliss, the paradise of pleasure,
The sacred harbour of that heavenly spright:

3. second: punning on the fraction of a minute (but the 'second hand' of a watch did not exist until the eighteenth century). *hand*: (1) script; (2) signature.
4. tide: (1) of the sea; (2) = temporal period.
5. assay: attempt something difficult: see *Am* 67. 5n.
7–8. decay . . . likewise: cf. *Am* 13. 6 and 8nn, *Am* dedicatory sonnet 2. 14n.
8. eke: also.
9. devise: arrange.
11. rare: (1) distinguished; (2) exceptional.
12. glorious: cf. *FQ*, 2. 1. 32 (on the Red Cross knight: 'enrolled is your glorious name/In heavenly registers above the sun'), echoing Revelation 20:12 (one's works written in 'the book of life').
14. later: contemporary form of *latter*; hence *later life* = [our] last years; also, the last years of the world.
Sonnet 76 The body as garden again (*Am* 64 headnote), focusing on the bosom as (implied) shield of the heart (*Am* 73): cf. Tasso, *Rime*, ed. Solerti, 3. 133, no. 94 ('Non son si belli i fiori'): Scott 1927: 192, 195.
1. fraught: stored, filled (*OED* fraught *ppl a* 2 cites *HHB*, 224 as its second instance).
3. bower of bliss: *bower* = abode and bedroom; recalls intemperate Acrasia's Bower of Bliss at *FQ*, 2. 12. 42–87. *paradise of pleasure*: a tautology because *paradise* means 'a garden of pleasure': *SC June* 10 gloss. On the two sorts of pleasure, see *Am* 72. 7n.
4. harbour: (1) abode; (2) arbour, bower (*OED* harbour *sb* 2, b, first citation 1563). *spright*: original spelling retained: cf. *Am* 1. 7n and, for the heart and the soul, *Am* 50. 7n and 62. 13.

How was I ravished with your lovely sight, 5
   And my frail thoughts too rashly led astray,
   Whiles diving deep through amorous insight
   On the sweet spoil of beauty they did prey!
And 'twixt her paps (like early fruit in May
   Whose harvest seemed to hasten now apace), 10
   They loosely did their wanton wings display,
   And there to rest themselves did boldly place:
Sweet thoughts, I envy your so-happy rest
   Which oft I wished, yet never was so blessed.

5. *ravished . . . sight*: half-serious half-parodic use of language of neo-Platonic *raptus*: *Am* 3. 12n.
6. *rashly*: hastily: he should satisfy himself with her breasts when they are married: Proverbs 5: 19.
7. *insight*: mental vision, superior to external (physical) vision, hence suggesting (and parodying) the Platonic and neo-Platonic abstract (of Beauty, etc.): *OED* insight *sb* 1, 1. See Wind 1967: 50 noting that for Ficino knowledge culminates in pleasure, which is of a higher order than vision. *Amorous insight* also puns on *amorous incite*, the spurring of amorous desire which becomes superior to bestial passion only through having Beauty as its origin and Pleasure as its goal: Wind 1967: 46.
8. *spoil*: *Am* 69. 13n.
9. *paps*: breasts. *May*: associated with love because of the rites of Flora celebrated in early May: Ovid, *Fasti*, 5. 183–378.
11. *loosely*: (1) unconstrainedly; (2) immorally. *wanton*: (1) undisciplined; (2) lewd. *wings*: these 'thoughts' are perhaps the *Amoretti* (winged Cupids) themselves; and cf. *Am* 72. 1.

SONNET 77

Was it a dream, or did I see it plain? –
A goodly table of pure ivory,
All spread with junkets, fit to entertain
The greatest prince with pompous royalty,
'Mongst which there in a silver dish did lie   5
Two golden apples of unvalued price,
Far passing those which Hercules came by,
Or those which Atalanta did entice:

Sonnet 77 Metaphorical revision of *Am* 76's bosom into banquet table, symbol of the communion of the immortals: Wind, E. 1948 *Bellini's Feast of the Gods*, Harvard U.P., Cambridge, Mass.
1–2. dream . . . ivory: hinting at the mediaeval dream vision but mainly drawing on Macrobius, *Commentary on the Dream of Scipio*, 1. 3. 17–20: the soul, floating free of the sleeping body, gazes at truth through a veil: when truth is perceived, the veil is said to be made of (transparent) horn; but sometimes the veil remains opaque, concealing truth, in which case it is said to be ivory (the symbolism derives from *Aeneid*, 6. 893–6 where the gate of ivory lets through dreams that are false in the light of day). The Bower of Bliss is entered through an ivory gate: *FQ*, 2. 12. 44–6. *Ivory* is also dedicated to Venus (*Am* 15. 10n); and note that the (male) beloved's 'belly [is] like white ivory' at Song of Solomon 5: 14; while 4: 16 reinforces the idea of the feast of love: 'let my well-beloved come to his garden, and eat his pleasant fruit'.
2. table: (1) in the modern sense; (2) tablet for writing memoranda, etc. on: *Hamlet*, 1. 5, 'the table of my memory' (so that, like the winged thoughts, it is a sign of the *Amoretti* themselves, inscribed and printed on a white background).
3. junkets: (1) cream- or milk-based foods made and sometimes served in a junket or basket (relates to the breast imagery); (2) sweatmeats.
4. pompous: magnificent.
5. silver: purity: Psalm 12: 6 (God's words as silver).
6. golden apples: mythologically ambivalent (7–8) but emblems of the breasts via their connection with Venus: Valeriano 1602: 573–77. On p 574 he cites Philostratus, *Imagines*, 1. 6 on the numerous Loves (Amoretti) who gather apples, images of the innumerable desires of men: cf. Claudian, *Epithalamium of Palladius*, 10–15. For the apple as marriage, see Smith 1992: 97. *unvalued*: of inestimable value. *price*: *Am* 69. 7n.
7. Hercules: his eleventh labour was to fetch the golden apples, guarded by a dragon (symbol of sexual prohibition), from the far-western garden (cf. *Am* 76 headnote and 3n) of the daughters of Atlas and Hesperia known as the Hesperides: Fraunce 1592: 46–7.
8. Atalanta: advised by an oracle not to marry, she nevertheless agreed to marry the man who could beat her in a running race provided those who lost were killed. Hippomenes tricked her by dropping three golden apples (given him by Venus from the Hesperidean garden) on the track, which distracted her so that he won. Hippomenes and Atalanta were turned into lions for consummating their relationship in the temple of Cybele: Fraunce 1592: 44, 48 (noting that the apples signify incitement to cupidity, and lions, lust); Tooke 1713: 137–8.

Exceeding sweet, yet void of sinful vice,
  That many sought yet none could ever taste, 10
  Sweet fruit of pleasure brought from paradise
  By Love himself, and in his garden placed:
Her breast that table was so richly spread;
  My thoughts the guests which would thereon have fed.

SONNET 78

Lacking my love, I go from place to place
  Like a young fawn that late hath lost the hind,
  And seek each-where where last I saw her face
  Whose image yet I carry fresh in mind.
I seek the fields with her late footing signed, 5
  I seek her bower with her late presence decked:
  Yet nor in field nor bower I her can find,
  Yet field and bower are full of her aspect.
But when mine eyes I thereunto direct,
  They idly back return to me again; 10
  And when I hope to see their true object,
  I find myself but fed with fancies vain:
Cease, then, mine eyes, to seek herself to see,
  And let my thoughts behold herself in me.

9. *void . . . vice*: but the Atalanta myth suggests it and anticipates ll. 11–12.
11–12. fruit . . . placed: the apples of Venus conflated with the fruit of the Fall (Genesis 3: 6; and on paradise = pleasure see *Am* 76. 3n), emblem of concupiscence (Latin *malum* = apple; *malus* (adjective) = evil).
Sonnet 78   An absence sonnet (*Am* 52 headnote; cf. *Am* 87–9) that is also a revision of *Am* 67 via Horace, *Odes*, 1. 23 (where Chloe shuns the lover 'like a fawn seeking its timid mother': Spenser's borrowing startlingly focuses the lover's dependence). In view of the sensuality of *Am* 76–7, note that distress at physical absence was, to neo-Platonists, a clear sign of the lover's failure to reach a sufficient level of abstraction: 'to escape the torment caused by absence and to enjoy beauty without suffering, with the help of reason the courtier should turn his desire completely away from the body to beauty alone . . . creat[ing] it in his imagination as an abstract distinct from any material form': Castiglione, *Courtier*, 4: 338 in the context of instructing the courtier 'who is no longer young' in the arts of love: note Spenser's age at *Am* 60.
4. image: *Am* 45. 11n.
5. late . . . signed: at Horace, *Odes*, 1. 23. 2 the mountains are 'untrodden' (*avius*); but the signs of the hind's absence here recall *Am* 75. 2n (and note that *trade* at *Am* 74. 1 can, in connection with the letters of her name, mean track or footprints: *OED* trade *sb* I. 2).
8. aspect: presence (Latin *aspectus*).
12. fancies: imaginings.

SONNET 79

Men call you fair, and you do credit it
    For that yourself ye daily such do see;
    But the true fair (that is, the gentle wit
    And virtuous mind) is much more praised of me:
For all the rest, however fair it be,   5
    Shall turn to nought and lose that glorious hue;
    But only that is permanent and free
    From frail corruption that doth flesh ensue.
That is true beauty: that doth argue you
    To be divine and born of heavenly seed,   10
    Derived from that fair Spirit from whom all true
    And perfect beauty did at first proceed.
He only fair, and what He fair hath made:
    All other fair, like flowers untimely, fade.

SONNET 80

After so long a race as I have run
    Through faery land, which those six books compile,
    Give leave to rest me (being half fordone),
    And gather to myself new breath awhile.

Sonnet 79 For the contrast between external and 'true fair', cf. 1 Peter 3: 3–4, opposing bodily apparel to 'the hidden man of the heart, which consisteth in the incorruption of a meek and quiet spirit': Jacobs 1983: 187–90. Scott 1927: 195 compares Tasso, *Rime*, ed. Solerti, 3. 142, no. 102 ('Vergine illustre').

1. credit: (1) believe; (2) bring repute to (the idea of fairness): *OED* credit *v* 5 (first citation 1596).

3. wit: understanding.

6. hue: *Am* 53. 6n.

8. ensue: follow (supersede).

10. born . . . seed: *Am* 61. 6 and n.

11–12. Spirit . . . beauty: cf. *HHB*, 8–13, where 'immortal Beauty' is 'with' the Holy Spirit.

14. flowers . . . fade: proverbial: Smith 1970: 109. *untimely*: out of their due season. *fade*: wither.

Sonnet 80 *1. race*: allies him with Hippomenes: *Am* 77. 8n; note also the Pauline image of the Christian's race, as at Hebrews 12: 1.

2–3. faery . . . fordone: the courtly world of *FQ* with its central idea of Gloriana as Queen of Faery now parallels *Am* 79's topic, 'fairness'. Note the claim that *FQ*'s 6 extant books were completed by this time (1594), though not published until 1596; and the stated intention to continue the epic. Cf. *Am* 33.

2. compile: construct: *OED* compile *v* II. 6 citing *FQ*, 3. 3. 10 and this instance.

3. half fordone: half dead (*OED* fordo *v* 1, 7; fordone *ppl a* cites *FQ*, 1. 5. 41 as its first instance).

4. new breath: suggesting 'inspiration' (a breathing into).

Then, as a steed refreshed after toil, 5
    Out of my prison I will break anew,
    And stoutly will that second work assoil
With strong endeavour and attention due.
Till then, give leave to me in pleasant mew
    To sport my Muse and sing my love's sweet praise, 10
    The contemplation of whose heavenly hue
My spirit to an higher pitch will raise:
But let her praises yet be low and mean,
    Fit for the handmaid of the Faery Queen.

SONNET 81

Fair is my love, when her fair golden hairs
    With the loose wind ye waving chance to mark;
    Fair when the rose in her red cheeks appears,
Or in her eyes the fire of love does spark;
Fair when her breast, like a rich-laden bark 5

5–7. steed . . . assoil: echoing *FQ*, 3. 12. 47 (last stanza in the original, 1590, text): 'But now my team begins to faint and fail,/All woxen weary of their diurnal toil:/Therefore I will their sweaty yokes assoil/At this same furrow's end, till a new day'. But the shire horse is also (1) Pegasus, horse of poetic inspiration and origin of the fountain of the Muses, Hippocrene (*SC April* 42 gloss), and (2) the horse of the passions (*SC December* 63–4n) which the poet must outgrow in order to complete the epic.

6. prison: stall: perhaps recalling the image of the stallion breaking his tether and galloping from his stall at *Aeneid*, 11. 492–3: Scott in *Var* 2. 451.

7. stoutly: valiantly. *assoil*: *Am* 11. 9n.

9. mew: the prison (of his libido) now changes, via winged Pegasus, into a cage for moulting hawks, symbol of confinement and transformation: *OED* mew *sb* 2, 1.

10. sport: entertain.

12. pitch: (1) height which falcon reaches before swooping on its prey (*OED* pitch *sb* 1 IV. 18, first citation 1591); (2) musical: cf. *SC October* 50 gloss and *Epith* 9n (*OED* sense 23, first citation 1597).

13. mean: (1) common; (2) moderate.

14. handmaid: servant.

Sonnet 81 A blazon (*Am* 15, 64 headnotes) influenced by Petrarch, *Rime*, 90 and Tasso, *Rime*, ed. Solerti, 2. 25–6, no. 17 ('Bella è la donna mia'): Scott 1927: 195.

1. Fair: pun developing from 'faery': *Am* 80. 2–3n. *golden hairs*: *Am* 73. 3n.

2. loose: (1) random (first *OED* citation 1681); (2) unchaste. *mark*: observe.

3. rose: *Am* 64. 6n.

4. eyes . . . spark: *Am* 7. 1, 3nn; Castiglione, *Courtier*, 4: 334: the fire of pleasure upon first seeing the beloved is increased by the 'spirits' glinting from her eyes.

5–6. breast . . . merchandise: reversion to the capitalist metaphor of *Am* 15.

With precious merchandise, she forth doth lay;
Fair when that cloud of pride (which oft doth dark
Her goodly light) with smiles she drives away;
But fairest she when so she doth display
    The gate with pearls and rubies richly dight   10
    Through which her words so wise do make their way
    To bear the message of her gentle spright:
The rest be works of Nature's wonderment,
But this the work of heart's astonishment.

SONNET 82

Joy of my life, full oft for loving you
    I bless my lot that was so lucky placed;
    But then the more your own mishap I rue
    That are so much by so mean love embased:
For had the equal heavens so much you graced   5
    In this as in the rest, ye mote invent
    Some heavenly wit, whose verse could have enchased
    Your glorious name in golden monument.
But since ye deigned so goodly to relent
    To me, your thrall, in whom is little worth,   10
    That little that I am shall all be spent
    In setting your immortal praises forth,
Whose lofty argument, uplifting me,
    Shall lift you up unto an high degree.

7. pride: Castiglione, *Courtier*, 4: 329: Morello says that beauty makes women proud; Bembo replies that this is merely a response to the transgression of due limits by the (older) lover.
7–8. dark . . . light: neo-Platonism again: e.g., *Am* 3.
10. pearls . . . rubies: *Am* 15. 8–9n. *dight*: *SC April* 29 gloss.
11. words: Castiglione, *Courtier*, 4: 336: the kiss is a union of souls, not bodies (cf. *Am* 64. 1n) and the 'rational lover' knows, too, that the mouth is the 'channel for words, which are the interpreters of the soul'.
13. wonderment: *Am* 69. 12n.
14. astonishment: *Am* 3. 10n.
Sonnet 82 *3. mishap*: misfortune.
4. embased: *Am* 13. 3n.
5. equal: equitable, impartial.
6. mote: *Am* 33. 4n. *invent*: discover.
7. enchased: (1) set (in a precious metal); (2) engrave.
8. your . . . monument: but see *Am* 17.
13. argument: subject.
14. degree: rung (on the Christian/Platonic ladder of virtue and spiritual ascent: cf. *Am* 13. 10).

SONNET 83

My hungry eyes, through greedy covetise
  Still to behold the object of their pain,
  With no contentment can themselves suffice
  But having, pine, and having not, complain:
For lacking it, they cannot life sustain;   5
  And seeing it, they gaze on it the more,
  In their amazement like Narcissus vain,
  Whose eyes him starved: so plenty makes me poor.
Yet are mine eyes so filled with the store
  Of that fair sight that nothing else they brook,   10
  But loathe the things which they did like before,
  And can no more endure on them to look:
All this world's glory seemeth vain to me,
And all their shows but shadows, saving she.

SONNET 84

Let not one spark of filthy lustful fire
  Break out that may her sacred peace molest;
  Ne one light glance of sensual desire
  Attempt to work her gentle mind's unrest;
But pure affections bred in spotless breast,   5
  And modest thoughts breathed from well-tempered sprites,
  Go visit her in her chaste bower of rest,
  Accompanied with angelic delights.
There fill yourself with those most joyous sights
  The which myself could never yet attain: 10

Sonnet 83 Reprints *Am* 35 with the one substantive variant: *seeing* instead of *having* (l. 6). See headnote and *Am* 35 notes. But now the Narcissus situation suggests the frustration of the betrothed, near (but not yet near enough) to sexual fulfilment: Kaske 1978: 275–6.

Sonnet 84 Scott 1927: 192, 195 compares Tasso, *Rime*, ed. Solerti, 2. 194, no. 120 ('Uom di non pure fiamme').
3. *light*: wanton.
5. *pure . . . breast*: the heart is seat of the affections (*Am* 50. 7n); note that the male lover appropriates the *spotlessness* of *Am* 65. 14n.
6. *modest*: another female quality attributed to the male: *Am* 13. 3n. *thoughts*: ct. the *thought* of *Am* 2. 1. *well-tempered*: balanced (cf. *Am* 13. 4n). *sprites*: emitted from the eyes (l.3), so cf. *Am* 81. 4n.
7. *bower of rest*: bedroom. Cf. *Am* 76. 3n.
8. *angelic*: ct. the bodily lust of l. 1.
9–10. *fill . . . attain*: cf. the feasting of *Am* 76–7.

But speak no word to her of these sad plights
Which her too-constant stiffness doth constrain.
Only behold her rare perfection,
And bless your fortune's fair election.

SONNET 85

The world (that cannot deem of worthy things),
   When I do praise her, say I do but flatter:
   So does the cuckoo, when the mavis sings,
   Begin his witless note apace to clatter.
But they that skill not of so heavenly matter,   5
   All that they know not, envy or admire:
   Rather than envy, let them wonder at her,
   But not to deem of her desert aspire.
Deep in the closet of my parts entire
   Her worth is written with a golden quill,   10
   That me with heavenly fury doth inspire,
   And my glad mouth with her sweet praises fill:
Which, whenas Fame in her shrill trump shall thunder,
   Let the world choose to envy or to wonder.

11. plights: (1) offences (*OED* plight *sb* 1, 2: a mediaevalism); (2) states (*OED* sb 2, II. 4); (3) punning on *plight* = fold, pleat (*sb* 2, sense I. 1), which is *constrained* by her *stiffness* = moral strength (*OED* stiffness 3) as well as aloofness.
13. rare: *Am* 75. 11n.
14. election: choice (the fact of having been chosen), with hints of the Calvinistic sense of chosen for salvation without reference to one's apparent merit, behaviour, etc. Cf. *free will* in *Am* 10. 4n.
Sonnet 85 Renwick compares Ronsard, *Hélène*, 1. 10.
1. deem: judge.
3. cuckoo: *Am* 19. 1n. *mavis*: song thrush associated with spring and love: Chaucer, *Sir Thopas*, stanza 11; cf. *Epith*, 81. The lover rejects the cuckoo of *Am* 19, remembering its connection with adultery.
4. witless: foolish; lacking in intellect (as manifested, presumably, in his two-note song). *clatter*: talk idly and/or rapidly.
5. skill: understand.
6. all that: all those things which. *envy*: one of Spenser's pet hates: cf. *SC* dedicatory poem 5n and *Am* 86. *admire*: view with surprise.
8. deem of: celebrate: *OED* deem *v* 10; poetic usage only: last citation 1547. *desert*: excellence.
9. closet . . . entire: secret place of my whole body (*entire* = undivided, wholly one, first attributed by *OED* entire *a* 5 to *FQ*, 1. 7. 33; see also sense 7b, private). Cf. *Am* 6. 11n.
10. quill: pen made from feather (thus uniting the birds and poetic creativity again); but *inspire* (11) suggests the meaning *musical pipe*: *SC June* 67n.
11. heavenly fury: divine possession, inspired by her *worth*.
13. Fame . . . trump: *SC* Dedicatory Epistle, p. 18n.

SONNET 86

Venomous tongue, tipped with vile adder's sting
  Of that self kind with which the Furies fell
  Their snaky heads do comb, from which a spring
  Of poisoned words and spiteful speeches well:
Let all the plagues and horrid pains of hell   5
  Upon thee fall for thine accursed hire
  That, with false-forged lies, which thou didst tell,
  In my true love did stir up coals of ire,
The sparks whereof let kindle thine own fire
  And, catching hold on thine own wicked head,   10
  Consume thee quite that didst with guile conspire
  In my sweet peace such breaches to have bred:
Shame be thy meed, and mischief thy reward,
  Due to thyself that it for me prepared.

SONNET 87

Since I did leave the presence of my love,
  Many long weary days I have outworn,
  And many nights, that slowly seemed to move
  Their sad protract from evening until morn:

Sonnet 86 By ending the sequence on notes of discord and absence, Spenser suggests their resolution in *Epith*. The 'poisoned words' of l. 4 also mark the irruption of the external, social, world into the lovers' solipsism: DeNeef 1982: 74–6. For Orphic implications, see Orphic Footnote to headnote above.

1–4. venomous . . . speeches: Envy was either accompanied by a snake or had snakes in her hair: Ripa 1603: 241–2. Cf. the iconography of the Blatant Beast at *FQ*, 6. 12. 28.

1. tongue: for the disembodied tongue of envy and slander, see *FQ*, 5. 9. 25–6.

2. self: same. *Furies*: the three Furies, also known as the Avengers, offspring of Night and Acheron, were Allecto, Tisiphone and Megaera; their function was to torment men with guilt and 'their hairs [were] hissing serpents' signifying 'that the conscience doth always gnaw, and bite the heart of the ungodly': Batman 1577: 21. *fell*: terrible.

3–4. spring . . . well: *SC June* 93–6 and *October* 108nn.

6. hire: payment.

7. lies: biographical background unknown; see Petrarch, *Rime*, 206 for a remote parallel.

8–12. coals . . . bred: fire is the traditional emblem of wrath, and cf. Song of Solomon, 8: 6: 'love is strong as death; jealousy is cruel as the grave: the coals thereof are fiery coals and a vehement flame'.

13. meed: here in its original meaning, wages (cf. *hire* at l. 6).

Sonnet 87 *2. outworn*: passed: *OED* outwear v 2 cites *FQ*, 3. 12. 29 as first instance.

4. protract: prolongation: *OED* cites one earlier instance, 1536.

For whenas day the heaven doth adorn, 5
   I wish that night the noyous day would end;
   And whenas night hath us of light forlorn,
   I wish that day would shortly reascend.
Thus I the time with expectation spend,
   And feign my grief with changes to beguile 10
   That further seems his term still to extend
   And maketh every minute seem a mile:
So sorrow still doth seem too long to last,
   But joyous hours do fly away too fast.

SONNET 88

Since I have lacked the comfort of that light
   The which was wont to lead my thoughts astray,
   I wander as in darkness of the night,
   Afraid of every danger's least dismay:
Ne aught I see, though in the clearest day, 5
   When others gaze upon their shadows vain,
   But the only image of that heavenly ray,
   Whereof some glance doth in mine eye remain;
Of which beholding the Idea plain,
   Through contemplation of my purest part, 10
   With light thereof I do myself sustain
   And thereon feed my love-affamished heart:

---

6. *night . . . end*: anticipating *Epith*, 278. *noyous*: troublesome.
7. *forlorn*: deprived (the verb was applied in various senses: *OED* forlese *v* 1).
10–11. *feign . . . extend*: imagine that I can (or: pretend to) [*feign*] cheat [*beguile*] my grief with change [of scenery, etc.], which seems to extend its duration still further. But the original spelling, *faine*, also suggests *fain* = wish (*OED* fain *v* 1; last citation *FQ*, 5. 12. 36).
12. *mile*: the time in which one might travel a mile: *OED* mile *sb* 1, 4 citing this as its last instance.
14. *But . . . fast*: proverbial: Smith 1970: 152.
Sonnet 88 For the neo-Platonic positive (which this sonnet half denies: 13–14n), see Castiglione as in *Am* 78 headnote. Renwick compares Petrarch, *Rime*, 130.
1–2. *lacked . . . astray*: the beloved, as the guiding light (cf. *Am* 3 and 78), controlled his straying thoughts.
4. *dismay*: dismaying influence (a nonce Spenserian use: *OED* dismay *sb* b; cf. *Am* 14. 11n).
7. *image*: *Am* 45. 11n.
8. *glance*: gleam, flash of light: *OED* glance *sb* 1, 3, with a suggestion of sense 1, swift oblique impact (as of an arrow: here, Cupid's as the 'heavenly ray'). Cf. *Am* 16. 5n.
9. *Idea*: *Am* 45. 7n.

But with such brightness whilst I fill my mind
   I starve my body and mine eyes do blind.

SONNET 89

Like as the culver on the bared bough
   Sits mourning for the absence of her mate,
   And in her songs sends many a wishful vow
   For his return that seems to linger late,
So I, alone now left disconsolate,   5
   Mourn to myself the absence of my love
   And, wandering here and there all desolate,
   Seek with my plaints to match that mournful dove.
Ne joy of aught that under heaven doth hove
   Can comfort me but her own joyous sight,   10
   Whose sweet aspect both God and man can move
   In her unspotted pleasance to delight:
Dark is my day whiles her fair light I miss,
   And dead my life that wants such lively bliss.

---

14. starve . . . blind: perhaps commendable asceticism; more likely, failure to handle the image rationally: it hasn't displaced the physical, and so absence still causes physical torment: *Am* 78 headnote. Note that 'gaze . . . shadows' (6) hints at Narcissus starving to death (*Am* 83).

Sonnet 89 Revising Petrarch, *Rime*, 353 and Tasso, *Rime*, ed. Solerti, 2. 439, no. 12 ('O vaga tortorella'): *Var* 2. 454.

1. culver: dove: *Am* 64. 10n and *SC November* 138n citing a line from Virgil's *Eclogue* 1, uttered by exiled Meliboeus, that the lover recalls here (exemplifying the dove's extreme fidelity in bereavement: Valeriano 1602: 223). The solitary dove is an ill omen for marriage (Scaliger tr. Bryce in Dubrow 1990: 279), and also an emblem of the man given to contemplation (Valeriano, p. 224).

1. bared: suggesting winter desolation consonant with the grief of Orpheus: *Epith* 16–18nn; Orphic Footnote to *Am–Epith* headnote above.

3. vow: prayer (French *voeu*); pledge of fidelity (the original text's *vew* is not a misprint but a form of the French word. *OED* vow *sb* list of forms records *veu*.).

6–8. Mourn . . . dove: an Orphic situation: cf. *Epith*, 17n.

6. Mourn: utter lamentations (to): *OED* mourn *v* 1, I. 1c (rare; one example from 1533; two from the eighteenth century).

7. desolate: note the punning rhyme: the root of *disconsolate* (l. 5) is Latin *solor* = I comfort; that of *desolate* is *solus* = alone.

8. plaints: *Am* 18. 7n. *match*: (1) equal; (2) ally myself in marriage to. *mournful*: grieving.

9. hove: linger, remain.

12. unspotted: *Am* 65. 14n. *pleasance*: ability to give pleasure.

14. wants: lacks. *lively*: belonging to a living person.

[Anacreontics]

[1]

In youth, before I waxed old,
  The blind boy, Venus' baby,
For want of cunning, made me bold
  In bitter hive to grope for honey:
But when he saw me stung and cry   5
He took his wings and away did fly.

[2]

As Dian hunted on a day,
She chanced to come where Cupid lay,
  His quiver by his head:
One of his shafts she stole away,
And one of hers did close convey   5

[1] *1. youth . . . old*: a further reminder of the lover's age (cf. *Am* 60, 78 headnote) and hinting at the commonplace that, though always young, Love is the oldest and strongest of the gods: Plato, *Symposium*, 178A–C, 195A–B; Hesiod, *Theogony*, 120–3.
2. blind . . . baby: for the iconography see *SC March* 33, 79 glosses; most traditions agreed that Venus was his mother, though there was less agreement about his father, Mars and Jupiter being favourite contenders: Tooke 1713:141–2.
3. cunning: wisdom: *OED* cunning *sb* 2 (last citation 1532).
4–6. hive . . . fly: the Cupid and the bee topos is the subject of [4], as well as of those *Am* concerned with love as 'bitter-sweet': see 26 headnote, 42. 2 and 71. 2nn; also, for Theocritus, *Idyll*, 19 where Cupid steals honey, *SC March* emblem n and Hutton 1941b repr. 1980.
4. honey: Miola 1980: 59 suggests that it symbolises the lover's goal because biblically it is the emblem of salvation and sustenance after tribulation (citing Deuteronomy 6: 3 among other texts); a sexual meaning is more likely: the lips of the beloved 'drop as honeycombs: honey and milk are under thy tongue' at Song of Solomon 4: 11; and Shakespeare's Lucrece talks of her rape thus: 'In thy weak hive a wandering wasp hath crept,/And sucked the honey which thy chaste bee kept' (*Rape of Lucrece*, 839–40; cf. 836: 'My honey lost').
[2] Translated from Marot, *Epigrams*, Book 3. 5, *De Diane* as [3] is of no. 24, *De Cupide et sa Dame*: Child in *Var* 2. 456.
1. Dian: Diana, moon goddess of virginity and the hunt: for her bow and arrows, see Batman 1577: 3.
4. One . . . away: cf. Panofsky's reading of Titian's 'Education of Cupid' in terms of the deprivation of the blindfolded god of his weapons in the interests of marriage and chastity (Panofsky 1962: 165–6); but note Wind 1967: 78–80: blind Cupid is a positive force, and the painting celebrates passion as the fulfilment of intellectual love.
5. close: secretly.

Into the other's stead:
With that Love wounded my love's heart,
But Dian beasts with Cupid's dart.

[3]

I saw in secret to my dame
How little Cupid humbly came,
   And said to her 'All hail, my mother'.
But when he saw me laugh, for shame
His face with bashful blood did flame,   5
   Not knowing Venus from the other:
'Then never blush, Cupid', quoth I,
   'For many have erred in this beauty'.

[4]

Upon a day, as Love lay sweetly slumbering
   All in his mother's lap,
A gentle bee, with his loud trumpet murmuring,
   About him flew by hap:
Whereof, when he was wakened with the noise,   5
   And saw the beast so small,
'What's this,' quoth he, 'that gives so great a voice
   That wakens men withal?
In angry-wise he flies about
   And threatens all with courage stout'.   10

---

6. *stead*: place.
7. *With that*: alluding to the virginal, Dianan (and disdainful) quality of the beloved in *Am*.
8. *Dian beasts*: her traditional function is to hunt the beasts of the passions; so that by wounding them with Cupid's dart of lust she infects them with bestial love in order to prevent it infecting mankind. Allegorically, the beloved has vanquished the lover's tendency to bestial love: i.e., the desire to seek fulfilment through the body alone rather than through the body as an image of the divine: Wind 1967: 138–9 quoting Pico.
[3] Celebrates the beloved as Venus (as in, e.g., *Am* 64, 77) to iconise her as the mysterious Venus–Diana composite: *SC April* emblem gloss.
[4] Derives from Theocritus, *Idylls*, 19 and Anacreon via Renaissance imitators including Alciati 1551: 122, Tasso, Ronsard, Thomas Watson's *Hecatompathia* (1582), sonnet 53 and Whitney 1586: 148: Hutton 1941b repr. 1980. The last two stanzas are original to Spenser.
3. *bee*: emblem of love's sting (bitterness in association with sweetness as at [1]. 4–6n and Wind 1967: 91n). See also *Am* 71. 2n.
4. *hap*: chance.
10. *courage stout*: fierce bravery, punning on strong erection (in allusion to the sting): *OED* courage *sb* 3c, and cf. *FQ*, 2. 12. 68.

To whom his mother (closely smiling) said,
   'Twixt earnest and 'twixt game:
'See, thou thyself likewise art little made,
   If thou regard the same;
And yet thou sufferest neither gods in sky   15
   Nor men in earth to rest,
But when thou art disposed cruelly
   Their sleep thou dost molest:
Then either change thy cruelty,
   Or give like leave unto the fly'.   20

Natheless, the cruel boy, not so content,
   Would needs the fly pursue,
And in his hand with heedless hardiment
   Him caught for to subdue;
But when on it he hasty hand did lay,   25
   The bee him stung therefore.
'Now out, alas!' (he cried) 'and wellaway!
   I wounded am full sore:
The fly that I so much did scorn
   Hath hurt me with his little horn'.   30

Unto his mother straight he weeping came,
   And of his grief complained,
Who could not choose but laugh at his fond game,
Though sad to see him pained.
'Think now,' quod she, 'my son, how great the smart   35
   Of those whom thou dost wound:
Full many thou hast pricked to the heart
   That pity never found;
Therefore henceforth some pity take
   When thou dost spoil of lovers make'.   40

---

11. *closely*: secretly.
15–16. *And . . . rest*: Plato, *Symposium*, 197C–E.
20. *fly*: generic noun for any winged insect.
23. *hardiment*: daring.
26. *therefore*: because of his action.
27. *wellaway*: alas.
30. *horn*: any pointed projection.
33. *fond*: foolish.
38. *found*: i.e., from Cupid.
40. *spoil . . . make*: (1) bring harm to; (2) make booty of.

She took him straight, full piteously lamenting,
  And wrapped him in her smock:
She wrapped him softly, all the while repenting
  That he the fly did mock.
She dressed his wound, and it embalmed well   45
  With salve of sovereign might,
And then she bathed him in a dainty well,
  The well of dear delight:
Who would not oft be stung as this,
  To be so bathed in Venus' bliss?   50

The wanton boy was shortly well recured
  Of that his malady,
But he soon after fresh again inured
  His former cruelty;
And since that time he wounded hath myself   55
  With his sharp dart of love,
And now forgets the cruel careless elf
  His mother's hest to prove:
So now I languish till he please
  My pining anguish to appease.   60

FINIS.

41–50. She . . . bliss: the lover is now identified with the complaining god, and Cupid with the bee: the beloved (as Venus) is imagined erotically rewarding him, in anticipation of the (chaster) consummation in *Epith*. Cf. *Am* 72. 9–10.
43. repenting: Cupid does the repenting.
45. embalmed: anointed.
46. salve: *Am* 50. 14, 65. 12nn.
47. well: cf. the fountain of libido in *FQ*, 2. 12. 60–8, parodying the chaste beloved as 'a fountain sealed' (Song of Solomon 4: 12). Only two of Spenser's sources as itemised by Hutton 1941b contain cures: in Ronsard, *Odes*, 4. 16, *Le petit Enfant Amour*, it is a kiss; in Watson, *Hecatompathia*, 53 'Herbs recured soon the wound'. But the joke may, in a characteristically Renaissance way, conceal a neo–Platonic/Orphic mystery of union: cf. Wind 1967: 169.
51. wanton: ungovernable. *recured*: cured.
53. inured: brought into effect: *OED* inure *v* 1, 4 (first citation 1589).
55–60. since . . . appease: ll. 41–50 have already fantasised the nature of the 'appeasement'.
57. elf: suggests malice: *OED* elf *sb* 2; also applied to insects: sense 3.
58. hest: bidding. *prove*: put to the test.
59. languish: *Am* 50. 1n.
60. pining: *SC January* 48n.

Epithalamion

[1]
Ye learned sisters which have oftentimes
Been to me aiding, others to adorn
Whom ye thought worthy of your graceful rhymes,
That even the greatest did not greatly scorn
To hear their names sung in your simple lays,   5
But joyed in their praise:
And, when ye list your own mishaps to mourn
Which death, or love, or Fortune's wreck did raise,

---

1. *learned sisters*: the nine Muses (*SC April* 41 gloss), often connected with the nine strings of Orpheus's lyre (16n below). Spenser translates Ovid's phrase *doctae . . . sorores* (*Fasti*, 6. 811, the penultimate line of this poem about calendar customs which ends in June, the month of Spenser's marriage).
2. *others*: the various aristocratic dedicatees of Spenser's poems, but especially Sidney, the dedicatee of *SC* and the subject of the elegy *Astrophel*, and the queen, as in *SC April* and *FQ*.
3–4. *graceful . . . greatly*: note the *traductio* (the turning of 'a word into many sundry shapes': Puttenham (1589) 3. 19 (p. 170)), and the pun, which introduces the three Graces appropriately early: cf. 103n and *Am* 74. 14n.
5. *simple*: (1) unostentatious; (2) guileless. *lays*: *SC April* 33 gloss.
6. *joyed*: rejoiced.
7. *list*: choose, punning on itemise. *mishaps*: as catalogued in Spenser's *Tears of the Muses* (in *Complaints* (1591); cf. l. 12 below) in which each Muse laments in turn the decline of her particular art.
8. *Fortune's wreck*: the ruin (*OED* wrack v 2, 3a) caused by Fortune. *raise*: cause, punning on produce a sound: *OED* raise v 1, 13b, citing *FQ*, 1. 11. 7 ('to my tunes thy second tenor raise') as first instance.

Your string could soon to sadder tenor turn,
And teach the woods and waters to lament   10
Your doleful dreariment:
Now lay those sorrowful complaints aside
And, having all your heads with garland crowned,
Help me mine own love's praises to resound,
Ne let the same of any be envied.   15
So Orpheus did for his own bride;
So I unto myself alone will sing:
The woods shall to me answer, and my Echo ring.

9. string . . . turn: cf., as well as the *FQ* instance just cited, *SC October* 50 gloss, *HHL*, 13–14. *Tenor* is a contemporary form of *tenure* = act of holding (i.e., the string in tension): *OED* tenure 1b. Spenser envisages a monochord tuned down because the lowest notes were the 'gravest': Gafurius (1969) 1. 2 (p 14). There are puns on *tenor* = (1) tone or mood; (2) voice adjacent to bass (*OED* tenor *sb* 1, I. 3, II. 4). For the Muses and stringed instruments, see *SC April* 103n; Ripa 1603: 347–9.
10. teach . . . waters: pastoral motif: *SC June*, 7–8, Virgil, *Eclogues*, 1. 4–5. Also recalls Orpheus's music as he grieved for Eurydice: Ovid, *Metamorphoses*, 10. 16–40 (16n below). In Spenser's *Virgil's Gnat*, 455–6 the woods respond to Orpheus's music.
11. dreariment: *SC November* 36 gloss.
13. garland: for the spelling, see *SC November* 75n, *February* 121n. For the Muses' garlands, see Ripa 1603: 346–9. Fowler 1970: 170 comments that they symbolise the circle of time that the poem celebrates structurally (and that the refrain's *ring* also evokes).
16. Orpheus . . . bride: for Orpheus, see *SC October* 28 gloss; his name meant 'best voice' (Friedman 1970: 89 citing Fulgentius). Spenser may recall Ovid, *Metamorphoses*, 10. 2–10 (where Orpheus summons Hymen, god of marriage, and he arrives bearing ill omens in anticipation of Eurydice's death by snake bite on the wedding day), or the more optimistic Orphic wedding in Claudian, *Epistle to Serena*, 1–33. Spenser identifies himself with the archetypal poet/singer, then revises the Orphic story into one of consummated marriage. For a less optimistic reading see Loewenstein 1986: 289–90. For Orphic mysteries in *Epith* see Orphic Footnote to headnote above.
17. myself alone: *SC June* 72n on Orpheus; also the dove in *Am* 89. 1–2, 6–8. In Claudian, *Epithalamium of Honorius and Maria*, 20, Honorius 'communed with himself' (*queritur secum*). Ct. *Am* 1. 13.
18. woods . . . ring: *SC June* 52n, and note the allusions to Narcissus in *Am* 35 and 83. Spenser anticipates his refrain at *FQ*, 1. 6. 14 (and cf. 1. 3. 8). For a list of precedents see *Var* 2. 460, but note especially Virgil, *Eclogues*, 10. 8 ('all the woods respond' to the song of Gallus's death through unfulfilled love); Claudian, *Epithalamium of Palladius and Celerina*, 23–5; and the echo that greets the dying Orpheus as he cries out Eurydice's name: Virgil, *Georgics*, 4. 523–7. For the connection between echo, permanence and fame, see Loewenstein 1984: 16–17; also Loewenstein in *SpE*, pp 231–2. I have retained the original's capitalisation (and non-capitalisation) of the initial letter of *Echo* throughout the refrain.

[2]
Early before the world's light-giving lamp
His golden beam upon the hills doth spread,   20
Having dispersed the night's uncheerful damp,
Do ye awake and, with fresh lustihead,
Go to the bower of my beloved love,
My truest turtle dove;
Bid her awake, for Hymen is awake   25
And long since ready forth his masque to move,
With his bright tead that flames with many a flake,
And many a bachelor to wait on him
In their fresh garments trim.
Bid her awake therefore, and soon her dight,   30
For, lo! the wished day is come at last
That shall, for all the pains and sorrows past,
Pay to her usury of long delight.

19. world's . . . lamp: the sun (common periphrasis).
22. lustihead: *SC May* 42n.
23. bower: *Am* 76. 3n.
23–5. beloved . . . awake: Song of Solomon 2: 10, 12 ('My well-beloved spake and said unto me, Arise, my love . . . .the time of the singing of birds is come, and the voice of the turtle is heard in our land'). The poet and his beloved make up a *pair* of doves (see *Am* 89), a good omen for marriage according to Scaliger tr. Bryce in Dubrow 1990: 279; ct. *Am* 89. 1n. The lines also fulfil *Am* 70. 5–14. The Muses take the part of the virgins who summon the bride with cries of 'Hymen' in Catullus, 61. 36–40. The awakening redeems the Eurydicean bride from the Hadean sleep of death that she was condemned to by the Orphic myth.
24. truest . . . dove: *Am* 89. 1n.
25–7. Hymen . . . tead: Hymen, the god of marriage, son of the Muse Calliope and hence brother of Orpheus (Claudian, *Epithalamium of Palladius*, 30–49, where he makes Echo resound from the rocks with his music: cf. 18n above and *SC April* 100 gloss), carried a pine torch (*tead*) to symbolise the flames of 'pure' passion: Virgil, *Ciris*, 439. His invocation in epithalamia was traditional: Scaliger tr. Bryce in Dubrow 1990: 277. The original's spelling *tead* echoes *taeda* at Catullus 61. 15 and is the preferred Spenserian form: *OED* tede *sb*.
26. masque: procession of attendants; the idea of the masque may have come from Marc-Claude de Buttet's *Epithalame aux Nosses de . . . Philibert . . . et de . . . Marguerite* (1559), 91 ff.: McPeek 1936: 185–6.
27. flake: spark or larger detached portion of flame.
28. bachelor: young knight following under his banner (*OED* bachelor 1) as well as 'unmarried man'.
30. dight: dress, adorn (*OED* dight *v* III. 10a: cf. *SC April* 29 gloss; sense 10b – to put on (apparel) – is a Spenserianism).
31. wished day: a classicism: *Var* 2. 462 citing, e.g., Catullus, 64. 31.
33. usury: increase.

And whilst she doth her dight,
Do ye to her of joy and solace sing, 35
That all the woods may answer, and your echo ring.

[3]
Bring with you all the nymphs that you can hear,
Both of the rivers and the forests green,
And of the sea that neighbours to her near,
All with gay garlands goodly well beseen. 40
And let them also with them bring in hand
Another gay garland
For my fair love, of lilies and of roses
Bound true-love wise with a blue silk riband.
And let them make great store of bridal posies, 45
And let them eke bring store of other flowers
To deck the bridal bowers;
And let the ground whereas her foot shall tread –

---

34. *dight*: prepare (herself) (sense 11). There are anticipatory hints here and at 30 of 'have sexual intercourse' (sense I. 4), activated by *usury* with its evocation of the assocation of sex, money and bride-bartering: the bedding of the bride is seen as the cancellation of a debt at 317–18: Leonard 1984: 89.

37. *nymphs*: *SC April* 37n, 120 gloss. *that . . . hear*: i.e., that can hear you.

38–9. *rivers . . . sea*: appropriate to the poem's topography (the wedding probably took place near the sea: *Epith* headnote above) and epithalamic symbolism generally: in Roman marriages water, the feminine element, complemented male fire (supplied by Hymen's torch): *Am* 55. 6n; Scaliger tr. Bryce in Dubrow 1990: 281. For local river nymphs in French epithalamia, see McPeek 1936: 192.

38. *forests green*: the territory of Diana as goddess of the hunt: anacreontics 2. 8n.

40. *goodly*: (1) notable for size or number (of the garlands: *OED* goodly *a* 2); (2) good looking, fair (of the nymphs: sense 1). *well beseen*: (1) well favoured (of the garlands: *OED* besee *v* II. 6); (2) well dressed (of the nymphs: sense 7).

43. *lilies . . . roses*: the flowers of Juno, goddess of marriage (also symbolic of the bride's virginity) combined with the flowers of Venus: *SC April* 136 gloss and 59n. In Claudian, *Epistle to Serena*, 9–10 doves bring garlands of roses and other flowers in celebration of Orpheus's wedding.

44. *Bound . . . riband*: emblem of marriage (the knot of love: *Am* 6. 14n; de Vries 1974: 385; Sir Thomas Browne, *Vulgar Errors*, 5. 22. 5). Blue is the colour of Juno's element, air: Ripa 1603: 121. The *riband* may also suggest the bridal girdle: one name of Juno is '*Cinxia*, from the girdle which the bride wore when about to marry; for this girdle was unloosed with Juno's good leave, who was thought the patroness of marriages': Tooke 1713: 106; cf. Martianus Capella, *Marriage of Philology and Mercury*, 2. 149.

45. *store*: hoard.

46. *store*: abundance.

For fear the stones her tender foot should wrong –
Be strewed with fragrant flowers all along, 50
And diapered like the discoloured mead.
Which done, do at her chamber door await,
For she will waken straight:
The whiles do ye this song unto her sing,
The woods shall to you answer, and your Echo ring. 55

[4]
Ye nymphs of Mulla which, with careful heed,
The silver-scaly trouts do tend full well,
And greedy pikes, which use therein to feed
(Those trouts and pikes all others do excel);
And ye likewise which keep the rushy lake 60
Where none do fishes take:
Bind up the locks, the which hang scattered light,
And in his waters (which your mirror make)
Behold your faces as the crystal bright
That, when you come whereas my love doth lie, 65

49. stones . . . wrong: Psalm 91: 11–12: 'For he shall give his angels charge over thee to keep thee in all thy ways. They shall bear thee in their hands, that thou hurt not thy foot against a stone' (cf. the angels at 229–33 below).
50. flowers: connecting the bride with Venus and Chloris-Flora, thus suggesting the transition from virgin to wife: *Am* 4. 11, 13nn.; *Am* 64 headnote; *SC March* 16 gloss.
51. diapered: adorned with various coloured patterns (usually diamond shaped): cf. heraldic *diapre* = surface (ground) painted with flowers, etc.: *OED* diaper *sb* II. 4b. Note sense 4c: specifically applied to flowers on the ground, first citation 1600. *discoloured*: of different colours.
56. Mulla: Spenser's name for the Awbeg, which marked the western and southern boundaries of his Kilcolman estate: *Colin Clout*, 104–55; Fukuda in *SpE*, p 110.
57–8. trouts . . . pikes: the *pike* suggest a male predatoriness which the rest of the poem excludes; *trout* signify female sexual availability in contemporary male discourse: Shakespeare, *Measure for Measure*, 1. 2: 'What's his offence?' 'Groping for trouts in a peculiar river.' 'What! is there a maid with child by him?' The lines thus introduce a fescennine (bawdy) element: *Epith* headnote.
58. use: are accustomed.
60–1. lake . . . take: the lake near Kilcolman castle: *Var* 2. 464–5.
62. Bind . . . locks: as a sign of chastity: *Am* 37. 6n. *light*: with hints of wanton[ly], and the hair reflected in the water as 'scattered light' (brightness).
63. mirror: Venus's emblem: Twycross 1972: 82–8; fish belong to Venus: *SC December* 81n (Pisces marks her exaltation as a planet).
65. whereas: where.

No blemish she may spy.
And eke ye, lightfoot maids, which keep the dore
That on the hoary mountain use to tower,
And the wild wolves which seek them to devour
With your steel darts do chase from coming near, 70
Be also present here
To help to deck her and to help to sing,
That all the woods may answer, and your echo ring.

[5]
Wake now, my love, awake, for it is time:
The rosy Morn long since left Tithon's bed, 75
All ready to her silver coach to climb,
And Phoebus 'gins to show his glorious head.
Hark how the cheerful birds do chant their lays
And carol of love's praise:
The merry lark her matins sings aloft, 80

66. *No blemish*: so that they match her in spotlessness: *Am* 89. 12n.
67. *eke*: also. *lightfoot*: *SC June* 26n. *dore*: the original spelling, and an available form for *deer* (*OED* deer, list of forms), making the usual editorial emendation to *deere* unnecessary. The creature is an emblem of Diana (*Am* 67. 7n); so these maids complement the Venerean nymphs to combine Diana and Venus again: anacreontics 3 headnote.
68. *hoary*: (1) white with frost (first *OED* citation 1573; cf. *SC February*, 79); (2) ancient (first *OED* citation 1609). *use to*: customarily. *tower*: (1) rise aloft, referring to the antlers; (2) climb (a hawking term).
69. *wolves*: still common then in Ireland: see *FQ*, 7. 6. 55 (where they are a force opposed to Diana) and *Colin Clout*, 318.
70. *darts*: anacreontics 2. 8n.
74–8. *Wake . . . birds*: see 23–5n above. McPeek 1936: 192–4 notes parallels in earlier Renaissance epithalamia.
75–6. *Morn . . . climb*: Aurora, the dawn goddess, fell in love with Tithonus and took him to the heavens, where she was granted immortality for him. She failed to request perpetual youth, however, and as he grew infirm he wished to die. Because this was impossible, she turned him into a grasshopper: Tooke 1713: 153–5 (another 'dark' image, like that of Orpheus, to prelude the wedding). In the Orphic *Hymn to Dawn* she is supplicated to illumine initiates: Athanassakis 1977: 101.
77. *Phoebus*: the sun god, leader of the Muses and god of poetry (thus heralding the bridegroom-poet): *SC April* 41 gloss.
78. *lays*: *SC April* 33 gloss.
79. *carol*: (1) sing joyously; (2) dance in a ring accompanied by singing (*OED* carol *v* 1), to reinforce the circular symbolism of the garlands (ll. 13, 40, 42).
80. *lark*: *SC November* 71n; *June*, 51–6. Spenser lists 5 birds because 5 is 'above all' the number of marriage: Plutarch, *Roman Questions*, 2 (263E–264B). *matins*: morning song (of birds): *OED* matin 2a, citing an instance from *c.* 1530; also hinting at the Protestant sense, the order for morning prayer.

The thrush replies, the mavis descant plays,
The ousel shrills, the ruddock warbles soft:
So goodly all agree with sweet concent
To this day's merriment.
Ah my dear love, why do ye sleep thus long,   85
When meeter were that ye should now awake
To await the coming of your joyous make
And harken to the birds' love-learned song
The dewy leaves among?
For they of joy and pleasance to you sing,   90
That all the woods them answer, and their echo ring.

[6]
My love is now awake out of her dreams,
And her fair eyes, like stars that dimmed were
With darksome cloud, now show their goodly beams
More bright than Hesperus his head doth rear.   95
Come now, ye damsels, daughters of delight,

---

81. *thrush*: song bird; also known as the *mavis*: *Am* 85. 3n.
82. *ousel*: blackbird (species of thrush) associated with the search for God when spring comes: cf. Dante, *Purgatorio*, 13. 123. *ruddock*: robin redbreast, noted for its song and connection with love: Shakespeare, *Two Gentlemen of Verona*, 2. 1 ('relish a love-song, like a robin redbreast').
83. *goodly*: beautifully: *OED* goodly *adv* 1 gives 1556 as date of last instance. *concent*: the original spelling, *consent*, was a familiar contemporary spelling for *concent* = harmony (*OED* concent *sb* 1), which is clearly the meaning here.
86. *meeter*: fitter.
87. *make*: (1) equal; (2) husband.
90. *pleasance*: delight (punning on the meaning *pleasure ground*: *OED* pleasance *sb* 1, 5).
92. *awake*: for the epithalamic awakening topos (and its connection with the dream vision) see Dubrow 1990: 50–7. *dreams*: the copy text reads *dream*. I follow most previous editors in emending for the rhyme.
95. *Hesperus*: name of Venus as the evening star (as the morning star she is Phosphorus/Lucifer). The name is used for morning star here because Hesperus was frequently invoked at weddings: e.g., Claudian, *Fescennine Verses*, IV. 1–2 (Hesperus, beloved of Venus, shines for the marriage) and cf. 288n below. Scaliger tr. Bryce in Dubrow 1990: 281 remarks that the morning star should be mentioned in epithalamia. For an astronomical reading of the passage, see Eade 1972: 174–5.
96. *damsels*: (1) female attendants (i.e., bridesmaids); (2) well-born maidens: *OED* damsel I. 1, 3. *daughters . . . delight*: phrase used of the Graces (l. 103) at *FQ*, 6. 10. 15, where they signify Venerean hilarity. Here it defines the bridesmaids.

Help quickly her to dight:
But first come ye, fair Hours (which were begot
In Jove's sweet paradise of Day and Night),
Which do the seasons of the year allot, 100
And all that ever in this world is fair
Do make and still repair.
And ye three handmaids of the Cyprian Queen,
The which do still adorn her beauty's pride,
Help to adorn my beautifullest bride; 105
And, as ye her array, still throw between
Some graces to be seen
And, as ye use to Venus, to her sing,
The whiles the woods shall answer, and your echo ring.

[7]
Now is my love all ready forth to come, 110
Let all the virgins therefore well await;
And, ye fresh boys that tend upon her groom,

97. *dight*: (1) dress; (2) prepare (cf. 34n).
98–102. *Hours . . . repair*: Spenser gives a similar non-classical pedigree at *FQ*, 7. 7. 45 (where they are offspring of Jove and Night and, as here, signs of wakefulness). Usually the daughters of Jove and Themis, they were three in number and attended Venus along with the Graces: cf. *The Honourable Entertainment . . . at Elvetham* (1591): the queen was greeted by six virgins, 'three . . . represented the three Graces, and the other three the Hours, which by the poets are feigned to be the guardians of heaven's gates . . . [they wore] flowery garlands on their heads, and baskets full of sweet herbs and flowers upon their arms': Nichols (1823) 3. 108. For the poetic tradition referred to, see Homer, *Iliad*, 5. 749–51. They embodied the seasons (originally three in number: Macrobius, *Saturnalia*, 1. 21. 13); in the Orphic *Hymn to the Horai* they are invoked to bring fertile growth [in understanding] to new initiates: Athanassakis 1977: 61. As embodiments of the sidereal hours (markers of the rising and setting of the planets) they were 24 in number: see Hieatt 1960: 32–8, 111–13.
103. *three . . . Queen*: the Graces, attendants of Venus (to whom 'was consecrated the island of Cyprus': Linche (1599), sig 2C 2v); they gather flowers for the wedding in Claudian, *Epithalamium of Honorius*, 202–3, and in the Orphic *Hymn to the Graces* they bestow prosperity: Athanassakis 1977: 81. See 3–4n above.
104. *pride*: magnificence.
107. *graces*: i.e., the manifestations of liberality listed by E.K. at *SC April* 109 gloss.
108. *use*: customarily.
111. *virgins*: the damsels of 96.
112. *boys*: for the bridegroom's attendants, cf. Jonson's *Hymenaei* (Orgel, S. (ed.) 1969 *Complete Masques*, p. 77).

Prepare yourselves, for he is coming straight.
Set all your things in seemly good array
Fit for so joyful day,   115
The joyfullest day that ever Sun did see.
Fair Sun, show forth thy favourable ray,
And let thy life-full heat not fervent be
For fear of burning her sunshiny face,
Her beauty to disgrace.   120
O fairest Phoebus, father of the Muse,
If ever I did honour thee aright,
Or sing the thing that mote thy mind delight,
Do not thy servant's simple boon refuse,
But let this day, let this one day be mine –   125
Let all the rest be thine.
Then I thy sovereign praises loud will sing,
That all the woods shall answer, and their echo ring.

[8]
Hark how the minstrels 'gin to shrill aloud
Their merry music that resounds from far,   130
The pipe, the tabor, and the trembling crowd,
That well agree withouten breach or jar!
But most of all the damsels do delight
When they their timbrels smite
And thereunto do dance and carol sweet   135

115. joyful day: translating Catullus, 61. 11, *hilari die*.
118. life-full: here, as at *FQ*, 6. 11. 46, the original spelling is the mediaeval *lifull*.
119. For . . . face: cf. Sidney, *Astrophil and Stella*, 22. *Sunshiny face* recalls Una at *FQ*, 1. 12. 23, and suggests Revelation 12: 1 (the 'woman clothed with the sun': Geneva gloss: 'a type of the true and holy Church').
120. disgrace: disfigure.
121. father: *SC April* 41 gloss.
124. boon: prayer, entreaty.
125. let . . . mine: version of the *carpe diem* motif: *Am* 70. 13–14n.
129. minstrels: music appears in stanza 8 because 8 is the number of the harmonious octave: Martianus Capella, *Marriage of Philology and Mercury*, 9. 950–1. *shrill*: utter shrilly (a favourite Spenserian word and *OED*'s first instance in this sense). *Shrill* = sharp, thus contrasting with the low notes of 9n above.
131. tabor: small drum, accompaniment to fife or *pipe*: cf. *SC May*, 22–3. *crowd*: fiddle with six strings, four bowed, the remainder plucked (hence *trembling* = agitated; though the word may refer to the vibration of the sound transmitted by the air: *OED* tremble *v* 2b).
134. timbrels: tambourines, usually played by women to accompany singing and dancing: *OED* timbrel *sb* 1, a.
135. carol: 79n above.

That all the senses they do ravish quite,
The whiles the boys run up and down the street,
Crying aloud with strong confused noise
As if it were one voice.
'Hymen, io Hymen' they do shout, 140
That even to the heavens their shouting shrill
Doth reach, and all the firmament doth fill;
To which the people standing all about,
As in approvance, do thereto applaud
And loud advance her laud. 145
And evermore they 'Hymen, Hymen' sing,
That all the woods them answer, and their echo ring.

[9]
Lo, where she comes along with portly pace,
Like Phoebe from her chamber of the east
Arising forth to run her mighty race, 150
Clad all in white that seems a virgin best.
So well it her beseems that ye would ween
Some angel she had been:
Her long loose yellow locks, like golden wire

136. ravish: in the neo-Platonic sense: *Am* 3. 12n; *SC October* 27 gloss.
140. Hymen: see 25–7n above; this is the traditional Graeco-Roman wedding cry: Catullus, 61. 119–21, where the 'boys . . . sing in measure "io Hymen . . ."'.
141. to . . . heavens: traditional motif: e.g., Claudian, *Fescennine Verses*, 4. 35: 'let this be the shout that echoes to the heavenly poles' (*haec vox aetheriis insonet axibus*).
144. approvance: approval; first *OED* instance 1592.
145. her: their: *SC May* 160 gloss. *laud*: praises.
148. portly: *Am* 5. 2 and 13. 1nn.
149. Phoebe: as a name for the moon, goddess of virginity, it means *bright, radiant*, and pairs her with her brother, Phoebus Apollo (77); cf. *SC April* 65 gloss.
150. mighty race: attributing to the feminine moon Psalm 19: 4–5: 'the sun . . . cometh forth as a bridegroom out of his chamber, and rejoiceth like a mighty man to run his race'.
151. white: Ripa 1603: 504: Virginity is a young woman . . . clothed in white'. *seems*: befits.
153. angel: *Am* 61. 5–8.
154. yellow . . . wire: *Am* 73. 3n; the bride is a Diana–Venus composite: anacreontics 3 headnote. *Wire* alludes to the metallic thread used in tapestry work: *OED* wire *sb* I. 1. The hair is *loose* to signify the sexual openness appropriate to a bride: *Proth*, 22–3; ct. the bound hair of *Am* 37.

Sprinkled with pearl, and purling flowers atween, 155
Do like a golden mantle her attire
And, being crowned with a garland green,
Seem like some maiden queen.
Her modest eyes, abashed to behold
So many gazers as on her do stare, 160
Upon the lowly ground affixed are;
Ne dare lift up her countenance too bold,
But blush to hear her praises sung so loud,
So far from being proud.
Natheless, do ye still loud her praises sing, 165
That all the woods may answer, and your echo ring.

[10]
Tell me, ye merchants' daughters, did ye see
So fair a creature in your town before? –
So sweet, so lovely, and so mild as she,
Adorned with Beauty's grace and Virtue's store, 170
Her goodly eyes like sapphires shining bright,
Her forehead ivory white,
Her cheeks like apples which the sun hath rudded,
Her lips like cherries charming men to bite,

155. pearl: attribute of Diana–Phoebe, hence emblem of virginity: Agrippa (1651) 1. 24 (p. 54). Pearls were common in royal and aristocratic head-dresses, as in the Rainbow portrait of Elizabeth I. *purling . . . atween*: flowers (garlands of which are emblems of Virginity: Ripa 1603: 504–5) are looped (*purling*) between the pearls: *OED* purl *v* 1, 2.
157–8. garland . . . queen: see 13n and cf. Una (= Oneness, Truth, Elizabeth I, etc.) at *FQ*, 1. 6. 13 and 1. 12. 8 (where she is 'a goodly maiden queen' crowned with 'a garland green'). *Green* symbolises virginal potential about to flower into womanhood, as in the Chloris/Flora myth: *SC April* 122 gloss; *August*, 68.
159–61. modest . . . ground: *Am* 13. 3n; Catullus, 61. 79.
164. proud: not the pride of *Am* 5. 2n but wrongful self-esteem.
167. merchants' daughters: places the bride in a context of bourgeois capitalism; but the following blazon, derived from the Song of Solomon and thus identifying her with the Song's bride/Church, depends mainly on pastoral images. See *Am* 15, 64, 76–7 and, for pejorative associations of merchants, *Am* 15. 1n.
170. store: 46n.
171. sapphires: *Am* 15. 7n.
172. ivory: *Am* 15. 10 and n.
173. apples: Venerean: *Am* 77. 6n. *rudded*: reddened: *OED*'s first example after Langland.
174. cherries: conventional comparison: cf. Sidney's blazon 'What tongue can her perfections tell', 37–9 (*Old Arcadia*, Book 3); de Vries 1970: 94.

Her breast like to a bowl of cream uncrudded, 175
Her paps like lilies budded,
Her snowy neck like to a marble tower,
And all her body like a palace fair,
Ascending up with many a stately stair
To Honour's seat and Chastity's sweet bower. 180
Why stand ye still, ye virgins, in amaze
Upon her so to gaze,
Whiles ye forget your former lay to sing,
To which the woods did answer, and your echo ring?

[11]
But if ye saw that which no eyes can see – 185
The inward beauty of her lively spright
Garnished with heavenly gifts of high degree –
Much more then would ye wonder at that sight,
And stand astonished like to those which read
Medusa's mazeful head. 190

175. uncrudded: *crud* = normal variant of *curd*; but this is *OED*'s only instance of *uncrudded*.
176. paps: breasts (especially the nipples). *lilies*: 43n; as the flower of Juno, goddess of marriage, it is associated with breast milk (Jonson's note to *Hymenaei*, 199 (Orgel S. (ed.) 1969 *Complete Masques*), thus anticipating the bride's childbearing role (382–406 below).
177. marble: as the traditional material of pillars (Song of Solomon 5:15 has legs of marble; the neck is 'a tower of ivory' at 7: 4), it prepares for the *palace* of 1. 178.
179. stair: conspicuous feature of the late Elizabethan prodigy house and hence emblematic of wealth: Summerson, J. 1970 *Architecture in Britain 1530–1830* (Harmondsworth: Penguin), pp. 93–5.
180. seat: i.e., the lady's mind. Cf. Alma's castle, *FQ*, 2. 9. 44–8.
181. amaze: *Am* 3. 7n; perhaps hinting at the lady-as-love-object at the centre of a maze: Senn, W. 1986 'The Labyrinth Image in Verbal Art: Sign, Symbol, Icon?', *Word and Image* 2: 219–30; Doob (1990) ch. 5. Note *mazeful* at 190 below.
186. inward beauty: cf. *Am* 79. *spright*: *Am* 1. 7n.
187. Garnished: (1) adorned; (2) accompanied as by a retinue. *gifts*: *Am* 61. 8n.
189. read: SC dedicatory poem 11n.
190. Medusa's . . . head: when the sea-god Neptune defiled the temple of Minerva (goddess of wisdom and chastity) with Medusa, Minerva transformed her hair into snakes and gave her the power to turn those who gazed on her into stone (hence *astonished*, l. 189) as a punishment for the alluring power of her beauty. The head was subsequently enshrined in Minerva's shield in defence of chastity: Petrarch, *Triumph of Chastity*, 119; cf. *Rime*, 197. In other words, spiritual beauty is awesome. *Mazeful* = bewildering is a Spenserian coinage: *OED*, citing this line.

There dwells sweet Love and constant Chastity,
Unspotted Faith and comely Womanhood,
Regard of Honour and mild Modesty:
There Virtue reigns as Queen in royal throne
And giveth laws alone, 195
The which the base affections do obey
And yield their services unto her will;
Ne thought of thing uncomely ever may
Thereto approach to tempt her mind to ill.
Had ye once seen these her celestial treasures 200
And unrevealed pleasures,
Then would ye wonder, and her praises sing,
That all the woods should answer, and your echo ring.

[12]
Open the temple gates unto my love,
Open them wide that she may enter in; 205
And all the posts adorn as doth behove,
And all the pillars deck with garlands trim,

191–3. Love . . . Modesty: list of traditional female virtues: *Chastity* is the married woman's equivalent of the girl's virginity; for *unspotted Faith*, cf. *Am* 65. 14n (bride as Church in Song of Solomon); for *Womanhood*, cf. *FQ*, 4. 10. 52 (where she is a companion of Venus); for *Honour* as the reward of virtue, see Ripa 1603: 202; for *Modesty*, see 159–61n above. The bride/Church analogy derives directly from the Marriage Service: 'matrimony . . . represent[s] the spiritual marriage and unity betwixt Christ and His Church' (*Prayer-book* 1559: 126).

194–5. Virtue . . . alone: see Ripa 1603: 510–12 and cf. Sidney, *Astrophil and Stella*, 9 (Stella's face as 'Queen Virtue's court'). The meaning is: she alone gives. . . .

196. affections: the lower passions, rational control of which is the practice of moral virtue in its basic Aristotelian sense: *Nicomachean Ethics* 2. 6. 10–12.

197. will: in conjunction with reason should direct the soul to good but, corrupted by the Fall, often yielded to the influence of the immoderate passions.

200–1. celestial . . . pleasures: cf., e.g., *Am* 22 and 24 on the beloved's saintly quality and her heaven-bestowed gifts, and *Am* 65. 14 and 72. 7nn for the Platonic implications of pleasure.

204. Open . . . gates: Isaiah 26: 2 ('Open ye the gates that the righteous nation, which keepeth the truth, may enter in') – the opening of 'a song . . . wherein is declared, in what consisteth the salvation of the Church' (Geneva chapter headnote). Cf. 157–8 and 191–3nn and Psalm 24: 7, 9 ('Lift up your heads ye gates, and be ye lift up ye everlasting doors'). Note, too, Catullus, 61. 76: *Claustra pandite ianuae* (Open wide the bolted gates).

206. posts adorn: cf. *SC May*, 11–14; Claudian, *Epithalamium of Honorius*, 208–9 (where door posts are decorated with Venerean myrtle).

For to receive this saint with honour due
That cometh in to you.
With trembling steps and humble reverence 210
She cometh in before the Almighty's view:
Of her, ye virgins, learn obedience,
When so ye come into those holy places
To humble your proud faces.
Bring her up to the high altar, that she may 215
The sacred ceremonies there partake
The which do endless matrimony make;
And let the roaring organs loudly play
The praises of the Lord in lively notes,
The whiles with hollow throats 220
The choristers the joyous anthem sing
That all the woods may answer, and their echo ring.

[13]
Behold – whiles she before the altar stands,
Hearing the holy priest that to her speaks
And blesseth her with his two happy hands – 225
How the red roses flush up in her cheeks

208. saint: *Am* 22. 4n and 61. 2, 7. The wedding takes place on St Barnabas's day (265–6n below), so she displaces him.
212. obedience: another female virtue (Ripa 1603: 363–4); Spenser anticipates the obedience demanded of a wife: see *Am* 67. 12n.
215. altar: although the more Protestant 'Lord's table' is used throughout the Communion liturgy in the *Prayer-book* 1559: 92, 98–9, 102–3, 'altar' appears in the Geneva Bible (e.g., 1 Corinthians 9: 13), so we need not suspect Catholic bias.
217. endless matrimony: the poem's central line (217/433). *Endless* because (1) the ceremony validates the injunction 'whom God hath joined together, let no man put asunder' (*Prayer-book* 1559: 124); (2) according to a Protestant poetic commonplace, marriage yields immortality through children; (3) the elect will be married to Christ eternally: Revelation 19: 7–9. Cf. *timely* at 425n. *make*: are the essential criteria of (*OED* make *v* I. 24) punning on the noun *make* = husband/wife.
218. roaring: sounding loudly in revelry: *OED* roar *v* 1b (first citation 1584). King 1990: 175 argues that the presence of an instrument confirms the non-Puritan nature of the ceremony. *organs*: the plural denoted the single instrument: *OED* organ *sb* 1, I. 1b.
220. hollow throats: i.e., wide-open mouths.
221. anthem: song sung antiphonally by the choristers split into the sides *cantores/decani* : *OED* anthem *sb* 1.
225. happy: propitious: *OED* happy *a* 3.
226. red roses: the pagan gift to the bride (43n above) now becomes the emblem of modesty: 191–3n above and *FQ*, 2. 9. 41–3.

And the pure snow with goodly vermeil stain
Like crimson dyed in grain,
That even the angels, which continually
About the sacred altar do remain, 230
Forget their service and about her fly,
Oft peeping in her face that seems more fair
The more they on it stare.
But her sad eyes, still fastened on the ground,
Are governed with goodly modesty 235
That suffers not one look to glance awry
Which may let in a little thought unsound:
Why blush ye, love, to give to me your hand,
The pledge of all our band?
Sing, ye sweet angels, 'alleluia' sing, 240
That all the woods may answer, and your echo ring.

[14]
Now all is done: bring home the bride again;
Bring home the triumph of our victory;

227. *vermeil*: vermilion red. Cf. *FQ*, 2. 12. 45; *Proth*, 33.
228. *dyed . . . grain*: i.e., fast dyed; used of red and purple: *OED* grain *sb* 1, III. 10.
229–30. *angels . . . altar*: at Holy Communion before the consecration the priest says the *Sanctus* 'with angels and archangels, and with all the company of heaven' (*Prayer-book* 1559: 102). For Spenser's fondness for angels, see *FQ*, 2. 8. 1–8 (where the angel is like Cupid) and 5. 9. 28–9. In *Epith* they displace the winged Cupids or *amoretti* of the preceding sonnets and anacreontics: *Am* 16. 6n.
234–7. *But . . . unsound*: cf. *Am* 13, 21.
234. *sad*: steadfast: *OED* sad *a* I. 2.
237. *unsound*: morally corrupt. *OED*'s suggestion that it means not soundly based in reasoning (unsound *a* 5, citing this line as a first instance) seems unlikely.
238. *give . . . hand*: as this is near the end of the marriage ceremony (242), probably the moment when, rings having been exchanged, the priest 'join[s] their right hands together and say[s], Those whom God hath joined together, let no man put asunder' (217n above). (Spenser omits reference to the readings and Communion that follow the marriage.) In contrast, as Orpheus lost Eurydice she stretched out her powerless hands towards him: Virgil, *Georgics*, 4. 498.
239. *pledge . . . band*: sign of our bond, punning on *band* = ring (*Am* 1. 3n).
240. *Sing*: perhaps recalling the angels' 'alleluia' before the marriage of the Lamb: Revelation 19: 1, 3.
243–4. *triumph . . . gain*: the language of Petrarch's *Triumph of Love*: cf. *Am* 20. 3n and 69 headnote.

Bring home with you the glory of her gain –
With joyance bring her, and with jollity.   245
Never had man more joyful day than this,
Whom heaven would heap with bliss:
Make feast, therefore, now all this livelong day.
This day forever to me holy is:
Pour out the wine without restraint or stay –   250
Pour not by cups but by the bellyful:
Pour out to all that wull,
And sprinkle all the posts and walls with wine,
That they may sweat, and drunken be withal.
Crown ye god Bacchus with a coronal,   255
And Hymen also crown with wreaths of vine;
And let the Graces dance unto the rest
(For they can do it best),
The whiles the maidens do their carol sing,
To which the woods shall answer, and their echo ring.   260

[15]
Ring ye the bells, ye young men of the town,
And leave your wonted labours for this day:

---

245. joyance: enjoyment, festivity; Spenserian coinage.
248. livelong: (1) in the usual intensive sense (this very long); (2) just possibly, enduring, ever-lasting, in reference to the day's monumental quality as embodied in the poem's 24 stanzas (see 433n): if so, it anticipates and antedates Milton's apparently unique use of this sense: *OED* livelong *a* 2.
250. stay: (1) self-control; (2) stopping.
251. bellyful: alluding to Bacchus's 'paunch' (255n) and to Comus, god of revelry and the belly: Ben Jonson, *Pleasure Reconciled to Virtue* (1618), opening description (Orgel, S. (ed.) 1969 *Complete Masques*, p. 263).
252. wull: common contemporary form of *will*: *OED* will *v* 1, list of forms 4.
253. sprinkle: Claudian, *Epithalamium of Honorius*, 209–10 (sprinkling with nectar); *FQ*, 1. 12. 38. A fertility spell according to Scaliger tr. Bryce in Dubrow 1990: 275.
255. Bacchus: the god of feasting and wine, traditionally portrayed 'with a grand paunch . . . and crowned with an ivy garland' (Batman 1577: 11–12) and/or vine leaves (Tooke 1713: 66–7). Scaliger recommends his invocation in epithalamia: tr. Bryce in Dubrow 1990: 276. Venus is his companion: Orphic *Hymn to Aphrodite*, 7 (Athanassakis 1977: 73).
256. Hymen: 25–7n above; but note that he was also said to be the son of Bacchus and Venus: Tooke 1713: 141. Usually crowned with marjoram: Catullus, 61. 6–7.
257. Graces: 103n above.
259. carol: 79n above.
262. wonted: customary.

This day is holy: do ye write it down,
That ye forever it remember may.
This day the Sun is in his chiefest height 265
With Barnaby the bright,
From whence, declining daily by degrees,
He somewhat loseth of his heat and light
When once the Crab behind his back he sees.
But for this time it ill ordained was 270
To choose the longest day in all the year,
And shortest night, when longest fitter were:
Yet never day so long, but late would pass.
Ring ye the bells to make it wear away,
And bonfires make all day, 275
And dance about them, and about them sing,
That all the woods may answer, and your echo ring.

[16]
Ah, when will this long weary day have end,
And lend me leave to come unto my love?

265–6. Sun . . . bright: according to the Elizabethan calendar (see *SC* General headnote, pp. 9–10), St Barnabas's Day – one of the relatively few saints' days retained by the reformed English Church – coincided with the longest day (solstice). The prayer-book calendar, e.g., listed Barnabas for 11 June, the sun entering Cancer for the 12th, the summer solstice for the 13th (*Prayer-book* 1559: 199); more learned sources calculated the solstice at around midnight 11/12 June: Fowler 1970: 162–3n.
266. Barnaby . . . bright: echoing the proverbial 'Barnaby bright, Barnaby bright,/The longest day and the shortest night': Smith 1970: 35; Hone (1826) 1. 772.
267. by degrees: (1) gradually; (2) with reference to the sun's progress through the circle of the heavens. See Fowler 1970: 168 for its relevance to the 23 ½ degrees of the sun's midsummer declination in relation to *Epith*'s 23 ½ stanzas.
269. Crab . . . back: probably colloquial: feels him pushing him on (through the zodiac and the year); but perhaps the stars comprising the zodiacal sign Cancer (265–6n) are 'behind' the sun's 'back' in the sense they comprise a backdrop to him: Campbell 1987: 200–1.
271. To . . . year: a long line where, on the model of most of the other stanzas, we would expect a short one: Hieatt 1961: 119.
273. never . . . pass: proverbial: Smith 1970: 68.
275. bonfires: 'The *summer solstice* has been celebrated throughout all ages by the lighting up of fires': Hone (1826) 1. 823.
278. when . . . end: Claudian, *Epithalamium of Honorius*, 14–15: 'the suffering lover complains at the delay; the long days seem as though they stood still' (*incusat spes aegra moras longique videntur/stare dies*).

How slowly do the hours their numbers spend! 280
How slowly does sad Time his feathers move!
Haste thee, O fairest planet, to thy home
Within the western foam:
Thy tired steeds long since have need of rest.
Long though it be, at last I see it gloom, 285
And the bright Evening Star with golden crest
Appear out of the west:
Fair child of Beauty, glorious lamp of Love,
That all the host of heaven in ranks dost lead,
And guidest lovers through the night's dread, 290
How cheerfully thou lookest from above,
And seemest to laugh atween thy twinkling light
As joying in the sight
Of these glad many which for joy do sing,
That all the woods them answer, and their echo ring. 295

280. numbers: alluding (1) to the arithmetic of the passing hours; (2) to the poem's numerology (headnote); (3) to the poem's metrics.
281. sad: (1) as at 234n: i.e., inexorable; (2) melancholy in allusion to Time conflated with personifications of Saturn, patron of melancholy: Panofsky (1962) ch 3. *feathers*: Time's wings, symbolising the seasons, were a mediaeval invention: Panofsky, *ibid*.
282. fairest planet: the sun.
284. steeds: for the horses that draw the sun's chariot, see Ovid, *Metamorphoses*, 2. 47–318.
285. gloom: become dark: *OED*'s first instance of this sense (gloom *v* 1, 2b).
286–92. Evening . . . light: 95n above; Catullus, 62. 1–37. McPeek 1936: 202–3 notes similarities with Bion, *Idyll* 9 (as imitated by Ronsard), and Buttet.
286. crest: suggesting its brightness (the word was applied to 'blazing stars': *OED* crest *sb* 1, 1c).
287. west: my emendation. All texts read *east*, which raises an insoluble astronomical puzzle because Venus appears in the west at sunset. It is clear that the printer mistook *west* for *east*: see Hieatt 1960: 24–5 and Eade 1972: 175–6.
288. Fair . . . Beauty: because Hesperus is a name for Venus. *glorious*: brightly shining. *lamp of Love*: Bion, *Idylls*, 9. 1: 'Hesperus, golden lamp of the lovely daughter of the foam [Venus]'; Catullus, 62. 1–2 (Hesperus is raising his long-awaited light). There may be a hint of the lamp of conjugal vigil, which was lit when the bride was put to bed and remained lit all night: Scaliger tr. Bryce in Dubrow 1990: 284.
289. all . . . lead: because it is visible before the other stars; *host of heaven* = stars is in Jeremiah 8: 2 (Geneva).
290. And . . . dread: metrically awkward. Editors have suggested emending *through* to *thorough* or *night's* to *nightes* (*Var* 2. 721).
294. many: company (which reflects on earth the *host* of 289).

[17]
Now cease, ye damsels, your delights forepast:
Enough is it that all the day was yours.
Now day is done, and night is nighing fast:
Now bring the bride into the bridal bowers.
Now night is come, now soon her disarray,   300
And in her bed her lay:
Lay her in lilies and in violets,
And silken curtains over her display,
And odoured sheets, and arras coverlets.
Behold how goodly my fair love does lie   305
In proud humility,
Like unto Maia whenas Jove her took
In Tempe, lying on the flowery grass,

296–7. Now . . . yours: as virgins (96, 111 above), the damsels yield the bride to Venus and Diana–Lucina (372–89).
298–9. Now . . . bride: Catullus, 61. 115–16: 'the day passes; come forth, newly-married one' (*sed abit dies:/Prodeas, nova nupta*) and 179: 'let her come now to her husband's bed' (*iam cubile adeat viri*).
299. bowers: bed chambers.
300. disarray: the function of the matrons (*bonae feminae*) in Catullus 61. 182–3, which included loosening the bridal girdle: Scaliger tr. Bryce in Dubrow 1990: 284–5; cf. 44n above.
301. bed: 399n below.
302. lilies . . . violets: Statius, *Silvae*, 1. 2. 19–23 (Love and Grace scatter flowers and perfumes, roses, and lilies mixed with violets); for *lilies* see 176n above; in Claudian, *Epithalamium of Palladius*, 118–20 violets are Venerean and a bridal gift.
303. silken curtains: detail from Claudian, *Epithalamium of Honorius*, 211–12, as is the perfume (l. 210): see also Claudian, *Epithalamium of Palladius*, 121–3. *display*: spread out.
304. arras: richly-embroidered tapestry (named from Arras in northern France). Cf. the elaborate marriage-bed cover at Catullus, 64. 50–266. It was conventional to describe the bed-cover as the site (and screen) of consummation: Scaliger tr. Bryce in Dubrow 1990: 275.
306. proud humility: the oxymoron recalls that she combines opposites (e.g., of Venus and Diana: 154n), reminding us that as she yields to her husband she retains the pride of *Am* 5. 2n: cf. 164n above.
307–10. Maia . . . brook: Jupiter, king of the gods, begot Mercury on Maia, daughter of Atlas and one of the Pleiades, on Mount Cyllene in Arcadia (Ovid, *Fasti*, 5. 85–8. *Tempe* in Thessaly is the home of Daphne's father Peneus (Ovid, *Metamorphoses*, 1. 568–82; the Boeotian spring *Acidale* belonged to Venus: Servius on *Aeneid*, 1. 720 (Servius (1881–7) 1. 199–200): cf. *FQ*, 4. 5. 5 and 6. 10. 5–9. Spenser conflates the myth of Maia – the origin of the name *May* (the month of flowers: *Fasti*, 5. 85–6, 103, 183) – with allusions that recall Petrarch's Laura and the attempted rape of Daphne (*Am* 28 headnote) and Venus.

'Twixt sleep and wake, after she weary was
With bathing in the Acidalian brook.
Now it is night, ye damsels may be gone
And leave my love alone;
And leave likewise your former lay to sing:
The woods no more shall answer, nor your echo ring.

[18]
Now welcome, Night, thou Night so long expected,
That long day's labour dost at last defray,
And all my cares, which cruel Love collected,
Hast summed in one, and cancelled for aye:
Spread thy broad wing over my love and me
That no man may us see,
And in thy sable mantle us enwrap
From fear of peril, and foul horror free.
Let no false treason seek us to entrap,
Nor any dread disquiet once annoy
The safety of our joy;
But let the night be calm and quietsome,
Without tempestuous storms or sad affray,
Like as when Jove with fair Alcmena lay

313. leave: stop.
314. no more: on the negative refrain, see headnote.
315–27. Now . . . affray: there are overtones of the Orphic concept of Night's blackness as the equivalent of ultimate wisdom and the universal first cause: Pico della Mirandola, *Orphic Conclusions*, 15 (*Opera omnia*, Basel 1572; 2 vols; 1. 107). The Orphic *Hymn to Night*, 2 calls Night Venus: Athanassakis 1977: 7.
315. so . . . expected: the slowness of night's arrival was an epithalamic topos: Scaliger tr. Bryce in Dubrow 1990: 281.
316. defray: pay off (night is the reward for the day's labour).
317. cares: the beloved's cruelties listed in *Am.* 10, 12, 23, 25, etc. The Orphic *Hymn to Night*, 6 says that her gentleness abolishes cares: Athanassakis 1977: 9.
318. summed . . . one: the year of torment (*Am* 60) is answered by the wedding and the year symbolised in *Epith*'s 365 long lines.
319–21. wing . . . mantle: for the iconography of Night, including her black (*sable*) robe, see Ripa 1603: 360–3.
322. From . . . free: recalling Evensong's third collect: 'defend us from all perils and dangers of this night' (*Prayer-book* 1559: 51).
326. quietsome: quiet; Spenserian nonce use: *OED*.
327. sad: calamitous: *OED* sad *a* 5f. *affray*: terror: *OED* affray *sb* 2 citing *FQ*, 1. 3. 12.
328–9. Jove . . . groom: Hercules of Tiryns was the son of Alcmena (wife of Theban King Amphitryon) by Jupiter: Tooke 1713: 332–3. The night of his begetting was three times as long as usual (ct. *Epith*'s solstitial day): Spenser,

When he begot the great Tirynthian groom;
Or like as when he with thyself did lie   330
And begot Majesty:
And let the maids and young men cease to sing,
Ne let the woods them answer, nor their echo ring.

[19]
Let no lamenting cries nor doleful tears
Be heard all night within nor yet without;   335
Ne let false whispers breeding hidden fears
Break gentle sleep with misconceived doubt.
Let no deluding dreams nor dreadful sights
Make sudden sad affrights;
Ne let house fires, nor lightning's helpless harms,   340
Ne let the Puck, nor other evil sprights,
Ne let mischievous witches with their charms,
Ne let hobgoblins (names whose sense we see not)
Fray us with things that be not.
Let not the screech owl, nor the stork, be heard;   345

Mother Hubberd's Tale, 1297–9; *FQ*, 3. 11. 33. Orphically, Hercules banishes harm and evil: *Hymn to Herakles*, 14–16 (Athanassakis 1977: 23).
330–1. like . . . Majesty: a puzzle. Majesty, namer of May according to one tradition (Ovid, *Fasti*, 5. 11–52, a cosmogonic passage; cf. 307–10n above), was the daughter of Honour and Reverence (*Fasti*, 5. 23–5); but Macrobius, *Saturnalia*, 1. 12. 17, notes a Tusculan deity called Majesty who corresponds to Jove, and Ripa 1603: 305 says that Majesty originates with Jove.
334–52. Let . . . ring: the banishing of harm was traditional in epithalamia: e.g., Claudian, *Epithalamium of Honorius*, 191–3; Sidney's 'Let mother Earth' (*Arcadia*, third eclogues), 64–90. But this list reads more like the false night fears that are dispelled by the true, Orphic, night: *Hymn to Night*, 14 (Athanassakis 1977: 9).
334–5. cries . . . within: not just of general woe (e.g., at the wedding of Proserpina and Pluto 'lamentation subsided': Claudian, *Rape of Proserpine*, 2. 330), but of the bride herself, whose 'outcry . . . [upon] feeling the first forces of her stiff and rigorous young man' was an expected part of epithalamic ritual: Puttenham (1589) 1. 26; cf. Scaliger tr. Bryce in Dubrow 1990: 285.
339. affrights: terrors: first citation *FQ*, 2. 3. 19 (*OED* affright *sb*).
340. helpless: allowing no remedy; that cannot be helped: Spenserian meaning (*OED* helpless *a* 4 citing only *FQ*, 1. 4. 49, 1. 7. 39).
341. Puck: mischievous spirit or goblin, in mediaeval period identified with the devil: *OED* Puck *sb* 1.
343. hobgoblins . . . not: hobgoblins are demons of lust: Agrippa (1651) 3. 19 (p. 404). For a list of names see Muir, K. (ed.) 1952 New Arden *King Lear*, Appendix 7.
345–6. owl . . . raven: *SC June* 23 gloss, 24n. 'The screech owl is always unlucky': Agrippa (1651) 1. 54 (p. 112); the stork is unclean (Leviticus 11: 19)

Nor the night raven that still deadly yells;
Nor damned ghosts called up with mighty spells;
Nor grisly vultures make us once affeared;
Ne let the unpleasant choir of frogs still croaking
Make us to wish their choking: 350
Let none of these their dreary accents sing,
Ne let the woods them answer, nor their echo ring.

[20]
But let still Silence true night watches keep
That sacred Peace may in assurance reign,
And timely Sleep (when it is time to sleep)   355
May pour his limbs forth on your pleasant plain
The whiles an hundred little winged loves,

and unchaste (Agrippa, 1. 55 (p 118)). It is also the bird of vigilance (Valeriano 1602: 171), so that if 'heard' something would be wrong. Most tellingly, though, Agrippa, 3. 18 (p. 400) itemises owls and storks as evil spirits or devils. Ct. the birds at 78–82.

347. damned . . . spells: see Agrippa (1651) 3. 42.

348. vultures: presaging death: Agrippa, 1. 55 (pp. 117–18).

349. frogs: generally evil in Spenser (e.g., *FQ*, 1. 1. 20; 3. 10. 59), they have 'jarring voices' in *Virgil's Gnat*, 230. They signify 'the spirits of devils' (Revelation 16: 13–14) and are infernal (Juvenal, *Satires*, 2. 150).

353. Silence: depicted as a woman with finger to her lips (the Roman goddess Angerona: Macrobius, *Saturnalia*, 3. 9. 4) or as a man with the same gesture (Harpocrates: Valeriano 1602: 291). S/he stands sentinel because Orphic Night (315–27n) must be worshipped in silence: Wind 1967: 53–4n, 276–7.

354. Peace: usually depicted with a cornucopia of flowers etc. to signify abundance and fertility: Ripa 1603: 375. Demeter/Ceres bestows Peace in the Orphic *Hymn to Eleusinian Demeter*, 4, 19 (Athanassakis 1977: 57). *assurance*: (1) confidence; (2) a guarantee of peace: *OED* assurance I. 1b (continues the military metaphor of 353).

355. Sleep: a winged young man, also with a cornucopia, this time filled with scents, the cause of sleep: Ripa 1603: 464–5. Brother to Death, he is invoked to protect the initiates in the Orphic *Hymn to Sleep* (Athanassakis 1977: 107).

356. plain: the antecedent to *your* might be Night (Renwick 1929: 239–40), in which case it means (1) the expanse of the sky, symbolised by Night's mantle (319–21n above); (2) plain cloth (Night's mantle again): *OED* plain *sb* 1, 9; (3) lamentation (*OED* plain *sb* 2), so that *pleasant plain* = the normal night-time noises and murmurings. But if *your* refers to the bride, then *plain* has sense 3 and refers to the bride's reluctance at sexual penetration which is quietened by sleep.

357–9. winged . . . bed: Cupids, or *amoretti*, suggesting that the desires of *Amoretti* are now fulfilled. They displace the angels of 229–30n and the birds of ill omen of 345–6, 348. *Doves* belong to Venus (*Am*. 64. 10n); for Cupid's vari-coloured (*diverse-feathered*) wings, see *SC March* 79 gloss.

Like diverse-feathered doves,
Shall fly and flutter round about your bed
And, in the secret dark that none reproves, 360
Their pretty stealths shall work, and snares shall spread,
To filch away sweet snatches of delight
Concealed through covert night.
Ye sons of Venus, play your sports at will,
For greedy Pleasure, careless of your toys, 365
Thinks more upon her paradise of joys
Than what ye do, albeit good or ill.
All night, therefore, attend your merry play,
For it will soon be day:
Now none doth hinder you that say or sing, 370
Ne will the woods now answer, nor your Echo ring.

[21]
Who is the same which at my window peeps?
Or whose is that fair face that shines so bright?
Is it not Cynthia, she that never sleeps,
But walks about high heaven all the night? 375
O fairest goddess, do thou not envy
My love with me to spy:
For thou likewise didst love (though now unthought),
And for a fleece of wool, which privily
The Latmian shepherd once unto thee brought, 380
His pleasures with thee wrought.
Therefore to us be favourable now;
And sith of women's labours thou hast charge,

---

364. play . . . will: Catullus, 61. 207, where the bridegroom is advised 'sport as you will' (*ludite ut lubet*).
365. Pleasure: *Am* 72. 7n and 76. 3 and 7nn. *toys*: games.
372–3. Who . . . bright: translating Buttet, *Epithalame*, 533–4: *Mais quelle grande clarté ai-je vu ondoyer/Contre ces vitres-là?* ('But what great brilliance have I seen rippling against these window panes?'): McPeek 1936: 209.
374. Cynthia: *SC April* 82 gloss; also a *persona* for Queen Elizabeth, whom Spenser invokes, with courtly wit, to bless his marriage. Cf. *Am* 80.
378–81. For . . . wrought: for the moon goddess and Endymion, see *SC July* 64 gloss. For the fleece, see Servius on Virgil's *Georgics*, 3. 391 (Servius (1881–7) 3. 307–8). In conjunction with the moon as goddess of childbirth (383n), it also recalls Scaliger on the fleece that was placed under the new bride when bedded: tr. Bryce in Dubrow 1990: 277.
378. unthought: not thought about or remembered: *OED*'s first citation in this sense (unthought *ppl a* 2).
383. sith . . . charge: as Lucina, Diana is the goddess of childbirth.

And generation goodly dost enlarge,
Incline thy will to effect our wishful vow, 385
And the chaste womb inform with timely seed
That may our comfort breed:
Till which we cease our hopeful hap to sing,
Ne let the woods us answer, nor our Echo ring.

[22]
And thou, great Juno – which with awful might 390
The laws of wedlock still dost patronise,
And the religion of the faith first plight
With sacred rites hast taught to solemnise;
And eke for comfort often called art
Of women in their smart – 395
Eternally bind thou this lovely band,
And all thy blessings unto us impart.
And thou, glad Genius, in whose gentle hand

384–7. generation . . . breed: epithalamic topos: e.g., Catullus, 61. 207–21. Cf. the Marriage Service: 'assist with thy blessing these two persons, that they may both be fruitful in procreation of children': *Prayer-book* 1559: 126.
384. enlarge: increase (*OED* enlarge *v* I. 4).
386. timely: favourite Spenserian word; usually means opportune (355, 404, 425); here = early (*OED* timely *a* 1) in reference to the hope that a (male) child would be conceived on the wedding night: Puttenham (1589) 1. 26 (p. 42).
388. hopeful hap: good fortune which inspires hope in us (i.e., the child). Answers *mishaps* (l. 7).
390–1. Juno . . . wedlock: as the goddess of marriage, she was known as Juno Pronuba: Valeriano 1602: 239. She has been anticipated earlier: 43, 44 and 176nn.
390. awful: awe-inspiring.
391. patronise: preside over as guardian deity: *OED*'s first citation in this sense (patronize *v* 1b).
392. the . . . plight: the religion (= state of life bound by vows: *OED* religion 1) of the faith first pledged between man and woman (i.e., Adam and Eve in paradise: 'matrimony . . . is an honourable state, instituted of God in paradise': *Prayer-book* 1559: 122). The etymology of *religion* from *religare* = to bind is exploited at l. 396.
394–5. eke . . . smart: Juno, too, was known as Lucina, goddess of childbirth: Ovid, *Fasti*, 2. 435–52.
395. smart: pain.
396. band: 239n above.
398. Genius: god of generation, male complement of the Juno, who anciently embodied the spirit of the child-bearing wife: Nitzsche 1975: 9–10. Cf. *FQ*, 3. 6. 31–2. *gentle*: *tender*, but playing on etymological root, Latin *gentilis* = born into the same family.

The bridal bower and genial bed remain
Without blemish or stain, 400
And the sweet pleasures of their love's delight
With secret aid dost succour and supply
Till they bring forth the fruitful progeny,
Send us the timely fruit of this same night.
And thou, fair Hebe, and thou, Hymen free, 405
Grant that it may so be:
Till which, we cease your further praise to sing,
Ne any woods shall answer, nor your Echo ring.

[23]

And ye, high heavens, the temple of the gods,
In which a thousand torches flaming bright 410
Do burn, that to us wretched earthly clods
In dreadful darkness lend desired light;
And all ye powers which in the same remain
More than we men can feign,
Pour out your blessing on us plenteously, 415
And happy influence upon us rain
That we may raise a large posterity
Which from the earth (which they may long possess
With lasting happiness)

---

399. genial bed: the Latin phrase, *lectus genialis*; i.e., the marriage bed for the begetting of children: Nitzsche 1975: 9; Scaliger tr. Bryce in Dubrow 1990: 283; Catullus, 64. 47–51. *Progeny* (403) is the last of the puns generated by *Genius*.

405. Hebe: goddess of youth, daughter of Juno: Tooke 1713: 101; Scaliger (tr. Bryce in Dubrow 1990: 276) recommends that she be invoked in epithalamia because of her marriage to Hercules (328–9n) which all the gods attended. *Hymen*: 25–7 and 256nn above. As the son of Bacchus he is *free* (Latin *liber*) since one of Bacchus's names is *Liber* (from Latin *libare* = pour a drink offering). See Nitzsche 1975: 140n on Genius, Liber, and *liber* = freeing of seed.

409–12. And . . . light: Hymen's torch (27) now yields to the stars; the imagery is Platonic: *Am* 3 and notes. The Orphic *Hymn to the Stars* addresses their sacred light, holy daimons, 'fiery' brilliance and the paths that they mark out for mortals: Athanassakis 1977: 13.

411. clods: human beings understood as being made of earth: *OED*'s first citation in this sense (clod *sb* 4). Cf. *Am* 13. 6n.

413. powers: astrological 'virtues'; possibly also the daimons guarding each planetary sphere, later conflated with Christian angels: *HHB* 82–98nn.

414. feign: imagine.

416. influence: astrological sense.

Up to your haughty palaces may mount 420
And, for the guerdon of their glorious merit,
May heavenly tabernacles there inherit
Of blessed saints for to increase the count.
So let us rest, sweet love, in hope of this,
And cease till then our timely joys to sing: 425
The woods no more us answer, nor our echo ring.

420–3. Up . . . count: Spenser refers to the Heavenly Jerusalem (Revelation 21, 22), echoing 22: 12 ('my reward is with me, to give to every man according as his work shall be'): cf. Romans 2: 6–7: '[God] will reward every man according to his works: That is, them which through patience in well-doing, seek glory, and honour, and immortality, everlasting life'. The Geneva gloss on *glory* states for those of an Arminian persuasion: 'Glory which followeth good works, which he layeth not out before us, as though there were any that could attaine to salvation by his own strength, but, by laying this condition of salvation before us, which no man can perform, to bring men to Christ, who alone justified the believer'.
420. haughty: high (*OED* haughty *a* 3, first instance 1570).
421. guerdon: reward.
422. tabernacles: dwelling places; sign of divine presence at Revelation 21: 3 (immediately after the bridal New Jerusalem has appeared, so that God's presence is mediated through the female, as Spenser's posterity are): 'Behold, the Tabernacle of God is with men, and he will dwell with them: and they shall be his people'. *inherit*: in the Marriage Service, the prayer which preceded the beginning of Communion ended: 'O Lord, bless them both, and grant them to inherit thy everlasting kingdom' (*Prayer-book* 1559: 126).
423. saints: the faithful elect: at the Day of Judgement '[God] shall come to be glorified in his saints' (2 Thessalonians 1: 10). See *SC July* headnote.
424. this: the succeeding short line, with a rhyme word, appears to be missing, as also at 271: see Hieatt 1960: 62, 66–8 and, for a modification of his numerological explanation, Fowler 1970: 167–8.
425. timely: not just opportune (386n), but suggesting the poem's preoccupation with time through its numerological structure, etc. now seen in relation to the end of time at the Day of Judgement (hence *rest* (424) = remain, but also [eternal] sabbath: cf. *Am* 63. 14n).

[24]
Song, made in lieu of many ornaments
With which my love should duly have been decked
Which, cutting off through hasty accidents,
Ye would not stay your due time to expect,   430
But promised both to recompense:
Be unto her a goodly ornament,
And for short time an endless monument.

FINIS.

427–33. Song . . . monument: the envoy, as at the end of *SC*; cf. *Am* 69. For its structural function, see Hieatt 1960: 31–59; Fowler 1970: 161–73, 180–2. The *accidents* it refers to, and which appear either to have caused the marriage to be brought forward, or to have frustrated Spenser's plans, remain unexplained. But Hieatt 1960: 47–50 offers a reading in terms of astronomical symbolism.
427. ornaments: presumably poems (even the abruptly-terminated *Am*: Neuse 1966: 164); perhaps other gifts Spenser was unable to provide.
429. cutting off: (1) the ornaments have been brought to a premature end; (2) *Epith* is itself truncated.
430. Ye . . . expect: the song would not *stay* (= delay or remain) to *expect* (= await, anticipate) its *due* (= proper) time: for the latter phrase's association in Spenser with birth after due gestation, see Hieatt 1960: 48–9.
431. But . . . recompense: but promised [in yourself] to be recompense both to the bride and for the missing ornaments.
433. short time: (1) the duration of the world versus eternity; (2) the 24 hours of the wedding day; (3) the lives of the lovers (as in Catullus, 5. 5–6: night's perpetual sleep follows our brief day). *monument*: *Am* 69. 10.

Amoretti and *Epithalamion*: Textual Notes

The copy text is the octavo edition of 1595 (see *Am–Epith* headnote), the only edition in Spenser's lifetime. It was printed quite carefully and, as is the case with some of the *SC* quartos, exists in corrected and uncorrected forms, the corrections having been incorporated during the printing process. There are no textual problems affecting a modernised edition with the exceptions of:

(1) *above* at *Am* 71. 9. The copy text reads *about*, a reading that is preserved by Dunlop in Oram *et al.* (eds) 1989: 643 and Prescott in Maclean and Prescott 1993: 616. I follow most modern editions (including Renwick's and *Variorum*) in emending to *above* because: (i) there is no reason for Spenser to have abandoned his rhyme scheme, which is otherwise strictly adhered to throughout *Am*; (ii) a compositor could easily have misread *about* for *aboue* (the way it would have been written in the manuscript); (iii) the reason for *not* emending seems to be that *about* suits the sense better (Dodge in *Var* 2: 720 and Prescott as above, p. 657). But it doesn't: Spenser clearly wrote *above*, employing it in the sense of 'on the surface' (*OED* above *adv* and *prep* B 2, giving two citations, the last 1523).

(2) *dore* at *Epith* 67 (see footnote).

(3) *dreams* at *Epith* 92 (see footnote).

Four Hymns,

made by
Edmund Spenser

Headnote

Hymn: 'The gods of the gentiles were honoured by their poets in hymns, which is an extraordinary and divine praise, extolling and magnifying them for their great powers and excellency of nature in the highest degree of laud [praise], and yet therein their poets were after a sort restrained: so as they could not with their credit [belief, faith] untruly praise their own gods. . . . But with us Christians, who be better disciplined, and do acknowledge but one God Almighty, everlasting, and in every respect self-sufficient . . . reposed in all perfect rest and sovereign bliss. . . . To him we cannot exhibit overmuch praise, nor belie him any ways': Puttenham (1589) 1. 12.

    The '*Fowre Hymnes*, made by Edm. Spenser' were published, together with a new edition of *Daphnaida*, by William Ponsonby in 1596. They are among Spenser's last poems, situated between *Amoretti and Epithalamion* (1595) and *Prothalamion* (also 1596). Even if we do not go as far as Cheney (1994) ch. 5 and see them as announcing a new vocation in religious verse (the fulfilment of *SC October*'s statement that poetry should 'fly back to heaven apace' (84), thus adding an Augustinian spoke to the Virgilian career wheel which had terminated in epic), they are nevertheless significant expressions of Spenser's philosophy of love, human and divine. And because of the place love held in Renaissance thought, that means that they are statements about his view of the universe; for Plato's well-known *Timaeus* dialogue had asserted that the elemental contraries of which the universe was made (earth, water, air, fire) were bound together by friendship, or love. Another main inspiration for the *Hymns* is the *Symposium*, together with Marsilio Ficino's *Commentary* on it; while much of the content of *HL* and *HB* especially can be glossed from Baldassare Castiglione's Platonist courtesy book *Il Cortegiano* (see *Am–Epith* headnote and accompanying bibliography). Additional sources include the Bible; the writings of the Church Fathers; and Petrarch and his followers. A summary of sources may be found in *Var* 1: 662–76; Fletcher 1911a, b; Bennett 1931; Bhattacherje 1935; Ellrodt 1960; Welsford 1967; Bieman 1988; and a useful discussion of Spenser's Platonism in general is offered by Quitslund in *SpE*, pp. 546-8.

Precedents for the *Four Hymns* are literary rather than liturgical, for although, among the Greeks, a hymn was originally a song in praise of a god and had a liturgical function, hymns appear soon to have developed into purely literary texts while retaining their religious subject-matter. Thus the *Homeric Hymns* seem to be literary only and, whatever their liturgical origin, the *Orphic Hymns* (see 'Orphic Footnote' to *Am–Epith* headnote above) were read as literary texts very early on. Later ancient literary hymns include those of Callimachus, Proclus and Prudentius. Among modern practitioners who influenced Spenser, Marullo (fifteenth century) and Vida and Ronsard (both sixteenth century) are the most important, Ronsard in particular combining pagan/philosophical and Christian topics in a manner that obviously invited Spenser's attention and imitation: Rollinson, P. B. 1969 'The Renaissance of the Literary Hymn', *Renaissance Papers 1968*: 11–20; Rollinson 1971 'A Generic View of Spenser's *Four Hymns*', *Studies in Philology* 68: 292–304.

Each of Spenser's hymns has an identical and conventional structure: invocation; cosmogony; elaboration of named topic; visionary conclusion. The subject of *HL* is the power of Love (or Cupid), in the universe and over the lover, for good or ill. There are echoes here of the Petrarchan lover of *Am*. *HB* is dedicated to Venus, Cupid's mother, who was identified by the neo-Platonists as Beauty; but the *Hymn* is not so much a paean to Beauty in the abstract as it is an invitation to women to celebrate their beauty by bestowing it upon men. Its climax is a plea to Venus to grant the lover his mistress's favour. *HHL* returns to Cupid, but this time the heavenly Cupid recognised by the neo-Platonists. He is also the Orphic Eros who was identified with Christ (*HHL* 1n), so that this *Hymn* describes how divine love operates in the universe: it led God to create man to replace the gap left by the fallen angels; it sent itself in the incarnate form of Christ to redeem mankind after man's own fall in the Garden of Eden. The poet considers Christ's commandment that we must love our neighbour as ourself, then proceeds to a meditation on Christ's life culminating in a vision of the earthbound soul inspired with a vision of the divine glory. Finally, *HHB* discusses Beauty as a universal principle originating in, and emanating from, God. Inviting us to prostrate ourselves before Him, the poet nevertheless takes refuge from the blinding strength of the divine brightness by focusing on Sapience who, as 'the sovereign darling of the deity', sits in his bosom: it is she who can finally bestow the grace that ravishes the loving human soul, enabling it to forget all earthly commitments in 'that sovereign light . . . even the love of God'.

The *Four Hymns*, then, juxtapose secular and religious in a manner familiar to Renaissance thought: erotic against heavenly Cupid; the Venus of generation and female beauty against Wisdom, image of, and gateway to, the Beauty of the Godhead. Yet the relationship between the *Hymns* is more complex than this summary makes it sound.

For one thing, scholars now generally dismiss as largely fictional Spenser's statement in the dedicatory epistle that the first pair were merely the product of youthful exuberance which he had tried, and failed, to withdraw from publication: they are, clearly, an integral part of a carefully-developed argument (Bennett 1931: 49-57; Ellrodt (1960) ch. 1; Bieman in *SpE*, pp. 315-16). But while the outline of that argument is evident enough, the view that the pairs *HL* and *HB* on the one hand, and *HHL* and *HHB* on the other, chart a vertical climb up a neo-Platonic ladder from earthly to celestial beauty (Fletcher 1911a; Lee 1928; Bennett 1931), is unsatisfactory because it fails to account for the precise nature of the parallels between the *Hymns*. It does not, for instance, explain the identification between *HB* and *HHL* as suggested by their identical line total (see below). The slightly more fluid notion that the two sets of hymns comprise a mutually reflective diptych seems nearer the mark (Bjorvand 1975, who also, at pp. 30-1, hints at a typological relationship between the pairs: earthly love and beauty are a foreshadowing of heavenly, as the Old Testament is of the New; the latter is comprehended through the former if not attained through it).

In short, the binding of the two pairs of hymns through cross-reference and parallel is so intimate and all-pervasive that we understand their purpose best if we recognise that they manifest this simple truth: for Spenser, there are no absolute disjunctions in the universe. It may contain opposites, but those opposites are *linked* to each other. For Spenser, as with all humane Platonists, illumination is attained through a careful process of understanding, not by cavalier and arrogant rejection.

The total of hymns, four, obviously evokes the four elements that comprise the universe according to ancient and Renaissance belief: as noted above, the universe permeated by love is one of their main topics. Moreover, the system of parallels that binds the hymns together is reminiscent of the way the elements – esentially so different from each other – are held together by shared qualities (of heat, cold, moisture and dryness). In addition, the hymns relate to each other in chiastic, or mirror (ABBA), fashion – a structural feature that alludes to the concord of the elements via the (supposedly) Pythagorean saying *philotēs isotēs, isotēs philotēs* (friendship is equality, equality, friendship: ABBA) which was interpreted as an expression of elemental union (see Fowler 1964: 24-6). For their line totals reveal the following near-symmetry: *HL*, 307 (A); *HB*, 287 (B); *HHL*, 287 (B); *HHB*, 301 (A). This, of course, adds to the complexity of the *Hymns*' interrelationship by suggesting that, cutting across the pairing *HL-HHL/HB-HHB*, is the additional pairing *HL-HHB* and *HB-HHL*.

All four hymns also share a common stanzaic structure and rhyme scheme: seven lines of iambic pentameters (with a few metrical variations) rhyming ababbcc: in other words, the rhyme-royal stanza which was particularly associated with formal topics. Spenser had employed a variant of the stanza in the elegy for Douglas Howard, *Daphnaida* (1591), where the total of lines per stanza carried one of the main meanings of the number seven, mutability and death. It is therefore tempting to assume that the stanzaic repetitions of seven are symbolic in the *Four Hymns* as well; though the contrasted nature of their subject-matter (two hymns devoted to earthly matters and the 'pagan' deities Cupid and Venus; two devoted to heavenly matters, Christ and Divine Wisdom) dictates that the number is used more discriminatingly: in the first two it does indeed signify the mutability and limitation of the created world (their main topic); but in the last two it transcends those meanings to become the number of eternal rest (the sabbath which succeeds the six days of creation in the biblical account: Genesis 2: 1–3); of Christ's seven last words on the cross (the crucifixion is described at *HHL*, 148–61 and 239–52); of the seven gifts of the Holy Spirit (the last gift is Wisdom, the subject of *HHB*: see Tuve 1966: 85–6 and, for the meanings of seven, Agrippa (1651) 2. 10. Bjorvand 1975 comments on some of the numerological aspects.)

But, in the end, the *Hymns* speak above all of Spenser's dedication to the feminine (however time-bound and patriarchal his attitudes may seem to be by radical feminist standards). Against the backdrop of *FQ*'s disillusionment with court politics, the *Hymns* – dedicated to two aristocratic females and dated from Greenwich, where the queen was in residence with her court – reveal passionate idealism, explicitly directed at the feminine as a principle, implicitly directed (once again) at the queen. For whatever else the Sapience who appears in the last section of *Hymn* 4 is, her regal robes signal her as an ideal manifestation of Elizabeth I, a further (re)vision of *FQ*'s distant super-heroine, Gloriana (as Fletcher 1911b: 474–5 astutely noticed). In the *Hymns* as in *Am*, then, monarch and personal beloved – Elizabeth I and Elizabeth Boyle – are inseparable. And so are monarch and God. Various sources have been sought for Spenser's Sapience (see *Var* 1. 558–64; Ellrodt (1960) chs 9–11; Welsford 1967: 52–8, 170–1; Quitslund 1969). She assimilates elements of the Jungian *anima* (female soul within the male: Jung, C. G. 1964. *Man and his Symbols* (Aldus Books: London), pp. 177–88) as encoded in traditional (male) myth (and cf. Oates 1984: 160); of the enthroned Virgin Mary (important because of Marian aspects in the cult of Elizabeth: Wilson 1939: 200–8); of Platonic Wisdom, as in *Phaedrus*, 250D–E ('Wisdom would arouse an amazing love if we were to see an image of her through our eyes'); of the Platonic heavenly Venus (Fletcher 1911b: 461; Bennett 1931: 43–4. Ficino, *Commentary on Plato's 'Symposium'*, 2. 7. (Ficino 1944: 142–3) identified her as the intelligence in God's first creation, the Angelic Mind, that embraces the glory of God.) She also recalls the Hebraic Shekinah (Saurat, D. 1926 'La "Sapience" de Spenser et la Schekhina de la Cabale', *Revue de Littérature Comparée* 6: 5-15). But above all she reveals Spenser's acquaintance with the Wisdom of Proverbs 8–9 – who existed 'from the beginning, and before the earth' (8: 23) – and of the apocryphal Old Testament Book of Wisdom (see Osgood, C. G. 1917 'Spenser's Sapience', *Studies in Philology* 14: 167–77. For further background, see Manley, F. (ed.) 1963 *John Donne: The Anniversaries* (Johns Hopkins Press: Baltimore), pp. 20–40; Rice 1958; and E. Ruth Harvey in *SpE*, p. 626.) Despite the fact that she was – in popular as well as learned Christian typology – identified with Christ (Geneva gloss on Proverbs 8: 30: '... this wisdom, even Christ Jesus, was equal with God his father'; and see Fletcher 1911b on her earlier identification with the Holy Spirit), what matters to Spenser is the fact that she is female. Like Milton – who in this as in so many other things may have followed his lead – he regarded her as distinct from Christ, a manifestation of deity in her own right (Fowler, note to *Paradise Lost*, 7. 8–12 in Carey, J. and Fowler, A. D. S. (eds) 1967 *The Poems of John Milton*, p. 775; see also Bennett 1931: 44–5 citing Ficino's commentary on Benivieni, 1. 4, where Wisdom is the neo-Platonic Logos distinct from Christ). Sapience, then, is not only the *telos* of the *Hymns*. She is the clue to, and at the heart of, Spenser's mystic apprehension of the feminine, and of the feminine in God (Galyon 1977).

Select bibliography

Note: this is a bibliography of works cited in short form in *Four Hymns* headnote and notes; it excludes works already listed under *SC* and *Am–Epith*.

Alpers, P. 1967 *The Poetry of 'The Faerie Queene'*. Princeton, N.J.
Bennett, J. W. 'The Theme of Spenser's *Fowre Hymnes'*. *Studies in Philology* 28: 18–57
Bjorvand, E. 1975 'Spenser's Defence of Poetry: Some Structural Aspects of the *Fowre Hymnes'*. In *Fair Forms: Essays in English Literature from Spenser to Jane Austen* (ed. M.-S. Røstvig). Cambridge
Fletcher, J. B. 1911a 'Benivieni's Ode of Love and Spenser's "Fowre Hymnes"'. *Modern Philology* 8: 545-60
Fletcher, J. B. 1911b 'A Study of Renaissance Mysticism: Spenser's "Fowre Hymnes"'. *Publications of the Modern Language Association of America* 26: 452–75
Galyon, L. R. 1977 'Sapience in Spenser's "Hymne of Heavenly Beautie"'. *Fourteenth-Century English Mystics Newsletter* 3. 3: 9–12
Henkel, A. and Schöne, A. 1967 *Emblemata: Handbuch zur Sinnbildkunst des XVI. und XVII. Jahrhunderts*. Supplement 1976. Stuttgart
Hutton, J. 1966 'Spenser's "Adamantine Chains": A Cosmological Metaphor'. In J. Hutton 1980 *Essays on Renaissance Poetry* (ed. R. Guerlac). Ithaca and London, pp. 169–91
Jung, C. G. 1968 *Psychology and Alchemy*. 2nd edition. London
Lee, R. W. 1928 'Castiglione's Influence on Spenser's Early Hymnes'. *Philological Quarterly* 7: 65–77
Oates, M. I. 1984 *'Fowre Hymnes*: Spenser's Retractations of Paradise'. *Spenser Studies: A Renaissance Poetry Annual* 4: 143–69
Quitslund, J. A. 1969 'Spenser's Image of Sapience'. *Studies in the Renaissance* 16: 181–213
Quitslund, J. A. 1985 'Spenser and the Patronesses of the *Fowre Hymnes*: "Ornaments of All True Love and Beauty"'. In *Silent but for the Word: Tudor Women as Patrons, Translators, and Writers of Religious Works* (ed. M. P. Hannay). Kent, Ohio, pp. 184–202
Rice, F. Jr 1958 *The Renaissance Idea of Wisdom*. Cambridge, Mass.
Tuve, R. 1970 *Essays by Rosemond Tuve: Spenser, Herbert, Milton* (ed. T. P. Roche, Jr). Princeton, N.J.
Tuve, R. 1940 'Spenser and Some Pictorial Conventions'. In Tuve 1970.

Dedicatory epistle

To the Right Honourable and Most Virtuous Ladies, the Lady Margaret, Countess of Cumberland, and the Lady Mary, Countess of Warwick.

Having, in the greener times of my youth, composed these former two *Hymns* in the praise of Love and Beauty, and finding that the same too much pleased those of like age and disposition (which, being too vehemently carried with that kind of affection, do rather suck out poison to their strong passion than honey to their honest delight), I was moved by the one of you two most excellent Ladies to call in the same. But, being unable so to do by reason that many copies thereof were formerly scattered abroad, I resolved at least to amend and, by way of retractation, to reform them, making instead of those two *Hymns* of earthly (or natural) Love and Beauty, two others of heavenly and celestial: the which I do dedicate jointly unto you two honourable sisters as to the most excellent and rare ornaments of all true love and beauty, both in the one and the other kind, humbly beseeching you to vouchsafe the patronage of them, and to accept this my humble service in lieu of the great graces and honourable favours which

---

Address: Margaret, the third daughter of Francis Russell, second Earl of Bedford, married George Clifford, Earl of Cumberland on 24 June 1577. *Mary* is generally agreed to be an error for *Anne*, the eldest daughter, widow of Leicester's brother, Ambrose Dudley, Earl of Warwick, who had died in 1590: *Var* l. 508; Bieman in *SpE*, p. 315. But if we recall that Anne is praised as *Theana* in *Colin Clout*, 492-503 alongside her 'sister dear,/Fair Marian' (probably Margaret, says Quitslund 1985: 195), it would seem that Quitslund (p. 282n) is right to suggest that *Mary* is either a pet name for, or middle name of, Anne, just as *Marian* was a family name for Margaret. *Colin Clout*'s *Marian* is the clue to the strong possibility that Margaret was known as a double of her sister (Mary + Anne); *Mary* shows that Anne may have been regarded likewise. The sisters were differentiated yet one, like the two Venuses to whom he compares the sisters in the dedication. On Anne, see also Tuve, 'Spenserus' in Tuve 1970: 139–62.

1–3. *youth . . . disposition:* suggests the traditional equation of lust and youth.

5. *poison*: a commonplace: Ellrodt 1960: 14.

8. *copies . . . abroad*: i.e., in manuscript.

9. *retractation*: in the Augustinian sense of treating again (revising) rather than recanting: *OED*. *reform*: revise.

10–11. *earthly . . . celestial*: Plato's distinction between the earthly, procreative, Aphrodite (Venus) Pandemos and the heavenly Aphrodite Ourania: *Symposium*, 180D–181C.

ye daily show unto me, until such time as I may by better means yield you some more notable testimony of my thankful mind and dutiful devotion.
    And even so I pray for your happiness.
    Greenwich this first of September,
        1596.
        Your Honours' most bounden ever
        in all humble service,
                Ed[mund] Sp[enser]

An Hymn in Honour of Love

[1]
Love, that long since hast to thy mighty power
Perforce subdued my poor captived heart
And, raging now therein with restless stour,
Dost tyrannise in every weaker part:
Fain would I seek to ease my bitter smart   5
By any service I might do to thee,
Or aught that else might to thee pleasing be.

[2]
And now, to assuage the force of this new flame
And make thee more propitious in my need,
I mean to sing the praises of thy name,   10
And thy victorious conquests to aread
By which thou madest many hearts to bleed
Of mighty victors, with wide wounds imbrued,
And by thy cruel darts to thee subdued.

---

21. *Greenwich*: the Court was in residence at this date.
1–21. *Love . . . sing*: lover's complaint to Cupid in the tradition of Ovid, *Amores*, 1. 2 and many mediaeval and post-mediaeval writers. May particularly echo Jerome Benivieni's *Canzone della Amore celeste e divino*, stanza 1: Fletcher 1911a: 547.
3. *stour: SC January* 51 gloss.
8. *new flame*: attribute of Venus and lust: Tervarent (1958) cols 183–5; possibly autobiographical; more likely part of the characterisation of the poet as fictional young lover.
11. *aread*: (1) declare; (2) interpet; (3) proclaim through the power of supernatural inspiration.
13. *imbrued*: blood-stained.
14. *darts*: traditional weapons of Cupid: *SC March* 79 gloss; *FQ*, 4. 10. 55.

[3]
Only, I fear my wits (enfeebled late 15
Through the sharp sorrows which thou hast me bred)
Should faint, and words should fail me to relate
The wondrous triumphs of thy great godhead:
But if thou wouldst vouchsafe to overspread
Me with the shadow of thy gentle wing, 20
I should enabled be thy acts to sing.

[4]
Come then, 0 come, thou mighty god of love,
Out of thy silver bowers and secret bliss,
Where thou dost sit in Venus' lap above,
Bathing thy wings in her ambrosial kiss 25
That sweeter far than any nectar is:
Come softly, and my feeble breast inspire
With gentle fury kindled of thy fire.

[5]
And ye, sweet Muses, which have often proved
The piercing points of his avengeful darts; 30

17. *faint*: become feeble.
18. triumphs: cf. Petrarch's *Triumph of Love* and the triumphal masque of Cupid at *FQ*, 3. 12. 7–26.
20. *gentle*: (1) noble; (2) soft to the touch: *OED* gentle *a* 1,5. *wing*: the usual ancient title for Cupid was 'Winged One': Plato, *Phaedrus*, 252C. Also recalls Psalm 36: 7: 'How excellent is thy mercy, O God! therefore the children of men trust under the shadow of thy wings'.
22–7: *Come ... inspire*: echoing Rabanus Maurus's eighth-century hymn to the Holy Spirit, *Veni, Creator Spiritus*.
23–4. *silver ... lap*: cf. 273–86 below and *Am* anacreontic 4. 41–50. For *silver* in an erotic context, see *Am* 77. 5 and n; but this Cupid, in opposition to the first, is Anteros or Sacred Love, who impels the lover to virtue: Panofsky 1962: 126–8; his position in his mother's lap suggests the innumerable mediaeval and later depictions of the infant Christ in the lap of the Virgin.
25–6. *ambrosial ... nectar*: *SC November* 195 gloss.
28. *fury*: poetical rapture (*SC October* headnote and Argument). In conjunction with the invocation to Venus at *HB*, 15–21, reminds us (in preparation for *HHL*, *HHB*) that the fury (or frenzy) inspired by Venus 'doth by a fervent love convert, and transmute the mind to God': Agrippa (1651) 3. 49 (p. 507). See also 226 below and *HB* l-3nn.
29. *Muses*: the Muses, traditionally virgins, but mothers of enough children to suggest that they suffered from (*proved*) love's power (*SC April* 41 gloss; Tooke 1713: 220), 'nourishers of the soul' and guides of the mind (Orphic *Hymn to the Muses*, 5–6: Athanassakis 1977: 99), sing at the wedding of Cupid and Psyche (Apuleius, *Golden Ass*, 6. 24), and that of Mercury and Philology:

And ye, fair nymphs, which oftentimes have loved
The cruel worker of your kindly smarts:
Prepare yourselves, and open wide your hearts
For to receive the triumph of your glory,
That made you merry oft when ye were sorry. 35

[6]
And ye, fair blossoms of Youth's wanton breed,
Which in the conquests of your beauty boast,
Wherewith your lovers' feeble eyes you feed,
But starve their hearts, that needeth nurture most:
Prepare yourselves to march amongst his host, 40
And all the way this sacred hymn do sing,
Made in the honour of your sovereign king.

   * * * *

[7]
Great god of might, that reignest in the mind,
And all the body to thy hest dost frame;
Victor of gods, subduer of mankind, 45
That dost the lions and fell tigers tame,
Making their cruel rage thy scornful game,
And in their roaring taking great delight:
Who can express the glory of thy might?

[8]
Or who alive can perfectly declare 50
The wondrous cradle of thine infancy,
When thy great mother, Venus, first thee bare,

Martianus Capella, 2. 117–27 (Stahl, W. H. *et al.* (eds) 1977, 2. 40–5).
36. *wanton*: lively (*SC November* 79n); amorous.
38–9. *eyes . . . hearts*: hints at Narcissus as used in *Am* 35 and 83. For *eyes* and *starve*, see *Am* 35. 1 and 8nn.
43–5. *Great . . . mankind*: a commonplace; see *Am* anacreontics 1. 1n; Ficino, *Commentary*, 1. 1 (Ficino 1944: 124–5).
44. *hest*: bidding; *frame*: fashion.
46. *lions . . . tame*: a commonplace based on the idea that love is all-powerful (*FQ*, 4. 10. 42) and that the rage of love is greater than that of beasts: Cupid rides on a lion at *FQ*, 3. 12. 22 (cf. Alciati 1551: 115), and at 4. 10. 46 lions and tigers roar in response to love's call.
50–6. *Or . . . peers*: Venus (i.e., Beauty) was Cupid's mother (*Am* anacreontics, 1. 2n) in the sense that he was fathered by Plenty/Resource and conceived by Poverty on Venus's birthday: i.e., Love desires Beauty (Venus); he is poor because he doesn't possess her and resourceful in his attempts to do so:

Begot of Plenty and of Penury,
Though older than thine own nativity;
And yet a child, renewing still thy years, 55
And yet the oldest of the heavenly peers?

[9]
For, ere this world's still-moving mighty mass
Out of great Chaos' ugly prison crept
(In which his goodly face long hidden was
From heaven's view, and in deep darkness kept), 60
Love – that had now long time securely slept
In Venus' lap, unarmed then and naked –
'Gan rear his head, by Clotho being waked;

[10]
And taking to him wings of his own heat,
Kindled at first from heaven's life-giving fire, 65
He 'gan to move out of his idle seat:
Weakly at first, but after, with desire
Lifted aloft, he 'gan to mount up higher

Symposium, 203B–D. For the paradox of Cupid's age/youth, see *Am anacreontics* 1. 1n and Ficino, *Commentary*, 5. 10 (Ficino 1944: 178).
56. *peers*: equals (i.e., gods).
57–91. *For . . . might*: creation myth composed from ancient and neo-Platonic commonplaces: Ellrodt 1960: 101; Tuve in Tuve 1970: 49–63 (cf. *HB*, 29–54; contrast the largely biblical accounts at *HHL*, 22–35 and *HHB*, 29–105). In Hesiod, *Theogony*, 116ff. Chaos is followed by Earth and beautiful Love (cited *Symposium*, 178B); and *Timaeus*, 32C describes how the four elements are bound together through love (though Spenser is possibly influenced by the primacy of Love in the Orphic cosmogony: Orphic *Hymn to Protogonos*; the Orphic *Argonautica* (Vian 1987), 12–16, 421–5; *Proth* 42–4n). See also Ficino, *Commentary*, 1. 3, which begins by citing the Orphic *Argonautica* (Ficino 1944: 125–9). Ovid's more familiar account (*Met*. 1. 5–75) omits Love.
63. *Clotho*: the Fate who holds the distaff from which the thread of life was spun (*SC November* 148 gloss). The Fates represent Necessity (e.g., Orphic *Hymn to the Fates*, 18 (Athanassakis 1977: 81); and Ficino, *Commentary*, 5. 11 (Ficino 1944: 179–80) notes that historically Love precedes Necessity, though among God's creation the reverse is true.
64–5. *wings . . . fire*: the heat of Cupid/Love's own ardour (see Benivieni, 48–52, cit. Fletcher 1911a: 548–9); but Spenser might also imagine it as originating with the divine fire as embodied in the seraphim (*HHB*, 94–5n). Note also that fire is the highest of the four elements and hence impels mankind to quest for divine Beauty: see diagrams in Heninger (1977) ch. 3.

And, like fresh eagle, make his hardy flight
Through all that great wide waste, yet wanting light. 70

[11]
Yet wanting light to guide his wandering way,
His own fair mother, for all creatures' sake,
Did lend him light from her own goodly ray:
Then through the world his way he 'gan to take –
The world that was not till he did it make, 75
Whose sundry parts he from themselves did sever,
The which before had lain confused ever.

[12]
The earth, the air, the water, and the fire
Then 'gan to range themselves in huge array,
And with contrary forces to conspire 80
Each against other by all means they may,
Threatening their own confusion and decay:
Air hated earth, and water hated fire,
Till Love relented their rebellious ire.

69. fresh eagle: an eagle that has been reborn through purging itself with solar fire and then bathing in water; according to mediaeval lore, an emblem of spiritual rebirth through the power to contemplate God: Ansell Robin 1932: 159–62. Cf. Ps 103: 5 ('thy youth is renewed like the eagle's') and Isaiah 40. 31 ('But they that wait upon the Lord, shall renew their strength: they shall lift up the wings, as the eagles'). But in Spenser's *Visions of Bellay*, sonnet 7, the eagle flies to the heat and light of God and is destroyed for its presumption.
70. yet . . . light: Genesis 1: 2 ('and darkness was upon the deep').
73. her . . . ray: as the morning star, Venus is Lucifer the light-bringer who precedes the sun: *Epith* 95n. In Ficino, *Commentary*, 6. 17, beauty is nothing but light (Ficino 1944: 211, speaking of the sun).
75–98. The . . . inspire: especially close to Plato's *Timaeus*, 31C–32C, *Symposium*, 188A; and see also Ficino, *Commentary*, 3. 2. The elements are described in their hierarchical order, lowest first (78); the *contrary forces* (80) reconciled by *loved means* (86; i.e., mediating qualities imposed through Love's agency) are the qualities inherent in each element which oppose and yet link it to its adjacent elements: earth is cold and dry; water, cold and moist; air, moist and warm; fire, warm and dry. Thus, earth is contrary to water because the one is dry and the other moist, but linked through love imposed by their shared quality, coldness.
84. relented: abated (*OED* relent *v* 1, 4, rare, and citing instances from *FQ* as last examples), with overtones of sense 1, softened under the influence of heat (i.e., Love's heat is greater than that associated with anger).

[13]
He then them took and, tempering goodly well 85
Their contrary dislikes with loved means,
Did place them all in order and compel
To keep themselves within their sundry reigns,
Together linked with adamantine chains:
Yet so, as that in every living wight 90
They mix themselves and show their kindly might.

[14]
So ever since they firmly have remained,
And duly well observed his behest,
Through which now all these things that are contained
Within this goodly cope – both most and least – 95
Their being have, and daily are increased
Through secret sparks of his infused fire
Which in the barren cold he doth inspire.

[15]
Thereby they all do live, and moved are
To multiply the likeness of their kind, 100
Whilst they seek only, without further care,
To quench the flame which they, in burning, find:
But man, that breathes a more immortal mind,
Not for lust's sake but for eternity
Seeks to enlarge his lasting progeny. 105

85. *tempering*: balancing: *Am* 13. 4 and 21. 2nn.
89. *adamantine chains*: image of the durability of the bonds between the elements, derived by Spenser from French sources and perhaps directly from Baif's *Les Muses* which, drawing on the Orphic *Argonautica*, has Orpheus singing a cosmogonic hymn to Love which contains a '*chaine adamantine*': Hutton 1966 (in ed. 1980) and cf. *Am* 42. 10 and n.
90–1. *in ... might*: living creatures (*wights*), too, have an elemental mixture in them in the form of the four humours (black bile corresponding to earth; phlegm to water; blood to air; yellow bile to fire): see Klibansky *et al.* 1964. When well balanced, health prevails: *kindly* = (1) natural; (2) thriving; (3) benevolent (*OED* kindly *a* I. 1, II. 4, 5).
95. *cope*: the canopy or vault of heaven, apparently first abbreviated to *cope* by Spenser here: *OED* sense 7 b.
98. *inspire*: (1) breathe into; (2) kindle.
99–105. *moved ... progeny*: in *Symposium*, 208E–209E Diotima tells Socrates that some men procreate to satisfy lust (the *flame* of l. 102), whereas others are impelled by (homoerotic) love of Beauty to beget spiritual offspring. Spenser's lines are in the spirit of the former and of *Epith* 409–23: the Protestant concept of marriage elevates heterosexual love so that one can populate heaven with the

[16]
For, having yet in his deducted spright
Some sparks remaining of that heavenly fire,
He is enlumined with that goodly light
Unto like goodly semblant to aspire;
Therefore in choice of love he doth desire   110
That seems on earth most heavenly to embrace:
That same is Beauty, born of heavenly race.

[17]
For sure, of all that in this mortal frame
Contained is, nought more divine doth seem,
Or that resembleth more the immortal flame   115
Of heavenly light, than Beauty's glorious beam.
What wonder, then, if with such rage extreme
Frail men, whose eyes seek heavenly things to see,
At sight thereof so much enravished be?

[18]
Which, well perceiving, that imperious boy   120

souls of one's offspring (hence 1. 100 echoes God's exhortation to man and the creatures to multiply according to their kinds: Genesis 1: 21–2, 28).
106. deducted: (1) derived (from heaven); (2) reduced, attenuated: *OED* deduct *v*, 4, 7. *spright*: *Am* 1. 7n.
108. enlumined: archaic; used by E.K. in *SC* Dedicatory Epistle; last cited *OED* instance from *FQ*, 5 proem.
109. semblant: likeness. *aspire*: the original spelling, *aspyre*, contains a pun on Greek *pyr* = flame, emblem of aspiration and of the fire moving the soul. Cf. *Am* 6. 8n.
111. That: that which.
111–12. most . . . Beauty: *Symposium*, 209.
117. rage: violent (sexual) appetite: *OED* sense 6.
119. enravished: transported with delight; *OED* cites this as first instance. Cf. *Am* 3. 12n for neo-Platonic overtones.
120–6. Which . . . grief: return to the effects of Eros/Cupid (as opposed to Anteros): 23–4n above. In the rest of the *Hymn* the poet puzzles over the conflicting impulses – for ill and for good – endured by the heterosexual lover much as he does in *Am*.
121. empoisoned: Ovid's description of Cupid's golden and leaden arrows (*Metamorphoses*, 1. 466–71) was developed into an elaborate allegory in the *Roman de la Rose*, where five gold arrows represent the beneficent effects of love and five iron arrows, shot from a black bow made from the 'bitter-fruited tree', signify love's anguish: pride, villainy poisoned with felony, shame, despair, and faithlessness (de Lorris and de Meun (1962), 4. 100–3, 129–39). Spenser follows with a characteristic depiction of the effects of love melan-

Doth therewith tip his sharp empoisoned darts
Which, glancing through the eyes with countenance coy,
Rest not till they have pierced the trembling hearts,
And kindled flame in all their inner parts
Which sucks the blood, and drinketh up the life   125
Of care-full wretches with consuming grief.

[19]
Thenceforth they plain, and make full piteous moan
Unto the author of their baleful bane;
The days they waste, the nights they grieve and groan,
Their lives they loathe, and heaven's light disdain;   130
No light but that whose lamp doth yet remain
Fresh burning in the image of their eye
They deign to see and, seeing it, still die.

[20]
The whilst thou, tyrant Love, dost laugh and scorn
At their complaints, making their pain thy play: 135
Whilst they lie languishing like thralls forlorn,
The whiles thou dost triumph in their decay;
And otherwhiles, their dying to delay,
Thou dost enmarble the proud heart of her
Whose love before their life they do prefer.   140

[21]
So hast thou often done (ay me the more!)
To me, thy vassall, whose yet-bleeding heart
With thousand wounds thou mangled hast so sore
That whole remains scarce any little part.
Yet, to augment the anguish of my smart,   145
Thou hast enfrozen her disdainful breast
That no one drop of pity there doth rest.

choly: cf. Chaucer, *Knight's Tale*, 1 (A). 1359–76; Castiglione, *Courtier*, 3: 274–6 and 4: 326–7; also *HB* 57–63n.
122. eyes: *Am* 7. 1, 3 and 81. 4nn.
127. plain: lament.
128. baleful: (1) painful (*SC January* 27n); (2) deadly. *bane*: (1) poison; (2) murderer.
131–3. No ... die: *Am* 88 headnote and nn.
133. still: continually. *die*: pine with passion (first *OED* citation of this sense 1591: die *v* I. 7a).
137. decay: (1) downfall; (2) decline.
139. enmarble: Spenserian coinage; cf. *Am* 51. 2, 6, 8nn.
141–68. So ... deem: the lover's pains are paralleled (and superseded) by those

[22]
Why, then, do I this honour unto thee
Thus to ennoble thy victorious name,
Since thou dost show no favour unto me, 150
Ne once move ruth in that rebellious dame
Somewhat to slack the rigour of my flame?
Certes, small glory dost thou win hereby
To let her live thus free, and me to die.

[23]
But if thou be indeed (as men thee call) 155
The world's great parent, the most kind preserver
Of living wights, the sovereign lord of all,
How falls it, then, that with thy furious fervour
Thou dost afflict as well the not-deserver
As him that doth thy lovely hests despise, 160
And on thy subjects most dost tyrannise?

[24]
Yet herein eke thy glory seemeth more
By so hard handling those which best thee serve,
That ere thou dost them unto grace restore
Thou mayest well try if they will ever swerve, 165
And mayest them make it better to deserve
And, having got it, may it more esteem;
For things hard gotten men more dearly deem.

[25]
So hard those heavenly beauties be enfired,
As things divine least passions do impress, 170

of Christ in *HHL*, 141–68: Nelson, W. 1963 *The Poetry of Edmund Spenser: A Study* (Columbia U.P., New York), pp. 101–2.
151–4. Ne ... die: cf. the complaints against the beloved at, e.g. *Am* 30, 31, 32.
151. ruth: pity.
156–7. world's ... all: caption to Ficino, *Commentary*, 3. 1 (Love ... is the Creator and Teacher of Everything).
162–8. Yet ... deem: Cupid's testing of the lover by making the woman hard to win is the topic of, e.g., *Am* 5, 6 and Castiglione, *Courtier*, 3: 262–4.
162. eke: also.
169–72. So ... steadfastness: those beauties are hard to inflame just as divine things are least susceptible to the influence of passion; the more steadfast they are, the more they are to be admired: cf. *Am* 55, 57, 61, 63.
169. enfired: this is *OED*'s first instance in the sense inflame with passion: enfire *v*, 2. *hard* = (1) difficult; (2) obdurate: cf. 139n above.

The more of steadfast minds to be admired,
The more they stayed be on steadfastness:
But base-born minds such lamps regard the less
Which at first blowing take not hasty fire:
Such fancies feel no love, but loose desire.   175

[26]
For Love is lord of truth and loyalty,
Lifting himself out of the lowly dust
On golden plumes up to the purest sky
Above the reach of loathly sinful lust,
Whose base affect, through cowardly distrust   180
Of his weak wings, dare not to heaven fly
But, like a mouldwarp, in the earth doth lie.

[27]
His dunghill thoughts (which do themselves inure
To dirty dross) no higher dare aspire;
Ne can his feeble earthly eyes endure   185
The flaming light of that celestial fire
Which kindleth love in generous desire
And makes him mount above the native might
Of heavy earth up to the heavens' height.

[28]
Such is the power of that sweet passion   190
That it all sordid baseness doth expel,
And the refined mind doth newly fashion
Unto a fairer form, which now doth dwell

172. stayed: *Am* 59. 11.
173–5. But . . . desire: Castiglione, *Courtier*, 3: 263: some men prefer to fall for the provocative and inviting woman.
176–82. For . . . lie: contrast *Am* 72 and nn. For *golden plumes* see *HHL* 1n. Miller 1988: 75 equates them with the poet's *golden quill* of *Am* 85.
180. affect: (1) desire; (2) innate disposition.
182. mouldwarp: mole, associated with blindness and idolatry: Isaiah 2: 20 ('At that day shall man cast away his silver idols and his golden idols . . . to the moles and to the backs [bats]'); *mould* suggests the earth of the grave and hence mortality: *OED* mould *sb* 1, 2.
183–4. His . . . dross: *SC October* 37n.
183. inure: accustom.
187. generous: noble-minded.
190–6. Such . . . light: the noble-minded lover moves beyond external physical beauty to a mental image (193–4) of the beloved which reflects heavenly Beauty: see *Phaedrus*, 249D–250C and *Am* 78 headnote; also *Am* 88. 13–14n and anacreontics 2. 8n on *image* and *Am* 7. 1n on *mirror*.

In his high thought, that would itself excel:
Which he, beholding still with constant sight,   195
Admires the mirror of so heavenly light,

[29]

Whose image printing in his deepest wit
He thereon feeds his hungry fantasy,
Still full, yet never satisfied with it:
Like Tantal' that in store doth starved lie,   200
So doth he pine in most satiety;
For nought may quench his infinite desire
Once kindled through that first-conceived fire.

[30]

Thereon his mind affixed wholly is,
Ne thinks on aught but how it to attain: 205
His care, his joy, his hope is all on this,
That seems in it all blisses to contain,
In sight whereof all other bliss seems vain:
Thrice-happy man (might he the same possess)
He feigns himself, and doth his fortune bless.   210

[31]

And though he do not win his wish to end,
Yet thus far happy he himself doth ween
That heavens such happy grace did to him lend
As thing on earth so heavenly to have seen –
His heart's enshrined saint, his heaven's queen,   215
Fairer than fairest in his feigning eye,
Whose sole aspect he counts felicity.

[32]

Then forth he casts, in his unquiet thought,
What he may do her favour to obtain:

197. wit: mind, understanding.
198. fantasy: faculty by which one apprehends an image.
200. Tantal' . . . lie: Tantalus was plunged into a lake in the underworld with a branch of fruit overhanging, unable to drink or eat, as a punishment for revealing divine secrets: *FQ*, 2. 7. 57–60. Traditionally an emblem of greed (Whitney 1586: 74), he partially deconstructs the spiritual quest he is invoked to describe. Note that *store, starved* (38–9n above) and *pine* (together with greed) recall Narcissus at *Am* 35.
210. feigns: imagines.
217. sole aspect: unrivalled appearance.
218. casts: resolves: *SC February* 125n.

What brave exploit, what peril hardly wrought, 220
What puissant conquest, what adventurous pain
May please her best and grace unto him gain:
He dreads no danger, nor misfortune fears;
His faith, his fortune, in his breast he bears.

[33]
Thou art his god, thou art his mighty guide: 225
Thou, being blind, lettest him not see his fears,
But carriest him to that which he hath eyed
Through seas, through flames, through thousand swords and
    spears;
Ne aught so strong that may his force withstand,
With which thou armest his resistless hand. 230

[34]
Witness Leander in the Euxine waves,
And stout Aeneas in the Trojan fire;
Achilles pressing through the Phrygian glaives,

220. hardly: with difficulty. For the bravery of the lover, see, e.g., Castiglione, *Courtier*, 3: 255–6.
226. blind: Cupid's blindness was usually interpreted as a sign of lovers' folly and sensuality; here, Spenser draws on the Orphic tradition of blind Cupid as the guide to union with the divine: 'The soul . . ., being converted, and made like to God, is so formed of God, that it doth above all intellect, know all things by a certain essential contract of divinity: therefore *Orpheus* describes love to be without eyes, because it is above the intellect': Agrippa (1651) 3. 49 (p. 507). The passage follows shortly after the one quoted at 28n above. But Spenser's fervent lover is devoted to a woman as the image of Beauty rather than to God (248–9n below). Hence the ambiguity of the *feign* (216, 240): imagine *and* depict falsely.
230. resistless: irresistible.
231. Leander: lover of Hero of Sestos, priestesss of Venus, he swam the Hellespont (not the Euxine sea) nightly to be with her, guided by her lamp, emblem of the flame of passion: Ovid, *Heroides*, 18. 177–8 (and *Heroides*, 19). The subject also of a poem by the Greek poet Musaeus (*c*. 500 A.D.), the tale celebrates sensual (not spiritual) love. The Marlowe/Chapman poem was not published until 1598.
232. Aeneas: demonstrated love of family by returning through burning Troy to rescue them. Secular love again (Aeneas carrying his aged father on his back became an emblem of 'mutual help': Alciati 1551: 173); but note the spiritual overtones of the fact that Aeneas is guided by his mother, Venus, who parts the mist dulling his mortal vision so that he can see the sacked city: *Aeneid*, 2. 589–804.
233. Achilles: angry with the Greek general Agamemnon, he refused to fight; but when his friend Patroclus was killed by Hector, his love and grief impelled

And Orpheus daring to provoke the ire
Of damned fiends to get his love retire: 235
For both through heaven and hell thou makest way
To win them worship which to thee obey.

[35]
And if, by all these perils and these pains,
He may but purchase liking in her eye,
What heavens of joy then to himself he feigns. 240
Eftsoons he wipes quite out of memory
Whatever ill before he did aby:
Had it been death, yet would he die again
To live thus happy as her grace to gain.

[36]
Yet when he hath found favour to his will, 245
He nathemore can so contented rest,
But forceth further on, and striveth still
To approach more near, till in her inmost breast
He may embosomed be, and loved best:
And yet not best, but to be loved alone; 250
For love cannot endure a paragon.

[37]
The fear whereof, O how doth it torment
His troubled mind with more than hellish pain,
And to his feigning fancy represent

him to fight for revenge: *Iliad*, 18–22. He is one of the honoured lovers at *Symposium*, 179E (cf. 208D). *Glaives* = spears.
234. *Orpheus*: *SC October* 28 gloss, *Epith* 16n. Excluded from the list of noble lovers at *Symposium*, 179D because he entered Hades alive, thus perhaps confirming the worldly implications of Spenser's list (but see 243n).
235. *retire*: return (*OED* retire *v* III. 9c, first instance 1600).
240. *feigns*: *Am* 87. 10–11n.
242. *aby*: endure (archaic: *OED* aby *v* 3 cites only Chaucer and Spenser for this sense).
243. *Had ... again*: Alcestis, unlike Orpheus, did die in order to regain her beloved; Orpheus saw only the shadow of his loved one in Hades: had he embraced death, he would have met her true self: Wind 1967: 156–7 citing Pico, commenting on *Symposium*, 179D.
246. *nathemore*: never [the] more: obsolete word revived by Spenser: *OED*, citing *FQ*, 1. 8. 13 and *HB*, 155.
248–9. *till ... be*: at least partly sensual, as at *Am* 76–7.
251. *paragon*: rival.
252–65. *The ... hell*: catalogue of the psychological effects of love melancholy complementing its physical manifestations at 12ln above (see also the love tor-

Sights never seen, and thousand shadows vain,   255
To break his sleep and waste his idle brain:
Thou that hast never loved canst not believe
Least part of the evils which poor lovers grieve:

[38]
The gnawing envy, the heart-fretting fear,
The vain surmises, the distrustful shows,   260
The false reports that flying tales do bear,
The doubts, the dangers, the delays, the woes,
The feigned friends, the unassured foes,
With thousands more than any tongue can tell,
Do make a lover's life a wretch's hell.   265

[39]
Yet is there one more cursed than they all –
That canker-worm, that monster, Jealousy,
Which eats the heart and feeds upon the gall,
Turning all love's delight to misery
Through fear of losing his felicity.   270
Ah, gods, that ever ye that monster placed
In gentle love, that all his joys defaced.

[40]
By these, O Love, thou dost thy entrance make
Unto thy heaven, and dost the more endear
Thy pleasures unto those which them partake: 275
As after storms, when clouds begin to clear,
The sun more bright and glorious doth appear,
So thou thy folk, through pains of purgatory,
Dost bear unto thy bliss and heaven's glory.

ments at Ovid, *Amores*, 1. 2 and *FQ*, 3. 12. 24–6). The lover's mental hell is his punishment for refusing to die into love, the equivalent of Orpheus's barren exile in Thrace after failing to regain Eurydice: Ovid, *Metamorphoses*, 10. Note that the *shadows* are banished at *HHB*, 291.

259. *envy*: literally *gnawing*: Whitney 1586: 4 has 'Envy eat[ing] her heart': Ripa 1603: 241–2 has her left breast devoured by a serpent.

263. *unassured foes*: foes on account of whom one is insecure.

266–72. *Yet . . . defaced*: Jealousy was often identified iconographically with Envy: cf. Brooks-Davies 1977: 50 on *FQ*, 1. 4. 30–2 and, for the gnawed heart, 259n above. See the horrific analysis through the person of Malbecco at *FQ*, 3. 9 and 10, especially 10. 53–60.

268. *gall*: associated with the bitterness of jealousy: *FQ*, 3. 10. 59; Alpers 1967: 222–6.

[41]
There thou them placest in a paradise
Of all delight and joyous happy rest,
Where they do feed on nectar heavenly-wise
With Hercules and Hebe and the rest
Of Venus' darlings, through her bounty blessed;
And lie like gods in ivory beds arrayed,
With roses and lilies over them displayed.

[42]
There with thy daughter Pleasure they do play
Their hurtless sports without rebuke or blame,
And in her snowy bosom boldly lay
Their quiet heads, devoid of guilty shame,
After full joyance of their gentle game.
Then her they crown their goddess and their queen,
And deck with flowers thy altars well beseen.

[43]
Ay me, dear lord, that ever I might hope,
For all the pains and woes that I endure,
To come at length unto the wished scope
Of my desire, or might myself assure
That happy port for ever to recure:
Then would I think these pains no pains at all,
And all my woes to be but penance small.

280–6. There ... displayed: a sensual paradise recalling those of *Am* 63. 11, 76. 3 and 77. 11–12nn.
282. nectar: 25–6n above. Drunk by the guests at the wedding of Cupid and Psyche: Apuleius, *Golden Ass*, 6. 24.
283. Hercules ... Hebe: Hercules was married by Zeus to Hebe, goddess of youth, after his death: Ross 1648: 151; *Epith* 405n.
285. ivory: Venerean: *Am* 15. 10, 77. 1–2.
286. roses ... lilies: *Epith* 226 and 43 and 302nn respectively.
287. Pleasure: offspring of Cupid and Psyche after their heavenly marriage: Apuleius, *Golden Ass*, 6. 24. Neo-Platonically, desire and love (two meanings of Eros/Cupid) united with soul (Psyche), spurred on by Beauty, gain Pleasure: Wind 1967: 46–52; cf. *Am* 65. 14, 72. 7 and 76. 7nn. But the meaning is closer to the idealisation of chaste love in *Epith*.
293. beseen: appointed, furnished.
296. scope: goal.
298. recure: gain, win (last *OED* example of this sense 1509: recure *v* 4b).

[44]
Then would I sing of thine immortal praise
An heavenly hymn such as the angels sing,
And thy triumphant name then would I raise
'Bove all the gods, thee only honouring,
My guide, my god, my victor, and my king.   305
Till then, dread lord, vouchsafe to take of me
This simple song, thus framed in praise of thee.

FINIS.

An Hymn in Honour of Beauty

[1]
Ah whither, Love, wilt thou now carry me?
What wontless fury dost thou now inspire
Into my feeble breast, too full of thee?
Whilst seeking to aslake thy raging fire
Thou in me kindlest much more great desire,   5
And up aloft above my strength dost raise,
The wondrous matter of my fire to praise

[2]
That, as I erst in praise of thine own name,
So now in honour of thy mother dear
An honourable hymn I eke should frame,   10
And with the brightness of her beauty clear

303–4. name . . . gods: because of his power and primacy as at 57–98nn above; but he will be supplanted by Christ in *HHL*.
307. framed: fashioned.
1–3. Ah . . . thee: Bjorvand and Schell (Oram *et al*. 1989: 706) compare Horace, *Odes*, 3. 25. 1–2 ('Bacchus, whither do you force me, filled with your ecstasy?'). Spenser replaces the Bacchic/Dionysian *fury* with the higher one of love (Agrippa (1651), 3. 46–9, e.g., lists the furies or frenzies in the following ascending order: Muses, Dionysius, Apollo, Venus and Cupid).
2. wontless: unaccustomed. *fury*: *HL* 28 and 226nn.
4. aslake: mitigate (rare word judging by the few *OED* instances).
7. matter: subject (i.e., Beauty).
8. erst: formerly.
9. mother: Venus, mother of Cupid, neo-Platonically identified with Beauty: *HL* 50–6n above.
10. eke: also.

The ravished hearts of gazeful men might rear
To admiration of that heavenly light,
From whence proceeds such soul-enchanting might.

[3]
Thereto do thou, great goddess, queen of Beauty,   15
Mother of Love and of all world's delight,
Without whose sovereign grace and kindly duty
Nothing on earth seems fair to fleshly sight –
Do thou vouchsafe with thy love-kindling light
To illuminate my dim and dulled eyne,   20
And beautify this sacred hymn of thine

[4]
That both to thee (to whom I mean it most),
And eke to her (whose fair immortal beam
Hath darted fire into my feeble ghost
That now it wasted is with woes extreme),   25
It may so please that she at length will stream
Some dew of grace into my withered heart
After long sorrow and consuming smart.

*   *   *   *

12. ravished: *Am* 3. 12n. *gazeful*: gazing intently (Spenserian coinage: *OED* cites only this and *FQ*, 4. 10. 28).
13. admiration: *Am* 3. 1, 10nn. *heavenly light*: Beauty as a manifestation of the divine; planetary Venus as the evening star guiding the earthly lover: *Epith* 288n.
14. enchanting: (1) enrapturing (in the neo-Platonic sense of ravishing: *OED* sense 3); (2) spell-binding in the secular sense.
16. Mother ... delight: the echo of Lucretius' invocation to the generative Venus Pandemos (*HL* 50–6n) – 'delight of men and gods, nourishing Venus' (*On the Nature of Things*, 1. 1–2) – sets the tone for *HB*, which is largely concerned with beauty as manifested in the earthly, mortal, beloved.
17. kindly duty: function in relation to nature and birth (*OED* kindly *a* I; duty *sb* 5). Cf. (as analogue, not source) the *Vigil of Venus* (*Pervigilium Veneris*), st. 17 ('she commanded the world to know the ways of birth'; in Loeb *Catullus* 1968: 358–9).
20. eyne: eyes.
23–5. her ... extreme: the earthly beloved (*HL* 8n); so that *ghost* is the tormented male suffering from love melancholy: *HL* 121, 252–65nn.
27. grace: *Am* 2. 12n.
28. smart: affliction.

[5]
What time this world's great work-master did cast
To make all things such as we now behold, 30
It seems that he before his eyes had placed
A goodly pattern to whose perfect mould
He fashioned them as comely as he could,
That now so fair and seemly they appear
As naught may be amended anywhere. 35

[6]
That wondrous pattern, wheresoe'er it be –
Whether in earth laid up in secret store,
Or else in heaven (that no man may it see
With sinful eyes for fear it to deflower) –
Is perfect Beauty, which all men adore, 40
Whose face and feature doth so much excel
All mortal sense that none the same may tell.

[7]
Thereof as every earthly thing partakes
Or more, or less, by influence divine,
So it more fair accordingly it makes, 45
And the gross matter of this earthly mine
Which clotheth it, thereafter doth refine,

29–42. *What ... tell*: cf. *HL* 57–91 and n. *Pattern*, as in Plato's *Timaeus*, 28 etc.
29. *work-master*: often applied to God in sixteenth and seventeenth century; also recalls Plato's *demiurge* (constructor): e.g., *Timaeus*, 29B. *cast: HL* 218n.
32–3. *goodly ... could*: cf. *Genesis* 1: 26 ('Furthermore God said, Let us make man in our image according to our likeness').
36–40. *That ... Beauty*: Bennett 1931: 31–2 cites Pico's *Commento* on Benivieni's *Canzone* on Beauty as the sum of the archetypal Ideas.
37. *store*: (1) plenty; (2) reserve; (3) place for storage.
40. *adore*: Spenser suggests merely that this is instinctive; Plato, *Phaedrus*, 250C–D attributes it to the memory of divine Beauty retained by the pre-existent soul.
43–9. *Thereof ... empight*: it was a neo-Platonic commonplace that matter was ugly and reguired redemption by beauty, which imposed form on it; physical beauty was, in addition, a sign of moral virtue: cf. Castiglione, *Courtier*, 4: 325–6 on physical beauty as the result of an influx of divine goodness which illuminates the object it inhabits, attracting the gaze and desire of others with its light; also 4: 330–2.
46. *gross ... mine*: the matter is earth, dug from the earth: cf. Genesis, 2: 7 ('The Lord God also made the man of the dust of the ground').

Doing away the dross which dims the light
Of that fair beam which therein is empight.

[8]

For through infusion of celestial power 50
The duller earth it quickeneth with delight,
And life-full spirits privily doth pour
Through all the parts, that to the looker's sight
They seem to please. That is thy sovereign might,
O Cyprian queen, which, flowing from the beam 55
Of thy bright star, thou into them dost stream.

[9]

That is the thing which giveth pleasant grace
To all things fair, that kindleth lively fire,
Light of thy lamp which, shining in the face,
Thence to the soul darts amorous desire 60
And robs the hearts of those which it admire:
Therewith thou pointest thy son's poisoned arrow
That wounds the life and wastes the inmost marrow.

[10]

How vainly, then, do idle wits invent
That beauty is nought else but mixture made 65
Of colours fair, and goodly temperament
Of pure complexions, that shall quickly fade

49. *empight*: implanted (a favourite with Spenser: *OED s.v.*).
51. *quickeneth*: animates.
52. *life-full spirits*: correspond in the macrocosm to the vital spirits that were believed to link soul to body; Ficino identified them as one spirit, light: Welsford 1967: 155. *privily*: secretly.
55. *Cyprian queen*: Venus, born near and worshipped particularly in Cyprus: Hesiod, *Theogony*, 173–210.
56. *star*: l3n above.
57–63. *That ... marrow*: cf. Castiglione, *Courtier*, 4: 325–7: beauty encourages desire in the lover who makes the mistake of thinking that the desire must be fulfilled carnally. If he does fulfil it so, the gap between achievement and beauty as it was imagined leads to love melancholy (pallor, lamentation, the desire for death, etc.). For the *poisoned arrow* (62) see *HL* 12ln.
64–70. *How ... disposition*: beauty is particularly manifest when it inhabits a well-proportioned, symmetrical, and harmoniously coloured countenance (Castiglione, *Courtier*, 4. 325–6). But Ficino, *Commentary*, 5. 3 (Ficino 1944: 167–9) agrees that in itself it is more than this; and see Fletcher 1911a: 554 citing Pico.
66. *temperament*: balance (of elements): cf. *Am* 13. 4n.
67. *complexions*: humours, the equivalent in the body of the cosmic elements: *HL* 75–91n.

And pass away, like to a summer's shade;
Or that it is but comely composition
Of parts well measured, with meet disposition.   70

[11]
Hath white and red in it such wondrous power
That it can pierce through the eyes unto the heart,
And therein stir such rage and restless stour
As naught but death can stint his dolour's smart?
Or can proportion of the outward part   75
Move such affection in the inward mind
That it can rob both sense and reason blind?

[12]
Why do not, then, the blossoms of the field
(Which are arrayed with much more orient hue,
And to the sense most dainty odours yield)   80
Work like impression in the looker's view?
Or why do not fair pictures like power show,
In which oft-times we Nature see of Art
Excelled, in perfect limning every part?

[13]
But, ah! believe me, there is more than so   85
That works such wonders in the minds of men:
I, that have often proved, too well it know;
And whoso list the like assays to ken
Shall find by trial, and confess it then,

70. *meet*: fitting. *disposition*: arrangement of parts.
71. *white ... red*: the traditional colours of female beauty: e.g., Sir John Davies, *Hymns of Astraea*, 12. 6–10.
73. *stour*: HL 3n.
74. *stint*: stop. *smart*: 28n above.
75–7. *Or ... blind*: the answer is 'no' as at 64–70n above. Nevertheless, the body was proportioned to the measures of the cosmos and contained an equally harmonious soul: the idea originated with the *Timaeus* and became a commonplace: e.g., Agrippa (1651) 2. 27 (entitled *Of the proportion, measure, and harmony of man's body*) and 28 (*Of the composition and harmony of the human soul*).
79. *orient*: bright, glowing.
84. *limning*: painting.
85. *more ... so*: than the beauty of the face (71).
87. *proved*: experienced.
88. *assays*: trials. *ken*: understand.

That beauty is not (as fond men misdeem) 90
An outward show of things that only seem.

[14]
For that same goodly hue of white and red
With which the cheeks are sprinkled, shall decay,
And those sweet rosy leaves so fairly spread
Upon the lips, shall fade and fall away 95
To that they were, even to corrupted clay:
That golden wire, those sparkling stars so bright,
Shall turn to dust and lose their goodly light.

[15]
But that fair lamp, from whose celestial ray
That light proceeds which kindleth lovers' fire, 100
Shall never be extinguished nor decay
But, when the vital spirits do expire,
Unto her native planet shall retire:
For it is heavenly born and cannot die,
Being a parcel of the purest sky. 105

[16]
For when the soul (the which derived was
At first out of that great immortal Spright
By whom all live to love) whilom did pass
Down from the top of purest heaven's height
To be embodied here, it then took light 110
And lively spirits from that fairest star
Which lights the world forth from his fiery car:

90. fond: foolish. *misdeem*: mistakenly judge.
92–8. For . . . light: see Ficino, *Commentary*, 5. 3 (nothing ages more swiftly than beauty; Ficino 1944: 168). The corruption argument is usually used to seduce the beloved: *Am* 70 headnote and 13–14n.
94. leaves: sheets of thinly-beaten metal (e.g., gold leaf), and continuing the metallurgic/alchemical metaphor started in *assays* . . . *trial* (88–9) with its implications of testing the purity of gold. *Rosy* recalls that the rose signified not just Venerean beauty but also mutability: Valeriano 1602: 581–2.
97. golden wire: *Epith* 154n.
99. lamp: the soul.
102. vital spirits: 52n above.
103. native planet: in the lady's case, presumably Venus.
105. parcel: part.
106–12. For . . . car: the soul, made in God's image, passes through the region of the sun: Benivieni, *Canzone*, st. 6: Fletcher 1911a: 553–5.
112. car: chariot.

[17]

Which power retaining still, or more or less,
When she in fleshly seed is eft enraced,
Through every part she doth the same impress 115
According as the heavens have her graced,
And frames her house, in which she will be placed,
Fit for herself, adorning it with spoil
Of the heavenly riches which she robbed erewhile.

[18]

Thereof it comes that these fair souls, which have 120
The most resemblance of that heavenly light,
Frame to themselves most beautiful and brave
Their fleshly bower, most fit for their delight,
And the gross matter by a sovereign might
Tempers so trim that it may well be seen 125
A palace fit for such a virgin queen.

[19]

So every spirit, as it is most pure
And hath in it the more of heavenly light,
So it the fairer body doth procure
To habit in, and it more fairly dight 130
With cheerful grace and amiable sight;
For of the soul the body form doth take,
For soul is form, and doth the body make.

[20]

Therefore, wherever that thou dost behold
A comely corpse with beauty fair endued, 135
Know this for certain: that the same doth hold

---

114. seed: offspring. *eft*: afterwards. *enraced*: implanted (*OED* cites only three examples, the first dated 1577, and two more from Spenser).
117. house: i.e., the body.
120–6. Thereof . . . queen: 43–9n above.
122. Frame: create. *brave*: handsome.
125. Tempers: cf. 66n above. *trim*: appropriately.
126. palace . . . queen: suggesting the idea of the body as temple of the holy spirit (1 Corinthians 6: 19), but the phrasing recalls *FQ*, 2. 9, the castle of Alma (castle = body; Alma, a crowned 'virgin bright', = the rational soul: stanzas 18–19).
130. habit: dwell. *dight*: dress.
135. corpse: (living) body; but the sense dead body was well established, reminding us of the corruptibility of matter. *endued*: invested with.

A beauteous soul, with fair conditions thewed,
Fit to receive the seed of virtue strewed.
For all that fair is, is by nature good:
That is a sign to know the gentle blood. 140

[21]
Yet oft it falls that many a gentle mind
Dwells in deformed tabernacle drowned,
Either by chance, against the course of kind,
Or through unaptness in the substance found,
Which it assumed of some stubborn ground, 145
That will not yield unto her form's direction,
But is performed with some foul imperfection.

[22]
And oft it falls (ay me the more to rue)
That goodly beauty, albe heavenly born,
Is foul abused, and that celestial hue – 150
Which doth the world with her delight adorn –
Made but the bait of sin and sinners' scorn;
Whilst everyone doth seek and sue to have it,
But everyone doth seek but to deprave it.

[23]
Yet nathemore is that fair Beauty's blame, 155
But theirs that do abuse it unto ill:
Nothing so good but that through guilty shame
May be corrupt and wrested unto will.
Natheless, the soul is fair and beauteous still,

---

137. fair ... thewed: having good qualities.
140. gentle: noble (i.e., excellent through its heavenly origins).
141–7. Yet ... imperfection: when the discrepancy occurs, it is through the recalcitrance of matter, which the soul cannot form: Bhattacherje 1935: 34–5 cit. *Var* 1. 531.
143. kind: nature.
147. performed: made.
148–54. And ... it: on the misuse of beauty see 57–63n.
148. falls: happens.
153. sue: court: *OED* sue *v* I. 15 citing *FQ*, 6. 8. 20 ('sude and sought') as first instance of this sense.
155. nathemore: see *HL* 246n.
158. corrupt: corrupted. *will*: carnal appetite: *OED* will *sb* 1, I. 2.
159–61. Natheless ... take: the soul's incorruptibility is discussed by Sir John Davies, *Nosce Teipsum* (1599), 473–580; and see Reid in *SpE*, pp. 665–6.

However flesh's fault it filthy make, 160
For things immortal no corruption take.

[24]
But ye, fair dames, the world's dear ornaments,
And lively images of heaven's light,
Let not your beams with such disparagements
Be dimmed and your bright glory darkened quite; 165
But, mindful still of your first country's sight,
Do still preserve your first-informed grace,
Whose shadow yet shines in your beauteous face.

[25]
Loathe that foul blot, that hellish firebrand,
Disloyal lust, fair Beauty's foulest blame, 170
That base affections, which your ears would bland,
Commend to you by love's abused name
But is, indeed, the bondslave of defame,
Which will the garland of your glory mar,
And quench the light of your bright shining star. 175

161. For . . . take: 1 Corinthians 15: 42 ('The body is sown in corruption, and is raised in incorruption'), 53–4 ('For this corruptible must put on incorruptible', etc.): the chapter is read at the Burial Service: cf. 135n.
162–8. But . . . face: cf. Castiglione, *Courtier*, 4: 334 (beauty is a ray of the divinity that is dishonoured when linked with corruptible matter). The *fair dames* are (1) women in general; (2) the poems' dedicatees.
163. lively: living.
164. disparagements: indignities; but also implying *OED*'s sense 1: the dishonour entailed by marriage to one of inferior rank (last instance 1585).
165. glory: Am 27. 2n.
166. first country: heaven: Platonist (*Phaedrus*, 249–51; Macrobius, *Commentary on the Dream of Scipio*, 1. 9. 1: the origin of souls is from the sky [*de coelo*]) and Christian (Hebrews 11: 13–16: faith guided the Jewish Fathers: 'And if they had been mindful of that country, from whence they came out, they had leisure to have returned. But now they desire a better, that is an heavenly').
167. informed: inspired (by a formative principle).
170. blame: hurt: *OED* blame sb 5 citing only two instances, one from Spenser (*FQ*, 1. 2. 18).
171. bland: flatter: rare by-form of blandish; *OED* bland *v* 2, cites only two examples, the last 1505.
173. defame: (1) dishonour; (2) slander.
174. garland . . . glory: 1 Peter 5: 4 ('And when that chief shepherd shall appear, ye shall receive an incorruptible crown of glory').

[26]
But gentle love, that loyal is and true,
Will more illumine your resplendent ray,
And add more brightness to your goodly hue
From light of his pure fire which, by like way
Kindled of yours, your likeness doth display,   180
Like as two mirrors, by opposed reflection,
Do both express the face's first impression.

[27]
Therefore, to make your beauty more appear,
It you behoves to love, and forth to lay
That heavenly riches which in you ye bear,   185
That men the more admire their fountain may;
For else, what booteth that celestial ray
If it in darkness be enshrined ever,
That it of loving eyes be viewed never?

[28]
But, in your choice of loves, this well advise,   190
That likest to yourselves ye them select,
The which your form's first source may sympathise,
And with like beauty's parts be inly decked:
For if you loosely love without respect,
It is no love, but a discordant war,   195
Whose unlike parts amongst themselves do jar.

176. *gentle*: noble (as opposed to sensual and dishonourable).
178. *hue*: appearance.
181–2. *Like ... impression*: touch is the sense of the sensual lover; sight that of the noble lover (Castiglione, *Courtier*, 4: 334); hence the lover imprints the likeness of the beloved on his soul, which becomes a mirror reflecting the beloved's image: Ficino, *Commentary*, 2. 8 (Ficino 1944: 146) following Plato, *Phaedrus*, 255C–D (but Spenser refers to heterosexual, not homosexual, love). This mental image was regarded as more beautiful than the physical reality.
185. *heavenly*: literally: 166n. Note also the neo-Platonic belief that souls descended through the planetary spheres (Macrobius, *Commentary on the Dream of Scipio*, 1. 12) and that love is truly reciprocal only between those who are astrologically compatible: Ficino as in 181–2n.
186. *fountain*: origin.
187. *booteth*: avails.
190. *advise*: consider.
191. *likest ... yourselves*: consonant with the mirror metaphor; cf. Ficino, *Commentary*, 6. 6, which also considers love between those born under the same star (197–203).
193. *inly*: inwardly.
194. *loosely*: lasciviously. *respect*: discrimination.

[29]

For love is a celestial harmony
Of likely hearts composed of stars' concent,
Which join together in sweet sympathy
To work each others' joy and true content,   200
Which they have harboured since their first descent
Out of their heavenly bowers, where they did see
And know each other here beloved to be.

[30]

Then wrong it were that any other twain
Should in love's gentle band combined be,   205
But those whom heaven did at first ordain
And made out of one mould the more to agree:
For all that like the beauty which they see
Straight do not love; for love is not so light
As straight to burn at first beholder's sight.   210

[31]

But they which love indeed look otherwise,
With pure regard and spotless true intent,
Drawing out of the object of their eyes
A more refined form, which they present
Unto their mind, void of all blemishment,   215
Which it reducing to her first perfection,
Beholdeth free from flesh's frail infection.

[32]

And then conforming it unto the light,
Which in itself it hath remaining still
Of that first sun, yet sparkling in his sight,   220
Thereof he fashions in his higher skill
An heavenly beauty to his fancy's will

---

198. composed of: arranged in accordance with. *concent*: harmony, concord.
205. band: bond; see also *Am* 1. 3n.
206. those . . . ordain: 'Almighty God, which, at the beginning did create our first parents Adam and Eve, and did sanctify and join them together in marriage . . .' (Marriage Service; *Prayer-book* 1559: 126).
207. mould: pattern.
209. light: frivolous.
211–17. But . . . infection: cf. Castiglione, *Courtier*, 4. 338 ct. *Am* 78 headnote above; also 4: 334 (when a man sees a beautiful woman and he responds to her in spirit, his eyes seize on her image and carry it to his heart).
218. conforming: shaping, harmonising.
220. sun: 106–12n above.
221. skill: knowledge.

And, it embracing in his mind entire,
The mirror of his own thought doth admire:

[33]
Which, seeing now so inly fair to be 225
As outward it appeareth to the eye,
And with his spirit's proportion to agree,
He thereon fixeth all his fantasy,
And fully setteth his felicity,
Counting it fairer than it is indeed, 230
And yet indeed her fairness doth exceed.

[34]
For lovers' eyes more sharply sighted be
Than other men's, and in dear love's delight
See more than any other eyes can see
Through mutual receipt of beams bright, 235
Which carry privy message to the spright,
And to their eyes that inmost fair display
As plain as light discovers dawning day.

[35]
Therein they see, through amorous eye-glances,
Armies of Loves still flying to and fro, 240
Which dart at them their little fiery lances,
Whom, having wounded, back again they go,
Carrying compassion to their lovely foe:
Who, seeing her fair eyes' so sharp effect,
Cures all their sorrows with one sweet aspect. 245

[36]
In which how many wonders do they read
To their conceit that others never see,
Now of her smiles (with which their souls they feed
Like gods with nectar in their banquets free),

223. *entire*: completely.
224. *admire*: *Am* 3. 1n.
228. *fantasy*: (1) imagination; (2) delusion of oneself by false images.
232–45. *For . . . aspect*: commonplaces illustrated by Castiglione, *Courtier*, 3: 268–9. Note that the lover now retreats into praise of physical beauty.
240. *Armies of Loves*: *Am* 16. 6; *Epith* 357–9n.
245. *aspect*: look.
246. *read*: describe, declare.
247. *conceit*: understanding; also imagination (*OED* senses I. 2, III. 7b).
248–9. *souls . . . nectar*: cf. *HL* 25–6, 282nn.

Now of her looks, which like to cordials be; 250
But when her words embassade forth she sends,
Lord, how sweet music that unto them lends!

[37]
Sometimes upon her forehead they behold
A thousand Graces masking in delight;
Sometimes within her eyelids they unfold 255
Ten thousand sweet belgards, which to their sight
Do seem like twinkling stars in frosty night;
But on her lips like rosy buds in May
So many millions of chaste Pleasures play.

[38]
All those, O Cytherea, and thousands more 260
Thy handmaids be, which do on thee attend
To deck thy beauty with their dainties' store,
That may it more to mortal eyes commend,
And make it more admired of foe and friend;
That in men's hearts thou mayest thy throne install, 265
And spread thy lovely kingdom over all.

[39]
Then 'Io triumph', O great Beauty's queen:
Advance the banner of thy conquest high,
That all this world, the which thy vassals been,
May draw to thee, and with due fealty 270

---

250. *cordials*: heart stimulants: *Am* 50. 12n.
251. *embassade*: on an embassy: *OED* embassade 4 (citing this as second of two instances only).
254. *Graces*: cf. *Am* 40. 3–4n and the multiple graces that adorn Belphoebe's eyelids at *FQ*, 2. 3. 25. *masking*: performing as in a masque (*Epith* 26n).
256. *belgards*: lovely/loving looks; apparently coined by Spenser from Italian *bel guardo* for Belphoebe (*FQ*, 2. 3. 25 again).
257. *twinkling . . . night*: Chaucer's Friar, *General Prologue*, 269–70: 'His eyen twynkled in his heed aryght,/As doon the sterres in the frosty nyght'.
259. *chaste Pleasures*: *Epith* 365n; *HL* 287n.
260. *Cytherea*: Venus, so named because of her cult on the Greek island of Cythera.
262. *store*: abundance.
267. Ovid, *Amores*, 1. 2. 34 ('the crowd shall sing with one voice [to Cupid] "io Triumph"'); *Epith* 140n.
268. *Advance*: lift up.
269. *all . . . been*: cf. *FQ*, 4. 10. 47.

Adore the power of thy great majesty,
Singing this hymn in honour of thy name,
Compiled by me, which thy poor liegeman am.

[40]
In lieu whereof grant, O great sovereign,
That she whose conquering beauty doth captive 275
My trembling heart in her eternal chain
One drop of grace at length will to me give,
That I – her bounden thrall – by her may live,
And this same life (which first fro me she reaved)
May owe to her, of whom I it received. 280

[41]
And you, fair Venus' darling, my dear dread,
Fresh flower of grace, great goddess of my life,
When your fair eyes these fear-full lines shall read,
Deign to let fall one drop of due relief
That may recure my heart's long-pining grief, 285
And show what wondrous power your beauty hath,
That can restore a damned wight from death.

FINIS.

274. lieu: place.
276. chain: *Am* 37. 6n.
277. grace: *Am* 2. 12–13.
279. reaved: stole forcibly.
281. dear dread: cf. the address to the queen at *FQ*, 1 proem 4 as 'dearest dread'.
285. recure: cure. *pining*: *Am* anacreontics 4. 60n.
287. wight: *HL* 90–1n.

An Hymn of Heavenly Love

[1]
Love, lift me up upon thy golden wings
From this base world unto thy heaven's height,
Where I may see those admirable things
Which there thou workest by thy sovereign might
Far above feeble reach of earthly sight,   5
That I thereof an heavenly Hymn may sing
Unto the god of love, high heaven's king.

[2]
Many lewd lays (ah, woe is me the more!)
In praise of that mad fit which fools call love
I have, in the heat of youth, made heretofore,   10
That in light wits did loose affection move.
But all those follies now I do reprove,
And turned have the tenor of my string
The heavenly praises of true love to sing.

1. Love . . . wings: cf. *HL*, 64–5, 69, and 176–82nn. The *golden wings* recall those of *HL*, 178–9, but now the subject is love of Christ. *Golden wings* are an attribute of the Orphic Protogonos (= 'first born'), 'egg-born, rejoicing in his golden wings' (Athanassakis 1977: 11), who was identified with Eros/Cupid: Athanassakis, pp 114–15 citing Aristophanes, *The Birds*, 693–9 on golden-winged Eros: cf. *HL* 57–91n, *Proth* 42–4n, and Guthrie, W. K. C. 1952 *Orpheus and Greek Religion*, 2nd edn (London: Methuen), p. 95. This Eros is a cosmic prime mover far removed from the Cupid of human desire; by l. 7 he has become identified with Christ himself (on Orphic Protogonos/Eros as Christ, see Hutton 1966 in ed. 1980: 181).

8. Many . . . lays: the hyperbole of the *persona* offering a retraction for the sake of his argument in imitation of Petrarch, as at *Rime*, 364 ('love held me burning . . . now I reproach my life for so much error . . . and render my last parts to you, high God, penitent and sorrowing'). *Lewd* = (1) unlettered; (2) unchaste; (3) not of a religious nature.

11. affection: passion, lust.

12. reprove: reject (*OED* sense 1).

13. And . . . string: *Epith* 9n. *Turned* not *tuned* (*pace* Todd in *Var* 1. 713) because Spenser refers to a tuning peg on, e.g., a lute.

[3]
And ye that wont with greedy vain desire 15
To read my fault and, wondering at my flame,
To warm yourselves at my wide sparkling fire,
Sith now that heat is quenched, quench my blame,
And in her ashes shroud my dying shame:
For who my passed follies now pursues 20
Begins his own, and my old fault renews.

*   *   *   *

[4]
Before this world's great frame, in which all things
Are now contained, found any being place;
Ere flitting Time could wag his eyas wings
About that mighty bound which doth embrace 25
The rolling spheres and parts their hours by space,
That high eternal power, which now doth move
In all these things, moved in itself by love.

[5]
It loved itself because itself was fair
(For fair is loved); and of itself begot, 30
Like to itself, his eldest son and heir,
Eternal, pure, and void of sinful blot,
The firstling of his joy, in whom no jot

16–17. flame ... fire: thus turning themselves into moths, traditional emblems of love's self-destructive power: Henkel, A. and Schöne, A. (1967) cols 910–11. Contrast their burnt wings with those of Love (1. 1).
18. Sith: since.
22–35. Before ... crowned: the idea originates with *Timaeus*, 29A but is closer to, e.g., Pseudo-Dionysius, *On the Divine Names*, 4. 10 (Collins in *Var* 1. 539). See also Agrippa (1651) 3. 8. With this creation account, cf. *HB* 29–42 and n.
22. frame: structure.
24. flitting: swiftly moving; favourite Spenserian word: *OED* flit *a. Time ... wings*: *Epith* 281n. *Wag* = move; *eyas* = young untrained hawk; used first by Spenser to mean *youthful*: *OED* eyas 2 (contrast Love, who is already fully fledged).
25–6. About ... space: the *primum mobile*, or outermost sphere which, in the Ptolemaic system, enclosed all the other spheres. It was notionally divided into 24 hours which were allocated to the planets as markers of their rising and setting: *Epith* 98–102; Hieatt 1960: 33–4.
31. eldest ... heir: Christ. Cf. John 1: 1 ('In the beginning was that Word', where the Word is Christ); Romans 8: 29 ('that he might be the first born among many brethren'). Note the identification of the Orphic 'first born' with Christ: 1n above.

Of love's dislike, or pride, was to be found,
Whom he therefore with equal honour crowned. 35

[6]
With him he reigned before all time prescribed,
In endless glory and immortal might,
Together with that third from them derived,
Most wise, most holy, most almighty Spright,
Whose kingdom's throne no thought of earthly wight 40
Can comprehend, much less my trembling verse
With equal words can hope it to rehearse.

[7]
Yet, O most blessed Spirit, pure lamp of light,
Eternal spring of grace and wisdom true,
Vouchsafe to shed into my barren spright 45
Some little drop of thy celestial dew
That may my rhymes with sweet infuse imbrue;
And give me words equal unto my thought
To tell the marvels by thy mercy wrought.

[8]
Yet being pregnant still with powerful grace, 50
And full of fruitful love that loves to get

34. love's dislike: aversion to love.
39. Most . . . Spright: the third member of the Christian Trinity, the Holy Spirit.
43–4. O . . . true: echoes the traditional invocation: *Veni, sancte Spiritus: Veni, lumen cordium . . . Lava quod est sordidum* (Come Holy Spirit; come, light of hearts . . . wash clean what is corrupt). *Wisdom* is the last of the gifts of the Holy Spirit, opposite of commitment to the flesh (Tuve 1966: 101); but it is named here to announce the Wisdom tradition that is the focus of *HHB*. See also the apocryphal book of Wisdom, ch 7.
46–7. drop . . . imbrue: *SC June* 93–6n. The Holy Spirit – identified particularly with love because it is the means by which divine love reaches mankind (Welsford 1967: 163 citing Aquinas) – is invoked because it 'worketh so mightily by the preaching of the word' (Geneva gloss on John 16: 8) and reveals 'the deep things of God' to us (1 Corinthians 2: 10). *Infuse*, a rare form of *infusion*, = especially the imparting of divine grace (*OED* infusion 2a); *imbrue* = saturate (with moisture): *OED* imbrue *v* 5; contrast the usage at *HL* 13n.
50–3. Yet . . . brood: God as a brooding bird goes back at least to the Church Fathers, but is influenced by the Orphic notion of primal chaos as an egg (1n above). *Pregnant* alludes to the originally Orphic and Hermetic notion that God was hermaphroditic: 'God is most replenished with the fruitfulness of both sexes . . . out of the Divinity of *Orpheus* [Apuleius] produceth this verse of *Jupiter*: *Jove is both male and female, immortal*': Agrippa (1651) 3. 8 (p. 362).
51. get: beget.

Things like himself and to enlarge his race,
His second brood – though not in power so great
(Yet full of beauty) – next he did beget:
An infinite increase of angels bright, 55
All glistering glorious in their Maker's light.

[9]
To them the heaven's illimitable height
(Not this round heaven, which we from hence behold,
Adorned with thousand lamps of burning light
And with ten thousand gems of shining gold) 60
He gave as their inheritance to hold,
That they might serve him in eternal bliss
And be partakers of those joys of his.

[10]
There they in their trinal triplicities
About him wait, and on his will depend, 65
Either with nimble wings to cut the skies
When he them on his messages doth send,
Or on his own dread presence to attend,
Where they behold the glory of his light
And carol hymns of love both day and night. 70

[11]
Both day and night is unto them all one,
For he his beams doth still to them extend
That darkness there appeareth never none;
Ne hath their day, ne hath their bliss, an end,
But there their termless time in pleasure spend: 75

56. *glistering*: sparkling.
59. *lamps*: the stars; the angels live beyond the *primum mobile* of 25–6n.
64. *trinal triplicities*: recalls *FQ*, 1. 12. 39. The angelic hierarchy was divided into three sets of three on the authority of Pseudo-Dionysius, *Celestial Hierarchies* (from God outwards the order goes: Seraphim, Cherubim, Thrones; Dominations, Virtues, Powers; Princedoms, Archangels, Angels).
66–7. *nimble ... send*: the angels (from Greek *angelos* = messenger) run errands. The phrasing recalls the angelic vision at *FQ*, 2. 8. 1–2; the fact that they carol *hymns* suggests the hymnic role of the poet.
71–5. *Both ... spend*: the Heavenly Jerusalem has no need of sun or moon 'for the glory of God did light it: and the Lamb is the light of it. . . . And the gates of it shall not be shut by day: for there shall be no night there': Revelation 21: 23, 25.
72. *still*: always.
75. *termless*: having no temporal or spatial limits.

Ne ever should their happiness decay,
Had not they dared their Lord to disobey.

[12]

But Pride, impatient of long-resting peace,
Did puff them up with greedy bold ambition,
That they 'gan cast their state how to increase 80
Above the fortune of their first condition,
And sit in God's own seat without commission:
The brightest angel, even the Child of Light,
Drew millions more against their God to fight.

[13]

The Almighty, seeing their so bold assay, 85
Kindled the flame of his consuming ire,
And with his only breath them blew away
From heaven's height, to which they did aspire,
To deepest hell and lake of damned fire,
Where they in darkness and dread horror dwell, 90
Hating the happy light from which they fell.

[14]

So that next offspring of the Maker's love,
Next to himself in glorious degree,
Degendering to hate, fell from above
Through pride (for pride and love may ill agree), 95
And now of sin to all ensample be:
How, then, can sinful flesh itself assure,
Sith purest angels fell to be impure?

[15]

But that eternal fount of love and grace,
Still flowing forth his goodness unto all, 100

78–84. But ... fight: the chief archangel Lucifer (light bringer: named at Isaiah 14: 12) persuaded a proportion of the other angels to rebel against God: Revelation 12: 3–9. The details of the tale accrued later.
82. commission: authority.
85. assay: endeavour, attack.
87. only breath: breath alone (implying Holy Spirit and breath as at l. 110). For the fallen angels' fate, see 2 Peter 2: 4 and Jude 6 and, for the *lake*, Revelation 21: 8.
94. Degendering: degenerating: *OED* cites four examples including this, spanning 1539–97 only.
97. assure: *Am* 58 headnote and 1n.

Now seeing left a waste and empty place
In his wide palace through those angels' fall,
Cast to supply the same, and to install
A new unknown colony therein
Whose root from earth's base groundwork should begin.   105

                    [16]
Therefore of clay – base, vile, and next to nought,
Yet formed by wondrous skill and by his might
According to an heavenly pattern wrought
Which he had fashioned in his wise foresight –
He man did make, and breathed a living spright   110
Into his face most beautiful and fair,
Endued with wisdom's riches, heavenly, rare.

                    [17]
Such he him made that he resemble might
Himself, as mortal thing immortal could,
Him to be lord of every living wight.   115
He made by love out of his own like mould,
In whom he might his mighty self behold;
For love doth love the thing beloved to see,
That like itself in lovely shape may be.

                    [18]
But man, forgetful of his Maker's grace   120
No less than angels (whom he did ensue),
Fell from the hope of promised heavenly place
Into the mouth of Death, to sinners due;
And all his offspring into thraldom threw,

103. Cast: resolved. *supply*: make up the deficiency (of).
104. colony: witty because the word derives from Latin *colonus* = tiller of the soil, and man is made from earth.
106–19. Therefore ... be: follows the biblical account in Genesis 2: 7 (man of dust with spirit breathed into him) and 1: 27 ('God created the man in his image'): influenced also by the legend of Prometheus' creation of man from clay (Ovid, *Metamorphoses*, 1. 76–86; his name means 'fore-thinker': cf. Spenser's *wise foresight*); the Hermetic account in *Poimander*, 1. 12 (the first Mind begot Man, a being like himself, carrying his likeness); and *Timaeus*, 29A the creator wants everything to be as good as he is.
112. Endued: HB 135n.
115. lord ... wight: Genesis 1: 26, 28.
116. mould: (1) pattern; (2) earth.
121. ensue: follow.
122–3. Fell ... Death: Genesis 3.

Where they for ever should in bonds remain 125
Of never dead, yet ever-dying, pain

[19]
Till that great Lord of love, which him at first
Made of mere love, and after liked well,
Seeing him lie like creature long accursed
In that deep horror of despaired hell, 130
Him wretch in dool would let no longer dwell,
But cast out of that bondage to redeem,
And pay the price, all were his debt extreme.

[20]
Out of the bosom of eternal bliss,
In which he reigned with his glorious sire, 135
He down descended, like a most demiss
And abject thrall, in flesh's frail attire,
That he for him might pay sin's deadly hire,
And him restore unto that happy state
In which he stood before his hapless fate. 140

[21]
In flesh at first the guilt committed was,
Therefore in flesh it must be satisfied:
Nor spirit, nor angel (though they man surpass)
Could make amends to God for man's misguide,
But only man himself, who self did slide. 145
So, taking flesh of sacred Virgin's womb,
For man's dear sake he did a man become.

128. mere: pure.
130. despaired: hopeless (last *OED* instance in this sense 1581).
131. wretch: substantive or adjective. *dool*: grief.
133. price: 1 Corinthians 6: 20 ('For ye are bought for a price'). *all*: even though.
134–5. Out . . . sire: ct. *HL*, 61–3.
136–8. He . . . hire: Philippians 2: 7–8 ('But he made himself of no reputation, and took on him the form of a servant, and was made like unto men, and was found in shape as a man. He humbled himself, and became obedient unto the death, even the death of the cross'); Romans 6: 23 ('The wages of sin is death: but the gift of God is eternal life, through Jesus Christ our Lord').
136. demiss: humble.
141–2. In . . . satisfied: 1 Corinthians 15: 21 ('For since by man came death, by man came also the resurrection of the dead').
144. misguide: irregularity (this is *OED*'s first citation).

[22]
And that most blessed body, which was born
Without all blemish or reproachful blame,
He freely gave to be both rent and torn   150
Of cruel hands who, with despiteful shame
Reviling him, that them most vile became,
At length him nailed on a gallow tree,
And slew the just by most unjust decree.

[23]
O huge and most unspeakable impression   155
Of love's deep wound, that pierced the piteous heart
Of that dear Lord with so entire affection
And, sharply launching every inner part,
Dolours of death into his soul did dart,
Doing him die that never it deserved,   160
To free his foes that from his hest had swerved.

[24]
What heart can feel least touch of so sore launch,
Or thought can think the depth of so dear wound,
Whose bleeding source their streams yet never staunch,
But still do flow and freshly still redound,   165
To heal the sores of sinful souls unsound,
And cleanse the guilt of that infected crime
Which was enrooted in all fleshly slime?

151. despiteful: (1) insulting; (2) malicious.
152. vile: vilely (from Latin *vilis* = (1) base; (2) cheap, of small price: cf. 138). Cf. Matthew 27: 39 ('And they that passed by, reviled him . . .').
154. just: Acts 3: 14 ('But ye denied the Holy one and the just, and desired a murderer to be given you'); cf. Acts 7: 52.
155–68. O . . . slime: modulation of Cupid's secular arrows (*HL* 121n) via John 19: 34 ('But one of the soldiers with a spear pierced his side, and forthwith came there out blood and water'; Geneva gloss: 'Christ being dead upon the cross, witnesseth by a double sign, that he only is the true satisfaction, and the true washing for the believers').
158. launching: piercing.
159. Dolours: pains.
161. hest: *HL* 44n.
162. launch: shot; but also a spelling variant of lance = spear (155–68n).
165. redound: overflow.
167. infected: morally/spiritually corrupted: *OED*'s first date for this sense is 1570; it also cites *FQ*, 1. 10. 25 ('infected sin').
168. fleshly slime: favourite Spenserianism: e.g., *FQ*, 2. 10. 50, 3. 6. 3.

[25]
O blessed well of love, O flower of grace,
O glorious morning star, O lamp of light;   170
Most lively image of thy father's face,
Eternal King of glory, Lord of might,
Meek Lamb of God before all worlds behight,
How can we thee requite for all this good?
Or what can prize that thy most precious blood?   175

[26]
Yet nought thou askest in lieu of all this love
But love of us for guerdon of thy pain.
Ay me, what can us less than that behove?
Had he required life of us again,
Had it been wrong to ask his own with gain?   180
He gave us life, he it restored lost;
Then life were least, that us so little cost.

[27]
But he our life hath left unto us free:
Free that was thrall, and blessed that was banned;

169–73. O ... God: litany drawing on various biblical sources: *well of love*: John 4: 14 ('the water that I shall give him shall be in him a well of water, springing up into everlasting life'); *flower of grace*: revision of *HB*, 282 under influence of, e.g., John 1: 16 ('And of his fullness have all we received, and grace for grace'); *morning star*: Revelation 22: 16 ('I Jesus . . . am . . . the bright morning star'); *lamp of light*: revising *HB*, 59 (and cf. 43 and n above) via John 1: 9 ('This was that true light'; Geneva gloss: 'Who only and properly deserveth to be called the light, for he shineth of himself and borroweth light of none'); *lively image*: Hebrews 1: 3 (Christ is 'the engraved form of [God's] person'); *King of glory*: Psalm 24: 7–10; *Lord of might*: cf. Ephesians 6: 10 ('be strong in the Lord, and in the power of his might'); *Lamb of God*: John 1: 29 ('Behold that Lamb of God, which taketh away the sin of the world').
173. behight: (1) promised; (2) named; a Spenserian usage: *SC April* 120 gloss.
175. prize: (1) fix the value of; (2) be the price of (nonce meaning: *OED* cites only this line: sense 2b): cf. *price* at 133n above.
177. love of us: our love. *guerdon*: recompense.
178. behove: be proper to.
180. gain: interest.
183–5. life ... loving: Galatians 5: 13–14 ('ye have been called unto liberty: only use not your liberty as an occasion unto the flesh, but by love serve one another. For all the Law is fulfilled in one word, which is this, Thou shalt love thy neighbour as thy self'; Geneva gloss on *liberty*: 'being delivered from the slavery of sin and the flesh').
184. banned: cursed, formally anathematised: *OED* ban *v* II (the modern sense – prohibit – is not historically possible).

Ne aught demands but that we loving be 185
As he himself hath loved us aforehand,
And bound thereto with an eternal band,
Him first to love that us so dearly bought,
And next, our brethren to his image wrought.

[28]
Him first to love great right and reason is, 190
Who first to us our life and being gave;
And after, when we fared had amiss,
Us wretches from the second death did save;
And last the food of life, which now we have,
Even himself in his dear sacrament 195
To feed our hungry souls unto us lent.

[29]
Then next, to love our brethren, that were made
Of that self mould and that self Maker's hand
That we, and to the same again shall fade,
Where they shall have like heritage of land 200
However here on higher steps we stand;
Which also were with self-same price redeemed
That we, however of us light esteemed.

189. *to*: in.
193. *second death*: either death itself (the first death being the fall into sin): Revelation 20: 14; or damnation: Revelation 21: 8.
194–6. *food . . . lent*: the Eucharist, initiated by the Last Supper: e.g., Matthew 26: 26–9: 'Jesus took the bread . . . and break it, and gave it to the disciples, and said, Take, eat: this is my body'. The Geneva gloss carefully explains the Protestant position: this is not transubstantiation (change of substance, bread into flesh) but 'a figurative speech . . . the bread . . . is the sign and sacrament [i.e., symbol: *OED* sense 3b] of his body'. See also John 6: 35: 'I am that bread of life: he that cometh to me shall not hunger'.
196. *lent*: gave.
197. *love*: 183–5n and John 13: 34, 15: 17 ('love one another').
198. *mould*: 116n, and note *OED* mould *sb* 1 sense 2: earth of the grave.
199. *That we* = as we. *same . . . fade*: Genesis 3: 19 (because of his disobedience man shall return to the earth from which he came).
201. *However . . . stand*: even though we may [while alive] have a superior social standing.
202–3. *Which . . . esteemed*: they were redeemed for the same price as we were however much we scorn them.

                    [30]
And were they not, yet since that loving Lord
Commanded us to love them for his sake,   205
Even for his sake, and for his sacred word,
Which in his last bequest he to us spake,
We should them love, and with their needs partake;
Knowing that whatsoe'er to them we give,
We give to him, by whom we all do live.   210

                    [31]
Such mercy he by his most holy rede
Unto us taught and, to approve it true,
Ensampled it by his most righteous deed,
Shewing us mercy (miserable crew)
That we the like should to the wretches show,   215
And love our brethren; thereby to approve
How much himself, that loved us, we love.

                    [32]
Then rouse thyself, O earth, out of thy soil,
In which thou wallowest like to filthy swine,
And dost thy mind in dirty pleasures moil,   220
Unmindful of that dearest Lord of thine:
Lift up to him thy heavy clouded eyne,

207. *last bequest*: John 15: 17 (see 197n), uttered as Jesus prepares to depart from earth.
208–10. *We ... live*: Matthew 25: 40 ('in as much as ye have [clothed and fed] the one of the least of these my brethren, ye have done it unto me').
211–17. *Such ... love*: Luke 6: 36 ('Be ye therefore merciful, as your Father also is merciful').
211. *rede*: counsel.
213. *Ensampled*: exemplified.
218–21. *Then ... thine*: parallels *HL*, 176–89. *Earth* is man, 'of the earth, earthly' (1 Corinthians 15: 47; Geneva gloss: 'wallowing in dirt, and wholly given to an earthly nature'). *Soil*: the mud wallowed in by a wild boar (*OED* soil 3 I. 1). *Swine*: 2 Peter 2: 22 ('the sow that was washed [is returned] to the wallowing in the mire'); also, swine are the biblical symbol of ignorance (Matthew 7: 6: pearl before swine, where *pearl* is 'the most precious heavenly doctrine': Geneva gloss) and evil (Matthew 8); but Spenser also recalls the story of Ulysses' companion Gryllos (Greek for pig) who refused to be changed from pig back to man: *FQ*, 2. 12. 86–7.
220. *moil*: muddy, soil.
222–3. *Lift ... behold*: Job 22: 26 ('lift up thy face unto God') combined with the creation of man in Ovid, *Metamorphoses*, 1. 85–6: 'he gave to man an uplifted face and commanded him to stand erect and turn his gaze to heaven' (cf. *Am* 13. 2n).

That thou his sovereign bounty mayest behold,
And read through love his mercies manifold.

[33]
Begin from first, where he encradled was   225
In simple cratch, wrapped in a wad of hay,
Between the toilful ox and humble ass;
And in what rags, and in how base array
The glory of our heavenly riches lay
When him the silly shepherds came to see,   230
Whom greatest princes sought on lowest knee.

[34]
From thence read on the story of his life,
His humble carriage, his unfaulty ways,
His cankered foes, his fights, his toil, his strife,
His pains, his poverty, his sharp assays,   235
Through which he passed his miserable days,
Offending none, and doing good to all,
Yet being maliced both of great and small.

[35]
And look at last how of most wretched wights
He taken was, betrayed, and false accused;   240
How with most scornful taunts and fell despites
He was reviled, disgraced, and foul abused;
How scourged, how crowned, how buffeted, how bruised;
And lastly, how 'twixt robbers crucified
With bitter wounds through hands, through feet and side.

[36]
Then let thy flinty heart that feels no pain   246
Empierced be with pitiful remorse,
And let thy bowels bleed in every vein

225–31. Begin . . . knee: the nativity, as in Matthew 1, 2 and Luke 2. Luke 2: 7 (Geneva) says Mary 'laid him in a cratch' (= manger; common term for Jesus's crib: *OED* sense 1b).
230. silly: innocent.
235. sharp assays: piercing tribulations.
238. maliced: (1) injured; (2) regarded with malice.
241. fell despites: cruel disdain.
242. reviled: 152n.
243–5. How . . . side: e.g., Matthew 27: 28–39.
246. flinty heart: Romans 2: 5 ('thine hardness, and heart that cannot repent').

At sight of his most sacred heavenly corse
So torn and mangled with malicious force,   250
And let thy soul, whose sins his sorrows wrought,
Melt into tears, and groan in grieved thought.

[37]
With sense whereof whilst so thy softened spirit
Is inly touched and humbled with meek zeal
Through meditation of his endless merit,   255
Lift up thy mind to the author of thy weal,
And to his sovereign mercy do appeal:
Learn him to love, that loved thee so dear,
And in thy breast his blessed image bear.

[38]
With all thy heart, with all thy soul and mind,   260
Thou must him love, and his behests embrace:
All other loves, with which the world doth blind
Weak fancies, and stir up affections base,
Thou must renounce and utterly displace,
And give thyself unto him full and free   265
That full and freely gave himself to thee.

[39]
Then shalt thou feel thy spirit so possessed
And ravished with devouring great desire
Of his dear self that shall thy feeble breast
Inflame with love, and set thee all on fire   270
With burning zeal through every part entire,
That in no earthly thing thou shalt delight,
But in his sweet and amiable sight.

---

256. *weal*: welfare.
259. *breast . . . image*: ct. *HB*, 211–31.
262–4. *All . . . renounce*: Luke 18: 29–30 ('Verily I say unto you, there is no man that hath left house, or parents, or brethren, or wife, or children for the kingdom of God's sake, Which shall not receive much more in this world, and in the world to come life everlasting').
263. *affections*: passions.
267–87. *Then . . . above*: cf. the instructed man's vision of the essence of Beauty, unimpeded by the body, in *Symposium*, 210–11. The *blinded eyes* (280) recall Orphic Cupid: *HL* 226n.
271. *part entire*: inward part: Spenserian usage: *OED* entire *a* II. 11. Cf. *Am* 6. 11 and 85. 9nn.

[40]
Thenceforth all world's desire will in thee die,
And all earth's glory on which men do gaze   275
Seem dirt and dross in thy pure-sighted eye,
Compared to that celestial Beauty's blaze,
Whose glorious beams all fleshly sense doth daze
With admiration of their passing light,
Blinding the eyes and lumining the spright.   280

[41]
Then shall thy ravished soul inspired be
With heavenly thoughts, far above human skill,
And thy bright radiant eyes shall plainly see
The Idea of his pure glory, present still
Before thy face, that all thy spirits shall fill   285
With sweet enragement of celestial Love,
Kindled through sight of those fair things above.

FINIS.

---

279. passing: surpassing.
280. lumining: illuminating.
282. skill: *HB* 221n.
284. Idea: *Am* 88. 9 and n. The Platonic sense of archetype (or, here, essence) is to the fore: meditation on the image of the earthly beloved (*HB* 211–17n) is displaced in *HHL* by meditation of almost Catholic intensity on the internalised image of Christ which leads to an essential vision of the ascended Christ in glory. *still*: 72n.
286. enragement: rapture (in the neo-Platonic sense): Spenserian coinage: *OED*.

An Hymn of Heavenly Beauty

[1]
Rapt with the rage of mine own ravished thought
Through contemplation of those goodly sights
And glorious images in heaven wrought,
Whose wondrous beauty, breathing sweet delights,
Do kindle love in high-conceited sprights: 5
I fain to tell the things that I behold,
But feel my wits to fail and tongue to fold.

[2]
Vouchsafe, then, O thou most almighty Spright,
From whom all gifts of wit and knowledge flow,
To shed into my breast some sparkling light   10
Of thine eternal Truth, that I may show
Some little beams to mortal eyes below
Of that immortal Beauty there with thee,
Which in my weak distraughted mind I see;

[3]
That with the glory of so goodly sight   15
The hearts of men – which fondly here admire
Fair-seeming shows, and feed on vain delight –
Transported with celestial desire
Of those fair forms, may lift themselves up higher,

---

1. Rapt . . . thought: *HHL* 286n; *Am* 3. 12n; and cf. the visionary madness in Plato, *Phaedrus*, 249–50.
3. glorious: (1) illustrious; (2) brilliant.
5. high-conceited: of a high understanding.
6. fain: (1) rejoice; (2) desire.
8. Spright: the Holy Spirit (*HHL* 43–4, 46–7nn).
9. wit: Understanding, the penultimate gift of the Holy Spirit associated with a state of mystical rapture: Tuve 1966: 101 (cf. *HHL* 43–4n); John 14: 26 ('the holy Ghost . . . shall teach you all things').
11. Truth: the Holy Spirit is 'the Spirit of truth' at John 14: 17.
14. distraughted: (1) driven to madness (first *OED* citation 1592); (2) pulled in various directions (Spenserian usage).
16. fondly: foolishly.
19. fair forms: revises *HL*, 193.

And learn to love with zealous humble duty 20
The eternal fountain of that heavenly Beauty.

* * * *

[4]
Beginnning, then, below, with the easy view
Of this base world subject to fleshly eye,
From thence to mount aloft by order due
To contemplation of the immortal sky, 25
Of the sore falcon so I learn to fly,
That flags awhile her fluttering wings beneath,
Till she herself for stronger flight can breathe.

[5]
Then look who list, thy gazeful eyes to feed
With sight of that is fair, look on the frame 30
Of this wide universe, and therein read
The endless kinds of creatures which by name
Thou canst not count, much less their natures aim:
All which are made with wondrous wise respect,
And all with admirable beauty decked. 35

20. zealous: ardently loving. *humble*: Matthew 5: 3 ('Blessed are the poor in spirit, for theirs is the kingdom of heaven').
21. The . . . Beauty: neo-Platonic commonplace: Ellrodt 1960: 25.
22–5. Beginning . . . sky: mystical Christian version of the Platonic movement from specific to universal beauty: *Symposium*, 211C.
26. sore falcon: young unmoulted hawk still with its red plumage (*OED* sore *a* 2).
27. flags: moves feebly: first citations in this sense attributed to Spenser: *OED* flag *v* 3.
28. breathe: take breath (note the bird-as-soul commonplace: *Am* 72. 1-2n).
29–77. Then . . . strive: cf. *HHL* 22–35n. But this account focuses specifically on the neo-Platonic (and especially Plotinian) notion of the perfection, beauty, and ineffable brightness of God which is perceived (and received) in more shadowy form as it emanates down into the created universe. Other than that, Spenser incorporates commonplaces of the Ptolemaic system.
29. list: will. *gazeful*: *HB* 12n.
30. frame: *HHL* 22n.
31. read: scrutinise, interpret (draws on the book of nature and book of the creatures topos: Curtius 1967: 319–26).
32–3. The . . . count: the notion of universal plenitude originates with Genesis 1: 20-4.
33. aim: conjecture.
34. respect: consideration.

[6]
First the earth, on adamantine pillars founded,
Amid the sea engirt with brazen bands;
Then the air, still flitting but yet firmly bounded
On every side with piles of flaming brands
Never consumed nor quenched with mortal hands; 40
And last, that mighty shining crystal wall,
Wherewith he hath encompassed this All.

[7]
By view whereof it plainly may appear
That, still as everything doth upward tend
And further is from earth, so still more clear 45
And fair it grows, till to his perfect end
Of purest Beauty it at last ascend:
Air more than water, fire much more than air,
And heaven than fire appears more pure and fair.

[8]
Look thou no further, but affix thine eye 50
On that bright, shiny, round, still-moving mass,
The house of blessed gods which men call Sky,
All sowed with glistering stars more thick than grass,
Whereof each other doth in brightness pass;
But those two most which, ruling night and day 55
As king and queen, the heavens' empire sway.

[9]
And tell me then, what hast thou ever seen
That to their beauty may compared be?

36–7. *First . . . bands*: 1 Samuel 2: 8 ('the pillars of the earth are the Lord: and he hath set the world upon them'); and see *HL* 89n (*adamantine*). The seas are placed *amid* the earth and their random force constrained: Ovid, *Metamorphoses*, 1. 30–45 in Arthur Golding's translation (1567); and cf. *FQ*, 4. 10. 35.
38. *air*: *HL* 75–98n for the elemental hierarchy; *flitting* = *HHL* 24n.
39. *piles*: lances, darts.
40. *with*: by.
41. *crystal wall*: the *primum mobile*: *HHL* 25–6n.
46. *his*: its.
50–63. *Look . . . seas*: general echo of Wisdom 13: 2–3.
52–3. *house . . . stars*: i.e., the sphere of the fixed stars, beneath which (and above earth) are the planetary spheres (the *gods* Venus, Mars, etc.). *Glistering*: *HHL* 56n.
55. *two*: sun and moon: Genesis 1: 16.

Or can the sight that is most sharp and keen
Endure their captain's flaming head to see? 60
How much less those, much higher in degree,
And so much fairer, and much more than these,
As these are fairer than the land and seas.

[10]
For far above these heavens which here we see,
Be others far exceeding these in light, 65
Not bounded, not corrupt, as these same be,
But infinite in largeness and in height,
Unmoving, uncorrupt, and spotless bright,
That need no sun to illuminate their spheres,
But their own native light far passing theirs. 70

[11]
And as these heavens still by degrees arise
Until they come to their First Mover's bound,
That in his mighty compass doth comprise
And carry all the rest with him around,
So those likewise do by degrees redound, 75
And rise more fair, till they at last arrive
To the most fair, whereto they all do strive.

[12]
Fair is the heaven, where happy souls have place
In full enjoyment of felicity,
Whence they do still behold the glorious face 80
Of the divine eternal majesty;
More fair is that where those Ideas on high

60. *captain's . . . head*: the sun.
64–77. *For . . . strive*: exemplifying the commonplace of the tripartite universe: the sublunary (earth up to the moon's sphere); the celestial (up to the *primum mobile*); the abode of God and the angels (the empyrean heaven).
69–70. *That . . . theirs*: Revelation 22: 5 ('they need no candle, neither light of the Sun: for the Lord God giveth them light').
71–2. *as . . . bound*: i.e., the planetary heavens beneath the *primum mobile*.
73. *comprise*: enclose.
75. *redound*: proceed (Spenserian meaning: *OED* sense 9).
78–81. *Fair . . . majesty*: a commonplace: e.g., 'the empyrean heaven [64–77n], which is the heaven of flame . . . is the place of the blessed spirits': Dante, *Convivio*, 2. 4. 1; 1 Corinthians 13: 12 ('but then shall we see face to face').
82–3. *Ideas . . . Plato*: *Phaedrus*, 247C–E.

Enranged be which Plato so admired,
And pure Intelligences from God inspired.

[13]
Yet fairer is that heaven in which do reign   85
The sovereign Powers and mighty Potentates,
Which in their high protections do contain
All mortal princes and imperial states;
And fairer yet whereas the royal Seats
And heavenly Dominations are set,   90
From whom all earthly governance is fet.

[14]
Yet far more fair be those bright Cherubins,
Which all with golden wings are overdight,
And those eternal burning Seraphins,
Which from their faces dart out fiery light.   95
Yet fairer than they both, and much more bright,
Be the Angels and Archangels, which attend
On God's own person without rest or end.

84. Intelligences: the spirits believed in ancient thought to guide the planetary spheres; by Augustine, Aquinas and others identified with angels.
85. Yet fairer: Christian truth supersedes that of the ancient theologians, however inspired. *reign*: includes the sense astrological power.
86–98. The ... end: see *HHL* 64n. Spenser appears to get the position of the *Angels and Archangels* wrong by putting them closest to God; but he merely follows Revelation 5: see 97–8n below. The functions of the various orders are described in Pseudo-Dionysius, *Celestial Hierarchies*, 7.
89. Seats: Thrones.
91. fet: derived.
92. Cherubins: the normal plural form, *cherubin* being the usual Elizabethan singular.
93. golden wings: Exodus 25: 18, 20 ('And thou shalt make two Cherubims of gold ... And the Cherubims shall stretch their wings on high'); the phrase assimilates *HHL* 1n.
94–5. burning ... light: *Celestial Hierarchies*, 7; Isaiah 6: 2 Geneva gloss: Seraphim are 'Angels, so called, because they were of a fiery colour, to signify that they burnt in the love of God'.
97–8. Angels ... end: Revelation 5: 11 ('I heard the voice of many Angels round about the throne ... and there were ten thousand times ten thousand, and thousand thousands'.) Spenser assumes that these will shine with God's glory; and the Geneva gloss explanation that these are 'the common order of Angels' guarantees that he doesn't make an elementary mistake, as has been supposed.

[15]
These thus in fair each other far excelling,
As to the highest they approach more near, 100
Yet is that highest far beyond all telling
Fairer than all the rest which there appear,
Though all their beauties joined together were.
How, then, can mortal tongue hope to express
The image of such endless perfectness? 105

[16]
Cease, then, my tongue, and lend unto my mind
Leave to bethink how great that Beauty is:
Whose utmost parts so beautiful I find,
How much more those essential parts of his,
His truth, his love, his wisdom, and his bliss, 110
His grace, his doom, his mercy, and his might,
By which he lends us of himself a sight.

[17]
Those unto all he daily doth display,
And show himself in the image of his grace
As in a looking glass, through which he may 115
Be seen of all his creatures vile and base
That are unable else to see his face –
His glorious face which glistereth else so bright
That the angels 'selves cannot endure his sight.

99. fair: fairness (beauty).
106–40. Cease . . . infirmities: the poet moves from utterance to the contemplation invited by God's manifestation of himself in his creation – 'the splendour and grace of his face, whether in the Angelic Mind, in the Soul, or in the material World, is to be called universal beauty. And the impulse towards it is to be called universal love': Ficino, *Commentary*, 5. 4 (Ficino 1944: 170); cit. Renwick 1929: 222–3.
108. utmost parts: the creation as (1) spatially distant from God and (2) his outer manifestation.
110–12. His . . . sight: it was a Christian commonplace that God manifests himself through nature and also his works.
111. doom: judgement.
115. looking glass: the Platonic mirror (e.g., *HL* 190–6n) yields to that of biblical tradition: e.g., 2 Corinthians 3: 18 ('But we all behold as in a mirror the glory of the Lord with open face, and are changed into that same image, from glory to glory . . .'); cf. 78–81n; also Exodus 33: 18–19 ('he said, I beseech thee, show me thy glory. And he answered, I will make all my good go before thee . . . for I will show mercy to whom I will show mercy . . .').

[18]
But we frail wights – whose sight cannot sustain 120
The Sun's bright beams when he on us doth shine,
But that their points rebutted back again
Are dulled – how can we see with feeble eyne
The glory of that majesty divine,
In sight of whom both sun and moon are dark, 125
Compared to his least resplendent spark?

[19]
The means, therefore, which unto us is lent
Him to behold, is on his works to look,
Which he hath made in beauty excellent,
And in the same (as in a brazen book) 130
To read enregistered in every nook
His goodness, which his beauty doth declare:
For all that's good is beautiful and fair.

[20]
Thence gathering plumes of perfect speculation
To imp the wings of thy high flying mind, 135
Mount up aloft through heavenly contemplation
From this dark world, whose damps the soul do blind,
And, like the native brood of eagle's kind,
On that bright Sun of Glory fix thine eyes,
Cleared from gross mists of frail infirmities. 140

123–4. how ... divine: Exodus 33: 20 ('Thou canst not see my face, for there shall no man see me, and live'; Geneva gloss: 'For Moses saw not his face in full majesty, but as man's weakness could bear').
127–33. The ... fair: Psalms 19: 1 ('The heavens declare the glory of God'); Romans 1: 20 ('For the invisible things of him ... are seen by the creation of the world').
130. book: 31n. *brazen* = durable, as in Horace, *Odes*, 3. 30. 1 (I have completed a monument more enduring than brass).
134. plumes: feathers. *speculation*: vision.
135. imp: engraft feathers in a deficient wing in order to improve flight (from falconry).
138. like ... kind: like the offspring of the native eagle: *HL* 69n and Red Cross's encounter with Contemplation at *FQ*, 1. 10. 46–8. At *Ruins of Time*, 421–7 similar imagery is associated with poetic fame.

[21]
Humbled with fear and awe-full reverence,
Before the footstool of his majesty
Throw thyself down with trembling innocence,
Ne dare look up with corruptible eye
On the dread face of that great Deity   145
For fear lest, if he chance to look on thee,
Thou turn to nought, and quite confounded be.

[22]
But lowly fall before his mercy seat,
Close covered with the Lamb's integrity
From the just wrath of his avengeful threat   150
That sits upon the righteous throne on high:
His throne is built upon eternity,
More firm and durable than steel or brass,
Or the hard diamond, which them both doth pass.

[23]
His sceptre is the rod of Righteousness,   155
With which he bruiseth all his foes to dust,
And the great dragon strongly doth repress
Under the rigour of his judgement just;
His seat is Truth, to which the faithful trust,

---

142. footstool: symbol of submission to God's sovereignty: Psalm 99: 5 ('fall down before his footstool: for he is holy'. The Geneva gloss reminds us that it is an emblem of divine presence and identifies it with the ark of the covenant.)
148. mercy seat: the covering of the ark of the covenant (which contained the tables of the law); it was made of gold with a cherub at each end: Exodus 25: 17–21 and cf. 93n. Symbol of God's presence (Psalms 80: 1: 'show thy brightness, thou that sittest between the Cherubims').
149–50. Close . . . threat: *HHL* 169–73n; Revelation 5: 6–7 where the Lamb (Christ) is the intercessor between man and God (Geneva gloss: 'Christ, the mediator between God, Angels and men').
149. integrity: sinlessness (*OED* sense 3a).
153–4. steel . . . diamond: cf. 130n; *SC December* emblem gloss; *Am* 9. 10n.
154. pass: surpass.
155. sceptre: Psalm 45: 6 ('Thy throne, O God, is for ever and ever: the sceptre of thy kingdom, is a sceptre of righteousness').
156. bruiseth: crushes.
157–8. And . . . just: Romans 16: 20 ('The God of peace shall tread Satan under your feet shortly'); Revelation 12: 9 ('And the great dragon that old serpent, called the devil and Satan, was cast out'); Genesis 3: 15 ('thou shalt bruise his heel').

From whence proceed her beams so pure and bright 160
That all about him sheddeth glorious light:

[24]
Light far exceeding that bright blazing spark
Which darted is from Titan's flaming head,
That with his beams enlumineth the dark
And dampish air, whereby all things are read; 165
Whose nature yet so much is marvelled
Of mortal wits that it doth much amaze
The greatest wizards which thereon do gaze.

[25]
But that immortal light which there doth shine
Is many thousand times more bright, more clear, 170
More excellent, more glorious, more divine,
Through which to God all mortal actions here,
And even the thoughts of men, do plain appear:
For from the eternal Truth it doth proceed
Through heavenly Virtue, which her beams do breed. 175

[26]
With the great glory of that wondrous light
His throne is all encompassed around,
And hid in his own brightness from the sight
Of all that look thereon with eyes unsound:
And underneath his feet are to be found 180

161–8. That ... gaze: cf. Ficino, *Commentary*, 2. 2 on the divine sun citing Pseudo-Dionysius and Plato, *Republic*, 6 (507E); *HHL* 169–73n; 69–70n above.
163. Titan's: the sun's.
165. read: 31n.
166. marvelled: wondered at.
167. amaze: *Am* 7. 1n.
168. wizards: sages.
172–3. all ... appear: 1 Chronicles 28: 9 ('For the Lord searcheth all hearts, and understandeth all the imaginations of thoughts').
174–5. Truth ... beams: see Ripa 1603: 499–501 for the sun as Truth's emblem; pp. 510–12 for Virtue with a sun over her heart.
176–9. glory ... unsound: 1 Timothy 6: 16 (God 'dwelleth in the light that none can attain unto, whom never man saw').

Thunder and lightning and tempestuous fire,
The instruments of his avenging ire.

[27]
There in his bosom Sapience doth sit,
The sovereign darling of the deity,
Clad like a queen in royal robes most fit   185
For so great power and peerless majesty,
And all with gems and jewels gorgeously
Adorned that brighter than the stars appear
And make her native brightness seem more clear.

[28]
And on her head a crown of purest gold   190
Is set in sign of highest sovereignty,
And in her hand a sceptre she doth hold,
With which she rules the house of God on high,
And manageth the ever-moving sky,
And in the same these lower creatures all,   195
Subjected to her power imperial.

[29]
Both heaven and earth obey unto her will,
And all the creatures which they both contain;

181–2. Thunder ... ire: traditional manifestations of divine power and wrath: Exodus 9: 23 ('and the Lord sent thunder and hail, and lightning upon the ground'; Geneva gloss on *lightning*: 'Hebrew, fire walked'); Revelation 4: 5 ('And out of the throne proceeded lightnings, and thunderings . . . and there were seven lamps of fire burning before the throne').

183–96. Sapience ... imperial: see headnote above. For the iconography, see Tuve 1940 in ed. 1970: 134–5. As the dedicatee Margaret, Countess of Cumberland, was known for her interest in alchemy (Quitslund 1985: 187, 190), Sapience may also recall the alchemists' mystic sister, the *anima* figure who held the key to the work: Jung (1968) fig. 140.

183–4. bosom ... deity: Proverbs 8: 30 ('Then was I with him as a nourisher, and I was daily his delight'); she is 'assistant of [God's] seats' at Wisdom 9: 4 (Douai-Rheims Bible, 1609).

188–9. brighter ... clear: Wisdom 7: 29–30 ('she is more beautiful than the sun, and above all disposition of the stars').

193. house ... high: Ecclesiasticus 24: 7 (Wisdom declares: 'I dwelt in the highest places').

195. in ... same: in doing that.

196. power imperial: Proverbs 8: 15 ('By me kings reign').

197–8. Both ... contain: Proverbs 8: 33 ('Hear instruction, and be ye wise, and refuse it not').

For of her fulness, which the world doth fill,
They all partake, and do in state remain 200
As their great Maker did at first ordain,
Through observation of her high behest,
By which they first were made and still increased.

[30]
The fairness of her face no tongue can tell,
For she the daughters of all women's race, 205
And angels eke, in beauty doth excel,
Sparkled on her from God's own glorious face,
And more increased by her own goodly grace,
That it doth far exceed all human thought,
Ne can on earth compared be to aught. 210

[31]
Ne could that painter (had he lived yet),
Which pictured Venus with so curious quill
That all posterity admired it,
Have portrayed this for all his mastering skill;
Ne she herself, had she remained still 215
And were as fair as fabling wits do feign,
Could once come near this beauty sovereign.

[32]
But had those wits (the wonders of their days),
Or that sweet Teian poet (which did spend

199–200. For . . . partake: Wisdom 1: 6, 7 ('The spirit of wisdom is gentle . . . the Spirit of our Lord hath replenished the whole world'): one of the texts that led to the identification of Wisdom with the Holy Spirit (superseded by Wisdom as Christ: *Var* 1. 560–1 and headnote above).
200. state remain: Proverbs 8: 29–30 ('when he appointed the foundations of the earth. Then was I with him').
204–10. fairness . . . aught: Wisdom 7: 26 ('She is the brightness of eternal light, and the unspotted glass of God's majesty, and the image of his goodness'); Ficino, *Commentary*, 6. 10 ('Wisdom is the most beautiful of all things'; Ficino 1944: 202).
211. painter: Apelles, whose painting of Venus rising from the waves was famous: e.g., Pliny, *Natural History*, 35. 36. 87, 91–2.
212. curious quill: intricate brush.
215. she: Venus.
219–20. Teian . . . praise: Anacreon (*Am* headnote 2), born in Teos, whose *Ode* 57 describes an engraving of Venus on a salver (and cf. *Ode* 5). Note the suggestion that we are dealing with the Platonic notion (*Republic*, 10) of art as imitation of reality.

His plenteous vein in setting forth her praise), 220
Seen but a glimpse of this which I pretend,
How wondrously would he her face commend
Above that idol of his feigning thought,
That all the world should with his rhymes be fraught?

[33]
How then dare I, the novice of his art, 225
Presume to picture so divine a wight,
Or hope to express her least perfection's part,
Whose beauty fills the heavens with her light,
And darks the earth with shadow of her sight?
Ah, gentle Muse, thou art too weak and faint 230
The portrait of so heavenly hue to paint.

[34]
Let angels, which her goodly face behold
And see at will, her sovereign praises sing,
And those most sacred mysteries unfold
Of that fair love of mighty heaven's king: 235
Enough is me to admire so heavenly thing
And, being thus with her huge love possessed,
In the only wonder of herself to rest.

[35]
But whoso may, thrice-happy man him hold
Of all on earth, whom God so much doth grace, 240
And lets his own beloved to behold:
For in the view of her celestial face
All joy, all bliss, all happiness, have place,
Ne aught on earth can want unto the wight
Who of herself can win the wishful sight. 245

---

220. *vein*: genius (*OED* sense 11).
221. *pretend*: (1) assert; (2) lay claim to.
224. *fraught*: *Am* 76. 1n.
230. *Muse*: a composite figure in Spenser: e.g., *FQ*, 1 proem; but here recalling Du Bartas's *La Muse chrétienne* (1574). Most important, she is female, and cannot compare with Sapience.
238. *only*: unique.
239. *thrice-happy*: supersedes *HL*, 209.
245. *wishful*: desired.

[36]

For she out of her secret treasury
Plenty of riches forth on him will pour,
Even heavenly riches, which there hidden lie
Within the closet of her chastest bower,
The external portion of her precious dower, 250
Which mighty God hath given to her free,
And to all those which thereof worthy be.

[37]

None thereof worthy be but those whom she
Vouchsafeth to her presence to receive,
And letteth them her lovely face to see, 255
Whereof such wondrous pleasures they conceive,
And sweet contentment, that it doth bereave
Their soul of sense, through infinite delight,
And them transport from flesh into the spright,

[38]

In which they see such admirable things 260
As carries them into an ecstasy,
And hear such heavenly notes and carollings
Of God's high praise that fills the brazen sky,
And feel such joy and pleasure inwardly,
That maketh them all worldly cares forget, 265
And only think on that before them set.

---

246. *secret treasury*: Baruch 3: 15 ('who has entered her treasure house?'; Jerusalem Bible).
248. *riches . . . lie*: Ephesians 3: 8–9 ('the unsearchable riches of Christ . . . the fellowship of the mystery . . ., which from the beginning of the world hath been hid in God, who hath created all things by Jesus Christ'); Proverbs 8: 21 as at 250n.
249. *bower*: chamber.
250. *dower*: dowry: combines Proverbs 8: 21 ('I . . . cause them that love me, to inherit substance') with Wisdom 8: 2 ('I resolved to have [Wisdom] as my bride'; Jerusalem).
252. *those . . . be*: possibly Calvinist, but a common biblical idea; and cf. Wisdom 8: 20 ('knowing I could not master Wisdom but by the gift of God'; Jerusalem).
255–9. *face . . . spright*: Wisdom 6: 13–14 ('Wisdom is clear, and such as never fadeth, and is easily seen of them that love her').
261. *ecstasy*: rapture of soul (neo-Platonic).
263. *brazen*: referring to the sound of angelic trumpets; first *OED* citation (sense 2).

[39]
Ne from henceforth doth any fleshly sense,
Or idle thought of earthly things, remain,
But all that erst seemed sweet seems now offence,
And all that pleased erst now seems to pain.   270
Their joy, their comfort, their desire, their gain,
Is fixed all on that which now they see:
All other sights but feigned shadows be.

[40]
And that fair lamp, which useth to inflame
The hearts of men with self-consuming fire,   275
Thenceforth seems foul and full of sinful blame;
And all that pomp to which proud minds aspire
By name of honour, and so much desire,
Seems to them baseness, and all riches dross,
And all mirth sadness, and all lucre loss.   280

[41]
So full their eyes are of that glorious sight,
And senses fraught with such satiety,
That in nought else on earth they can delight
But in the aspect of that felicity
Which they have written in their inward eye;   285
On which they feed, and in their fastened mind
All happy joy and full contentment find.

[42]
Ah, then, my hungry soul, which long hast fed
On idle fancies of thy foolish thought
And, with false beauty's flattering bait misled,   290

267–70. Ne ... pain: cf. the description of the ecstasy at 2 Corinthians 12: 2–4; also 1 Corinthians 13: 11–12 ('when I became a man, I put away childish things. For now we see through a glass darkly: but then shall we see face to face').
274. fair lamp: earthly female beauty: *HHL* 169–72n.
277–80. pomp ... loss: cf. the superiority of Wisdom to material wealth at Job 28: 15–20.
282. fraught: 224n.
284. aspect: *HB* 245n.
285. inward eye: *HHL* 267–87n; Wind 1967: 58 on the identification of closed eyes with initiation; Plato, *Symposium*, 219A (intellectual sight improves as external light wanes).
286. fastened: fixed steadfastly.

Hast after vain, deceitful shadows sought,
Which all are fled, and now have left thee nought
But late repentance through thy folly's prief:
Ah, cease to gaze on matter of thy grief,

[43]

And look at last up to that sovereign light,   295
From whose pure beams all perfect Beauty springs,
That kindleth love in every godly spright,
Even the love of God, which loathing brings
Of this vile world and these gay-seeming things;
With whose sweet Pleasures being so possessed,   300
Thy straying thoughts henceforth for ever rest.

293. prief: experience (*OED* proof *sb* II. 5).
300. Pleasures: superseding *HL* 287n.
301. rest: the eternal 'sabbath' also hinted at in *FQ*, 7. 8. 2; it resolves the *restlessness* of *HB*, 73. The omission of *finis* (as at the end of the previous three hymns) may be deliberate, suggesting the rest beyond mortality's limits.

Four Hymns: Textual Notes

Copy text is the handsomely printed quarto of 1596, the only edition during Spenser's lifetime. The only textual problems relevant to the present edition are the following:

HL
228. This very long line is divided in 1596 after *thousand*, with the following word, *swords*, slightly indented. There seems no reason to attach particular significance to this precise division; nor is there any reason to suppose that it is especially significant that the stanza is one line short of the normal total, 7.

HHB
165. And dampish] emended Hughes 1715; The dark & dampish (1596); The darke damp (1611 folio *Works*).
170. many thousand times more bright, more clear] folio reading; 1596 omits more bright. Renwick 1929 conjectures many thousand thousand times more clear.

Prothalamion

Or
A Spousal Verse made by Edmund Spenser.

In Honour of the Double Marriage of the two Honourable and Virtuous Ladies, the Lady Elizabeth and the Lady Katherine Somerset, Daughters to the Right Honourable the Earl of Worcester and espoused to the two worthy gentlemen, Mr Henry Guildford, and Mr William Petre, Esquires.

Headnote

Title: from Greek *pros* = before (in the temporal sense) + *thalamos* = bridal chamber: i.e., a pre-wedding song (or, engagement gift). Although the genre itself was known, the title was coined by Spenser on the model of *epithalamium*, the title-page explaining that it is a 'spousal verse' (*spousal* could mean either marriage or betrothal: *OED* sense 2; and see *FQ*, 1. 10. 4: 'Though spoused, yet wanting wedlock's solemnize'). The title-page also announces the occasion: *Proth* was written to celebrate the double betrothal (and forthcoming marriage) of Elizabeth and Katherine Somerset, eldest daughters of Edward Somerset (who had recently – 1589 – succeeded his father to become the fourth Earl of Worcester) to, respectively, Henry Guildford of Hemstead Place, Kent and William Petre (born 1575, son of Sir John Petre; his father was later created Baron Petre of Writtle and became a Roman Catholic convert): Renwick 1929: 224. The poem was published in 1596 as a single slim quarto bearing the imprint of Spenser's publisher, William Ponsonby. The fact that it had not been entered in the Stationers' Register has led to the inference that it was circulated privately among relevant families – an inference that should, perhaps, be dismissed, not only because virtually half of the books published at this period were not entered in the Register, but also because of the poem's obviously public nature.

As well as allusions to Ovid, Virgil, etc. as detailed in the notes, *Proth* is indebted to William Vallans's *A Tale of Two Swans* (1590: for parallels, see *Var* 2. 667–9) and, possibly, John Leland's *Cygnea Cantio* (1545) and the *De Connubio Tamae et Isis* (1586), a poem cited in fragments in William Camden's *Britannia* and which, like Leland's, follows the pattern of a river journey surveying sites of historic interest. *Proth* celebrates the betrothal in the form of a water fête: the brides' barge is rowed down the Lea, which enters the Thames opposite Greenwich (where the court was in residence during the summer of 1596); it then proceeds up the Thames to Essex House, where the brides are greeted by Essex and the bridegrooms. During their journey they are accompanied by court ladies (the 'nymphs'). Despite *Proth's* spring setting, the betrothal appears to have occurred in late August or September (Essex arrived at court after the Cadiz expedition on 11 August; the court left Greenwich on 1 October; the marriage took place at Essex House on 8 November 1596: Dan Norton cit. Fowler 1975: 60). The spring setting is thus symbolic, invoking the Chloris/Flora myth as a neo-Platonic allegory of the infusion of love, as well as in its more naturalistic significance as a statement of male capture of the virginal female (which is also underpinned by allusions to the rapes of Proserpina and of Leda and the attempted rape of Daphne: see 2, 13–14, 22, 24–8, 30, 32 nn and Rogers 1977).

Spenser's intrusion as melancholic malcontent (stanzas 1, 8) constitutes one of *Proth*'s most striking features, complemented as it is by a narrative progression which begins with the author's retreat, proceeds to pastoral vision, and terminates in historical eulogy and prophecy: Miller 1983: 217; Cheney 1990, 1994. We may agree with Cheney that this suggests a continuation of the impetus of *FQ* and registers an authorial concern with reconstituting his public role after his engagement with pastoral in Book 6, the last published book of the epic (1596). We may also agree that an Arthurian Essex is central to *Proth*, possibly even pointing the way for a continuation of the *FQ* in his favour (see Hieatt 1988, 1990, 1991). But we must also acknowledge that it does so in part by recording the difficulty felt by the middle-aged poet adapting to the younger generation of Elizabethans and the inevitably restless (even apocalyptic) mood of the 1590s, so that *Proth* is shot through with the nostalgia characteristic of its decade even as it traces the rise of the new men. The poem's narrative thus resides (1) in the poet's disillusionment with the court as it was, and as it received his *FQ* (in silence, with no additional pension or award) and (2) in his espousal of a future guaranteed by Essex, both as his patron and as the nation's salvation.

If this seems removed from the world of the Somerset daughters' betrothal, we must recall that *Proth* is a public work, the exoteric version of the private and personal *Epith*. The betrothal it celebrates is dynastic with national implications. Thus Somerset, the brides' father, was a Roman Catholic, yet also a favourite of the queen's (who remarked fondly on his ability to reconcile

Catholic fervour with the loyalty of a good subject: *DNB* citing Lloyd's *State Worthies* (1766)). This yields the clue that the poem is concerned with 'spousal' in specific and general senses: that the double betrothal of the male and female pairs enacts a tetradic model of concord that is the focus for a celebration of courtly religious union (Catholic subject with Protestant prince) testifying to the queen's magnanimous tolerance at precisely the moment when anti-Catholic fervour and Protestant triumphalism were at their height after Essex's defeat of the Spaniards at Cadiz (147n; this allies the subject of *Proth* with *FQ* 4, in which the book's themes of concord and friendship, symbolising personal union as an image of cosmic and national union, culminate in a river marriage of patriotic magnitude, glorifying as it does English history, learning and naval power through the wedding of Thames and Medway; the latter being the site of the new naval base at Chatham). Essex is the pivot between the poet (for whom Essex is Leicester's natural successor: 134–5 and 137–9nn) and the brides (whose father was a friend of Essex: Strong 1987: 27). As Hesperus he is an Arthurian hero (164–5n) linked to the world of Spenser's Arthurian epic and pointing to a reinvigoration of Elizabethan imperial and chivalric ideals. He is also, like Somerset and the dead Leicester, a Knight of the Garter, and the importance of the Order for the poem cannot be overestimated: it enters *Proth* explicitly at stanzas 8–9 by invoking Essex as the new 'flower of chivalry' who has displaced the discredited Knights Templar and followed in Leicester's footsteps by inhabiting (and renaming) Leicester House (134–5n). Essex and Leicester thus double each other as ghost and ghosted and (perhaps) the most important of *Proth*'s various sets of twins.

Moreover, Essex's triumphs against Spain will be sung (like *Proth* itself) 'Upon the bridal day, which is not long': *not* the 'bridal day' of the Somerset daughters; rather, the day some 9 days after that, 17 November, when the queen's accession and marriage to her realm were celebrated annually with knightly jousts led, until 1590, by the venerable Garter knight, Sir Henry Lee (159–60n; Yates 1975: 89–94, 100–11; Strong (1987) ch. 5), who may even be wittily hinted at in ll. 115–18. A national as well as court celebration, it was matched in the earlier part of the year by an equally public annual celebration that took place by the Thames, either at Whitehall or Greenwich, on 23 April: this was the grand Garter Feast, presided over by the monarch as head of the Order and attended by all available Knights. Do we not have here another clue to *Proth*'s seasonal symbolism? It is not just a spring poem but, with its numerous references to Chloris/Flora, an *April* poem (the rites of Flora were celebrated, according to Ovid, *Fasti*, 5. 185–6, from the end of April into the beginning of May) in part for the reasons adduced above but also to evoke the date of the Garter Feast.

Into this pattern of national and courtly eulogy is woven a particular intertextual strand involving Virgil's *Aeneid*, 8, the book in which Trojan Aeneas, having landed in Latium, is granted a prophetic vision of the founding of Rome and allies himself with King Evander and his son, Pallas. To the allusions recorded below (116, 164–5nn) may be added the assimilation of Essex to Hercules (148), which recalls the feast of Hercules and the account of his heroic destruction of Cacus at *Aeneid*, 8. 185–305, and Essex's descent from his 'high towers' (163), which evokes Aeneas's magnanimous and humble stooping as he enters his kinsman King Evander's low palace door (formerly entered by a stooping victorious Hercules) at *Aeneid*, 8. 362-8. The intertextual allying of Essex with Aeneas and Evander's son, Pallas (164–5n), together with the other parallels, affiliates *Proth* with its London ending with the *Aeneid* book which not only begins but also ends with a prophecy of Rome's creation and its imperial success under Augustus, and has as its concern an alliance that guarantees the safety of the empire of the west (*Aeneid*, 8. 147–50). The Elizabethan significance of this lies in the queen's claim (now voiced for propaganda purposes only) to be descended from Aeneas; the mythologisation of London as second Rome (or Troynovant); and the queen's consequent insistence that she had a claim to the papal empire, which was regarded as a continuation of the Roman empire founded by Augustus.

For those with more finely-attuned ears, King Evander – 'beset with years' (*rex obstitus aevo*: *Aeneid*, 8. 307) – presides as the voice of the old generation (equivalent in Virgil's text to dead Leicester and the ageing Queen Elizabeth in Spenser's), just as Aeneas and Pallas together evoke Essex as the incarnate future, a soldier courtier of such promise that he is a two-in-one, the supreme champion of Elizabeth's Protestant claim to the papal empire into the imaginable future. Not only that, he also transcends those two lesser 'gentle knights', the bridegrooms (169), to reach out to the Heavenly Twins, Castor and Pollux, the zodiacal sign Gemini. The point here is that they were the guardians of Rome (Tooke 1713: 352) and that their sister Helen was the cause of the Trojan war that led to Aeneas's flight to Latium in the first place: 42–4n; Ross 1648: 160–6.

Proth enacts its concern with the Twins structurally, since its 18-line stanzas recall the Ptolemaic star total for Gemini: Fowler 1964: 175 (the total would be used under slightly different circumstances in the Caroline masque: Brooks-Davies 1983: 100–1, 105, 119, 120, 122); while the poem's line total, 180, mimes the half-day semicircle (180°) of the sun's progress from morning (stanza 1) to evening (stanza 10): Fowler 1975: 66, and see his ch. 4 *passim* for further astronomical symbolism. These numerological features ally it with *Epith*, suggesting again Spenser's concern to insist on the cosmic significance of his themes. Yet, if Fowler is right about *Proth's* numerological structure – indeed, even if he is only partly right – the poem is a structural *tour de force* of considerably greater magnitude than *Epith*. One reason for this must be that Spenser was attempting to overgo even himself in the new mannerist style – the style that demanded that the art work be of considerable complexity but that all its difficulties should be concealed beneath a surface ease – in order to attract Essex's notice and his patronage (on mannerism, see Fowler 1970: 103–4 (who, however, argues for *Epith*'s greater mannerist complexity); on the patronage question, see Pitcher in *SpE*, p 254). Spenser effort may have been the greater because he knew that Essex was acquainted with John Donne. Some twenty years younger than Spenser, Donne had accompanied Essex on the Cadiz expedition and had, presumably, written some at least of his brilliantly revolutionary love lyrics by 1596 (we do not know what Spenser and Essex may have seen because the dating of many of Donne's poems is highly problematic). Whether *Proth's* stylistic difference from Spenser's earlier work reflects awareness of Donne's practice, or merely of the general direction poetry was going with the new poets, is impossible to say. The fact remains that, although *Proth* is, like *Epith*, a *canzone* (or ode) – but this time with stanzas of regular length,

Prothalamion 389

and without a *commiato* (see *Am–Epith* headnote, Verse Forms) – it is stylistically rather different from it and Spenser's other work: it still uses myth, but it avoids archaisms; introduces the fashionable malcontent figure (the author himself, in stanza 1); exploits occasionally problematic syntax (even in a modernised text stanza 1 takes some unravelling, as does stanza 8); and revels in particularly outrageous or riddling puns (tongueless River Lee as Sir Henry Lee at 11. 115–18; the birds/brides of the final stanza: see Textual Note and 176n).

Select bibliography

Note: this is a bibliography of works cited in short form in the headnote and notes; it excludes works already listed under *SC*, *Am–Epith* and *Four Hymns*.

Anglo, S. 1969 *Spectacle, Pageantry, and Early Tudor Policy*. Oxford
Berger, H. Jr 1965 'Spenser's *Prothalamion*: An Interpretation'. *Essays in Criticism* 15: 363–80
Cheney, P. 1990 'The Old Poet Presents Himself: *Prothalamion* as a Defense of Spenser's Career'. *Spenser Studies: A Renaissance Poetry Annual* 8 (1987): 211–38
Hieatt, A. K. 1988 'The Passing of Arthur in Malory, Spenser, and Shakespeare: The Avoidance of Closure'. In *The Passing of Arthur: New Essays in Arthurian Tradition* (ed. C. Baswell and W. Sharpe). New York, pp. 173–92
Hieatt, A. K. 1990 'The Projected Continuation of *The Faerie Queene*: Rome Delivered?' *Spenser Studies: A Renaissance Poetry Annual* 8 (1987): 335–42
Hieat, A. K. 1991 'Arthur's Deliverance of Rome? (Yet Again)'. *Spenser Studies: A Renaissance Poetry Annual* 9 (1988): 243–48
Miller, D. L. 1983 'Spenser's Vocation, Spenser's Career'. *ELH: A Journal of English Literary History* 50: 197–231
Norton, D. S. 1944 'Queen Elizabeth's "Bridal day" '. *Modern Language Quarterly* 5: 149–54
Peacham, H. (the Younger) 1612 *Minerva Britanna, or A Garden of Heroical Devises*. London
Rogers, W. E. 1977 'Proserpina in the *Prothalamion*'. *American Notes and Queries* 15: 131–5

Prothalamion

1

Calm was the day, and through the trembling air
Sweet-breathing Zephyrus did softly play –
A gentle spirit, that lightly did delay
Hot Titan's beams, which then did glister fair;
When I – whom sullen Care,   5
Through discontent of my long fruitless stay
In Prince's court, and expectation vain
Of idle hopes (which still do fly away
Like empty shadows), did afflict my brain –
Walked forth to ease my pain   10

---

1. trembling: (1) through heat haze; (2) through apprehension, since *air* is a feminine element (*Am* 55. 7n on *mollis aer*) and *Zephyrus* may mean harm.
2. Zephyrus: west wind of spring, signifying fruitfulness (ct. 1. 6; cf. 1. 104): Catullus 46. 1–3 ('Now spring brings back genial warmth; now the fury of the equinoctial sky is silenced by Zephyrus's pleasant breezes'); Petrarch, *Rime*, 310 ('Zephyrus returns, leading back fine weather, the flowers and the grass'). Associated also with the sanguinic temperament of youth and lust (*Am* 55. 7n), his rape of Chloris suggests a threat (13–14n below), though neo-Platonically it signifies the relationship between chastity, love and beauty: Wind 1967: 116–17. The Orphic *Hymn to Zephyros* addresses the zephyrs as bringing 'deathlike rest' as well as vernal sweetness: Athanassakis 1977: 103; cf. 37 and 42–4nn below on Orpheus and death and Orphism; also 'Orphic Footnote' to *Am–Epith* headnote.
3. gentle: (1) well-born, to accord with the poem's noble subject (cf. 1. 169); (2) courteous; (3) tender (the last two bringing to mind by contrast the rape of Chloris). *spirit*: (1) breath, breeze (Latin *spiritus*); (2) suggesting his daimonic character. *lightly*: (1) unchastely (*OED* light *a* 1, III. 14b); (2) merrily (sense VI. 21; contrast the poet's mood); (3) gently (sense II. 8). *delay*: mitigate, temper: *OED* delay *v* 2.
4. Titan's: the sun's: *SC July* 59 gloss. The pejorative aspects of the name are explained by the poet's disillusionment with the monarch (whose emblem is the sun), and *Psalm* 91: 6 (God's protection from 'the plague that destroyeth at noon-day'). *glister*: sparkle. *fair*: the original spelling, *fayre*, is almost homophonic with contemporary spellings of *fire* (*OED* fire *sb* list of forms).
5. Care: personified at *FQ*, 4. 5. 33–46, where he is a melancholic (*sullen*) emblem of discord. Melancholy opposes the sanguinic temperament: Peacham 1612: 126.
6–7. stay ... court: Spenser had the Kilcolman estate and a pension of £50 a year from Elizabeth, but hoped for more preferment. For a longer complaint, see *Mother Hubberd's Tale* (in *Complaints* 1591), 892–914; 1. 912 ('And will to court for shadows vain to seek') is echoed in *Proth*, 9.

Along the shore of silver-streaming Thames,
Whose rutty bank, the which his river hems,
Was painted all with variable flowers,
And all the meads adorned with dainty gems
Fit to deck maidens' bowers, 15
And crown their paramours
Against the bridal day, which is not long:
  Sweet Thames run softly, till I end my song.

2

There, in a meadow, by the river's side,
A flock of nymphs I chanced to espy – 20
All lovely daughters of the flood thereby,
With goodly greenish locks all loose untied

11. silver-streaming: begins a strand of imagery that implicates the swans (63) and the moon (121). Emblematic of purity (*Am* 77. 5n) and lunar (Agrippa (1651) 1. 24 (p. 54)), the silver balances the sunbeams of 1. 4 to suggest a combination of gold and silver that has overtones of alchemical fusion: Brooks-Davies 1983: 22–9, 85–123. *Thames*: the offspring of Thame and Isis (*FQ* 4. ll. 24–7), hence an emblem of union that anticipates the 'spousal' that is *Proth*'s subject.

12. rutty: *OED* rutty *a* 1 cites this line and glosses 'full of ruts'; but Drayton's *rut* = noise (of sea gods; cit. *OED* rut *sb* 4) is *à propos*: cf. *OED* rout *v* 2 : to roar (of the sea). Hence the banks are noisy with rushing water, which must be hushed (*run softly*). However: *rutty* is also a common form for *rooty*. *hems*: confines; but *OED* hem *v* 1, 1 (edge with an embroidered border) is paramount.

13–14. painted ... gems: *painted* = coloured (by any means); *variable* = diverse; *gems* = (1) jewels and (2) buds (*OED* gem *sb*, 4), so that the banks and meadows are like tapestries: compare *Epith* 51n and Penelope's needlework at *Am* 23. But *variable* recalls Ovid, *Fasti*, 5. 213–14: after being raped by Zephyrus, Chloris is given a garden of innumerable different flowers as recompense and renamed Flora: *SC April* 122 gloss, *Am* 4. 11, 13nn; 70. 5–6n. Hales in *Var* 2. 497 notes a similarity with the rape of Proserpine at *Fasti*, 4. 429–30: 'all the colours of nature were there, and the earth shone with the various painted flowers' (*tot fuerant illic, quot habet natura, colores,/pictaque dissimili flore nitebat humus*).

15. bowers: *SC August* 167n.

16. paramours: lovers, with chivalric connotations: *OED* paramour *sb* 2c.

17. Against: in anticipation of; *long*: far away (the line echoes *FQ*, 4. 4. 12: 'Against the tournament which is not long').

20. nymphs: water deities: *SC April* 37n. But Greek *nymphē* = daughter-in-law, bride (*OED* bride *sb* 1, headnote), so that they are a proleptic vision of the bride/birds at 37ff. See 23n.

21. flood: river.

22. goodly: beautiful. *greenish ... untied*: for unbound hair, see *Am* 37. 6n and *Epith* 154n. *Green* suggests fertility and, specifically, the mythological *green one*, Chloris: 13–14n.

As each had been a bride;
And each one had a little wicker basket
Made of fine twigs entrailed curiously, 25
In which they gathered flowers to fill their flasket,
And with fine fingers cropped full featously
The tender stalks on hie.
Of every sort which in that meadow grew
They gathered some: the violet pallid blue, 30
The little daisy that at evening closes,
The virgin lily and the primrose true,

23. *bride*: woman about to be married (*OED* bride *sb* 1 I. 1).
24–8. *And . . . hie*: flower gathering was an occupation associated with Flora's month, April: Ovid, *Fasti*, 5. 185–6; Fowler 1975: 69. Compare the Hours who approach the newly crowned Flora in *Fasti*, 5. 217–18: 'the Hours assemble . . . and gather our gifts in light baskets'. But the passage also recalls the rape of Proserpine (30, 32nn below) and contains other omens of loss of virginity because the flowers are presented to the men (34).
25. *entrailed*: entwined: *SC August*, 30. (*OED* cites only three examples, two of them from Spenser.) *curiously*: skilfully.
26. *flasket*: long shallow basket into which the flowers are transferred.
27. *fine*: delicate. *featously*: nimbly, elegantly: *OED* gives early seventeeth-century dates for last instances of both senses. The flower culling echoes the rape of Chloris, anticipating bridal loss of virginity in a ritual that is at once celebratory and elegiac.
28. *on hie*: with haste; variant of the phrase *in hie*, often used as a rhyme filler: *OED* hie *sb*.
30. *violet*: Venerean (*Epith* 302n), it is also associated with Chloris and signi-fies maidenly modesty: D'Ancona 1983: 94. It was one of the flowers being gathered by Proserpina's maidens before she was raped by Pluto: Ovid, *Fasti*, 4. 437. Cf. the flower blazon at *Am* 64. *pallid*: first *OED* examples from Spenser, who appears to connect it with death (here, death of the virgin self); though it is a conventional qualifier of *violets*: Virgil, *Eclogues*, 2. 47 (*pallentis violas*); Petrarch, *Rime*, 156, pale violets of love (*amorosette et pallide viole*).
31. *daisy*: = love: *SC June* 6–8n. Evening closure suggests virginal shyness on the wedding night.
32. *lily*: *Epith* 43, 302nn, *Am* 1. 1n. White lilies (*lilia alba*) were gathered by Proserpina before her rape: Ovid, *Fasti*, 4. 442. *primrose true*: primrose or cowslip, both either *primula vera* or *verbasculum* in Spenser's time: William Turner, *Libellus de Re Herbaria* (1538); *The Names of Herbs* (1548), facsimile, Britten, J. *et al.* (eds) 1965 (Ray Society: London), pp. 44, 79. Latin *ver* (sub-stantive) = spring; *verus* (adjective) = true. The alternative name *arthritica* (Turner 1538: 44) suggests a Spenserian – even Donnean – joke: it is 'good against' gout and joint-stiffness (Salmon (1678) 1. 5 (p. 125)) and so is unnec-essary for the nimble-fingered nymphs. Like the *violet* it is 5–petalled and so appropriate to marriage: *Epith* 80n. For the primrose of love, see Donne's 'The Primrose'.

With store of vermeil roses,
To deck their bridegrooms' posies
Against the bridal day, which was not long: 35
Sweet Thames run softly, till I end my song.

3

With that I saw two swans of goodly hue
Come softly swimming down along the Lee:
Two fairer birds I yet did never see.
The snow which doth the top of Pindus strew 40

33. store: abundance. *vermeil roses*: dedicated particularly to Venus: *SC April* 59n, *June* 6–8n. But the rose also signifies mortality and frailty: Valeriano 1602: 581–2.
34. bridegrooms' posies: or *poesies*, since the poem *Proth* itself may have been a gift from the bridegrooms: Fowler 1975: 65.
35. bridal: with the swans imminent, note that *bryd* is a mediaeval form for *bird* and that *bird* could mean maiden (*OED* bird I. 1d).
37–54. With . . . song: the stanza that introduces the two swans is particularly rich in puns (e.g., fair/foul [fowl]; Lee/Leda; snow/swan) and verbal doubling (see 41–6n).
37. swans: perhaps influenced by Vallans and Leland (see headnote). Emblematic of the brides because dedicated to Venus (Agrippa (1651) 1. 28 (p. 59)), whose chariot was drawn by a pair of swans: 63n below; emblem of the (female) soul's whiteness and purity (Valeriano 1602: 229–30; see 49–52n below) and, alchemically, of sublimated spirit: Jung 1968: 373. But because of its association with Orpheus as poet and god of mysteries, and with the poet-god Apollo (Valeriano 1602: 230–1), the swan becomes a symbol of Spenser himself as creator-poet and as brooder on his own mortality (the swan sings best before it dies: *SC October* 90 gloss and Spenser's *Ruins of Time*, 589–602, where a vision of the dead Sidney as an elegiac swan is juxtaposed with a vision involving the river Lee; cf. the melancholy of 5n). Valeriano 1602: 230 *s.v.* Musica says that the swan sings sweetest when Zephyrus (2n above) is blowing. The Thames, then as now, was famous for its swans; swans may also have featured decoratively on the brides' barges. The brides' mother's family claimed descent from the Swan Knight: Fowler 1975: 67 citing Dan Norton. *hue*: appearance.
38. down along: cf. 114–15; also Spenser's *Ruins of Time*, 135. *Lee*: *lea* means meadow; and *FQ*, 5. 2. 19 may suggest that *lee* could mean *river* (though there is no other evidence for this). But it is clear that in this *Proth* instance Lee = the tributary of the Thames which enters the river opposite Greenwich: the swans remain on the Lee until stanza 7, when they process through London to Essex House (Hieatt 1991, private communication. I have retained the spelling of the original; modern spelling for the river = Lea).
40. Pindus: traditionally used to signify a high mountain, in Horace, *Odes* 1. 12. 6 it resounds with Orphic music, while in Ovid, *Metamorphoses*, 1. 570 Peneus flows past it in the Thessalian vale of Tempe (see 78–80n below).

Did never whiter show;
Nor Jove himself, when he a swan would be
For love of Leda, whiter did appear;
Yet Leda was (they say) as white as he,
Yet not so white as these, nor nothing near: 45
So purely white they were
That even the gentle stream, the which them bare,
Seemed foul to them, and bade his billows spare
To wet their silken feathers, lest they might
Soil their fair plumes with water not so fair, 50
And mar their beauties bright
That shone as heaven's light
Against their bridal day, which was not long:
   Sweet Thames run softly, till I end my song.

41–6. Did . . . were: rhetorical device of ploce, or what Puttenham (1589) 3. 19 (p. 168) calls 'the doubler' (i.e., 'a speedy iteration of one word, but with some little intermission by inserting one or two words between'). The 'doubling' of *white* is appropriate to this poem of twinning at the point where the two swans are introduced; but its *five*-fold repetition recalls the number of marriage: 32n.

42–4. Jove . . . Leda: Jupiter metamorphosed himself into a swan so that he could rape Leda, wife of the Laconian King Tyndarus. Pregnant at the time by her husband, she gave birth to two eggs; out of one came the immortal pair, Pollux and Helen; out of the other, the mortal pair, Castor and Clytemnestra: *FQ*, 3. 12. 32; Tooke 1713: 350–3 (another version has the girls being born from one egg, the boys from the other). Wind 1967: 167–70 examines the myth as an Orphic allegory of generation (concord from discord) and connects Leda's egg(s) with the Orphic egg of creation, representing the Chaos from which birdlike (winged) Eros (Love) is born (on which, see also the Orphic *Hymn to Protogonos* (Athanassakis 1977: 11) and Aristophanes, *The Birds*, 693–99). The double twinning again relates to *Proth*'s subject; on Castor and Pollux, see 173–4n below.

48. to: compared to.

48–9. spare/To: refrain from.

49–52..lest . . . light: suggesting not just their virginal whiteness but the immaculacy of their heaven-descended souls: Valeriano at 37n. *Heaven's light* also hints at the transformation of the Jovian swan who raped Leda into the constellation Cygnus (Tooke 1713: 350): cf. *Am* 28 headnote and 32. 14n on metamorphosis in Spenser's poems dealing with sexual thresholds.

50. plumes: not just a periphrasis for *feathers*, but bunch of feathers grouped to suggest pride and dignity (i.e., the swans' tail feathers elevated above the water): *OED* plume *sb* 3.

4

Eftsoons the nymphs, which now had flowers their fill, 55
Ran all in haste to see that silver brood
As they came floating on the crystal flood:
Whom, when they saw, they stood amazed still
Their wondering eyes to fill,
Them seemed they never saw a sight so fair 60
Of fowls so lovely, that they sure did deem
Them heavenly born, or to be that same pair
Which through the sky draw Venus' silver team;
For sure they did not seem
To be begot of any earthly seed, 65
But rather angels, or of angels' breed.
Yet were they bred of summer's-heat, they say,
In sweetest season, when each flower and weed
The earth did fresh array:
So fresh they seemed as day – 70
Even their bridal day, which was not long:
   Sweet Thames run softly, till I end my song.

5

Then forth they all out of their baskets drew
Great store of flowers, the honour of the field,
That to the sense did fragrant odours yield, 75
All which upon those goodly birds they threw
And all the waves did strew,

---

55. *Eftsoons*: (soon) afterwards: *OED* eftsoons 3.
56. *silver brood*: conventional Elizabethan epithet (*OED* silver *a* II. 12 : 'having the whiteness or lustre of silver'); but cf. 11n above. *brood* = offspring, particularly when hatched from eggs; the last word in the punning bride/bird sequence (35n above).
58. *amazed still*: *Am* 7. 1n.
62–66. *Them . . . breed*: *Am* 61. 6n on heavenly lineage, but also hinting at the stellified Ledean swan (49–52n above).
63. *Venus' . . . team*: *team* = Latin *temo* (wagon); for Venus's chariot drawn by swans, see Ripa 1603: 51; Tervarent (1958) col. 81. Cheney 1990: 221–2 notes the contextual relevance of Venus's swans at *Aeneid*, 1. 390–6.
67. *summer's-heat*: the pun (characteristic of panegyric) on Somerset, the family surname, works best in the original spelling: *Somers-heat*.
68. *sweetest . . . flower*: hinting at spring and Flora: 13–14n.
69–70. *fresh . . . fresh*: (1) newly, brightly coloured (*OED* fresh *a* 2, 9); (2) untainted (sense 6).
74. *flowers . . . honour*: anticipating Essex at 150; *honour* has its Latin sense of ornament, beauty, as well as the more usual renown.
75. *sense . . . odours*: on perfume and marital ceremonial, see *Epith* 303n.

That like old Peneus' waters they did seem
When, down along by pleasant Tempe's shore,
Scattered with flowers through Thessaly they stream,   80
That they appear, through lilies' plenteous store,
Like a bride's chamber floor.
Two of those nymphs, meanwhile, two garlands bound
Of freshest flowers which in that mead they found,
The which presenting all in trim array,   85
Their snowy foreheads therewithal they crowned
Whilst one did sing this lay,
Prepared against that day –
Against their bridal day – which was not long:
   Sweet Thames run softly, till I end my song.   90

6
'Ye gentle birds – the world's fair ornament,
And heaven's glory – whom this happy hour
Doth lead unto your lovers' blissful bower:
Joy may you have, and gentle hearts' content

78–80. Peneus ... stream: cf. 40n above and *Epith* 307–10n. In the Ovid passage, Peneus is father of virginal Daphne: *Am* 28 headnote; but while Daphne's virginal state is appropriate here, the fact that she remains virginal is not: note that she is metamorphosed into a state of perpetual virginity through her father's power (*Metamorphoses*, 1. 543–52) but that he originally wanted her to marry (*ibid.*, 481–7: 'often the father would say, "Daughter you owe me a son-in-law; you owe me grandchildren" '). The embedded myth – perceived by Berger 1965: 353 – thus functions as an argument for marriage and obedience to patriarchal demands. The reference to flowers alludes to Catullus's epithalamic poem 64. 281–4 (flowers revealed by the spring wind on Peneus's banks brought as a wedding gift).
81. lilies: 32n above. But note that Greek *nymphaia* = water lily (cf. 20n).
82. bride's ... floor: *Epith* 302n.
85. trim: neat, beautiful.
86. foreheads ... crowned: to celebrate the fertility of the coming marriage; but the action of these shadowy doubles for the brides/birds harks back to the Daphne myth, enticing the birds to remain virginal: when metamorphosed, she, too, was crowned (albeit only with laurel leaves) on the banks of the Peneus (simultaneously her feet became roots: *Metamorphoses*, 1. 551; a teasing reminder of 1. 12 above).
87. lay: *SC April* 33 gloss.
91. gentle: 3n above.
92. glory: *Am* 17. 1, 27. 2nn.
93. blissful bower: with a witty sidelong glance at the seductive and pernicious Bower of Bliss in *FQ*, 2. 12.

Of your love's couplement; 95
And let fair Venus, that is queen of love,
With her heart-quelling son upon you smile
(Whose smile, they say, hath virtue to remove
All love's dislike, and friendship's faulty guile
For ever to assoil). 100
Let endless Peace your steadfast hearts accord,
And blessed Plenty wait upon your board,
And let your bed with pleasures chaste abound
That fruitful issue may to you afford
Which may your foes confound 105
And make your joys redound,
Upon your bridal day, which is not long:
   Sweet Thames run softly, till I end my song'.

7

So ended she; and all the rest around
To her redoubled that her undersong, 110
Which said 'Their bridal day should not be long';
And gentle Echo from the neighbour ground
Their accents did resound.

95. couplement: the fact of being coupled: *OED* cites only two instances before this, the earlier 1548 and referring to marriage. At *FQ*, 4. 3. 52 Spenser uses it to describe a double marriage ('mutual couplement').
97. heart . . . son: Cupid: e.g., Ovid, *Metamorphoses*, 1. 454–75. *quell*: (1) overcome; (2) destroy. *smile*: bless; but Venus is also the laughing goddess: *Am* 18. 12n.
98. virtue: power (in the sense of planetary influence).
100. assoil: clear up, resolve: *OED* assoil *v* II. 6 (in its various meanings a favourite Spenserian word).
101–2. Peace . . . Plenty: the coupling implies the fruitfulness bestowed by Ceres: *Am* 62. 4n. *accord* = reconcile, attune.
103–6. let . . . redound: cf. *Epith* 354–424.
104. That . . . afford: that it (the marriage bed) may grant you children.
106. redound: overflow, be plentiful: *OED* redound *v* I. 1, 2 (its original meaning relating to liquids is relevant to the river context); also return, re-echo (senses 4, 5): appropriate because of the refrain and ll. 110–13.
110. redoubled: re-echoed: *OED* redouble *v* 1, 4. But also (sense 1) suggesting arithmetical doubling to conform to *Proth*'s concern with 2s and 4s. *undersong*: subordinate song (i.e., to *Proth*): *SC August* 128n.
112. Echo: *SC June* 52n; *Epith* 18n; she introduces another metamorphic myth and (by implication) another flower related to the Proserpina myth (30, 32nn above), the daffodil, which was also being gathered by Proserpina when Pluto abducted her: Ross 1648: 307. *neighbour ground*: *SC January* 50 and *June* 52 glosses.
113. accents: words: *OED* accent *sb* 5.

So, forth those joyous birds did pass along
Adown the Lee, that to them murmured low 115
As he would speak (but that he lacked a tongue),
Yet did by signs his glad affection show,
Making his stream run slow.
And all the fowl which in his flood did dwell
'Gan flock about these twain, that did excel 120
The rest so far as Cynthia doth shend
The lesser stars. So they, enranged well,
Did on those two attend
And their best service lend
Against their wedding day, which was not long: 125
   Sweet Thames run softly, till I end my song.

8

At length they all to merry London came –
To merry London, my most kindly nurse,
That to me gave this life's first native source;
Though from another place I take my name, 130

114–15. along . . . Lee: 38n above.
116. lacked a tongue: in view of the complaint in stanza 1 (repeated in stanza 8), suggests the poet himself, offering symbolic gestures of congratulation but silenced to really significant utterance (cf. *Malfont* in *FQ*, 5. 9. 25–6, whose tongue is nailed to a post for speaking against the monarch; note that the river-poet's silence seems itself to cause the (poetic) 'stream [to] run slow'). But at *Aeneid*, 8. 86–9 the Tiber slows his course and makes his waves voiceless when Aeneas sacrifices to Juno (goddess of marriage: *Epith* 390–1, 394–5nn).
121. Cynthia: *SC April* 82 gloss; *Epith* 374n. *shend*: shame by superiority: *OED* shend *v* 1b (only instance of this particular meaning; usually = disgrace). Punning on *sheen* = shine (*Am* 15. 12n). There is clearly an allusion to the queen amongst her ladies, confirmed by the echo of Horace, *Odes*, 1. 12. 46–8 ('The Julian constellation shines among all as the moon among the lesser lights') and Vallans: Renwick 1929: 226 and Flower in *Var* 2. 668.
122. enranged: (1) ranked; (2) arranged (a word unique to Spenser: *OED*).
127. merry: pleasant. *London*: William Camden refers to Spenser as 'a Londoner born' in his obituary: Cummings 1971: 315–16.
128. kindly: (1) native; (2) rightful; (3) excellent; (4) benign. *nurse*: one who gives nourishment.
129. source: (1) point of origin; (2) fountain-head (to tie in with the river symbolism and the notion of poetic inspiration: *SC June* 93–6n).
130–1. Though . . . fame: Spenser repeats his claim to be related to the (in fact quite newly ennobled) Spencers of Althorp in *Colin Clout*, 536–51 (the Spencers themselves were wrongly connected with the ancient house of Despencer in a pedigree drawn up by the Clarenceux King of Arms in 1595: Strathmann in *Var* 2. 501–2). He dedicated *Muiopotmos, Mother Hubberd's Tale* and *Tears of the Muses* individually to three of the Spencer daughters.

An house of ancient fame.
There when they came whereas those bricky towers,
The which on Thames' broad aged back do ride,
Where now the studious lawyers have their bowers,
There whilom wont the Templar Knights to bide   135
Till they decayed through pride;
Next whereunto there stands a stately place,
Where oft I gained gifts and goodly grace
Of that great lord which therein wont to dwell,
Whose want too well now feels my friendless case.   140
But, ah! here fits not well
Old woes, but joys, to tell
Against the bridal day which is not long:
    Sweet Thames run softly, till I end my song.

The whole stanza (indeed, the poem, as it celebrates the transition from virgin to bride) is concerned with aetiology and mutation, ancient versus modern and the changes that bring the modern world about.
132. There when: when there.
134–5. lawyers ... Knights: the Temple, a short distance from Leicester House (137), was originally the London home of the great military Order of the Knights Templar. Founded in the twelfth century, they were named after Solomon's Temple in Jerusalem, where they had their headquarters as guardians of pilgrims to the city; they gained international influence as financiers and were eventually crushed by the Church on grounds of heresy. In England Edward II suppressed them and gave the Temple to the Knights of St John, who in turn leased it to the lawyers as what became known as the Inns of Court: Hales in *Var* 2. 502 (the brides' father, the Earl of Worcester, had been admitted a member of the Middle Temple in 1591). Spenser implicitly links the lost ancient knightly orders with the dead Robert Dudley, Earl of Leicester, and looks for their renovation as guarantors of Christendom through the new warrior Essex, Leicester's stepson and successor as Master of the Queen's Horse (stanza 9). As a Knight of the Garter, like Leicester and the brides' father, Essex belonged to the select army of knights that had, under Elizabeth, developed from their Roman Catholic mediaeval origins into a militant Protestant force epitomising Elizabethan 'chevalry' (so that, unlike the Templars, they had survived and adapted in a period of reform): Yates 1975: 108–9; Strong (1987) ch. 6. On Worcester's relationship with and commitment to Essex, see Strong 1987: 27–8.
134. bowers: rooms.
137–9. place ... dwell: Leicester House, London dwelling of the Earl of Leicester, Spenser's employer 1579–80 and original dedicatee of *SC* (see Woudhuysen in *SpE*, pp. 432–3), stood in the grounds of what had been the Outer Temple. Upon his death in 1588 it passed to Robert Devereux, second Earl of Essex, and was renamed Essex House.
138. goodly grace: courteous favour.
140. Whose ... case: my friendless case now feels his absence.
141. fits not: it is inappropriate.

9

Yet therein now doth lodge a noble peer, 145
Great England's glory and the world's wide wonder,
Whose dreadful name late through all Spain did thunder,
And Hercules' two Pillars standing near
Did make to quake and fear:
Fair branch of honour, flower of chivalry, 150
That fillest England with thy triumph's fame,
Joy have thou of thy noble victory,
And endless happiness of thine own name
That promiseth the same:
That through thy prowess and victorious arms 155
Thy country may be freed from foreign harms,
And great Elisa's glorious name may ring
Through all the world, filled with thy wide alarms,
Which some brave Muse may sing
To ages following 160
Upon the bridal day, which is not long:
  Sweet Thames run softly, till I end my song.

145. lodge: reside (without the modern sense of temporariness).
147. Spain: Essex, with Ralegh, Lord Thomas Howard, and Lord Howard of Effingham, successfully stormed, captured, and plundered Cadiz in June 1596, disabling in the process preparations for another Armada: note the tone of Protestant triumphalism (cf. 134–5n). The situation of Cadiz near the Straits of Gibraltar (known from antiquity as the Pillars of Hercules because they were thought to mark the western limit of the hero's travels) prompts an assertion of Elizabethan imperialism: Elizabeth I appropriated the Pillars from the Holy Roman Emperor Charles V as an emblem to assert her claim to empire as a descendant of the Roman emperors: Yates 1975: 23, 57–8, 102–3, 116–17. More specifically, they *quake and fear* because the emblem was also adopted by Charles's son, Philip II, who had instigated the defeated Armada of 1588.
150. honour . . . chivalry: *honour*: 74n above; *chivalry*: *SC* dedicatory poem 4n, here specifically alluding to the Garter. The whole line associates Essex with Spenser's Arthur at *FQ*, 1. 8. 26: 'Faire branch of noblesse, flower of chivalry' (Cheney 1990: 228).
153–4. name . . . same: French *devenir heureux* = become happy (punning on Essex's family name, *Devereux*).
158. alarms: calls to arms: *OED* alarm *sb* II. 4a.
159–60. Which . . . following: which Spenser (or another) may proclaim (even on the wedding day itself) so that succeeding ages may be familiar with them. But the *bridal day* here referred to may not be that of the Earl's daughters: their 8 November wedding date was near enough to the queen's accession day festival – which celebrated Elizabeth's marriage to England – for Spenser to mean the latter: Norton 1944; *SC November* headnote.

10

From those high towers this noble lord issuing
(Like radiant Hesper when his golden hair
In the ocean billows he hath bathed fair),   165
Descended to the river's open viewing
With a great train ensuing.
Above the rest were goodly to be seen
Two gentle knights of lovely face and feature
Beseeming well the bower of any queen,   170
With gifts of wit and ornaments of nature
Fit for so goodly stature
That like the twins of Jove they seemed in sight,
Which deck the baldric of the heavens bright.
They two, forth pacing to the river's side,   175

164–5. Hesper . . . fair: Hesperus as the morning star heralding love (*Epith* 95n); the name also hints at '*Essex*'/*heureux* and perhaps evokes the Arthurian associations of Hesperus, so that Essex is assimilated into a further aspect of Tudor chivalry: Anglo 1969: 79–81; 150n above; headnote above. The phrasing recalls Pallas as the morning star bathing in the ocean at *Aeneid*, 8. 589–91 (though Virgil uses Lucifer, which Spenser replaces with Hesperus to deflect current accusations of Essex's pride and ambition: Fowler 1975: 83). For the importance of *Aeneid*, 8 see headnote.
168. goodly: handsome.
169. gentle knights: the bridegrooms, Henry Guildford and William Petre: see headnote, and 3n above on *gentle*. The phrase is common (e.g., Chaucer, *General Prologue to the Canterbury Tales*, I (A) 72), but may echo *FQ*, 1. 1. 1, the future St George, patron saint of the Garter, as 'a gentle knight'. See174n.
172. goodly: notable, excellent.
173–4. twins . . . bright: Castor and Pollux, stellified as the constellation Gemini, traditional emblems of concord and immortality: Fowler 1964: 166–8; 42–4n above. As guardians of Rome (Ross 1648: 55–7) they relate to the *Aeneid* symbolism and the poem's assertion of Elizabethan imperialism (147, 164–5nn) and as friends of mariners (like the swans: Fowler 1975: 81–2) they are auspicious for future naval exploits by Essex and others: Ovid, *Fasti*, 5. 720 (Ovid celebrates them under June, the month of the Cadiz expedition). Traditionally portrayed as warrior horsemen, they accompanied Orpheus on the Argonautic expedition: *Am* 44. 1n.
173. in sight: when one saw them.
174. baldric = ornamented sword belt worn diagonally across breast from shoulder to under the opposite arm; used by Spenser to refer to the star-studded zodiacal belt: *OED* baldric *sb* 2 citing *FQ*, 5. 1. 11. Also suggests – perhaps as an abstract symbol or as a prophecy for the bridegrooms' future – the brilliant Garter collar, or the Garter itself: on which see Strong 1987: 32–3, 184–5.

Received those two fair brides, their love's delight,
Which, at the appointed tide,
Each one did make his bride,
Against their bridal day, which is not long:
   Sweet Thames run softly, till I end my song.   180

FINIS.

Textual note

The copy text is the 1596 quarto, the only edition printed during Spenser's lifetime. Two points are worth mentioning here: (1) *your* at 102 has been adopted from the folio *Works* of 1611 (it corrects *you* 1596); (2) *brides* at 176 is the 1596 and 1611 reading, but it has caused editorial head-scratching: see footnote and Marsh and Renwick as reported in *Var* 2: 722.

176. *brides*: the original reads 'Brides'. Renwick 1929: 242 prints *birds* after arguing (falsely: see Norton in *Var* 2: 722) that, as *bride* is spelled *bryde* throughout the poem, we have evidence of compositorial confusion in this line. But of course *brides* suggests *birds*, and *vice versa*: 35n. And see Hughes in *Var* 2: 666.
177. *tide*: time (of the betrothal ceremony; of the wedding itself); punning as well on the river's tide.

Appendix

'Fishes' hask': the Problem of *November*, line 16

The following lines have proved an interpretative stumbling block to editors and commentators alike:

> But now sad Winter welked hath the day,
> And Phoebus, weary of his yearly task,
> Ystabled hath his steeds in lowly lay
> And taken up his inn in Fishes' hask.
>
> (ll. 13-16)

Spenser (or, rather, Colin Clout) appears to be saying that the sun passes through the zodiacal sign Pisces in November, an error that is compounded by E.K.'s apparently incompetent gloss 'the sun reigneth, that is, in the sign Pisces all November'. But Pisces belongs to February where, in fact, we find it in *SC* itself since it presides over *February*'s woodcut (fig. 2) just as November's correct sign, Sagittarius, presides over the *November* woodcut (fig. 11). Did Spenser and E.K. make a mistake? Or, in line with the theory that pastoral coded darker (often political) material (see the quotation from Puttenham, Dedicatory Epistle, p. 23n above), is it a signal to probe for a deeper meaning?

W.L. Renwick, one of the most learned of *SC*'s annotators, suspected an oversight on Spenser's part resulting from his (hypothetical) repositioning of *November* which, he argued, was originally designed as the February eclogue. The 'Fishes' hask' reference is thus an uncorrected textual residue (Renwick 1930: 184). However, in view of the facts (1) that *November* sits happily enough in its eleventh place among *SC*'s twelve eclogues because eleven is the number of elegy (*November* headnote) and (2) that Spenser's knowledge of astronomy would not permit him to make such a mistake, we must suspect a meaning that would be available to the poem's early readers. We might even suspect that E.K. was in on this meaning. Better, then, to assume intention on E.K.'s part as well: his gloss is, one could argue, deliberately crass in order to nudge readers into considering what the lines may really signify.

McLane 1961 argued, in the course of his controversial allegorical reading of *SC* that followed Parmenter 1936 in detecting within the poem a continued, if necessarily oblique, attack on the marriage negotiations between Elizabeth and Alençon (see *January*, *March*, and *November* headnotes), that the sun, as the prime monarchical symbol, represents Elizabeth, now resident in the hask (basket) of the Fish, i.e., Alençon, who, as a Catholic, was obliged to eat fish on fast days (McLane 1961: 54).

Cain in Oram *et al.* (ed.) 1989: 188 cites Renwick and McLane without offering a solution of his own. He was rapidly followed by Richardson 1989 and Johnson 1990, both of whom offered interpretations. Indeed, Richardson's thoroughgoing astrological study of *SC* includes a full appendix on the topic. Richardson notes that the sun is indeed in a 'lowly lay' in November in that it is south of the celestial equator and descending towards the solstice; but that when in Pisces it is rising from that lay. Hence the passage has the sun simultaneously at the end of the ecclesiastical year (January to December) and at the beginning of the zodiacal year (March to February), in effect juggling the alternative years that E.K. directs attention to in his General Argument (and see *SC* General Headnote). But Richardson's conclusion is disappointing in merely noting that, seen as Colin's utterance, the lines register the mental disturbance caused by his love melancholy; and seen as a statement by Spenser, their invocation of a sun that is both descending and ascending has some application to the case of Dido, *November*'s subject, at once corporeally dead yet spiritually alive. Richardson's speculations on the word 'hask', however, are even more disappointing. On the evidence of E.K. and the *OED* a hask is a basket (see below for citations), and Richardson assumes that the sign Pisces is being alluded to by Colin/Spenser *as* a basket, admitting that there is no precedent for this. He then hazards the possibility that Spenser refers to Scorpio – appropriate to part of November – via a passage in Dante (*Purgatorio*, XVIII. 76-8) which, according to Richardson, 'says that the Moon in Scorpio made its stars appear to be "fashioned like a bucket all burning" ' (p. 505). However, as he admits (p. 506), the allusion to Scorpio requires a considerable amount of detective work to unveil, Dante's own words being rather less direct on this matter than Richardson at first implies:

> La luna, quasi a mezzanotte tarda,
>   facea le stelle a noi parer piu rade,
>   fatta come un secchion che tutto arda.

(In Bickersteth's virtually literal translation: 'The moon, almost at midnight pacing slow,/shaped like a copper bucket all ablaze,/made the stars seem less numerous to us': G.L. Bickersteth (tr.) 1981 *The Divine Comedy*, Oxford, pp. 390-1.) But of course a bucket isn't a basket, and we certainly could not guess from the *November* passage that Spenser was incorporating a rather abstruse reading of Dante into his eclogue; and so Richardson, after making this suggestion, takes refuge in Colin's confusion of intellect again.

The latest contributor to the debate, Johnson 1990: 200-1, accepts McLane 1961 and complicates him with a pun. *Hask* sounds like *hasp* = (1) clasp; (2) reel of yarn. Ignoring *hask*, he then proceeds to explain that Colin means either that the sun is caught by the fish (because in its clasp or embrace), or that the planetary sun pauses temporarily in the Knot of Pisces (this is the star Alpha Piscium; it marks the point at which the tails of the fishes comprising the constellation Pisces were traditionally imagined to be bound together by cords or lines: Allen, R. H. 1963 *Star Names: Their Lore and Meaning*, New York, p. 342). The significance of the latter would be that it sees the sun as about to leave Pisces for Aries, sign of the vernal equinox and hence of a spring rebirth predicated upon the queen's rejection of the Alençon marriage proposals. This is appropriate to *November* because it is the month of Elizabeth I's accession and the commemorative festivities surrounding it (*November* headnote).

Johnson's reading is ingenious and accords with the interpretative stance adopted in the present edition. The major – indeed, only – problem is that it requires Spenser to have written *hasp* when he so manifestly did not.

My own answer assumes, like Johnson's, that the political reading is correct; that, whatever *SC*'s other meanings, it registers a strong objection to the idea of a French marriage and that, in *November*, Dido 'is' Elizabeth-Elissa. My answer also assumes that the passage does not refer to the zodiacal sign alone but to its correlation with a particular astrological house and the aspect of life governed by that house – a possibility (I would say certainty if the passage is to make readily accessible sense) that no commentator has considered (table of correlations supplied below).

Let us return to Colin's lines and try to understand – with E.K.'s help and an awareness of lexical problems – what they say on a simple level: winter has shortened the days (but *welk* was a mediaevalism in this sense, and, according to *OED*, Spenser was the first to use it in a transitive application; so that a contemporary reader was already having to pause slightly: 13 gloss), and the sun, weary of his annual task, has stabled his horses 'in lowly lay', where *lay* = lodging or lair is another unusual word and possibly a Spenserian first (see 15 gloss). E.K. explains: 'according to the season of the month November when the sun draweth low in the south toward his tropic or return'. So far, no problem.

But then: he has 'taken up his inn in Fishes' haske'. 'Fishes' – italicised and with initial capital in the original texts – is obviously Pisces; 'hask' is a problem because it is apparently yet another Spenserian first: *OED* hask *sb* accepts E.K.'s gloss as its definition, supporting it with one from Florio in 1598 ('fisher's basket, or hask') and a final contemporary quote from Francis Davison which cribs from Spenser's *November*. *OED* cross-refers hassock *sb* I 3: 'A hassock, a basket made of twigs, or rushes' (citing John Baret's *Dictionary* (1573, 1580)). E.K.'s gloss is, of course, the infamous: 'the sun reigneth, that is, in the sign Pisces all November (a hask is a wicker pad wherein they use to carry fish)'. *Pad* itself is a variant of *ped* = lidded hamper or wicker pannier, current from the late 14th century; *OED's* first citation for *pad* in this sense is, again, E.K.'s gloss. *Inn* = astronomical habitation was not uncommon.

E.K.'s gloss is wrong in connecting Pisces with November, as everyone who has commented on the gloss has pointed out: the sun enters Pisces in February and Sagittarius in November (a fact depicted, as we have seen, in the appropriate woodcuts). Maybe, though, we should ignore E.K. for a moment. Colin/Spenser, after all, says something rather different: that the sun is residing 'in Fishes' hask'. What could this mean? First, we should recall that this passage is lexically rather problematic since its contemporary reader was grappling with three neologisms in four lines, though *hask* is clearly the most difficult word, punning as it does also on *haskard* = man of low degree and *haskardly* = base (thus reinforcing 'lowly lay'). The cluster of neologisms is, maybe, a signal to the reader to think about this passage carefully. And a moment's thought produces the suggestion that Colin/Spenser refers to Pisces's traditional correlation with the twelfth astrological house which governed the area of life associated with prisons. It was, after all, a commonly available fact that the twelve astrological houses and their areas of governance were correlated with the zodiacal signs and the planets in the following array (note that the signs appear in their annual sequence starting with the first spring sign, and that the planets appear in their normal order beginning with the furthest from earth):

	House of:	*Sign:*	*Planet:*
1	life	Aries	Saturn
2	wealth/riches	Taurus	Jupiter
3	brothers/sisters	Gemini	Mars
4	parents	Cancer	Sun
5	children	Leo	Venus
6	sickness	Virgo	Mercury
7	enemies/marriage	Libra	Moon

8	death		Scorpio	Saturn
9	travel/religion		Sagittarius	Jupiter
10	trade/honours		Capricorn	Mars
11	friendship		Aquarius	Sun
12	affliction/prison		Pisces	Venus

(Compare the similar table in Eade, J. C. 1984 *The Forgotten Sky A Guide to Astrology in English Literature*, Oxford, p 76.)

I suggest, then, that Colin is making an unproblematic statement to the effect that the sun is residing in the twelfth astrological house, correlated with Pisces, where he is suffering a particularly strong debility because this house was traditionally regarded as the worst (worse even than the eighth), implying the direst situation, in fact. Add this reading to the political one, and we get the following: the sun (Elizabeth) is, in the poetic cycle of Spenser's consideration of the implications of the proposed marriage for English Protestantism, at her lowest point, in a state of (astrological) debility; and the lowest point of all is marked by residence in the twelfth house, correlated with Pisces.

But what about 'hask'? Hassock = basket was new enough to be a puzzle, let alone hask itself; so presumably most readers needed E.K. to tell them that it is a basket for carrying fish in. Most obviously, therefore, 'Fishes' hask' is a periphrasis for 'Fishes' house'. But – because fish are only ever in a basket if they have been caught and trapped, and are usually left gasping and struggling when they are in one – hask becomes a symbol of confinement and affliction. In other words, hask confirms the significance of Pisces when correlated with the twelfth astrological house of affliction and prison (the queen is well and truly trapped if or when she marries Alençon; her [Protestant] people will suffer the direst affliction as a consequence). Moreover, the additional correlation of Pisces and the twelfth astrological house with Venus makes the additional point that Elizabeth is also the queen of love (see *April* headnote and the flower symbol of Colin's lay to Elisa): both as sun queen and as queen of love, therefore, she is at a nadir, imprisoned by circumstances her own making.

What, finally, of E.K.'s crassness? It is true that he does make some mistakes (usually lexical) in the glosses. Nevertheless, this is unlikely to be one of them unless he composed the gloss without checking the text (a possibility that maybe we shouldn't dismiss too readily). Assuming, though, that he wasn't that careless, why should he have perpetrated the error? First, consider the likelihood of his having made a slightly different – if still elementary – mistake: that he put 'sign' for 'house', and that what he thought he was saying was: 'the sun reigneth in the house [correlated with the sign] Pisces all November [the month belonging to the eclogue in which the queen's death is elegiacally commemorated]'. Or second, consider the (perhaps remoter) possibility, already mooted above, that he made such an obvious error in order to direct the reader back to meditate on a passage that was already prickling with difficult verbal signals; that the error was a mode of signalling Spenser's devious political intentions. I prefer the first suggestion; but what is important is that, for the first time, and thanks, initially, to the critics who pioneered our understanding of *SC*'s topical allegory, we now have a reasonable interpretation of the 'Fishes' hask' crux that overcomes most objections and doesn't demand that we accuse Spenser of carelessness or of astronomical or astrological ignorance.

Woodcuts to The Shepherds' Calendar: Figures 1–3

Ianuarie.

Februarie.

Marche.

Bibliography

Note: this list supplements the select bibliographies appended to the headnotes preceding the texts, which often contain the best criticism. *The Spenser Encyclopedia* (ed. Hamilton) (see below) contains articles on texts, topics, themes, historical background, etc. Items marked with an asterisk are especially recommended.

1. General

Alpers, P. J. 1969 *Edmund Spenser: A Critical Anthology*. Harmondsworth, Middlesex

Atkinson, D. R. 1937 *Edmund Spenser: A Bibliographical Supplement*. Baltimore

Berger, H. Jr 1968 *Spenser: A Collection of Critical Essays*. Twentieth Century Views. Englewood Cliffs, N.J.

*Bernard, J. 1989 *Ceremonies of Innocence: Pastoralism in the Poetry of Edmund Spenser*. Cambridge

*Berry, P. 1989 *Of Chastity and Power: Elizabethan Literature and the Unmarried Queen*. London

*Bloom, H. (ed.) 1986 *Modern Critical Views: Edmund Spenser*. New York

Carpenter, F. I. 1923 *A Reference Guide to Edmund Spenser*. Chicago

Cheney, D. 1983 'Spenser's Fortieth Birthday and Related Fictions'. *Spenser Studies: A Renaissance Poetry Annual* 4: 3–31

Craig, J. 1986 'The Queen, Her Handmaid, and Spenser's Career'. *English Studies in Canada* 12: 255–68

*Duffy, E. 1992 *The Stripping of the Altars: Traditional Religion in England 1400–1580*. New Haven and London

ELH 1970 *Critical Essays on Spenser from 'ELH'*. Baltimore

Ettin, A. V. 1984 *Literature and the Pastoral*. New Haven and London

Evett, D. 1990 *Literature and the Visual Arts in Tudor England*. Athens, Georgia

*Fowler, A. D. S. 1977 *Edmund Spenser*. Writers and Their Work. London
Giamatti, A. B. 1984 *Exile and Change in Renaissance Literature*. New Haven and London
Goldberg, J. 1990 *Writing Matter: From the Hands of the English Renaissance*. Stanford, California
*Hamilton, A. C. (ed.) 1972 *Essential Articles for the Study of Edmund Spenser*. Hamden, Connecticut
*Hamilton, A. C. et al. (eds) 1990 *The Spenser Encyclopedia*. Toronto and London
*Helgerson, R. 1983 *Self-Crowned Laureates: Spenser, Jonson, Milton and the Literary System*. Berkeley, Los Angeles and London
*Heninger, S. K. Jr 1974 *Touches of Sweet Harmony: Pythagorean Cosmology and Renaissance Poetics*. San Marino, California
Judson, A. C. 1945 *The Life of Edmund Spenser*. Baltimore
*King, J. N. 1989 *Tudor Royal Iconography*. Princeton, N.J.
Krier, T. M. 1990 *Gazing on Secret Sights: Spenser, Classical Imitation, and the Decorums of Vision*. Ithaca, New York
Lambert, E. Z. 1976 *Placing Sorrow: A Study of the Pastoral Convention from Theocritus to Milton*. Chapel Hill, North Carolina
Levin, H. 1969 *The Myth of the Golden Age in the Renaissance*. Bloomington, Indiana
Logan, G. M. and Teskey, G. (eds) 1989 *Unfolded Tales: Essays on Renaissance Romance*. Ithaca, New York
*Mallette, R. 1981 *Spenser, Milton and Renaissance Pastoral*. Lewisburg, Pennsylvania and London
Marinelli, P. 1971 *Pastoral*. The Critical Idiom. London
May, S. W. 1991 *The Elizabethan Courtier Poets: The Poems and Their Contexts*. Columbia, Missouri
McNeir, W. F. and Provost, F. 1975 *Edmund Spenser: An Annotated Bibliography* 1937–1972. Pittsburgh
Miller, D. L. 1990 'The Writing Thing'. *Diacritics* 20: 17–29
*Miller, J. T. 1986 *Poetic License: Authority and Authorship in Medieval and Renaissance Contexts*. Oxford
Miskimin, A. S. 1975 *The Renaissance Chaucer*. New Haven and London
*Nelson, W. 1963 *The Poetry of Edmund Spenser: A Study*. New York
Osgood, C. G. 1915 *A Concordance to the Poems of Edmund Spenser*. Washington
Patterson, A. 1991 *Fables of Power: Aesopian Writing and Political History*. Durham, North Carolina
Quint, D. 1983 *Origin and Originality in Renaissance Literature: Versions of the Source*. New Haven and London
Richardson, D. A. 1978 'Duality in Spenser's Archaisms'. *Studies in the Literary Imagination* 11: 81–98

Rose, M. 1968 *Heroic Love: Studies in Sidney and Spenser*. Cambridge, Mass.
*Rosenberg, D. M. 1981 *Oaten Reeds and Trumpets: Pastoral and Epic in Virgil, Spenser and Milton*. Lewisburg, Pennsylvania and London
Rosenmeyer, T. G. 1969 *The Green Cabinet: Theocritus and the European Pastoral Lyric*. Berkeley, Los Angeles and London
Rubel, V. L. 1941 *Poetic Diction in the English Renaissance: From Skelton Through Spenser*. New York
*Scheper, G. L. 1974 'Reformation Attitudes toward Allegory and the Song of Songs'. *Publications of the Modern Language Association of America* 89: 551–62
Shepherd, S. 1989 *Spenser*. Harvester New Readings. New York and London
Shire, H. 1978 *A Preface to Spenser*. London and New York
*Sinfield, A. 1983 *Literature in Protestant England, 1560–1660*. London and Totowa, N.J.
Smith, H. D. 1952 *Elizabethan Poetry: A Study in Conventions, Meaning, and Expression*. Cambridge, Mass.
Spenser Studies: A Renaissance Poetry Annual 1983–. New York
*Wall, J. N. 1988 *Transformations of the Word: Spenser, Herbert, Vaughan*. Athens, Georgia
*Waller, G. F. 1986 *English Poetry of the Sixteenth Century*. Harlow
Waller, G. F. 1993 *Edmund Spenser: A Literary Life*. Basingstoke and London

2. The Shepherds' Calendar

i. Editions

As well as the *Variorum* edition, and those cited under Maclean and Prescott 1993, Oram *et al.* 1989 and Renwick 1930 in the *SC* Select Bibliography, see:
Sommer, H. O. (ed.) 1890 *The Shepheardes Calender*. London
Herford, C. H. (ed.) 1895 *The Shepheardes Calender*. London
Dodge, R. E. N. (ed.) 1908 *Spenser: Complete Poetical Works*. Boston
de Sélincourt, E. (ed.) 1910 *Spenser's Minor Poems*. Oxford
Smith, J. C. and de Sélincourt, E. (eds) 1912 *Spenser: Poetical Works*. Oxford
Kellogg, R. and Steele, O. (eds) 1965 *Books I and II of 'The Faerie Queene', The Mutability Cantos and Selections from the Minor Poetry*. New York
Kermode, F. (ed.) 1965 *Spenser: Selections from the Minor Poems and 'The Faerie Queene'*. London
Spenser, E. *The Shepheardes Calender* 1579. Scolar Press facsimile 1968. Menston, Yorkshire

Heninger, S. K. Jr 1979 *The Shepheardes Calender* (1579). Scholars' Facsimiles and Reprints 329. Delmar, New York

ii. *Critical reading*

Alpers, P. J. 1972–3 'The Eclogue Tradition and the Nature of Pastoral'. *College English* 34: 352–71
*Alpers, P. J. 1985 'Pastoral and the Domain of Lyric in Spenser's *Shepheardes Calender*'. *Representations* 12: 83–100
Anderson, J. H. 1970 'The July Eclogue and the House of Holiness: Perspective in Spenser'. *SEL: Studies in English Literature 1500–1900* 10: 17–32
Berger, H. Jr 1969–70 'Mode and Diction in *The Shepheardes Calender*'. *Modern Philology* 67: 140–9
Bernard, J. D. 1981 'June and the Structure of Spenser's *Shepheardes Calender*'. *Philological Quarterly* 60: 305–22
Bond, R. B. 1981 'Supplantation in the Elizabethan Court: The Theme of Spenser's February Eclogue'. *Spenser Studies: A Renaissance Poetry Annual* 2: 55–65
*Bradford, A. T. 1974 'Mirrors of Mutability: Winter Landscapes in Tudor Poetry'. *English Literary Renaissance* 4: 3–39
Bristol, M. D. 1970 'Structural Patterns in Two Elizabethan Pastorals'. *SEL: Studies in English Literature 1500–1900* 10: 33–48
Brown, J. N. 1972–3 ' "Hence with the Nightingale Will I Take Part": A Virgilian Orphic Allusion in Spenser's "August" '. *Thoth* 13: 13–18
Brown J. N. 1975 'Elizabethan Pastoral and Renaissance Platonism'. *Journal of the Australasian Universities Language and Literature Association* 44: 247–67
Brown, M. 1984 'Spenserian Technique; *The Shepheardes Calender*'. *Yearbook of Research in English and American Literature* 2: 55–118
Cheney, D. 1989 'The Circular Argument of *The Shepheardes Calender*'. In Logan and Teskey (eds [see 1 above]), pp. 137–61
Cooper, H. 1974 'The Goat and the Eclogue'. *Philological Quarterly* 53: 363–79
DeNeef, A. L. 1976 'The Dialectic of Genres in *The Shepheardes Calender*'. *Renaissance Papers 1975*: 1–10
Dixon, M. F. N. 1977 'Rhetorical Patterns and Methods of Advocacy in Spenser's *Shepheardes Calender*'. *English Literary Renaissance* 7: 131–54
Doebler, B. A. 1982 'Venus-Humanitas: An Iconic Elizabeth'. *Journal of European Studies* 12: 233–48
*Durr, R. A. 1957 'Spenser's Calendar of Christian Time'. *ELH: A Journal of English Literary History* 24: 269–95

Farmer, N. 1986 'Spenser's Homage to Ronsard: Cosmic Design in *The Shepheardes Calender*'. *Studi di Letteratura Francese* 12: 249–63

Fowler, A. D. S. 1986 'The Beginnings of English Georgic'. In *Renaissance Genres: Essays on Theory, History, and Interpretation* (ed. B. K. Lewalski). Harvard English Studies 14. Cambridge, Mass., pp. 105–25

Friedland, L. S. 1937 'Spenser as a Fabulist'. *Shakespeare Association Bulletin* 12: 85–108, 133–54, 197–207

Fujii, H. 1974 *Time, Landscape and the Ideal Life: Studies in the Pastoral Poetry of Spenser and Milton*. Kyoto, Japan

Goldberg, J. 1989 'Colin to Hobbinol: Spenser's Familiar Letters'. *South Atlantic Quarterly* 88: 107–26

Greene, R. 1987 '*The Shepheardes Calender*: Dialogue, and Periphrasis'. *Spenser Studies: A Renaissance Poetry Annual* 8: 1–33

Greenlaw, E. A. 1911 '*The Shepheardes Calender*'. *Publications of the Modern Language Association of America* 26: 419–51

Greenlaw, E. A. 1913 '*The Shepheardes Calender*, II'. *Studies in Philology* 11: 3–25

*Hamilton, A. C. 1956 'The Argument of Spenser's *Shepheardes Calender*'. *ELH: A Journal of English Literary History* 23: 171–82

*Hamilton, A. C. 1982 ' "The Grene Path Way to Lyfe": Spenser's *Shepheardes Calender* as Pastoral'. In *The Elizabethan Theatre VIII* (ed. G. R. Hibbard). Port Credit, Ontario, pp. 1–21

Hardin, R. F. 1976 'The Resolved Debate of Spenser's "October" '. *Modern Philology* 73: 257–63

*Helgerson, R. 1978 'The New Poet Presents Himself: Spenser and the Idea of a Literary Career'. *Publications of the Modern Language Association of America* 93: 893–911

*Heninger, S. K. Jr 1962 'The Implications of Form for *The Shepheardes Calender*'. *Studies in the Renaissance* 9: 309–21

Herman, P. 1992 '*The Shepheardes Calender* and Renaissance Anti-Poetic Sentiment'. *SEL: Studies in English Literature 1500–1900* 32: 15–33

Hoffman, N. J. 1977 *Spenser's Pastorals: 'The Shepheardes Calender' and 'Colin Clout'*. Baltimore

Hume, A. 1969 'Spenser, Puritanism, and the "Maye" Eclogue'. *Review of English Studies* n.s. 20: 155–67

*Ingham, P. 1970–1 'Spenser's Use of Dialect'. *English Language Notes* 8: 164–8

Iser, W. 1984 'Spenser's Arcadia; The Interrelation of Fiction and History'. In *Mimesis in Contemporary Theory* (ed. M. Spariosu). Philadelphia, pp. 109–40

*Johnson, L. S. 1981 'Elizabeth, Bride and Queen: A Study of Spenser's "April" Eclogue'. *Spenser Studies: A Renaissance Poetry Annual*. 2: 75–91

*Kay, D. 1990 *Melodious Tears: The English Funeral Elegy from Spenser to Milton*. Oxford

Kennedy, W. J. 1985 'The Virgilian Legacies of Petrarch's *Bucolicum Carmen* and Spenser's *Shepheardes Calender*'. In *The Early Renaissance Virgil and the Classical Tradition* (ed. A. L. Pellegrini). Binghamton, New York, pp. 79–106

*King, J. N. 1986 'Spenser's *Shepheardes Calender* and Protestant Pastoral Satire'. In *Renaissance Genres: Essays on Theory, History, and Interpretation* (ed. B. K. Lewalski). Harvard English Studies 14. Cambridge, Mass., pp. 369–98

Lasater, A. E. 1974 'The Chaucerian Narrator in Spenser's *Shepheardes Calender*'. *Southern Quarterly* 12: 189–201

*MacCaffrey, I. G. 1969 'Allegory and Pastoral in *The Shepheardes Calender*'. *ELH: A Journal of English Literary History* 36: 88–109

*Mallette, R. 1979 'Spenser's Portrait of the Artist in *The Shepheardes Calender*'. *SEL: Studies in English Literature 1500–1900* 19: 19–41

Marx, S. 1985 *Youth Against Age: Generational Strife in Renaissance Poetry with Special Reference to Edmund Spenser's 'The Shepheardes Calender'*. Ph.D. New York

Marx, S. 1985 'Fortunate Senex: The Pastoral of Old Age'. *SEL: Studies in English Literature 1500–1900* 25: 21–44

*McCanles, M. 1982 '*The Shepheardes Calender* as Document and Monument'. *SEL: Studies in English Literature 1500–1900* 22: 5–19

McElderry, B. R. Jr 1932 'Archaism and Innovation in Spenser's Poetic Diction'. *Publications of the Modern Language Association of America* 47: 144–70

McLane, P. E. 1973 'Skelton's *Colyn Cloute* and Spenser's *Shepheardes Calender*'. *Studies in Philology* 70: 141–59

McNeir, W. F. 1977 'The Drama of Spenser's *Shepheardes Calender*'. *Anglia* 95: 34–59

*Miller, D. L. 1979 'Authorship, Anonymity, and *The Shepheardes Calender*'. *Modern Language Quarterly* 40: 219–36

Millican, C. B. 1939 'The Northern Dialect of *The Shepheardes Calender*'. *ELH: A Journal of English Literary History* 6: 211–13

*Montrose, L. A. 1979 ' "The perfect paterne of a poete": The Poetics of Courtship in *The Shepheardes Calender*'. *Texas Studies in Literature and Language* 21: 34–67

*Montrose, L. A. 1980 ' "Eliza, Queene of Shepheardes", and the Pastoral of Power'. *English Literary Renaissance* 10: 153–82

*Montrose, L. A. 1981 'Interpreting Spenser's February Eclogue: Some Contexts and Implications'. *Spenser Studies: A Renaissance Poetry Annual* 2: 67–74

*Montrose, L. A. 1983 'Of Gentlemen and Shepherds: The Politics of Elizabethan Pastoral Form'. *ELH: A Journal of English Literary History* 50: 415–59
*Moore, J. W. Jr 1975 'Colin Breaks His Pipe: A Reading of the "January" Eclogue'. *English Literary Renaissance* 5: 3–24
*Moore, J. W. Jr and Fletcher, S. 1982 'The "December" Eclogue and the Ending of the *Calendar*'. In *Spenser at Kalamazoo, 1982* (ed. R. J. Meyer and T. P. Roche Jr). Clarion, Pennsylvania, pp. 104–15
*Neville Davies, H. 1981 'Spenser's *Shepheardes Calender*: The Importance of November'. *Cahiers Elisabéthains* 20: 35–48
*Patterson, A. 1986 'Re-Opening the Green Cabinet: Clément Marot and Edmund Spenser'. *English Literary Renaissance* 16: 44–70
Pigman, G. W. 1985 *Grief and the English Renaissance Elegy*. Cambridge
*Rambuss, R. 1993 *Spenser's Secret Career*. Cambridge Studies in Renaissance Literature and Culture, 3. Cambridge.
*Sagaser, E. H. 1992 'Gathered in Time: Form, Meter (and Parentheses) in The *Shepheardes Calender*'. *Spenser Studies: A Renaissance Poetry Annual* 10: 95–107
Schleiner, L. 1985 'Spenser and Sidney on the Vaticinium'. *Spenser Studies: A Renaissance Poetry Annual* 6: 129–45
Shawcross, J. T. 1990 'Probability as Requisite to Poetic Delight; A Re-View of the Intentionality of The *Shepheardes Calender*'. *Studies in Philology* 87: 120–7
Shore, D. R. 1976 'Colin and Rosalind: Love Poetry in The *Shepheardes Calender*'. *Studies in Philology* 73: 176–88
Shore, D. R. 1979 'Morrell's Earthly Paradise and the Varieties of Pastoral in Spenser's "July" Eclogue'. *English Studies in Canada* 5: 1–15
*Shore, D. R. 1985 *Spenser and the Poetics of Pastoral: A Study of the World of Colin Clout*. Kingston and Montreal
Smith, B. R. 1980 'On Reading The *Shepheardes Calender*'. *Spenser Studies: A Renaissance Poetry Annual* 1: 69–93
Spiegel, G. S 1980 'Perfecting English Meter: Sixteenth-Century Criticism and Practice'. *Journal of English and Germanic Philology* 79: 192–209
Staton, W. F Jr 1962 'Spenser's "April" Lay as a Dramatic Chorus'. *Studies in Philology* 59: 111–18
*Steinberg, T. L. 1973 'E.K.'s *Shepheardes Calender* and Spenser's'. *Modern Language Studies* 3: 46–58
*Thornton, B. 1991 'Rural Dialectic: Pastoral, Georgic, and The *Shepheardes Calender*'. *Spenser Studies: A Renaissance Poetry Annual* 9 (1988): 1–20
*Tylus, J. 1988 'Spenser, Virgil, and the Politics of Poetic Labor'. *ELH: A Journal of English Literary History* 55: 53–77

Vink, J. 1987 'A Concealed Figure in the Woodcut to the "January" Eclogue'. *Spenser Studies: A Renaissance Poetry Annual* 7: 297-8
*Walker, S. F. 1979 ' "Poetry is/is not a cure for love": The Conflict of Theocritean and Petrarchan Topoi in *The Shepheardes Calender*'. *Studies in Philology* 76: 353-65
Waters, D. D. 1974 'Spenser and Symbolic Witchcraft in *The Shepheardes Calender*'. *SEL: Studies in English Literature 1500-1900* 14: 3-15
*Weiner, A. D. 1988 'Spenser and the Myth of Pastoral'. In C. Hulse, A. D. Weiner, R. Strier 'Spenser: Myth, Politics and Poetry'. *Studies in Philology* 85: 378-411 pp. 390-406
Wrenn, C. L. 1943 'On Re-reading Spenser's *Shepheardes Calender*'. *Essays and Studies* 29: 30-49

3. Amoretti and Epithalamion

i. Editions

As well as the *Variorum*, Oram *et al.* (eds) 1989 (cited under *SC* Select Bibliography), Renwick 1929 (cited in *Am-Epith* Select Bibliography) and de Sélincourt 1910, Smith and de Sélincourt 1912, Kellogg and Steele 1965, and Kermode 1965 (cited under 2. i above) see:

Amoretti and Epithalamion, 1595. Scolar Press Facsimile. Menston, Yorks, 1968

Maclean, H. and Prescott, A. L. (eds) 1993 *Edmund Spenser's Poetry*. Norton Critical Edition. 3rd edition. New York and London (contains full text with notes, excluding only the dedicatory epistle and dedicatory sonnets).

ii. Critical reading

*Allman, E. J. 1980 '*Epithalamion's* Bridegroom: Orpheus-Adam-Christ'. *Renascence* 32: 240-7
*Anderson, D. 1985 ' "Unto My Selfe Alone": Spenser's Plenary Epithalamion'. *Spenser Studies: A Renaissance Poetry Annual* 5: 149-66
Baker-Smith, D. 1988 'Spenser's Triumph of Marriage'. *Word and Image* 4: 310-16
*Baroway, I. 1934 'The Imagery of Spenser and the Song of Songs'. *Journal of English and Germanic Philology* 33: 23-45
*Bates, C. 1991 'The Politics of Spenser's *Amoretti*'. *Criticism* 33: 73-90
Bennett, J. 1973 'Spenser's *Amoretti* LXII and the Date of the New Year'. *Renaissance Quarterly* 26: 433-6

Benson, R. G. 1972 'Elizabeth as Beatrice; A Reading of Spenser's *Amoretti*'. *South Central Bulletin* 32: 184–88

*Bernard, J. 1980 'Spenserian Pastoral and the *Amoretti*'. *ELH: A Journal of English Literary History* 47: 419–32

*Bieman, E. 1983 ' "Sometimes I ... mask in myrth lyke to a Comedy": Spenser's *Amoretti*'. *Spenser Studies: A Renaissance Poetry Annual* 4: 131–41

Chinitz, D. 1991 'The Poem as Sacrament: Spenser's *Epithalamion* and the Golden Mean'. *Journal of Medieval and Renaissance Studies* 21: 251–68

Cirillo, A. R. 1968 'Spenser's *Epithalamion*: The Harmonious Universe of Love'. *SEL: Studies in English Literature 1500–1900* 8: 19–34

Clemen, W. 1968 'The Uniqueness of Spenser's *Epithalamion*'. In *The Poetic Tradition: Essays on Greek, Latin, and English Poetry* (ed. D. C. Allen and H. T. Rowell). Baltimore, pp. 81–98

Cruttwell, P. 1966 *The English Sonnet*. Writers and Their Work. London

Cummings, L. 1964 'Spenser's *Amoretti VIII*: New Manuscript Versions'. *SEL: Studies in English Literature 1500–1900* 4: 125–35

Cummings, P. M. 1970 'Spenser's *Amoretti* as an Allegory of Love'. *Texas Studies in Literature and Language* 12: 163–79.

*Dasenbrock, R. W. 1985 'The Petrarchan Context of Spenser's *Amoretti*'. *Publications of the Modern Language Association of America* 100: 38-50

Dasenbrock, R. W. 1991 *Imitating the Italians: Wyatt, Spenser, Synge, Pound, Joyce*. Baltimore

*DeNeef, A. L. 1978 ' "Who Now Does Follow the Foule Blatant Beast": Spenser's Self-Effacing Fictions'. *Renaissance Papers 1978*: 11–21

Dunlop, A. 1980 'The Drama of *Amoretti*'. *Spenser Studies: A Renaissance Poetry Annual* 1: 107–20

*Forster, L. 1969 *The Icy Fire: Five Studies in European Petrarchism*. Cambridge

*Fowler, A. D. S. 1970 *Triumphal Forms: Structural Patterns in Elizabethan Poetry*. Cambridge

*Fowler, A. D. S. 1975 *Conceitful Thought: The Interpretation of English Renaissance Poems*. Edinburgh

Graves, R. N. 1986 'Two Newfound Poems by Edmund Spenser: The Buried Short-Line Runes in "Epithalamion" and "Prothalamion" '. *Spenser Studies: A Renaissance Poetry Annual* 7: 199–238

*Greene, R. 1991 *Post-Petrarchism: Origins and Innovations of the Western Lyric Sequence*. Princeton, N.J.

*Heninger, S. K. Jr 1986 'Sequences, Systems, Models: Sidney and

the Secularization of Sonnets'. In *Poems in Their Place: The Intertextuality and Order of Poetic Collections* (ed. N. Fraistat). Chapel Hill, North Carolina, pp. 66–94

Hill, W. S. 1972 'Order and Joy in Spenser's *Epithalamion*'. *Southern Humanities Review* 6: 81–90

*Hunter, G. K. 1973 'Spenser's *Amoretti* and the English Sonnet Tradition'. In *A Theatre for Spenserians* (ed. J. M. Kennedy and J. A. Reither). Toronto and Buffalo, pp. 124–44

Hyman, L. 1953 'Structure and Meaning in Spenser's *Epithalamion*'. *Tennessee Studies in Literature* 3: 37–41

John, L. C. 1938 *The Elizabethan Sonnet Sequences*. New York

Johnson, W. C. 1973 'Amor and Spenser's *Amoretti*'. *English Studies* 51: 217–26

*Johnson, W. C. 1976 ' "Sacred Rites" and Prayer-Book Echoes in Spenser's "Epithalamion" '. *Renaissance and Reformation* 12: 49–54

*Johnson, W. C. 1990 *Spenser's 'Amoretti': Analogies of Love*. Lewisburg, Pennsylvania and London

Kalil, J. 1973 ' "Mask in Myrth Lyke to a Comedy": Spenser's Persona in the *Amoretti*'. *Thoth* 13: 19–26.

*Kellogg, R. 1965 'Thought's Astonishment and the Dark Conceits of Spenser's *Amoretti*'. In *Renaissance Papers 1965* (ed. G. W. Williams). Durham, North Carolina, pp. 3–13

Kesler, R. L. 1990 'The Idealisation of Women: Morphology and Change in Three Renaissance Texts'. *Mosaic: A Journal for the Interdisciplinary Study of Literature* 23: 107–26

King, J. N. 1986 'Milton's Bower of Bliss: A Rewriting of Spenser's Art of Married Love'. *Renaissance and Reformation*, n.s. 10: 289–99

Kuin, R. 1987 'The Gaps and the Whites: Indeterminacy and Undecidability in the Sonnet Sequences of Sidney, Spenser, and Shakespeare'. *Spenser Studies: A Renaissance Poetry Annual* 8: 251–85

Leavell, L. 1986 'And Yet Another Ring of Echoes in Spenser's "Epithalamion" '. *South Central Review* 3: 14–26

*Lever, J. W. 1966 *The Elizabethan Love Sonnet*. 2nd edition. London

*Lewis, C. S. 1936 *The Allegory of Love: A Study in Mediaeval Tradition*. Oxford

MacArthur, J. H. 1989 *Critical Contexts of Sidney's 'Astrophil and Stella' and Spenser's 'Amoretti'*. English Literary Studies 46. University of Victoria, B.C.

Marchand, Y. 1979–80 'Hypothesis for an Interpretation of the Later Poems of Edmund Spenser'. *English Miscellany* 28–9: 7–18

McNeir, W. F. 1965 'An Apology for Spenser's *Amoretti*'. *Die Neueren Sprachen* 14: 1–9. Reprinted in *Essential Articles for the Study of Edmund Spenser* (ed. A. C. Hamilton). Hamden, Connecticut, pp. 524–33

Miller, J. T. 1979 ' "Love Doth Hold My Hand": Writing and Wooing in the Sonnets of Sidney and Spenser'. *ELH: A Journal of English Literary History* 46: 541–58

Miller, P. W. 1970 'The Decline of the English Epithalamion'. *Texas Studies in Literature and Language* 12: 405–16

Mulryan, J. 1973 'The Function of Ritual in the Marriage Songs of Catullus, Spenser and Ronsard'. *Illinois Quarterly* 35: 50–64

*Neely, C. T. 1978 'The Structure of English Renaissance Sonnet Sequences'. *ELH: A Journal of English Literary History* 45: 359–89

*Neuse, R. 1966 'The Triumph over Hasty Accidents: A Note on the Symbolic Mode of the "Epithalamion" '. *Modern Language Review* 6l: 161–74

Okerlund, A. N. 1982 'The Rhetoric of Love: Voice in the *Amoretti* and the *Songs and Sonets*'. *The Quarterly Journal of Speech* 68: 37–46

Pearcy, L. T. 1981 'A Case of Allusion: Stanza 18 of Spenser's "Epithalamion" and Catullus 5'. *Classical and Modern Literature* 1: 243–54

Ricks, D. M. 1972 'Persona and Process in Spenser's *Amoretti*'. *Ariel* 3: 5–15

*Rose, M. 1968 *Heroic Love: Studies in Sidney and Spenser*. Cambridge, Mass.

Scott, J. G. 1929 *Les Sonnets Elizabéthains*. Paris

Smith, H. 1961 'The Use of Conventions in Spenser's Minor Poems'. In *Form and Convention in the Poetry of Edmund Spenser: Selected Papers from the English Institute* (ed. W. Nelson). New York, pp. 122–45

*Turner, M. 1988 'The Imagery of Spenser's *Amoretti*'. *Neophilologus* 72: 284–99

Villeponteaux, M. A. 1988 ' "With her own will beguyld": The Captive Lady in Spenser's *Amoretti*'. *Explorations in Renaissance Culture* 14: 29–39

Warkentin, G. 1990 'Spenser at the Still Point: A Schematic Device in "Epithalamion" '. In *Craft and Tradition: Essays in Honour of William Blissett* ed. H. B. de Groot and A. Leggatt. Calgary, pp. 47–57

*Wells, R. H. 1984 'Poetic Decorum in Spenser's *Amoretti*'. *Cahiers Elisabéthains* 25: 9–21

Young, F. B. 1973–4 'Medusa and the *Epithalamion*: A Problem in Spenserian Imagery'. *English Language Notes* 11: 21–9

Yuasa, N. 1961 'A Study of Metaphor in Spenser's *Amoretti*'. *Studies in English Literature* (Tokyo) 37: 165–86

See also *Cheney 1993, *King 1990, *Tufte 1970 in *SC* Select Bibliography

4. Four Hymns

i. Editions

See the editions listed under 3. i above with the exclusion of Kellogg and Steele, Kermode, and Maclean and Prescott. In addition, see Welsford 1967 (in *Am–Epith* Select Bibliography) and:

Winstanley, L. (ed.) 1907 *Spenser: The Fowre Hymnes*. Cambridge

ii. Critical reading

Bennett, J. W. 1935 'Spenser's *Fowre Hymnes*: Addenda'. *Studies in Philology* 32: 131–57

Bjorvand, E. (ed.) 1973 *A Concordance to Spenser's 'Fowre Hymnes'*. Oslo

*Blondel, J. 1976 'Allégorie, éros et religion dans *The Fowre Hymnes*'. In *Imaginaire et croyance: Etudes de poésie anglaise*. Grenoble, pp. 49–56

Collins, J. B. 1940 *Christian Mysticism in the Elizabethan Age*. Baltimore

*Comito, T. 1977 'A Dialectic of Images in Spenser's *Fowre Hymnes*'. *Studies in Philology* 74: 301–21

*DeNeef, A. L. 1974 'Spenserian Meditation: The *Hymne of Heavenly Beautie*'. *American Benedictine Review* 25: 217–34

Jayne, S. R. 1972 'Attending to Genre: Spenser's *Hymnes*'. *Spenser Newsletter* 3: 5–6

*Johnson, P. 1972 *Form and Transformation in Music and Poetry of the English Renaissance*. New Haven and London

*Mulryan, J. 1971 'Spenser as Mythologist: A Study of the Nativities of Cupid and Christ in the *Fowre Hymnes*'. *Modern Language Studies* 1: 13–16

Padelford, F. M. 1914 'Spenser's *Fowre Hymnes*'. *Journal of English and Germanic Philology* 13: 418–33

Padelford, F. M. 1932 'Spenser's *Fowre Hymnes*: A Resurvey'. *Studies in Philology* 29: 207–32

*Rogers, W. E. 1983 *The Three Genres and the Interpretation of Lyric*. Princeton, N.J.

Smith, P. R. 1977 'Rhyme Linking Techniques in Spenser's *Fowre Hymnes*: Another Aspect of Elizabethan Rhymecraft'. *The Claflin College Review* 2: 39–48

Stewart, J. T. 1957 'Renaissance Psychology and the Ladder of Love in Castiglione and Spenser'. *Journal of English and Germanic Philology* 56: 225–30

Szőnyi, G. E. 1982 'A Synthesis of Renaissance Love Theories: The Compositional Structure of Edmund Spenser's *Fowre Hymnes*'. *Papers in English and American Studies* 2: 241–68

See also *Cheney 1993 in *SC* Select Bibliography and *Bieman 1988 and *Ellrodt 1960 under *Am–Epith* Select Bibliography.

5. Prothalamion

i. Editions

As under 3. i.

ii. Critical reading

Cain, T. H. 1978 *Praise in 'The Faerie Queene'*. Lincoln, Nebraska
*Fujii, H. 1976 'A Reading of Spenser's *Prothalamion*'. *Poetica: An International Journal of Linguistic-Literary Studies* (Tokyo) 4: 50–9
Halio, J. L. 1961 ' "Prothalamion", "Ulysses", and Intention in Poetry'. *College English* 22: 390–4
*Herendeen, W. H. 1981 'Spenserian Specifics: Spenser's Appropriation of a Renaissance Topos'. *Medievalia et Humanistica* 10: 159–88
*Herendeen, W. H. 1986 *From Landscape to Literature: The River and the Myth of Geography*. Duquesne Studies: Language and Literature Series 7. Pittsburgh
*Hollander, J. 1987 'Spenser's Undersong'. In *Cannibals, Witches, and Divorce: Estranging the Renaissance* (ed. M. Garber). Baltimore, pp. 1–20
*Hollander, J. 1988 *Melodious Guile: Fictive Patterns in Poetic Language*. New Haven and London
*Manley, L. 1982 'Spenser and the City: The Minor Poems'. *Modern Language Quarterly* 43: 203–27
Norton, D. S. 1944 'The Bibliography of Spenser's *Prothalamion*'. *Journal of English and Germanic Philology* 43: 349–53
Norton, D. S. 1951 'The Tradition of Prothalamia'. In *English Studies in Honor of James Southall Wilson* University of Virginia Studies 4. Charlottesville, Virginia pp. 223–41
Patterson, S. R. 1979–80 'Spenser's *Prothalamion* and the Catullan Epithalamic Tradition'. *Comitatus* 10: 97–106
Prager, C. 1976 'Emblem and Motion in Spenser's *Prothalamion*'. *Studies in Iconography* 2: 114–20
Rogers, W. E. 1977 'The *Carmina* of Horace in "Prothalamion" '. *American Notes and Queries* 15: 148–53
Smith, J. N. 1959 'Spenser's "Prothalamion": A New Genre'. *Review of English Studies* n.s. 10: 173–8
West, M. 1974 'Prothalamia in Propertius and Spenser'. *Comparative Literature* 26: 346–53

*Wine, M. L. 1962 'Spenser's "Sweete *Themmes*": Of Time and the River'. *SEL: Studies in English Literature 1500–1900* 2: 111–17
*Woodward, D. H. 1962 'Some Themes in Spenser's *Prothalamion*'. *ELH: A Journal of English Literary History* 29: 34–46

See also *Cheney 1993 and *Fowler 1975 in *SC* Select Bibliography; *Helgerson 1983 under 1 above; Bieman 1988, Leonard 1984 and *Schenck 1988 in *Am–Epith* Select Bibliography; Graves 1986 under 3. ii above.

Index of First Lines

A shepherd's boy (no better do him call) 31
After long storms' and tempests' [...] 263
After so long a race as I have run 279
Ah, Colin, whether on the lowly plain 215
Ah, for pity! Will rank Winter's rage 39
Ah whither, Love, wilt thou [...] 340
Ah, why hath Nature to so hard a heart 239
Arion, when through tempest's cruel wrack 245
As Dian hunted on a day 287

Be nought dismayed that her unmoved mind 220
Being myself captived here in care 273

Calm was the day, and through the trembling air 390
Colin, my dear, when shall it please thee sing 173
Coming to kiss her lips, such [...] 264
Cuddy, for shame, hold up thy [...] 159

Daily, when I do seek and sue for peace 224
Dark is the day when Phoebus' face is shrouded 215
Diggon Davy, I bid her god day 142
Do I not see that fairest images 253

Fair bosom fraught with Virtue's richest treasure 275
Fair cruel, why are ye so [...] 252
Fair eyes, the mirror of my [...] 221
Fair is my love, when her [...] 280
Fair proud, now tell me why should fair be proud 237
Fair ye be sure; but cruel and unkind 257

Fresh Spring - the herald of love's mighty king 270

Go, little book: thyself present 16
Great wrong I do, I can it not deny 241

Happy, ye leaves, whenas those [...] 216
How long shall this like-dying [...] 235

I joy to see how, in your drawen work 271
I saw in secret to my dame 288
In that proud port, which her so goodly graceth 226
In vain I seek, and sue to her [...] 232
In youth, before I waxed old 287
Innocent paper – whom too [...] 251
Is it her nature, or is it her will 247
Is not thilk same a goatherd proud 113
Is not thilk the merry month of May 81
It fell upon a holy eve 132
It was upon a holiday 58

Joy of my life, full oft for loving you 281

Lacking my love, I go from [...] 278
Leave, lady, in your glass of [...] 249
Let not one spark of filthy lustful fire 282
Like as a huntsman after weary chase 267
Like as a ship that through [...] 241
Like as the culver on the bared bough 286
Lo, Colin, here the place, whose pleasant site 103
Lo, I have made a *Calendar* for [...] 199
Long languishing in double malady 252
Long while I sought to what I might compare 223
Love, lift me up upon thy golden wings 354

Love, that long since hast to thy mighty power   325

Mark when she smiles with [...]   246
Men call you fair, and you do credit it   279
More than most fair, full of [...]   222
Most glorious Lord of life that, [...]   268
Most happy letters, framed by [...]   273
My hungry eyes, through greedy covetise   242, 282
My love is like to ice, and I to fire   239

New Year, forth looking out of Janus' gate   218

Of this world's theatre in [...]   255
Oft when my spirit doth spread her bolder wings   272
One day, as I unwarily did gaze   229
One day I sought with her heart-thrilling eyes   225
One day I wrote her name upon [...]   274

Penelope, for her Ulysses' sake   234

Rapt with the rage of mine own ravished thought   368
Return again, my forces late dismayed   227
Rudely thou wrongest my dear heart's desire   219

See how the stubborn damsel [...]   238
Shall I then silent be, or shall I speak   248
Since I did leave the presence of [...]   284
Since I have lacked the comfort of that light   285
So oft as homeward I from her depart   254
So oft as I her beauty do behold   256
Sweet is the rose, but grows upon a briar   236
Sweet smile, the daughter of the queen of love   245
Sweet warrior, when shall I have peace with you   258

Tell me, good Hobbinol, what gars thee greet   65
Tell me, Perigot, what shall be [...]   129
Tell me, when shall these weary woes have end   243
The doubt which ye misdeem, fair love, is vain   265
The famous warriors of the [...]   269
The gentle shepherd sat beside a spring   188
The glorious image of the Maker's beauty   262

The glorious portrait of that [...]   230
The laurel leaf, which you this day do wear   238
The love which me so cruelly [...]   247
The merry cuckoo, messenger [...]   231
The painful smith, with force of fervent heat   240
The panther, knowing that his spotted hide   255
The rolling wheel that runneth often round   230
The sovereign beauty which I [...]   218
The weary Year his race now [...]   262
The world (that cannot deem of worthy things)   283
There grew an aged tree on the green   44
They that in course of heavenly spheres are skilled   261
Thilk same Kid (as I can well devise)   90
This holy season, fit to fast and pray   233
Thomalin, why sitten we so   56
Thrice-happy she that is so [...]   260
To all those happy blessings which ye have   266
Trust not the treason of those smiling looks   250

Unquiet thought, whom at the first I bred   217
Unrighteous Lord of love, what law is this   224
Up, then, Melpomene, thou mournfullest Muse of nine   176
Upon a day, as Love lay sweetly slumbering   288

Venomous tongue, tipped with vile adder's sting   284

Was it a dream, or did I see it plain   277
Was it the work of Nature or of Art   232
Weak is the assurance that weak flesh reposeth   259
What guile is this, that those her golden tresses   244
When I behold that beauty's [...]   235
When those renowmed noble peers of Greece   248
When my abode's prefixed [...]   250

Ye dainty nymphs, that in this blessed brook   67
Ye learned sisters which have [...]   291
Ye tradeful merchants that, with weary toil   228
Ye waste-full woods, bear witness of my woe   136

Index to the Introduction and Commentary

Aaron, 126
Abel, 125
Achilles, 63, 168–9, 336–7
Acrisius, 266
Actaeon, 267
Aeneas, 64, 99, 126, 172, 188, 336, 387–8, 398
Aeschylus, 127
Aesop, 21, 38, 41, 52, 54, 98, 144, 160
ages of man, 39
Agrippa, H.C., 4, 104, 109, 128, 170, 173, 176, 180, 185, 192, 202, 228, 229, 246, 253, 264, 274, 301, 311–12, 322, 326, 336, 340, 344, 356, 393
Agrippa, M.V., 36
Alcaeus, 20
Alcestis, 337
alchemy, 75, 249, 345, 377, 391, 393
Alciati, A., 40, 147, 161, 166, 230, 288, 327, 336
Alcmena, 310
Alençon, Duc d', 7, 8, 9, 16, 30, 38, 46, 49, 54, 55, 61, 64, 77–9, 100, 102, 128, 172, 173, 187, 188, 404, 405, 407
Alexander the Great, 108, 167, 168–9
Allen, D.C., 242
Allen, R.H., 405
Alpers, P.J., 338
Amphitryon, 310
Anacreon, 205, 288, 378
Andromache, 99
angels, 222, 223, 305, 315, 322, 328, 357, 371, 372, 380
Angerona, 312
Anglo, S., 401
anima (Jungian), 322, 377
Anne Boleyn, Queen, 68
Ansell Robin, P., 93, 217, 252, 329
Apelles, 378
apocalypse, 39–40, 113, 122, 125, 146, 386
Apollo, 22, 35, 63, 74, 75–6, 110, 165, 180, 223, 238, 241, 296, 300, 340, 393
Apollodorus, 78, 124, 125, 186
Apollonius Rhodius, 248–9
Aptekar, J., 94
Apuleius, 326, 339, 356
Aquinas, St Thomas, 356, 372
Arachne, 271

Arber, E., 19
archaism, 19, 20, 21, 38, 53, 169
Aretino, P., 36
Argonauts, 248–9, 401
Argus, 126, 151, 167
Arion, 245
Ariosto, L., 3, 162
Aristophanes, 354, 394
Aristotle, 127, 167, 303
Arruntius Stella, 36
Art and Nature, 232, 378
Arthur, King, 77, 386, 387, 401
Ascanius, 99
Ascham, R., 19, 77,
Astraea, 64, 129, 141
astral immortality, 181
astrological houses, 405–7
Astyanax, 99
Atalanta, 277–8
Athanassakis, A.N., 186, 207, 296, 298, 306, 310, 311, 312, 315, 326, 328, 354, 390, 394
Atlas, 98, 277, 309
Augustine, St, 124, 319, 324, 372
Augustus, 64, 158, 162, 168, 388
Aurora, 296
Ausonius, 76, 184
Aylmer, J., 112

Bacchus/Dionysius, 131, 165, 170, 306, 315, 340
Baïf, J.–A. de, 179, 330
Barber, C.L., 83
Barnett, R., 44
Bartholomew's Day (St) massacre, 100
Batman, S., 61, 284, 287, 306
Bawcutt, P., 177
Bednarz, J.P., 85
Bellona, 170–1
Benivieni, J., 322, 325, 328, 342, 345
Bennett, J.W., 320, 321, 322, 342
Berger, H., Jr, 49, 167, 184, 396
Bersuire, P., 123
Bhattacherje, M., 202, 320, 347
Bible, the (books cited) 4, 8, 28, 29, 33, 35, 38, 40, 43, 44, 45, 47, 48, 64, 68, 80, 81, 84, 85–90, 93, 95, 98, 99, 102, 108–9, 112, 115, 117, 118, 119,

122–6, 144, 145, 147, 151, 152, 160,
  161, 177, 178, 181, 186, 193, 194,
  199, 204, 209, 216–17, 220, 223, 224,
  226, 228, 229, 233, 237, 242, 243,
  250, 255, 259, 261, 263–9, 270–2,
  274–9, 284, 287, 293, 295, 298, 300,
  301, 302, 308, 312, 316, 319, 321,
  322, 326, 328, 329, 331, 342, 346,
  348, 355–66, 368–78, 380–1, 390
Bickersteth, G.L., 405
Bieman, E., 207, 217, 218, 320, 321, 324
Bion, 55, 61, 172, 182, 308
bishops (objections to), 87
Bjorvand, E., 321, 322, 340
Boccaccio, G., 23, 27, 61, 63, 76–7, 172
Bongo, P., 4, 64, 102, 223, 261, 273
Bono, B.J., 74
Book of Common Prayer, 10, 203, 204, 207,
  216, 234, 261, 265, 266, 267, 268, 296,
  303–5, 307, 310, 314, 316, 348, 350
Botticelli, S., 68
Boyden, D.D., 70
Boyle, E., 5, 201, 205, 206, 274, 322
Braden, G., 238
Brant, S., 8, 30, 38, 141, 158
Bridget, St, 115
British myth, 64, 125–6, 388, 400
Britten, J., 392
Brooks–Davies, D., 49, 64, 70, 75, 79, 103,
  110, 137, 178, 207, 220, 223, 256,
  263, 338, 388, 391
Brown, J.N., 64–5, 204, 207
Browne, Sir Thomas, 294
Brutus, founder of Britain, 64, 126, 188
Bryce, J., 206, 286, 293, 294, 297, 306,
  308, 309, 310, 311, 313, 315
Bryskett, L., 241
Buchanan, G., 207
Burghley, William Cecil, first Baron, 85
Bush, D., 32
Butler, C., 4,
Buttet, M.C. de, 207, 293, 308, 313

Cacus, 387
Cadiz, 400, 401
Cain, T.H., 64–5, 99, 158, 176, 200, 207,
  404
calendar, 9–10, 27–9, 166, 203–4, 206,
  218–19, 233, 262, 291, 307
Calendar of Shepherds, The, 24
Callisto, 242
Calvin, J., 82
Calvinism, 50, 203, 204, 224, 270, 283, 380
Camden, W., 386, 398
Campbell, G., 307
Campbell, L. B., 99
canzone, 209–10, 389

Capp, B., 24
Casady, E., 202
Castiglione, B., 202, 264, 278, 280–1, 285,
  319, 332, 333, 334, 336, 342, 343,
  348, 349, 350, 351
Castor, 388, 394, 401
Catherine, St, 124
Catullus, 206, 207, 210, 271, 293, 298,
  300, 301, 303, 306, 308, 309, 313,
  314, 315, 317, 390, 396
Caxton, W., 53, 183
Celtic Britons, 109, 123
censorship, 148
Cerberus, 161
Ceres, 263, 264, 312, 397
Chapman, G., 264, 336
Charles V, Holy Roman Emperor, 400
Chaucer, G., 9, 16, 18, 23, 34, 46, 48, 51,
  53, 55, 62, 76, 80, 89, 93, 98, 100,
  102, 107, 110, 119, 121, 125, 126,
  154, 155, 169, 179, 186, 191, 195,
  196, 199–200, 242, 253, 274, 283,
  332, 337, 352, 401
Cheney, P., 137, 167, 168, 272, 319, 386,
  395, 400
chivalry, 16, 71, 387, 399, 401
Chloris, 61, 77, 83, 219, 295, 301, 386,
  387, 390, 391, 392
Churchyard, T., 141
Cicero, 19, 20, 97, 110, 168–9, 170, 185, 197
Circe, 237
Clarke, R.A., 44
Claudian, 207, 277, 292, 293, 294, 297,
  298, 300, 306, 307, 309, 311
Clytemnestra, 394
Coiro, A., 52
Colonna, G., 201
Collinson, P., 85
Comes, N., 74
comets, 196–7
Comus, 306
Constable, H., 209
constellations, extra-zodiacal (*see also* zodiac):
  Caput and Cauda Draconis, 197;
  Corona borealis, 123, 139; Crater,
  123; Cygnus, 394–5; Delphinus, 245;
  Ursa Major, Ursa Minor, 242
Cooper, H., 172
Cooper, T., 52, 55, 112
creation myths, 235, 328–30, 342, 355–6,
  359, 370–1
Cullen, P., 8, 105
Cummings, R.M., 205, 398
Cupid/Eros, 55, 57, 62–3, 160, 196, 201,
  206, 208, 219, 221–2, 224, 229, 231,
  258, 266, 276, 285, 287–90, 305, 312,
  320, 321, 325–6, 327, 328, 331, 333,

Index

336, 339, 340, 352, 354, 361, 366, 394, 397
Curtius, E.R., 35, 38, 40, 162, 217, 255, 369
Cybele, 277
cycles, historical, 39

D'Ancona, M.L., 68, 103, 236, 264–5, 392
Danaë, 266
dance of death, 178
Daniel, A., 136
Daniel, S., 209
Dante Alighieri, 3, 201, 217, 234, 242, 297, 404–5
Daphne, 76, 238, 241, 309, 386, 396
Davies, Sir John, 230, 344, 347
Davies, R., 141
Davison, F., 406
de Cetina, G., 136
de Lorris, G. and J. de Meun, 227, 231, 331
De Neef, A.L., 284
de Vries, A., 103, 131, 192, 228, 236, 272, 301
Desportes, P., 228, 230, 233, 239, 251, 252, 261, 269
Deucalion, 241
dialect, 16, 19, 34, 38, 72–3, 82, 89, 92, 119
Diana, 64, 75, 78–9, 124, 205, 223, 229, 242, 267, 287–8, 294, 296, 300, 301, 309, 313
Dido, 102, 172
Diodorus Siculus, 108, 124
Dodge, R.E. Neil, 261, 318
Dog star, 123
Donne, J., 102, 205, 216, 388, 392
Douai priests, 141, 149
Drayton, M., 110, 209, 228, 391
Druidism, 44, 49
Du Bartas, G. de Saluste, 379
Du Bellay, J., 3, 5, 21, 35, 45, 173, 207, 225, 228, 269
Dubrow, H., 203, 206, 207, 286, 293, 294, 297, 306, 308, 309, 310, 311, 313, 315
Duncan–Jones, K., 19
Dunlop, A., 203–4, 234, 260, 262, 318
Durling, R.A., 201
Durr, R.A., 10

E.K., 5, 8, 9, 10–12, 20, 26, 30, 36, 51–4, 63, 68, 73–8, 109, 110, 112, 122, 123, 125, 126, 127, 136, 139, 153, 156, 171, 183, 184, 185, 186, 197, 298, 331, 403–7
Eade, J.C., 206, 261, 297, 308, 407
Echo, 105, 397
Edward II, 399
Edward VI, 80
Edwards, C.R., 243

eirenic prophecy, 90
elements, the four, 223, 256, 294, 321, 328–330, 343, 390
Eliot, Sir Thomas, 62
Elizabeth I, 7, 10, 16, 31, 32, 38, 46, 54, 55, 61, 62, 64–5, 68, 70, 73–80, 90, 100, 102, 121, 128, 132, 141, 149, 162, 164, 172–3, 184, 187, 203, 205, 223, 228, 241, 262, 264, 273, 298, 301, 313, 322, 353, 387–8, 390, 398, 399–400, 401, 404, 405, 407
Ellrodt, R., 202, 320, 321, 322, 324, 328, 369
elves, 109
Elyot, Sir Thomas, 252
Endymion, 124, 313
Epimetheus, 235, 241
epithalamia, 206, 208, 210, 293, 294, 296, 297, 311, 315
Erasmus, 11, 51, 54, 97, 248
Eros: see Cupid
Essex, Robert Devereux, second Earl of, 386–8, 395, 399–400, 401
Estienne, H., 205, 207
Euripides, 184
Eurydice, 5, 106, 167, 207, 208, 292–3, 305, 338
Eusebius, 96
Eustathius, 63
Evander, King, 387–8

fable tradition, 52 (*see also* Aesop)
fairies, 109
Fall of man, 45, 90, 102, 232, 252, 259, 278, 303, 359–60, 363
Fates, the Three, 185–6, 328
Faustus, 146
Ferguson, G., 264, 265
festivals/feast days, 61, 80, 83, 132, 167, 172, 173, 206, 263, 269, 276, 304, 307, 387, 400, 405
Ficino, M., 202, 221, 222, 243, 262, 274, 276, 319, 322, 327, 328, 329, 333, 343, 345, 349, 373, 376, 378
Fletcher, G., 264
Fletcher, J.B., 320, 321, 322, 324, 328, 343, 345
Flora, 61, 80, 83, 219, 270, 276, 295, 301, 386, 387, 391, 392, 395 (*see also* Chloris)
Florio, J., 54, 406
flower gathering, 298, 392
Fowler, A.D.S., 55, 64–5, 80, 123, 187, 204, 206, 207, 220, 264, 292, 307, 316, 317, 321, 322, 386, 388, 392, 393, 401
Foxe, J., 85
Francis I, King of France, 75, 187, 193, 196
Fraunce, A., 98, 277

Freccero, J., 243
Friedland, L.S., 46
Friedman, J.B., 207, 292
Friedman, L.J., 227
Fukuda, S., 204, 295
Fulgentius, 292
Furies, the Three, 186, 284
fury (inspirational), 170, 326, 340

Gafurius, F., 167, 292
Galathea, 235
Galyon, L.R., 322
Garter, Order of the, 5, 387, 399–400, 401
Gascoigne, G., 46, 77, 175, 185
Gellius, A., 21
gentility, 40, 314
George, St, 70, 401
Gesualdo, A., 222
Gibbs, D., 233
gifts of the Holy Spirit, 356, 368
Giorgio, F., 207
Goldberg, J., 137, 159, 160
Golden Age, 64
Golding, A., 83, 167, 370
Gombrich, E.H., 139
Gordon, D.J., 207
Gower, J., 62, 126, 186
Graces, the Three, 34, 68, 70, 76–7, 110, 203, 208, 246, 274, 291, 297, 298, 306, 352
Greene, T.M., 207
Gregory XIII, Pope, 10
Greville, F., 209
Grindal, E., 41, 80, 83, 85, 112, 121, 126, 127, 141
Guildford, H., 385, 401
Guthrie, W.K.C., 354

Hamilton, A.C., 8
Hankins, J.E., 202
Hardison, O.B., 217
Hardy, T., 5
Harington, J., 45
Harmonia/Harmony, 55, 128
Harpocrates, 312
Harvey, E. Ruth, 322
Harvey, G., 11, 18, 34, 36, 74, 102, 109, 156
Hazard, M. E., 204, 254
Hebe, 186, 315, 339
Hector, 99, 168
Helen (of Troy), 73, 125, 269, 394
Helgerson, R., 228
Heninger, S. K., Jr, 8, 9, 10, 199, 256, 328
Henkel, A., 355
Henry VII, 46, 68, 75
Henry VIII, 68, 74, 80, 184
Hercules, 147, 161, 221, 248, 277, 310–11, 315, 339, 387–8
Hercules, Pillars of, 400
Herebus, 185
Herford, C.H., 122
Hermetica: *Poimander*, 359
Hermetism, 356
Hero, 336
Herodotus, 97
Hesiod, 74, 76, 186, 231, 235, 287, 328, 343
Hesperia, 277
Hesperides, 277
Hesperus, 197, 297, 308, 387, 401
Hibbert, C., 64
Hieatt, A. Kent, 62, 204, 206, 298, 307, 308, 316, 317, 355, 386
Hieatt, C., 272
Higginson, J.J., 8
Hippocrates, 63
Hippomenes, 277, 279
hobgoblins, 311
Hoffman, N.J., 8
Holinshed, R., 155
Homer, 8, 42, 63, 74, 76, 161, 168, 234, 237, 242, 298, 320, 337
homosexuality, 36, 330, 349
Hone, W., 307
Horace, 34, 104, 122, 125, 131, 154, 161, 170, 198, 199, 267, 278, 340, 374, 398
Hours, 208, 298, 392
Howard, Lord Thomas, 400
Howard, Charles, 400
Hughes, M.Y., 139, 179
Hume, A., 80, 99, 112
Hunter, G.K., 204
Hutton, J., 39, 90, 205, 287, 288, 290, 330, 354
hydra, 147
hymn, 319–20
Hymen, 292, 293, 294, 300, 315

idolatry, 73, 112, 126, 237, 334
Inns of Court, 399
Io: *see* Isis
Isis, 64, 68, 126, 167

Jacobs, E.C., 279
Jacobs, K.R., 279
Janus, 28, 30, 32, 218
Jason, 248–9
Jerusalem, Temple of, 399
Johnson, L. S., 8, 27, 34, 68, 105, 136, 172, 404–5
Johnson, W.C., 204, 221, 267
Jonson, B., 1, 207, 221, 298, 302, 306
Jung, C.G., 322, 377, 393
Juno, 78, 167, 242, 256, 269, 294, 302, 314, 315, 398

Index

Jupiter/Zeus, 74, 167, 235, 242, 245, 248, 266, 287, 298, 309, 310, 311, 339, 394
Juvenal, 170, 312

Kaske, C. V., 204, 205, 261, 269, 272, 282
Kastner, L.E., 233, 251, 252, 261, 269
Kennedy, J.M., 138, 200
King, J.N., 16, 20, 35, 44, 53, 68, 77, 80, 112, 123, 141, 203, 204, 304
Kirke, E., 10
Klibansky, R., 158, 330
Knights of St John, 399
Knights Templar, 387, 399
Knollys, L., 62
Knox, J., 82
Kostić, V., 202, 248, 255, 267, 273

Lactantius, 61
Lambarde, W., 109
Lane, R., 8, 76, 123, 141, 147, 172
Langland, W., 9, 80, 89, 109, 125, 141, 199
Larson, K., 204
Latona, 75–6
Lavater, L., 96
Leander, 336
Leda, 386, 394–5
Lee, Sir Henry, 387, 389
Lee, R.W., 321
Leicester, Lord Robert Dudley, Earl of, 7, 8, 16, 30, 62, 168, 185, 215, 387–8, 399
Leland, J., 386, 393
Lemmi, C.W., 74
Leonard, C.A., 243, 294
Levarie, J., 205
Lievesay, J.L., 255
Linacre, T., 68
Linche, R., 61, 78, 219
Livy, 19
Lloyd, H., 151
Loewenstein, J., 204, 292
Long, P.W., 45
Lotspeich, H.G., 63, 238
Luborsky, R.S., 31, 38, 55, 159, 173, 183, 188
Lucan, 45, 171
Lucifer, 197, 297, 328, 358, 401
Lucina, 313, 314
Lucretius, 246, 341
Lydgate, J., 16, 18, 51, 52, 53, 107, 154, 169, 183, 194, 263

MacLachlan, H., 64, 77
Maclean, H., 200, 264, 318
Macrobius, A.A.T., 10, 21, 27, 28, 29, 32, 61, 219, 223, 277, 298, 311, 312, 348, 349

Maecenas, 162, 168
Maia, 61, 309
Mallette, R., 73
Manley, F., 322
mannerism, 4
Mantuan (Battista Spagnoli), 8, 23, 41, 80, 101, 112, 118, 123, 124, 141, 154, 166, 170
Margaret, Countess of Cumberland, 324, 377
Marino, G.B., 207
Marlowe, C., 146, 336
Marot, C., 9, 23, 30, 35, 38, 64, 75, 78, 80, 155, 172, 175, 177, 179–81, 183, 186–90, 192, 193, 195–6, 287
Marotti, A.F., 204
marriage, 203, 206, 207, 216, 221, 241, 256, 259, 261, 264, 265, 266, 268, 277, 287, 291–4, 302, 303, 304, 308, 314, 315, 316, 326, 339, 350, 386, 395, 396, 397, 398, 400, 401
Mars, 55, 77, 168, 170, 224, 225, 287
Martial, 36
Martianus Capella, 128, 294, 299, 327
Martz, L.L., 259
Marullo, M., 320
Mary, Blessed Virgin, 68, 75, 132, 155, 173, 184, 263, 264, 265, 322, 326, 365
Mary Tudor, 80, 85, 141, 149, 156
McLane, P.E., 8, 30, 41, 64, 73, 80, 112, 126, 141, 156, 172, 404, 405
McPeek, J.A.S., 207, 293, 294, 296, 308, 313
McQueen, J., 4
Medusa, 302
melancholy, 158, 176, 187, 192, 308, 331–2, 337, 341, 386, 390, 393, 404
memory aids, 233
Mercury, 32, 167, 237, 326
metamorphosis, 238, 241, 394, 396, 397
Meyer–Baer, K., 178
Michel, G., 8, 30, 38, 158, 309
Midas, 110
mid-point symbolism, 55, 65, 112, 122, 158, 206–7, 304
Miller, D.L., 200, 334, 386
Milton, J., 306, 322
Minerva, 170, 269, 271, 302
Minos, 260
Miola, R.S., 205
misrule, lord of, 41, 83
modes (musical), 167, 168
Mohl, R., 109
Moschus, 62, 172, 177, 179, 182
Moses, 126
Muir, K., 311
Mulcaster, R., 190

Musaeus, 110, 336
Muses, 70, 74, 76, 106, 158, 165, 171, 180, 217, 280, 291–3, 296, 326, 340, 379
Mustard, W.P., 26, 63, 77-8, 97, 126, 186

Narcissus, 105, 106, 157, 187, 204, 221, 241, 243, 282, 286, 292, 327, 335
Navarre, Marguerite de, 267
Neale, J. E., 30, 54,
nectar, 186, 326, 338
Needham, Sir Robert, 214
Negro, A. di, 27
Nelson, W., 202, 333
neo-Platonism, 68, 77, 79, 124, 158, 164, 169, 186, 202–3, 205, 207, 208, 216, 218, 219, 221, 226, 234, 236, 237, 238, 246, 248, 249, 266, 272, 274, 276, 278, 281, 285, 290, 300, 320, 321, 328, 331, 339, 340–1, 342, 349, 367, 369, 380, 386, 390
Neptune, 302
Neumann, E., 271
Neuse, R., 317
Neville Davies, H., 173
Nichols, J., 77, 156, 298
Nicolas, H., 156
Niobe, 75–6
Nisus, 260
Nitzsche, J.C., 214-15
Nohrnberg, J., 269
Norbrook, D., 41, 49, 53, 80, 199
Norton, D., 386, 393, 400, 402
numerology, 3–4, 40, 64, 80, 102, 128, 158, 165, 172–3, 187, 199, 202, 203–4, 206, 223, 242, 261, 273, 295, 299, 307, 308, 310, 316, 321–2, 387–8, 392, 394, 397

Oates, M.I., 322
ode, 210, 389
Odysseus/Ulysses, 32, 234, 237, 364
Orgel, S., 207, 221, 298, 302, 306
Orpheus, 5, 106, 137, 162, 169, 186, 204, 206, 207–8, 248–9, 286, 291, 292–4, 296, 305, 330, 337, 338, 390, 393, 401
Orphism, 61, 74, 105, 107, 207–9, 236, 258, 284, 290, 292, 296, 298, 306, 310–11, 312, 315, 320, 326, 328, 330, 336, 354, 355, 356, 366, 390, 393, 394
Oruch, J.B., 24, 63, 110, 169
Osgood, C.G., 321
Ovid, 35, 36, 55, 59, 61, 62, 65, 74, 75–7, 103, 106, 110, 126, 137, 151, 156, 157, 166, 167, 170, 171, 172, 192, 198, 199, 226, 230, 234, 238, 241, 242, 245, 254, 260, 276, 291, 292, 308, 309, 311, 314, 325, 328, 331, 336, 338, 352, 359, 364, 370, 386, 387, 391, 392, 393, 396, 397, 401
Owen, A.L., 44

Pallas, 170
Pallas, son of Evander, 387–8, 401
Pan, 32, 74–5, 96–7, 110, 126, 184, 187, 196
Pandora, 235, 240, 241, 262
Panofsky, E., 55, 63, 123, 222, 224, 231, 235, 259, 262, 271 287, 308, 326
paradise, 102, 108–9, 252, 264, 275
Paris, 63, 125, 128, 139, 269
Parmenter, M., 8, 172, 185, 404
pastoral, 187, 386; elegy, 172; theories of, 8, 22, 26, 403
patriarchy, 396
Patterson, A., 30, 31, 38, 52, 141, 196
Paul, St, 93, 226
Pausanias, 243
Peacham, H., 256, 390
Pegasus, 80, 280
Penelope, 32, 234, 244, 271, 391
Peneus, 238, 309, 393, 396
Perion, J., 36
Persephone/Proserpina, 182, 186, 386, 391, 392, 397
personifications:
  Beauty, 320, 327, 328, 330, 334, 336, 339, 341, 342; Care, 390; Constancy, 46; Contention, 46; Deceit, 93, 94; Envy, 16, 45, 284, 338; Error, 217; Fame, 18, 106, 239; Fortune, 40, 230, 259, 291; Genius, 314–15; Honour, 303, 311; Innocence, 220; Jealousy, 338; Majesty, 311; Misery, Earthly, 224; Modesty, 226, 303; Night, 35, 185, 186, 208, 298, 310, 312; Obedience, 304; Old Age, 195; Opportunity, 271; Peace, 208, 312; Penance, 44; Philology, 326; Pleasure, 266, 272, 276, 339; Plenty, 327; Poverty, 327; Reverence, 311; Sapience/Wisdom, 320, 321–2, 356, 377–9, 381; Shamefastness: *see* Modesty; Silence, 208, 248; Sleep, 208, 312; Sorrow, 32; Time, 259, 271, 308; Truth, 376; Virginity, 300, 301; Virtue, 376
Pervigilium Veneris, 341
Petrarch, 3, 23, 26, 32, 33, 68, 69, 73, 76, 80, 136, 168–9, 170, 172, 201–2, 203, 205, 217, 218, 220, 222, 224, 225, 226, 229, 230, 231, 233, 235, 238, 239, 241–2, 243, 244, 246, 254, 257, 261, 267–8, 285, 286, 302, 305, 319, 320, 326, 354, 390, 392
Petre, Sir John, 385

Petre, W., 385, 401
Phaethon, 180
Philip II, King of Spain, 400
Philomela/Philomena, 137, 175, 180, 185
Philostratus, 170, 191, 277
Philpot, J., 123
Phoebe: *see* Diana
Phoebus: *see* Apollo
Pico della Mirandola, 207, 209, 288, 310, 337, 342, 343
Piers, J., 80
pilgrimage, 44
Pindar, 97, 169
Pitcher, J., 388
planets, 349, 355, 371–2, 397: Mars, 261, 370; moon, 223, 370–1, 391, 404; sun, 261, 293, 308, 329, 345, 370–1, 376, 390, 404, 405-6; Venus, 261, 295, 329, 341, 345, 370
Plato, 167, 202: *Alcibiades*, 36; *Ion*, 170, 191, 272; *Laws*, 166–7, 261; *Phaedo*, 167, 186; *Phaedrus*, 160, 169, 218, 272, 322, 326, 334, 342, 348, 349, 368, 371; *Republic*, 376, 378; *Symposium*, 224, 287, 289, 319, 324, 328, 329, 330, 331, 337, 366, 369; *Timaeus*, 4, 167, 319, 328, 329, 342, 355, 359
Platonism, 61, 158, 164, 191, 218, 224, 243, 249, 276, 303, 315, 320, 367, 373 (*see also* neo-Platonism)
Plautus, 61
Pléiade, La, 3, 128, 139, 179, 228
Pliny (C. Plinius Secundus), 78, 86, 127, 169, 180, 192, 228, 236, 255, 378
Plotinus, 369
Plutarch, 96, 169, 295
Pluto, 392, 397
Politianus, A. (Politian), 55, 62, 68, 236
Pollio, A., 19
Pollux, 394, 401
Polydorus, 184
Polymnia, 76
Polyxena, 63
Ponsonby, W., 35, 201, 214, 319, 386
Pontano, G., 207
Porphyry, 219, 234, 242, 246, 372
Prescott, A.L., 30, 173, 200, 264, 267–8, 270, 318
Procne, 185
Prometheus, 98, 235, 241, 359
Propertius, 62
Proserpina: *see* Persephone
Protestantism, 7–8, 9, 16, 21, 30, 35, 38, 44, 45, 46, 55, 64, 77, 80, 82, 85, 89, 90, 100, 112, 124, 125, 126, 132, 141, 159, 172, 187, 202–3, 204, 206, 208, 295, 304, 316, 321, 330, 363, 387–8, 399, 400, 407
Pseudo-Dionysius, 355, 357, 372, 376
Psyche, 266, 326, 338, 339
Ptolemy, 71, 80, 223, 261, 273, 355, 369
Puck, 311
Puttenham, G., 9, 19, 23, 27, 73, 99, 100, 199, 206, 223, 291, 311, 314, 319, 393, 403
Pygmalion, 235, 254
Pyrrha, 241

quintessence, 257
Quintilian, 170
Quitslund, J.A., 202, 222, 320, 322, 324, 377

Rabanus Maurus, 326
Rabelais, F., 11
Ralegh, Sir Walter, 205, 400
Ramus, P., 156
Reid, R.L., 347
Renwick, W.L., 32, 36, 99, 101, 109, 151, 171, 214, 222, 226, 230, 269, 283, 285, 312, 318, 373, 385, 398, 402, 403
Resnikov, S., 40
revolution periods (planetary), 261
Rice, F., Jr, 322
Richard III, 75
Richardson, J. M., 38, 64–5, 71, 125, 158, 404–5
Ripa, C., 16, 18, 35, 93, 106, 123, 131, 180, 220, 224, 226, 239, 248, 256, 272, 292, 294, 300, 301, 303, 304, 310, 311, 312, 338, 376, 395
river marriage, 124, 386, 387, 391
Robertson, J., 110, 172, 203
Robinson, J., 126
Roche, T.P., Jr, 204, 238
Rogers, W.E., 386
Rollinson, P.B., 320
Roman Catholicism, 7–8, 9, 30, 38, 45, 49, 53, 80, 82, 89, 95, 98, 100, 112, 121, 123, 126, 146, 149, 154, 156, 187, 188, 203, 385, 386–7, 399
Romulus, 28
Ronsard, P., 3, 55, 59, 179, 205, 238, 283, 288, 290, 308, 320
Ross, A., 98, 243, 249, 266, 267, 339, 397, 401
Røstvig, M.-S., 173, 187
Ryden, M., 71

Sacks, P.M., 176
Sackville, T., 30, 32
saints, 82, 112, 132, 316
Sallust, 19
Salmon, W., 78, 124, 228, 236, 264
Sannazaro, J., 9, 23, 136, 172

Sansovino, F., 9
Saturn, 158, 176, 180, 192, 219, 308
Saurat, D., 322
Saxons, 109, 123, 155
Scaliger, J.C., 206, 286, 293, 294, 297, 306, 308, 309, 310, 311, 313, 315
Scattergood, J., 35
Schell, R., 340
Schenck, C.M., 207
Schleiner, L., 11
Schöne, A., 355
Scott, J.G., 202, 218, 219, 226, 232, 235, 239, 250, 252, 255, 257, 267, 272, 273, 275, 279, 280, 281
Scylla (and Charybdis), 242, 257
Scylla (daughter of Nisus), 260
Seneca, 77, 122, 184
Senn, W., 302
senses, the five, 236, 264, 349
Servius, 78, 309, 313
sestina, 128, 136
Seymour, Sir Thomas, 45
Shakespeare, W., 3, 73, 110, 160, 177, 179, 180, 202, 203, 205, 208, 209, 231, 236, 237, 271, 277, 287, 295, 297, 311
Shapiro, M., 136
Shearman, J., 4
Shekinah, 322
Shrewsbury, John Talbot, first Earl of 109–10
shrines, 112, 124
Shumaker, W., 208
Sidney, M., 220
Sidney, Sir Philip, 1, 3, 8, 16, 18, 22, 30, 62, 69, 110, 136, 137, 172, 202–3, 207, 209, 241, 253, 254, 274, 291, 299, 301, 303, 311, 393
Singleton, H., 7
Skelton, J., 16, 30, 35, 52, 80
Smith, B., 277
Smith, B.R., 9, 31, 155
Smith, C.G., 22, 43, 51, 147, 221, 230, 231, 232, 233, 236, 237, 239, 240, 242, 245, 248, 250, 253, 254, 258, 259, 260, 261, 262, 263, 270, 279, 285, 307
Smith, H., 112
Smith, Sir Thomas, 36, 156
Socrates, 186
Solerti, A., 218, 219, 226, 232, 248, 250, 252, 257, 267, 272, 273, 275, 279, 280, 281, 286
Solomon, King, 399
Somerset, Elizabeth and Katherine, 385–7, 400
sonnet form, 209
Spanish Armada, 400
Spenser, E., 1–5, 30, 51, 52, 53, 56, 66, 73, 77–8, 80, 82, 92, 93, 103, 112, 126, 127, 154, 156, 163, 168, 169, 172, 183, 187, 190, 196, 199, 202–3, 204–5, 206, 207, 208, 215, 220, 227, 231, 232, 235, 239, 241, 249, 252, 261, 271, 274, 275, 278–9, 283, 288, 291, 292, 295, 305, 316, 317, 320–21, 328, 330, 336, 337, 343, 346, 352, 368, 369, 372, 379, 385, 388, 390, 392, 393, 394, 397, 398, 399, 400, 401, 403–6, 408: 'lost' works, 24, 63, 110, 169, 186, 269; *Amoretti and Epithalamion*, 3, 4, 5, 61, 68, 104, 105, 110, 157, 167, 168, 182, 201–318, 319, 322, 326, 327-39, 341, 345, 350–3, 355, 367–9, 386, 388–92, 395–8, 401; *Astrophel*, 39, 215, 241, 291; *Colin Clout's Come Home Again*, 5, 295, 296, 324; *Complaints*, 5, 30, 390; *Daphnaïda*, 319, 321; *The Faerie Queen*, 1, 2, 5, 34, 35, 39, 42, 44, 52, 61, 69, 78–9, 94, 107, 110, 116, 124, 154, 160, 162, 164, 168, 171, 172, 195, 196, 204, 205, 214, 215, 216, 217, 222, 225, 229, 233, 241, 251, 253, 257, 260, 262, 264, 266, 269, 270, 277, 280, 283, 284, 288, 291–2, 296, 299, 301, 302–5, 309, 311, 312, 322, 325, 326, 327, 329, 331, 335, 337, 338, 341, 346, 347, 348, 352, 353, 357, 361, 364, 370, 374, 382, 385–7, 390–1, 394, 396, 397, 398, 400, 401; *Four Hymns*, 5, 35, 158, 164, 169, 202, 209, 218, 221, 222, 223, 226, 247, 266, 267, 279, 292, 315, 319–83; *Mother Hubberd's Tale*, 311, 390, 398; *Muiopotmos*, 5, 398; *Prothalamion*, 3, 5, 80, 209–10, 304, 319, 328, 354, 385–402; *The Ruins of Rome*, 45, 221, 269; *The Ruins of Time* 5, 374, 393; *The Shepherds' Calendar*, 2–200, 202, 215, 216, 217, 220, 222, 230, 233, 236, 246, 248, 249, 250, 258, 260, 262, 264, 265, 269, 272, 275, 280, 283, 284, 286–8, 290, 291–6, 298–301, 303, 312–13, 316, 319, 325, 326, 327, 331, 332, 334, 335, 337, 356, 362, 375, 390–3, 396–400, 403–8; *Tears of the Muses*, 30, 74, 76, 158, 160, 165, 262, 291, 398; *Three . . . Letters*, 97, 186; *Virgil's Gnat*, 186, 292, 312; *Visions of Bellay*, 329
Spenser, J., 109
Spitzer, L., 55
Stahl, W.H., 327
Stanyhurst, R., 183
Statius, 36, 207, 309

Index

Stewart, S., 125, 129
Strong, R., 46, 68, 75, 78, 387, 399, 401
Stubbes, P., 84
Stubbs, J., 7
Summerson, J., 302
Surrey, Henry Howard, Earl of, 73, 78, 209, 253
symbols:
adamant, 247, 330, 370; alder tree, 180; anchor, 35; ape, 54, 86; apple, 105, 128–9, 139, 269, 277–8, 301; arrows, 288, 331, 343, 361; bagpipe, 30; ball, 40; bay tree, 68, 76, 180 (*see also* laurel); bear, 131; bee, 191, 208, 246, 271–2, 287–8, 290; beech tree, 30; bird, 272, 273, 356, 369, 393; blindness, 336, 366, 381; brass, 266, 374–5; bride (as Church), 64, 68; bridle, 66; bubble, 43; building, 233, 346; bull, 144; carnation, 71, 78, 264–5; cockatrice, 252; colours, 75, 81, 178, 273, 294, 300, 301, 391; columbine, 71, 265; cowslip, 71; crystal, 223; cuckoo, 231, 283; cypress, 185, 236; daffodil, 243, 397; daisy, 103, 392; deer, 216, 267–8, 296; diamond, 223, 247, 375; dog, 16; dove, 179, 265, 286, 292–3, 312; dragon, 277; eagle, 329, 374; egg (Orphic), 354, 356, 394; eglantine (sweet briar), 45–6, 236, 272; elder tree, 180; ermine, 68; fir tree, 78, 236; fish, 166, 192, 216, 295; flames/fire, 220, 221, 231, 234, 256, 293, 294, 307, 325, 329, 331, 336, 355, 372, 377; Fleece, Golden, 248–9; bridal, 313; flight, 169; flint, 231; fox, 93, 94, 99, 149; frog, 312; girdle, 42; glass, 224; gold, 228, 229; gorse, 236; grasshopper, 160, 296; hair, 66, 244, 300, 391; hare, 190; hawthorn, 83; honey, 287; honeysuckle, 272; horse, 191; hunt, 251, 267; ivory, 228, 277, 301, 339; ivy, 131, 170, 306; jasmine, 265; kingcup, 71; knot, 221, 265, 268, 294; ladder/stair, 164, 227, 281, 302, 321; lamb, 70, 220; lark, 177; laurel, 238; lightning, 222, 223; lily, 45, 78, 216, 265, 294, 302, 309, 392, 396; lion, 113, 123, 188, 232, 277, 327; marjoram, 306; mask, 256; maze, 221, 302; mirror, 221, 334, 349, 373; mole, 334; moly, 237; moth, 355; myrtle, 303; nightingale, 46, 137, 175, 177, 185, 192, (*see also* Philomela); oak tree, 38, 44–5, 46, 115, 179, 220; olive tree, 77–8, 180; owl, 104, 192, 311–12; pansy, 71; panther, 255;
peacock, 59; pearl, 228, 301, 364; Pillars of Hercules, 400; primrose, 68, 71, 392; raven, 104; robin redbreast, 297; rose, 46, 64, 73, 75, 103, 202, 236, 264, 294, 309, 345, 393, *see also* eglantine); rosemary, 179; ruby, 228; sapphire, 228, 301; ship, 242, 257; silence, 248; silver, 229, 277, 326, 391; spider, 271; spring, 165; steel, 230, 375; stone, 256; stork, 311–12; storm, 245, 250; strawberry, 265; sun, 123, 223, 233, 249, 299, 376, 390, 404, 405–6, 407; (*see also* Apollo); swallow, 61, 189; swan, 169, 391, 393, 401; swine, 364; sword (rusty), 168; thorns, 45; thrush, 283, 297; thunder/thunderbolt, 245, 377 tiger, 131, 255, 257, 327 toad, 192; torch, 293, 315; trumpet, 18, 239; vine, 131; violet, 68, 309, 392; water, 242, 243, 256, 257, 267, 294, 329; weaving, 234; wheel, 40, 230; wolf, 88, 149, 156
syncretism (Renaissance), 182
Syrinx, 32, 68, 74–5, 167
Syrus, P., 51, 60

Tacitus, 61
Tantalus, 184, 335
Tasso, T., 3, 202, 218, 219, 226, 232, 248, 250, 252, 255, 257, 267, 272, 273, 275, 279, 280, 281, 286, 288
Tempe, 393
temperaments, the four, 256, 390
Terence, 196
Tereus, 137, 185
Tervarent, G. de, 43, 59, 70, 77, 78, 80, 105, 106, 131, 180, 190, 220, 222, 223, 232, 256, 265, 271, 273, 325, 395
Thiébaux, M., 189, 267
Themis, 298
Theocritus, 23, 26, 36, 59, 61, 64, 67, 73, 124, 128, 131, 139, 166, 172, 175, 177, 179, 181, 197, 207, 287–8
Theodontius, 76–7
Theognis, 100
Thompson, C., 204
Tiberius, 36
Titans, 124, 390
Tithonus, 296
Tooke, A., 74, 76, 228, 277, 287, 294, 296, 306, 315, 326, 394
topoi: absence, 254; astronomy as pathway to God, 199; awakening, 297; book of nature, book of the creatures, 369; *carpe diem*, 270, 299; drowning, 175; evening, 35; generation in marriage, 314; locus amoenus, 102, 103; night's

slow arrival, 310; 'no more', 177; portrait, 230; theatre of world, 255; youth/age, 38, 40
Trapp, J.B., 252
triumph, 122, 232, 239, 305, 325, 387, 400
Tufte, V., 64, 207
Turberville, G., 112, 123, 124, 141
Turner, J., 45
Turner, W., 392
Tuve, R., 44, 126, 264, 322, 324, 328, 356, 368, 377
twins/twinning, 387-8, 394
Twycross, M., 295
Tyndale, W., 112
typology, 321, 322
Tyrius, M., 36

Valeriano, P., 169, 245, 255, 257, 267, 271, 272, 277, 286, 312, 314, 345, 393, 394
Valla, L., 19
Vallans, W., 386, 393, 398
Van Dorsten, J., 19
Venus, 38, 42, 55, 64, 68, 70, 71, 77–80, 103, 104, 128, 139, 168, 190, 192, 197, 202, 205, 223, 224, 225, 228, 231, 233, 236, 244, 245, 246, 247, 251, 254, 258, 261, 264, 265, 269, 272, 277–8, 287–8, 290, 294, 295, 296, 298, 300, 303, 306, 308, 309, 310, 312, 320, 321, 322, 324, 325, 327, 329, 336, 339, 340–1, 343, 352, 378, 392, 393, 395, 397, 407
vestiarian controversy, 126
Vian, F., 207, 328
Vida, 320
Virgil, 8, 26, 30, 53, 76, 158, 168, 184, 196, 199, 319, 386: *Aeneid*, 21, 22, 23, 62, 78–9, 99, 161, 162–3, 171, 172, 186, 197, 257, 277, 280, 286, 336, 387–8, 395, 398, 401; *Ciris*, 293; *Eclogues*, 18, 23, 30, 32, 35, 36, 38, 52, 57, 62, 64, 66, 105, 106, 110, 111, 131, 139, 141, 158, 162, 166, 168, 169, 170, 172, 174, 178, 179, 180, 181, 187, 292, 392; *Georgics*, 23, 78, 106, 162, 167, 168, 292, 305, 313
Vulcan, 55, 170, 235

Waldman, L., 11

Walker, D.P., 208
Wall, J.N., 126, 132
Waller, G., 203
Walsingham, Sir Francis, 30
Warkentin, G., 205, 210
Warner, M., 263
watchfulness, 151–2
Watson, T., 288, 290
Webster, J., 204
Wells, R.H., 173, 184
Welsford, E., 206, 320, 322, 343, 356
Whitaker, V.K., 80
Whitney, G., Jr, 45, 61, 86, 215, 257, 267, 271, 288, 335, 338
Whitney, G., Sr, 215
Wickert, M.A., 206
Wilkins, E., 68, 75
Wilson, E.C., 68, 75, 129, 139, 322
Wind, E., 30, 61, 66, 77, 79, 124, 129, 169, 191, 202, 207, 208, 209, 218, 224, 236, 244, 247, 272, 274, 276, 277, 287–8, 290, 312, 337, 339, 381, 390, 394
Winternitz, E., 30
Woods, S., 210
Worcester, Edward Somerset, fourth Earl of, 385–7, 399
Wordsworth, W., 9
Woudhuysen, H.R., 7, 9, 16, 399
Wright, A., 44
Wyatt, Sir Thomas, 42, 52, 73, 78, 209, 241, 261, 267

Xenophon, 36

Yates, F.A., 16, 64, 78, 141, 162, 172, 188, 208, 232, 233, 241, 255, 387, 399, 400
Young, J., 66, 80, 124, 156

Zephyrus, 77, 219, 270, 390, 391, 393
Ziegler, G., 234
zodiac, 401, 404: Aries, 40, 61, 405; Cancer, 219, 307; Capricorn, 219; Gemini, 80, 388, 401; Leo, 113, 123; 196; Libra, 141; Pisces, 38, 184, 295, 403–7; Sagittarius, 403, 406; Scorpio, 158, 404–5; Taurus, 64, 197; Virgo, 64, 128–9, 132, 139, 141; signs per month tradition, 128